# HOW TO MAKE EARLY AMERICAN & COLONIAL FURNITURE

**Other TAB books by the author:**

No. 788 *Handbook of Practical Boat Repairs*
No. 860 *The Woodworker's Bible*
No. 894 *Do-It-Yourselfer's Guide to Furniture Repair & Refinishing*
No. 910 *How To Make Your Own Built-In Furniture*
No. 937 *Modern Sailmaking*
No. 1004 *The Upholsterer's Bible*
No. 1008 *Woodworking with Scraps*
No. 1044 *The Woodturner's Bible*

No. 1114
$12.95

# HOW TO MAKE EARLY AMERICAN & COLONIAL FURNITURE

BY PERCY W. BLANDFORD

TAB BOOKS

BLUE RIDGE SUMMIT, PA. 17214

FIRST EDITION

FIRST PRINTING—JANUARY 1979



Printed in the United States of America



**Library of Congress Cataloging in Publication Data**

Blandford, Percy W.
How to make Early American furniture.

Inclues index.
1. Furniture making—Amateurs' manuals. 2. Furniture, Early American. I. Title.
TT195.B59 684.1'0974 78-26896
ISBN 0-8306-9843-4
ISBN 0-8306-1114-2 pbk.

Cover photograph from *Early American Life* magazine, reproduced courtesy The Early American Society, Inc.

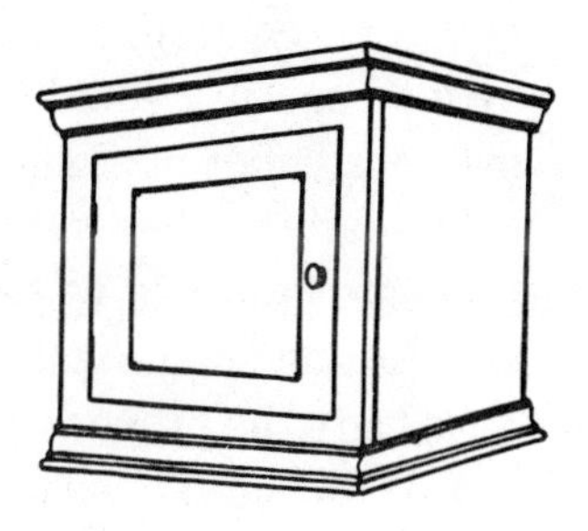

# Preface

The first American settlers from Europe arrived in their new homes with a knowledge of furniture they had used in the old country, but they had to start by making their homes and furnishing them, using the plentiful supply of wood around them, but with usually only a meager kit of tools and often very limited skill in using them. This meant that some of the first furniture was primitive, and that is the name applied to surviving pieces. However, these very early examples should not be dismissed as unworthy of attention, as some have qualities worth reproducing.

Furniture which followed had more attention and skill given to it after the first pioneer days had passed. The designers and craftsmen were in a different situation from others who had stayed at home among long-established ways. Instead, they were opening up a new field of furniture building based on new concepts. Fitness for purpose was a prime aim. This very desirable attribute of any furniture had been overlooked by some designers in Europe, where striving for novelty may have been the main aim. Usually, anything designed to perform a task in the best possible way acquired a beauty of its own, without applied decoration. Obviously, there may by carving, veneering, inlaying, or other decorative touches, but if the design is wrong, no amount of decoration will make it right.

Furniture that best suits a particular purpose does not go out of date. Some of those early pieces of furniture can still be used in a modern home. In some cases, where the original use is no longer required, as with a washstand, the item will still serve for a new use—in this case as a side table in a bedroom, or maybe a buffet in a dining room.

The early craftsmen worked with basic tools. The things they constructed had to be made without the aid of power tools. Glues and metal fastenings were mostly of poor quality, so parts had to be properly jointed. This meant that their work was made in a craftsmanlike tradition, without shortcuts that go with mass-produced furniture today. Such work is ageless. A few modern cabinetmakers continue to make furniture in this way professionally, but such skill is expensive and the number of men able to engage in the work are few. This is where a keen amateur craftsman can keep a tradition alive, by making furniture in the time-honored way. And what better examples to take than the furniture which is our own heritage? That is what this book is all about.

Furniture of the days of British rule is described as "Colonial" while that made after Independence is "Early American." There was no sudden change, and furniture design evolved with steady progress. There are some influence from the other side of the Atlantic. Most settlers arrived with ideas from England and nearby European countries, but some groups wanted to make their furniture in a style they remembered from other countries, not necessarily very far apart. The Pennsylvania Dutch (German), with their bright painting may be particularly distinctive, and the Shakers produced the ultimate in simplicity, but there are other early characteristics of particular groups. In time there was more of a blending of designs, and the best features became adapted, so there was less distinction between the products of several areas.

News of furniture developments in the old countries came across the Atlantic. Designs were brought over. Particularly when special woods were imported, some of the European designs were followed and then adapted. By the time of Chippendale and other famous cabinetmakers, the best furniture in their styles was exceptionally good, but not of a type for an amateur with limited skills to reproduce.

This book is about the furniture that led up to those days. The author believes that an amateur woodworker of moderate skill, and with only a modest tool kit, should be able to find examples to make that will be within his skill and enable him to progress to some of the more ambitious types.

The furniture described forms a selection only. It is possible to adapt designs. A low cupboard may be heightened so its use is changed from kitchen storage to clothes hanging. A design with parts in solid boards may be altered to paneled parts. Variations in this way were practiced by early craftsmen. Many methods of construction can be seen following through a variety of pieces of furniture. Once these techniques have been mastered, special designs can be made, with a fair chance that someone in the past would have made something similar.

The furniture in this book is described mainly as authentic reproductions. It may be that some amateur furniture makers will decide not to strive for absolute authenticity. This is particularly so in broad panels, such as backs of cabinets. The modern treatment would be plywood, instead of building up from many thin boards. The choice is yours.

The designs used are all either identical with existing old pieces of furniture or based on a type in which there were variations. When furniture was made singly, there were many changes to suit needs or the available wood, so if changes are made, without drastically altering a design, there is scope for individual treatment without the work being spoiled as a reproduction.

In most cases there is no specific wood quoted. Some pieces of furniture were made to the same design in different places with different woods, and the same could be done today. There is general guidance to the woods that were available and probably chosen in particular areas.

All measurements given are in inches. The lists of material are given for guidance and are generally sufficiently accurate, but wood was often used in a size it happened to be, as there was no power saw to rip it down, and avoiding too much physical labor was obviously desirable. Wood of odd sizes can be used. If two parts which would be power sawn to the same size today are made slightly different, where this does not affect appearance or use, the work is likely to be more like the original. If the insides of old furniture is examined, uneven and rough edges where they do not matter are quite common.

Visiting museums or collections of old furniture will provide ideas for many other items of furniture to copy. Comparing old furniture seen with examples in this book will show what variations are possible.

The author believes that Colonial and Early American furniture offers very satisfying designs to be used by the modern amateur to exercise his growing skill. Probably in no other way can he learn the traditional processes that are at the base of true woodworking craftsmanship.

Percy W. Blandford

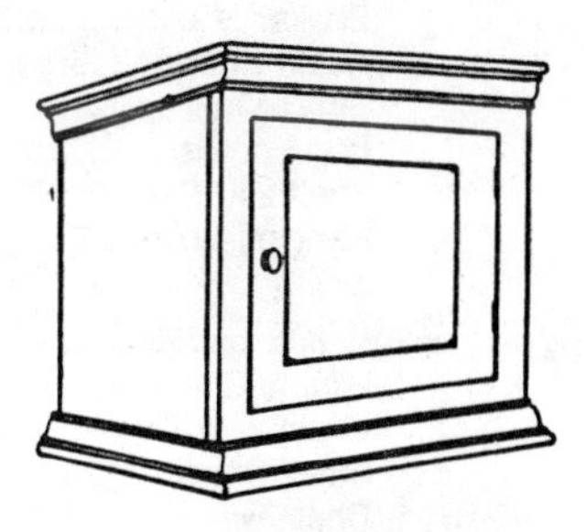

# Contents

# Furniture Wood

Man has attended to his creature comforts by making furniture almost from the earliest times. Some of it was very primitive, but as tools developed so did the quality of furniture. This applied to man all over the world, and the early residents of the American continent must have produced furniture of various sorts. Some of the lost civilizations of South America apparently progressed to a high standard of design and craftsmanship, but there is little evidence of much sophisticated furniture making by the early residents of North America.

Explorers from Europe must have introduced furniture from their homelands, but if the Vikings, Irish, and other early peoples who arrived on the American continent made furniture during their stays, we know little of it today, probably because their settlements did not last long. Wood does not last for centuries under everyday conditions, and such peoples as the Vikings did not produce records that included written and drawn matter. They relied on history passed on by word of mouth, and that is not a good way to record details of furniture construction.

Furniture worth reproducing did not appear until the arrival of peoples with a determination to settle. Columbus, Cabot, and others set immigration in motion at the end of the fifteenth century. Many European nations were in the exploration business, and their attempts to get a foothold in America brought differing ideas of furnishings as the settlers tried to reproduce things that they remembered from home. French and Spanish influence in the south brought designs markedly different from those used by English, Dutch, and other settlers farther north. The types of trees available for conversion to furniture also influenced furniture making. The near-tropical hardwoods of the south happened to be more like those familiar to the French and Spanish, while the northern trees were of the hardy types suited to temperate climates.

The furniture of the northern states had the most lasting influence on the designs of the settled parts of North America, with the English influence having more effect than any tendencies due to other European settlers, because of their preponderance and greater numbers. Other cultures had effects, and these will be seen later in the book, but as designs developed and became American rather than ex-European, the many originals blended into a hole that was recognizable as something new, but incorporating facets of the originals that were found to be suitable for the new conditions.

All this was an ongoing process and still is, without clearly marked breaks, but for convenience of description we need to define periods. "Colonial period" must mean that period from the first settlements, while the settlers were colonists of another nation, up to 1776 and independence from English rule. After that it is convenient to describe furniture as "Early American" for the period when most work was done with hand tools. This is up to the beginning of the Industrial Revolution in the middle of the nineteenth century. With factory facilities then furniture could be produced by mass-production methods and a craftsman did not see a job through from start to finish, but he exercised what skill he had doing only a part of the work. This did not mean the end of the individual craftsman, but mass-produced furniture was cheaper and the choice of the majority of people, so individual craftsmanship became only available to the more wealthy.

Mass production of furniture continues to today, but methods of a century in wood techniques have had to give way to plastics and manufactured boards since the end of World War II. The Industrial Revolution caused a recognizable break with furniture that had gone before, but there is no comparable obvious division between Colonial and Early American furniture. They have a family likeness, and differences are more the effects of natural evolution than abrupt alterations. Tools and equipment improved. With improvements in communications and transport, woods were imported or came from distant parts of the continent. Methods of seasoning improved. Better materials and improved tools, with some mechanization, produced better furniture.

In the earliest days of settlement in Eastern America and again as man pushed West, furniture had to have an immediate practical use and little or no intentional aesthetic value. This was made from wood available locally, worked with the few tools available to a pioneer woodworker, many of which were primarily for much rougher carpentry. Such furniture is often described as "Primitive." This may not exactly be a period, but it marked the early stages of furniture in particular areas as they were settled.

Northern settlers had to contend with a harsh climate and not very profitable activities, so wealth came slowly, if at all. Much of their furniture making was by their own hands. A farmer tackled most things and made his own furniture, usually with the minimum of tools. Specialist craftsmen came later. The Southern settlements, with better climate, farms with crops more easily turned into money, and quick development of towns around harbors, were able to import furniture and employ craftsmen to specialize in woodworking, so luxury was tied to utility in much of their furniture, with ornament and decoration being important.

## DESIGN

"Primitive" is not necessarily a description of something makeshift for limited use. Fitness for purpose is often one of the most important features of good design. There is often a beauty in something which has been designed to do a job properly, without the need for added decoration. Good proportions can be all that are needed to make something look attractive. The Shaker religious philosophy of rejecting vanity is seen in their furniture, which is all severely plain, yet much of it is very attractive, due to being functional and nicely proportioned.

Another type of furniture, usually of comparatively plain construction, is that of the Pennsylvania Dutch (more correctly *Deutsche*, meaning German), which is embellished with bright colors and patterns.

More advanced furniture showed influence of the great designers, particularly such names as Chippendale, Sheraton, and Hepplewhite, who not only made fine furniture in England, but published books of designs, some of which found their way across the Atlantic to the New World. By then American furniture was finding traits of its own. While good designs have a following anywhere, local influences are bound to be important. Craftsmen and designers learn from experience—their own and that of others—and appreciate what is good in design and adapt it to their own ways. Such is progress.

When a hand craftsman makes things it is unlikely that any two items will be alike. This is one of the attractions of individual craftsmanship and was even more so in the days of early settlers, when what was made may have had to be designed to suit particular pieces of wood available. If a craftsman had in mind a piece of wood, say ¾ in. thick and a piece was available ⅞ in. or 1 in., he did not put in the considerable hand labor of planing it down, but used it as it was. If shelves were wanted 6 in. wide and a board 7 in. wide was available, that might be just as acceptable without cutting. On another occasion a similar thing might have been made with 5 in. boards to suit available stock.

This means that in considering reproducing furniture from the days of hand work, there is no virtue in carefully measuring to fine limits unless the work is intended as a museum specimen or an exact replica for historical reasons. If it is something that would have been made many times over, possibly by a great many craftsmen, it is safe to assume that variations in sizes would have been considerable, and any modern reproduction using similar woods and methods of construction would be as good a copy as one made to within 1/16 in. of the measurements of a particular specimen.

The original craftsman's ideas of design probably were on the lines of, "If it looks right, it probably is right." He gained a feeling for good proportions, probably without being able to analyze his reasons. If something is to be made in the style of an old piece of furniture without having an actual specimen or drawing to follow, there are a few rules that will provide guidance.

Having measurements the same in two or more directions does not usually produce a good looking shape. This means that a circle and a square (Fig. 1-1A and B) are better avoided. An ellipse is generally more pleasing than a circle (Fig. 1-1C). Any rectangle should produce a better looking shape than a square, and various proportions are needed to

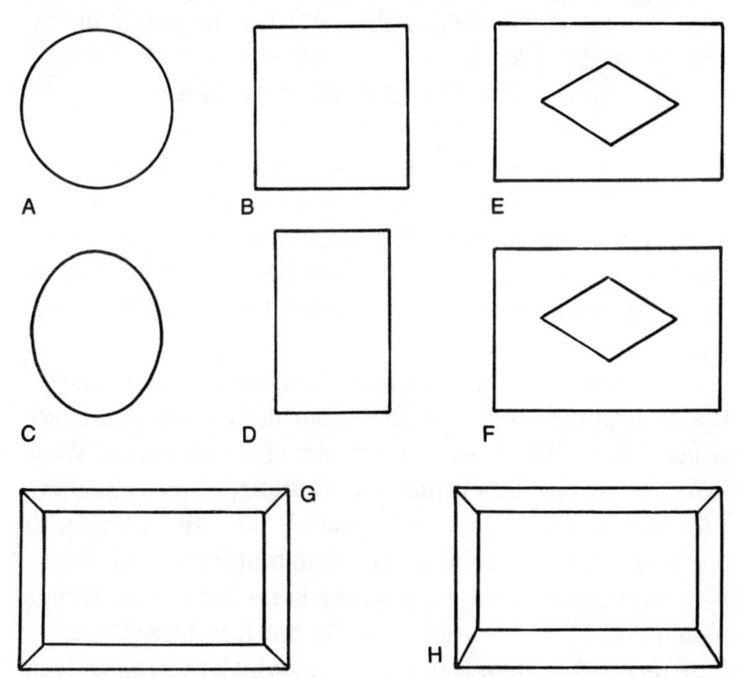


Fig. 1-1. A circle (A) or a square (B) are not as pleasing as an ellipse (C) or a rectangle (D). If decoration is placed exactly central (E) it looks low and is better placed above the center (F). This also applies to a border, where the lower part may look narrow (G) and is better wider (H).

suit what is being made, but there is a *golden proportion* that comes from way back into antiquity. Our Colonial craftsman may not have known of it, but by his feeling for a good shape, he often arrived at it. This golden rule says that the most pleasing rectangular shape has sides in the proportions $1:\sqrt{2}$. For practical purposes this means that the rectangle is 1½ times or slightly less in length than it is wide (Fig. 1-1D).

Another design point to consider is never to make a design symmetrical on a vertical surface. If you put a pattern exactly in the center it will appear to be below center (Fig. 1-1E). It is better, for the sake of appearances, to put it decidedly *above* center (Fig. 1-1F). This is more marked if the inner shape produces an even border. The bottom border will appear narrow (Fig. 1-1G). It is better to make the bottom border definitely wider (Fig. 1-1H). This is seen in paneled doors. In framed pictures, the frame of the same width all round is disguised by making the bottom of the picture mount wider than the sides and top.

With a three-dimensional piece of furniture, the various panels are better rectangular than square, although an occasional square will not matter. Such a piece of furniture will be more often viewed at an angle. Individual shapes have to contribute to the whole. This means that the height and a diagonal measurement are better not the same—legs could be higher or lower, or one of the horizontal measurements altered a little.

These rules are only guides to good design. It is safer to follow them than to ignore them, but design is not an exact science. Art is a feeling and we do not all feel the same. What looks good to one person may seem unsatisfactory to another. To a certain extent taste can be trained. What seemed right to one generation may be unattractive to a later one. The Victorians were preoccupied with decoration and would not accept plain wood. Modern furniture design has gone the other way. If there is a moral to this, it is that we should please ourselves in selecting a design to reproduce, but we must always maintain the general style of that other day. For instance, a Colonial style televison cabinet should be unthinkable, but a nicely proportioned Early American side table should be just as useful today as it was to our forefathers, and just as attractive as a piece of decoration if properly made.

## MATERIALS

Those early craftsmen worked in wood as it came from the tree. It may have been cut to get the best effect from grain markings, and it was seasoned by air drying for several years, but the cabinetmaker did his work in that wood, aided by glue, screws, and nails. If he wanted a wide board and no tree would cut that width, he glued pieces edge to edge. If he wanted a piece for the bottom of a drawer, it was carefully cut thin from solid wood.

Today we have a great many manufactured boards. The one that has had the most effect on furniture this century is plywood, but that has only appeared after the Industrial Revolution. The makers of the furniture that interests us did not have it. Variations on this are blockboard and stripboard. Hardboard is made from wood and appears in some furniture. Particleboard or chipboard, made from pieces of wood embedded in resin, is veneered or covered with plastic to make much modern furniture. Most of these modern materials give us large panels of even character and density, with a regular thickness and mostly no tendency to warp or shrink. All this is fine and a mark of progress, but we have to remember that we have to come back to wood, and wood only, if a reproduction is to have the mark of authenticity.

How true to the original a piece is to be depends on the maker. An enthusiast will not be satisfied with anything except a piece of craftsmanship made of exactly the same materials as the original. This means using the same woods and building them up to width where necessary. It also means choosing an animal glue instead of a modern synthetic one and any nails would be cut instead of machine made. Another maker may decide to keep the general appearance correct, but for a back and a drawer bottom he chooses plywood. Is he doing wrong? If he is making something to please himself and to use in his own home, he is at liberty to make the item of any material he wishes. If he is commissioned to make a reproduction for display or sale, he is doing wrong, unless the other party agrees to the divergence from the original design.

The would-be reproducer of old furniture may come up against a problem of supply. It may not be possible to get a particular wood, or it may no longer be available in the sizes wanted. Fortunately, searching will usually produce what is wanted, even if the local lumberyard says it is impossible. Old and discarded furniture will often produce boards that can be used again. Although the piece of furniture that appeals to you may be made of a particular wood that now proves to be impossible to get, you may be able to use another wood without losing authenticity, if it is of a type that would have been available. Obviously, some exotic wood from Africa would not do, but another native wood should be acceptable. A carpenter in another part of the country or just a few miles away might have used a very different wood for a similar thing.

Akin to the choice of woods is the choice of tools. Tool details are given elsewhere, but there are some general considerations. How much mechanization did the original craftsman have? This depends on the date. When most settlers left Europe, some logs were converted to boards with pit saws, but there were frame saws powered by water wheels or horses. There were no planers and thicknessers. There may have been some rather crude drilling machines. There were certainly lathes producing good work, powered by water, treadle, or an assistant turning a wheel. At first the American cabinetmaker only had the tools he brought with him. His methods had to revert to a century or so earlier than the methods being used at home by the craftsmen who had not emigrated. This meant splitting wood instead of cutting boards. Early conversion of wood was crude, but pit saws and water-powered frame saws were not long in coming into use.

A modern woodworker need not hesitate to use power to cut and plane wood, but it must then be dealt with so all signs of this preparatory work are eradicated. Although craftsmen showed considerable skill in making furniture entirely by hand, there could not be the machinelike precision possible with modern equipment. In any case a board might not come up to size all over, and an inaccurate part might be arranged where it is usually hidden. This means that reproduction work is better for not being perfect, particularly in things like regular thickness or the perfection of a surface that is now fairly easy with power planing and sanding, but might not have been attained with the original hand methods. This does not apply to things like dovetail joints. The old-time craftsman took a pride in his joints. He aimed at perfection there, and usually achieved it, even if wood flatness and thickness showed variations.

## WOOD CONVERSION

There are several ways of converting a log to useful pieces of wood in the form of boards. This applies whether the cutting is done with a pit saw by hand work, with a saw frame powered by water, horses, or steam, or in a modern sawmill. The simplest cuts are parallel and described as "plain sawing" or "through and through." There may be flat surfaces cut top and bottom for ease in controlling the log, but otherwise the log is cut into a number of parallel slabs (Fig. 1-2A). The pattern of grain across the boards varies according to their distance from the center of the log. This affects both appearance and stability of the cut wood.

With wood that gets its beauty from the pattern of the grain, the boards farther from the center can be expected to have a better surface appearance. Against that is the risk of warping and twisting. Sap in the tree has to be dried out by seasoning. The wood will shrink during this process, but this is not uniform. It is more in the direction of the lines of grain in end view than across them. This means that a board cut radially will become a little thinner, but is unlikely to distort (Fig. 1-2B). A board farther out shows grain lines becoming increasingly near parallel to a surface. A convenient way to consider the effect of shrinkage in this case is to think of the grain lines trying to straighten (Fig. 1-2C). In some woods that have been carefully seasoned the amount of distortion is slight and can be corrected by planing, but in other cases the warping may be enough to make the board useless for anything except narrow strips.

Grain in the length of a log is not parallel even if the log is a fairly uniform cylinder. A new layer of grain is formed with each year of growth and this is affected by weather conditions, swaying of the tree, and soil conditions. This lack of mechanical uniformity provides much of the beauty of wood, but it means that its characteristics can vary along a board, so different degrees of shrinkage can cause warping and twisting.

Some woods are most attractive when they show what is often described as "figuring" or "silver grain." This marking is due to medullary rays, which radiate from the center of the tree towards its outside. The rays occur in all trees, but they are not usually visible to the unaided eye. In other woods they appear as attractive markings across the normal grain lines if a board is cut parallel with them. This is called "quarter sawing." To get exact radial cuts means being wasteul (Fig. 1-2D). Fortunately, the silver grain will still show in boards that are not truly radial, so it is possible to cut more economically and still get a majority of boards that show some silver grain.

One way is to first cut the log into 90° quadrants (Fig. 1-2E) and cut boards from this with only the center cut truly radial (Fig. 1-2F). Many of the wide boards may then be expected to show silver grain. Another way is to take a quarter log and make cuts parallel with one side (Fig. 1-2G). This will produce a few boards with silver grain. Other boards may still have interesting normal grain markings, but no visible silver grain. A way of getting more boards with silver grain is to cut a few boards parallel with the side of a quadrant, then turn what is left to make a few more cuts parallel with the other side (Fig. 1-2H). These will be narrower, but should have silver grain markings on their surfaces.

Even with woods that do not show silver grain, quarter sawing will produce boards with less risk of warping. When buying wood for reproduction furniture, you may have to take the wood as it comes from the lumberyard. It is unlikely that you will be able to specify quarter-sawn boards for most woods, but if you examine the yard stock, the lines of grain on the end of a board will show which part of the log section it came from. Even when parallel boards are cut across a log, the

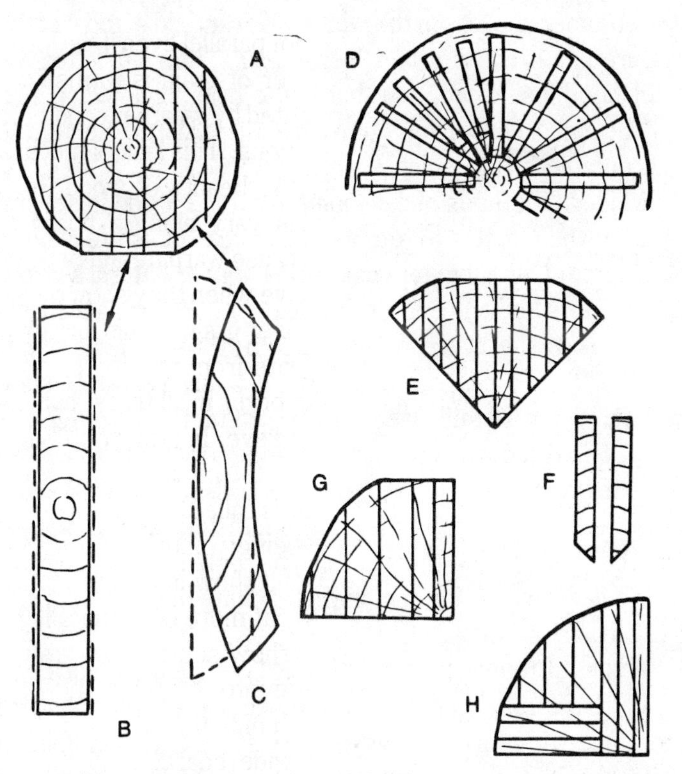

Fig. 1-2. A log cut across (A) produces boards that keep their shape (B) if from the center or may warp if from further out (C). Cutting the boards radially (D) avoids warping, but is wasteful and alternative ways (E-H) give many boards cut near the radius.

ones near the center are the equivalent of quarter-sawn. If you can find pieces where the end grain lines are approximately at right angles to the board surfaces, you will have wood that is unlikely to warp; if it is a type where silver grain may be expected, this is your best chance of seeing it.

If you have the means of power sawing and machine planing, it is often a good policy to obtain wood in larger sections than you need for a particular project; then you can take into account grain direction when you reduce it to the size you want.

## SEASONING

The life blood of a tree is its sap, which may be regarded as unwanted moisture in the wood. There is more sap present in the summer and less in the winter. Getting rid of most of the moisture is a process called "seasoning." Trees felled in the winter need less drying, so that is the traditional felling season. The aim of seasoning is to reduce the moisture content to an acceptable level, which is around 15%.

Modern methods of seasoning treat the wood in several ways, but the effect is to remove the excess moisture in quite a short time. Our ancestors used *air drying* or natural seasoning. If wood is left long enough it will eventually dry, and that is all there is in the process. The length of time necessary is considerable and can run into a great many years. Despite this, air drying is still used. Many craftsmen consider the quality of air dried wood is markedly superior to that which has been seasoned by any of the quick methods. Although waiting many years to use wood may seem difficult, once the initial period has been given, the wood can be replenished as some of the first is drawn off for use, and seasoning that way may not be regarded as delay.

A rule of thumb for air drying is "one year for each one inch of thickness," but this has to be varied according to experience with particular woods. Most air drying is done in flat stacks with the cut boards separated by battens, so air can circulate. There may be a roof to keep off rain and snow, but air has to be free to enter all round.

Lumber from a reputable yard can be expected to have been properly seasoned, but it is good policy to buy wood some time ahead of using it, so it can be stored to complete seasoning in the shop atmosphere or in conditions where the finished piece of furniture will be. Furniture used in a centrally heated room tends to dry out to less than the usual seasoned moisture content. This means that if made as received there is a risk of shrinking or warping with possible splits after it has been in use for some time. If the wood has been allowed to settle in an equivalent atmosphere before being made into furniture it should remain more stable in your finished product.

## FLAWS

Wood is a natural material. As a tree grows, many things happen to it that affect boards which may eventually be cut from it. Branches spread from the trunk. At the junction of every branch there is a knot in a board cut past that point. If it is a tree growing alone, branches are likely to grow from quite low on the trunk, and knots may be expected at any point. In a forest all trees aim to climb upwards ahead of competitors to get the maximum benefit from the sun. This means a forest tree can be expected to have a longer and straighter trunk, and branches will only occur much higher. Some of the greater forest trees yield boards that are knot-free for considerable lengths. In any case, the tendency to grow branches and therefore produce knots varies between different species.

Knots are not necessarily a bad thing. If the knot is a sound "bound" one that forms a definite part of the wood structure, it may be regarded as a decorative feature. A loose "dead" knot can be identified in most woods by a black outline, even if it is not already free to move. This obviously does not contribute any strength and boards with dead knots might have a use in an out of the way place or be cut around to make smaller parts.

"Checks," "splits," and "shakes" are names given to various cracks in wood. Some cannot be avoided. Checks may open along the grain at the ends of boards during seasoning. Ends often have to be sawn off or narrower pieces cut to avoid the checks. This can happen in the ends of boards during seasoning. Ends often have to be sawn off or narrower pieces cut to avoid the checks. This can happen in the ends of boards stored in the shop. Sometimes if you cut across a board, slight checking may start from the new end, but not usually enough to matter.

Shakes occur in the growing tree and cannot usually be detected until it is felled. They are splits due to the twisting and bending of the trees. A shake may follow the curve of the grain or radiate from the center. Nothing can be done about it, except cut around it. Damage to a tree may cause a split. This can happen in handling after felling. Less common are splits due to frost. Coniferous trees may have "pitch pockets," which are like shakes, but full of resin, that do not show until the wood is cut into boards. For structural work they do not have a significant effect on strength, but there is no satisfactory way of obscuring a resin pocket on a finished surface.

In a section of a tree the *heartwood* near the center is better, stronger, and more durable than the *sapwood* around the outside. In some woods the difference is very marked, both in appearance and in durability. Using the wrong part of the tree for an external construction could mean rot in a few years instead of a reasonably long life. Not all woods are affected in this way. In some of the slower growing hardwoods there is nothing to choose in characteristics between heartwood and sapwood, so any part of the tree section can be used.

Outside the wood is the bark, which has no furniture use and any boards with a "waney edge" still holding bark or showing its outline should be trimmed far enough in to remove the obviously weak part immediately under the bark. However, it is interesting to make use of wood that shows uneven outlines or contains flaws. In modern lumber production boards with shakes, loose knots, and other flaws are discarded. If this wood can be obtained it is possible to cut around the problem areas in the way our forefathers did and get pieces that may have more interesting grain than in the straightforward parts of the tree that are necessary to make use of sophisticated conversion equipment.

## WOOD SPECIES

Wood is available all over the world. Compared with many other things used by man, it is easy to extract from its source and convert to use. It is one of the natural products we use that replenishes itself in a comparatively short time. Things like fossil fuels do not regenerate with a speed to be of use to modern man, with his prolific consumption of these materials, but trees may grow to be of use in a few generations.

The wide distribution of trees in all kinds of situations and climates means that the types available run into thousands worldwide. Even in a comparatively small country like England, the supply and variety of woods was considerable, so woodworkers were able to ply their craft with wood that they did not have to go far to find. Elsewhere in Europe forests were larger and the available woods were plentiful. Some of these woods found their way into other countries and around the time of the first settlements in America, European craftsmen were becoming familiar with woods other than those grown nearby. During Colonial times, exploration was going on in other parts of the world. Commerce was established and there was trade in new woods, particularly from the Tropics and Africa in particular. This meant that furniture was beginning to be made from woods previously unknown. Much of this was used for the furniture of the great master cabinetmakers.

The immigrant craftsman arrived in America to find trees in great variety and profusion. He could recognize some as being of the same species as those he knew at home, but there were a great many others, which he had to learn to know and find uses for. England took away large numbers of trees for the masts of her fighting sailing ships, but there seemed an unlimited supply, and there were many species besides those that would make masts. Wood was there, suitable for furniture, implements, house construction and all the needs of a people setting up a new civilization. It did not take long to discover the woods most suitable for particular purposes, both utilitarian and decorative.

Woods have scientific classifications, and these names are needed for positive identificaiton when two woods seem almost the same, but for general identification there are common names, although these vary between communities and users. The pioneer woodworkers who produced the furniture that interests us sometimes used names that were based on woods they had known at home, but were not in fact the same. In some cases the name has stuck—for instance, there are American oaks that would not be recognized as such elsewhere.

Wood is broadly divided into *softwoods* and *hardwoods*, which seem clear definitions, except they do not really define relative hardness or softness, as some hardwoods are softer than some softwoods. The names actually indicate the type of tree. Coniferous trees with needles produce softwoods. Hardwoods come from the broad-leafed trees. Most softwood trees are evergreens. Hardwood trees lose their leaves in the winter.

Hardwood and softwood trees may grow in many climates, but the softwoods used for woodworking grow mostly in the northern temperature parts of North America, Europe, and Asia. Hardwoods have a wide distribution. Some of the more attractive ones for cabinetwork are tropical. Nearly all wood will float in water, but there are exceptions. Lignum vitae and greenheart are very hard and heavy woods that will not float. Even harder is black ironwood *(Krugiogendron ferrum)*, which grows in Southern Florida and Centeral America. At the other extreme another Central America wood is balsa (*Ochroma*), which is technically a hardwood, but is softer and lighter than most softwoods.

Early settlers in most parts of the country found a variety of hardwoods, and these were mostly used for furniture, but softwoods generally offer easier working conditions, particularly when a man's muscles were the only source of power for his tools, so softwoods were used for many things, particularly when quick results rather than durability were important.

## SOFTWOODS

White pine grew plentifully and was much used. The trees grew high, with long straight trunks, so boards of sound wood in long lengths were possible. Such things as benches and tables could be made without waste or the need to cut around flaws. Much of this softwood was used quite thick to compensate for its lesser strength, which was then quite adequate.

Cedar, usually described as red, was another plentiful softwood. Types varied according to locality, with Carolina being considered superior to Virginia, which was supposed to be better than New England, but much cedar furniture was made from the last version of the wood and shipped to other parts of settled America. The aromatic oil that exudes, particularly from the knots, was valued as a moth deterrent in clothes chests.

Other softwoods, variously described as pines, firs, and larches, were used when available. Some of them have characteristics and appearances similar to white pine. In reproduction work it may be necessary to accept a softwood that may not be exactly the same as originally used. Cypress (*Taxodium distichum*) with its greasy feel and sour smell has uses where a resistance to heat and moisture is valuable, but not in normal furniture. Douglas fir, sometimes called Columbian pine, Douglas pine, or Oregon pine (*Pseudotsuga taxiflora*) has modern uses in plywood, but its long straight grain made it more suitable for large structures than for furniture. Redwood, with many other names (*Pinus sylvestris*), was an alternative to white pine. Spruce *(Picea Excelsa)* was considered inferior and only of use for rougher work.

## HARDWOODS

For more durable furniture the choice has to be a hardwood. The uses of some of the native hardwoods became more specialized than in some furniture made in the Old World, where the tendency was to make something like a chair of the same species of wood throughout. Woods were chosen for their characteristics and there might be three or four different woods in one piece of furniture.

The woods available governed what was used in the first instance, but there began to be an interchange of woods overland, and even more from sea transport. As life became more settled and the demand was for better and more fashionable furniture, ships that traded with the West Indies or South America returned with tropical hardwoods that could be made into furniture comparable with some of the best then being made in Europe. However, the country carpenter and furniture maker was mostly dependent on what grew around him and this varied according to his region, as can be seen in the lists below, although there was some overlap and some trees grew outside the specified regions.

**Northern Region.** Ash, aspen, basswood (*Tilia Americana*), yellow birch (*Betula lutea*), butternut, cherry, elm, hickory, locust, hard maple (*Acer saccharum*), oak, walnut.

**Central Region.** White ash (*Fraxinus Americana*), basswood, beech, buckeye, chestnut, cottonwood, American elm (*Ulmus Americana*), hackberry, shagbark hickory (*Quercus Alba*), sycamore, yellow poplar (*Liriodendron tulipifera*), American walnut (*Juglans nigra*).

**Appalachian Region.** Ash, beech, red oak (*Quercus rubra*), hard maple, white oak.

**Southern Region.** Ash, basswood, beech, birch, cottonwood (*Populos dildoides*), elm, hackberry, hictory, locust, maple, red oak and cherry-bark oak, pecan, sweet and red gum (*Liquidambar styraciflua*), sycamore, tupelo gum (*Nyassa aguatica*), black willow (*Salix nigra*).

Some of the woods that were used for Colonial and Early American furniture are listed below, but these are samples and those early woodworkers used whatever came to hand.

**Ash** (*Fraximus exelsior*). This is a white/grey wood with a rather coarse straight grain and little tendency to warp. It is tough and fibrous, with a springiness that made it favored for cart shafts and handles of tools like hammers. It could be steamed for bending and used in this way for curved parts of chairs. Common ash is not very durable in exposed conditions, but the species called "white ash" is better at resisting decay.

**Basswood, or lime** (*Tilia Americana*). A near white wood from the tulip tree. The softwood shows little grain marking and has few knots. Wide boards were used for chests. It is easily worked and was used for carving. Large boards could be shaped into chair seats.

**Beech.** Close-grained, stable, and easily worked. Much used for planes and similar tools. Color varies between reddish brown and white. Turns well on a lathe. Can be steam bent.

**Birch.** Tends to be brittle and can crack; this brown wood makes furniture and its wide boards were used as panels. With a suitable stain it matches mahogany. Does not bend and may split if nailed without pre-drilling.

**Butternut, or white walnut.** Not a very strong wood, but used in furniture, being easily worked.

**Cherry**. This fruit wood could not be obtained in very wide boards, but its deep reddish heartwood and pinker sapwood gave it an attractive appearance for making furniture. Age enhances the appearance. Frequent tool sharpening was necessary to get a good finish.

**Chestnut** (*Castanea sativa*). This is the wood of the sweet chestnut, not the horse chestnut. It looks similar to English oak, but does not have any obvious silver grain when quarter-sawn. Its main use was for structural parts of drawers and cabinets.

**Elm** (*Ulmus*). Common elm has a confused brown grain with a resistance to splitting. Large trees produced wide boards, many of which were used for chair seats. Besides furniture it has uses in wagon building and boat building. Rock elm (*Ulmus thomasi*) and wych elm (*Ulmus glabra*) are straighter-grained, hard, strong and suitable for steam bending.

**Hickory**. A very hard wood suitable for steam bending and used for the bows at the backs of chairs and similar applications. A springy wood with very similar characteristics to ash, but with closer, harder and more attractive grain. Hickory had many applications in wagon building and this demand caused a shortage.

**Locust**. Another chair seat wood, this very hard wood dries from a tan to a grey/yellow color and is very durable, although it does not take nails readily.

**Mahogany.** This is a name covering a range of woods, not native to Northern America, but it was a popular furniture wood in Europe and supplies came into America by the beginning of the seventeenth century. Spanish or Cuban mahogany (*Swietenia mahogani*) was a rich brown and the well known furniture wood. Honduras mahogany, or baywood (*Swietenia macrophyela*) was lighter in weight and color but otherwise similar.

**Maple**. Varieties are known as "rock maple," "hard maple," and "sugar maple." This is strong and hard with a great many woodworking applications as well as many parts of furniture. Some of the twists in a tree produced special grain formations, such as "bird's eye maple," which was used in veneers.

**Oak** (*Quercus*). The dark brown open-grained English oak was famous for building fighting sailing ships, also much medieval furniture. It is the oak most suitable for quarter sawing to show silver grain. This, and other oaks, can be cleft or split, so it allowed cleaving with a froe or axe as an alternative to sawing in the length. Red oak *(Quercus rubra)* has similar characteristics, but with a reddish tinge in the color. White oak is another variety. All parts and kinds of furniture have been made of oak. Quarter-sawn oak may be described as "wainscot oak," from its use in the paneling around a room, or from an earlier German word for a wagon side.

**Poplar, yellow or canary wood** (*Liriodendron tulipfera*). An even close-grained yellow/white wood, similar to basswood, with which it is sometimes confused.

**Sycamore** (*Acer pseudoplatanus*). This is related to the plane tree and has been confused with it in history. The white/yellow hardwood is close-grained with ripples often apparent in the grain. It has a clean look and has been used for equipment and furniture associated with food, because of its hygienic appearance. Turns well. "Fiddle-back" markings make it suitable for veneers.

**Walnut** (*Juglans nigra*). Brown/purple close-grained wood that finishes to an attractive surface. A stable wood that is easy to work. Outside of America this is "American black walnut" to distinguish it from the lighter colored European walnut.

# Tools and Techniques

The modern woodworking shop, whether its user is amateur or professional, is becoming increasingly mechanized. Electric power is convenient and lends itself to the use of tools that have their own motors. While some tools are fixed, others are portable and take their built-in small motors with them. The overall effect is to take much of the drudgery out of routine tasks and make the performing of accurate and often intricate work comparatively easy. Of course, there is nothing wrong with this and it is a welcome sign of progress in technique, but it leads to a dependence on power, and many modern craftsmen turn to power tools for even the simplest task, so their attitude toward craftwork is very different from the days when the workman had to provide power with his muscles to make any tool work.

The makers of Colonial and Early American furniture did their work almost entirely by hand. Sawyers converted the logs to boards, which were then seasoned before being supplied to the man at the bench. From there on it was his problem to take a rough-surfaced piece of wood, that might have warped or split, and convert it into furniture by using his hand tools. He had to scheme the best way to cut the parts he needed, so as to avoid flaws and benefit from the way of the grain. He would also be considering how to do this with economy of effort. He was close to the wood he was using and developed an affinity and feel for wood in its different species. He knew from the choice of wood and how it behaved under the first strokes of the plane, what its characteristics were and what sort of finish he could expect to get.

Much of this feeling for wood is lacking in modern methods. Someone else has converted the wood and it has been artificially seasoned. Any part with flaws has been discarded, long before the wood comes into the hands of the cabinetmaker. So far as it is possible to be, wood supplied is a substance of uniform size and quality bought by the length. The opportunity to take a piece of wood in its early stages and make use of twisted grain, adapt designs to suit, and arrange construction to feature unusual grain markings is no longer ours. Wood for making furniture is almost as much a factory product as cloth sold by the yard. This is a pity for anyone wanting to make reproduction furniture, but it is still possible to produce worthwhile results. If anyone has an opportunity to obtain wood from an earlier stage in its conversion, getting authentic appearances is that much easier and more interesting.

If he wishes, a copier of early furniture may go back to those hand methods. This may give him much satisfaction, but what he produces may look no different from a similar thing made by another craftsman who takes advantage of modern power tools as well as hand tools. The skill comes in using power tools without this being discernable in the finished piece of furniture. This means that finishing stages should be by hand. Power tools may lessen the labor of early stages and get parts close to finished sizes, but there should be enough wood left for hand tool work to completely obliterate any evidence of power tools.

## POWER TOOLS

It is reasonable in modern furniture making to use a power planer and thicknesser to get wood to size and smooth surfaces, then follow with power sanding. You do not need to have a great experience of examining furniture to see from the wood when this was the way it was treated. A power planer leaves a good surface, but it is different from the surface left by hand planing. The rotating cutters hitting the surface leave ridges across the wood. With hasty work they may be very obvious, but with sharp cutters and slowly fed wood, the effect is much smoother although the discerning eye can detect the method used. Power sanding may obliterate the machine plane marks, but it suffers from being too good for period furniture. The surface is very uniformly smooth, in a way that would be almost impossible to achieve by hand work. Obviously, evidence of these modern methods in a copy of an original of 200 years ago would destroy some of its authenticity and diminish the satisfaction to be got from it by its maker and owner.

If the available wood has to be brought to size to suit the cutting list for the furniture being made, this can be done with a table or other power saw and power planing can be used to smooth the surfaces, but a little should be left for completion by hand planing. In effect, this gets the wood to the stage that the old-time craftsman did with his jack plane, although accuracy is likely to be much greater.

The tool to follow is a smoothing plane. It need not be a traditional wooden one, but a modern metal plane, such as the Stanley 4 or 4½, is suitable. Its purpose is to remove enough of the surface to destroy any evidence of machine planing. If in the process it slightly destroys some of the perfection of machine planing, that is not a fault for this type of work. If a straightedge or square is put across an original article, it is possible to detect how the craftsman was aiming at precision but did not quite make it. This is a feature of work that is exclusively by hand—accuracy to a stage that was adequate for the intended purpose was all that was needed. If a surface, such as a quality table top, had to be flat to look right, time was spent getting it accurate, but if such quality was not vital in something of less importance, the standard worked to was not as high.

Machine work may get something close to perfection with little effort on the part of the operator. While this is a desirable attribute in much modern cabinetmaking, there are parts of older furniture that did not have such exactness of finish, and perfection in a part of a reproduction that would not have had it in an original could be too obvious evidence of machine work.

Power saws of various types can be used. Originally, general sawing was with hand saws and a backsaw was the general-purpose saw for cutting on the bench. Most woodworkers have one, but it would be advisable to make more use of it in reproduction work. It is possible to make some of the traditional types of joints with power tools, but the marks left on the wood by a circular saw or a band saw are different from those left by hand sawing. In most cases the sawn edge will get further treatment or be hidden, but if evidence of the use of power saws is to be avoided, it is advisable to get into the habit of making more use of a backsaw.

## HANDWORK

When woodwork was all done by hand it was customary to plane one surface and one edge at right angles to it and mark them as the "face side" and "face edge" with a traditional pencil marking (Fig. 2-1A). Other marking and measuring was arranged to use these as data. A try square was always used against one of these faces. If there was to be a saw cut across the grain, the fibers were first severed with a knife (Fig. 2-1B). The knife line was "squared around" all four faces for a cut right through. With power tools this sort of working is not

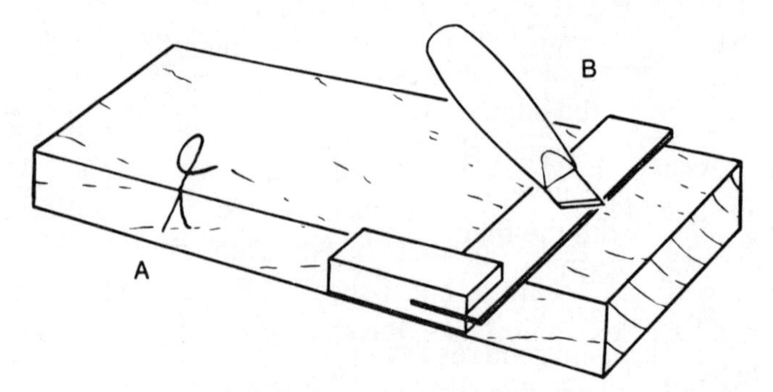


Fig. 2-1. The face side and edge are traditionally marked (A). Lines at right angles are marked with a try square and knife (B).

so important, but when working on reproduction furniture, adoption of these methods helps in getting accuracy with the greater use of hand tools, as well as influencing your attitude to the work, so you get more of a feeling akin to that of the original craftsman.

Many woods do not yield as smooth a surface as may be required from planing. A power sander may do all that is necessary to finish this smoothly on modern furniture, but the handworking craftsman followed planing by scraping, particularly on parts of hardwood with grain that tore up whichever way it was planed. Quite often this was an interesting feature included for the sake of appearance. There are hooked scrapers available today and others with the scraper blade mounted in a body like a plane or spokeshave. Earlier workers had similar tools, but they usually depended on a scraper that was just a rectangular piece of tool steel of the type used in saw blades.

Mastery of such a scraper is a big help in finishing period furniture. The method of sharpening this and the blades mounted in bodies is unusual, but not difficult. The edge of the scraper should be straight and at right angles to the sides (Fig. 2-2A). It can be filed, but it should be rubbed smooth on a flat oilstone (Fig. 2-2B). The next step is rubbing with a hard piece of steel, which may be a round burnisher (Fig. 2-2C) or it can be done with an ordinary gouge or chisel. The object is to turn over the edge, by angling the rubbing a little one way and then the other (Fig. 2-2D). The amount turned over may be quite slight, and felt rather than seen. Scraping is done by pushing or pulling the scraper over the wood surface at an angle that causes the turned edge to cut (Fig. 2-2E). It is usual to bend the sheet steel scraper slightly so the cutting edge meets the wood at a slight curve. If the scraper is to be pushed, it is held at the sides with the thumbs pushing the center forward to a curve (Fig. 2-2F).

Scraping can be done diagonally to the grain or in any direction that gets good results. The scraper should be angled so it removes very thin shavings. If the waste comes away as dust and the angle is right, that is a sign that the edge is blunt.

It can be restored several times by first rubbing the burr straight, using the burnisher on the flat surfaces (Fig. 2-2G), then turning it over again (Fig. 2-2D). When this no longer works, sharpening is started again from the beginning.

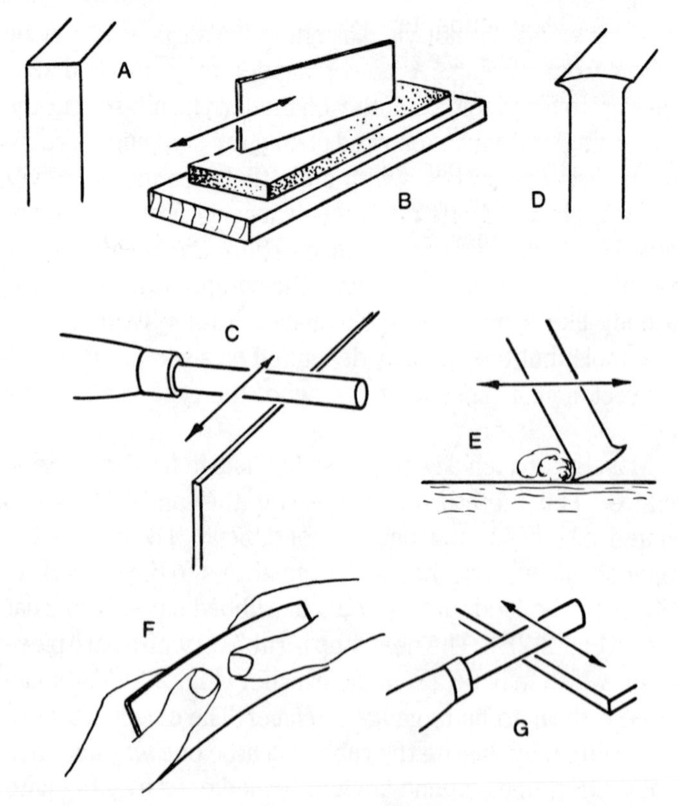


Fig. 2-2. A steel scraper starts with a square edge (A) rubbed on an oilstone (B), then a hard steel burnisher (C) turns over the edges (D) to give a cutting action (E). This is helped by curving the scraper (F). When worn, the edge is rubbed flat with the burnisher (G) and sharpening started again.

## SHAPING

Shaped outlines can be cut with a saber saw or a band saw. Originally these shapes were cut with a framed bow saw, a keyhole saw or other narrow hand saw. As the surface is likely to be treated by further tool work it is improbable that any of the regular and distinctive power sawing surface will remain. Nearly all these outlines were smoothed with a spokeshave, but this was the wooden type with a low-angled cutter (Fig. 2-3A) and not the higher-angled cutter more like a plane in a metal body (Fig. 2-3B). The older type is pleasanter to use and gives a good finish. One or more should be obtained, if possible. Modern hand shaping is more likely to be done with a filing action, using either a woodworking rasp or a Surform tool. These are acceptable on reproduction work, but care is needed to follow with enough sanding to remove all marks they make. Very little filing of wood was done by hand craftsmen. This was partly because the craftsman considered wood should be cut and not just rubbed away, and partly because the only files and rasps available were rather inefficient tools.

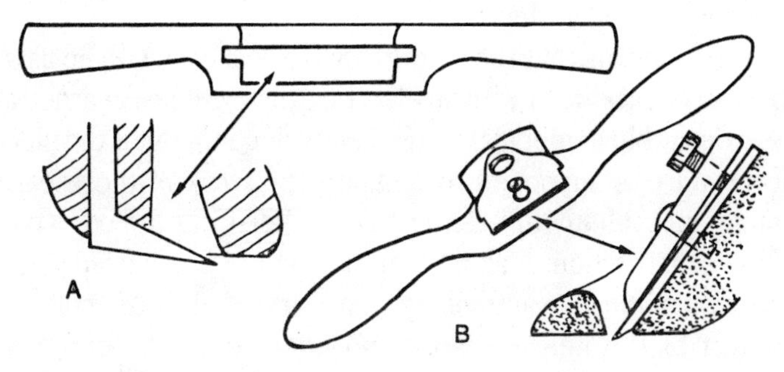


Fig. 2-3. A traditional wooden spokeshave has a low cutting angle (A). A modern one has a higher angle (B) like a plane.

There has to be more chisel work in shaping and making joints than may be needed in modern furniture. Modern chisels and gouges cut in the same way as those of 200 years ago, so there is nothing wrong in using them and leaving surfaces from them. There may have to be more chisels available than needed for modern work, as traditional joints have to be cut and cleaned up, with the different constructions involved. Extra chisels worth having are long thin paring types, perferably with beveled edges, and one or two stout mortise chisels.

A problem comes in the production of grooves, dadoes, and rabbets. Most of us have power tools that make these cuts easily and accurately. If it is a side of a joint into which another part will fit and the method of cutting is not obvious, there is nothing wrong with using a power tool, but if it is something that will be visible, like a rabbet forming part of a decorative edge, the power part of the work should only remove the bulk of the waste and the job be finished with a rabbet plane, or there should be scraping and sanding in the recess enough to remove evidence of power cutting.

One of the biggest differences between the tool kit of the Colonial carpenter and the modern woodworker was in the means of making holes. Right up to the Industrial Revolution, the quality and efficiency of hole making equipment was not as high as the tools available for other woodworking processes. It needed engineering thought and factory methods to produce drills and the means of driving them to make good clean holes of many sizes and depths.

This means that the smooth cylindrical hole with no flaws that can be produced with an electric drill might be regarded as very desirable in modern furniture production, but if the piece of furniture is supposed to emulate the work of those early immigrant craftsmen, it is too good. If holes are drilled as part of the construction, making part of a joint or being filled with a screw, a modern exact hole is what is needed. If the hole will be part of the finished work and open to view, something should be done to roughen and make it slightly inaccurate. Drilling with a center bit in a brace may give a better look than using a rapidly-rotating bit in an electric drill. Hand drilling from one side until the point shows through, then turning over and drilling back into it, should produce a more authentic appearance.

## FINISHES

Abrasives play a large part in modern woodworking. Power sanders of various types do useful work. There were abrasives in the early days, but they were neither plentiful nor good. There was also a different attitude to woodworking craftsmanship. There was a pride in getting a finish from the tools. The surface left from a sharp plane or chisel might be followed by scraping, but in much furniture that was all. Some old furniture that has survived may now have a smooth mellow sheen, but that is more likely to be the effect of long use and some later owner's application of polish, than any original treatment.

This means that any reproduction should have a good tool finish and any sanding be by hand and kept to a minimum. Power sanding is best avoided. Early sanding was with sand, and the name has survived, although modern abrasives are many things, but not sand. Powdered glass was also used. There were sheets of abrasive paper with the sand or glass spread on glue, but abrasive powders were also used on a cloth pad, sometimes wet. Modern hand sanding is best done with abrasive paper wrapped around a block. Traditionally this was a block of cork, but it can be wood, preferably faced with a piece of stiff rubber or other material with a slightly greater resiliance than wood. Sand *with* the grain, to avoid marks that may show through any finish. Slight rounding of corners is acceptable. Any sanding of end grain should be thorough, but not such that it gives the appearance of power sanding.

It is necessary to decide what final appearance is required. When the things we are considering were first made, the cabinetmaker aimed to give the work as good an appearance as possible. If it has now been in use for a century or more, it will have acquired the patina of age; it will show signs of use; it may have evidence of damage; it will have that well worn appearance we expect. What do we expect of a reproduction? Do we want to make something comparable to the work as first produced or do we want to make something that looks old? Only the maker and user can decide. It seems a form of mild cheating to pass off something made now as being old. It is very unlikely to pass scrutiny and be accepted as an old piece of work. Trying to pass a reproduction as a genuine antique could bring trouble with the law.

Nevertheless many people find furniture with an old appearance attractive, although they know it is of recent construction. Others prefer a reproduction that looks like the original probably did when new. This latter attitude seems to be the preferable one for the maker to adopt. If he wants to make it look old, there are ways of "distressing" it.

## GLUES, SCREWS, AND NAILS

Coupled with tool work are fastenings and fittings, findings or hardware. The only glue used in the original work was produced from animal bones, hoofs, and sometimes fish. This was melted in a two-part glue pot, with water in the outer container and the glue in the inner one, so the glue was never overheated. It was a foul-smelling mixture. If obtained from another supplier and not made by the carpenter, it came in resinlike slabs to be broken up and melted. The glue has a reasonable strength under dry conditions, but would lose its hold when wet. However, there is much furniture from times earlier than Colonial days still sound and with elaborate veneer decorations undamaged, all secured with this sort of glue.

Such glue is not obsolete, but very nearly so, and getting any may be difficult. There are more recent glues that are basically the same, but more refined so the smell is less objectionable and application is easier. Some can be used direct from the can, but the better ones need moderate heating in hot water. Anyone wishing to make glued joints as near as possible in the same way as the original workers, will find these glues suitable.

Most modern glues are synthetic and mostly stronger than those earlier types. Some are either water resistant or fully waterproof. These are obviously desirable features, but not consistent with the characteristics that the original craftsman had in his adhesive. However, in most constructions the glue is not obvious when the work is finished and the use of a modern glue should not detract from the appearance and effectiveness of the article of furniture. It should produce greater strength. There are some experts who can identify the adhesive from an exposed glue line, so if the work is to pass any scrutiny, it might be better to use a traditional glue in a place like an exposed dovetail corner joint, where fairly extensive glue lines are visible.

Lack of trust in glue and a reluctance to use it can be seen in the way some furniture was designed and assembled so that joints interlocked. Joints were sometimes made with one piece of wood passing through another and then spread by wedging, so even without glue the mechanical layout resists separation. These and other joints are described in the next chapter.

Screws were known, but early ones were without points, and the threads were not as clean as modern ones. They were probably not very plentiful. Consequently, much early woodwork was without screws. Fortunately, the surface appearance was much the same as today, so if modern screws are used (slotted and not Phillips heads) they should look right. Steel screws should look sufficiently like the early iron ones. Modern brass screws are yellower than early ones. Bronze screws look more like older brass.

Nails are more of a problem, although it is only the heads which show. Round wire nails have been in use for a long time, but they do not go back further than the Industrial Revolution. Earlier iron nails were individually forged or cut from sheet metal. On the surface the appearance was a plain rectangle, without any of the pattern seen on some machine-made nails. Such nails can still be obtained from specialist suppliers, but it may be possible to file the heads of other nails to give an acceptable appearance on the surface.

It was only in less important work that nail heads were left on the surface. Otherwise they were punched below the surface and the hole filled with a stopping. This means that almost any nail could be used in that reproduction, but a rectangular head punched in leaves a rectangular hole at the surface, not a round one, so it is worthwhile filing a piece of iron to make a punch with a rectangular end to give an authentic look after driving in the nail.

In some cases nails were forged with decorative heads which were left standing on the furniture. It is possible to buy reproduction nails for this purpose, but an alternative is to make the joint with any nail, which is punched and covered with a head filed to shape on a short stub. It can be held in with epoxy glue.

Much hardware was wrought iron, made by a local smith. Some copies can be bought. It would be unwise to spoil the work by using modern hardware. Early hinges were rather crude. Most extended over the surface to provide a grip, and were often given decorative outlines. Modern butt hinges to mount in the thickness of the wood came later. Metal handles mostly had flat brass plates filed to a pleasing shape, with wire bails fixed to bolts or other simple arrangements. More elaborate handles were imported.

To avoid metalwork many handles were of wood, either bars or turned knobs. Pictures of period furniture should be examined to see the styles made.

There were no mass-production fittings. Where handles or other items of hardware bolted through, nuts were individually made and not the hexagonal or square patterns standardized today. Shapes were usually only roughly squared.

# Joints

It is in the way parts of an assembly are joined that cabinetwork made by hand methods differs most from things made with the help of power tools. Much modern work has quite satisfactory methods of assembly that have been developed to suit techniques appropriate to machines of various sorts. Even today there are different methods of construction between furniture made in factories and that made by individual workers. Factories have large and expensive machines, while the individual craftsman has portable power tools and less advanced shop tools. Even the simplest equipped modern woodworking shop has equipment that the carpenter of 200 years ago would regard as so advanced and sophisticated that he could not comprehend much of it.

This means that anyone wanting to make reproductions of early furniture should do some rethinking. The original craftsman joined his wooden parts in ways that were suited to his hand tools. Many of the joints also took into account the fact that they had to provide strength and security without such a dependence on glue as is possible today. Dowels were not unknown, but they were made individually and there was no ready supply of quantity-produced ones, so doweling did not play as big a part in construction as it does today. Other joints were cut in the solid wood to serve the same purpose and the mortise and tenon joint was commonest in many situations where a modern assembly would be with dowels.

It may be possible to use dowels or power tool joints in some reproduction furniture in places where they would not be apparent, but for most articles of period furniture, traditional joints should be chosen. The original craftsman had to do quite a lot of heavy chopping with chisels and mallet. His modern counterpart can lessen the labour by removing waste with a power drill or other tool, but finishing the joint will usually have to be by hand. Tenons can be cut with a circular saw, sides of dovetails may be cut with a band saw, a router can remove waste from a groove or dado, but what is important is that the finished joint has the same form as it would have done when made entirely by hand.

Anyone unfamiliar with traditional hand-made joints may find it worthwhile to spend some time practicing joints on scrap pieces of wood, before moving on to make furniture using these methods. If a specimen joint is made completely by hand, the problems of the original worker can be appreciated. It will also be possible to think of ways of using any available power tools to ease the labor of cutting the multiplicity of joints there may be in the cabinetwork being planned. There is really no virtue in reverting to solely hand methods if a modern power aid can make the work easier and often more accurate. Obviously, it would be wrong to go so far as to alter the visible joints to suit power and get an incorrect appearance. There are some modern versions of older joints that have been adapted to suit power, and the appearance is no longer the same, as will be seen in some examples later.

## EDGE JOINTS

One problem in the days before manufactured boards of reasonable width was the making up of narrower pieces to get the size required for such things as table tops and the backs of cabinets. The width of available boards depends on the size of the tree. Wide boards were probably more generally available then than they are now. Care was taken in conversion to keep a board as wide as possible, where today it is more likely to be ripped down to a standard width. Even with the widest boards, edge joints were essential in many cases. Some woods, such as some choice varieties from fruit trees, were no more than 6 in. wide in any case, so widths had to be made up for many pieces of furniture.

The simplest edge-to-edge joint is a glued one. Both edges have to be perfect right angles if the surfaces are to finish in the same plane (Fig. 3-1A). The hand worker used a "shooting" or "shuting" board to hold the wood and on which he slid his long trying or shuting plane (Fig. 3-1B). If a power planer is available, edges can be planed true with little trouble, but there are some points to watch. A machine-planed surface does not take glue as well as a hand-planed one. Glue gets a grip by entering the pores of the wood and power planing tends to close many of them. It is advisable to follow power planing of edges to be glued with a skim over of a hand plane.

There is a tendency for edge joints to open at the ends, if they weaken at all. As a guard against this, edges should be planed very slightly hollow; then a bar clamp arranged centrally will press the ends of the joint together (Fig. 3-1C). Other useful devices are "pinch dogs" (Fig. 3-1D), which were used by early carpenters and are still available. Driving one into each end of a joint uses a wedge action to press the boards together (Fig. 3-1E).

So far as possible, boards should be arranged so they compensate for each other's tendency to warp. If grain lines are through the thickness there is unlikely to be much movement, but with the curves of grain about the same way as the surfaces of the boards, arranging pieces opposite ways will make any overall warping minimal (Fig. 3-1F).

Although a simple glued joint should have adequate strength for many purposes there are ways of further stiffening it. Dowels may be arranged between the parts (Fig. 3-1G). Groove the dowels to let air and surplus glue ooze out, and make the holes slightly deeper than needed so the dowels do not hit the bottoms before the surfaces are tight.

An interesting version of doweling used in early construction was "secret slot screwing," and this is just as useful

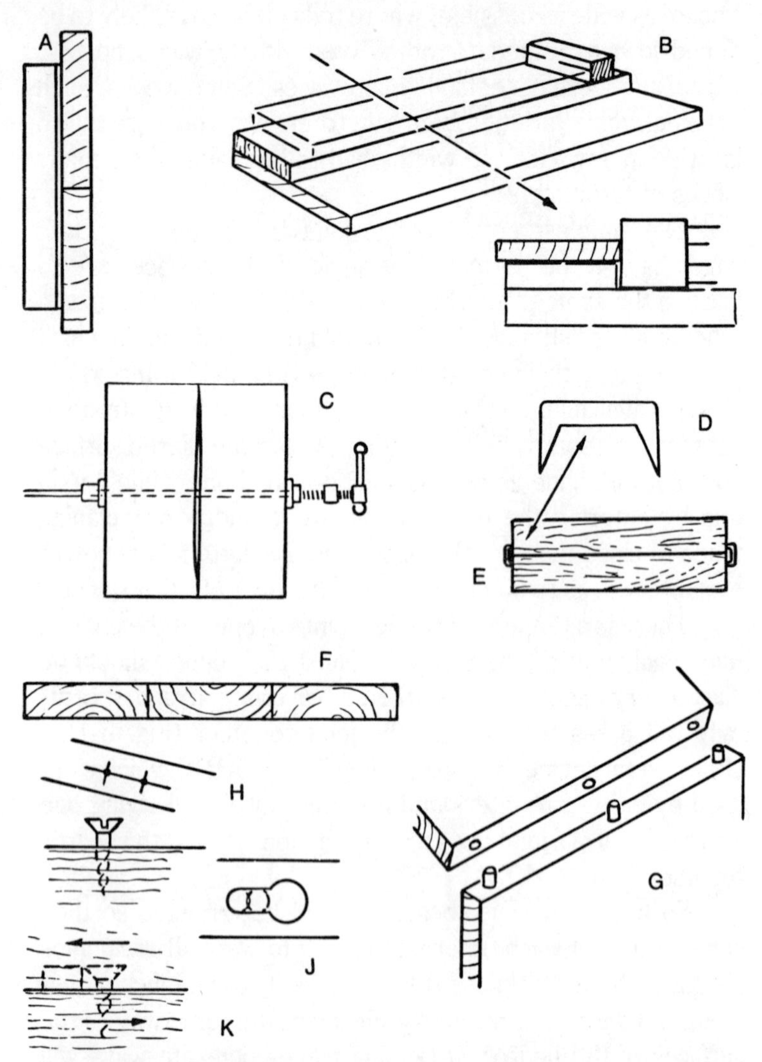


Fig. 3-1. Boards joined to make up width should assemble flat (A) and a shuting board (B) helps to guide the plane to get the edges square. Planing edges hollow (C exaggerated) gets joint ends tight. Dogs (D) are alternatives to clamps to pull joints together (E). Any risk of warping is minimized if grain directions are alternated (F). Dowels strengthen joints (G). Secret slot screwing (H-K) is another way of strengthening and closing joints.

today. Stout screws are driven at intervals into one edge, until the heads are ¼ in. to ⅜ in. above the surface. Their positions are marked on the other piece, with additional centers about ½ in. away (Fig. 3-1H). Holes large enough to clear the heads are drilled at these positions, and a slot is made from each to the other positions, started by drilling a series of holes of a size to clear the neck of each screw (Fig. 3-1J). A trial assembly is made by inserting the screw heads in their mating clearance holes, then one board is driven along the other. The screw heads will cut their way along as their necks pass along the slots (Fig. 3-1K). Knock the boards back and dismantle them. Give each screw a tightening quarter turn. Apply glue and knock the joint together again. Tightening the screws will have put on just that little more clamping thrust.

Joints are made today with splines in plowed grooves (Fig. 3-2A). The spline is quite often plywood. If this is used, it would not do for the plywood to be visible in furniture copied from something belonging to the days before plywood. There could be a cross-grained piece of solid wood at each exposed end of the plywood joint.

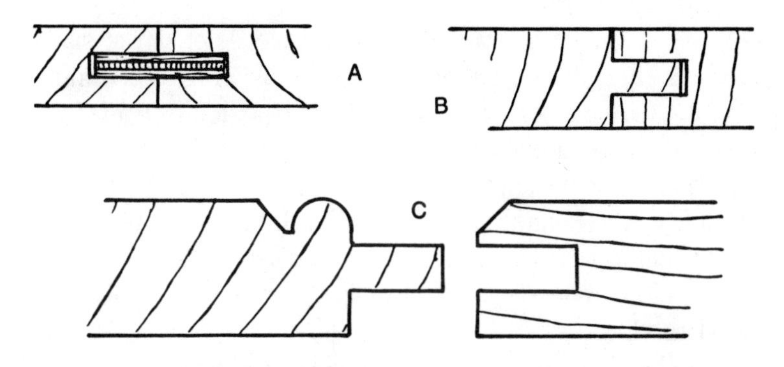


Fig. 3-2. Tongue and grooved joints may be close and glued (A and B), but they may be beaded for decoration and assembled dry to allow for expansion and contraction (C).

Similar to this is a *tongue and groove* joint (Fig. 3-2B). Matching planes were used for Early American furniture. Such a joint was glued to make a solid joint, but a variation of it was used to allow for expansion and contraction when many boards had to be used to make a back for something broad, like a hutch. The joints were left without glue, but the ends of the boards were nailed or screwed. The exposed side of the joint was made less severe by working a bead on the edge of one piece and a matching bevel on the other (Fig. 3-2C). The joint could then open and close appreciably and still look attractive.

Matching planes are no longer made, although they may sometimes be found amongst old tools, but the parts of these joints can be made with power tools. This type of backing to open shelving is necessary and preferable to any sort of more recent flat sheet material if the result is to look authentic.

## HALVING JOINTS

When two pieces of wood cross each other at or near the same level, they have to be notched into each other in a *halving* or *half lap* joint. The crossing does not have to be at right angles; an example of a diagonal crossing comes in some bottom rails of a rectangular table. The crossing does not have to be within the length of both pieces of wood, but can be at the end of one or at a corner between the two, although there are usually better joints for these situations.

The simplest half lap joint has two pieces of similar size crossing (Fig. 3-3A), either flat or on edge (Fig. 3-3B) in a *cross lap*. If one meets the other in a T-shape, it is a *middle lap* (Fig. 3-3C). At a corner it is an *end lap* (Fig. 3-3D). If the pieces are of different thicknesses, it is stronger to not cut much from the thinner part (Fig. 3-3E). If there may be a pull on the center part of a middle lap joint, it can be given a dovetail shape, either one (Fig. 3-3F) or both sides (Fig. 3-3G) to resist the load.

In the traditional hand cutting method, the two parts are prepared and the face surfaces marked. The width of each piece is marked on the other, using the actual pieces of wood instead of measuring with a rule. These lines are squared around the wood with a pencil. A marking gauge is set to half the thickness and used to mark both sides of both pieces, with its stock against the face side each time. What is to be cut out of each piece is marked (Fig. 3-4A). Where the saw cuts are to come the fibers are severed by going over the pencil lines with a knife. A fine back saw is used and kept on the waste side of the line. For small work this can usually be done by eye, but for larger work a chisel cuts a guiding groove inside the knife line (Fig. 3-4B).

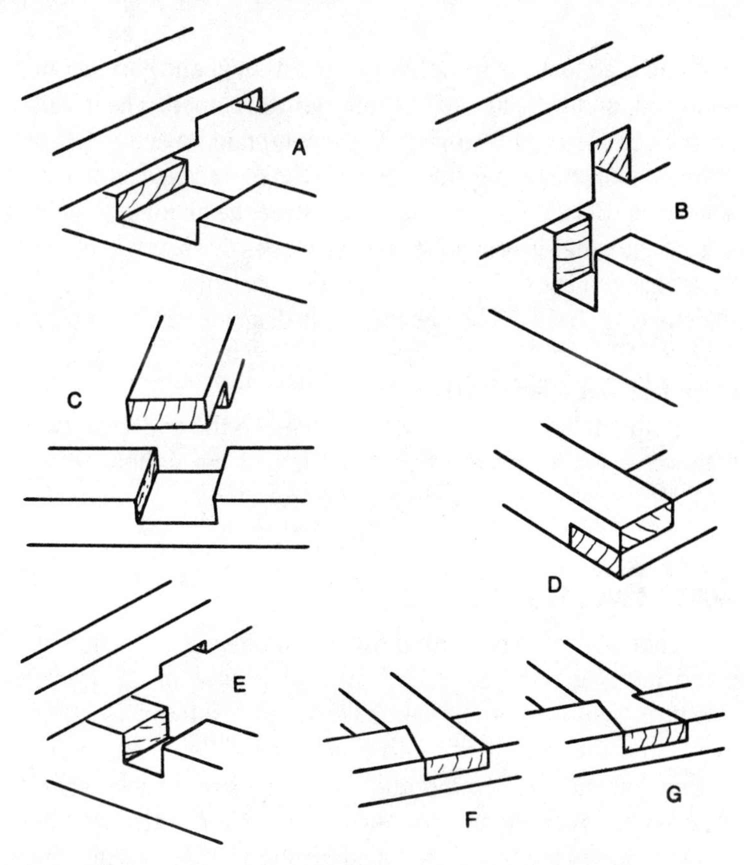


Fig. 3-3. There are many variations on the crosslap joint in traditional furniture. Basically half is cut from each crossing piece (A) and B), but the joint may come at the end of one piece (C) or at a corner (D). For different sizes (E) the cut is uneven. Dovetail shapes (F and G) will resist pull.

After sawing down the side of each groove, the waste is removed with a wide chisel, working upwards in turn from each side, to get down to the gauge lines (Fig. 3-4C), then cuts are made straight across (Fig. 3-4D).

Even when power tools are available, it is probably wisest to mark out in the same way and saw across the grain with a handsaw, but the waste may be removed with a router. The best joint is a drive fit, that finishes level on the face sides. It is better to make the cut-out parts very slightly hollow than to have the centers high.

With other cross laps, marking out may be adapted to suit a diagonal crossing or thick and thin pieces, but the method of working is almost the same. With a middle lap, one part has an open end, and with an end lap both parts are open. These can be cut completely by sawing. The open-ended piece is left a little too long and it is gauged around the end as well as on the sides (Fig. 3-4E). A cut is made across at the shoulder. Hand sawing the other way is done in three stages to ensure keeping to the gauged lines. The first cut is diagonal into one side and the end (Fig. 3-4F). The second cut is diagonal the other way (Fig. 3-4G), and the third one straight through, so the waste piece falls out (Fig. 3-4H).

With a table saw it is possible to make the end grain cut with one pass, using the fence and height adjustment (Fig. 3-4J). If there is a small amount of excess length on the end, this can be planed level after the joint has been glued.

## MORTISE AND TENON JOINTS

This type of joint, with a tongue of one piece projecting into a cavity in another piece, has a wider use in traditional furniture than any other joint. The tenon is the projecting piece, and the hole it fits into is a mortise (less frequently spelled "mortice"). Some of the applications of the joint have been taken over in modern furniture with dowels, mainly because dowel joints are more adaptable to mechanical production methods.

When there was no good reason for doing otherwise the mortise in a straightforward joint was made one-third the width of the wood or to the width of the mortise chisel nearest to this.

In the basic *full* mortise and tenon joint between pieces of wood of the same thickness, the tenon goes right through (Fig. 3-5A). If the tenon does not go through, it is a *stub* mortise and tenon joint (Fig. 3-5B). If the tenoned part is thinner, it may be a *bare-faced* mortise and tenon joint (Fig. 3-5C).

If the two pieces meet at a corner and the joint is open, it is more likely to be called a *bridle* joint. Neither this nor the end lap joint have much place in good quality cabinetwork. Instead, there is a *haunched* mortise and tenon joint. This can be

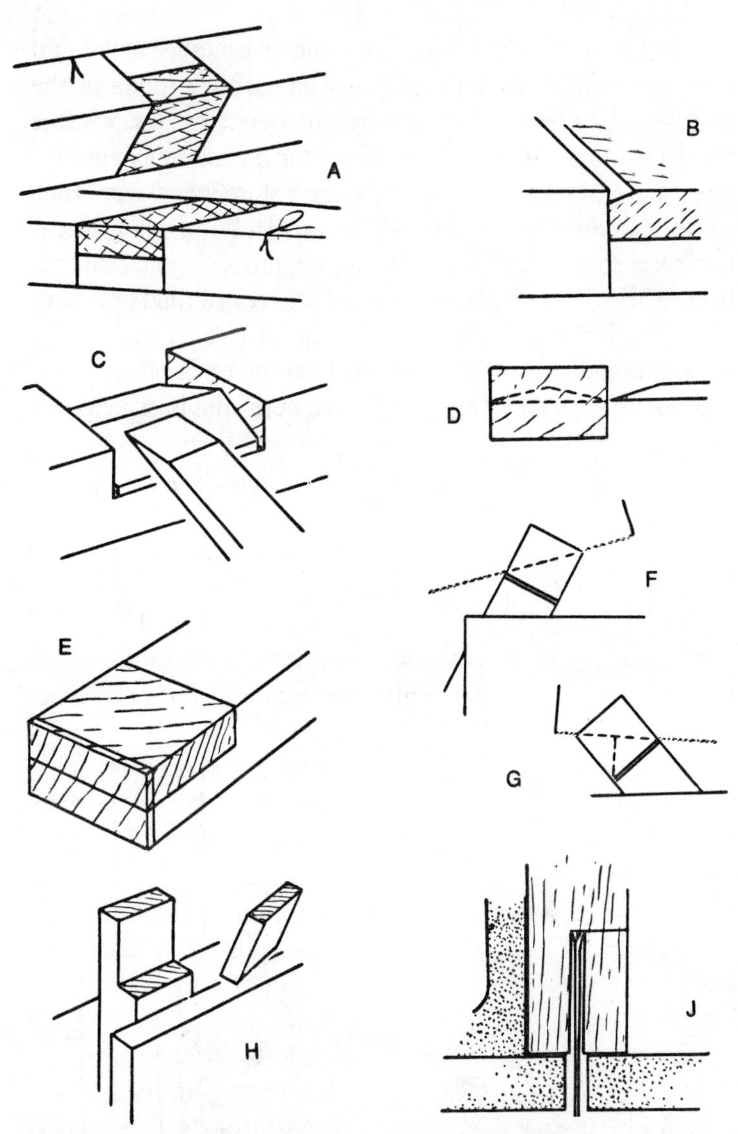


Fig. 3-4. For hand cutting crosslap joints the parts are marked (A), a chisel slice inside the line (B) guides the saw. Waste is chiseled from both sides (C and D). An end is sawn (E-H) in stages. A table saw will cut accurately (J).

worked in two ways. In one, the tenon is cut back so a short stub goes into a groove and is visible in the finished joint (Fig. 3-5D). This may be used when the frame is grooved to take a panel, but otherwise it is better to taper the haunch (Fig. 3-5E).

A full mortise and tenon joint may be merely glued, but examples will be found that are wedged. The ends of the mortise are beveled outwards slightly. In one method wedges are driven outside the tenon (Fig. 3-5F). In another method there are saw cuts made in the tenon before it is driven, then wedges driven into these cuts (Fig. 3-5G). If the tenon is near square, a single wedge may be driven into a diagonal saw cut (Fig. 3-5H). In all cases, the ends of the wedges and tenon are cut off and planed level. A stub tenon can be tightened by *fox-tail wedging*. Saw cuts are made in the ends of the tenon and wedges inserted (Fig. 3-5J), so as the joint is driven they

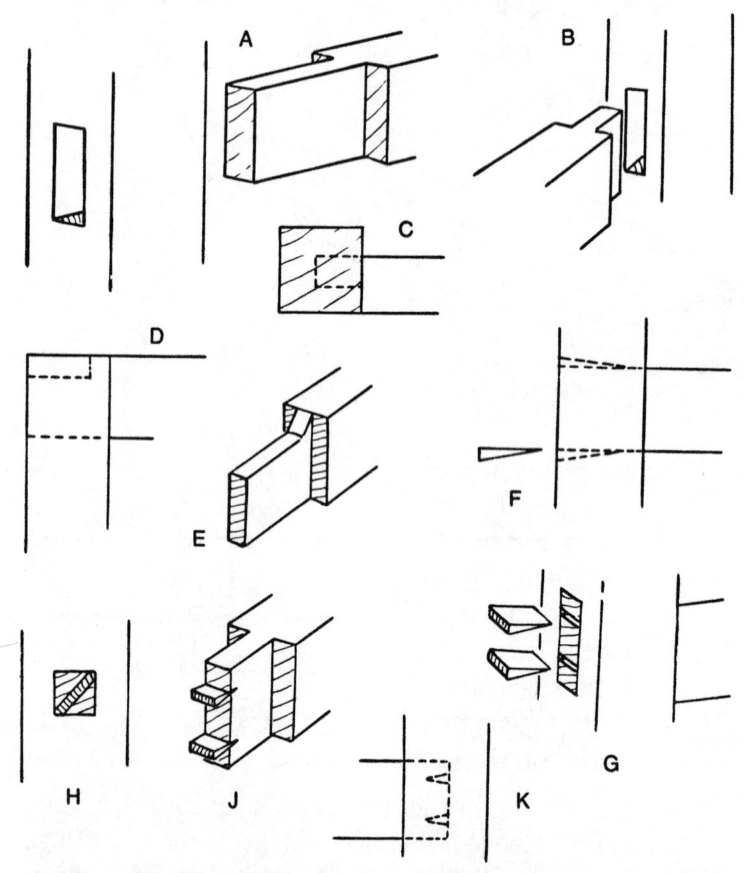


Fig. 3-5. The mortise and tenon joint (A-C) was the most used means of fastening wood parts together. At a corner it may be haunched (D and E). Strengthening is by wedging (F-H). Foxtail wedging (J and K) can be used if the tenon does not go through.

spread the end of the tenon against the bottom of the mortise (Fig. 3-5K).

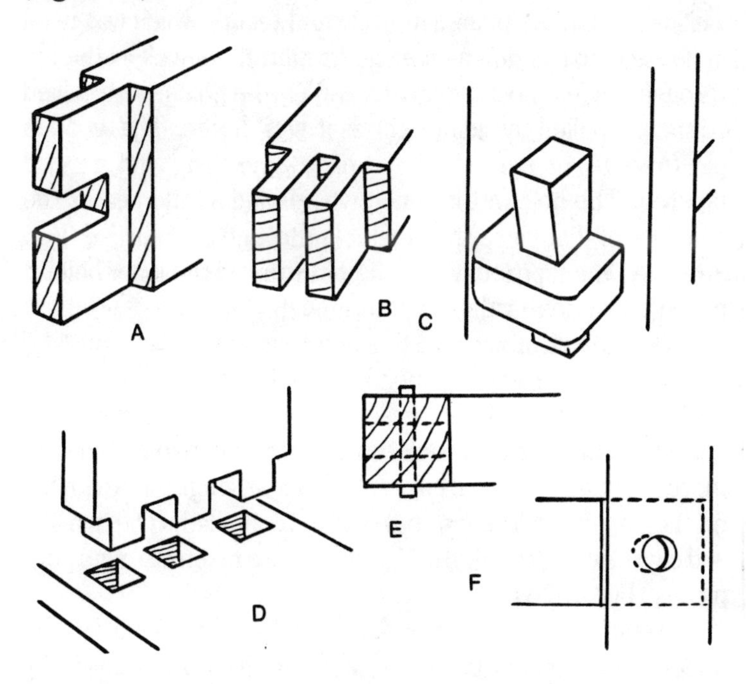


Fig. 3-6. Multiple tenons (A and B) are used for wide boards. A tenon may go through and be wedged (C). Many tenons can go across a board (D). Dowels or pegs (E and F) can pull a joint together.

Mortise and tenon joints can be adapted in many ways. If a wide board is to be tenoned, as with the rail under a table top into a leg, there are two or more full-length tenons, with a short piece between (Fig. 3-6A). If this was not done, so much would be cut from the leg for a wide tenon that it would be weakened. If the rail is thick, rather than wide, two or more tenons alongside each other (Fig. 3-6B) are stronger than one thick one. *Tusk* tenons that go right through and are locked with a key, peg, or wedge (Fig. 3-6C) go back to medieval days and were more common in some middle European countries than in Britain, but they may be found in some Colonial furniture. If a wide board joins another wide board, one way of joining them is with a series of mortise and tenon joints (Fig. 3-6D).

Clamps were not very plentiful nor efficient, and any joint that would pull itself tight without outside aid was welcomed. This is seen in the pinned mortise and tenon, which was used in house construction as well as furniture. As well as the pin through the joint locking it (Fig. 3-6E), the holes were drilled so the pin pulled the joint tight as it was driven. The wooden pin (*treenail* or *trunnel*) was made over long and its end tapered. The hole in the tenon was drilled a little nearer the shoulder of that piece than the hole through the mortise (Fig. 3-6F). As the tapered end of the pin entered the inner hole, it pulled the tenon farther into the mortise.

Both parts of any mortise and tenon joint were marked out from the face sides. A mortise gauge had two pins adjustable in relation to each other, so both lines could be marked in one pass. An ordinary gauge can be used with two settings if a mortise gauge is unavailable. A little extra length was allowed on the end of a full tenon, but a stub tenon had to be marked and cut the correct length. All marks were taken all round both pieces (Fig. 3-7A).

Tenons are cut in the same way as described for the open-ended parts of lap joints, but cuts have to be made by hand sawing on both sides. To ensure accuracy lengthwise cuts are made diagonally before cutting through. There may have to be some paring with a chisel, but be careful not to take off too much. Pay particular attention to the angles between the cross-grain and end-grain cuts—any particles of waste wood there would prevent the joint closing properly.

Tenons can be cut conveniently with a table saw in a similar way to that described for lap joints, but in two passes.

Mortises were chopped out with a thick mortise chisel and a mallet. It is more convenient to drill out much of the waste and leave chisel work to the final cuts. The drill should be slightly smaller in diameter than the width of the mortise. As many holes should be drilled as can conveniently be fitted in the length (Fig. 3-7B). Drill from both sides of a through mortise to minimize the risk of splintering or breaking out. Leave some wood to be removed by chisel at the end grain parts of the mortise.

Remove waste wood with a chisel no wider than the mortise, chopping between the holes and levering chips out, but be careful not to damage the wood that will show outside the joint. Work from both sides of a through mortise. If necessary, use a wider chisel to trim the sides of the opening. Do not trim the ends of the mortise until all other parts are finished, then pare vertically to remove the final waste (Fig. 3-7C).

The traditional craftsman always made a point of not making a trial assembly. He argued that this would wear the joint loose. He preferred to trust his skill in getting it right first time. He had a point, but anyone with less experience may test

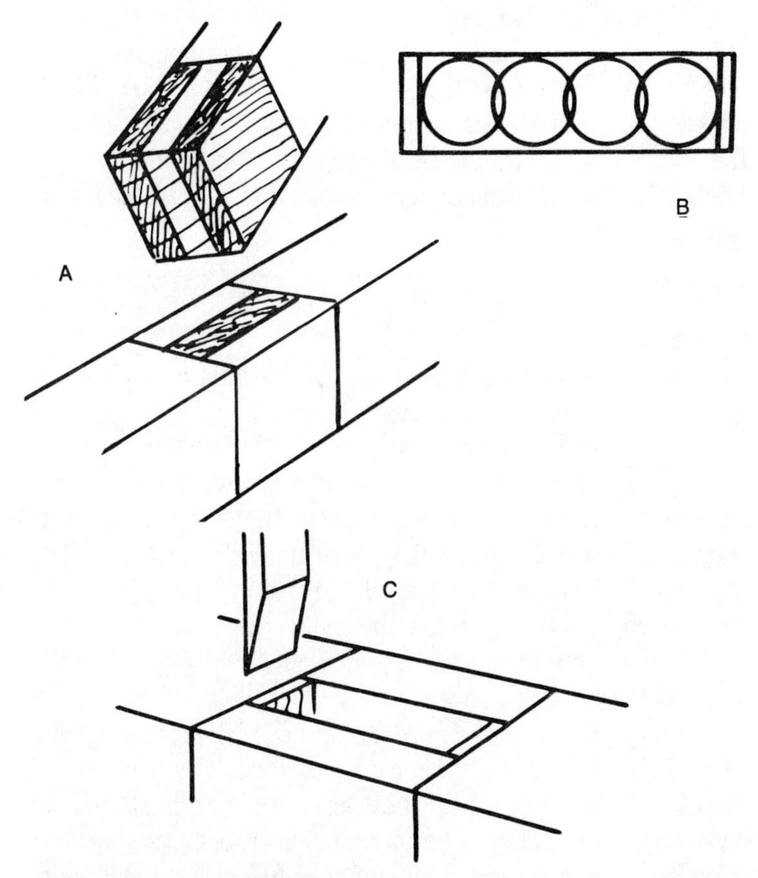


Fig. 3-7. The mortise and tenon are marked to match (A). Some mortise waste can be drilled (B), then the shape finished with a chisel (C).

a joint at least part way before applying glue and driving it together.

Haunches are a simple matter of sawing, but if a mortise is to be made near the end of a piece of wood, it is advisable to leave a few inches of spare wood there until after cutting out, to prevent the risk of the short grain breaking through during drilling and chopping with a chisel. Wide tenons may need careful paring with a chisel. The tool particularly intended for this is the low-angled rabbet plane, called a "shoulder plane" from its use in trimming the shoulders of tenons.

## SHELF JOINTS

In the simplest construction the end of a shelf rested on a strip of wood glue, nailed or screwed to the upright part. This might be satisfactory in the reproduction of a primitive block of shelves, but for better construction the shelf was grooved into the upright, in what is now usually called a "dado joint," but the original craftsman probably called it by the English name of "housing joint."

In its simplest form there is a groove across the upright as wide as the thickness of the shelf and deep enough to support it without weakening the other part (Fig. 3-8A). For extra strength there could be a strip of wood underneath (Fig. 3-8B). Where fastenings through the end would spoil appearances, nails or screws were driven diagonally from below (Fig. 3-8C). This *through dado* or *housing joint* may not be considered pleasing at the front and for a better appearance a *stopped dado* is used (Fig. 3-8D), with just a short width of the shelf notched around the end of the dado. Another way to improve appearance is to have the shelf wider than the upright (Fig. 3-8E). If both sides of the joint would be visible, it can be stopped at the back as well.

A normal dado joint does not offer any resistance to a pull. This can be rectified by using a dovetail form. For thick wood there can be beveling top and bottom (Fig. 3-8F), but for most constructions it will only be on one side, usually the bottom (Fig. 3-8G). A further refinement, needing greater skill, but providing maximum tightening, has the dovetail part tapered,

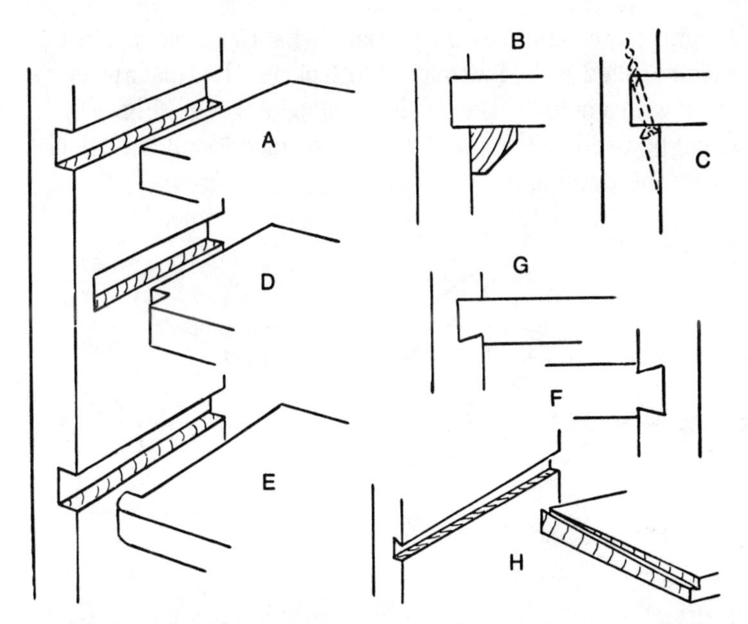


Fig. 3-8. The dado or housing joint (A) may be strenghtened (B and C). Stopping the dado (D) or overlapping the shelf (E) improves the front appearance. Dovetail variations (G-H) lock the parts together.

so the joint tightens as the shelf is driven in from the back (Fig. 3-8H).

For hand cutting the dado is marked out in a similar way to that described for a half lap, with a chiseled bevel inside the cut lines as a guide for the backsaw; then the bulk of the waste is removed with a chisel (Fig. 3-9A). For hand sawing a stopped dado it is necessary to cut away the far end with chisels before sawing. This is done for about 1 in., carefully paring out to the full width, but leaving a small pad at the end (Fig. 3-9B) to take the inevitable knocks from the end of the saw. This cutaway part allows the sides of the dado to be sawn with a limited movement, then the waste chiseled out, and that pad trimmed to size last of all.

Although it is possible to get the bottom of a housing joint flat with a chisel, it is a help to use a router. This may be the modern power tool of that name, which might cut the dado completely without sawing, if guides are used. The name *router* is also applied to a hand tool, with a projecting cutter to level the bottom of the groove. There are metal versions to be bought, but it is interesting to make what those early cabinet makers called an "old woman's tooth plane." It is just a piece of wood with a hole to take a chisel held by a wedge (Fig. 3-9C). It can be used in a dovetail dado by turning to cut at an angle under the overhang.

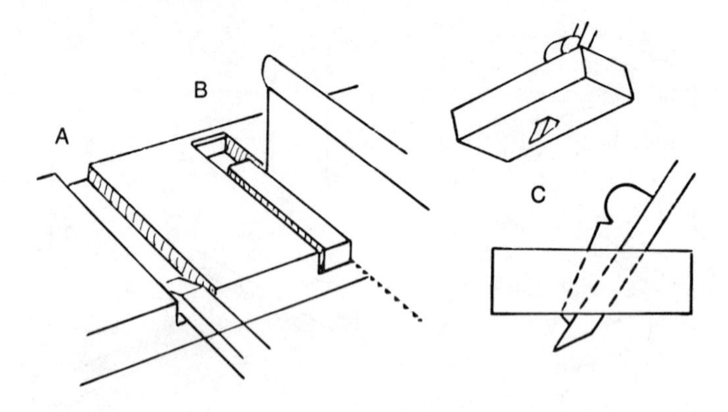


Fig. 3-9. Dadoes are sawn and chiseled (A and B). A router (C) cleans and levels the groove.

## DOVETAIL JOINTS

Hand-made dovetail joints were the pride of the old-time cabinetmaker, from before the days of settlement in America. The ability to make neat and accurate dovetails indicated mastery of his craft. Sometimes the joints were made unnecessarily complicated and difficult, probably to show off skill. Exposed dovetail joints have become a feature of some types of furniture. In others, they can still be seen, although not on the more exposed surfaces. Others were completely hidden in the finished work, but the craftsman who took a pride in his work put them there knowing they were the strongest way to make the joint, although only he knew at the end that they were there.

In a simple *through dovetail joint* the *tail* is the part that is shaped and the projections each side of the sockets are *pins*. In the simplest form two strips are joined with a single dovetail at a corner (Fig. 3-10A). The angle of the side of a dovetail was probably found by experience, but if old work is examined the angle will be found to be about 1 in 8 (Fig. 3-10B) in hardwood and broadened to about 1 in 6 maximum for softwood (Fig. 3-10C).

Glue strength is poor on end grain and very much better on side grain. The only places where side grain meets side grain is between the sides of the tails and pins, so that is where the greatest strength is. This means that in joining wide boards a joint made with a large number of dovetails will have more side glue area and be stronger than one with fewer. Obviously there are practical considerations, but if old work is seen with a great many dovetails on something like a drawer side, they were there for strength and not just to show the skill of the cabinetmaker.

Dovetails were cut entirely by hand. There is no modern way that similar dovetails can be made throughout with power tools. It is possible to make dovetails by machine and there is a device that can be powered by an electric drill. These are perfectly satisfactory dovetails for modern work, but unfortunately they have one feature that would make them look wrong in reproduction work. Machine-made dovetail joints have the pins and tails the same width (Fig. 3-10D). A hand craftsman does not make them that way and never did. The pins are always narrower than the tails (Fig. 3-10E). How

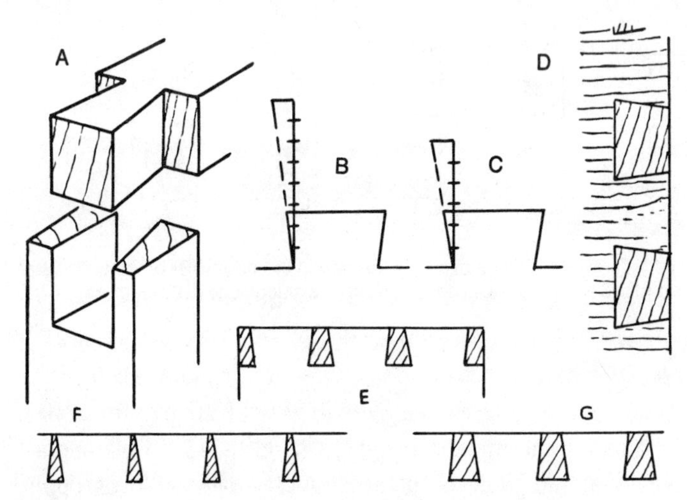


Fig. 3-10. Dovetails are the traditional cabinetmaking joints, with angles to suit the wood (A-C). Mechanical dovetails have the pins and tails the same size (D), but hand cut dovetails have narrow pins (E-G).

much narrower depends on the particular worker, but there was a phase when dovetail joints in the higher class work were made with pins that had sides almost meeting at a point (Fig. 3-10F). There seemed no good reason for this and the joints were difficult to cut, so they only showed off skill. They could not have been as strong as slightly wider pins. This means that in reproduction work it is better to have moderately narrow pins, perhaps about one-quarter the width of the tails (Fig. 3-10G), unless the original in one with minimal width pins and truth in the copy is desired.

If wide boards are joined with dovetails, it is usual to keep the tails and pins a uniform size, which means experimenting to get sizes that will divide into the width (Fig. 3-11A), but some work will be found with narrower tails toward the edges of the boards (Fig. 3-11B) or there may have to be a tail of a special width to accept a groove (Fig. 3-11C) or a half tail at a bottom to hide an insert (Fig. 3-11D).

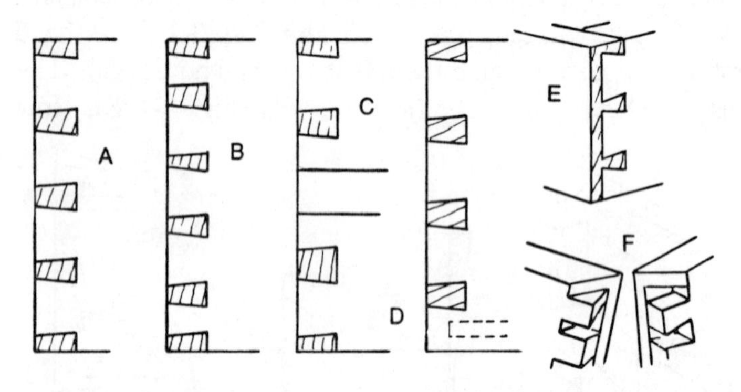


Fig. 3-11. Dovetails may be even (A), narrow at the edges (B) or spaced to suit other joints (C and D). Special dovetails may be hidden one (E) or both ways (F).

In many parts of furniture the joint has to be a *stopped* or *half blind* dovetail. The ends of the tails are hidden. Its form can be thought of as a through dovetail with a flap extension. It is a common joint on a drawer front (Fig. 3-11E). Pulling out a drawer of an old piece of furniture will usually show stopped dovetails at the front and through dovetails at the back. Half tails will usually be found to cover where the drawer bottom is fitted.

The other cabinetmaking dovetail joint is a *blind* or *miter* one. Externally the joint shows a miter, with no pins or tails visible, due to the dovetailed part being enclosed by extensions that meet each other when the joint closes (Fig. 3-11F). This is a difficult joint to cut as there is not much scope for sawing and most of the shaping has to be done by careful work with chisels.

To make a simple through dovetail joint with a few pins, the parts should be marked to length, but cut with a little waste left on the ends. This should not be much or it may make cutting difficult, but if less than 1/16 in. is left, it allows the ends to be planed level after the joint has been assembled. The angles of the dovetails can be marked with an adjustable bevel, or a piece of sheet metal can be made into a template (Fig. 3-12A). A wooden one can be made with plywood (Fig. 3-12B). Mark the width of each piece on the other and square these marks around (Fig. 3-12C). Divide the dovetail part suitably and mark all the dovetails. It may be helpful to pencil on the parts that have to be cut away (Fig. 3-12D).

Saw down the sides of the tails, keeping the saw kerf on the waste side of the line. This can be done by hand with the wood held in a vise or a band saw can be used. Some of the waste may be removed by other cuts (Fig. 3-12E). The rest of the waste has to be chopped out with a bevel-edge chisel. This should be done a little at a time from each side, getting both sides cut almost back to the line before hand paring with the chisel just to the line (Fig. 3-12F). Be careful not to leave the center of the wood higher than the outside.

Put the dovetail part in position over the other piece. Use the lines marking the insides of the joint as guides. Use a finely sharpened pencil or a scratch awl to mark each side of the dovetails (Fig. 3-12G). Square these marks down the sides of the wood. Pencil on the waste parts and saw by hand, on the waste sides of the lines.

Some of the waste can be removed by sawing, but if a band saw is used, have the wood with the narrow sides of the openings upwards to reduce the risk of cutting into the pins (Fig. 3-12H). The rest of the waste has to be cut out with a chisel, but remember the tapers of the pins and be careful of cutting into them.

Some cabinetmakers prefer to work the other way round and mark the dovetail shapes on the end of the piece that will have the pins. This is sawn and chiseled, then used to mark the dovetail piece. Working this way gives wider openings to mark through and would be advisable if the work has extremely narrow pins, but for most work it is probably better to cut dovetails first.

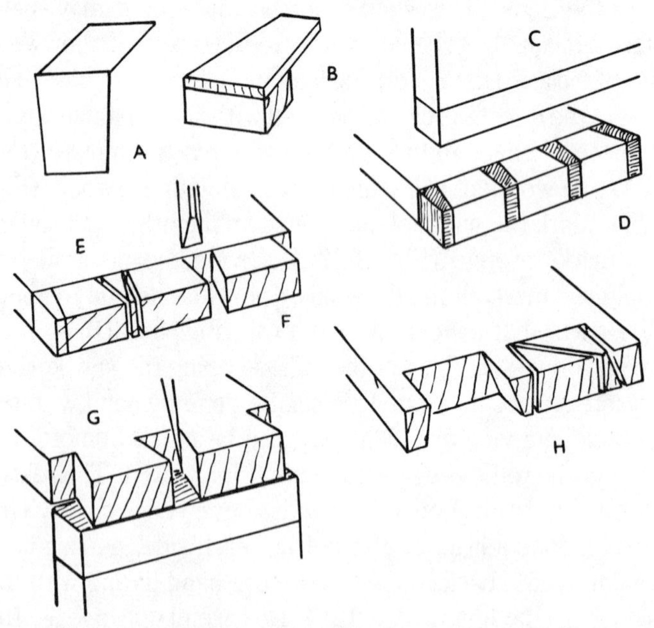


Fig. 3-12. Templates help with making dovetail angles (A and B). The dovetails may be marked before the pins (C and D), the waste sawn and chiseled out (E and F), then the pins marked (G) and some waste sawn (H).

A skilled man trusts his craftsmanship and does not make a trial assembly, but applies glue and drives the joint together, preferably with a strip of wood to spread the pressure of mallet or clamp.

If several joints have to be the same, as they would at the four corners of a chest, it is possible to get them all the same by marking out on one piece only at first. Lengths and thicknesses of wood are marked for all corners, but two pieces can be held together and the sides of the dovetails cut, using the markings on the front piece only. If the second piece is turned end for end and the other end put behind the first, its dovetails can be sawn by using the saw through the first cuts. The same can be done with the fourth corner. Further work is then done on each joint separately.

With a stopped dovetail joint the part with the dovetails is made first. In this case it should be cut to exact length. The amount it overlaps the other piece is marked on it (Fig. 3-13A). That piece may have a slight extra piece of waste left to be planed level later. The shapes of the dovetails are marked on it and squared down the surface, with waste parts penciled (Fig. 3-13B). It is possible to saw only a small amount (Fig. 3-13C). Be careful not to saw too far on either surface. Some of the waste can be removed with a chisel used at the same angle as the sawing (Fig. 3-13D).

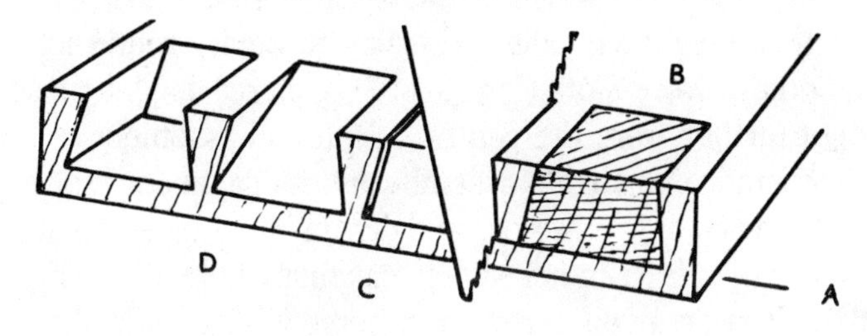


Fig. 3-13. If the dovetail is stopped (A) it can be marked (B), partially sawn (C), then finished with a chisel (D).

Further waste has to be cut out with chisels, first across the grain to sever the fibers, then along the grain and at the sides of the pins. A narrow chisel is needed to tilt for the cross-grain cuts beside the pins, so as not to cut too far into the bottom of the recess.

It is important to remove all waste from the internal angles of the joint. The inner edges of the dovetails can be beveled slightly to reduce the risk of them fouling the bottoms of the cut-outs and preventing tight assembly.

## OTHER JOINTS

A great many other hand-made joints will be found in early furniture, but many of them are adaptions of those just described and their cutting is obvious.

Nailed joints may not be quite as obvious as they appear on the surface. They were often driven at alternate angles to give a dovetail effect for greater strength (Fig. 3-14A). If a screw head was to be hidden it was more likely to be counterbored and covered with a wooden plug than to be merely deeply countersunk and covered with stopping, because there probably was no satisfactory stopping available. There were no plug cutters for making round wood plugs from similar wood to that being plugged. There may have been hand-cut round plugs, although sometimes the plug was square or diamond shaped in a chiseled hole (Fig. 3-14B).

If several boards were used to make up a width of something to be used in kitchen or wash house, the effects of damp had to be allowed for. Stout battens were put across the underside to prevent warping, but to allow for expansion and contraction, only the middle screw was through a round hole. All the others were slots (Fig. 3-14C) of increasing length as they got further from the center on a broad assembly.

For a more important assembly in less damp conditions, the batten was tapered across and driven into a tapered dado slot and its ends trimmed after maximum tightening (Fig. 3-14D). For an even stronger assembly without nails or screws, the batten had a dovetail section (Fig. 3-14E).

Not all assemblies could have battens. One method of resisting warping was a variation of the tongue and groove joint (sometimes called a *bread board joint*), with the tongue in the end grain of the wide piece mating with a groove in the narrow piece with its grain across (Fig. 3-14F). This might be a table or cabinet top with a molded edge worked all round.

One corner joint that is fairly common today, but has no place in reproductions of old furniture, is the *combed joint* with projections from each part fitting between those of the other part, something like straight-sided dovetails. This is a joint for machine production.

Although hinges produced in the earliest Colonial days were crude and usually fitted on the surface, as designs progressed to better quality furniture, the usual hinges were then *butt hinges*. The better ones were solid brass made by extrud-

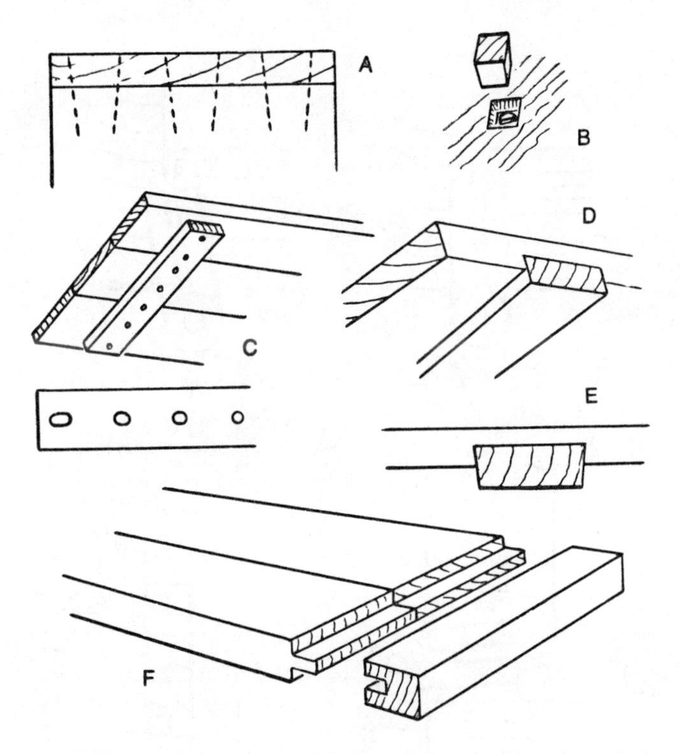


Fig. 3-14. Nails may be driven dovetail fashion (A) for strength, and punched and plugged for neatness (B). A wide assembly can have slots for screws to allow for expansion (C). To prevent warping a cleat may be let in (D and E) or tongued across an end (F).

ing. Cheaper ones were of sheet metal wrapped around the pin. Cabinetmakers had special ways of letting butt hinges into the edges of cabinet doors. Sometimes the parts were let equally and squarely into the door and post (Fig. 3-15A), but more often the two parts were set at an angle. The important consideration, in any case, is the position of the pivot point through the pin. The door must swing clear about this as it is opened. With the door flush or set back from the post, the hinge was let in at an angle, so the pivot was over the edge of the door and not the post (Fig. 3-15B). The same sort of angled mounting was used when the door overlapped the cabinet side (Fig. 3-15C).

With nothing like plywood and other manufactured boards available, panels had to be solid wood, so designs had

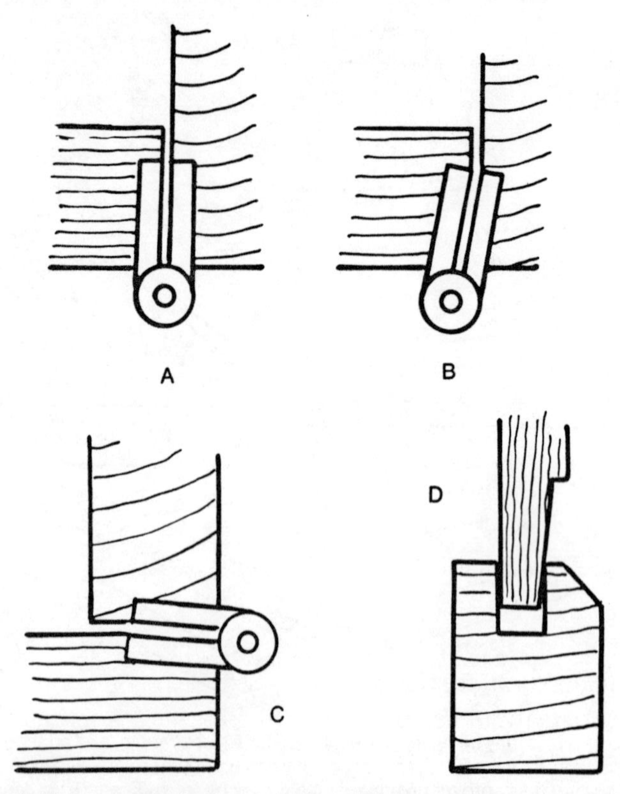


Fig. 3-15. Hinges may be let in evenly (A), but many old cabinetmakers angled them (B and C). Panels should not reach the bottoms of plowed grooves, so there is space for expansion (D).

to be arranged to allow for panels of reasonable size by building framed structures to enclose them. This produced an attractive appearance, but a solid wood panel of perhaps 12 in. width might be expected to expand and contract up to ¼ in., and this had to be allowed for. With most woods, movement in the length of the grain was negligible, so joints in that direction could be tight. Joints in the width were grooves, made deeper than the panel was expected to go, to permit movement (Fig. 3-15D). No glue was used and the panel edge formed a push fit.

# Special Processes

Although a would-be maker of reproduction furniture may have a good general knowledge of woodworking using hand and power tools, there are special techniques appropriate to some older furniture that are not so widely practiced today and therefore may not be so well known. This chapter is intended to provide some general instructions as guidance to anyone with a modest woodworking capability. If more detailed instructions are needed, there are many complete books on each of the subjects.

The woodworker of a century or more ago, working without the mechanical aids available today, used his general skill to make properly jointed and designed pieces of furniture, which were often sufficient in themselves, but he had some skills and facilities that allowed him to decorate and embellish his work, in ways which were probably ahead of the general woodworking of which he was capable. This meant that these techniques were used to show his skill and the fact that he was up to date in his design and thinking. The results are characteristically attractive examples of the work of the period.

Some of these special processes are: veneering, carving, turning, and molding. None of them are essential constructionally, but they improve the appearance of the furniture on which they are worked. In a few cases the process is carried to excess and the thing becomes over-ornate by modern standards, but in general the added work has been applied with restraint.

## VENEERING

A veneer is a very thin slice of wood, which has to be glued to a solid backing. Veneers have been cut in many ways. Some cut by saw were comparatively thick—as much as ⅛ in. Others cut by knife are much thinner—1/25 in. or 1 mm. Some veneers are cut on a sort of lathe, with a broad knife slicing off a layer around the circumference of a log. It is this type which has made the production of plywood possible. Examination of the surface of a piece of plywood will show a grain pattern that is due to cutting that way. Other knife-cut veneers are cut across the wood, so the width of the veneer is limited by the width of the board. It is this last type which were, and still are, used mainly for applying to furniture.

Veneers can be cut from woods that are also used in solid form, but they are also cut from woods with attractive grain markings that would be unsuitable for solid construction. Veneers also make possible the cutting through many times of a decorative curl or other feature of the grain, so it can be applied many times to furniture, where it could only be featured once if the wood had been used solid.

Veneering as sometimes practiced today differs in several ways from the traditional methods, which should be used on reproduction furniture. The ground is often plywood and for modern work this is a good choice, but it would be inappropriate in a copy of piece of Colonial furniture except, possibly, in a situation where there could be no evidence in the finished work that plywood had been used. There is also the choice of glue. Much modern work is done with impact adhesive, which was not available for the original furniture and is considered to have some drawbacks by experts.

Traditional veneering is now sometimes described as "hammer veneering" because the principle tool used is called a "veneer hammer," although it is not a hammer of the type that is swung. Some veneer hammers look like ordinary hammers with a wooden handle and a round head at one side, which is actually used as a second handle, and a very broad cross peen at the other side. This cross peen is thin and rounded, and may be up to 4 in. wide (Fig. 4-1A). It is more usual to have a veneer hammer made of wood with a brass or aluminum face, which is about ⅛ in. thick and up to 4 in. long, set in a hardwood stock with a handle wedged to it (Fig. 4-1B). This is preferable to the iron hammer. Iron will react with the tannic acid in some woods and cause staining. In any case the lower edge should be straight and smoothly rounded, with any sharpness at the ends taken off.

Veneer can be cut with a knife, and for many purposes this is the tool to use, drawn along a steel straightedge for straight cuts. However, even with a thin razorlike section to the knife, the edge left on the veneer will be slightly beveled (Fig. 4-1C). In some cases this does not matter, but if an upright cut is wanted, it is better to use a saw. This is made in several versions, but the important part is a thin saw blade about 3 in. long, with very fine teeth without set. Usually the edge is curved in its length. The saw may be double-edged and one convenient version has a handle attached to a cranked tang, so the hand is kept away from any guiding board and the tool can be reversed (Fig. 4-1D). Some of these saws are made with the edge thinned to a knife edge, which defeats the object of having a saw, by leaving beveled edges. That type is best avoided.

There are no other special tools. A low-angle block plane is used for trimming off excess veneer at edges. A hand scraper is needed to finish surfaces, particularly to remove glue or paper there.

The glue used should be animal or fish type, sometimes described as "hide" glue. Suitable glue may be bought in sheets, which have to be broken into small pieces with a hammer, or in pearls, which are small grains or balls ready for melting. Since the glue is all-important in veneering, care is needed in its preparation and use. New glue is softened by soaking in water. The excess water is then poured off and the glue put into the inner container of a double glue pot.

There are double glue pots with electrical heaters thermostatically controlled. There are other simpler types to stand over a gas flame, or even a fire (Fig. 4-1E). It is even possible to do a limited amount of work with an arrangement of two cans of different sizes, with wire handles (Fig. 4-1F). The important thing is to keep the inner container surrounded by water, so the glue itself does not boil or burn.

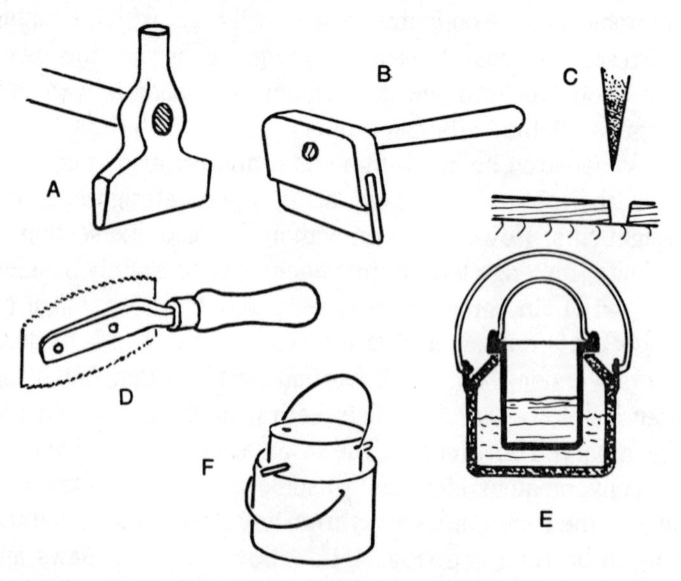


Fig. 4-1. A veneer hammer (A and B) is used to press veneer down. A knife leaves an angled edge (C), but a veneer saw (D) cuts squarely. Hot glue is prepared in a double container (E and F).

When the glue is melted it may need water added. It can be stirred with a piece of wood. The right consistency is found by experience. It should flow from a brush, but not like water—it should be more like honey or syrup. The consistency will vary during prolonged use and heating, so it must not be assumed that if it is right on one occasion, it will still be the same an hour later. Long heating causes evaporation of the water, so there may have to be more dilution.

If possible, use a brush for the glue that does not have any metal in the mounting of the bristles, then there cannot be any risk of staining of some woods.

Like other glued work, it is the edges which are most likely to come away. Veneers, as supplied, tend to curl if they are not kept in a press or under weights. If veneer is glued in place with its concave side downwards, its natural tendency to curl will help to keep the edges pressed down. If the new dry veneer is remaining flat, it can be moistened both sides to see which way it may try to curl.

Some veneered work is arranged as a pattern. This was called "marquetry" and much of it was geometric in form, with beauty coming from the use of grain patterns to get effects. The name now seems to be applied more to the use of veneers to build up a picture, using the color and grain of different woods for pictorial effects. Much of either form of marquetry can call for a considerable amount of patience in fitting the parts closely. Practice work for furniture should be in covering surfaces and edges with single pieces or very simple patterns. This is what was done, in any case, on much veneered Colonial and Early American furniture.

Although veneering is normally done on surfaces first, with edges following, the technique is best understood by dealing with an edge. Cut a strip of veneer slightly wider than the edge to be covered. Do not make it very much wider, or the excess glue outside exposed to the air will dry quicker and may cause the veneer to curl away. The strip can be cut with a knife along a steel straightedge, or the veneer saw can be used with a piece of wood as a guide.

Hot glue is not very sticky, but as it cools its stickiness increases, until it sets when it is cold, although the greatest strength takes about 24 hours to build up. This means that you need to work fast while the glue is still liquid. It is possible to soften the glue again with heat, if necessary. However, with an edge, reheating should not be necessary.

Apply glue to the edge first. Some workers then put the strip of veneer on the edge, face side down, and quickly apply glue to the surface and turn it over quickly and press down with the hammer. The advantage claimed is that the glue picked up helps the hammer slide easily. The alternative is to put the strip on some paper, face down, and apply glue there, so the face side remains dry. The hammer is held with its rounded edge straight down and is drawn along with good pressure to squeeze the glued surfaces together and force out any air bubbles or excess glue (Fig. 4-2A). A straight pull with the pressure from one hand is probably all that is needed on an edge. Some workers prefer to push, but so long as the pressure is there, the direction does not matter.

If the glue is allowed to get too cold before the veneer is positioned, heat can be applied with an electric domestic iron. Ideally, an old one is kept for the purpose. If an old flat iron, to be heated over a flame or on a hotplate, can be found, this may give it a new and useful life. The iron is rubbed over the veneer to transfer heat and quickly followed by the veneer hammer.

Some of the excess veneer and glue can be removed from the edge with a knife. Be careful cutting the end that the knife is not used in a way that would lift unsupported veneer. Dipping the knife in hot water helps it clear excess glue without becoming coated with glue. Leave trimming to exact size until the job has stood for 24 hours, then the edge can be treated with a sharp block plane, angled so cuts are towards the solid wood (Fig. 4-2B), to reduce the risk of grain breaking out.

If plywood is veneered, it is advisable to let veneer grain and top ply grain cross at an angle (Fig. 4-2C). The crossing need not be at right angles. If particleboard is veneered, there is no grain, so any direction is possible. Veneer laid with the grain on plywood may develop cracks later. If the ground is solid wood, it is better to lay the veneer with its grain in the same direction as that below it (Fig. 4-2D). Expansion and contraction of the two layers are then likely to match. If the ground wood is thick it should resist any tendency to warp due to adding the veneer. If it is thin and unsupported over a large area, it is advisable to veneer the opposite side as well, so any stresses set up by gluing are balanced and the wood will not pull out of shape.

Veneering a surface follows the same sequence as described for an edge. The veneer is moistened and both the ground and it are coated with glue. Position the veneer by laying it with a curving action from one end (Fig. 4-2E). Use the hammer with a zig-zag action and plenty of pressure near the center (Fig. 4-2F). The way the veneer was laid will reduce trapped air to a minimum, but the first work is to get any air out at the edges by working from the middle. Keep the hammer close to right angles to the grain at all times.

Not much can be rubbed down with the hammer before the glue gets too cool. Iron over a part to soften the glue, then work over that with the veneer hammer and plenty of weight. Reheat an adjoining part and move on to that. Let heated and worked parts overlap and progress towards the edges. Air and excess glue has to be persuaded to orogress to and escape from the edges.

If the veneer is not wide enough to cover the ground in one piece, or there is to be a pattern made up of adjoining

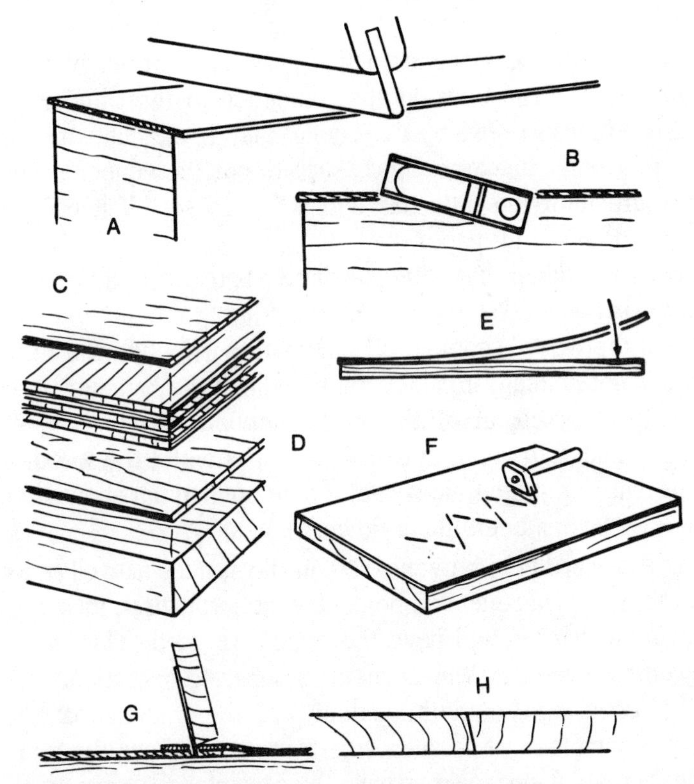


Fig. 4-2. Veneer is rubbed down with a hammer (A) and trimmed with a block plane (B). Grain usually crosses plywood (C), but is the same way on solid wood (D). Veneer is lowered on (E) to avoid air bubbles and the hammer used from the center out to get the joint close (F). Sawing overlapping veneers at an angle (G) gets a close butt joint (H).

parts, the meeting edges are best cut in position. One piece is laid, then the other piece also laid with about ½ in. overlap (Fig. 4-2G). The two pieces are cut through together. If the saw and its guide board are tilted slightly, that will allow for the amount of wood removed by the thickness of the saw (Fig. 4-2H). If necessary, reheat the work, so the waste piece on top can be taken away, then the top veneer lifted to allow the waste piece underneath to be removed. More reheating and work with the hammer should make the pieces lay down with a very close joint. It may help to put a strip of paper along the joint until the glue has set. It may be stuck down with the ordinary glue, or a piece of self-adhesive masking tape may be satisfactory. Paper and excess glue can be removed by scraping.

Some of the more attractive grain in a veneer may be associated with a considerable tendency to twist and curl. Getting this sort of veneer to lay flat may be difficult with the hammer only. It may be necessary to put the veneer under pressure until the glue has had a day to set. If it can be clamped, put stout paper over the surface, with a stiff board above, and clamp that. The alternative is to put weights over the board.

If the work is completed and an area is found where the glue is not holding, it can be reheated and the hammer used over the affected part. If there is an air bubble and this cannot be persuaded to come out through the pores of the wood, a short cut along the grain will let the air out and not show after the veneer has been stuck down.

If a board is to be veneered on the surface as well as its edges, the surface should be done completely first, including leaving to harden and have the edges trimmed. This is followed by veneering the edges as a separate operation.

Veneering is sometimes done with the grain the narrow way. Examples will be seen where the edges have the grain lines across. A surface may have the central panel surrounded by a frame with the grain directed towards the center and mitered corners. The method of laying and trimming adjoining pieces is as described, but care is needed in the use of the hammer, which should be as near as possible at right angles to the grain it is covering for most of its work, otherwise the fibers may be stretched across the grain. If the veneer does not crack during laying, it may open later, due to the cross-grain stresses.

## CARVING

Carving as a means of decoration or artistic expression in wood is a craft that goes back a long way. The work can range from a few cuts in an otherwise plain piece of work to intricate figures, foliage, and three-dimensional work in which the carving is more important than the structure it is a part of. Many early American furniture makers used carving to add style and decoration to things that were otherwise purely functional. If they had artistic ability they were able to cut representations of animals, leaves and similar things in lifelike form, but in most cases the practical ability was there, but the craftsman was not an artist. In that case he followed an existing pattern by someone else or, more often, used formalized and geometric designs. Properly applied, these can be quite effective.

In the Old World, wood carving and wood turning were specialized crafts, with enough work available to keep men occupied exercising their particular skills on furniture that was otherwise made and completed by a cabinetmaker. The cabinetmaker usually had some knowledge and facility for carving and turning, but it was not until he emigrated that he was called on to see production right through with his own hands. This meant that the earlier American furniture makers may have been feeling their way with carving, which was limited by few special tools being available. Wood carving tools are mostly gouges and chisels, but their variety ran into hundreds, particularly in Victorian times, when many pieces of furniture were expected to be carved all over.

Much of the carving by early cabinetmakers was done with the tools also used for cutting joints and other general woodworking. This usually meant a few chisels of various widths, very few gouges and maybe a few knives. As the tools were mostly bigger than the usual carving tools, carved work was either bold or limited to simple cuts.

Some of the simple cuts were in patterns now often called "chip carving." This is based on triangles, which can be made entirely with a chisel, aided by a pointed knife. In the basic cuts a triangle is penciled and the chisel pressed in two sides, angled towards the corner where they meet (Fig. 4-3A). The chisel is pared from the other side to the point (Fig. 4-3B). The corner has to be a right angle for the usual square-ended chisel to be used. Otherwise the chisel end can be sharpened askew or the final cut made with a knife, if the angle is more acute than a right angle. In any case the point of a knife may be needed to clear the corner. These triangles are built into a pattern in many ways. A series in alternate directions makes a border (Fig. 4-3C), where the effect comes from shadows cast by diagonal light.

A further step is to let three triangles meet, sinking to a point at the meeting corners. The shape is drawn and a knife used to cut along the lines from the center outwards (Fig. 4-3D). A chisel pares each triangle towards the center, progressively getting deeper (Fig. 4-3E).

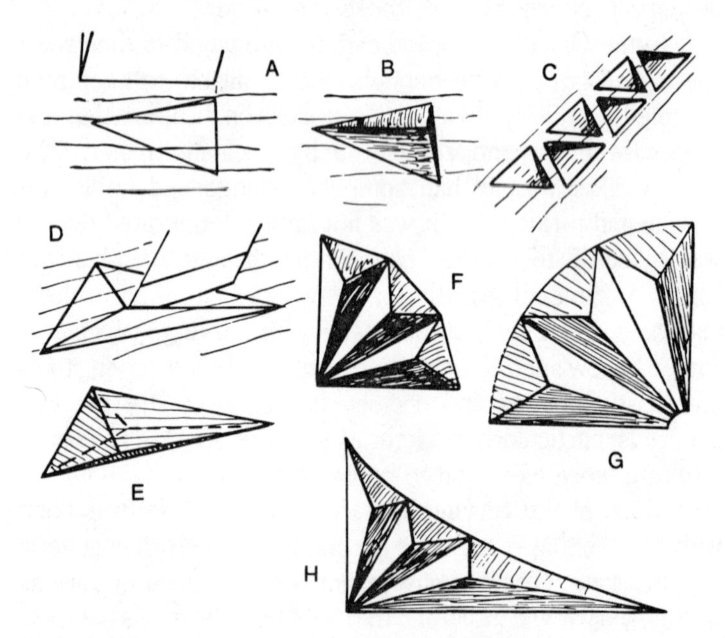


Fig. 4-3. In chip carving, triangles are cut (A-C) and arranged in patterns. If cut to the center (D and E), they can be combined into fan patterns (F-H).

The shapes do not have to be all straight lines. A simple pattern can be built up from straight-sided meeting triangles (Fig. 4-3F), but the outside edges can be curved to a fan pattern (Fig. 4-3G) or with a concave curve at corner (Fig. 4-3H). Old furniture will show a variety of patterns that were cut in this way, with only simple tools.

It is unnecessary to obtain an elaborate collection of carving tools to work on most reproduction furniture. Only later examples that were based on European originals at the time of great popularity of carving, would call for a profusion of carving tools to make properly. Modern makers of carving tools have limited their range considerably, so if new tools are to be bought, only the most popular shapes can be obtained.

Carving tools are made like common firmer gouges and chisels, but rather lighter. Wooden handles with metal ferrules are preferred to plastic. The tool has a tang into the handle and a bolster to press against and resist hitting with a mallet (Fig. 4-4A). Gouges are sharpened with a bevel on the outside, without any break between the ground and honed angles. It is usual to sharpen inside so there is a light angle there as well (Fig. 4-4B), unlike tools for general use, where such an angle is avoided and the inside kept absolutely straight.

Carving gouges are in widths from 1/16 in. to 1 in. in twelve steps, but within each width were as many as nine different *sweeps*, meaning curves from nearly flat to deep U shapes (Fig. 4-4C). Only a very limited number, mostly around the middle sizes and average shapes, are now available. Besides straight patterns, there are gouges curved in the length (Fig. 4-4D). For getting into awkward places a gouge may be a spoon bit type (Fig. 4-4E).

A deep narrow gouge is worth having. It was called a "veining tool," from its use in outlining veins of leaves, but it is a good tool for cutting in any outlines. Another tool for similar work is a "V-tool" or "parting tool," with a V section, sharpened on the outside like a double chisel (Fig. 4-4F). These were made in widths from 1/16 in. to 1 in. and in at least three angles of about 40°, 60°, and 90°. One parting tool of average size should do all that is required of it today.

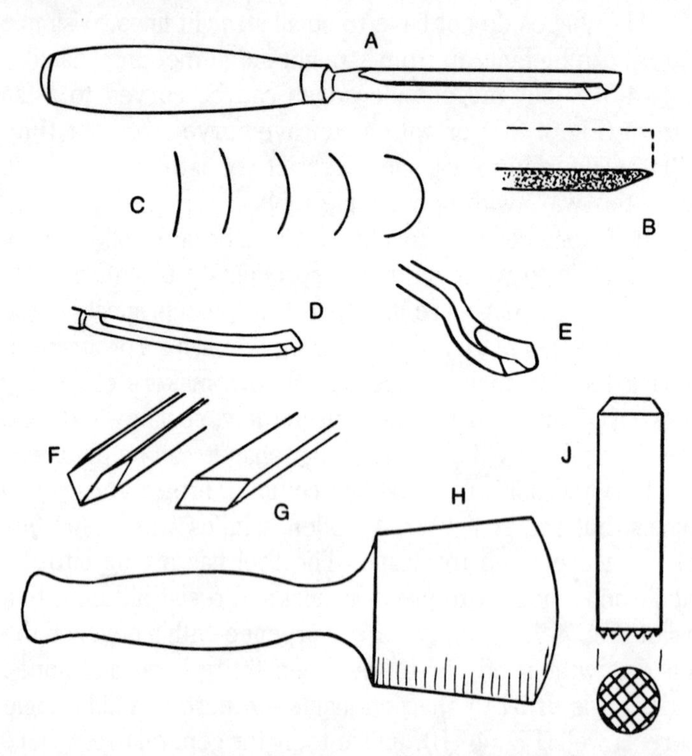


Fig. 4-4. Most carving is done with gouges of many sections (A-C) and shapes (D and E). A V-tool (F) cuts grooves and carving chisels may have skew ends (G). The traditional mallet is round (H). Backgrounds may have punched designs (J).

Carving chisels are much less used than gouges and most work can be done with general-purpose chisels. Carving chisels are thinner and in widths from ½ in. to 1 in. They may have the second bevel similar to a gouge and may be given skew ends (Fig. 4-4G). Chisels are made curved in the length and in spoon and other bit types for getting into awkward places.

Much carving is done with hand pressure only, but for harder woods and heavier cuts there has to be a mallet. Any mallet already available can be used, but a carver prefers one with a round head (Fig. 4-4H).

An expert carver took a pride in his cut backgrounds and generally preferred not to use punches to decorate the background. Early American furniture makers who did their own carving, often punched backgrounds to show up the work done on raised parts. If original backgrounds are examined it will be seen that home-made punches were used, being merely iron rods filed across the end (Fig. 4-4J).

Carving is mostly done with two hands on the tool. The hand gripping the handle provides direction and thrust. The other hand over the blade provides pressure and is ready to restrict when a cut reaches its intended limit or shows signs of going too far. Gouges are used, so their points are always kept above the surface of the wood, otherwise grain will break out. Deeper cuts are made in stages. So far as possible cuts are made diagonally across the grain (Fig. 4-5A). A cut straight along the grain might generate a split.

Much of the carved work on period furniture is comparatively low relief and worked on surfaces. After drawing the main outlines it is usually best to cut down the backgrounds. This is first outlined with a veiner or parting tool (Fig. 4-5B), then the waste cut away with a fairly broad gouge of shallow sweep (Fig. 4-5C). If there is much wood to be removed a power router could be used, but this should not be taken to the full depth, then there is scope for hand tool work to finish. Be careful that router cutter marks do not show around the outline, and avoid leaving the background so uniformly level that it has obviously been done by machine.

The raised part of relief carving should show an overall carved appearance. It would look wrong if parts of it remained flat and level with the surrounding uncarved parts. This means that any curved section should be complete and not left with a flat top (Fig. 4-5D). Leaves and similar things should be given an undulating section (Fig. 4-5E). Veins are outlined and carefully curved, so adjoining parts curve and blend in (Fig. 4-5F).

Outlines are strongest if they curve into the background (Fig. 4-5G). They are more distinct if cut at an angle or upright (Fig 4-5H). If the carved part is intended to stand out, they can be undercut. An upward curving edge of a leaf may appear to be much higher above the background than it is, if undercut (Fig. 4-5J). Of course, undercutting may leave a weak edge, so this should only be done when it is a strong wood or the

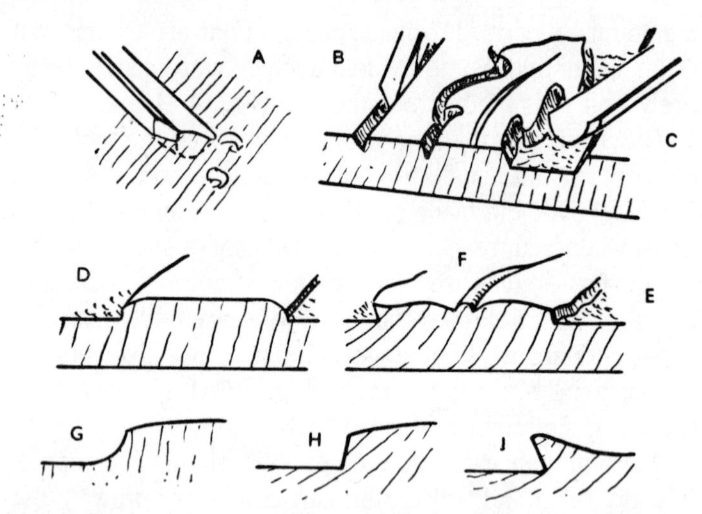


Fig. 4-5. Most carving cuts are diagonal to the grain (A). Outlines are cut and backgrounds lowered (B and C), then surface shaping done (D-F). The way edges are cut (G-J) controls the degree of shadow produced.

grain is across the cut. Undercutting along the grain leaving lengthwise fibers in a thin section, may cause crumbling or breaking some time after the work has been completed.

Carving tools should be kept sharp so they produce a good surface. It is usual to leave carving untouched by abrasives. There may occasionally be a need for the use of a file or rasp. Little files on narrow extending shafts that serve as handles, and called "rifflers," are the carver's tools for getting into difficult places, but they would have had little use on Colonial furniture and are unlikely to have been in the cabinetmaker's tool kit. Surfaces are smoothed by careful paring and are not sanded. If tool marks show, that does not matter and are characteristic of carved work.

Most carved decoration on early furniture is simple. The steps in its working can usually be visualized, so a reproduction can be tackled in the same way. It will be necessary to decide at what stage carving is to be done. Obviously, it would be unwise to have comparatively delicate carving knocking about the bench on a piece of wood requiring other work on it. It would also usually be unwise to wait until assembly had been completed, when it might be difficult to support the wood being worked on or manipulate tools properly because of other parts of the assembly.

With most pieces of furniture it is advisable to cut all joints and have the parts that are to be carved ready for assembly, so nothing more than perhaps a light cut with a smoothing plane will follow, then carving is done. Usually, it is possible to temporarily clamp the wood on the bench top. This is better than putting it in the vise, as the solid bench top below the wood gives good support when cuts are made with the aid of a mallet.

Details of carving patterns are given with particular pieces of furniture later in the book, but anyone unused to carving should try working a few practice patterns on scrap wood of the type to be used. Although softwood may be easy to cut, it does not permit very fine or complicated work, as parts of the pattern must have some substance if grain is not to break out. Hardwoods are more usual for detailed carving. Open-grained hardwood, such as oak, has a long history of very fine ecclesiastical carving, but it is not so easy to carve delicately as a more closely grained hardwood, such as beech.

## TURNING

A wood-turning lathe does not have to be a very complicated machine, and it will still function adequately if it lacks precision in much of its construction. This is seen in some of the quite crude lathes still used by some not-so-primitive peoples, such as Asians, who produce well-made things for the tourist trade. Lathes have been known for a very long time. At the time of the early American settlements, European lathes were treadle operated or power was provided by helpers turning a large wheel; but not long before, the usual type was a pole lathe, where a rope from a springy bow was passed around the work and taken down to a treadle. A push with the foot revolved the work and the bow provided a return stroke. Cutting could only be done on the down stroke. It is probable that much of the first American turning was done on improvised lathes of this type.

There is no need for anyone reproducing early turning to revert to such a basic lathe, but the fact that wood was turned in this way means that it was all comparatively simple. It would be wrong to include very fine detail in wood turning intended to reproduce work of the earliest Colonial type. Nearly all the turned work in early furniture is what is often called "spindle turning." This means parts that are long rather than thick. Early turners did not have the facilities for making things of large diameter in relation to their length, like bowls and very bulbous feet. Instead, their products were table and chair legs or decorative spindles—all of which have diameters much less than their lengths. Such work can be done on the simplest lathe. Small work can be turned on a lathe powered by an electric drill. Larger pieces can be made on a simple lathe, preferably with a capacity up to 30 in. between centers, so it will accommodate the usual length of table leg.

A lathe takes its power at a *headstock*, usually with a belt drive from a treadle or electric motor. The spindle extends and carries a *driving center*, which is an arrangement with a central spike and teeth to engage with the wood being turned (Fig. 4-6A). This is mounted on a *bed*, which can be in several forms, but usually has to parallel parts of metal or wood. On this slides a *tailstock*, the main purpose of which is to support a plain center in line with the headstock center. The plain center provides the bearing on which the other end of the wood revolves. The tailstock can be locked at any position on the bed to accommodate various lengths of wood (Fig. 4-6B). The Colonial turner probably called the headstock a "fixed poppet" and the tailstock a "sliding poppet."

The only other essential is a *toolrest*, which can be fixed at any position on the bed and usually has a T-shaped top that may be adjustable in height (Fig. 4-6C).

Wood turning is done with gouges and chisels. It is not a case of gouges for curved work and chisels for straight work. In general, gouges are the roughing tools and chisels are the finishing ones. There can be considerable leverage on a tool when it cuts into the work and turning tools are longer than their bench equivalents. As the tool is never hit, it tangs into its handle without a bolster. The tool blade may be about 10 in. long and the handle extends a like amount. Fortunately there does not have to be a large variety of turning tools.

Gouges are from about ¼ in. up to as a much as 1½ in., but most roughing can be done with a ¾ in. gouge; then a ¼ in. one can supplement it for closer curves. Chisels are in similar sizes, but almost everything can be done with just a ½ in. one, although an additional narrower one is useful.

The end of a turning gouge is beveled on the outside and given a curved outline, called "spindle nosed" or "finger nail ended" (Fig. 4-6D). An expert may have other outlines, but this serves for all spindle turning. The end of a chisel is angled and sharpened on both sides equally (Fig. 4-6E). The amount it is cut on the skew is not important.

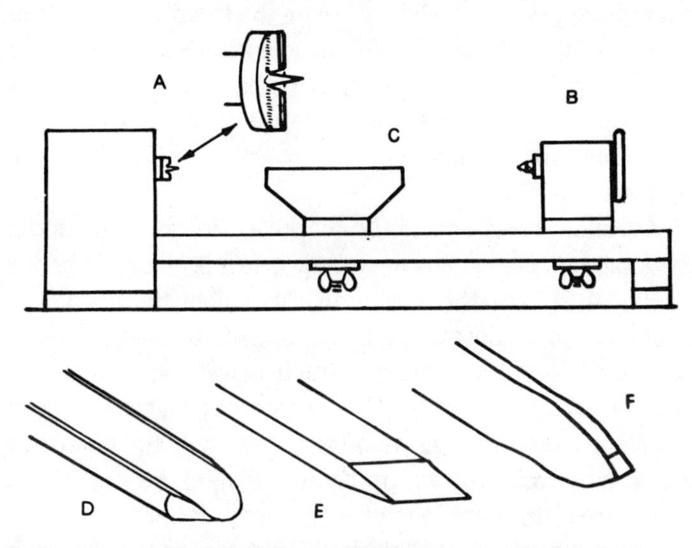


Fig. 4-6. A lathe revolves the work with a driving center (A). The other end is supported by a tailstock (B) and work is done on a toolrest (C). First shaping is with a gouge (D); smoothing is with a chisel (E). A parting tool (F) cuts straight in.

It helps to have a *parting tool* (different from the tool of the same name used for carving). This is a sort of narrow chisel, deeper than it is wide and narrowed behind the cutting edge (Fig. 4-6F). Its use is to push straight into the revolving wood to cut down a recess or part the wood right through.

To make something like a stool leg, square wood is chosen an inch or so overlength. The center of each end is found and a dent made with a center punch. It may help to make a shallow saw cut across the dent for the teeth of the driving center to engage (Fig. 4-7A). In most power-driven lathes the square wood can be mounted in the lathe and turned immediately, but if the power is not great or there is a fear of wood breaking out during the first cuts, corners can be planed off to make the wood approximately octagonal (Fig. 4-7B). In any case, the wood is pressed on to the driving center and the tailstock brought up tightly, with a spot of lubricant on its center. The toolrest is adjusted to be reasonably close to the work and with its top edge slightly below center height.

The first job is to make the wood round, without bothering about the final shape. This is done with a gouge. Have one hand pressing down on the tool over the toolrest. The other hand should be at the end of the handle and usually near your side for steadiness. It will probably be best for the hand over the toolrest to grip with the fist on top, at first, but later there will be occasions when it is more convenient to only have the thumb on top.

Advance the gouge to the work. At first have it almost horizontal, but as it begins to cut, tilt it so it is giving more of a slice (Fig. 4-7C). Do this at several places along the wood. You do not have to withdraw the gouge at each position, but you can slide it along the toolrest. Practice will soon show how heavy a cut can be made and what rate of progress you can make along the work. The wood will apparently be round, but if you stop the lathe you will probably find there are still flats on it. Continue to turn until the wood is round. It helps to get the tailstock end down to a full circle and use that as a guide while turning the rest of the wood.

You can now get the shape very roughly formed with the gouge, leaving enough for finishing. Calipers are needed for checking diameters. They can be the precision spring bow type, but many turners use simple ones with friction joints (Fig. 4-7D). Inside calipers are rarely needed.

Have a drawing of the intended leg or spindle available. If it is a leg, it is usually convenient to have its foot at the tailstock end. Allow a little waste there, then mark other key positions by holding a pencil on the toolrest (Fig. 4-7E). Use the gouge to get the wood close to size, checking with the calipers and remarking with pencil if necessary.

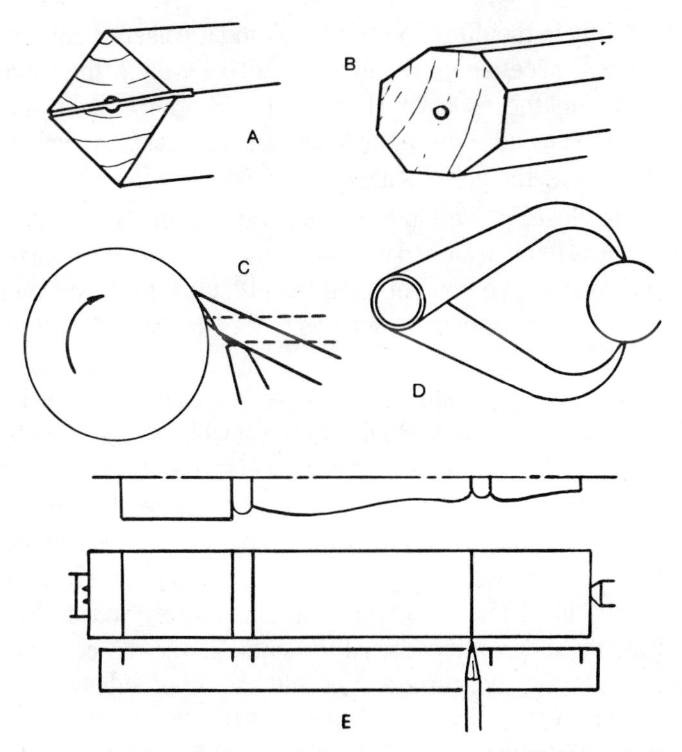


Fig. 4-7. The driving end of wood to be turned is prepared with a saw cut and center punch dot (A). Corners can be planed off (B). The work revolves towards the tool, which tilts up to cut properly (C). Calipers are useful for checking sizes (D). A marked strip of wood can be used with a pencil to mark the wood (E) for shaping.

Mark positions with a chisel held on edge with its longer point downwards and thrust straight into the revolving wood (Fig. 4-8A). Grasp with both hands in the same way as for a gouge. This will cut into the wood. The surface left from a gouge is quite rough. It is made smooth by a slicing action with a chisel. It should not scrape, but waste wood should come away in definite shavings.

The chisel is held firmly with both hands and sloped towards the direction it is to cut, with the lower corner leading. Its position is adjusted so one bevel is in contact with the revolving wood. Aim to cut with the center of the edge. The long point must be kept clear of the wood at all times. If the short point enters the wood, it is not as serious. Tilt the tool slightly in the direction it is to go and it will start cutting. As it does, slice along by moving the tool, still at the same angle, along the toolrest (Fig. 4-8B). Stop the lathe and examine the wood. Where the gouge leaves a surface comparable to a saw, the chisel leaves a surface more like planing.

The chisel is used in the same way on curved surfaces, but always cut from high to low—from thick parts to thin parts. On a convex curve you cut from the outside into the hollows (Fig. 4-8C). On a concave part you work into the hollow (Fig. 4-8D).

Much turning includes *beads*, either alone or in series (Fig. 4-8E). They are worked with the chisel. Outline them by cutting straight in with the long corner of the chisel. Now treat each side of a bead in the same way as described for turning any curved surface. Have the short corner in the direction you wish to cut, but with the usual small bead you do not have to slide the chisel along the toolrest, but merely roll it (Fig. 4-8F). In a series of beads, all the cuts on one direction are made, then the tool turned over and the other sides cut.

With parts of varying diameter it is sometimes convenient to cut in with the parting tool where an angle comes in the outline. This shows where the limits of each size are. The parting tool does not leave a very good surface on the exposed crossgrain. This can be smoothed with the chisel point downwards, but angled so one of the sharpening bevels is pointing straight in (Fig. 4-8G).

The finish from the tools should be quite good, but there may have to be some sanding. Bring the toolrest out of the way, so abrasive paper cannot catch on it. Hold the paper underneath the revolving work. Keep it moving, so as to get different parts of the paper in contact as well as to cover different parts of the wood, otherwise heat is built up and may cause scorching marks.

A turned part can be cut to length with the parting tool. At the tailstock end a stool or table leg can be turned slightly hollow by angling the tool as it enters. At the other end it may be necessary to part in so far and use a chisel to smooth the end before parting further and cutting off.

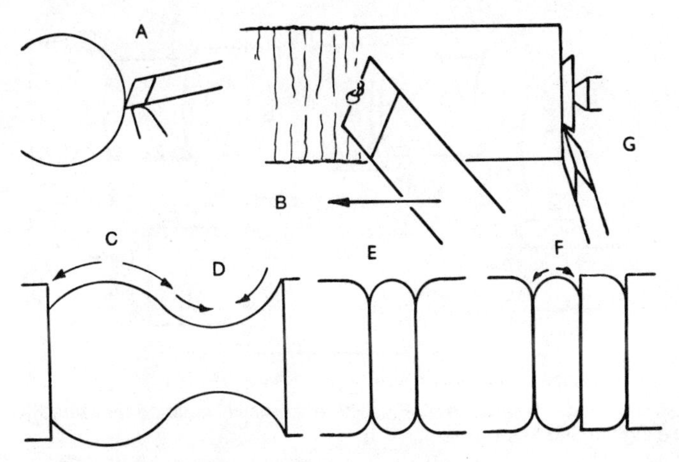


Fig. 4-8. The point of a chisel cuts lines (A), but it slices along to smooth a surface (B). It should always cut curves from high to low (C) and D). Beads are cut similarly (E and F). A straight cut in (G) trims an end.

Turned work has to be joined to other parts of the furniture. Table legs often have square tops for mortise and tenon joints to be made. This calls for careful centering so the leg does not run out of true and produce an eccentric turned part. It also calls for careful cutting where the square part blends into the round, otherwise corners may break out. Angle the gouge to cut from what will remain square towards the rounded part and do any work with the chisel in the same way.

In some cases a dowel is turned on the end of a spindle to mate with a hole in a flat part of the furniture (Fig. 4-9A). If this can come at the end towards the tailstock, it is possible to drill a hole in a scrap piece of wood and use that as a gauge to test the dowel for size (Fig. 4-9B). If dowels come at both ends of the work, that at the other end can be tested with calipers (Fig. 4-9C), but it is always better to use a hole when possible. Cut a slight bevel on the end as the final work on a dowel (Fig. 4-9D), to help it enter its hole.

## MOLDING

In nearly every way we are better equipped than those woodworkers of over 200 years ago. We can do most of the same work with much less effort and with a much greater

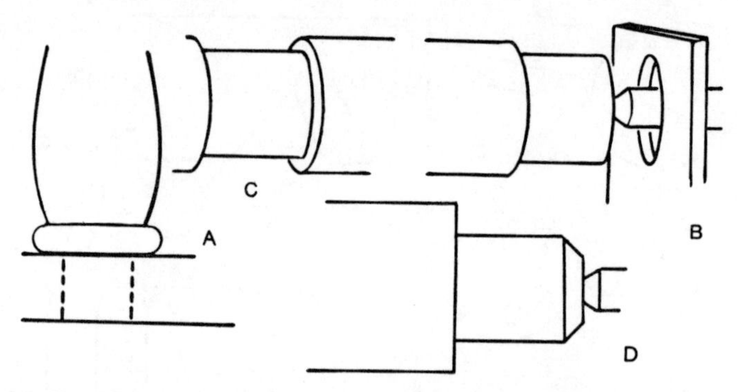


Fig. 4-9. Turned parts assemble with doweled ends (A). A hole in scrap wood acts as a gauge (B) at an end. Elsewhere the dowel must be measured (C). Tapering the end helps assembly (D).

degree of accuracy. However, there is one aspect of woodworking in which they were better equipped than we are today—the hand cutting of moldings. It is possible to make molding with suitable cutters on a spindle, but not everyone has those facilities. Some combination planes are still made with a range of molding cutters, but these are expensive. The old-time cabinetmaker had a number of molding planes. They are no longer made and it is difficult to find used versions in working condition.

It is possible to form many moldings by working in steps and using several planes. Fortunately most of the moldings to be reproduced are fairly simple. The pioneer cabinetmakers did not have the tools nor the inclination to use complication for complication's sake, when something simpler would be just as effective.

Molding planes were made of wood, with a cutting iron narrowed to a stem held with a wedge in a slot. The sole of the plane and the edge of the iron were shaped to produce the molding shape required. In many cases the tool was used at an angle on the edge of a board and the intended angle was marked on the end (Fig. 4-10A). Plane soles were reinforced with harder wood or metal, particularly where a narrow part had to be provided.

Besides full molding planes there were *hollows* and *rounds*, made in the same way. The name indicates the shape cut, so a plane with a rounded bottom is a hollow. Much of the work of a round can be done with a flat-bottomed plane, but if any hollows can be obtained, they are useful tools in reproduction work.

One of the simplest moldings is a bead. This can be worked with an ordinary plane, followed by sanding, on the edge of a piece of wood (Fig. 4-10B). A *cocked bead* stands above the surface (Fig. 4-10C). It was sometimes worked separately and let into a rabbet (Fig. 4-10D). This would be the best method today.

An *ovolo* molding may be found around the edge of a table top. In its simplest form it is part of a circle (Fig. 4-10E), or it may be elliptical (Fig. 4-10F). Without a suitable molding plane it can be worked by cutting two rabbets and planing some of the corner off (Fig. 4-10G), followed by careful work with a rabbet plane and sanding.

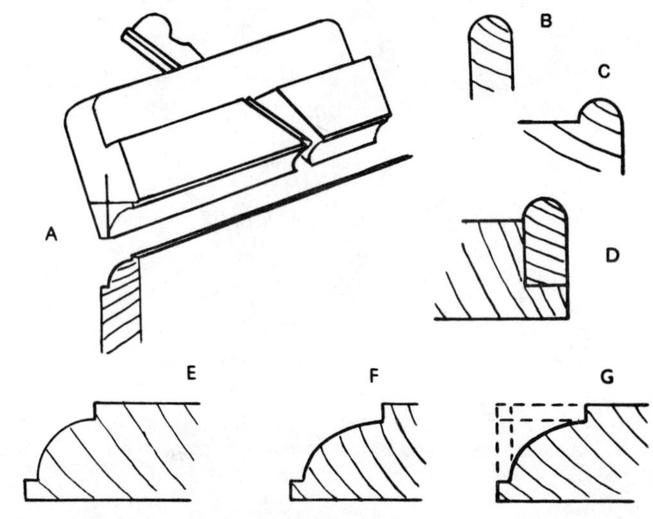


Fig. 4-10. Much early furniture had molded edges, hand cut (A), with beads (B-D) or more complex patterns (E-G).

The *ogee* is a much used molding, appearing in many variations, but the important feature is the double curvature section. There may be a common ogee (Fig. 4-11A) or a reversed ogee (Fig. 4-11B) and either may be combined with quirks and beads. With a suitable molding plane any of these forms is easy, otherwise the shape has to be worked in stages.

A full-size section can be drawn on paper and sequence of cuts planned. Some of the waste can be removed with a simple chamfer (Fig. 4-11C). A convex curve can be shaped with an ordinary plane. A plow or circular saw can be used to cut into the hollow (Fig. 4-11D). Even if a suitable hollow plane is available, this serves as a guide to keep the cut straight. Otherwise it is possible to tilt a rabbet plane in the cut and remove more waste, then use coarse abrasive paper around a shaped piece of wood to true the shape (Fig. 4-11E).

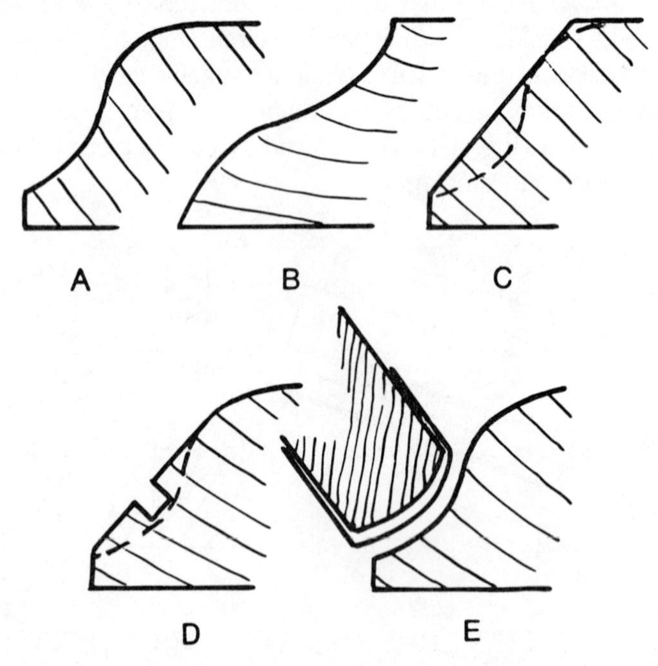


Fig. 4-11. Double curves (A and B) can be made by progressive planing and sanding (C-E).

Many other molding sections can be copied by similar sequences of cuts. If beads have to be cut with narrow gaps alongside, it is often possible to cut in with a circular saw (Fig. 4-12A) or use a cutting gauge. A rabbet plane then bevels the wood (Fig. 4-12B) to leave enough clearance for using the same plane to round the bead section (Fig. 4-12C). A further step is a bead worked on a corner section (Fig. 4-12D). Several beads (called "reeds" if away from an edge) can be worked in a similar way if no suitable plane is available. Narrow grooves are cut, then a little taken off each side of the cut with a rabbet plane progressively until each bead can be shaped (Fig. 4-12E).

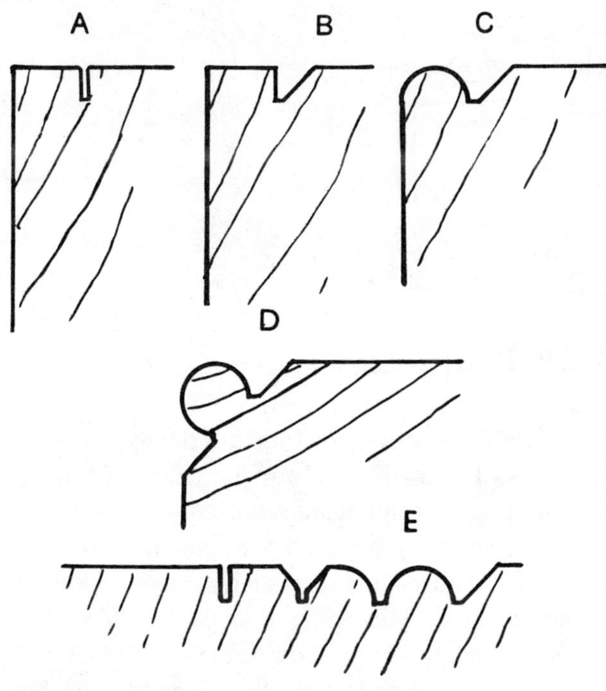


Fig. 4-12. Beads are made with progressive saw and plane cuts, whether on an edge (A-D) or a surface (E).

Moldings of a great many sections were used. The majority are based on classical forms, going back to Greek and Roman days, but some will be found to merely follow the particular craftsman's ideas. If moldings are examined the most pleasing ones will be found to have all or most curves based on parts of an ellipse and not on sections of circles. For instance, an ogee can be made with one quarter circle hollow blending into another quarter circle round. This looks better if one is to a very different radius from the other, but the whole thing looks even better if the two curves are parts of ellipses.

# Simple Projects

The term *furniture* embraces all sorts of things used about the home, besides the obvious tables and chairs, with the cupboards and storage items needed for convenience and comfort. There are many things on the fringe, but many are made in the same way and include wooden items used in the kitchen or washhouse, or even in the yard or garden. Many of these are simple and compact, so they require little material, and some will serve as things to make by beginners, who hesitate to risk their ability, or lack of it, on a large piece of furniture where a mistake could be costly.

This chapter includes simple items of true furniture, as well as associated items of interest, which are made in the same way and provide scope for practice as well as worthwhile results. Many of them are based on Colonial desgins, dating from those early days when the urgent need was for furniture that would serve a purpose, but did not necessarily have much applied decoration. Later examples incorporate these original designs, but as more time became available, the finish became more decorative. The earlier pieces were made by settlers for their own use, so skill in design and execution varied. Later examples were more likely the products of specialists serving the needs and desires of customers.

Consequently many of the examples could be finished plainly, or be made more ornate and decorated in several ways. In any case, providing nothing was used that would not have been available to an early craftsman, the result should be authentic. It may even be acceptable to use a modern synthetic finish, if protection of a much used item is more important than keeping strictly to the original standards.

Some of these simple items lend themselves to production from wood bought machine-planed all round and their simplicity almost invites quantity-production, but care is needed to hand plane and avoid a finished product that is so precise that machine production is obvious.

## STOOL FROM ONE BOARD

This is an example of the basic nailed construction for stools and related small pieces of furniture (Fig. 5-1A). Obviously, several sizes are possible, but the example is schemed to cut from a board planed to 7 in. by ⅝ in. and would be simplest to make in pine or other softwood, although it would look better of oak or walnut if intended to take its place in a living room. Softwood might be more appropriate for kitchen use, although a painted finish, possibly with brightly colored decoration, would indicate the Pennsylvania Dutch style.

Cut the main parts to length, with a little surplus for trimming later. The sides are cut down the middle of the board. Plane their edges true and do any hand planing necessary to all parts. Make a full-size drawing of one end of the stool (Fig. 5-1B). This gives you the angles. For stability the bottoms of the legs should extend to come directly under the ends of the top.

Cut the top and sides to size. Bevel the ends of the sides. Use an adjustable bevel and pencil to mark the positions of the legs on the inner surface of the side.

Mark out the legs, but do not cut them to length yet. The cutouts are made by first drilling a hole and making saw cuts into it (Fig. 5-1C). Clean the cuts by paring with a chisel. Mark the joints where the sides will fit, using the actual pieces of wood to get the sizes and the adjustable bevel at the same setting as it was for the sides (Fig. 5-1D) to get the angles correct. Use a knife to mark across the grain, then cut on the waste sides of the lines with a fine saw. With careful cutting there may be no need for further treatment; otherwise carefully pare with a chisel.

Mark and cut the tops and bottoms of the legs to the correct angles. Take sharpness off the edges of the feet by lightly chamfering. A block plane is convenient for this. Enough surplus at the top can be left for a few leveling plane strokes to be made after the sides are attached to the legs.

Nail the sides into the recesses in the leg. Glue may be used as well. The nails could have decorative heads, but it is probably better to punch nails below the surface and cover them with stopping. Common or box nails might be used in softwoods, but the smaller headed finishing nails do not leave such a large hole to fill after punching. Assemble the stool on a level surface and see that all four legs are touching it. Check for squareness, either by using a try square across the tops of the legs, or by measuring diagonals (Fig. 5-1E). Let the glue set, then plane the upper surfaces level, if necessary.

The top is shown with a cutout (Fig. 5-1F) to serve as a hand hold for carrying the stool. It is not essential, but it is convenient and a decorative feature. The ends are holes, then the sides can be drawn freehand. Several holes can be drilled in the waste part, then the shape cut with chisels and gouges, or a jigsaw will follow the lines. Thoroughly sand inside the cutout and round its edges.

Nail the top to the underframe, with glue in the joints. Drive the nails in dovetail fashion along the sides. As there would be little grip for nails in the end grain of the legs, one central nail into each leg is enough and the sides can be relied on to provide strength (Fig. 5-1G).

Level adjoining surfaces where necessary and sand all exposed parts. The original stools would probably have been left with hand plane marks showing, but edges would have been well rounded. For a natural hardwood finish that would look best, but if softwood is to be painted it is better to sand the surfaces level.

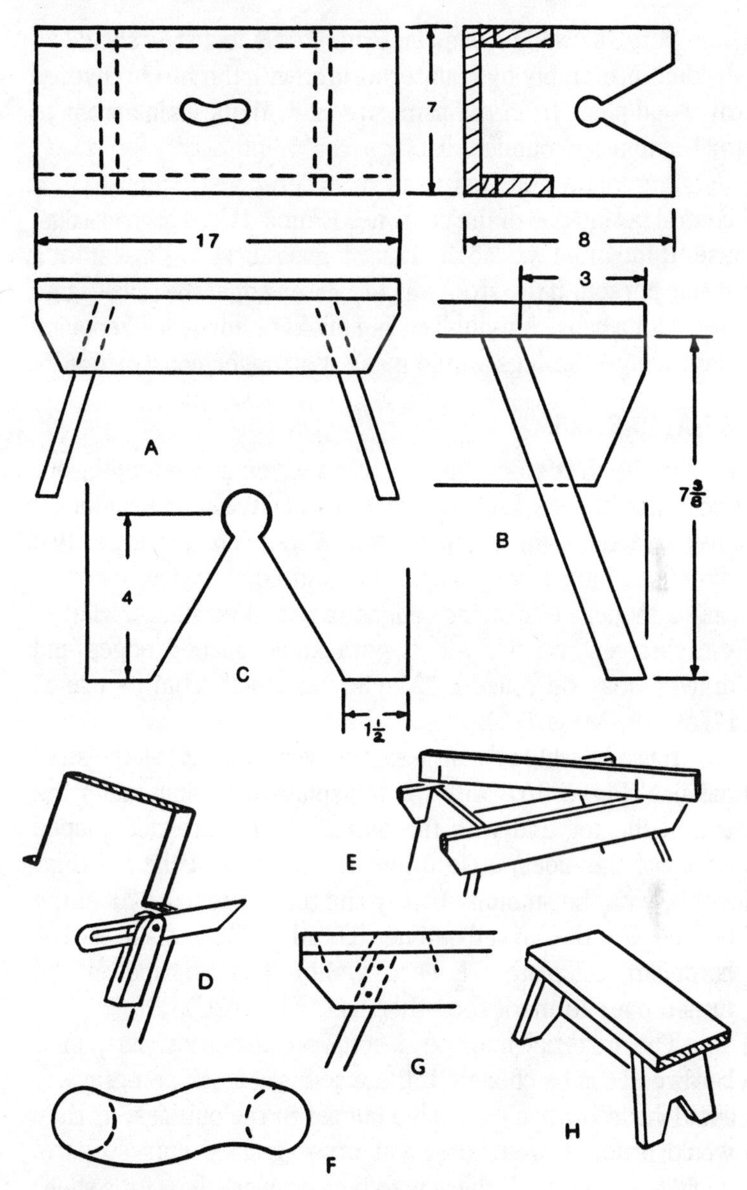


**Materials List 5-1**

Stool from One Board

| | | |
|---|---|---|
| 1 | Top | 7 × 17 × 5/8 |
| 2 | Legs | 7 × 8 × 5/8 |
| 2 | Sides | 3 3/8 × 17 × 5/8 |

Fig. 5-1. Stool from one board.

Screws could be used instead of nails, but they should be hidden, preferably by counterboring, with the heads covered by wood plugs from the same wood, with its grain across to match that surrounding it.

A variation on this form of nailed construction uses a central rail instead of the side ones (Fig. 5-1H). This had a dual use. If the stool was about 12 in. high it served as a seat for a young person. If the stool was turned on edge, the rail became a seat for a baby. Although nailing might be adequate, tenoning the rail into the legs would make a stronger construction.

## SPLAYED STOOL

In the first stool the legs are splayed in the length, but there would be an improvement in stability and appearance if they splayed in the width as well. Too much splaying in two directions introduces complications in edge angles, but with only a moderate splaying, edges may still be right-angled to the surfaces. Such a stool, with some shaped edges and drawer, may be called a "Mayflower stool" from its use at Plymouth, Mass.

It is advisable to draw a side view of at least half the stool full-size (Fig. 5-2A), with the leg splayed to come under the end of the top and with the outline of the intended shaped edges of the sides. Also draw an end view of the leg (Fig. 5-2B), with the amount of splay and the shape to be cut at the bottom. For the curved outlines it is advisable to make card or hardboard templates. Each can show half a shape and be turned over to mark the other half (Fig. 5-2C).

The material may be a softwood, such as pine, or a hardwood can be chosen. If the wood is soft or open-grained, avoid incorporating excessive curves in the outlines, as they would produce weaknesses at cross-grained cuts so parts might break away. If there is to be a drawer, allow for a shelf, as included in the material list.

Mark out the two legs, using the full-size drawing as a guide to sizes and using the template for the shape to be cut out at the bottom. Cut the angles across with a jigsaw or a coping saw (Fig. 5-2D). Clean up the shapes with a chisel or rasp and finish by sanding. If there is to be a drawer the shelf will provide stiffness in a nailed construction, but if the stool is to be made without this, it would be stronger to allow for the sides to be let into the legs, in a similar way to the rails in the first stool, but to only about half their thickness.

The shelf is the part that controls sizes. Battens across its ends serve as guides for the drawer (Fig. 5-2E). The angle of the shelf end and the side of a batten can be found from the drawing. The sides of the shelf and the ends of the battens must also be beveled to match the splay in the width of the legs. Mark where the shelf comes on each leg. Glue and nail it in position. Check that the assembly stands level and the splay of the legs is the same. If the splay is not exactly the same as the drawing, it is more important that both legs splay the same amount.

Mark out the sides. Top edges will be beveled slightly at angles to be found by checking against the assembly. Mark the shaped edges from the template. See that the wide part will bear over the side of a leg. The curve may have to be adjusted if the leg splay is not exactly as first drawn. Cut the curved shapes with a bandsaw or jigsaw and clean up the edges. Both parts can be fixed to the legs if there is not to be a drawer. If there is to be one, only fix the rear piece.

Put the front part in position and mark on it the inside edges of the battens and the top edge of the shelf. Mark the height the opening for the drawer is to come (Fig. 5-2F). Cut out the opening. The vertical edges are cut squarely, but top and bottom have to be at an angle to suit the splay of the leg sides (Fig. 5-2G).

Fix that side to the legs. Cut a drawer side to width and slide it through the opening. The back of the drawer can be cut at the same angle as the stool side, but that is unnecessary. It can be upright, so its top edge strikes the far side (Fig. 5-2H). Mark the angle of the front edge (Fig. 5-2J) on the side. That side serves as a guide to the finished size of the drawer.

How the drawer is made depends on the preference of the maker. Most of the original drawers in this type of stool were nailed together with a thin piece of wood nailed on as

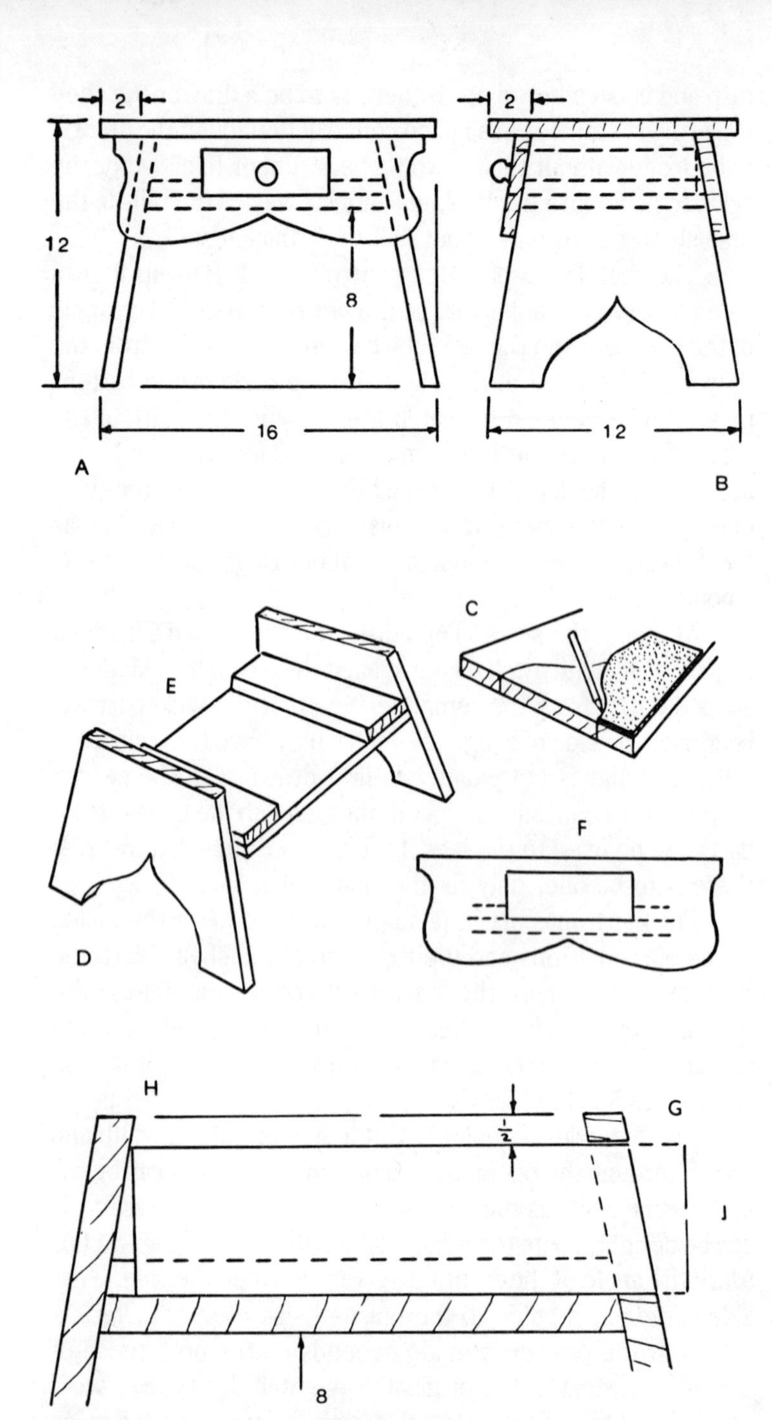


Fig. 5-2. Splayed Mayflower stool. (Continued on next page.)

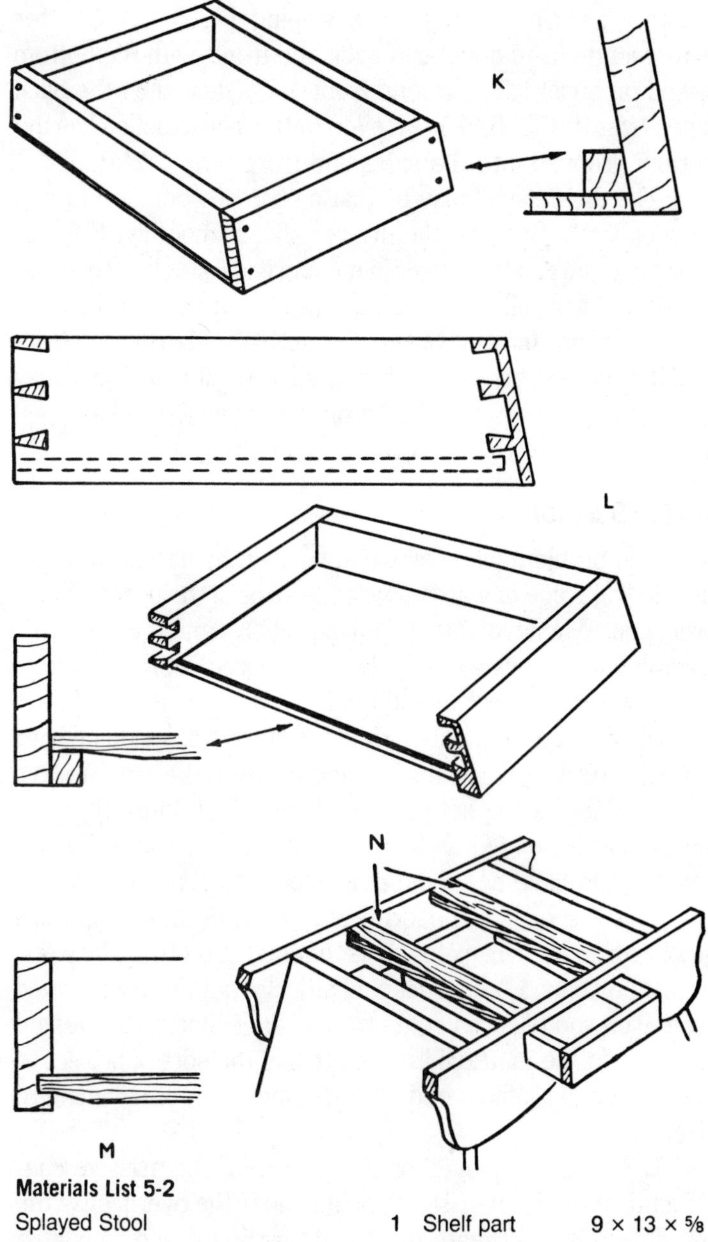


**Materials List 5-2**

Splayed Stool

| | | |
|---|---|---|
| 1 | Top | 12 × 16 × 5/8 |
| 2 | Legs | 12 × 12 × 5/8 |
| 2 | Sides | 5 × 15 × 5/8 |
| 1 | Shelf part | 9 × 13 × 5/8 |
| 2 | Shelf parts | 3½ × 9 × 5/8 |
| 1 | Drawer part | 9 × 9 × ¼ |
| 4 | Drawer parts | 2½ × 9 × 5/8 |

bottom—just a box with the front sloping (Fig. 5-2K). A better construction used dovetails, back and front, with the bottom raised on small fillets around front and sides, then the back taken over it (Fig. 5-2L). An even better construction has the bottom grooved into the sides and front (Fig. 5-2M).

The drawer pull may be just a strip of wood or a turned wooden knob. See that the drawer slides smoothly. Plane to fit, if necessary. The drawer in most original stools of this type tilted as it was pulled out. If it is to slide out without the front dropping there may be *kickers* put across under the top (Fig. 5-2N). The top should overhang slightly all round and may have its edges rounded. Nail it on with punched and stopped nails or use screws counterbored and plugged.

## TENONED STOOL

One problem when all wood was cut by hand—from the tree-felling stage onwards—was the sizes of the boards finally produced. When wood was cut laboriously from the log with a pitsaw, thicknesses were likely to be more than the furniture maker would like, but he did not have the means of reducing them easily. Consequently some furniture was made heavier and with thicker wood than would normally be used today. This produced a characteristic style and a structure that was simple and depended on bulk to give rigidity, where thinner wood would have needed a more complex construction.

This is seen in some forms and seats, or most simply in a stool with no framing except legs tenoned into a top. The wood should be about 1½ in. thick and any close-grained hardwood type. Top and legs can come from a single board. Suggested sizes are in the material list, but this is the sort of project to plan to suit available wood with the minimum of trimming to size.

Legs can be splayed or upright—with the massive construction there is less risk of tipping due to the overhang of the top (Fig. 5-3A). Prepare the wood for the top and both legs, with a little extra on the length. The simplest construction has all the parts parallel-sided, but there can be some profiling of the top and the legs. The legs should be cut back to produce feet in any case, so that there is less risk of the stool wobblıng (Fig. 5-3B).

Mark the tenons on the tops of the legs, allowing them to be long enough to project through a short distance. Their width should be a little more than the thickness of the wood. Unless it is a very wide stook, two should be enough (Fig. 5-3C). Mark the positions of the legs on the top and take the lines around so they are on top and bottom surfaces (Fig. 5-3D). If there is to be any profiling of outlines, the joints should be marked out first, while there are straight edges to put a try square against and to gauge from.

Upright legs will have tenons and mortises marked across squarely. If the legs splay this bevel will have to be allowed for when laying out the joints (Fig. 5-3E).

Remove the waste from the legs by sawing, but keep the thickness of saw kerfs on the waste sides of the lines. Much of the waste in the mortises can be removed by drilling, either one large hole or several near the outline. It is advisable to drill back from both sides to reduce the risk of grain breaking out. If holes have to be taken right through, have scrap wood close against the far side.

Working from both sides is important when dealing with splayed legs, as the outlines on the two surfaces are not directly opposite. Pare with chisels from opposite sides, in any case.

Make diagonal saw cuts in each tenon for about three-quarters of its depth and prepare wedges from the same wood ready to drive into them. As the wedges will show and may be regarded as a decorative feature, arrange their directions symmetrically (Fig. 5-3F). The assembly can be glued, but original specimens were put together dry. With the tenons driven as tightly as possible into the mortises, support the stool on a strong surface—the ground rather than a springy bench—and drive in the wedges. If glue has been used, give it time to set, then cut off the projecting ends of tenons and wedges, and plane them level.

An alternative to straightforward planing, with or without profiled edges, is to treat the wood as if leveled with an adze

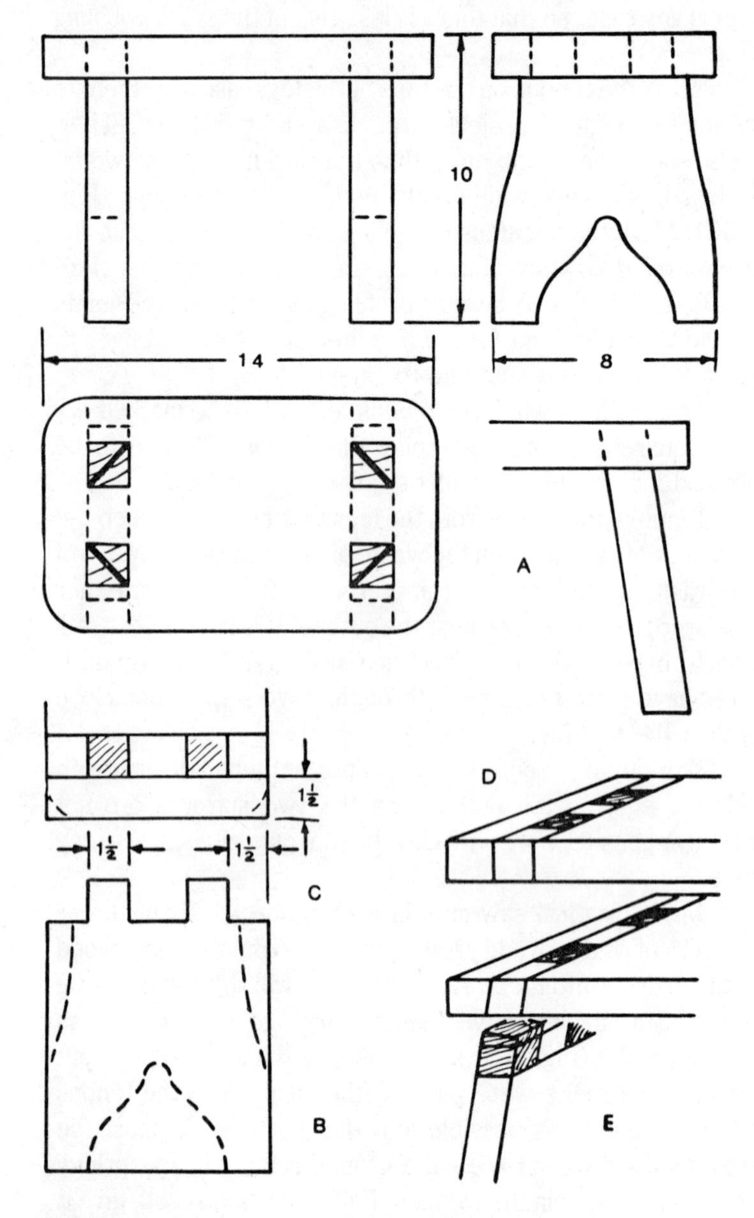


**Materials List 5-3**

Tenoned Stool

| | | |
|---|---|---|
| 1 | Top | 8 × 14 × 1½ |
| 2 | Legs | 8 × 10 × 1½ |

Fig. 5-3. Tenoned stool. (Continued on next page.)

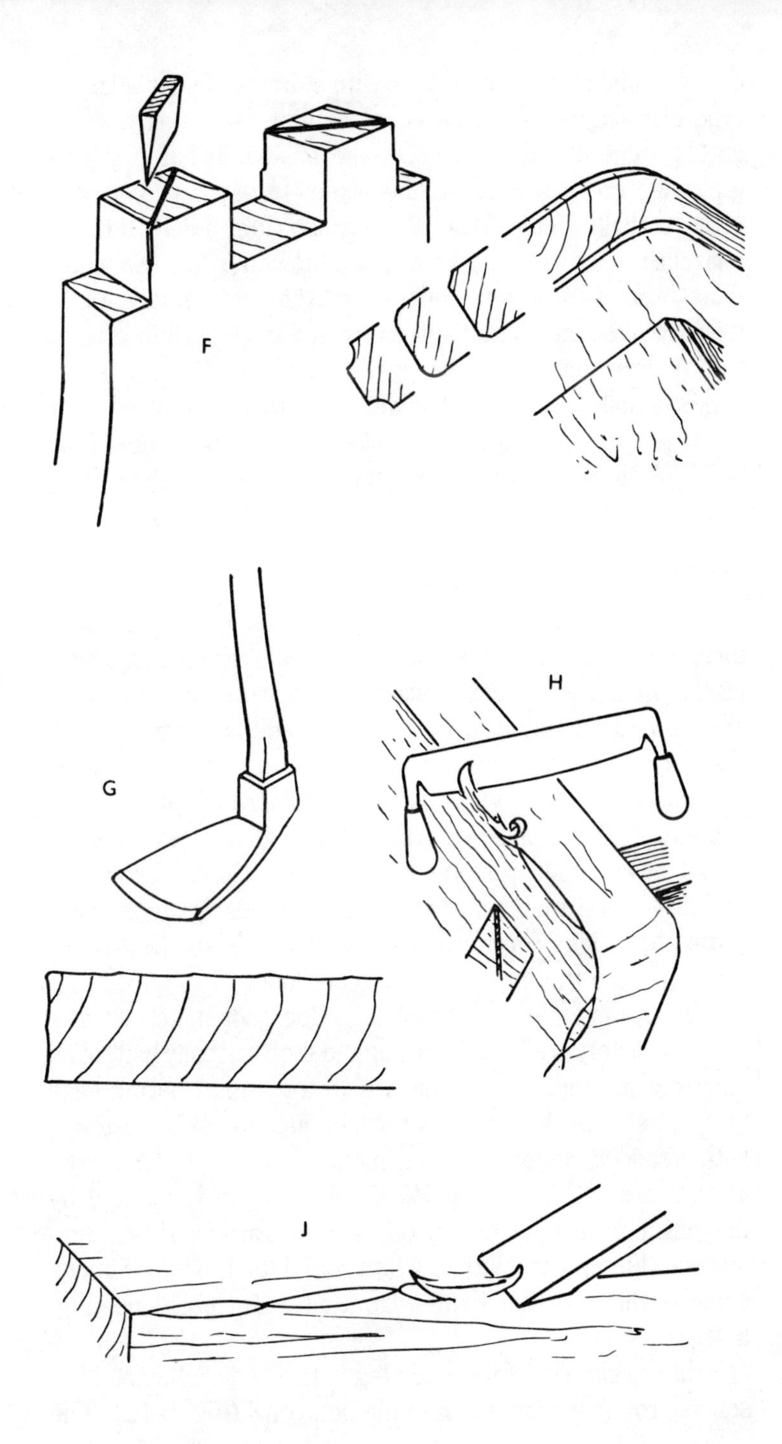
F
G
H
J

and trimmed around the edges with a drawknife. An adze is a type of swinging cutting tool, something like an ax with the cutting edge at right-angles to the handle. It has a slightly gougelike cross section to the blade. In use it is swung to remove shallow chips from the surface (Fig. 5-3G). If one is unavailable, a similar effect can be obtained by using a smoothing plane with a well rounded cutter set coarsely, or by working over the planed surface with a large shallow gouge.

A drawknife would be used to chamfer the edges in a series of hollows comparable with the surface produced by an adze. A drawknife is a broad blade with two handles (Fig. 5-3H). A similar effect can be obtained by using a spokeshave or a broad chisel used bevel downwards (Fig. 5-3J).

## PEG-LEGGED STOOL

We accept that any floor is level and any piece of furniture, whatever the number of legs, will stand reasonably firmly. In the early days, when floors were of earth or of unseasoned roughly hewn logs, they might be far from level. Four or more legs require a flat surface to rest on if they are not to wobble. Three legs do not have this trouble and will rest without wobbling on any surface. Sawing trestles for use in woodland and milking stools for use in a dirt-floored cowshed use this tripod method of support. Many early stools were given three legs for normal household use so they would accommodate themselves to uneven floors.

An arrangement of three legs does not match up to a square top very well, so three-legged stools usually had round or hexagonal tops. Those shapes of top do not permit easy framing, so tops were mostly thick enough to hold their shape without added woodwork. This meant a thickness of at least 1 in. and preferably nearer 1½ in. A hexagon is marked by drawing a circle and stepping off the radius around the circumference (Fig. 5-4A). With this or a round top the leg positions come on lines to the center from alternate positions (Fig. 5-4B).

In the simplest form each leg is tapered slightly and left square, roughly rounded or made octagonal (Fig. 5-4C). The top is brought down to a round dowel of a size to suit the holes in the top. It is inadvisable to reduce the tops of the legs too much. As a rough guide the holes through the top should be about the same diameter as the thickness of the top (Fig. 5-4D). Drill a hole of this size in a piece of scrap wood and use it as a gauge while shaping the tops of the legs. Allow some excess length on each leg for trimming after passing through the top and leveling the bottoms after fixing.

If the stool is to look right, it is important that all three legs slope outwards at the same angle. If a drilling machine is available the stool top can be supported on an angled block so the drill approaches each position at exactly the same direction. Otherwise, a piece can be cut to stand on the top as an angle gauge, while a try square is stood at right angles to it. If an assistant watches from one side and you sight over the drill at right angles to him, it should be possible to direct an electric drill or a bit brace sufficiently near the correct angle each time (Fig. 5-4E).

Make a saw cut in the dowel part of each leg. Drive each leg so this cut is across the grain of the top, then when each wedge is driven, any burst effect on the top is taken in the direction best able to resist it (Fig. 5-4F). The assembly can be made dry or glue may be used. Cut off the projecting leg tops and the wedges and plane level.

The best way to get the legs level and of equal length is to make up a temporary assembly that works like an engineer's surface gauge. Have a solid block of wood with a smooth level bottom and a strip of wood standing up at one side, with a pencil through it at the height needed (Fig. 5-4G). Invert the stool on a smooth surface, then use the height gauge to mark as far as possible around each leg (Fig. 5-4H) indicating where to cut off.

This produces a rather basic stool and the primitive appearance may be regarded as a good reproduction of one of the earliest types. Several things can be done to obtain a better appearance. The top of hexagonal shape may have its edges molded. If a lathe of suitable capacity is available, the top may be turned. Turned legs are appropriate and were

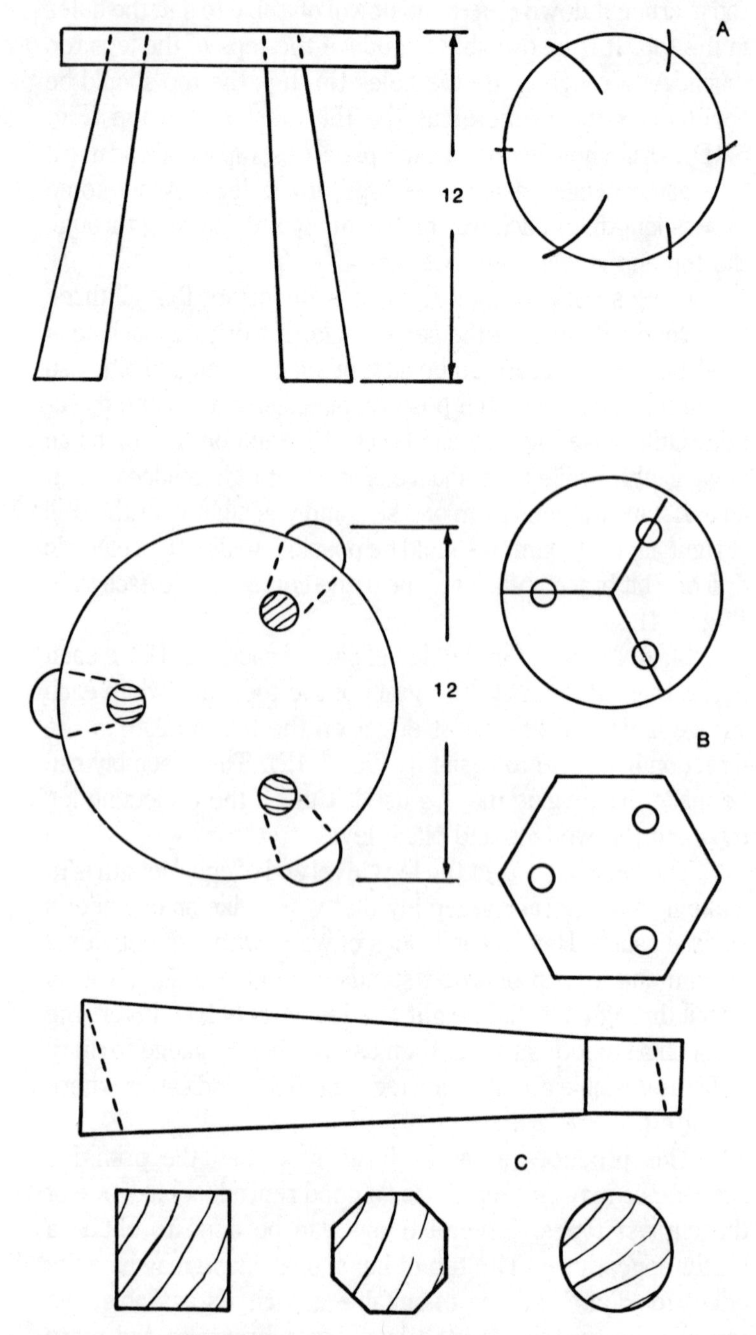


Fig. 5-4. Peg-legged stool. (Continued on next page.)

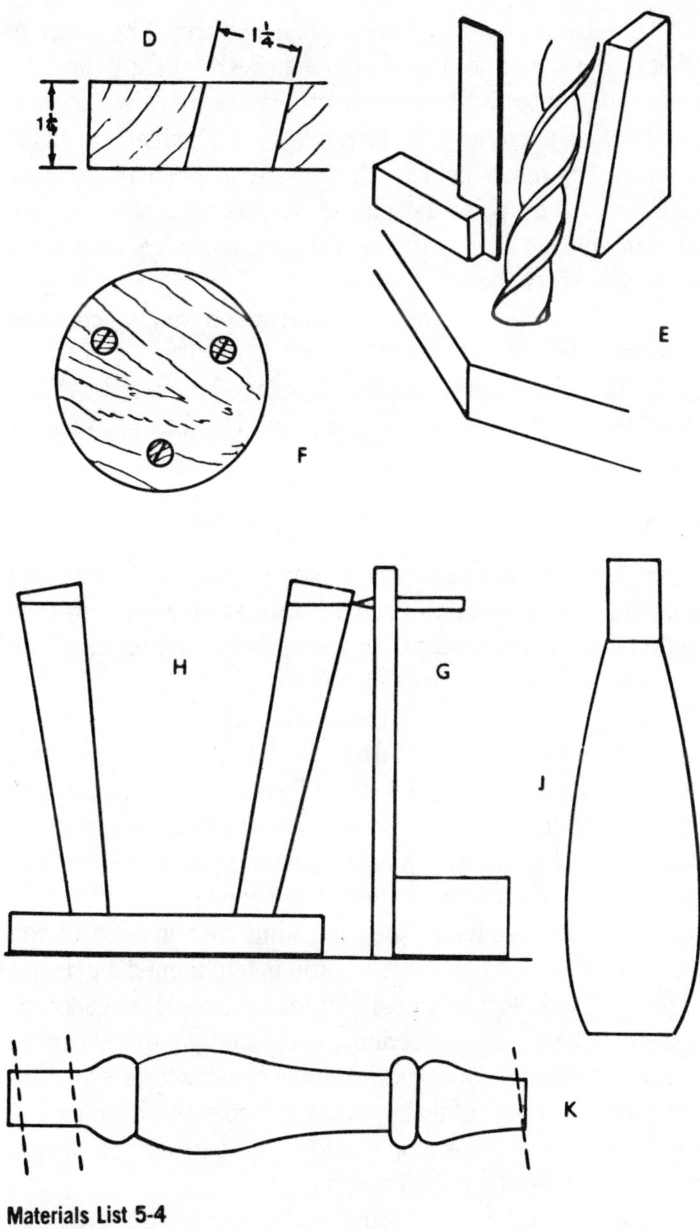


**Materials List 5-4**

Peg-Legged Stool

| | | |
|---|---|---|
| 1 | Top | 12 × 12 × 1¼ |
| 3 | Legs | 2 × 13 × 2 |

often used, ranging from fairly plain outlines (Fig. 5-4J) to those of more complicated form (Fig. 5-4K). In any case the top is tapered to the hole size, otherwise there would be a difficult angle to cut next to the dowel end. The feet may finish as balls, but more usually they were allowed to be near parallel, so they could be cut across, as described for the simple stool, and slight variations in trimming to get them level would not affect the final pattern.

Of course, this method of construction was not confined to three-legged stools. A rectangular top was fitted with four legs in the same way, with each leg splayed cornerwise. Such a stool would not be appropriate as a yard bench or a stand for plant pots.

## BENCH

Stools were made longer to serve as benches for more than one. Construction can be the same as for a stool, providing there is enough stiffness to prevent the top sagging. With the tenoned stool construction the top would have to be stiff enough in itself, due mainly to thickness, but the other types should get enough stiffness from the other lengthwise parts.

The bench described here follows a Shaker design, intended to be purely functional but getting its beauty from its proportions (Fig. 5-5A). Many variations are possible. The original had the legs bracketed to the top, but a stiffer construction would come from using long rails instead of the brackets. Rails are needed if the top is lengthened and is not stiff enough to hold its shape under load. It would be inappropriate in a Shaker reproduction to mold edges or otherwise decorate the bench, but the method of construction is basic to designs used by other furniture makers, so shaping outlines or otherwise adding decoration would not necessarily be wrong, but could not be described as Shaker.

The top is a plain rectangle. As it is not to have any shaping, care is needed to finish edges squarely and plane the ends truly, otherwise discrepancies may show. This also applies to the legs. Although machine sawing and planing will help in getting accuracy, particularly if top and legs are first machined in one length, follow by hand planing to remove machine marks.

The bottoms of the legs have semi-circular cutouts, with edges left square in cross section (Fig. 5-5B). If brackets or braces are to be used, they should be fixed to the legs before fixing them to the top.

The simplest construction has the brackets profiled and fixed with screws, sunk deeply and covered with wood plugs (Fig. 5-5C). Adjust the depth of counterboring so the screw ends will almost go through the legs and arrange the holes slightly staggered so screw points do not meet. Use glue as well as screws. Note that the grain of the brackets is across. They can be fixed slightly high on the legs and their tops planed level and checked at right angles to the legs as a final preparation before fixing to the top.

A better way of making and fixing the brackets is to let each pair be in one piece of wood. This notches into the top of the leg, preferably with the leg grooved to let the bracket in, making a sort of combined half lap and dado joint (Fig. 5-5D). A closely fitting glued joint should not need screws as well.

If rails are to be used instead of brackets, they are made and fixed in the same way and are, in effect, brackets extended until they join (Fig. 5-5E).

The top can be fixed with screws in counterbored holes driven downwards into the legs and brackets or rails (Fig. 5-5F). If it is prefered that there should be little evidence of fastenings on the top surface, screws can be driven diagonally from below through the brackets (Fig. 5-5G) and deeply counterbored if rails are used (Fig. 5-5H). There may still have to be screws downwards into the tops of the legs, but they can be avoided if strips of wood are fixed as cleats to the inner surfaces and screwed both ways (Fig. 5-5J). Ideally, all screws are sunk below the surface and covered with plugs, but it would not matter if the screws through the cleats remain on the surface.

## CRICKET

The idea of three legs for stability extended from the milking stool to more attractive stools for use indoors. One

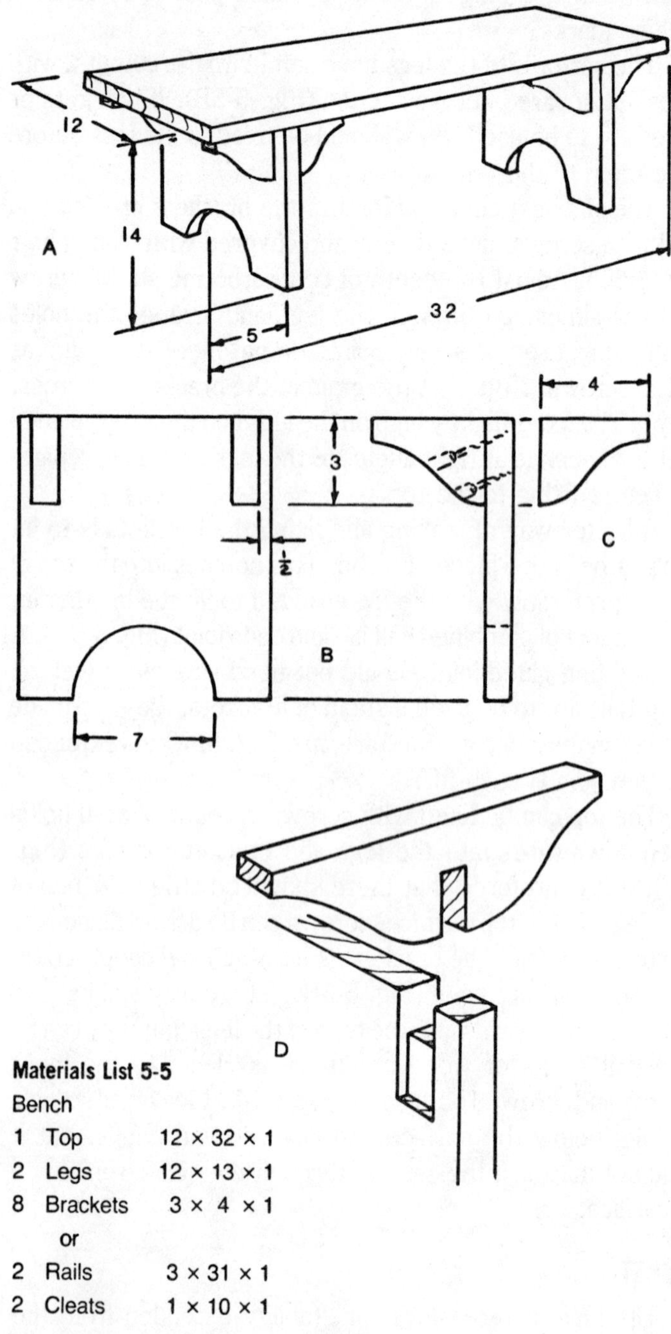


**Materials List 5-5**

Bench

| | | |
|---|---|---|
| 1 | Top | 12 × 32 × 1 |
| 2 | Legs | 12 × 13 × 1 |
| 8 | Brackets | 3 × 4 × 1 |
| | or | |
| 2 | Rails | 3 × 31 × 1 |
| 2 | Cleats | 1 × 10 × 1 |

Fig. 5-5. Bench. (Continued on next page.)

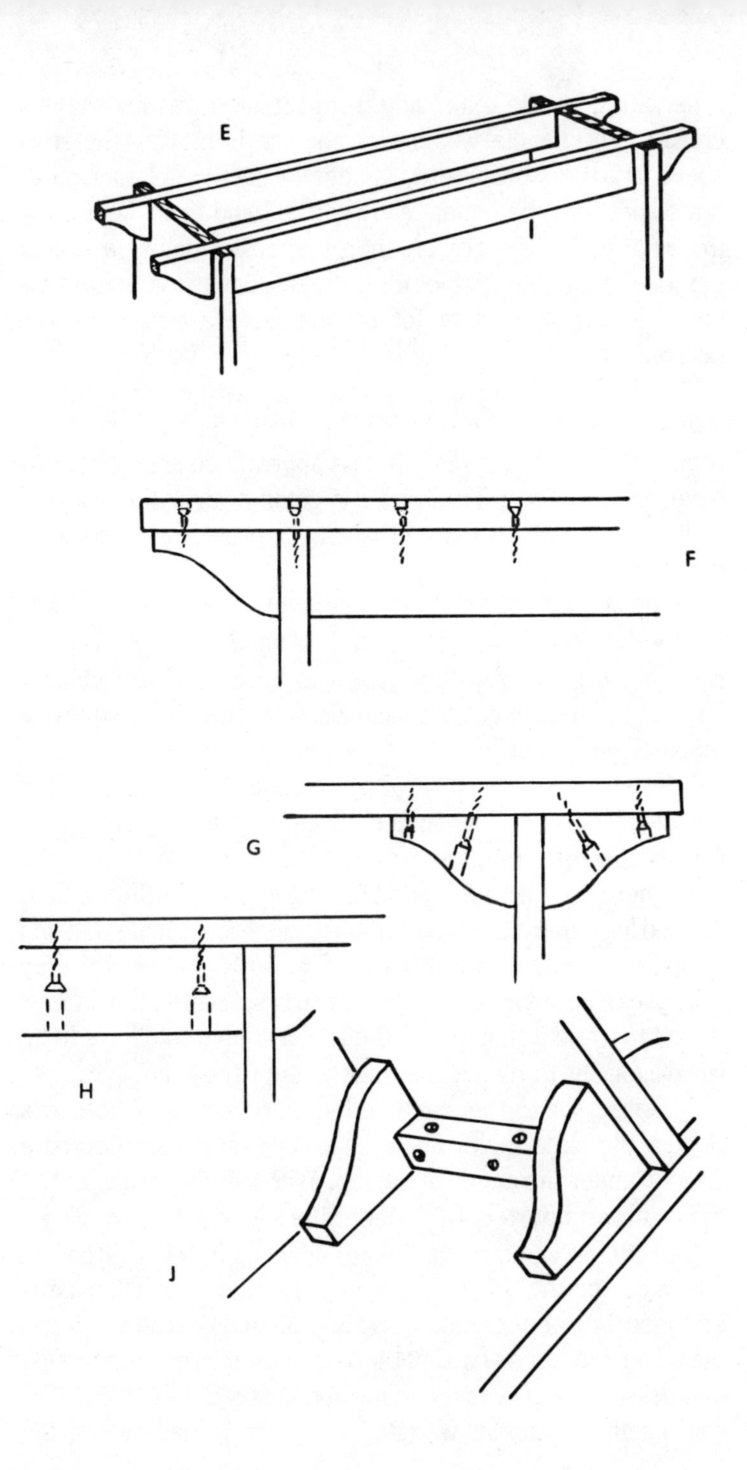
E
I
F
G
H
J

type with a handle extending from the side was known as a cricket. The handle was a convenience in moving the stool about, but the stools were also used near the fire to support hot dishes and the handle allowed the hand to be kept away from the heat. The cricket then served for dishes a similar purpose to the metal trivet for kettles and pots taken from the fire. They may account for the phrase, "a cricket on the hearth."

In its simplest form the cricket top has the handle part of it (Fig. 5-6A). It is made of fairly thick wood for strength and to reduce the risk of warping, but its appearance is lightened by beveling the edges. The handle is given a curved outline and well rounded by whittling and sanding to provide a comfortable grip (Fig. 5-6B).

An alternative top has a separate handle turned and doweled in (Fig. 5-6C). Many kinds of handles are possible if a lathe is available. Another type can be carved and given a hooked end to prevent the hand sliding off and be fixed with a tenon (Fig. 5-6D).

The legs are arranged with one under the handle end and two at the far end. The simplest legs are made octagonal, by planing the corners off square section wood, tapering to the top, where the end is rounded to plug into a hole (Fig. 5-6E). Turned legs are made in patterns to match the handle, but it is advisable to round the bottoms (Fig. 5-6F), otherwise they will have to be cut across diagonally to rest level on the floor. It is best to avoid a shoulder at the top, as this would have to be cut diagonally to match the underside of the other part.

Drilling the top needs to be done carefully so all three legs slope at the same angle. Their outer edges at the bottom come directly under the edges of the top. With a drilling machine the top can be supported on a tapered block. For hand drilling a piece of scrap wood cut to the intended angle can be stood on the wood and the drill or brace kept parallel to it. The joint is stronger the deeper it goes, so holes should be made well into the wood, but not so far that there is a risk of breaking through or cracks developing in the thin wood above. This is a joint that will benefit from foxtail wedging. A saw cut is made across the

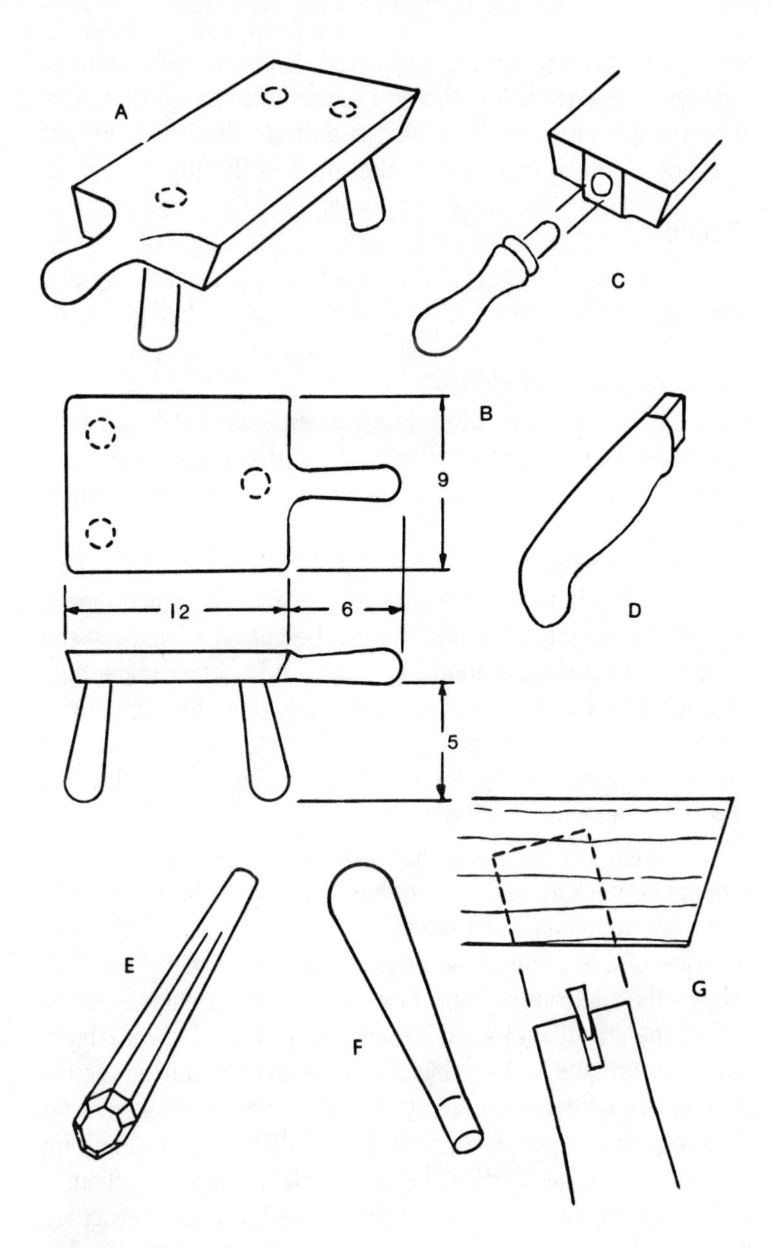


**Materials List 5-6**

Cricket

1 Top 9 × 18 × 1⅛

3 Legs 1½ × 8 × 1½

Fig. 5-6. Cricket.

end of the leg and a wedge inserted, large enough to spread the leg end when it hits the end of the hole (Fig. 5-6G). This assembly is prepared with glue and driven into the hole with the line of the wedge across the grain of the top.

## TABOURET

An item coming between a stool and a small table can still have similar uses to those of the first owners, being suitable for sitting on, while also making a coffee table. The usual arrangement has four legs and the top is either round or octagonal. There are three-legged versions, but this means the underframing cannot be halved and the top is made hexagonal or round, to match the leg arrangement. The example has four legs and the usual framing (Fig. 5-7A).

Size may depend on the available wood for the top, which will probably have to be made up in width by gluing pieces together. Although a round top can be cut on a bandsaw and carefully smoothed around the edges, it is better made on a lathe, but it would have to be a lathe equipped for mounting a faceplate on the outboard end to accommodate the size. An attractive appearance is more easily obtained by hand working, if an octagonal shape is chosen.

It is the underframing that takes the strain, so these parts should be thick enough to provide deep joints. A full-size side view of one leg and part of the top should be drawn, with the outside of a leg under the edge of the top (Fig. 5-7B). This shows the angle in the joint. For a leg made without the aid of a lathe, the strongest joint is a thick tenon. For a leg 2 in. thick, the tenon should be 1 in. thick. This means that the leg section is a square with its corners off (Fig. 5-7C) and not taken as far as a regular octagon, as this would cut into the tenon. The joint should be laid out and cut before working the leg section.

The underframing parts are halved where they cross (Fig. 5-7D) and their ends cut back under the top. The leg tenons can go right through the underframing and could be strengthened by wedging. The legs and underframing assembly should be made up completely and the glue allowed to set before fitting the top.

The top could be fitted with screws downwards, with the holes plugged (Fig. 5-7E), but it would look better if screwing was from below (Fig. 5-7F). Modern glue in the joint would provide strength much greater than that originally used.

If turned legs are used, it would be possible to leave their tops square and make mortise and tenon joints similar to those for octagonal legs (Fig. 5-7G). If the legs are to be fully turned, there are two ways of dealing with the angled joint. If a leg end is shouldered to give a stout dowel end, the crossframe end is better if made deeper and the end angled (Fig. 5-7H).

The alternative, if the crossframing is to remain flat, is to turn the top of the leg with a short part parallel, above a dowel end that is made overlong. The shoulder has to be cut on the skew and this has to be done by hand. Put the dowel in its hole, so the turned shoulder rests on the surface. Cut a piece of scrap wood to a width that is the same as the greatest height the shoulder is above the surface. Use this as a gauge with a pencil. Move it around the leg to mark the line to be cut (Fig. 5-7J). Dismantle the joint and cut around this line with a saw and pare away the dowel shape to meet it.

The bottoms of the legs should be marked after assembly and cut to rest flat on the floor. Take off sharp edges by beveling all round.

## HANGING SHELVES

Some wall furnishings consist of two or more shelves between uprights with a crossbar to brace the assembly and provide a means of fixing to the wall. Many developments include elaborations in the way of decoration or the addition of doors, hooks, and other features, but a simple rack to the basic design will serve as a small bookcase, a display place for souvenirs, or somewhere to accommodate small items.

The wall shelves shown (Fig. 5-8A) can be made in hardwood and given a clear finish to feature the grain, or softwood could be used for a painted finish. Although a light construction is possible, original examples use fairly stout wood—upwards of ¾ in. This allows the dado joints to be cut deep enough to have good fits and adequate strength.

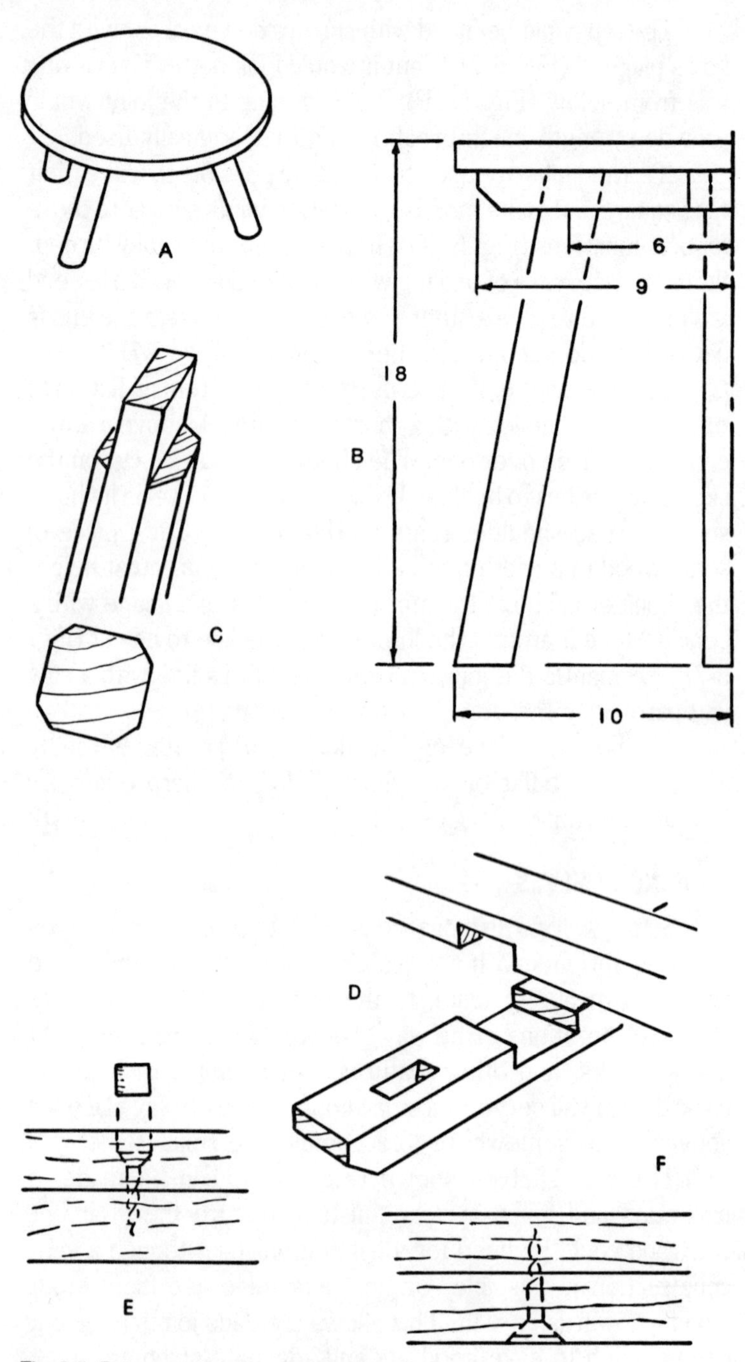


Fig. 5-7. Tabouret. (Continued on next page.)

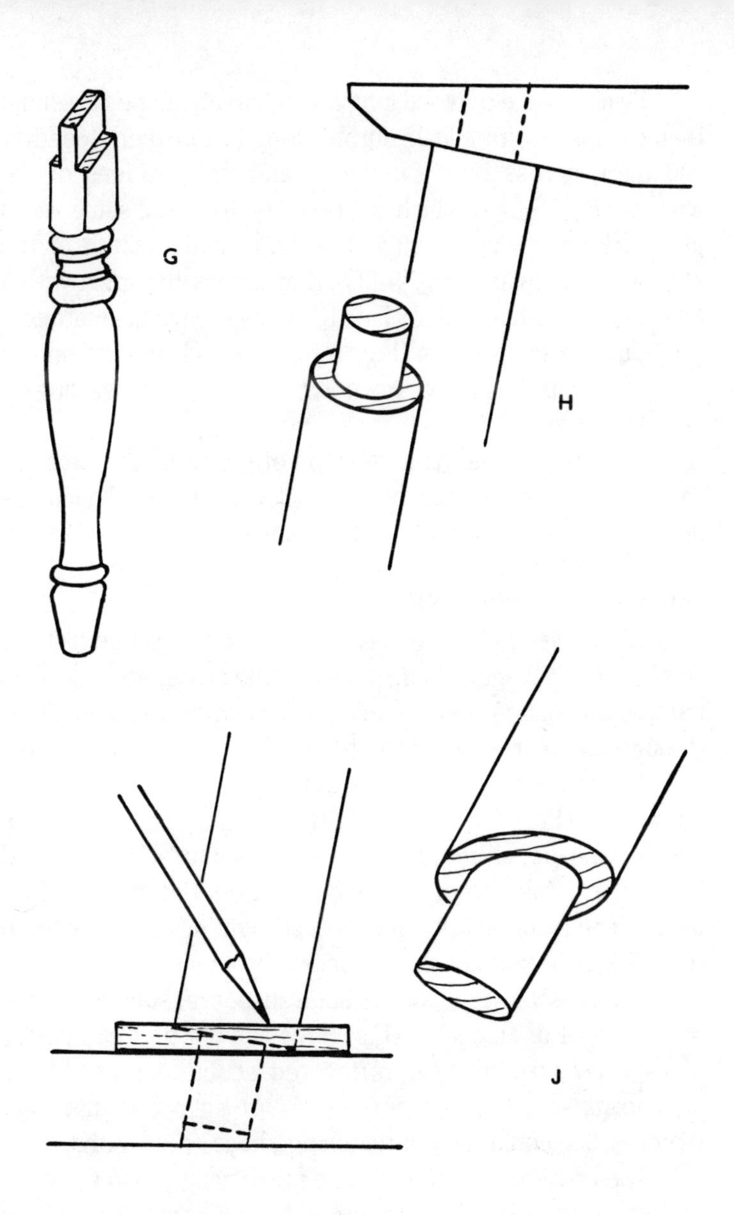


**Materials List 5-7**

Tabouret

| | | |
|---|---|---|
| 1 | Top | 20 × 20 × 1 |
| 2 | Top frames | 2½ × 18 × 1½ |
| 4 | Legs | 2 × 18 × 2 |

Plane a piece of wood long enough to make the two ends, then cut them with a little surplus length. Put them together and mark across both for length and the positions of the shelves (Fig. 5-8B), which can be made from the same width and thickness wood. Gauge the depth and breadth of the stopped dado joints (Fig. 5-8C). Cut across the grain with a knife and use the actual shelves to check the widths marked.

Cut the dado joints (Fig. 5-8D). Get clean cuts on the exposed front edges of the notched shelves by sawing to knife-cut lines.

The crossbar is made of wood of the same thickness as the other parts. It may be a parallel piece, or shaped, as described below. Its ends go into rabbets, which may be the same depth as the dado joints, or can be taken deeper to give a better bearing (Fig. 5-8E).

When the shelves are assembled, there can be nails or screws driven diagonally from below; the crossbar is screwed into the ends and other fastenings are driven upwards into it through the rear edge of the top shelf.

The top edges of the ends can be given a simple bevel or be shaped (Fig. 5-8F). The bottom edges can be given a matching shape, although if the assembly may also be wanted to stand on a table, there could be a cut-out to form feet (Fig. 5-8G). The front edges can be left straight or hollowing them (Fig. 5-8H) breaks up the hardness of outline.

The crossbar can have its edge shaped. A simple curve is better if part of an ellipse (Fig. 5-8J) and not part of a circle. Many early furnituremakers favored double curves, of the ogee form, so if the tops of the ends are shaped in that way, the crossbar could have a matching shape (Fig. 5-8K).

The crossbar provides scope for carving. In some cases this was quite elaborate, although if the maker was less artistic it may have been a chip carved diamond pattern (Fig. 5-8L) or some edge beveling (Fig. 5-8M).

Hanging can be done with screws—near the ends of the crossbar. If the crossbar is decorated and drilling for screws would spoil the appearance, there can be sheet metal plates, sometimes described as "mirror plates," fixed to the sides below the top shelf (Fig. 5-8N). If they project inwards, they will be less obvious and may be hidden by books. If there are only two shelves, a pair of hangings near the top should be sufficient, but for a multi-shelved assembly additional fixings will be necessary.

## DISPLAY WALL RACK

Many prized possessions, such as brassware, pewter-ware, or china could be displayed and were safer on a wall rack than on tables. Such racks were used in homes, taverns and public places and were developments of the basic shelves just described. Some New England wall racks featured sides that were deeply cut with decorative curves, as in the example shown (Fig. 5-9A). Construction is otherwise, similar to the previous example.

The curves in this case are based on parts of circles, but the outline is broken by small steps or quirks where the curves change direction (Fig. 5-9B). It is advisable to make a template of at least a section of a side, so all curves will match. Be careful not to reduce the wood above and below a shelf too much (Fig. 5-9C), or the short grain may break out, particularly if a softwood, such as pine, is used—as in many originals.

The dado joints may be stopped or cut right through and the shelves finish level or made wider with a curved corner (Fig. 5-9D). The joints should be cut before the curves are cut. With a band saw or jigsaw it may be possible to cut the profiles of both sides at the same time, so they match. If the saw will not take the double thickness, one side can be cut and used as a template to mark the other, then the two parts put together in a vise and the edges cleaned up with chisels, files and spokeshaves. Finish by sanding, using abrasive paper wrapped around shaped pieces of wood. Edges should be square across, except for slight rounding at the angles, enough to remove sharpness.

A simple rack consists of shelves and ends only and is hung with a cord from holes in the tops of the ends. This lacks rigidity as there is nothing to brace the shape except the comparatively narrow bearing areas of the dado joints. Such a

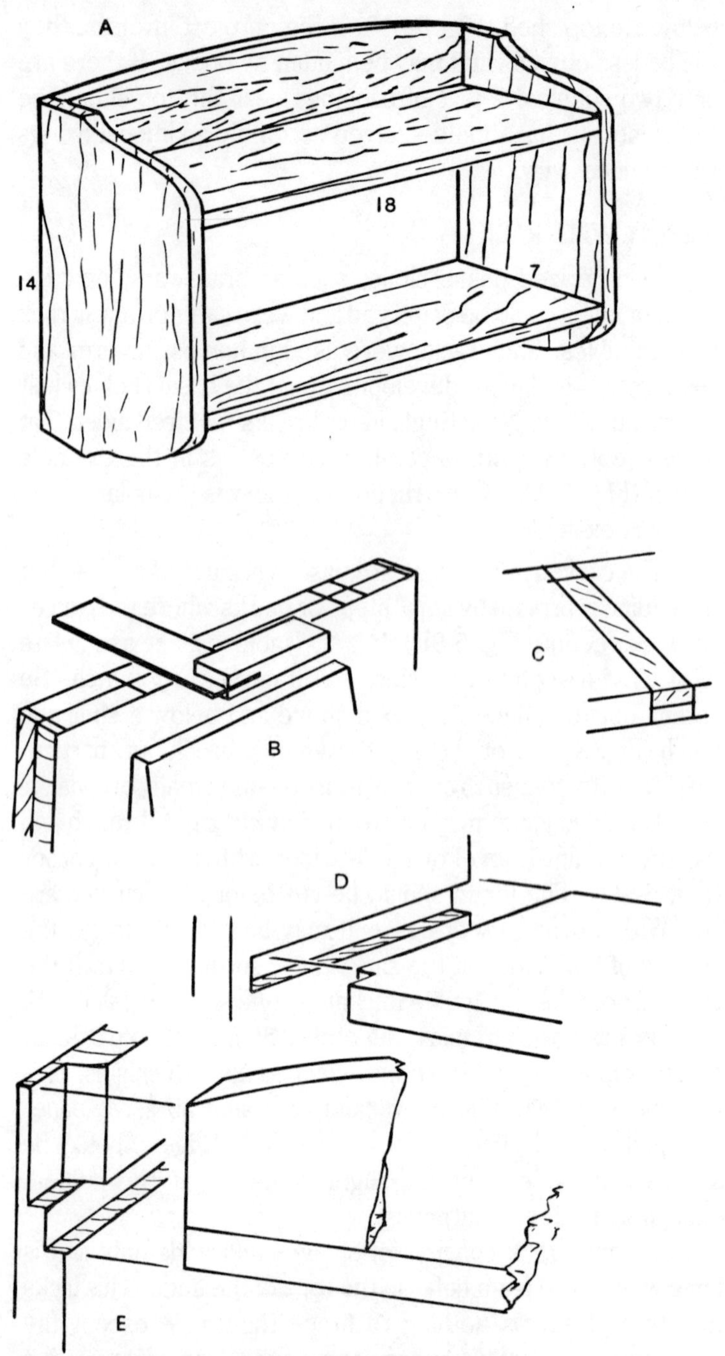


Fig. 5-8. Hanging shelves. (Continued on next page.)

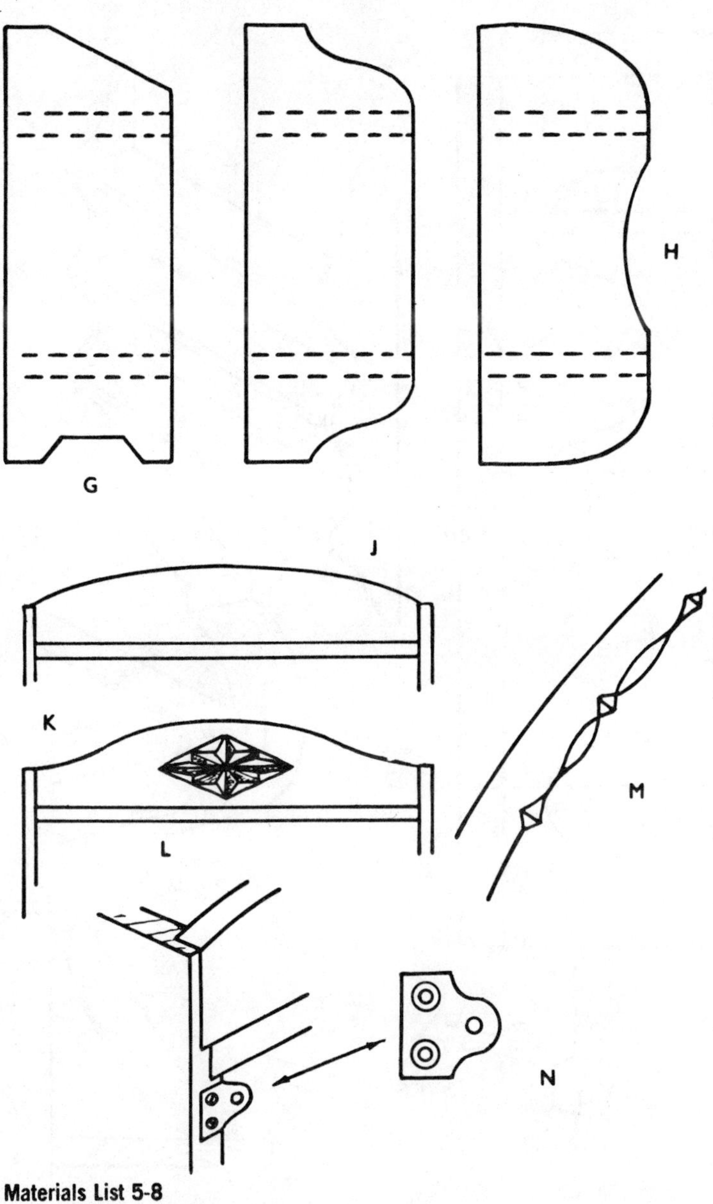


**Materials List 5-8**

Hanging Shelves

| | | |
|---|---|---|
| 2 | Ends | 7 × 14 × ¾ |
| 2 | Shelves | 7 × 18 × ¾ |
| 1 | Crossbar | 4 × 18 × ¾ |

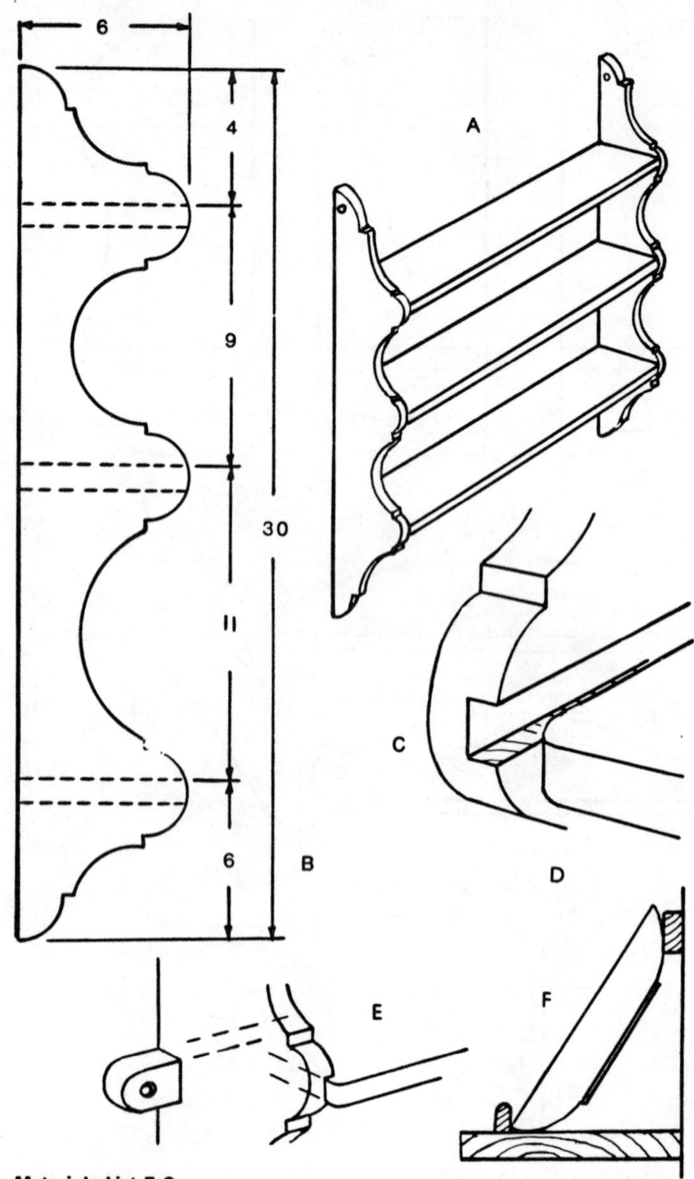


**Materials List 5-9**

Display Wall Rack

| | | |
|---|---|---|
| 2 | Sides | 6 × 30 × 1 |
| 2 | Shelves | 6 × 36 × 1 |
| 1 | Brace | 1½ × 40 × 1 |

hanging rack did not resist swaying if knocked, but examples of this type were used.

Some bracing can be provided by letting in a crossbar at one or all the shelves. The top one can extend, so fixing screws can go through the ends (Fig. 5-9E). Any shorter crossbars may be let in the same way as in the previous example. In a deep fitment an extending crossbar lower down can take another pair of fixing screws, so the rack is rigidly held to the wall. This is important if plates or other china are to rest against the wall. The whole back could be closed in with thin wood, or there could be crossbars where the china will rest and light strips of wood could be put near the shelf fronts to prevent plates slipping (Fig. 5-9F).

## SHAKER SHELVES

Another method of supporting shelves is to have the supporting boards at the back instead of the ends and use brackets. In this example the brackets are similar to those used in the bench and the two pieces of furniture would complement each other. The example is a two-shelf version intended to hang from hooks or pegs, so it could be taken down for cleaning or moving to another position (Fig. 5-10A).

The back boards are parallel strips of wood with their tops rounded and holes drilled for hanging. In one example made by Shakers the bottom is narrowed (Fig. 5-10B).

It would be possible to merely notch the shelves around the back boards, but they are more positively located and better supported by letting them into shallow dado grooves (Fig. 5-10C).

The brackets should extend far enough to support most of the width of the shelves. Apart from supporting, they will also provide some resistance to any tendency to warp. Cut the brackets so their grain is diagonal (Fig. 5-10D) for greatest strength. Screws can be driven through the back boards and it will be possible to avoid screw heads on the shelf tops by driving diagonally from below (Fig. 5-10E).

The ends of the shelves may be square, but they look better if given curves similar to those of the brackets. Ex-

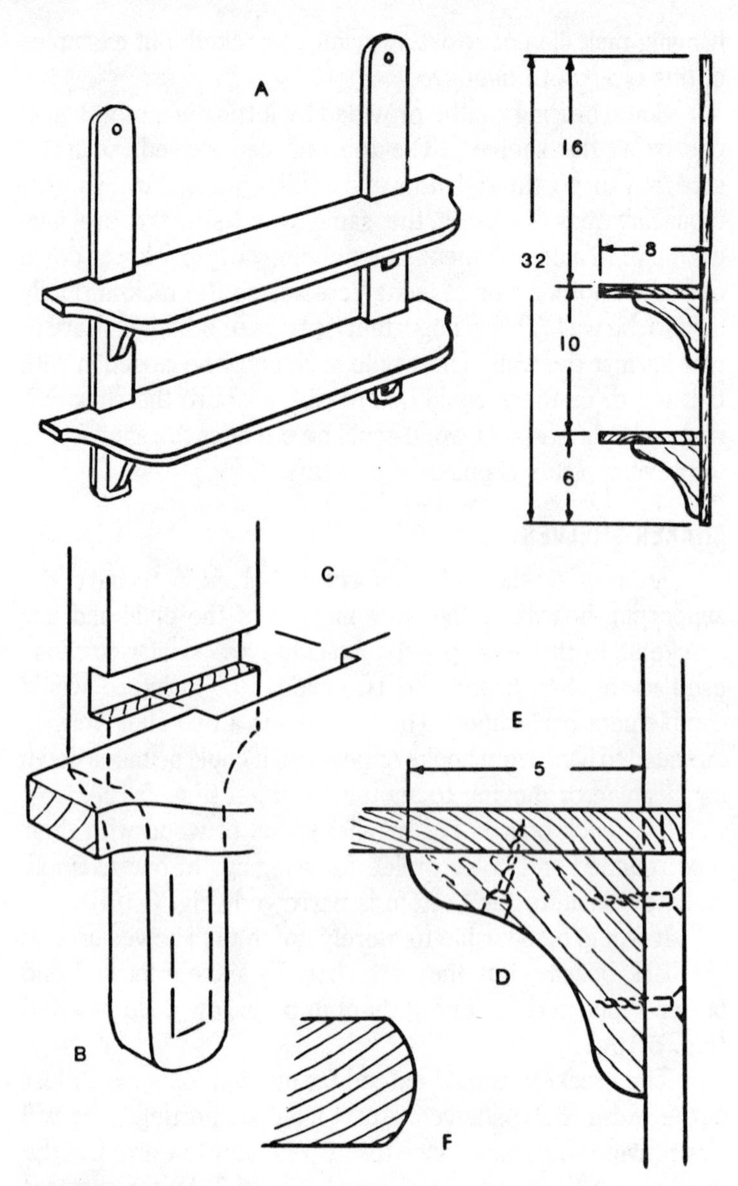


**Materials List 5-10**

Shaker Shelves

| | | |
|---|---|---|
| 2 | Back boards | 5 × 32 × 1 |
| 2 | Shelves | 7 × 40 × 1 |
| 4 | Brackets | 5 × 5 × 1 |

Fig. 5-10. Shaker shelves.

posed edges may be left square with just the sharpness rubbed off the angles, or they can be given curves, which look better and more authentic as part circles (Fig. 5-10F) than completely semi-circular edges.

## HUTCH SHELVES

Simple hanging shelves developed into more substantial pieces of furniture. Backs were closed, so there were matched boards or other arrangements of thin wood to hide the wall. One problem with open shelves is the settling of dust from above, and this may often have been a serious problem in early hastily erected dwellings. Putting a top on the rack did something to protect china and other things below. This might have been a plain board, but it progressed to a molded top. Other developments were special arrangements for stowage of particular items. Eventually, in many cases the hanging shelves became united with a standing cupboard or chest of drawers and the dresser or hutch cupboard had become a freestanding important piece of furniture without a connection to the wall. Complete items of this type are described later. The example here is of the transitional type, where the shelves still form a hanging unit (Fig. 5-11A).

Construction is similar to the previous examples. The shelves may extend to the edges of the sides, or be set back in stopped dados (Fig. 5-11B). There may be strips fixed to the shelves a short distance forward of the back edges to prevent plates sliding (Fig. 5-11C). An alternative is to make a slot in the shelf. This can be a plowed groove, that is then eased off to the rear with a rabbet plane (Fig. 5-11D).

Another treatment to a lower shelf is to provide a spoon slot (Fig. 5-11E). In the original construction this was provided by making a narrow strip of the same width as the shelf, then hold it off at intervals with spacer pieces. With a suitable router cutter it would be possible to work similar slots in the solid shelf (Fig. 5-11F), but those facilities were not available to the original cabinetmakers, so it may be better to use the built-up method.

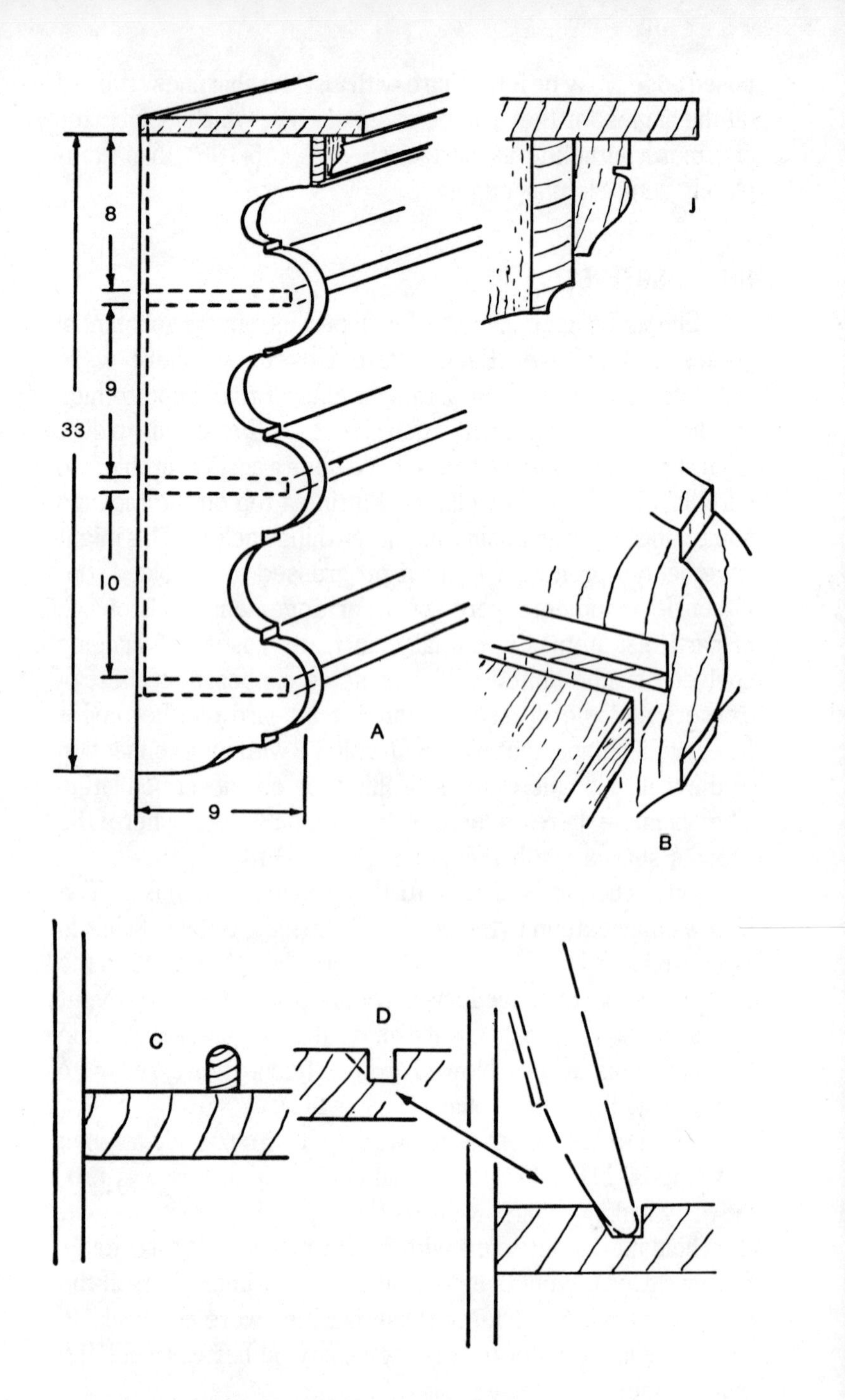


Fig. 5-11. Hutch shelves. (Continued on next page.)

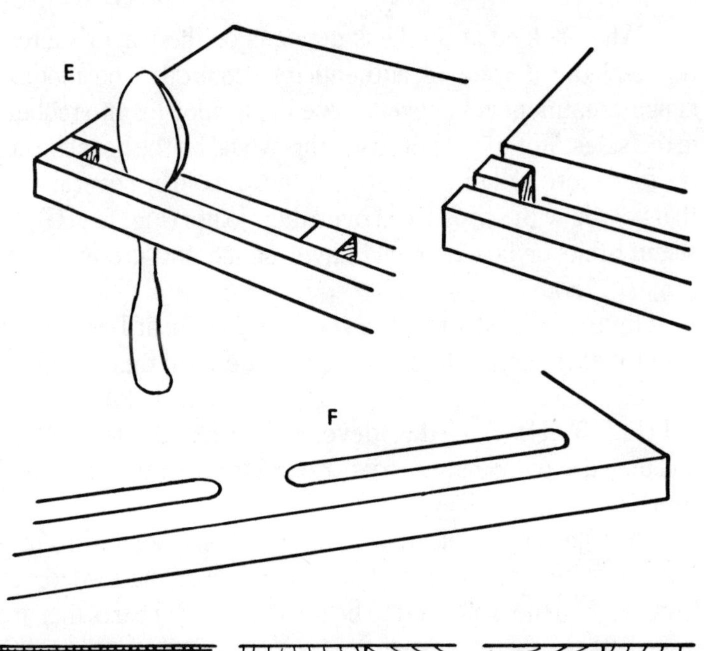


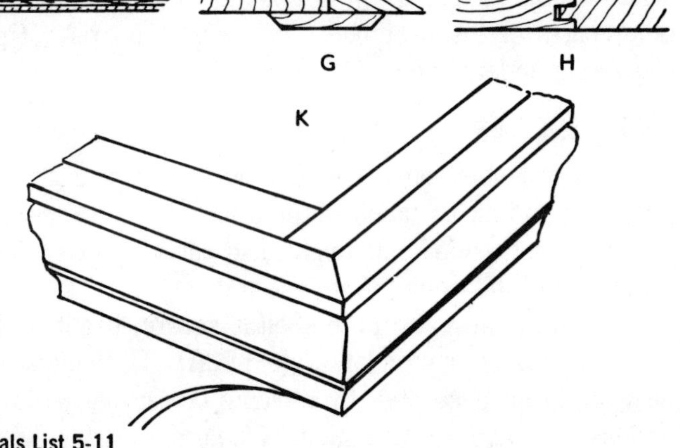


**Materials List 5-11**

Hutch Shelves

| | | |
|---|---|---|
| 2 | Sides | 9 × 33 × 1 |
| 3 | Shelves | 8 × 30 × 1 |
| 1 | Top | 12 × 30 × 1 |
| 1 | Rail | 3 × 30 × 1 |
| 1 | Back, built up | 30 × 30 |
| 1 | Molding | 1¼ × 2 × 30 |
| 2 | Moldings | 1¼ × 2 × 12 |

What is done at the back depends on the maker's intention and the degree of authenticity required. The modern simple treatment is to have a piece of plywood let into rabbets in the sides. For many purposes this would be the best choice, but for a more authentic treatment there could be several wide thin boards with strips fixed over their joints (Fig. 5-11G), or slightly thicker boards could have tongue and groove joints (Fig. 5-11H).

In its simplest form the top is a plain board with a rail under it at the front. In a more elaborate form there can be a molded edge to the top and a length of molding below it on the rail (Fig. 5-11J). A further development has the rail molded and the strip of molding carried around to cover the ends (Fig. 5-11K).

A large hanging piece of furniture when loaded with china can be quite heavy, particularly if made of hardwood, so fastenings to the wall need to be strong, and the parts that are drilled for the fastenings should be very securely attached to other parts of the assembly, so there is no risk of parts separating under strain.

## SMALL SHELVES

A small shelf on a single bracket had a main use in supporting a lamp or candle in the place where it could spread its light most usefully. It might also carry a pot or vase of flowers, and this could be its use today.

In its simplest form the shelf is square, has its corners beveled or is semi-circular (Fig. 5-12A). The edges of the shelf could be decorated by molding or carving. A bracket underneath supports the shelf by bearing against the wall. Some shelves were made without backs extending behind the bracket. Instead there was a narrow back nailed to the shelf and extending above, then the bracket merely rested against the wall. Two screws or nails through the back supported the assembly (Fig. 5-12B). The edge of the bracket should complement the edge of the shelf, being curved if that is curved and decorated in a similar way.

In its simplest form the bracket is held to the shelf by nails or screws from above (Fig. 5-12C). A better joint is a dado, and the strongest version is a tapered dovetail dado (Fig. 5-12D). This locks the shelf and bracket together and reduces any risk of the shelf warping.

In another form the back extends far enough below the shelf to join to the bracket. This is made like the first shelf, but the back is screwed into the bracket (Fig. 5-12E). This can be made without the back projecting above the shelf level and the screws into the wall go through the back just below the shelf (Fig. 5-12F). This type offers scope for carving. The bracket can be any shape from a simple triangle to a carved scroll, with the back and shelf similarly carved (Fig. 5-12G). The easiest furniture brackets were rather plain, but those intended for supporting lamps in the more opulent homes of the settled later years were decorated by carving and some were veneered.

Similar small shelves were fitted into corners. To get a sufficient area to stand something on it is insufficient to make the shelf a triangle. It is better to come out at right angles to the wall first, before cutting across, or make the shelf outline semi-circular or part of an ellipse, so there is a useful area forward of the line of a simple triangle (Fig. 5-12H).

For most shelves sufficient support is provided by brackets along each wall (Fig. 5-12J). They overlap and are nailed together at the corner, so they have to be laid out with similar shapes, but one is cut back enough to let the other pass behind it for nailing. The edges can be decorated in a way that matches the shelf. As they will bear against the wall their rear surfaces should be flat and any rounding or beveling kept to the exposed edges (Fig. 5-12K).

The brackets can extend upwards to form backs sufficiently high to prevent anything on the shelf marking the wall, or taken up far enough to be decorated like the lower parts. Appearance is better if the arrangement is not symmetrical. There may be more below than above (Fig. 5-12L) or the other way round. The shelf may be held by nails through, although it will be better let into dado joints. The parts then have to be assembled in sequence, with the shelf into the dado in the narrower support first, and the second support overlapped and glued and nailed on finally.

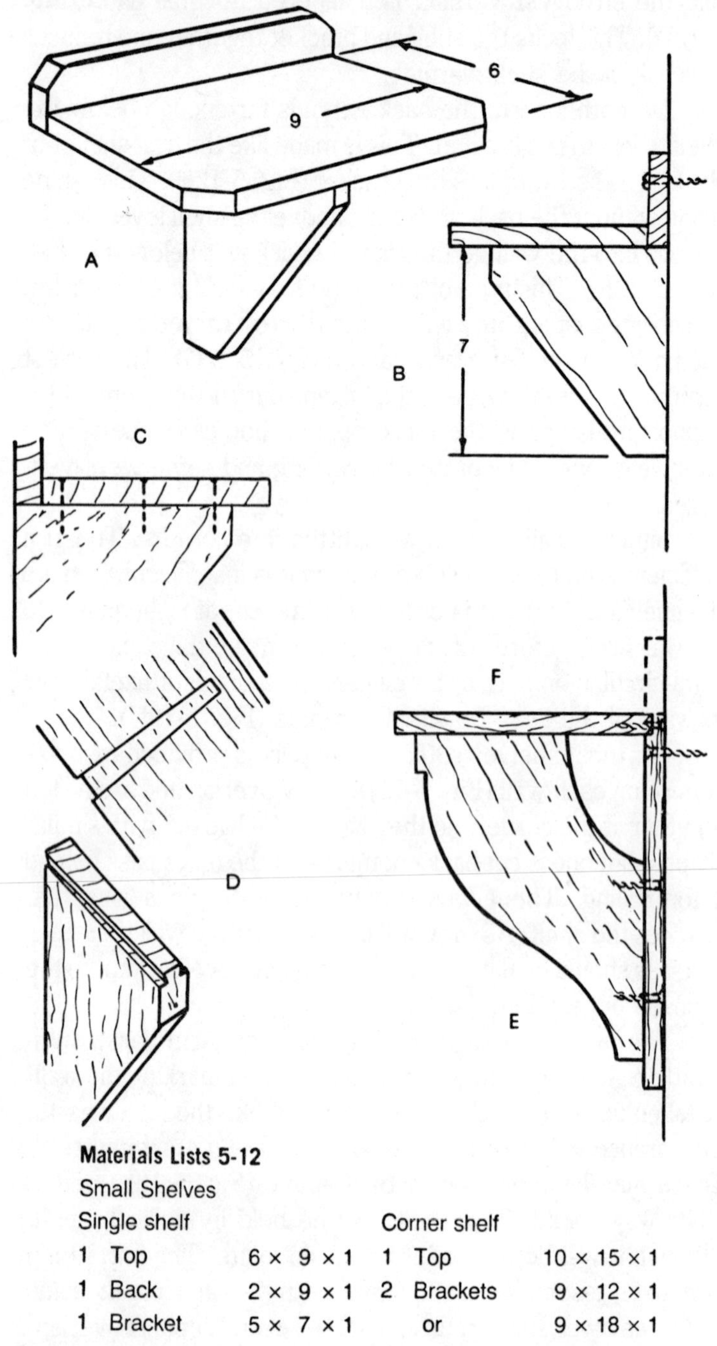


**Materials Lists 5-12**

Small Shelves

| Single shelf | | | Corner shelf | | |
|---|---|---|---|---|---|
| 1 | Top | 6 × 9 × 1 | 1 | Top | 10 × 15 × 1 |
| 1 | Back | 2 × 9 × 1 | 2 | Brackets | 9 × 12 × 1 |
| 1 | Bracket | 5 × 7 × 1 | | or | 9 × 18 × 1 |

Fig. 5-12. Small shelves. (Continued on next page.)

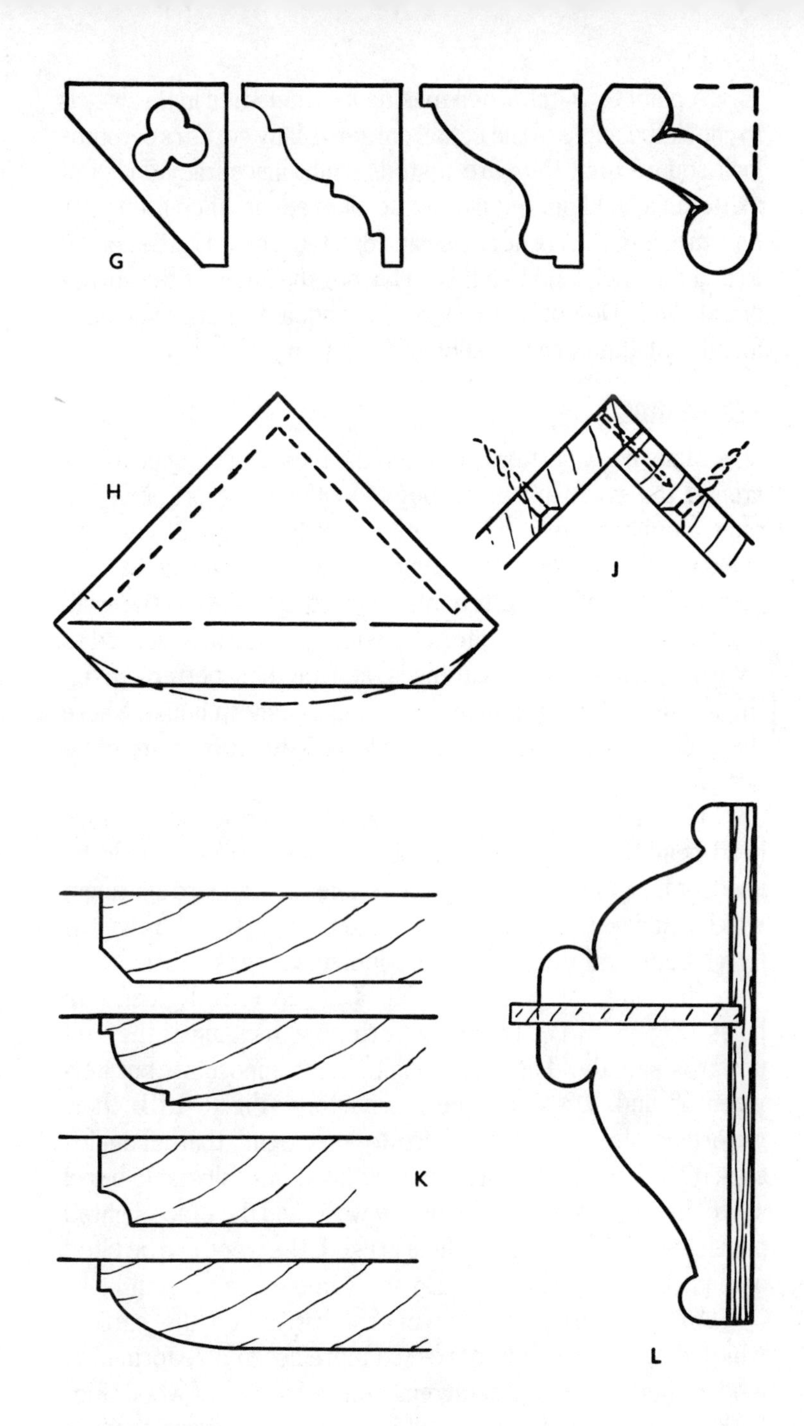
G
H
J
K
L

A point to watch when making a corner shelf in this way is to check the angle of the actual corner. Many corners of rooms look square until they are tested. Slight inaccuracy does not matter in a building, but it must be allowed for when fitting any furniture into the corner. Use an adjustable bevel in the corner to find the angle and use this to lay out the angle of the corner of the shelf. Do not just rely on a try square, unless you have found that the corner really is a right angle.

## PEG BOARDS

Many early settlers provided the means of hanging things around the room by using pegs. In the most primitive arrangement, these were roughly whittled pegs driven into holes in the logs forming a cabin. A further step was to have pegs of better shape fitted into a board attached to the wall. Such pegs could be used for clothing, but they also served to hang harness, household utensils, and anything better kept off the ground. There are many rooms in a modern house where these pegs might have uses—children's bedrooms are obvious places.

The Shakers used boards around rooms at a little above head height, with pegs at regular spacings. These could be used for hanging racks with pairs of holes at standard spacings, which could be moved to different parts of the room, as well as for clothing and other things on individual pegs.

The simplest pegs are pieces of dowel rod glued into holes (Fig. 5-13A). They are better for hanging if they tilt upwards slightly. The exact angle is not important, but between 5° and 10° should be satisfactory (Fig. 5-13B). It is important, if a row of pegs are to look right, that all angles should be the same. If drilling is by hand, an adjustable bevel set to the angle can be stood by the wood and the brace sighted parallel to it. If a drilling machine is used, the wood can be tilted on a packing piece to maintain the same angle at each hole.

An alternative to a dowel that carries on the earliest whittled peg shape, but makes it a more acceptable form for a modern home is to use octagonal tapered pieces of wood (Fig. 5-13C). The wood is first planed to a taper in square section, then the corners planed off to produce an octagonal section. Absolute perfection is not important, but drawing a square and converting it to an octagon of the size of the large end of a peg helps in showing how much to plane off the corners. Draw the square and its diagonals (Fig. 5-13D), then measure half a diagonal and take that up to the sides, working from each corner in turn (Fig. 5-13E). These marks are the corners of a regular octagon (Fig. 5-13F). Round or chamfer the outer ends of the pegs. The small ends will probably drive into round holes without special treatment, but if a very hard wood is used the corners may have to be eased off the octagonal end.

Another peg is given a squared section and a shaped hooked end. The ends of pegs could be made round to fit into drilled holes, but it is more craftsmanlike to cut square mortises and make the pegs shouldered to fit against the board (Fig. 5-13G). If there are many pegs in a row a card template should be used for marking to keep shapes uniform. If there are only a few pegs, several may be cut at one time on a bandsaw or the first peg can be usd to mark the others.

Many Shaker pegs were turned and had a long mushroom shape, so the enlarged end retained whatever was hung on the peg without it being fixed at an upward angle (Fig. 5-13H). If a lathe is available, pegs of this type can be made, but they can be bought ready-made.

It may be sufficient to merely glue parallel pegs or tenons into holes, but the strongest joint comes from letting the end be slightly overlength, then a wedge is driven into a sawcut and the surplus cut off (Fig. 5-13J). This was the method used in many early assemblies, when glue was unavailable and a tight fit provided the only grip.

The back board needs to be thick enough to give an adequate area of support to a loaded peg. This depends on the intended loads and how far the pegs project, but 1 in. is a probable thickness. A heavy look can be reduced by molding the edges. For most purposes a straight board is all that is needed, but if the assembly is to be a clothing rack in the vicinity of furniture with shaped outlines, it can be shaped with a bandsaw or other tool to matching curves.

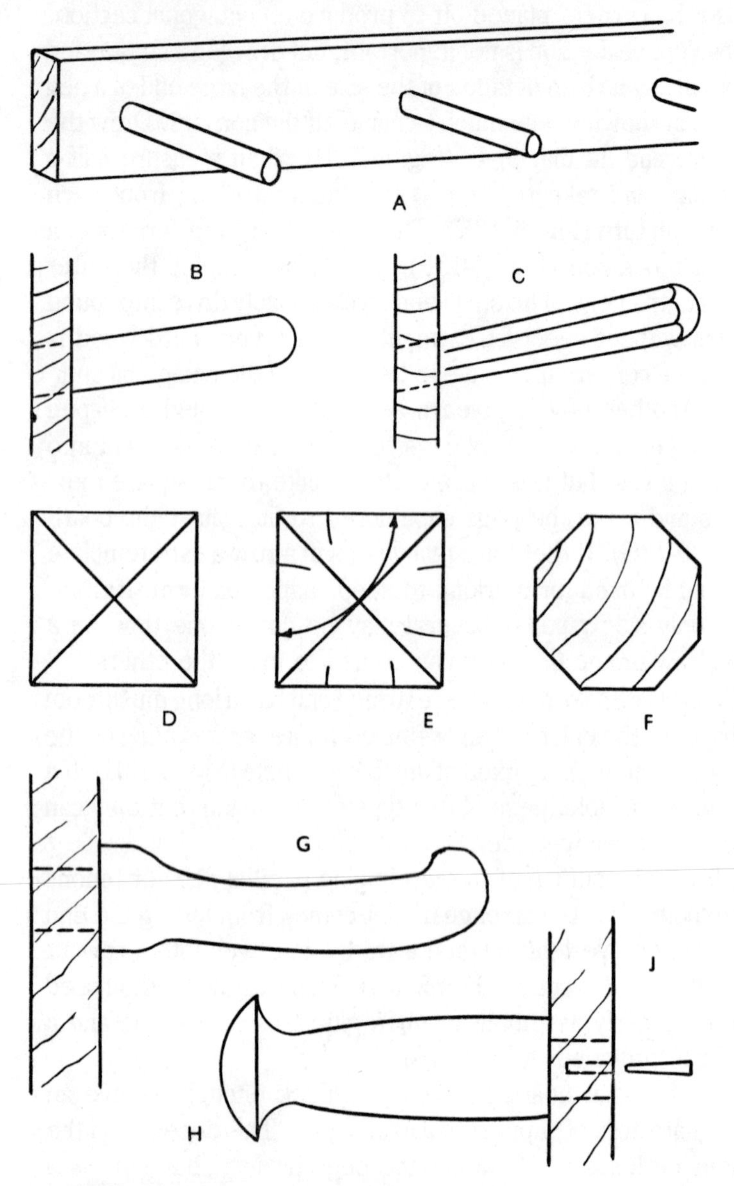


Fig. 5-13. Peg boards.

A peg which develops a sag, so it remains at a few degrees below horizontal after being used for a heavy load, does not look right. Although Shaker pegs and those with hooked ends may be satisfactory fitted into holes made square with the surface of the back board, it may be advisable to drill the holes or cut the mortises so the pegs slope up slightly in the first assembly. Only a slight angle is enough, but this will look level to a casual glance, while a downward slope will be much more apparent.

## SHELF AND CLOTHING RACK

In the days when the wearing of hats was more common, a hanging fixture that combined a row of pegs for coats and a shelf above for hats was important. One of these shelves (Fig. 5-14A) can still have many uses, even if the shelf now carries other things than hats. If the shelf is mounted so clothing can hang, it comes above eye level, and any decoration should be arranged with that view in mind. This means that a plain rectangular top could be molded around its edges, but with the work done around the lower edge (Fig. 5-14B) and the top edge left square or only slightly rounded. If plates may be stood on edge at the back of the shelf, a groove can be worked a short distance forward to take their rims (Fig. 5-14C).

There could be a back extending above the shelf, but a crossbar below the shelf will support it and provide a means of hanging, by drilling through for screws into the wall. Further screws can be taken through the peg rail. The top rail or crossbar can have screws into it from the shelf, but its ends are best tenoned into the brackets (Fig. 5-14D), although it is simpler to notch them in and screw from the back (Fig. 5-14E).

The peg rail can be fixed into the brackets in either of these ways, if it is to be kept within them. Another treatment carries the rail through the brackets far enough to extend almost as far as the shelf above and have another (possibly smaller) peg outside the bracket at each end (Fig. 5-14F). The rail may go through in its full thickness, but a stronger joint is made by notching it in a variation of a halving joint. Edges and ends of this rail, if it extends, can be molded to match the shelf, left square, or given a slight rounding or chamfer.

The edges of the brackets provide the main decorative feature. There must be sufficient wood left to provide strength, but otherwise it is possible to out a variety of outlines, from purely functional angles to ornate combinations of curves. The sections of classical moldings suggest shapes. It may be possible to have a bracket outline that is related to the molding of the shelf edge. The makers of original furniture of this type, who may not have had much artistic ability, tended to favor patterns that could be drawn with compasses, and a pattern for an edge was often built up from inward and outward circular curves, either directly linked or with angles between. Something of this type may be traditionally correct, but using curves that are like parts of ellipses may be more acceptable to modern ideas. Almost any shape that the maker finds pleasing can be satisfactory (Fig. 5-14G).

## HANGING BOXES

In the pioneer home many things were hung from the walls, as the safest place to keep them out of reach of animals and children, and still convenient for use. The simplest containers were very basic in outline and made from any wood available with little attempt at producing an attractive finish. Later boxes were made of more attractive wood and decorated either by shaped outlines or by carving or painting. Some boxes with painted decorations showing considerable artistic ability have survived.

Many early boxes are described as salt boxes, as this commodity, valuable to the early household, could be kept dry and safe in a hanging box, but boxes were also used for knives, soap, boot cleaning materials, clothes pins, and a great many other things.

The basic box was nearly always built with nails. Some later boxes had cut and glued joints, but reproductions can be nailed, preferably with the nails punched and stopped for a better finish. For a painted finish, a better surface results if screws are used and counterbored for wood plugs.

In most boxes there is a back piece extending above the box. This can have one or two holes for hanging on nails or hooks. In most cases the box was lifted down to a table when its contents were needed, so it was not fixed directly to the

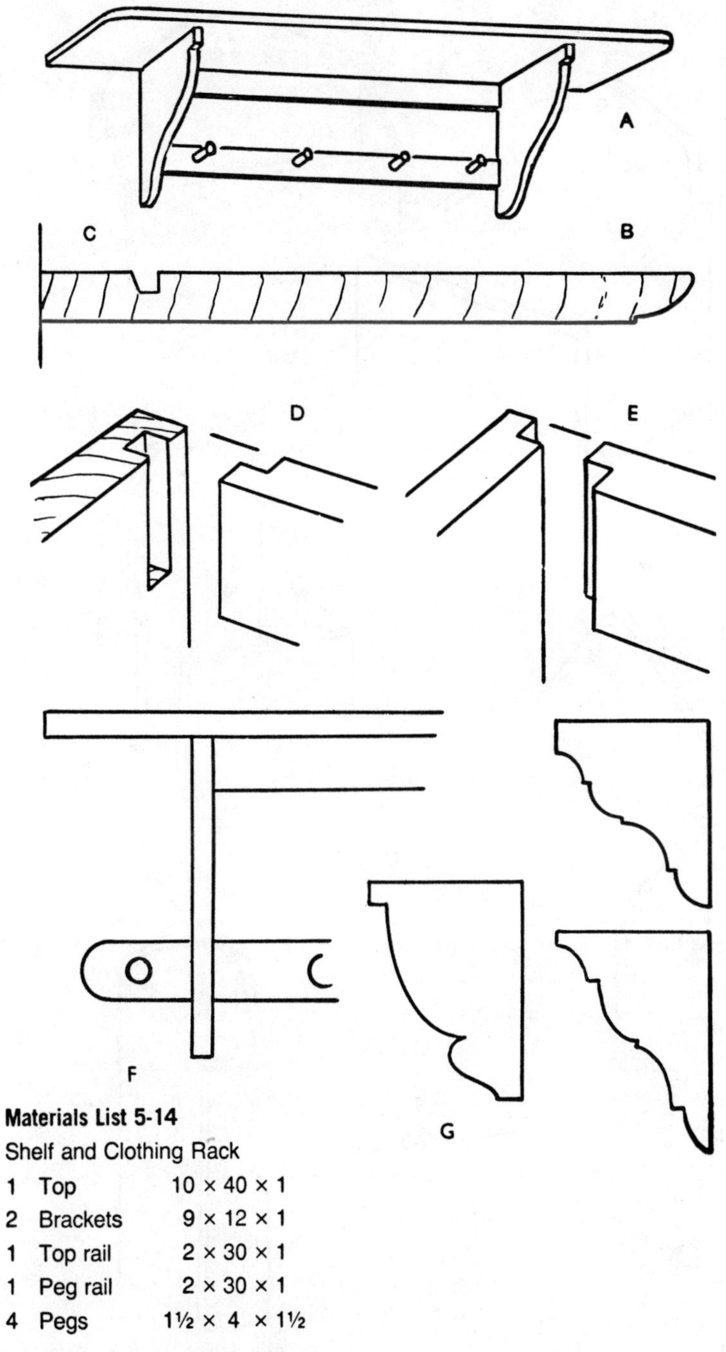


**Materials List 5-14**

Shelf and Clothing Rack

| | | |
|---|---|---|
| 1 | Top | 10 × 40 × 1 |
| 2 | Brackets | 9 × 12 × 1 |
| 1 | Top rail | 2 × 30 × 1 |
| 1 | Peg rail | 2 × 30 × 1 |
| 4 | Pegs | 1½ × 4 × 1½ |

Fig. 5-14. Shelf and clothing rack.

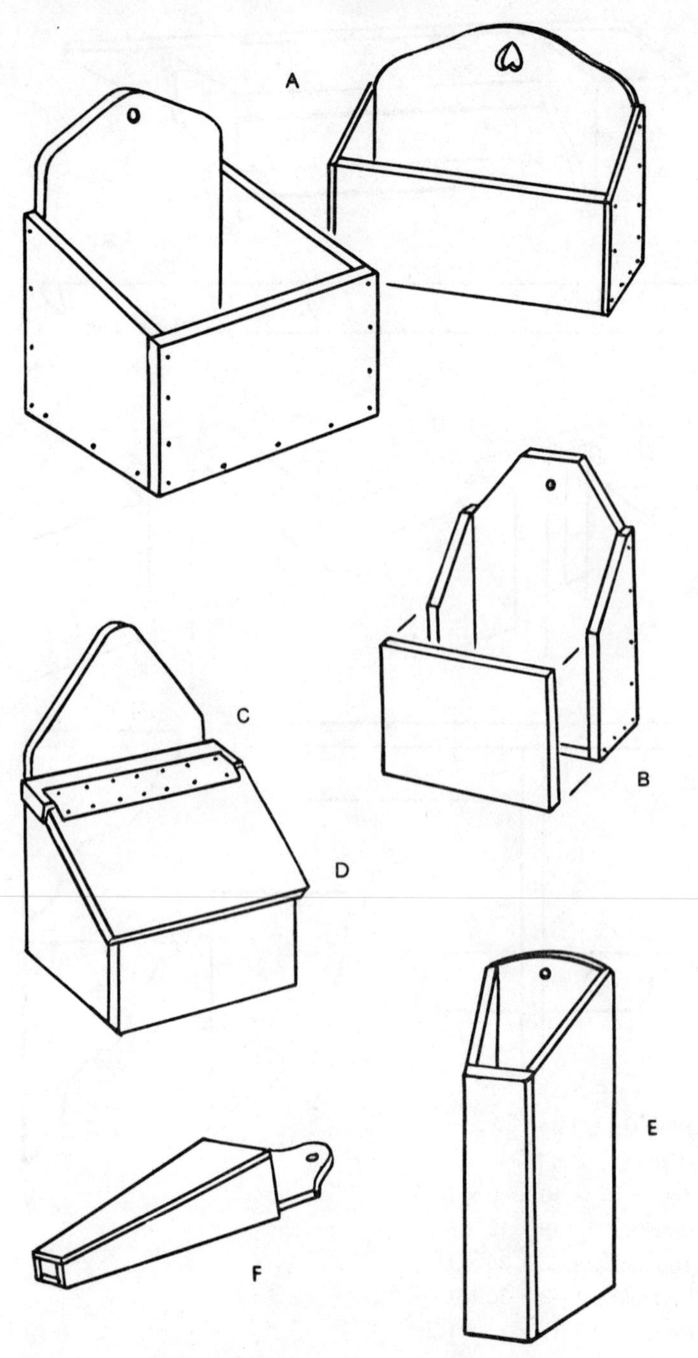


Fig. 5-15. Hanging boxes. (Continued on next page.)

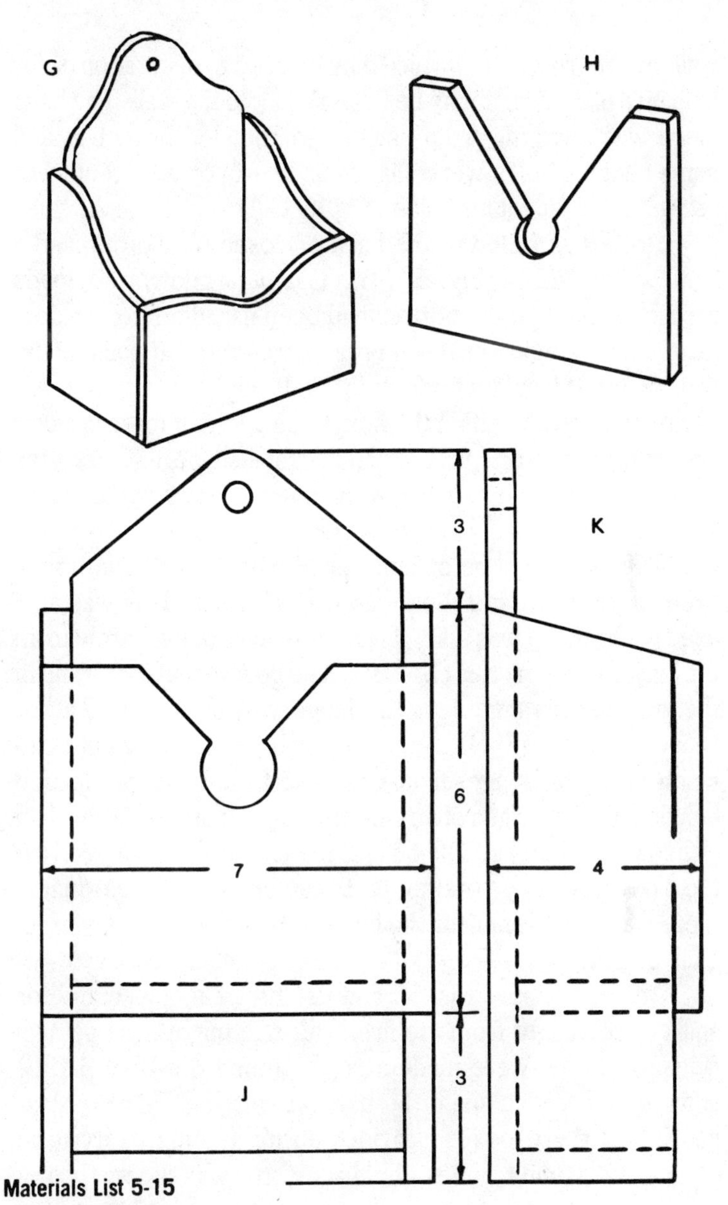


**Materials List 5-15**

Shoeshine Box

| | | |
|---|---|---|
| 1 | Back | 6 × 12 × ½ |
| 2 | Sides | 3½ × 9 × ½ |
| 1 | Front | 6 × 7 × ½ |
| 2 | Shelves | 3 × 6 × ½ |

wall. In a reproduction, which may be used as decoration or for holding a plant pot, it may be better to fix to the wall. The back piece was anything from angular to rounded in outline and some hanging holes were shaped as hearts or other outlines, as well as plain round holes (Fig. 5-15A).

Box sides nailed to the back enclosed the bottom and a front was nailed on (Fig. 5-15B). This put all downward loads across the nails. If the bottom had been nailed on from underneath, any weight on the box put strain on the nails in the direction that would withdraw them. It might not happen, but having the bottom within the box framing kept it more secure. An open-topped box with a near square shape was used for soap and loose things such as nails. If made long it was used for keeping knives out of reach of children.

The box could be strengthened with a narrow crossbar fixed to the back and the sides (Fig. 5-15C). This was also used when there was a lid. The sides came out squarely from the back to support this crossbar. The lid fitted against it and in the simplest arrangement the hinge was a piece of leather nailed on (Fig. 5-15D). Some larger boxes of later date had smith-made iron hinges fixed on the surface. In a reproduction box decorative hinges of an older pattern would be better than plain modern hinges. The lid and the crossbar should overlap the sides and the projecting parts can be rounded. Normally, there was no fastener for the lid, which stayed down under its own weight.

Another shape was tall and used for clay pipes and for spills to get a light from the fire. This box might have parallel sides, but some were made narrow to the front (Fig. 5-15E) and others flared in one or both directions (Fig. 5-15F). Making one of these boxes provides an interesting exercise in cutting and planing angles. Trial and error was the method of the first makers and is probably as good a way today, unless the maker is keen on geometry.

Most boxes were made straight across the front, but for easy reaching into some were shaped. This would not do for a material in particle form, such as salt, but for more substantial items, such as brushes, the front could be cut down (Fig

5-15G). In one pattern cuts were made into a drilled hole (Fig. 5-15H), in the reverse direction to the same idea used on stool legs.

Boxes were sometimes extended below to include a shelf (Fig. 5-15J). The shelf might also enclose a drawer, but it was more often open. One example is a box to hold shoe and boot cleaning materials, with the brushes standing up in a box with a cutaway front and the polish, paste, or dubbin on the shelf below (Fig. 5-15K).

# Boxes and Chests

The basic container for household goods is a box. Most of the early settlers arrived with their possessions in boxes and chests, made of heavy sectioned wood and stoutly constructed to stand up to the rigours of a sea voyage of those days. There were no equivalents of modern traveling cases. Those chests, with their lids, also served as seats, in the same way that generations before medieval dwellers in Europe often used chests as almost the only pieces of furniture in simpler homes. A chest has the advantage of fully enclosing the contents, and for things like bedding and spare clothing it will offer protection that is better than that provided by most other storage furniture. In an early home, where dust and dirt could not be avoided, this sort of protection for treasured items of special clothing and other things that only came out rarely, would have been important.

Chests and boxes varied in size and design, from larger ones, usually described as blanket boxes and often made of cedar because of its aromatic and clean preservative air, down to boxes for books, particularly the family Bible, candles, and trinkets. Chests developed so they became more suitable for secondary uses. A chest often had to stand on an earth floor, which might be damp, so ends or corners were extended to make legs to allow an air space under the bottom. If a chest was to be used as a seat, there was an advantage in adding a back, which might be of full height or a low one supported by the chest ends extended to form brackets.

A simple chest is more utilitarian than beautiful. A plain box with a lid may still have its uses and be worth making. Craftsmen favored chests for storing their tools, particularly in the days when a man might have to travel to a job in a cart with little springing over roads that were barely passable. A tool chest for storing equipment that does not have frequent enough use to justify fitting in racks behind the bench, yet needs to be kept in good condition, might be produced in an amateur craftsman's shop and stay there. There are some examples of old chests that are bare and well worn on the outside, but inside there are sliding compartments and drawers, and the underside of the lid is carefully veneered, usually with an elaborate marquetry design. This would have been a cabinetmaker's masterpiece. Towards the end of his apprenticeship he was expected to make something to prove his skill in his trade, and his tool chest was often the chosen example. In later life he was faced with a specimen of his best craftsmanship and a standard to live up to, every time he opened the lid of his tool box.

Some early examples of chests were quite plain in their construction, but they were decorated by carving and less frequently by veneering. Others were painted. Sometimes there was an overall treatment in one or two colors, but there are examples with skillfully painted designs, which may be geometric or stylized leaves and flowers, or someone with pictorial artistic skill has portrayed scenes on each face of the box. With this sort of decoration it is better if the chest starts quite plain, but it should be made of a close-grained wood that can be given a smooth surface, able to take several coats of the base paint that serves as the ground on which the decorative painting is done.

The construction of most chests was quite simple. Corners were often nailed through simple overlaps. The hand-forged iron nails had much rougher surfaces than modern wire nails, so they gripped the fibers of the wood quite well. A modern reproduction secured by nailing might be done with reproduction nails and the heads left level. If modern nails are used, they should be fairly long and be driven dovetail fashion, rather closer together, then punched below the surface and the heads covered with stopping. Bottoms were sometimes nailed on (Fig. 6-1A), but there was greater strength if the bottom was enclosed by the sides (Fig. 6-1B), as in the hanging boxes, described in Chapter 5.

Not much sheet metal was available, but where it was, bottoms and corners were reinforced by bent straps nailed on. These were sometimes simple rectangles (Fig. 6-1C), but if a blacksmith made the hinges and these straps he sometimes shaped the parts to similar outlines to give a more pleasing effect (Fig. 6-1D). That type of construction was used on chests of earlier days than the first settlements, but memories of older furniture may have provided the ideas for this sort of construction.

Corners were often dovetailed. Wide dovetails and pins are easier to cut than narrow ones and it is obvious in some early chests, particularly those made of softwood, that the easy way out was taken, either because of limited equipment available, little ability or the need to get results quickly. Later chests made of better woods usually have narrower dovetails and sometimes the pins between them were very narrow in the manner favored by cabinetmakers.

Resistance to pulling apart is provided in a dovetail joint by the shape of the dovetail. The joint cannot be separated in that direction without breaking the wood. In the other direction (which is the way the joint was assembled), strength depends on tightness or glue. It might have been thought that the greatest probable strains in use would have been to pull chest sides off ends and not ends off sides, but it is interesting to see in many old chests that the dovetails are cut in the sides, so the ends have the greatest resistance to coming apart (Fig. 6-1E). It is only when the sides flare outwards that dovetails are always found cut in the ends (Fig. 6-1F). This is probably because an angled dovetail joint is easier to lay out and cut that

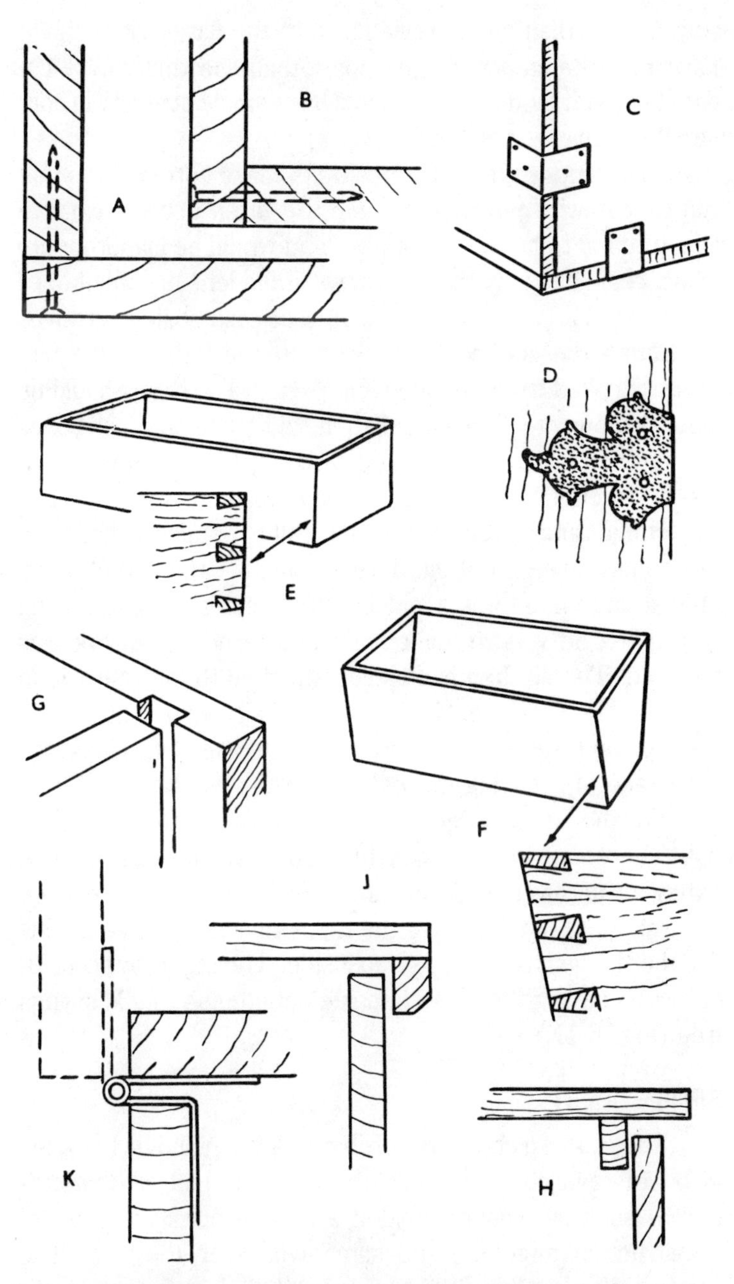


Fig. 6-1. In box construction bottoms were nailed on (A) or contained within the sides (B). Metal plates were used for strengthening (C and D). Exposed dovetails (E and F) were popular, but some corners were grooved (G). Lids fitted in (H) or over (J) a box. Some hinges were cranked to get the knuckle outside (K).

way, rather than an appreciation that the flared sides might have more tendency to pull apart than the ends. Well-cut dovetails with modern glue should have ample strength in both directions in any case.

The various types of notching to make corner joints that can be cut with power tools and are often used in wooden construction today were not used and would be inappropriate in any reproduction unless they were hidden. In some boxes the sides overlapped the ends. In that case shallow grooves were cut in the sides to positively locate the ends, but the joint was still nailed from outside (Fig. 6-1G). The dado should be quite shallow, or it might weaken the side. In many such boxes the extended sides were linked with crossbars to form handles, so strength was needed if heavy loads had to be lifted.

Hinges and fasteners were difficult to obtain and had to be made individually, if at all. This meant that the use of metal fittings often had to be avoided. The simplest way of dealing with a box lid was to make it lift off, so no metalwork was involved. The lid then had pieces attached to locate it within the box (Fig. 6-1H), or there was a rim all round to fit outside the box top (Fig. 6-1J). In both cases the added parts had the advantage of reducing the risk of the top warping.

For the lid of a large chest the hinges had to be substantial. There are chests with blacksmith-made strap hinged extending across the top and down the back. An outside hinge strap above is not wanted if the top is to also serve as a seat. Another hinge has the top strap inside. The important consideration is having the hinge knuckle outside, so the lid swings free (Fig. 6-1K).

## SIMPLE CHEST

The size of a chest was probably determined by the sizes of boards available, although the contents had to be considered, such as blankets folded a certain number of times. Construction might be the same whatever the size. The example shown (Fig. 6-2A) is a suitable height for sitting and the size should suit folded blankets and sheets. For that purpose aromatic red cedar would be a good choice of wood, but for use elsewhere the wood could match other furniture or be a strong hardwood for shop use.

If boards have to be joined to make up width, these glued joints should be dealt with first. It is advisable to stagger joints, so they do not meet at a corner (Fig. 6-2B). The overlapping corner joints then serve to clamp the board joints. Care is needed in planing the wood true. Sight along to check for twists. Be careful that all angles are right angles. In any construction with little embellishment slight variations from truth become very obvious. Cut the two ends to length and plane their cross-grain true, checking with a try square from the face edges and trying one end against the other. Mark the lengths of the sides, but they can remain slightly overlong until after nailing to the ends, and then be planed level (Fig. 6-2C). It is the top corners where most strain can be expected to come, so nails there can be closer and might be longer (Fig. 6-2D).

If the chest is to stand with its bottom on the floor, it will be better to enclose the wood within the sides and ends. In that case it is advisable to nail one side to both ends and use that assembly as a guide for the size of the bottom. Get one end of the bottom planed to a right angle to its side, then pull the three-part assembly to this and mark the other end and width. Fit the bottom into the one side and two ends before adding the second side (Fig. 6-2E).

The chest can be given a plinth, which is a border around the bottom. Besides improving appearance, it allows the bottom to be nailed on instead of let in. This is simpler, as it can be oversize and planed to match after fitting. The plinth then projects below the bottom and strengthens it with nails, while keeping it off the floor (Fig. 6-2F).

Another way of raising the bottom off the floor is to extend the ends to form legs. Although this could be done with the grain of the ends across, it is stronger for the legs, if the grain is upright. The ends need only project a few inches, then a V is cut in them so feet are formed (Fig. 6-2G). Much depends on the intended use of the chest. The box part could be shallower and the leg extensions longer. A very shallow

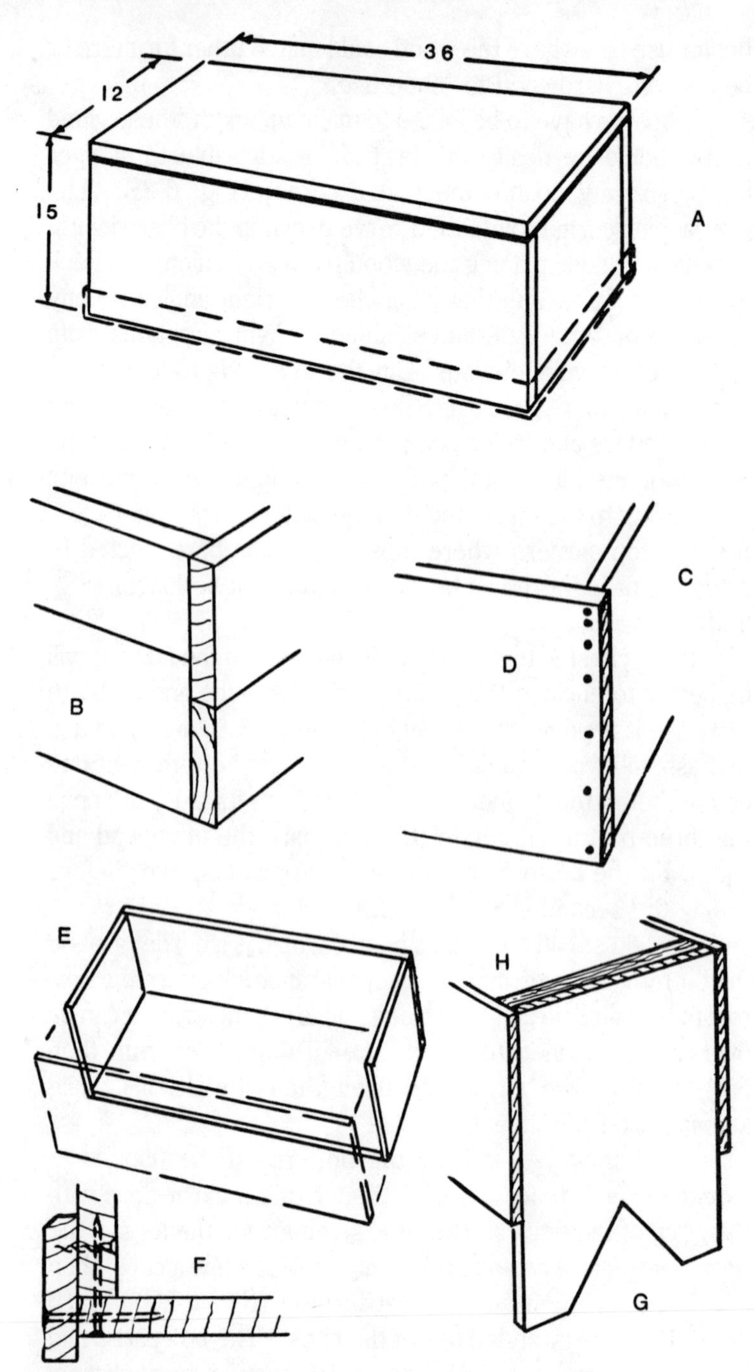


Fig. 6-2. Simple chest. (Continued on next page.)

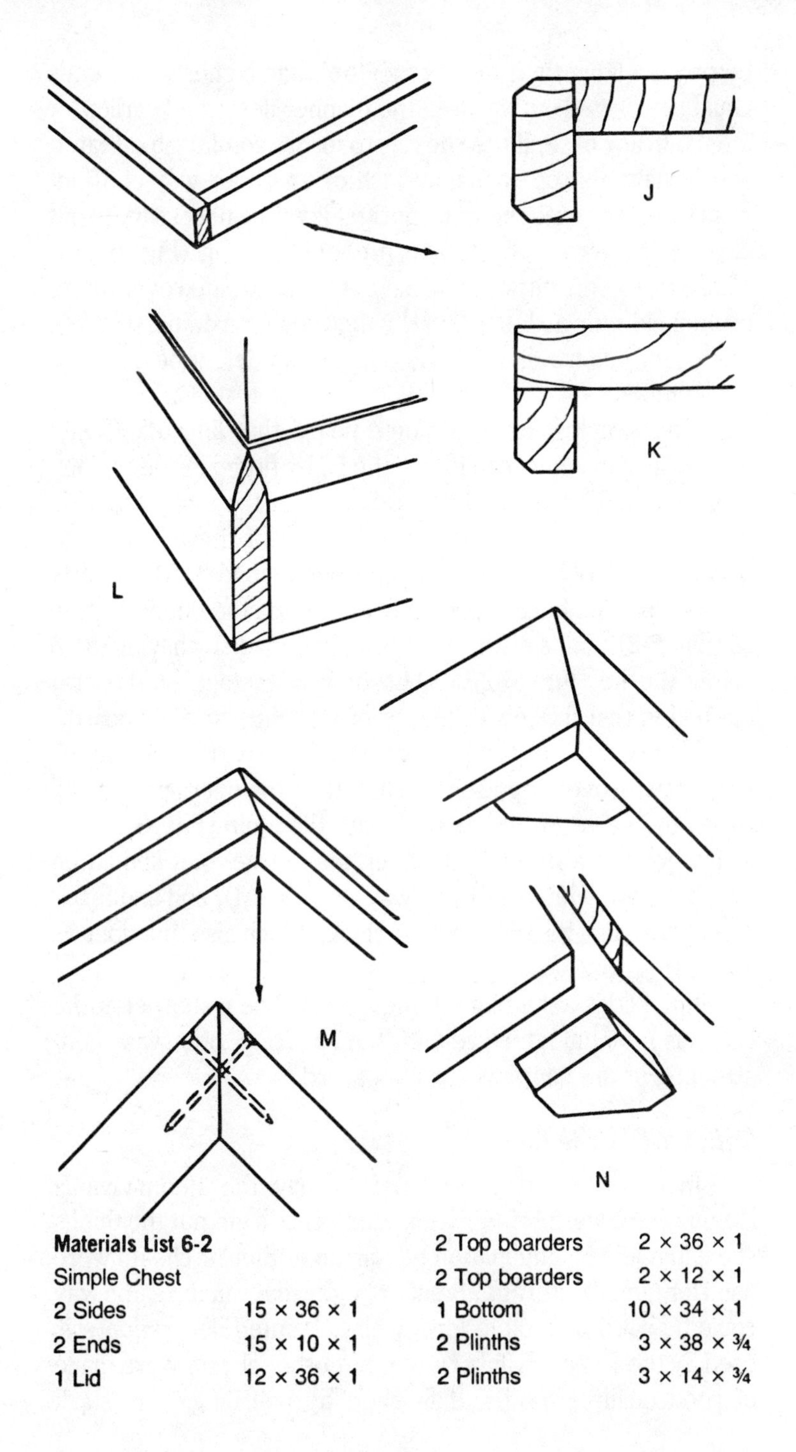


**Materials List 6-2**

Simple Chest

| | | | |
|---|---|---|---|
| 2 Sides | 15 × 36 × 1 | 2 Top boarders | 2 × 36 × 1 |
| 2 Ends | 15 × 10 × 1 | 2 Top boarders | 2 × 12 × 1 |
| 1 Lid | 12 × 36 × 1 | 1 Bottom | 10 × 34 × 1 |
| | | 2 Plinths | 3 × 38 × ¾ |
| | | 2 Plinths | 3 × 14 × ¾ |

box with a lid is then more of a stool than a chest. The ends could be splayed outwards in the manner described earlier for stools. In any case, if the chest is to form a comfortable seat, it should have its top within an inch or so either way of 15 in. from the floor. With the grain upright it will be necessary to put cleat strips across the top to prevent warping (Fig. 6-2H). These may come outside and have the lid extended over them, or be inside for a closer lid. Having these cleats outside lets them serve as handles, as the fingers can be put below them for lifting.

The simplest lid is a single board that lifts off. Cleats across near the ends can locate the lid by fitting inside the box (Fig. 6-1H). They should be made deeper than they are wide to give stiffness to resist any tendency of the lid to warp. Another type of lift-off lid has a border around it. Many early chests have the border pieces fixed around the outside of the lid (Fig. 6-2J), but a stronger assembly is made by having them below the lid (Fig. 6-2K). The only advantage of the first method is that it allows the use of a slightly smaller board.

The corners of the lid border and the parts making up a plinth can be overlapped and nailed, then the overlapped parts cut to the same profile as the parts they join (Fig. 6-2L). A neater joint is a miter, but under the lid the joint should be strengthened with a nail each way (Fig. 6-2M), and under the plinth there can be a reinforcing block, which also functions as a foot (Fig. 6-2N).

If the lid is to be hinged, there should be no border at the back, as it would interfere with the lid lifting, otherwise construction is the same as for a loose lid.

## CHEST WITH TRAYS

In some communities, particularly the Pennsylvania Dutch, there were bride's chests, in which a girl put the things she had made in anticipation of marriage. Similar chests were used for general storage. Smaller boxes made in the same way could be used on a table for jewelry. Painted decoration was used by the Pennsylvania Dutch, but other chests were made of good quality wood and finished by polishing. The stark outline of a rectangular box was broken by shaped feet and some molded edges.

The specimen (Fig. 6-3A) is of moderate size, but originals were in all sizes from those to be carried in one hand to blanket boxes. Corners could be nailed and the holes hidden with stopping, but dovetails are better. The bottom should be enclosed within the sides and ends. Plywood or other manufactured board might be used for the bottom, as its edges are covered and it would not be easily identified. Thinner material might have supporting battens underneath (Fig. 6-3B).

A plinth goes around the bottom with a small overlap and with much of the lower edge cut away to leave supports at the corners. Corners are mitered and there should be blocks inside to strengthen the joints and provide extra bearing surfaces on the floor (Fig. 6-3C). The top edge of the plinth could be molded, although a separate strip of molding may be fixed around, with glue and thin nails or pins (Fig. 6-3D).

The lid can be a single stout board, preferably cut with the end showing grain lines vertical, so there will be the minimum of risk of warping. The edge is molded and there should be strips around below this to provide a dust seal to the box, so the whole top should have enough overlap on the carcase of the chest to allow for this (Fig. 6-3E). The rear edge of the top is not molded, but should finish level with the box back, so it will swing up on its hinges.

Some of these chests had a single fixed compartment inside at one end. This did not interfere with reaching into the bottom of the box, but it provided a place for small items (Fig. 6-3F). In the best construction the side and bottom of the compartment are let into the sides and end of the chest (Fig. 6-3G). The grooves have to be made before the chest is assembled and the compartment parts put in before the second side is fitted. The side of the compartment should have its top edge well rounded in cross section and may be hollowed at the center.

An alternative arrangement has a liftout tray. In some chests this was full size, so it had to be lifted out to get at the lower part of the box (Fig. 6-3H). Compartments could be

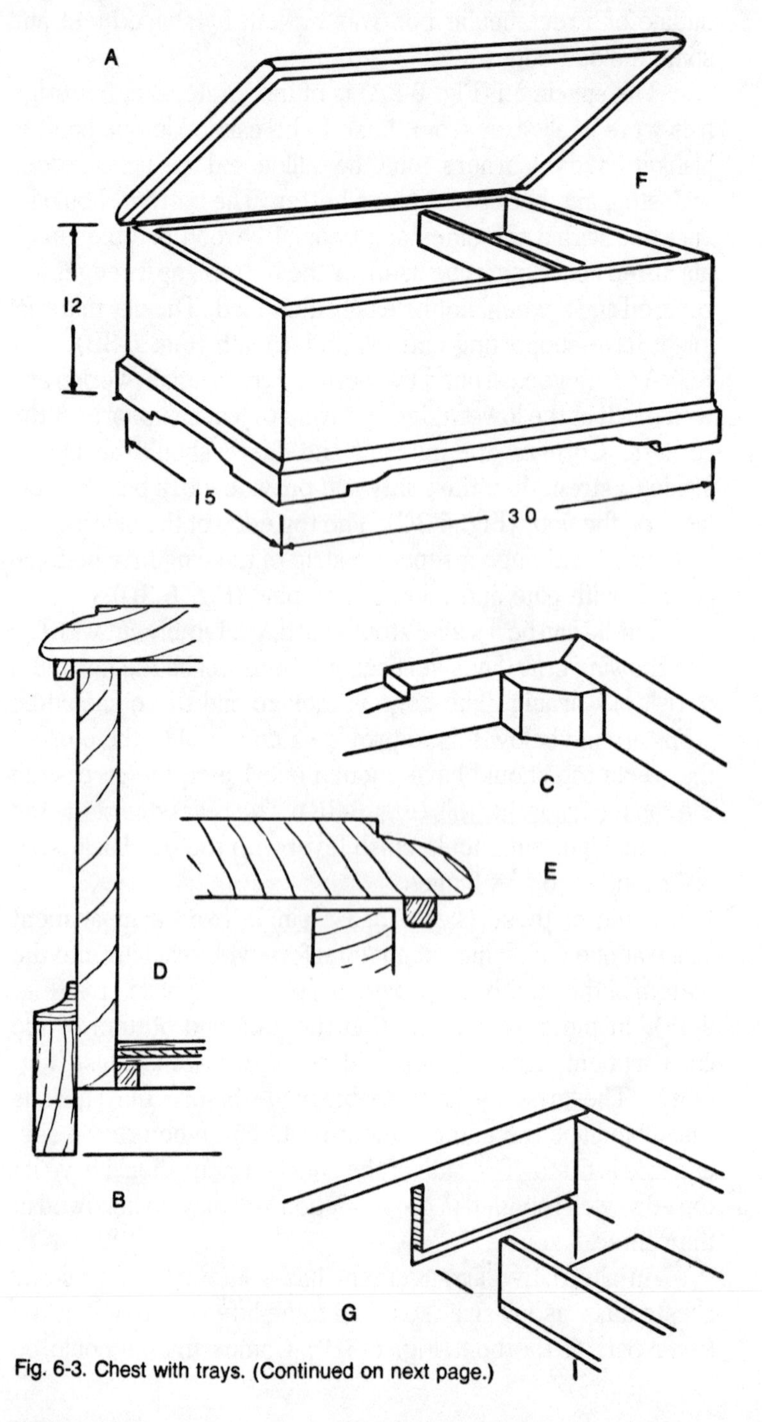


Fig. 6-3. Chest with trays. (Continued on next page.)

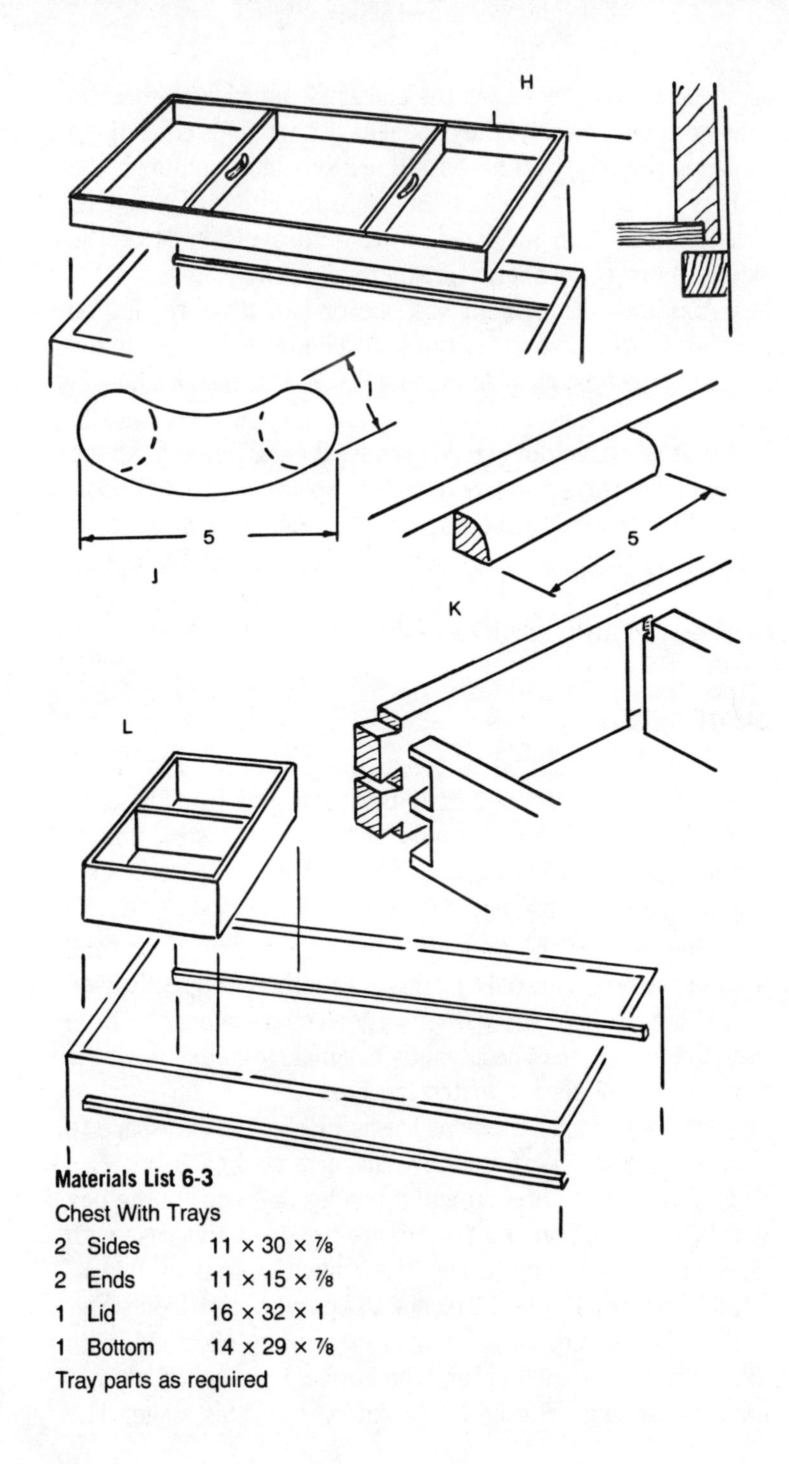


**Materials List 6-3**

Chest With Trays

| | | |
|---|---|---|
| 2 | Sides | 11 × 30 × 7/8 |
| 2 | Ends | 11 × 15 × 7/8 |
| 1 | Lid | 16 × 32 × 1 |
| 1 | Bottom | 14 × 29 × 7/8 |

Tray parts as required

arranged in this tray to suit the contents. If divisions could be arranged conveniently, they could have handholds cut in them for lifting (Fig. 6-3J), otherwise there should be cutouts in the ends of the tray or blocks fixed there for lifting (Fig. 6-3K). The tray rests on strips of wood across the ends or the sides—there is no need to fit them all round.

Another arrangement has one or two trays resting on lengthwise strips, so a tray can slide along to aid access to the bottom of the box, or be lifted out (Fig. 6-3L). Besides household use, this was a common arrangement in tool chests. Trays should have dovetailed corners if possible, and the top edges of the trays and any dividers should be rounded. Bottoms of trays would have been solid wood cut thin, but they could be plywood if they have their edges hidden by letting into rabbets. For jewelry or precision tools the bottoms of trays could be lined with cloth or rubber.

## SMALL CHESTS

The chest method of construction was used for quite small boxes, which might have been for sugar or salt, or to hold trinkets or jewelry. Some of these were scaled-down versions of chests already described, but there were others. The smaller sizes allowed different uses of wood.

One box had the framing of the lid a continuation of the body of the box (Fig. 6-4A). This is a method frequently used today, but none of the earlier larger chests appear to have used the technique. The advantage of making a box this way is that the lid will always match the box.

In the example the joint line is marked with a space to allow for the saw kerf and dovetails arranged each side of it (Fig. 6-4B). Joints are cut and the sides and ends of the box glued together. Top and bottom are fixed—in this case with glue and nails—and both can overlap slightly, to be planed off later. The top of this box is planed to a curve before fixing (Fig. 6-4C). The outside of the box is cleaned up all round, with excess wood planed level and the surfaces smoothed, except for final sanding. The lid is not cut off until this stage. The original makers cut around between the lines with a hand saw, but if a table saw is available, it is a simple matter to set the fence and go around the four faces. Unless it is obvious from grain markings, it may be advisable to mark the mating parts of lid and box, so they are put back together the right way.

The sawn edges have to be planed level and any surplus glue inside the box cleaned away. Two hinges are arranged at the back. There is no need for any sort of handle, but some of these boxes were given small turned knobs on the front of the lid and matching turned feet under the corners of the box (Fig. 6-4D).

A variation on this is made in the same way, except the top and bottom are allowed to project all round, then given molded edges (Fig. 6-4E). The back could be cut level so the lid would open some way, but if the lid projected there it could be arranged to act as a stop when the lid was vertical (Fig. 6-4F). Either box could be lined with velvet to make a jewelry case.

One way of avoiding the use of hinges, yet provide a secure lid instead of having it lift off, was to extend the ends of the box at least as high as the thickness of the lid. Sometimes the ends reached high enough to be fretted to form decorative handles (Fig. 6-4G). The lid fitted over the sides, but between the ends. The underside of its back edge was rounded and pivots were provided by nails through the ends (Fig. 6-4H).

A sliding lid was another secure type. This was seen in school children's pencil boxes, but the idea was also used in boxes for other purposes. In the simplest form the sides of the box were grooved and the lid shaped to slide in the grooves. Simplest was a V-cut (Fig. 6-4J), but a stronger lid edge comes from plowing a groove and beveling its top edge (Fig. 6-4K). In a simple box the end overlaps the sides and provides a stop for the lid, which passes over the other end and is either given a knob or a finger notch (Fig. 6-4L).

In a better box the lid also enters a groove in the end. To avoid marring the surface where a groove in the overlapping parts ran through, the top corners should be mitered for the depth of the grooves (Fig. 6-4M). This can be done whether the box has overlapped nailed corners or dovetail joints.

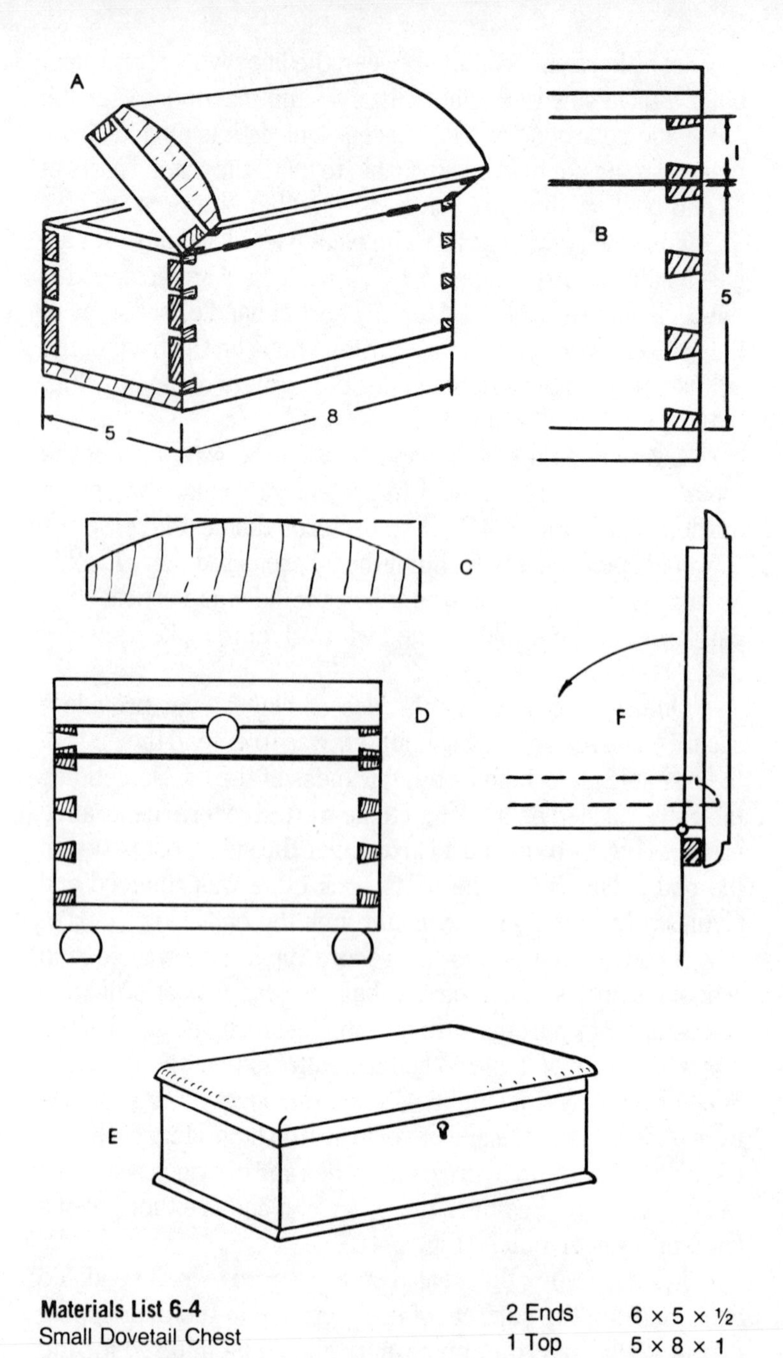


**Materials List 6-4**
Small Dovetail Chest

| | |
|---|---|
| 2 Sides | 6 × 8 × ½ |
| 2 Ends | 6 × 5 × ½ |
| 1 Top | 5 × 8 × 1 |
| 1 Bottom | 5 × 8 × ½ |

Fig. 6-4. Small chests with hinged and sliding lids. (Continued on next page.)

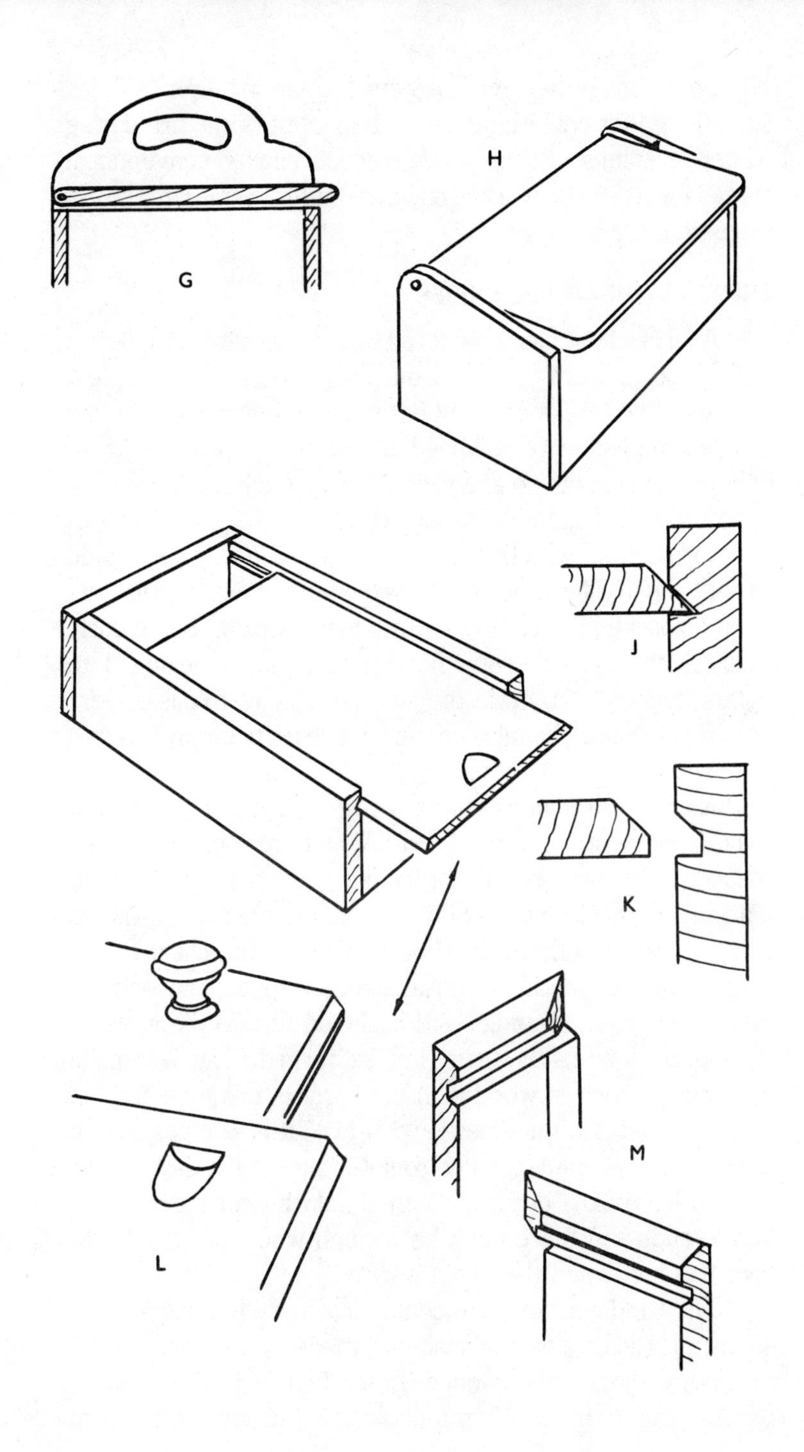
G
H
J
K
L
M

Small boxes became subjects for carving—probably as something that could be dealt with in front of the fire during winter evenings. Panels of leaves or similar conventional carved forms can be worked on lid and sides. Some later boxes were veneered.

## CHEST WITH EXTENDED SIDES

A large chest has to be lifted by two persons. Handles of various sorts were provided on plain chests. The simplest handles were blocks of wood extending a few inches. Better wooden handles were hollowed underneath to provide a grip. Others were cut out so a hand could go through and the fingers wrap around. Seamen's chests usually had stout blocks of wood projecting, with horizontal holes, so a loop of rope could pass through. The rope, which provided the actual grip, was often elaborately decorated with fancy knotting. Some early Colonial chests with rope handles may have belonged to sailors who had settled in the new country or to passengers who had seen such handles on the voyage to their new homes.

Another way of providing handles is to extend the sides and include a crossbar as a hand grip at each end. The crossbar could come near the top (Fig. 6-5A), where it might serve a secondary purpose as a rail for hanging towels or other cloths. If arranged lower down it allowed a higher lift. For stability in carrying, the position should be above half the chest height (Fig. 6-5B). It would be unsatisfactory to depend only on nailed ends to the handle, and it should fit into the sides to transfer the load safely. In its simplest form the handle is made of a square piece of wood with the corners taken off and the ends tenoned into the sides (Fig. 6-5C). It is also possible, if the sides are shaped suitably, to notch the handle through the sides (Fig. 6-5D), but not much should be cut away at the handle ends and there must be enough wood in the sides to take the load when the chest is lifted.

The handle has a more comfortable grip if it has a round section. It can be a parallel cylinder, made by hand planing and sanding, with its ends tenoned (Fig. 6-5E). If a lathe is available the handle can be decorated and the ends cut as dowels to fit holes in the sides (Fig. 6-5F). The center, which has to be gripped, should be without much decoration and be about 1¼ in. diameter for a good grip. The dowel ends can stop inside holes or pass right through and have their ends rounded where they project slightly.

The example of a large chest (Fig. 6-5G) could be varied in several ways, with different sizes or different arrangements of handles. Construction is generally similar to other chests, except for the extending sides. Cut the sides with some excess length and make the dado joints before doing any end shaping. The grooves should not be deeper than about one-third of the thickness of the wood. Use the ends as gauges for the width of the cuts, so the joints will be tight (Fig. 6-5H). Mark opposite sides together and check that the dados match when finished.

It is important for appearance that the end shapes are all the same. A card or hardboard template can be used, or one end can be laid out and cut, then used to mark around the ends of the opposite side. When they are cut, one of them can be used to mark around the opposite end of the first side.

If the handles are made by hand, prepare them square and cut the tenons, then plane off the corners. The pieces may be left with an octagonal section or other corners can be planed off and the wood rounded by sanding—first by pulling a strip of abrasive paper around the wood and finally by rubbing lengthwise. If the wood can be prepared in a lathe, it is simpler to turn dowel ends to fit drilled holes. In both cases the distances between the shoulders must match the width between the sides when the chest is assembled and this should be carefully checked by measuring or a trial assembly.

The handles have to be fitted at the same time as the chest is assembled. Fix the chest ends into one side and make and fit the bottom. Have the handles ready to glue in and fit them when the second side is added.

Chests can be made with the sides only extended enough to accommodate dado joints, but without handles between the sides. In some Colonial chests the extending pieces are rounded. In some the bottom also extends and is rounded

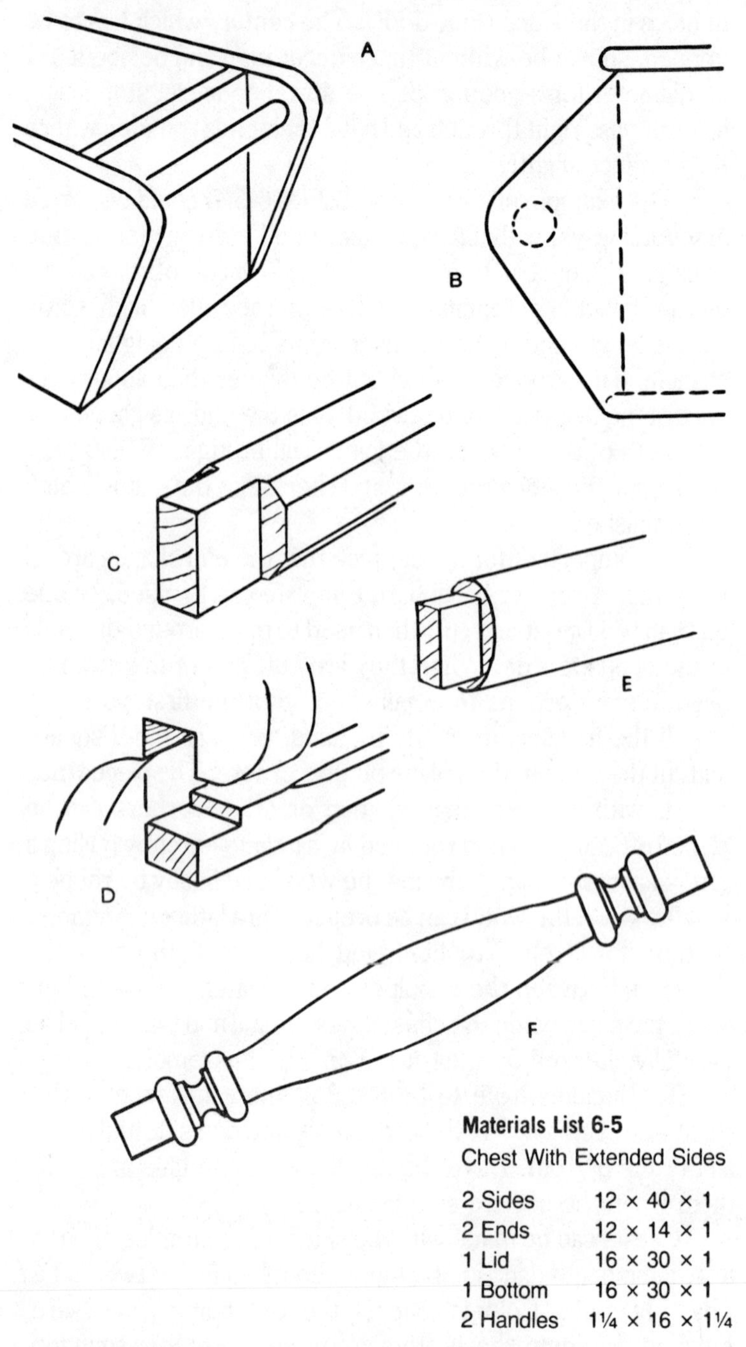


**Materials List 6-5**

Chest With Extended Sides

| | |
|---|---|
| 2 Sides | 12 × 40 × 1 |
| 2 Ends | 12 × 14 × 1 |
| 1 Lid | 16 × 30 × 1 |
| 1 Bottom | 16 × 30 × 1 |
| 2 Handles | 1¼ × 16 × 1¼ |

Fig. 6-5. Chest with extended sides. (Continued on next page.)

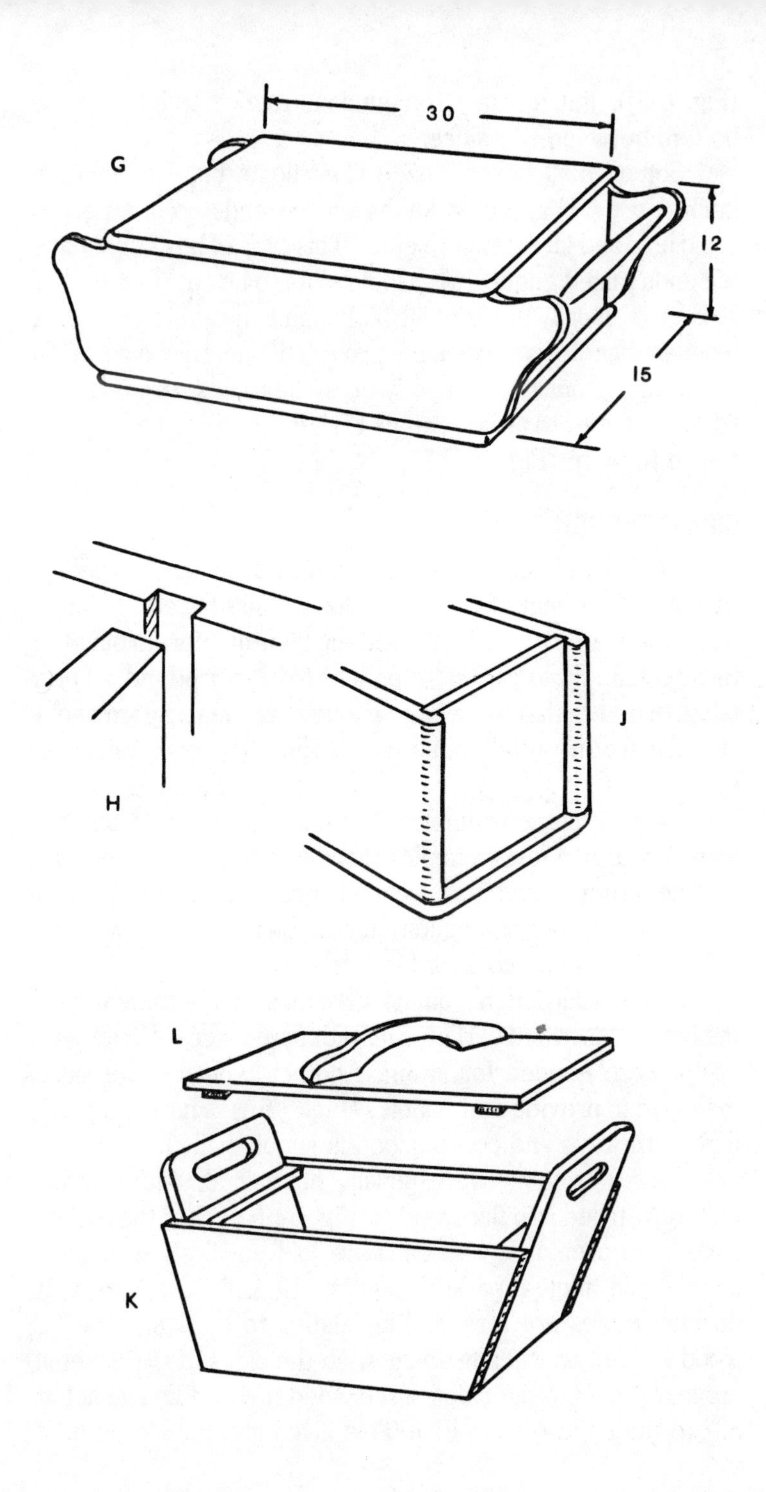

30
G
12
15
H
J
L
K

(Fig. 6-5J), but it is a stronger construction to enclose the bottom between the sides.

Some small boxes, made like chests but intended for kitchen use, were given knobs on the ends so one person could hold and lift from both ends. This type of box might have the ends raised enough for handle slots to be cut (Fig. 6-5K). Lids were usually made to lift, although some were hinged. A wooden handle was usually provided and this was often mounted diagonally, with fairly broad bearing surfaces on the lid, presumably to provide some resistance to any tendency of the lid to warp (Fig. 6-5L).

## DOUGH TROUGH

After dough for bread was mixed and kneaded it was left to rise before being formed into loaves and baked. A dough trough was a form of chest used for flour and for holding the rising dough. Sizes varied from those to be carried and put on a table, to others that were large enough to require a permanent place. A feature of all these was flaring. The ends might be upright, but the sides opened outwards to make the box wider at the top. In some examples the sides were upright and the ends flared. In a few examples there was flare both ways. To put the larger troughs at a convenient working height they were given legs or arranged to mount on a stool or low table. Lids then became working table tops.

Some small dough troughs were made in the same way as the boxes described earlier, but with flared sides. Handles or knobs were needed for lifting. Another type has the sides extended to provide four handles (Fig. 6-6A). There is a slight flare both ways and construction is simply nailed.

Larger troughs were usually dovetailed, with vertical ends dovetailed into flared sides (Fig. 6-6B). After the boards have been prepared, the ends are laid out first, with their lengths and angles marked together (Fig. 6-6C). Note that dovetail angles are arranged in relation to the length of the wood and not to the angled cuts, so the sides of the dovetail are at about 7° to the sides of the wood (Fig. 6-6D) and not at 83° to the edge (Fig. 6-6E). This gives greater strength. It may not be very different with a moderate flare, but when there is much of an angle, cutting dovetails in the second way results in too much weak "short" grain in each dovetail. Except for this the joints are laid out and cut in the same way as for a square corner—preferably with the dovetail part first and the other marked from it.

The lid is given a slight overlap all round and is located by battens across the ends in positions to locate the lid on the trough. If legs are built in they have to stand wide enough to hold the trough steady when used as a working table. One type is cut from stout solid wood, extending up the sides (Fig. 6-6F). The shapes can be band sawn. The tops of the extensions and the outer edges should be chamfered.

Crossbars share the weight of the box and they should be tenoned into the legs. The part of each leg that will be mortised should be arranged at right angles to the crossbar, to simplify marking and cutting the joint. Mortises may have gone right through in some early specimens, but if a dough trough is being made with a good finish to serve as a side table in modern surroundings, it might be better to have stub tenons finishing within the thickness of the leg (Fig. 6-6G).

Another way of supporting a trough to put the top at table height was to have a stool under it. This might be a separate item or it could be made so the bottom of the trough was also the top of the stool. The stool was made in one of the ways described earlier, but it was important that its feet stood wide enough to be steady under the wider top and this required some flaring of the legs (Fig. 6-6H).

Instead of the stool construction the support could be made more like a table (see Chapter 7). Athough quite low if the trough is deep, this can have table construction, but with the legs sloping outwards to give a steady base.

Although there is no need for a dough trough, as such, in a modern home, the pattern makes a convenient table with storage space underneath. If the full depth of a traditional trough is not required, there could be a shallowed bow with longer legs. It might be more convenient to hinge the lid than to arrange it to lift off. For use with dough the troughs were

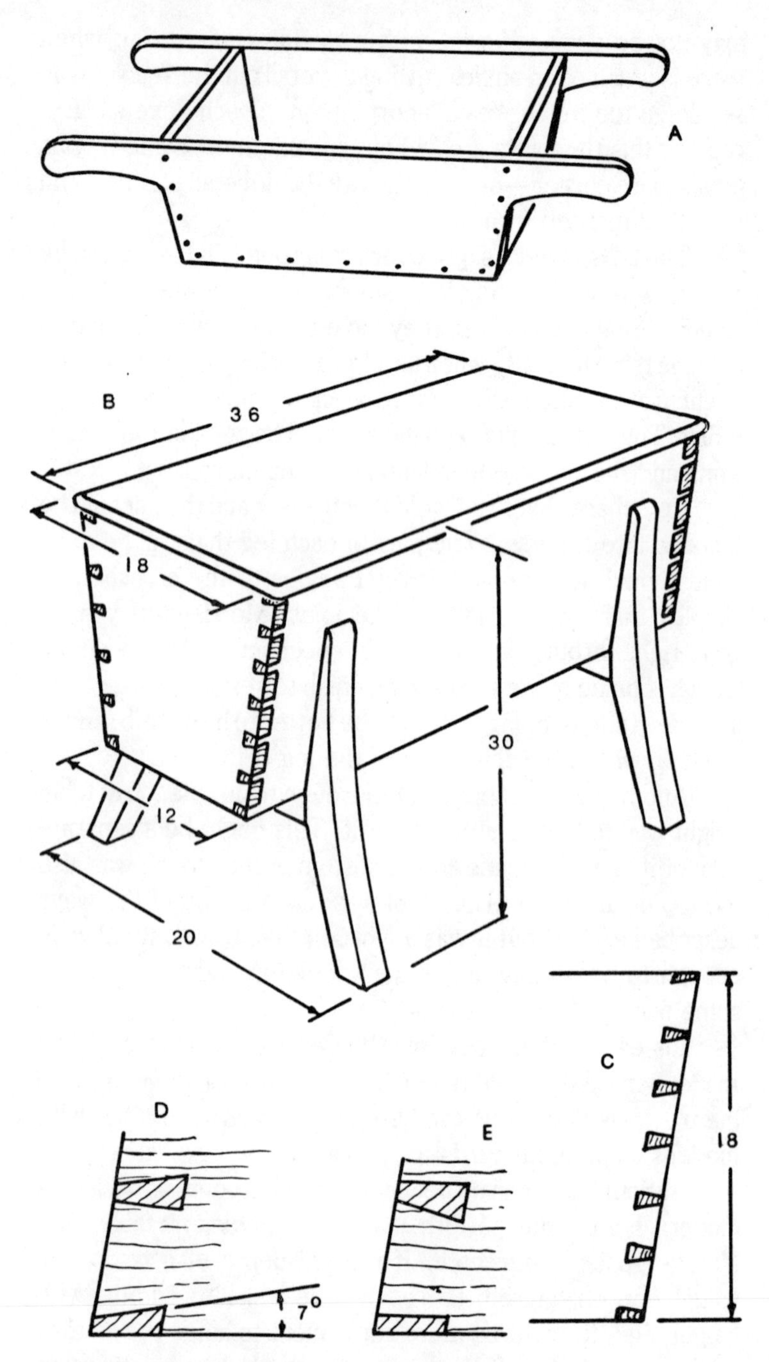


Fig. 6-6. Dough trough. (Continued on next page.)

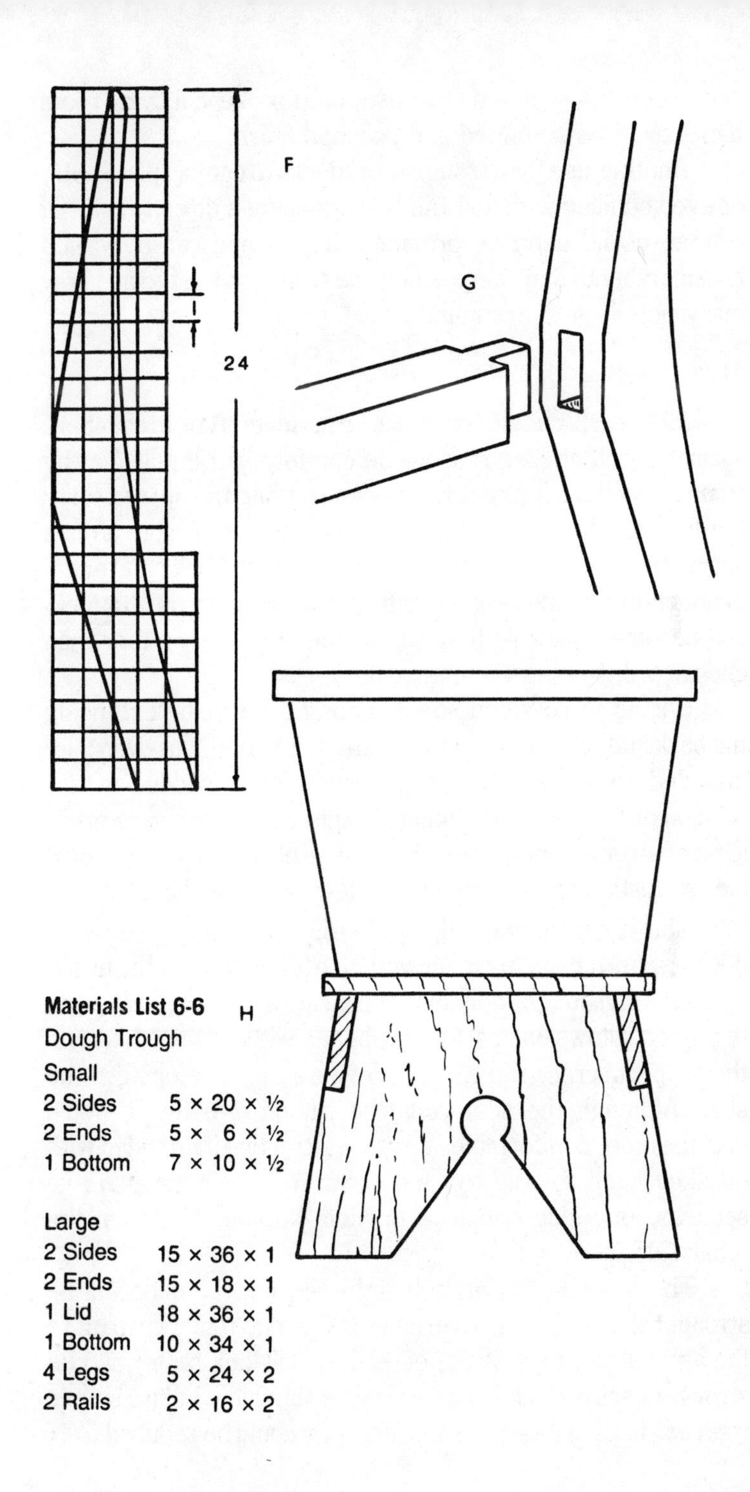


**Materials List 6-6**

Dough Trough

Small

| | |
|---|---|
| 2 Sides | 5 × 20 × ½ |
| 2 Ends | 5 × 6 × ½ |
| 1 Bottom | 7 × 10 × ½ |

Large

| | |
|---|---|
| 2 Sides | 15 × 36 × 1 |
| 2 Ends | 15 × 18 × 1 |
| 1 Lid | 18 × 36 × 1 |
| 1 Bottom | 10 × 34 × 1 |
| 4 Legs | 5 × 24 × 2 |
| 2 Rails | 2 × 16 × 2 |

bare wood and scubbed after use, but for use in a living room there could be a stained and polished finish.

Another use for a trough is outdoors to contain plant pots, or even be filled with soil and flowers planted directly in it. Of course, no lid need be provided. The shape can be varied considerably to suit the position the trough is to take and how many pots it is to accommodate.

## SEAT CHEST

Most early chests had to serve as seats. A plain chest put against a wall offered reasonable comfort, but if pulled away from the wall, as it might have been to bring the sitter nearer the fire, the lack of back support became noticeable after a short time. Chests developed into seats with backs and ends, eventually reaching heights sufficient to protect from draughts and become chairs with storage under the seat, rather than chests with seating accommodation.

Chests were given some seating comfort by extending the back and ends upwards. The amount varied, but even 9 in. provided some back support, particularly if padded with a cushion or blanket. Continuing straight up too high gave problems of strengthening and a high vertical back is uncomfortable, so further developments made more of a chair.

The chest shown (Fig. 6-7A) is made into a settle or double seat. It could be made with one lifting top and the inside without a division, but dividing the inside and having two parts to the top, allows one part to be opened without the other, and the support across the center prevents sag developing in the seat. Although the seat could be sat on directly, it would become more comfortable and more attractive if provided with fitted cushions for the top and back. With each made in two sections, one side could be opened without disturbing the other side.

The front has its grain lengthwise, but the ends will be stronger if their grain is vertical. If there is much shaping to the arms at the tops of the ends they will look better and be stronger if fairly thick—1 in. would be suitable—but if a simple rounding is all that is to be applied, they could be reduced to ¾ in. Both back and front can be glued and nailed in place or they could be extended enough to allow for dado joints (Fig. 6-7B). Dovetail joints are inappropriate since the vertical grain of the ends does not cut to make strong pins or dovetails. If dovetailed construction is preferred, the ends could be made cross grained and the arms made separately and doweled in place (Fig. 6-7C).

A central division can be fitted into dado slots. It is kept low enough to take a broader top to provide support under the meeting lids (Fig. 6-7D). In the original construction the division was probably nailed in directly without a dado.

The bottom shown was nailed underneath. Since this piece of furniture does not have to be carried about, maximum strength in the bottom is not so necessary. Bottoms were often made with the grain across the box and many boards used to make up the length (Fig. 6-7E). The projecting edges were rounded and blocks put under the corners to serve as feet. In a modern version the main area of the bottom could be plywood, framed around with solid wood and the plywood rabbeted in with the meeting edges covered by the box sides and ends.

The seat top is supported by battens across the ends at the same height as the center support. There is a rear strip full length at the back, nailed through the back and to the supports. The two seat parts that form lids rest on the supports and overhang the front slightly (Fig. 6-7F). It is advisable to put battens across to prevent warping, far enough in to clear the supports. The lids are hinged to the rear strip.

The upper extension of the back could be left straight or it might be shaped. If it is to be hidden by cushions, it might as well remain straight. Too much shaping or carving should be avoided, in any case, as this could prove uncomfortable to lean against. A flowing curve to match the ends would be suitable (Fig. 6-7G). Some of these seats had cut-out patterns in the back. Heart shapes were often used.

All exposed edges should be well rounded. The type of chest extended to a seat was common to many settlers, so the finish may be anything from a plain polish to painting with symbolic or pictorial decoration.

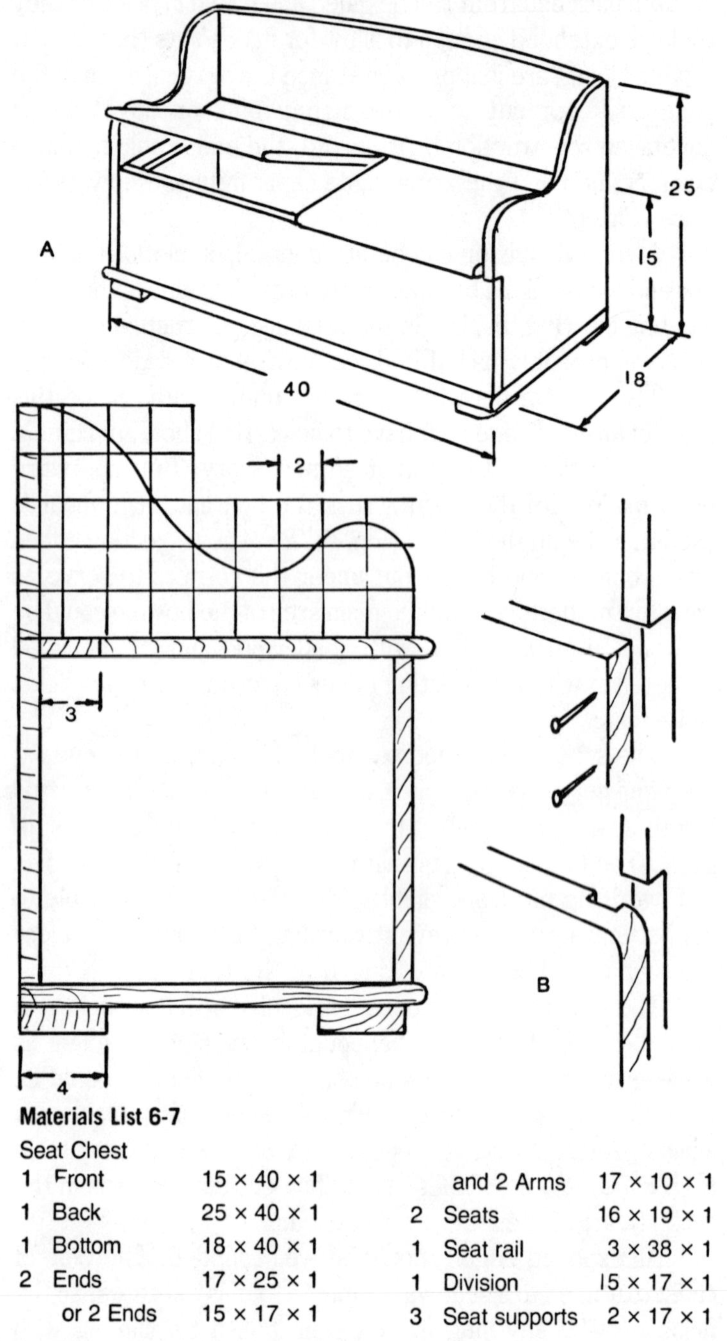


**Materials List 6-7**

Seat Chest

| | | |
|---|---|---|
| 1 | Front | 15 × 40 × 1 |
| 1 | Back | 25 × 40 × 1 |
| 1 | Bottom | 18 × 40 × 1 |
| 2 | Ends | 17 × 25 × 1 |
| | or 2 Ends | 15 × 17 × 1 |
| | and 2 Arms | 17 × 10 × 1 |
| 2 | Seats | 16 × 19 × 1 |
| 1 | Seat rail | 3 × 38 × 1 |
| 1 | Division | 15 × 17 × 1 |
| 3 | Seat supports | 2 × 17 × 1 |

Fig. 6-7. Seat chest. (Continued on next page.)

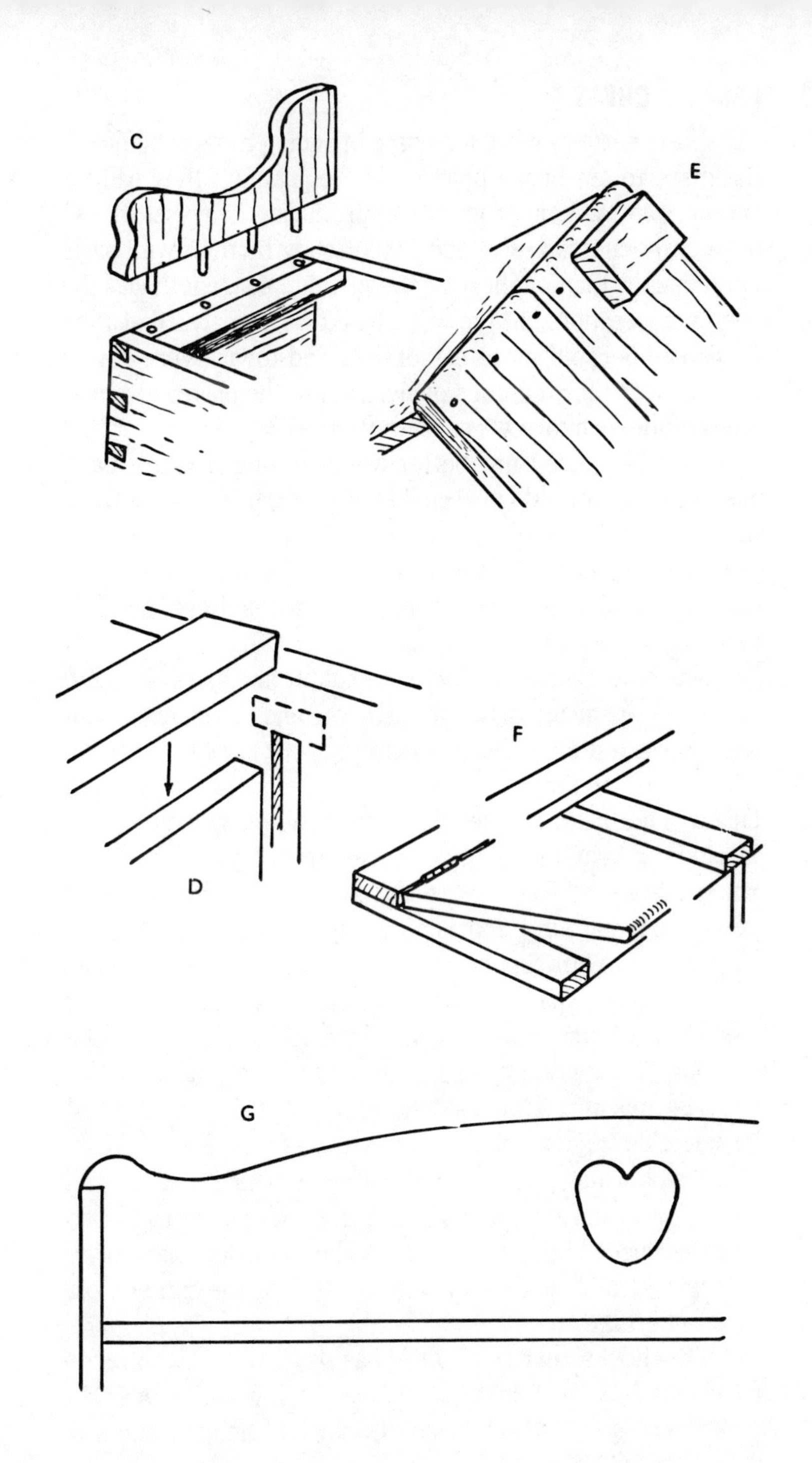
C
E
F
D
G

## PANELED CHEST

Early settlers were fortunate in finding trees of sufficient thickness to cut broad boards. The equipment they had for cutting was more appropriate to producing heavy stock, so most early chests are of quite stout construction, with parts often thicker than might really be justified if strength was the only consideration, but the wood had to be prepared that way. As people became more established and towns were set up with more of the amenities of civilization, the plain and sometimes crude furniture was not wanted. Alongside the demand for better furniture came better woodworking facilities. Sawmills were set up and wood could be provided of more delicate section. The cabinetmaker was able to equip his shop with more than the basic hand equipment, although for a very long time nearly all of the operations he performed depended on hand or foot power.

The newer furniture had to be lighter and better looking. Chests were still important in the home and cedar, in particular, was valued for making chests to store blankets and clothing. One type that evolved had the sides and ends paneled. This was not new; Medieval furniture had many examples of paneled construction. Without our modern plywood for wide panels there was an ever present problem of wide pieces of wood expanding and contracting with changes in moisture content due to atmospheric variations. Panels in a frame can be arranged so expansion and contraction across the grain can take place without affecting appearance. Variations in the direction of the grain are so slight as to be negligible.

The making of paneled furniture by hand called for a considerable amount of skill and some of it was hard work. With a modern table saw much of the work can be done with greater precision and much less labor. Other power tools also have their uses in this type of work, but a modern hand plow plane will do much of the grooving better than the earlier tools could undertake.

The chest shown (Fig. 6-8A) has single panels at the ends and sides made up of three similar panels. It would be possible to overlap assembled side panels on the ends in the same way as chests made from solid boards. Some chests were made this way, but this chest has corner legs. A point to watch if variations are made is that to get a pleasing appearance the faces of the legs, the upright stiles and the top rails should all be the same width on each side or end of the chest, but the bottom rail should be wider. If the bottom rail is kept the same width as the other faces, an optical illusion will make it look narrower and this spoils appearance. There may have to be variations to suit the widths of wood available for panels. Having a center side panel wider than the two that border it looks good, but a narrower center panel between wider panels is not as attractive.

The panels have raised centers. These should not be cut until after other parts are prepared, but it is necessary to examine the wood available and decide on sizes. The raised center of each panel is surrounded by what was called "fielding." This slight taper is fitted into a groove made deeper than needed for a close fit (Fig. 6-8B). As the wood expands or contracts it moves in and out of the groove. If the panels are ¾ in. thick it should be satisfactory to settle on grooves ⅜ in. wide throughout the assembly. The design is shown with all edges square. It is unwise to try to incorporate molding around the framing as this complicates the joints. All that is needed is for the sharpness (the *arrisses*) to be sanded off just before assembly, particularly along those edges that will frame the panels.

The top is the only part that can have its appearance relieved by molding (Fig. 6-8C). The legs are square, but inside the chest it looks better if they have the inner angle taken off (Fig. 6-8D). This might be cut right through so the feet are the same shape, or it could be stopped at the bottom to leave the projecting feet square.

Like any other cabinetmaking project consisting of a great many parts, preparation should be tackled systematically. It is advisable to collect the wood for all parts, then cut and plane at least the vital structural parts to width and thickness. There will be a few parts, like the bottom and panels, that will not be worked to size until they can be fitted into other parts, but they can be prepared to thickness.

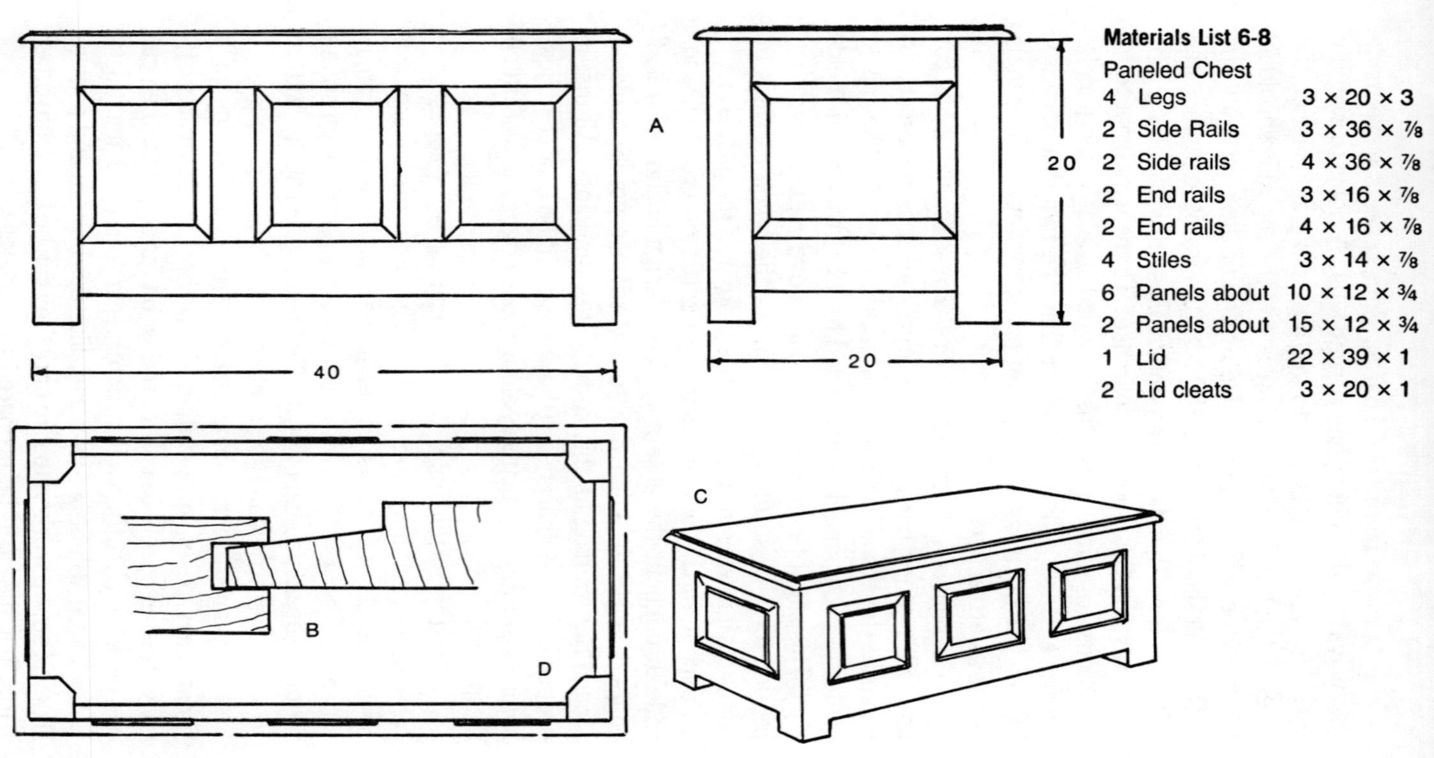


**Materials List 6-8**

Paneled Chest

| Qty | Part | Size |
|---|---|---|
| 4 | Legs | 3 × 20 × 3 |
| 2 | Side Rails | 3 × 36 × 7/8 |
| 2 | Side rails | 4 × 36 × 7/8 |
| 2 | End rails | 3 × 16 × 7/8 |
| 2 | End rails | 4 × 16 × 7/8 |
| 4 | Stiles | 3 × 14 × 7/8 |
| 6 | Panels about | 10 × 12 × 3/4 |
| 2 | Panels about | 15 × 12 × 3/4 |
| 1 | Lid | 22 × 39 × 1 |
| 2 | Lid cleats | 3 × 20 × 1 |

Fig. 6-8. Paneled chest.

The next work should be grooving. The legs, rails and stiles have similar grooves, which all need to be at the same distance from the front (face) surfaces (Fig. 6-9A). Joints could be doweled, but the early cabinetmaker always used mortise and tenon joints. By choosing ⅜ in. for the width of groove, that can also be used for the width of mortise, so simplifying the marking out and cutting of the joints. The top rails go about 1½ in. into the legs and are haunched to fit the grooves (Fig. 6-9B). The joints for the bottom rails can be similar, although a 4 in. width is better arranged with two tenons (Fig. 6-9C). Where the stiles go into the rails, that tenon is the width between the bottoms of the grooves (Fig. 6-9D).

With grooves cut where needed, put parts requiring similar distances to be marked together and mark across them with a try square, so all distances that have to match, will actually do so. Put the legs together. Mark across their length, but it is advisable to not cut the ends close to the marks until after other work has been done. Use the ends of rails as guides to their widths and mark the positions of the mortises (Fig. 6-9E). Marks on the legs can be used as guides for marking the stiles for their tenons—it is the distance between the shoulders which is important (Fig. 6-9F).

Mark the edges of the four lengthwise rails together and do the same with the four end rails. In all of these parts it is the distances between shoulders which are important and these should be cut around the wood with a knife. Slight variations in overall length affecting the tenons are not so important. Cut the tenons by hand or by using the table saw. Drill out some of the waste from the mortises and chop them to shape with a chisel. It is best to not make a complete trial assembly, as this may cause wear in the joints so they may not fit as closely in the final assembly.

Measurements from these parts will give the overall sizes of the panels. In the widths allow for the panels having about ⅛ in. clearance above the bottoms of the grooves. Lengths can be similar, but as later variations along the grain will be slight, the wood can be a closer fit that way.

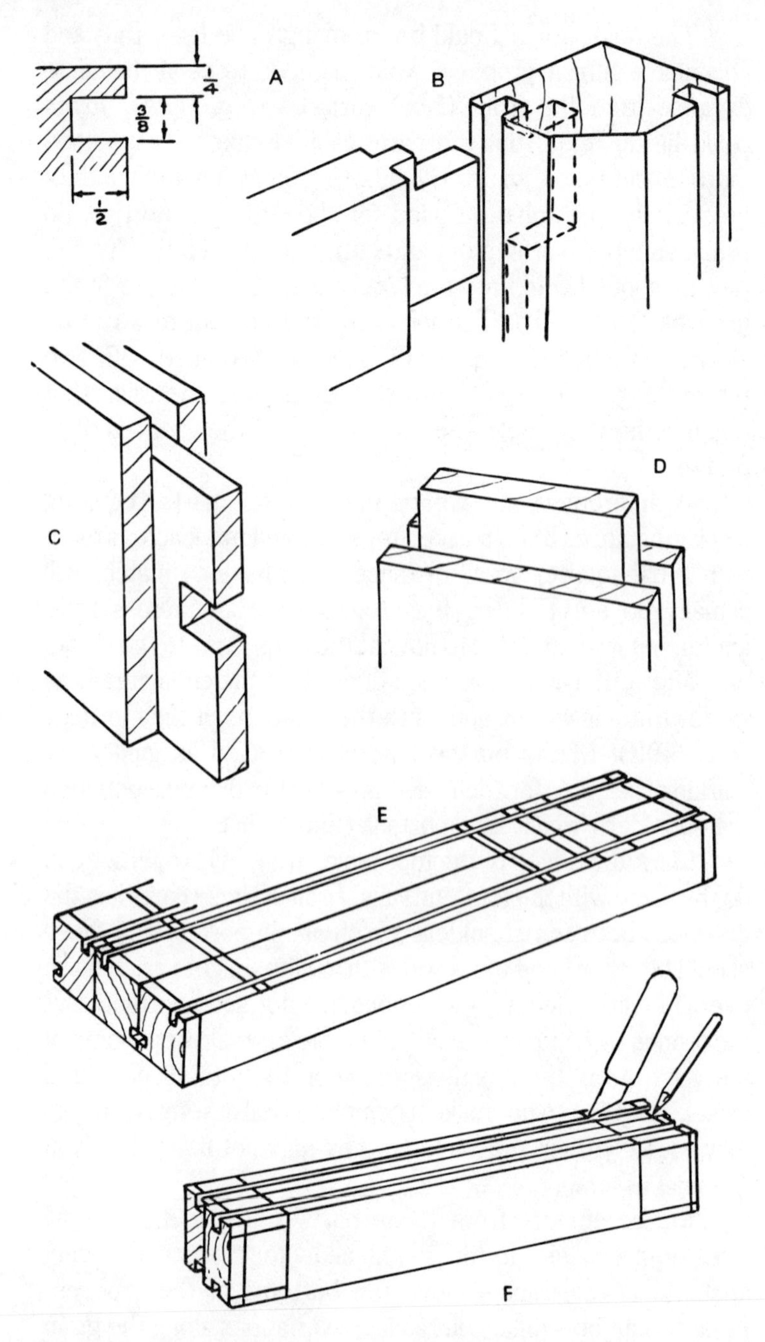


Fig. 6-9. Constructional details of a paneled chest, showing frame joints (A-F), panel details (G and H), the bottom (J) and lid shaping (K-M). (Continued on next page.)

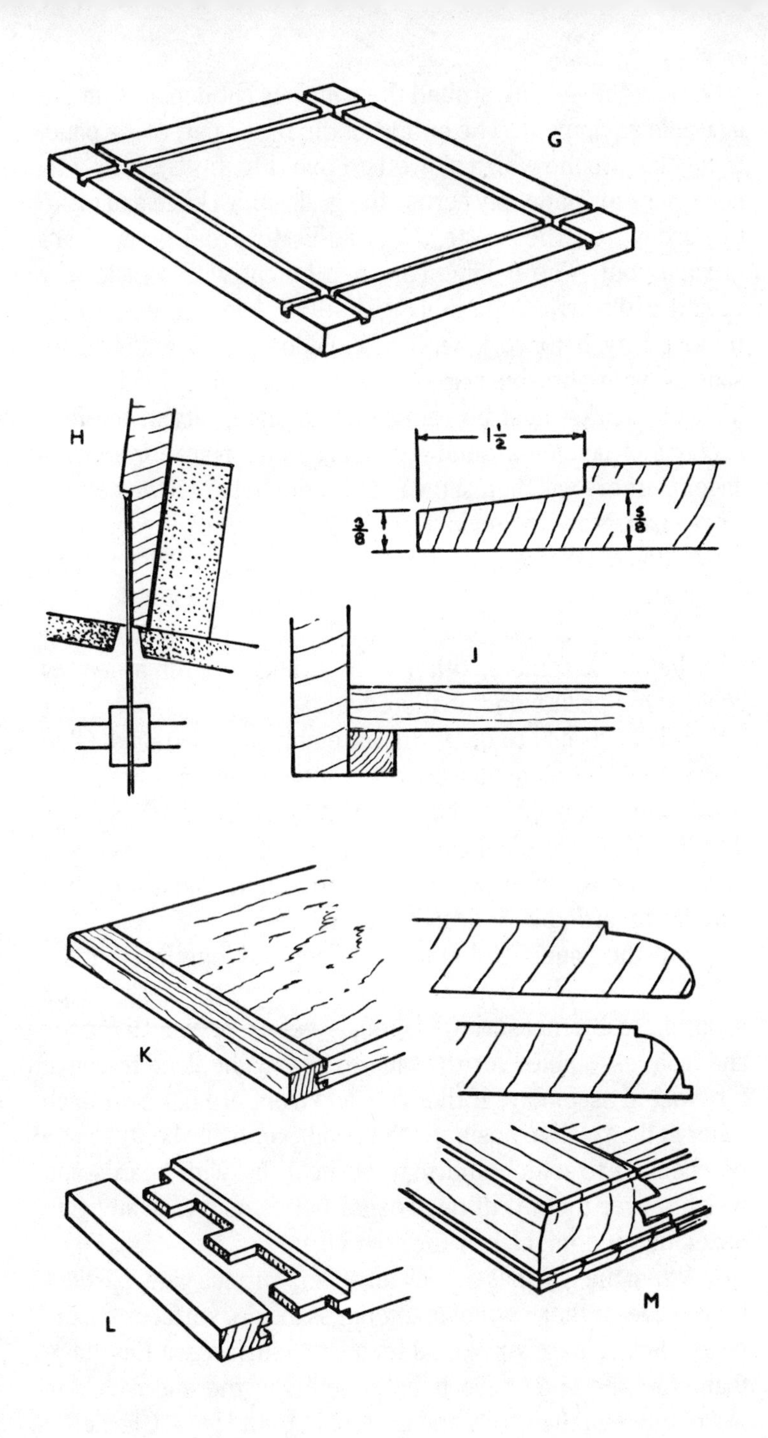
G
H
1 1/2
3/8
5/8
J
K
L
M

How the fielding around the panels is cut depends on the available equipment. The outline of the raised part of the panel is best cut around with a plowed groove (Fig. 6-9G). It may be necessary to cut deeply across the grain with a knife and make the groove on the waste side of this to avoid grain fibers breaking out. The fielding can then be cut with a table saw having a tilt arrangement (Fig. 6-9H). Allow a little to be removed by handwork with a shoulder plane, followed by sanding with abrasive paper wrapped around a wood block. Machine marks must be removed and uniformity of the four sections of fielding around a panel are important for appearance. Corners will then show neat miters between the bevels. These panels are the main decorative features of the chest, so they should be given as good a tool and sanded finish as possible.

If the chest is to be stained, the panels should be dealt with before assembly, otherwise shrinkage after assembly could show plain wood at the edges.

It is advisable to deal with assembly in two stages. Glue alone should be adequate, provided sufficient clamps are available. Some early chests had the joints secured with pegs or dowels. This can be done, particularly if it is necessary to move a clamp on after pulling a joint together. The dowel ends may be regarded as a design feature.

Put the panels and stiles between the lengthwise rails, then add the legs. With all these joints pulled close, check squareness by measuring diagonals before leaving the back and front assembled for the glue to set. Sight along to check for twisted assembly. If the back and front are put over each other in the relative positions they will eventually be, they can be checked to match and may be held flat with boards and weights over them. Put newspaper between in case any glue oozes out and might join the two parts.

When the glue has set, clean off any surplus glue, particularly inside. If there is any unevenness inside, surfaces should be leveled. It is easier to deal with inner surfaces at this stage than after the ends have been added. Put the end panels in place between their rails and assemble to the legs. Check the end assemblies for squareness. Have the chest standing so the four legs rest on a surface known to be flat. Measure diagonally across the tops of the legs to see that the chest is square in plain view. Stand well back and sight across the two ends and then the two sides to see there is no twist, then leave the assembly for the end glued parts to set.

The bottom fits inside. Solid wood was arranged with several boards having their grain across the box and resting on strips inside the bottom rails (Fig. 6-9J). If the rest of the chest is made of cedar for storing blankets or linen, it would be advisable to use thin cedar boards for the bottom, but for other purposes it might be plywood.

The lid could be a plain board, but it would need battens underneath to reduce warping, and this might be considered a rather crude and earlier method that would not match the more refined method of construction of the rest of the chest. The better method is to tenon on cleats across the ends. A cleat is a strip of wood with its grain across the direction of the grain of the top (Fig. 6-9K).

A groove across the cleat has a matching tongue on the top, which extends in two or three places to deeper tenons (Fig. 6-9L). How many tenons depends on the width, but in this case three should suit. To get a good fit it is simplest to have the cleat too long and too thick; then it can be worked to exact size after fitting. Molding around the top has to be carried around the cleat (Fig. 6-9M), which calls for care where lengthwise grain changes to end grain at the joints.

The lid should swing on three strong hinges, preferably of the strap type, bent to bring their knuckles outside. Although earlier chests rarely had locks, or were fitted with staples, this later type might have a proper box lock let into the front to engage with a plate under the lid. This ties in with the more advanced cabinetmaking standard of this chest compared with the earlier ones.

# Tables

Chests may have served as seats before chairs were made, but the furniture need next in importance was for working surfaces at a convenient height for use when standing or sitting. The need was particularly acute in the home for the preparation of food and then eating it. The simplest tables, in Colonial days and in earlier European days, were boards resting on any temporary support. The temporary supports became trestles or other folding devices, so when the table was not required, it and its supports could be put flat against a wall. A development of this was the takedown table, where the table and its supports made a fairly rigid and substantial structure, but they could be taken apart for storage and transport. This was an obvious advantage when a family expected to move westward from a temporary first home and furniture that could be packed compactly had advantages. There are surviving examples of very well made examples of this type of furniture, but there are others in which the features that were needed for folding are incorporated in tables with other parts that do not fold and prevent the first features being taken apart. This seems a transitional idea where design was not properly understood.

The obvious table would seem to be one with four legs arranged upright at each corner (Fig. 7-1A), but there are

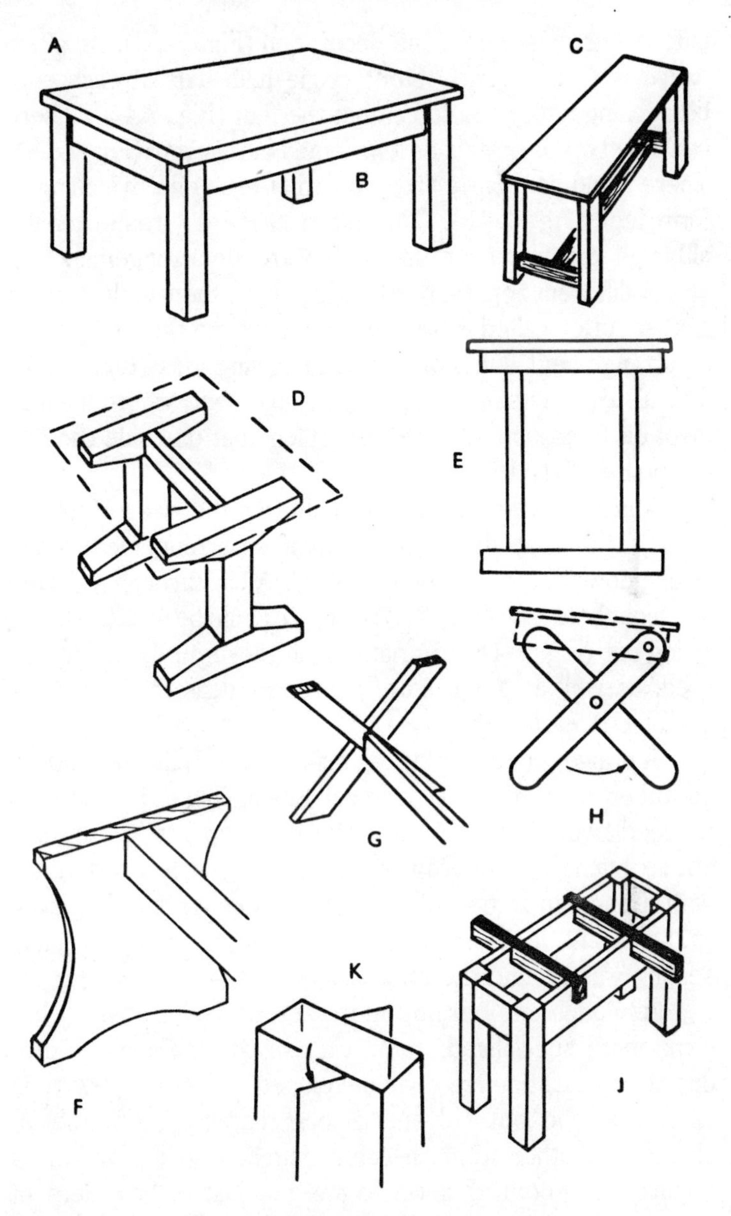


Fig. 7-1. Methods of table construction with legs (A-C), pedestals (D-F), sawbuck ends (G and H) and flap supports (J and K).

other forms. Such a table needs its legs bracing. One way is to have broad rails at the top (Fig. 7-1B). Another way is to join them with rails lower down, and these provided scope for different arrangements and decoration (Fig. 7-1C). An alternative is to have fairly stout single pedestals at each end, broadening under the top and at the feet (Fig. 7-1D). There could be two pedestals or legs joined in this way (Fig. 7-1E). There could be a fairly broad board at each end, widening to form feet (Fig. 7-1F). This often called a "trestle table," although it differs from the original trestle arrangement.

A different approach to legs is to have them in the form of a cross, often called a "sawbuck table," from the similarity to an arrangement common for hand sawing logs (Fig. 7-1G). This also lends itself to a folding arrangement, where the legs pivot on their joint and the top attached at one side can fold down (Fig. 7-1H).

Much thought was given to altering the sizes of tables, usually with drop flaps. In the common arrangement a flap swung downwards when not wanted. A bar through a slotted rail might hold it up (Fig. 7-1J) or there could be an extra leg to swing out (Fig. 7-1K). Variations on these methods are still used, as well as some more advanced ideas that were not available in earlier days.

A drawer under a table top makes a good place for cutlery and other things needed for a meal. Sewing tables had drawers for needlework items. For a normal fixed top table there could not be much depth of drawers or there would be interference with sitting, but some folding tables had deeper drawers, even to the extent of a nest of drawers, in the fixed supports and seating was around the raised flaps.

As conditions became more settled and craftsmen became more specialized, some very ornate tables were produced and a distinctive style developed, related to design as used in Europe, but with special local characteristics. Tables, chairs, and other items became matched so design was a feature of a room as a whole and not just of one piece of furniture.

## PLAIN TABLE

A simple four-legged table had many variations, and still has, and may be named according to its uses. A general-purpose table may be a kitchen table, made with a softwood top and the legs and underframing of hardwood for strength. A smaller near-square table was usually a lamp table and stood at a strategic place for light at night. It would make a good side table. A similar table, rather smaller than a kitchen table was often called a tavern table. In the simplest table the legs were square and parallel, but this gives a rather heavy appearance and it was usual to taper them slightly. Many legs were turned, with the upper part left square for jointing. Usually the legs were stout enough to be rigid and hold their shape without rails, but some of these tables have lower rails and stretchers which served as footrests.

If a table is to be used for purposes other than sitting to, it can be any size. A coffee table may be low, while one intended to carry a flower vase may be higher. The usual height for a table to be used with a normal chair has its top about 30 in. from the floor. There needs to be clearance under any rail of at least 24 in. so as not to impede the knees. This means that the thickness of the table top and the width of a rail under it should not exceed 6 in. and would be better if rather less. It is these considerations that have led to many tables having rails lower down, to serve as bracing, when the joints between the top rails and the legs might have been considered unlikely to stand up to the loads on them. With modern glues and carefully cut joints, joint strength should be much better. The example shown is of tavern table size, but other sizes are made in the same way (Fig. 7-2A).

The legs (Fig. 7-2B) are square and parallel slightly deeper than the rail joint. Leave some excess length at the top. Mark out all four legs together and take the lines all round. Tapers can be marked one way, but it is more convenient to cut the top joints before the legs are shaped. The traditional way of joining the rails is with mortise and tenon joints, having two parts in the depth (Fig. 7-2C). It might be satisfactory to substitute dowels (Fig. 7-2D), but for a table expected to get heavy use, mortise and tenon joints are stronger. Mark the rail ends together. Cut the joints before tapering the legs. With a suitable table saw it is possible to arrange a sliding fence to cut the tapers accurately so they only need lightly planing. Otherwise the tapers should be marked on opposite faces and the waste removed by sawing and planing. Leave some excess length on tops and bottoms of the legs until after the framing is assembled.

Care is needed to get all parts of a table assembled squarely. Lack of truth in any direction becomes very apparent to a viewer. Assembly should be in two stages. Make up opposite sets of legs and rails—usually the longer way. Put them together on a flat surface and check diagonals. Pull the joints tight with clamps, but nails or dowels can be driven inside the legs to hold them and the clamps removed (Fig. 7-2E). Assemble the second side in the same way and put it over the first side. See that both assemblies rest level and match. If there are any discrepancies, put them right before the glue has started setting.

When the glue in those joints has set, add the rails the other way. At this stage you have to check diagonals at the ends, then diagonals across the top, while the legs are standing on a flat surface. Sight across the rails in both directions and see there is no twist, then leave the assembly for the glue to set (Fig. 7-2F).

Further strength in the corners is provided by triangular fillets between the legs and rails (Fig. 7-2G). These are almost as deep as the rails and glue alone should be sufficient, although pins may be driven to prevent slipping. Level the tops of the legs with the rails. The whole surface should present a flat area to take the top. It can be tested by inverting on a flat piece of stout plywood or particleboard.

The top is made is up of several boards glued together. Overhang was often more in the length than the width. Edges might be cut square or round—or they could be molded. Elaborate molding would be inappropriate. Corners were well rounded for kitchen tables and even with side tables apparently square, the sharpness should be taken off.

The most basic table has the top nailed to the rails, possibly with the nails punched and stopped. It is better to fix from below so nothing shows on the top surface. *Pocket screwing* was used and this is still a good method. The screw goes diagonally upwards through the rail into the top, and pockets have to be cut with a gouge and chisel at intervals to let the screw head in (Fig. 7-2H). A simple way of cutting a pocket is to use a large diameter bit in a brace and enter it at right angles to the line the screw will take (Fig. 7-2J).

Fixing a top rigidly makes no allowance for expansion and contraction of a fairly wide top. One way of dealing with this is to use bottoms. These engage with grooves plowed in the rails before assembly. Buttons are screwed at intervals around the underside of the top with their extensions free to move in the grooves (Fig. 7-2K).

Some of the severity of appearance can be removed and better leg room provided by cutting away the undersides of the rails (Fig. 7-2L). This allows of rather deeper joints for greater strength at the legs, but the cutaway parts should not be too close to the legs, or there may be weakness due to short grain breaking out.

## TABLE WITH DRAWERS

If a table has to be used by people using chairs and having to put their legs underneath, any drawer has to be shallow, otherwise its framing and the rails will come too low. This means that it is possible to make a kitchen table with a drawer with space enough for cutlery, with an internal depth of about 2 in., but any more would be unsuitable. Many kitchen tables were made with these drawers at opposite ends and it is possible to frame up a table in this way, but cutting away end rails to admit drawers tends to weaken the structure, so good workmanship to make strong joints is essential.

If the table does not have to admit the knees of someone sitting on a chair, freedom of design is extended. Such tables may be for side use or they could be sewing tables. They might be lower as coffee tables today. A serving table in the dining room could have drawers deep enough to give useful capacity. If a table is made the same height as a dining table it could serve to extend that when needed, although it would not be suitable for sitting with legs under.

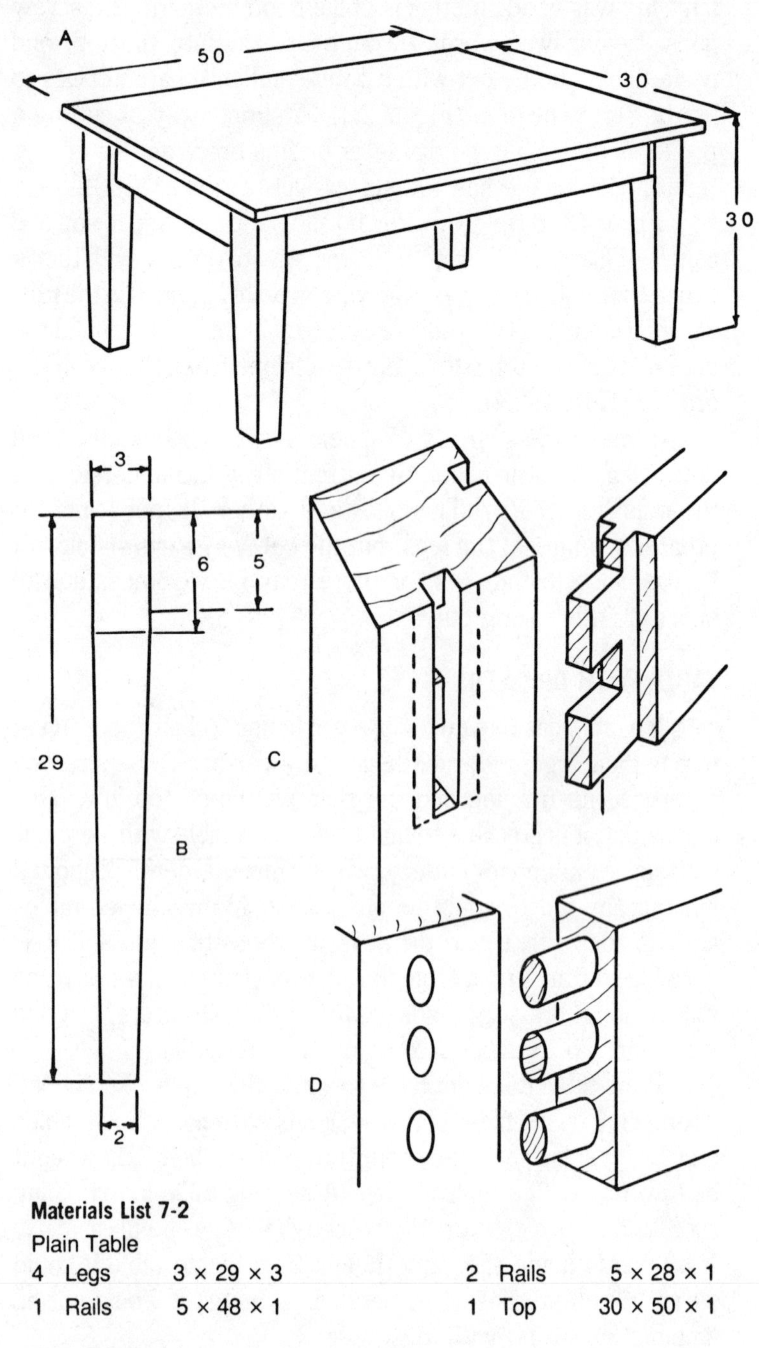


**Materials List 7-2**

Plain Table

| | | | | | |
|---|---|---|---|---|---|
| 4 | Legs | 3 × 29 × 3 | 2 | Rails | 5 × 28 × 1 |
| 1 | Rails | 5 × 48 × 1 | 1 | Top | 30 × 50 × 1 |

Fig. 7-2. Plain table. (Continued on next page.)

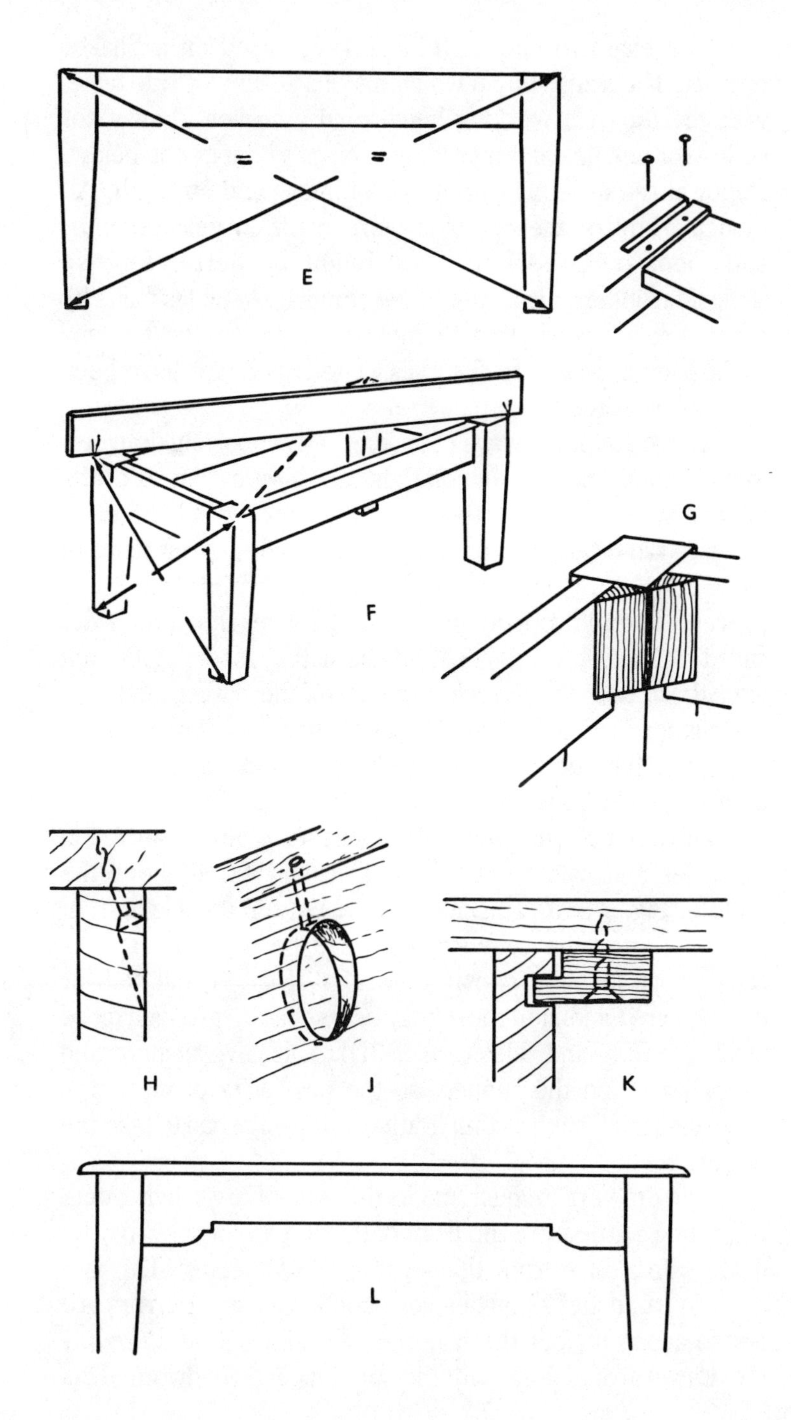
E
F
G
H
J
K
L

The example shown (Fig. 7-4) is based on a Shaker original. The sizes shown would make a sewing or side table, with the top at a working height and a shallow drawer for cutlery or needles and thread, as well as a deeper one below. Depth in the assembly produces stiffness and strength. Although many of these tables were made in pine or other softwood, polished hardwood might be better for use alongside modern furniture. Some comparable tables made by other colonial workers had molded edges to the top and shaped lower edges to the rails. The legs might have been turned below rail level.

There are many ways of making and supporting drawers. In much modern construction there are plastic runners or the drawer side is grooved to run on a strip of wood. All early drawers ran on the bottom edges of the sides, over strips of wood called "runners." As the drawer was withdrawn, it was prevented from dropping by a piece of wood above the side, called a "kicker" (Fig. 7-3A). If the actual assembly did not keep the drawer on its track in the width, there were guides on the runners (Fig. 7-3B). If reproduction furniture is to be authentic, this method of controlling the movement of each drawer should be used.

Drawer bottoms were often let into grooves plowed in the sides and front, but the back usually fitted above the bottom (Fig. 7-3C). This allowed the bottom to slide in from the back after the drawer joints had been glued. This is satisfactory for light construction, but if larger and heavier drawers are examined there may be a separate grooved piece inside the front and sides (Fig. 7-3D). This gave an increased bearing area on the runner, so the possibility of wear was much less than when a comparatively thin edge had to take the weight.

The drawers in much modern furniture have their fronts projecting a little from the front of the carcase or they may be made with a false front that overlaps the opening. This is a modern trend and simplifies construction as slight errors are not so apparent, but the majority of traditional furniture has the drawer fronts flush with the surrounding woodwork. This

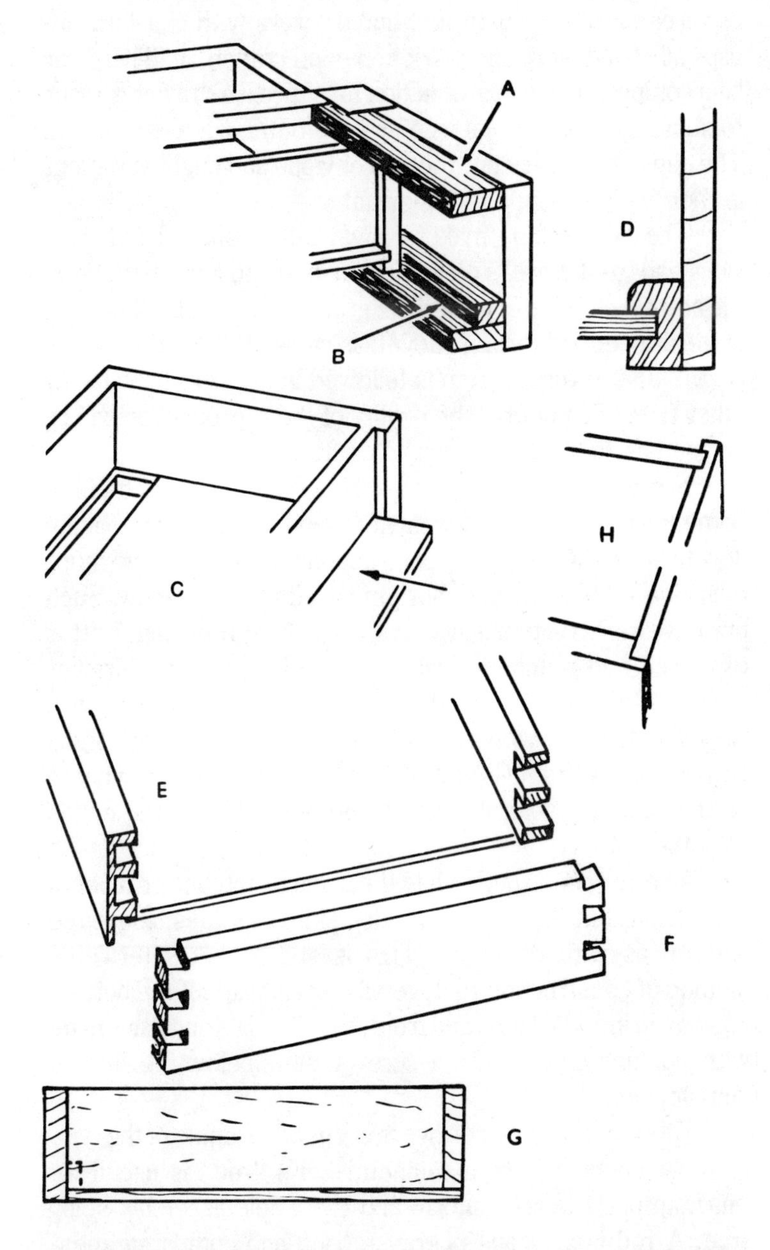


Fig. 7-3. Standard methods of traditional drawer construction. The drawer is prevented from tilting with a kicker (A) and is within guides (B). The bottom slides in grooves in the sides (C) or added pieces (D). Dovetails were usual (E and F). The bottom goes under the back (F). A simpler construction is notched and grooved (H).

requires more careful fitting, and drawers with equal narrow gaps all round were the mark of a good craftsman. There can be a compromise in reproduction furniture if a drawer is made to stand out a short distance and the outer edge is rounded. The gaps around are not then so obvious and slight variations in their widths is not so important.

The best cabinetmakers always dovetailed drawers. If sides and front were grooved for the bottom, a half dovetail at the bottom of a side enclosed the groove (Fig. 7-3E). The back of the drawer had through dovetails worked above the groove (Fig. 7-3F). If this system is followed in drawers for table or other type of furniture, the quality of the reproduction will be as good as the best by original craftsmen.

Not all early furniture makers were trained craftsmen. Sometimes their ability was not good enough for making dovetails. In the simplest construction a drawer was no more than a nailed box, with its bottom nailed on from below. Such primitive construction is not really worth reproducing. Better examples had notched corner joints. The simplest drawer then had the sides notched into the front, but the back was lapped and nailed, with the bottom nailed to sides, back and a strip inside the front (Fig. 7-3G). It is the bottom which bears on the runners, so nails have to be punched and the edges smoothed.

A better construction had the sides in notches or rabbets in the front, but the back was dadoed into the sides, above the bottom, as with dovetails. This is still a good alternative method of construction to dovetails, particularly if the bottom is grooved into the sides and front (Fig. 7-3H). Joints are made with glue and either nails or screws, sunk below the surface and stopped.

This table with two drawers is a good example of the type of construction where a cabinetmaker's "rod" is useful for ensuring parts being uniform and the whole assembly being true. A rod is a means of transferring and comparing measurements without having to frequently refer to rule. In this case the rod is used as a guide for all vertical measurements. The sizes given make a table with a comfortable working height (Fig. 7-4A). As a first step, draw one leg with the outlines of the top, the drawers and their rails (Fig. 7-4B). For the rails, use the sizes of the pieces of wood as they are and not what they should be, for drawing their locations. A wood width slightly more or less than the intended size will not matter if it is allowed for when laying out parts to which it will be attached. Transfer all the vital measurements to a straight piece of scrap wood that will serve as a rod (Fig. 7-4C). From this point mark rail positions and drawer depths from the rod and not by using a rule.

Mark out all four legs together. Leave a little surplus length at the top until after the joints have been cut. The sides and back are best tenoned into the legs (Fig. 7-4D), in the way described for the plain table. Dowels are not so satisfactory for these deeper rails, although they can be used.

The place of a front rail is made up by the two drawers and the three narrow rails that accommodate them. Select straight-grained wood for the narrow drawer rails as warping after assembly could interfere with the action of the drawers. The rails can join the legs with "barefaced" tenons (Fig. 7-4E). With a table of the sizes given there should be little risk of the rails warping, but if there is any doubt or the sizes are increased, there can be pieces from front to back at the centers of the two lower rails. Keep their lower edges level with the undersides of the rails. The top edges should be level with or below the top sides of the rail, so as not to interfere with the drawer above.

Make up the table framework in the sequence described for the plain table, getting back and front right, before adding the ends and checking diagonals. The top can be prepared, and tried in position, but do not fit it until after doing all the work associated with the drawers.

The table assembly can be used as a guide for first making the drawer fronts. They should be cut to fit with just a little clearance in the two openings. Lightly pencil marks to show which way they go. Make a drawer side. It should be of such a length that it butts against the back rail when the drawer front is level with the framework, if that is the chosen design, or projecting about ⅛ in., if the front is to be rounded. Allow for the chosen method of construction. The rear end of each side can be left slightly too long, so the finished drawer can be adjusted to get the drawer at exactly the right projection and parallel at the front.

Assemble the drawers completely and try them in their openings. Make up kickers, guides and runners to suit the drawers by testing them in position. Start at the top. There are plain kickers above the top drawer. Their thickness should be the same as the front rails. For the drawer it is important that the lower surface should be level with the underside of the top front rail. These kickers will also be used to take screws to secure the top, so the top surfaces should finish level with the tops of the side rails (Fig. 7-4F). The runners for the top drawer are also the kickers for the bottom drawer, so should be the same thickness as the middle front rail, projecting far enough to give a good bearing to the drawer and with a strip added level with the inner surfaces of the legs to act as guides (Fig. 7-4G). The bottom runner is a similar piece (Fig. 7-4H), but accuracy of its bottom surface is not so important.

There may have to be a little adjusting of the drawers to get an easy action and a good fit. Back to front adjustment is by planing off the rear ends of the sides. If you are unlucky and a side is too short, a piece of veneer or even paper can be glued on. Adjustment in the width is by planing the sides.

If the piece is to be authentic Shaker style, the top edges should be left square or given a slight radius (Fig. 7-4J). If the table is to go against a wall the rear of the top wood should be level with the legs. Fixing can be by inserting screws from below, through the kickers at the ends and through the top drawer rail. There could be pocketed screws in the back rail, although another way is to have a strip inside the back rail and screw upwards through that (Fig. 7-4K).

To prevent a drawer being pulled out accidentally there can be small pieces of wood to act as stops under the rail above the drawer (Fig. 7-4L). If a stop is kept thin it will bear against the back and stop the drawer, but if the front of the drawer is lifted to tilt the drawer up when in this position it can still be removed.

If a more decorative finish is required, the legs could be turned and the rails given shaped lower edges (Fig. 7-4M). The top could have its edges molded or the outline could be curved instead of straight.

There should be one or two knobs or handles on each drawer. Locate them slightly above half the depth of the front. For a Shaker design they should be plain turned wood, but ornamental metal (not plastic) handles can be used with a more decorative table design.

## DROP LEAF TABLE

Some tables that can be adjusted in size are intended for sitting around whether they are fully extended or in their reduced size, but another type is normally in its larger form for use, but the top can be reduced in size so the table may occupy less space when out of use. There are several ways of arranging this, but usually part of the top is arranged to fold downwards. When it is hanging down there is no space for a sitter's knees, so it is unsuitable for eating off when folded, although it may still serve for storage as a side table. The example shown (Fig. 7-5A) is based on an Appalachian original, but the type was common to many early households.

The table framework is made up in the same way as the plain table. Legs could be square and tapered, but lathes came early and many legs were turned. The drawing is of an original type (Fig. 7-5B). A drawer at one end is useful and easily incorporated. The main construction is basically similar to that of the table just described.

There are upper and lower drawer rails at one end. These are extended for at least the distance the drawer is to go by runners and kickers, with guides level with the inner surfaces of the legs (Fig. 7-5C). The drawer is stopped at the right position by small blocks of wood on the runners (Fig. 7-5D), but fitting these should be delayed until the drawer is made and put in position, then the blocks can be located to come against the drawer. It helps in stiffening the table to make the lower drawer rail wide, with twin tenons (Fig. 7-5E).

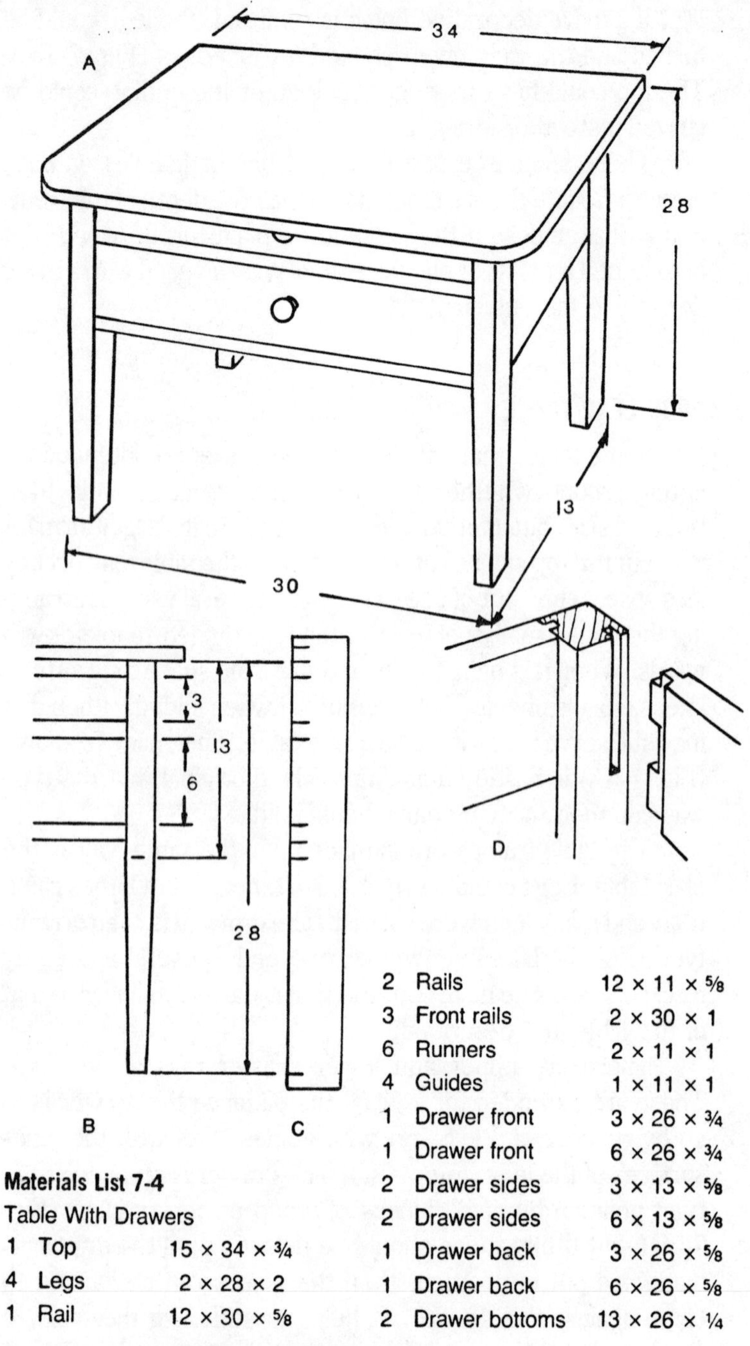


**Materials List 7-4**

Table With Drawers

| | | |
|---|---|---|
| 1 | Top | 15 × 34 × ¾ |
| 4 | Legs | 2 × 28 × 2 |
| 1 | Rail | 12 × 30 × ⅝ |
| 2 | Rails | 12 × 11 × ⅝ |
| 3 | Front rails | 2 × 30 × 1 |
| 6 | Runners | 2 × 11 × 1 |
| 4 | Guides | 1 × 11 × 1 |
| 1 | Drawer front | 3 × 26 × ¾ |
| 1 | Drawer front | 6 × 26 × ¾ |
| 2 | Drawer sides | 3 × 13 × ⅝ |
| 2 | Drawer sides | 6 × 13 × ⅝ |
| 1 | Drawer back | 3 × 26 × ⅝ |
| 1 | Drawer back | 6 × 26 × ⅝ |
| 2 | Drawer bottoms | 13 × 26 × ¼ |

Fig. 7-4. Table with drawers. (Continued on next page.)

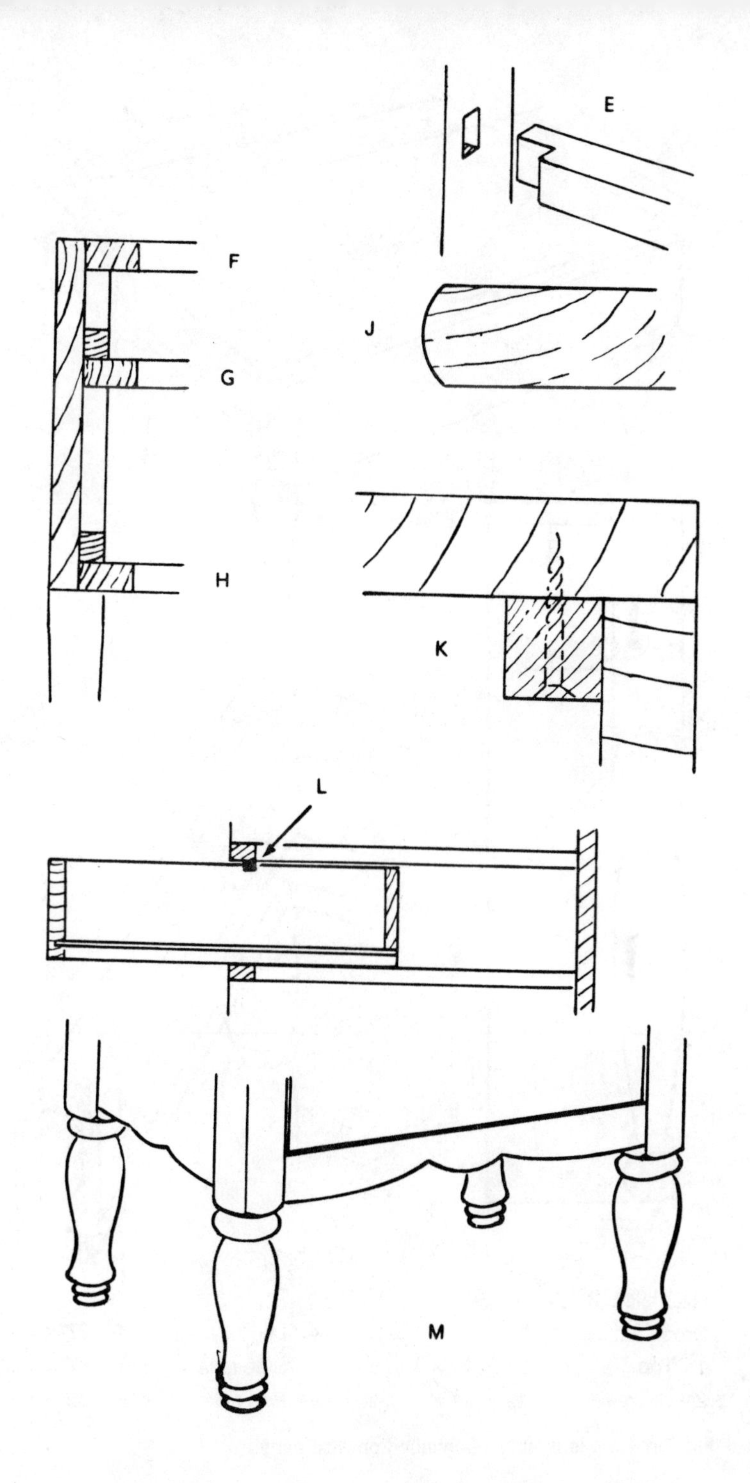
E
F
J
G
H
K
L
M

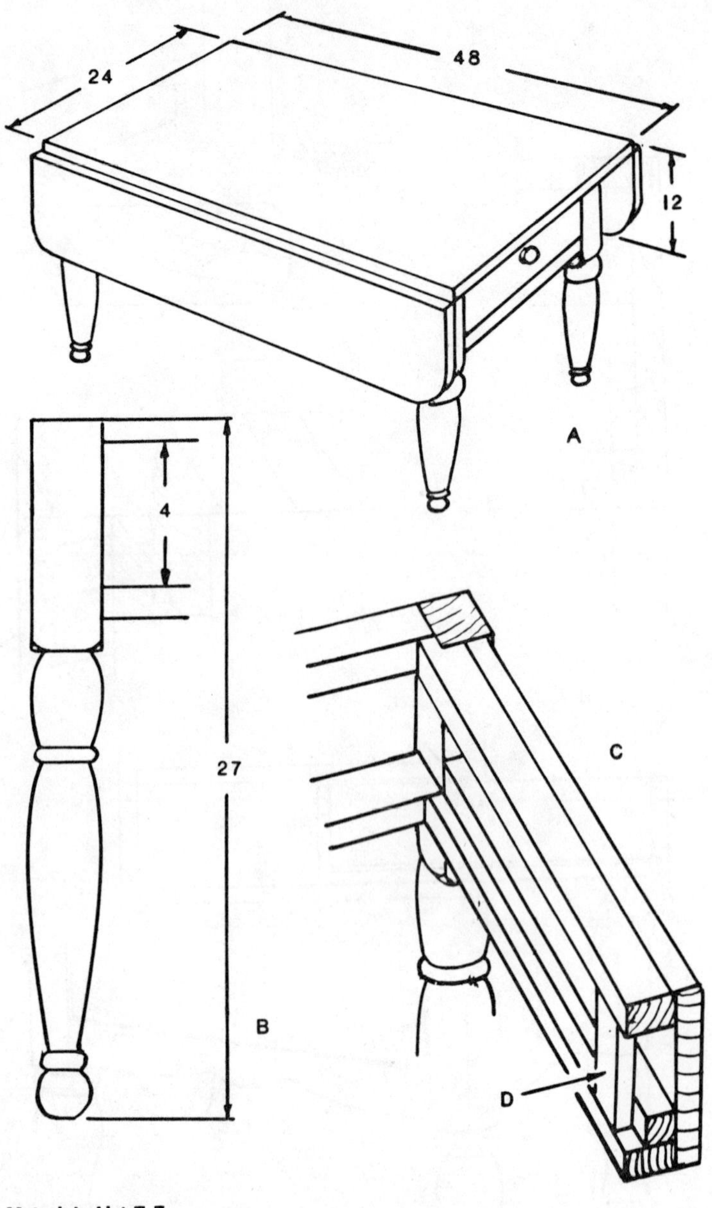


**Materials List 7-5**

Drop Leaf Table

| | | | | | |
|---|---|---|---|---|---|
| 1 | Top | 24 × 48 × 1 | 4 | Legs | 3 × 27 × 3 |
| 2 | Leaves | 12 × 24 × 1 | 2 | Side rails | 6½ × 47 × 1 |
| | | | 1 | End rail | 6½ × 23 × 1 |

Fig. 7-5. Drop leaf table. (Continued on next page.)

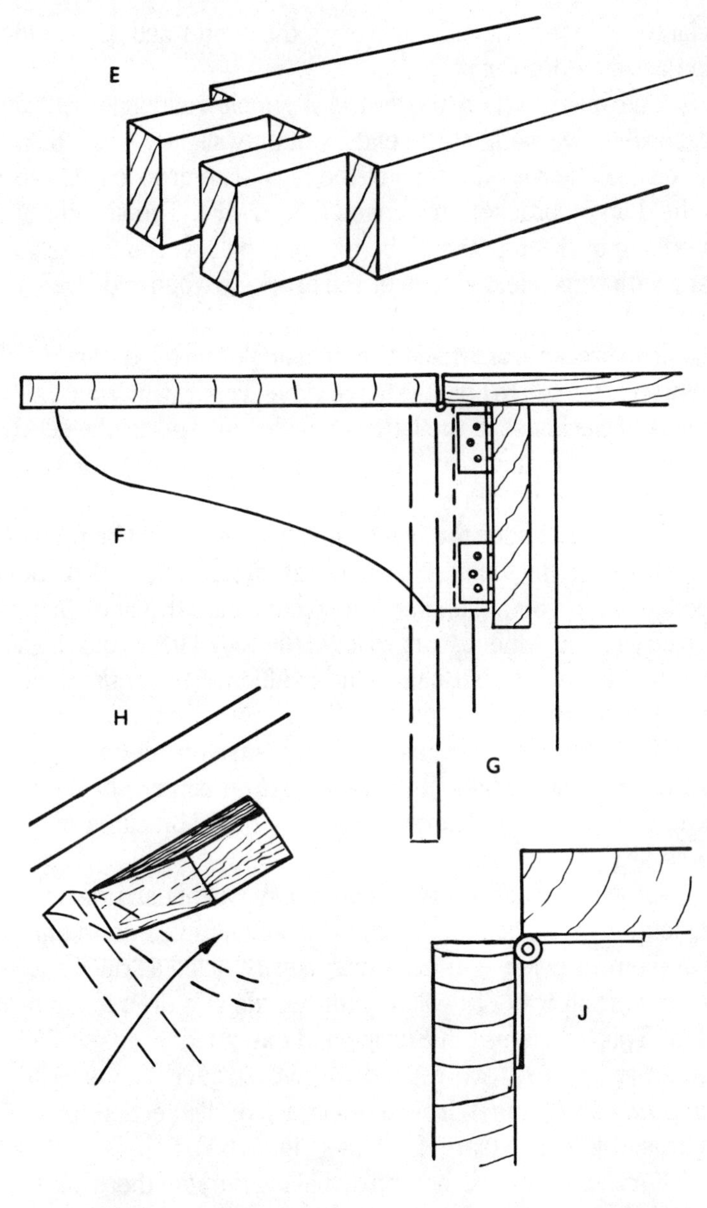


| | | | | | |
|---|---|---|---|---|---|
| 2 | Drawer rails | 2½ × 23 × 1¼ | 1 | Drawer front | 4 × 18 × 1 |
| 4 | Brackets | 6 × 12 × 1 | 2 | Drawer sides | 4 × 24 × ⅝ |
| 4 | Drawer runners | 2 × 24 × 1¼ | 1 | Drawer back | 4 × 18 × ⅝ |
| 2 | Drawer guides | 1 × 24 × 1 | 1 | Drawer bottom | 18 × 24 × ¼ |

A large table may have a rail across the center and this could also act as a drawer stop.

The main part of the top is a simple rectangle with a reasonable overhang at the ends, but only slightly wider than the distance across the tops of the legs. The drop leaves can be held up by brackets on hinges (Fig. 7-5F). The amount of overhang of the top should be enough to allow the leaves to hang with some clearance over the brackets when folded (Fig. 7-5G).

The brackets are made to a right angle and might theoretically be expected to hold the leaves level when swung out, but wear and slackness in the hinge knuckles, as well as the need for clearance to allow of moving the brackets, cause the leaves to sag slightly, unless something is done about it. Where a bracket comes under the leaf a small wedge should be fitted, longer and going deeper than is, at first, expected to be needed (Fig. 7-5H). The bracket swings on to this and can be moved as far as is necessary to level the top. There could be a stop on the wedge, but usually it is sufficient to continue the deep part of the wedge parallel for a short distance.

In the simplest arrangement the leaves hang on hinges and have square edges (Fig. 7-5J). Three hinges should be located so they do not come in the way of the brackets when these are swung out.

Although square-edged boards may have been practical, the joint was not beautiful, and many cabinetmakers brought with them knowledge of what was usually called a "rule joint" as the normal way of dealing with boards in a drop leaf tabletop. This was in use in Europe and extended hinges, called "back-flap hinges," were used to give stronger joints. The name *rule joint* comes from a similarity of the section to the joint used in some two-fold rules (Fig. 7-6A).

For the traditional method of making the joint there had to be hollow and round planes, but a modern way of forming the shapes could be with a spindle molder or suitable router cutters. When the table top is up the edges should meet closely, and the leaf should follow the curve as it swings down so there is little gap showing and the meeting surfaces have a molded look (Fig. 7-6B). A back-flap hinge is designed to be used with its knuckle upwards and the two parts can swing back to a right angle, which is further than normal hinges will go. The knuckle is notched into the wood so it comes at the center of the curve molded on the edge (Fig. 7-6C). If an ordinary hinge is used, it will have to be arranged with the knuckle downwards and the action will not be quite as accurate when the parts move in relation to each other (Fig. 7-6D).

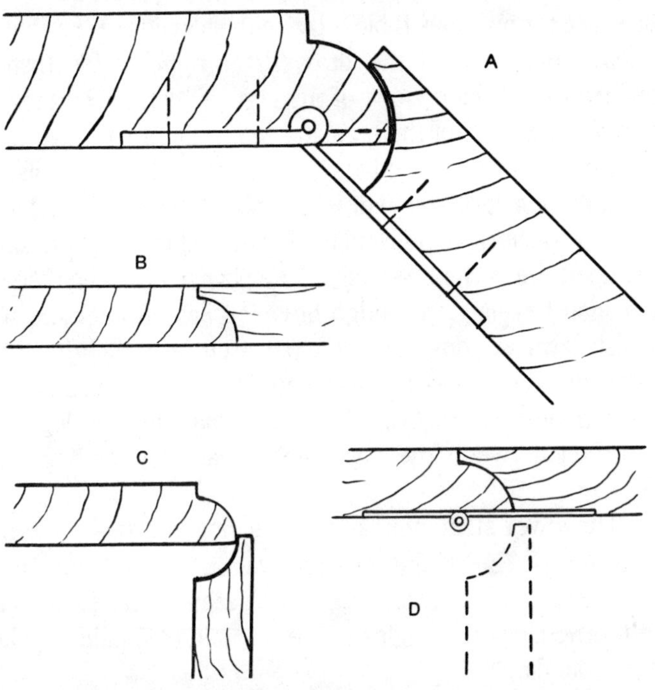


Fig. 7-6. A rule joint for a drop flap, showing the relative positions of the parts.

## DEEP LEAF TABLE

If a drop leaf table is to take up the minimum space when folded, the center part has to be narrower and the flaps wider. If the leaves are very wide and the center very narrow there is a loss of stability on four legs only, so the flap supports incorporate extra legs, as in the next example. But many early tables have the width of the top divided approximately into three, and the four legs are heavy, with stout lower rails—all of which help to keep the table stable. The legs were also slightly splayed, but this could not be very much if they were not to interfere with the hang of the leaves (Fig. 7-7A). This table has the top overhanging enough at the ends to accommodate a sitter's knees and the raised flaps are wide enough to give knee clearance at the sides, so the top rails are fairly deep for rigidity. One or two drawers can be fitted at the ends. They can be deep, yet still allow for the strength of deep lower drawer rails. Drawer construction and fitting is similar to that described for previous tables, but with splayed legs it is better to leave the ends of the drawers at right angles than to conform to the slight slope of the legs. There can be tapered fillers on the sides of the legs and the runners will have to be arranged with beveled edges to fit against the long rails.

If the legs are splayed, it is advisable to make a full-size end view to check angles and the location of rails and the joints they need. Legs can be square. The plainness can be relieved by wagon beveling (the edge beveling named after the way English farm wagons had their parts cut away). Where the rails come the edges are left square, but beveling is done between these places (Fig. 7-7B). Alternatively, the legs may be turned between the parts left square for jointing (Fig. 7-7C).

The lower stretcher rails have simple mortise and tenon joints (Fig. 7-7D). If the legs are wagon beveled, the upper angles of the stretchers could be treated in the same way. With turned legs the angles of the stretchers should be taken off by rounding.

Support for the leaves can be arranged in one of two ways. The side rails may be notched to take loose cross rails, arranged about one-quarter of the length from each end. These rails are kept separate and pushed in place when needed (Fig. 7-7E). They were sometimes hung by straps under the table, hidden by the lowered flaps.

Another way is to use brackets, which could be on hinges as in the previous table, but a variation is to use central brackets pivoting on crossbars. The crossbars are notched into the top and bottom edges of the front and rear top rails

(Fig. 7-7F). They should be made of close-grained hardwood as they have to take a load on the short grain at their ends. The table top and the crossbars must extend far enough to allow the brackets to pivot on dowel pins (Fig. 7-7G). The back of a bracket is rounded and the top is notched to clear the end of the crossbar. The shaped part has its edges rounded and a similar wedge arrangement should be put under each leaf to allow for leveling in the raised position.

The meeting edges between the leaves and the center of the top may be left square or worked as a rule joint, as in the previous example. The outer corners of the leaves should be rounded—slightly, if the general effect is to be square, or with large sweeps if a rounded effect is preferred. The outer edge can be left square, given a slightly curved section, or molded, but it is important that whatever pattern is used it follows around the three parts smoothly, so finishing work on the edge of the top is best done after assembly and with the leaves raised.

Although it may seem obvious for the leaves to swing down, where gravity helps to keep them in the folded position, there have been tables of this type made where one flap swings upwards. Such a table can be moved against a wall, with the upturned flap up the wall and the other down. The table can then be used as a sideboard or serving table, or regarded as a storage place for many kitchen or dining room articles, with the upturned flap acting as a background, to show off the display and prevent items falling off the back of the table.

## GATE LEG TABLE

For a table to reduce to the most compact width when not needed, the center part has to be narrower than the flaps. If it stands on four legs, they have to be close together in the width. Stability when the flaps are up is unsatisfactory unless additional support from the floor is provided. Furniture designers in many places seem to have gotten over this problem in similar ways without reference to each other, using swinging assemblies to take an extra leg out to each side to come under

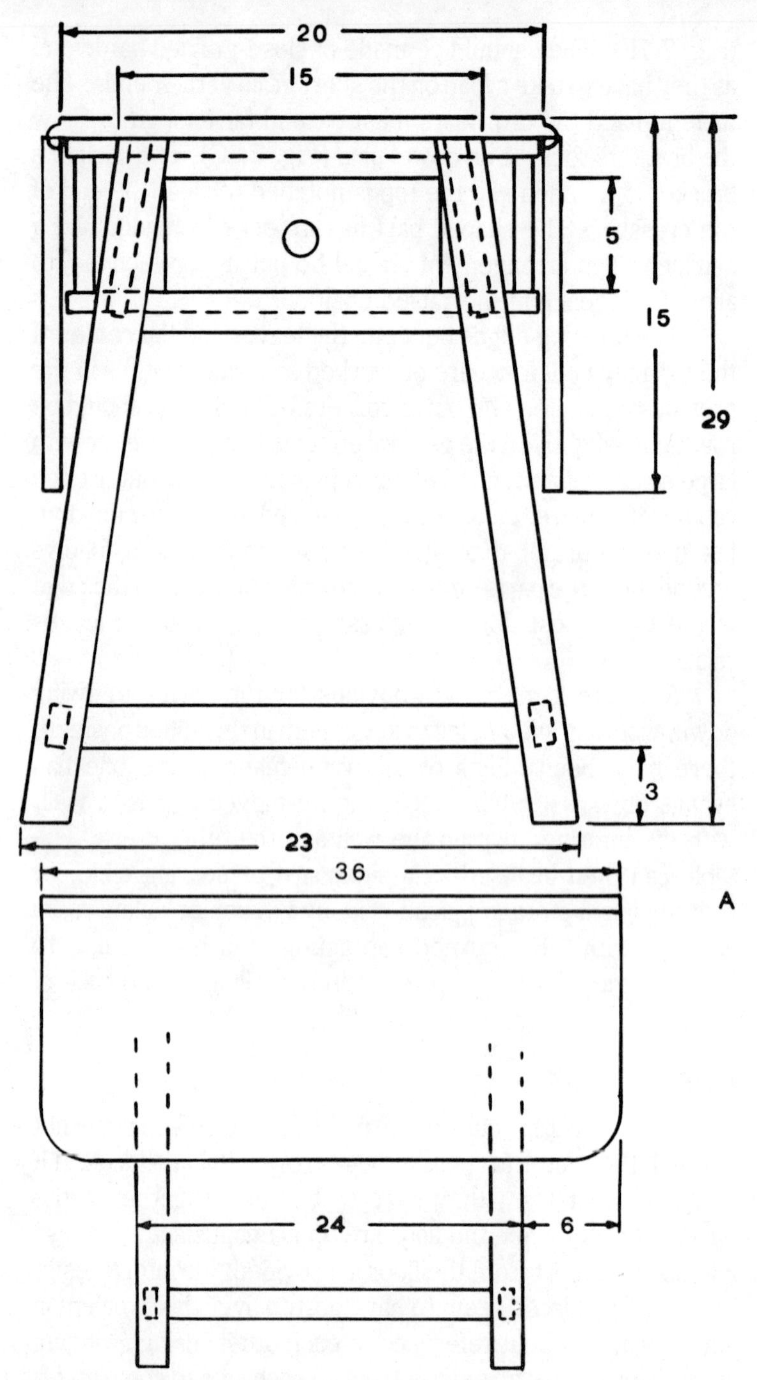

Fig. 7-7. Deep leaf table. (Continued on next page.)

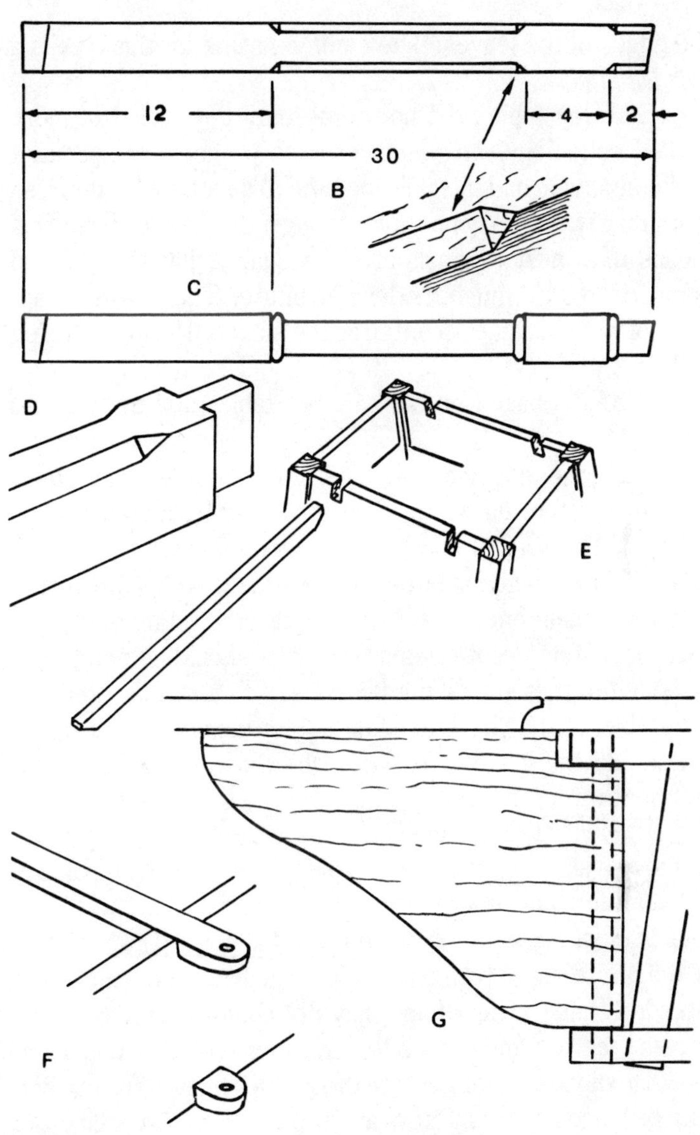


**Materials List 7-7**

Deep Leaf Table

| | | |
|---|---|---|
| 1 | Top | 20 × 36 × 1 |
| 2 | Leaves | 15 × 36 × 1 |
| 4 | Legs | 2 × 30 × 2 |
| 2 | Side rails | 8 × 23 × 1 |
| 1 | End rail | 8 × 15 × 1 |
| 2 | Drawer rails | 1½ × 15 × 1½ |
| 2 | Brackets | 7 × 12 × 1 |
| 2 | Bracket rails | 2 × 20 × 1 |
| 4 | Bottom rails | 2 × 23 × 1 |

Drawer parts, as required

the edges of the leaves. The common name for this type is a *gate leg table*.

Gate leg tables did not come until the period of more settled conditions, so they were the products of specialist craftsmen, who had the skill and time to devote to better class work than was usually possible amongst the first settlers. This means that most originals are of a quality that would stand comparison with much modern furniture. The first development of what became accepted as the standard form of gate leg table in America was in New England, and the specimen drawn (Fig. 7-8A) is based on old gate leg tables still to be found there.

The general layout uses a central section which is about one-third of the full width. The top could be rectangular or elliptical. The comparatively narrow central assembly has two gatelike parts swinging out to support the leaves, with legs to match the main ones and a similar pillaster acting as a pivot each side. If different sizes are used, it should be noted that the side top rails should not be as deep as might be used in a plain table, as they have to be drilled for the dowel pin hinges. These and the lower rails should be thick enough to retain sufficient strength after notching for the swing legs.

The legs are square and should be the same size at upper and lower joint positions. To avoid a heavy look the parts in between and the feet are turned on most originals. There are a total of eight pieces to be turned with matching patterns. The best approach is to turn one leg after making a drawing of the intended shape. The outline may not conform exactly to the drawing, as you find curves that are more pleasing under the tool than those on paper. From the first leg make a rod marked with distances and diameters at various points. An outline can be drawn back from the edge (Fig. 7-8B). Some turners cut the edge to make a template to put against the wood, but having the diameters to set calipers to and a drawing to work parallel to is probably a better guide to uniformity.

The feet may be finished completely, but leave some excess length at the top until after joints are cut. Notice tha the rails for the gate legs are closer together than the main rails, and the square parts are long enough to allow for this, with all legs having squares of the same length (Fig. 7-8C).

To suit the action of the gate legs, the side rails come flush with the outsides of the legs, so are conveniently made with "barefaced" tenons (Fig. 7-8D). The end rails need not be flush with the leg surfaces, but they will match the others if made this way. Extra rigidity may be obtained by having the top end rails deeper than the side ones. As the ends show whether the table is open or folded, these rails can be decorated with carving or by shaping the lower edges (Fig. 7-8E).

The upper and lower long rails should be marked out together so the pivot holes and the half lap notches match. As the distance between the pivots and half lap cuts must match the gate legs, cutting the joints should be delayed until each gate leg can be assembled and tried in place.

Each gate leg has lighter rails tenoned into the pillaster and leg (Fig. 7-8F). As with the rest of the table framing, be careful to assemble the parts flat and at right angles, checking with a try square and measuring diagonals. Although it is possible to use doweled joints instead of mortise and tenons throughout the table, traditional methods are stronger and more authentic. Mortises can have small dowels across for additional strength, but a glued joint that fits closely should have ample strength without dowels. If clamps have to be removed for use elsewhere before glue has set, there can be nails driven across the mortises from the least obvious side, then punched below the surface and covered with stopping.

Holes for the hinge dowel pins need to be truly at right angles to the rails. Drilling by machine should ensure this, but if drilling has to be by hand the hole positions should be marked around the wood and the holes drilled halfway from each side, so slight inaccuracies can be expected to cancel out in the center of the wood. A gate leg should be put in position and marked through the rail holes. The pillaster lengths should make a close fit between the upper and lower main rails. Check in the assembly that the gate leg feet are level with the feet of the main legs. Since it is the top of the gate leg that

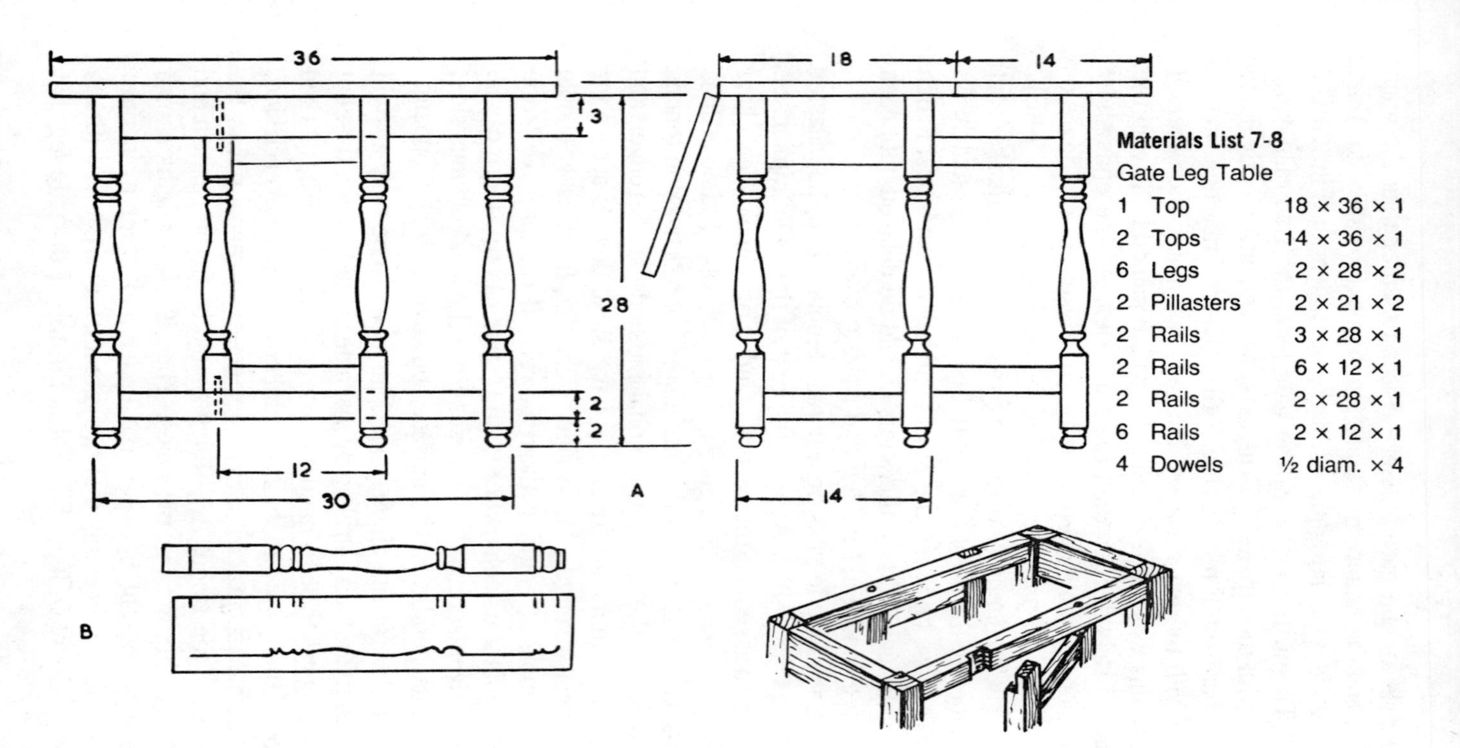


**Materials List 7-8**

Gate Leg Table

| | | |
|---|---|---|
| 1 | Top | 18 × 36 × 1 |
| 2 | Tops | 14 × 36 × 1 |
| 6 | Legs | 2 × 28 × 2 |
| 2 | Pillasters | 2 × 21 × 2 |
| 2 | Rails | 3 × 28 × 1 |
| 2 | Rails | 6 × 12 × 1 |
| 2 | Rails | 2 × 28 × 1 |
| 6 | Rails | 2 × 12 × 1 |
| 4 | Dowels | ½ diam. × 4 |

Fig. 7-8. Gate leg table. (Continued on next page).

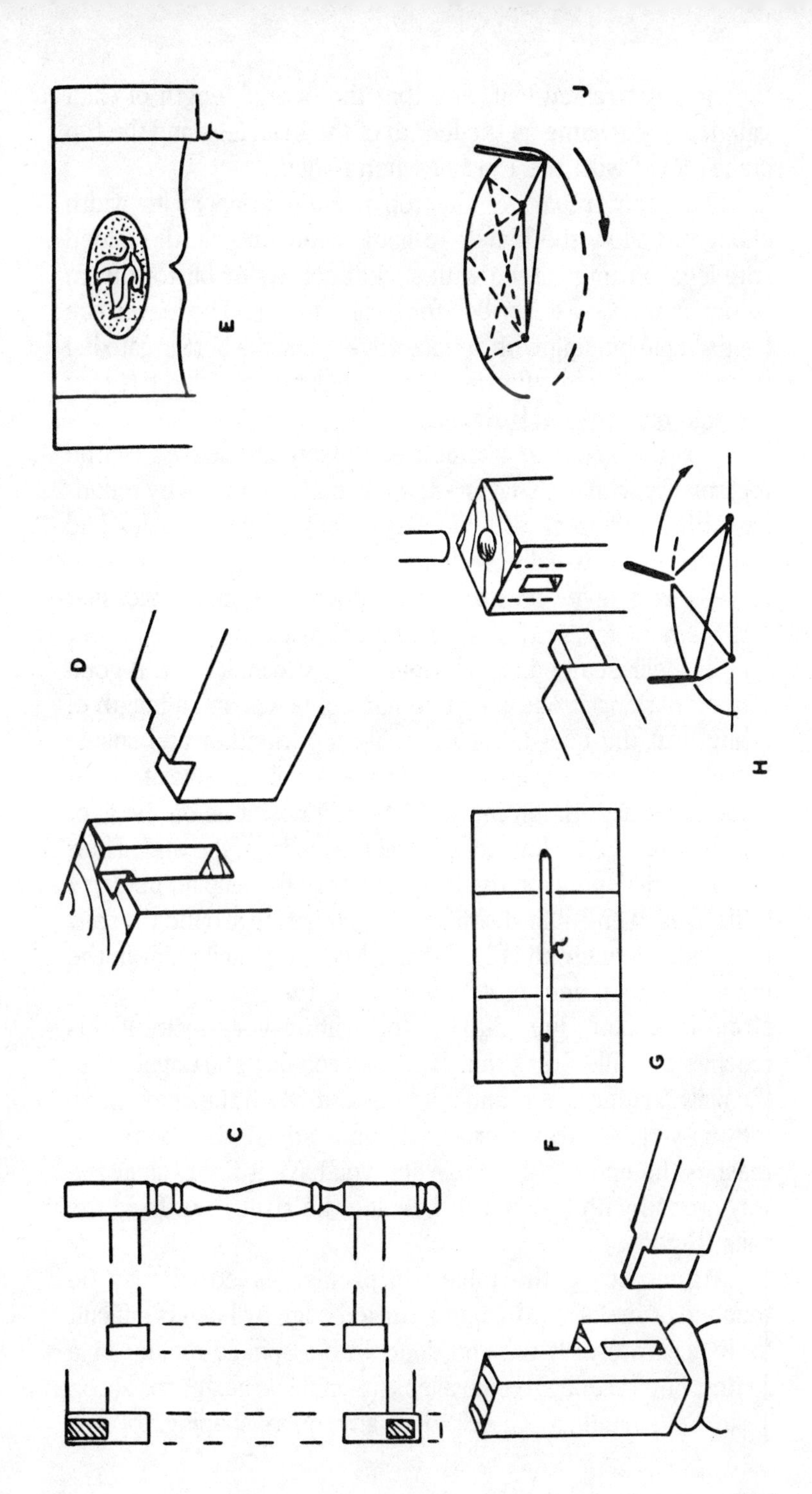
C
D
E
F
G
H
J

supports the raised leaf, see that the overall length of each gate leg is the same as the length of the main legs and the top comes level with the top rail when folded.

The center part of the top must overlap in its width enough to allow the leaves to hang freely outside the folded gate legs. Fitting can be with socket screws or buttons from below, in the way described for earlier tables. The leaves can have simple hinging with square edges, but the better gate leg tables had rule joints for the better appearance with the rest of the high-quality construction.

For the greatest useful area on top, the leaves can be rectangular with the sharpness taken off the corners by rounding with a radius of a few inches. Many of these tables had elliptical tops, usually with the greater length across the leaves. This gives an attractive appearance and a pleasant arrangement for setting several meal places.

The ellipse needs to be regular if it is to look right. A good way of marking it out uses two nails, a pencil and a length of string. Put the boards for the table top together and upside down. Draw a centerline across them. A suitable size of ellipse is found by experimenting with the nail positions on the line. Put the nails on the line at equal distances from the end. Their position will depend on the proportions of the ellipse, but try 1 ft. from each end at first. Make a loop of string around the nails to extend to one end (Fig. 7-8G). Put the pencil point in the end of the loop and work it around to the side, keeping the string loop taut (Fig. 7-8H). You will be very lucky if this reaches the side first time. If it goes too far, start again with the nails farther apart, and if it does not reach the side, move the nails closer together. Each time adjust the loop so it reaches the end of the line. When you have it right, go all the way around with the pencil, keeping the string taut from the nails (Fig. 7-8J).

After cutting the table top profile, its edges may be rounded or molded. Molding a curved edge by hand is difficult to do accurately. It may be done with a spindle molder or a router, but if these are unavailable it would be better to rely on a simple rounding. Check that any edge shaping follows through smoothly at the top joints. Finishing at these positions might be better left until after the final assembly. A gate leg support has a longer reach than a swinging bracket, so the possibility of a leaf sagging is less, but it may be advisable to include a slim wedge under a leaf to allow for wear. There may also be a small wood block to act as a stop when the extended leg comes under the center of the leaf.

## SWIVEL-TOP TABLE

One way of arranging a tabletop with drop leaves, without brackets, gate legs, or other supports for the leaves, is to have the top swiveling on the framework, which is narrow and long. The leaves hang down when the top assembly is crosswise, but if the leaves are lifted level and the top turned through a right angle, they will be held up by resting on the ends of the framework. The top parts are best joined with backflap hinges, but if ordinary hinges are used, the top can be raised on packings so the hinges clear the framework as it is turned. Metal pivots were made and modern versions can be bought, but a bolt type and a wooden pivot are described here.

Although this type of table could stand on upright legs, a more stable form has the legs splayed in both directions. The example shown is a small side table, but the method could be used for a table of any size. This example gets its stiffness from wide top rails only. With straight-grained wood for the legs and good mortise and tenon joints, preferably doweled through, the result is a graceful rigid table (Fig. 7-9A).

The compound angles due to splaying the legs both ways need not cause difficult work if tackled systematically. The angles in both directions need not be the same. There could be more splay in the width than the length, but setting out is simpler if the angle is the same both ways. Make a full-size drawing of a leg and one corner. It is helpful if the top line is at least as long as half the length of the side rail.

When a framework is splayed in two directions the view of a leg from above remains a right angle, but the actual section of a leg becomes a diamond shape. With a wide splay this becomes increasingly important if joints are to fit properly and the angles to which the wood for the legs has to be planed must be found geometrically. With a double splay of only a few degrees, as in this example, the difference between a theoretically correct section and a square sectoin is very slight. By using barefaced tenons in the rail joints the slight difference between the fit of front and back shoulders of each joint is avoided, so the legs can be made to square sections.

Each leg is square and parallel to a point below where the rails will come, then there is a slight taper on each side to the bottom (Fig. 7-9B). The legs look even more graceful if the outer corner is rounded, starting with only a slight curve at the top of the taper and continuing to a quarter circle at the foot (Fig. 7-9C). Allow a little excess length at top and bottom of each leg.

Set an adjustable bevel to the angle shown in (Fig. 7-9D). Lock it at that. It is the only angle other than a right angle you will have to test, but it should be the same throughout.

Mark the wood for the two side rails. Plane the top edges to the angle of your adjustable bevel. The bottom edges can remain at right angles. Put the two pieces together and mark across their edges the length between shoulders and a further 1 in. at each end for the tenons. Mark the shoulders on the outer surfaces with a knife and the ends of the tenons with a pencil, using the adjustable bevel (Fig. 7-9E). Cut the pieces to length, mark the widths of the tenons and cut away the waste. Shape the tenons (Fig. 7-9F).

Mark the mortises to match the tenons and cut them. Do the same with the short rails. Do not try any of the joints at this stage. The rails have to be fairly deep to provide stiffness. They can be left full width or their central areas can be reduced, either by cutting back with plain curves or with a decorative outline. It may be preferable to leave the end rails full depth and only reduce the side rails. In any case, leave a good width of full-depth ends so as not to weaken the joints with short grain.

The best way to tackle assembly is to first make up the two sides, ignoring the splay in the other direction, then add the short rails to join the sides. The joints have to be pulled tight and two packing blocks should be made for the bar clamp to squeeze on. While the clamp is still on, drill through for a dowel into each extending tenon (Fig. 7-9G). Check the two side assemblies on each other. Turn one over on the other. This will show if the splay is the same at each corner. Let the glue set before proceeding.

All four joints the other way should be made together since the meeting surfaces will not be quite at right angles due to the double splay. Make a dry trial assembly with the tenons only entered a short distance. This will show that they are not entering quite squarely and it may be necessary to pare the side of each tenon slightly with a chisel to get a neat fit. Having done that, apply glue and clamp the joints, preferably pulling each end tighter a little at a time to keep the shape uniform. Dowel through in the same way as at the sides, and the corners at the top are at right angles, by using a try square and by checking diagonals.

The beveled top edges of the rails will show how much to cut off the tops of the legs. Measure down each leg the same amount and make a mark on the outer corner for the foot. Use a long straight board as a guide to mark where the legs are to be cut (Fig. 7-9H). Round the edges of these cuts.

The top can be made up from three boards, preferably with rule joints and backflap hinges, but the meeting edges can be cut square and plain hinges used for a simpler construction. If sizes different from those shown are used, the center part should be long enough to have a slight overhang on the framework, but its width must be enough to allow the leaves to hang without touching the splayed legs. The proportions are best if the ends of the framework come more than halfway under the raised leaves when the top is turned to give the full area.

The top shown has square corners and plain edges, but it could be treated in any of the ways described for the tops of earlier tables. Many of these tables had round tops. Others were elliptical. Hanging curved leaves have a pleasing appearance. Edges could be rounded or molded. Much shaping goes better with turned legs, and a plainer treatment is all that is needed with the legs shown.

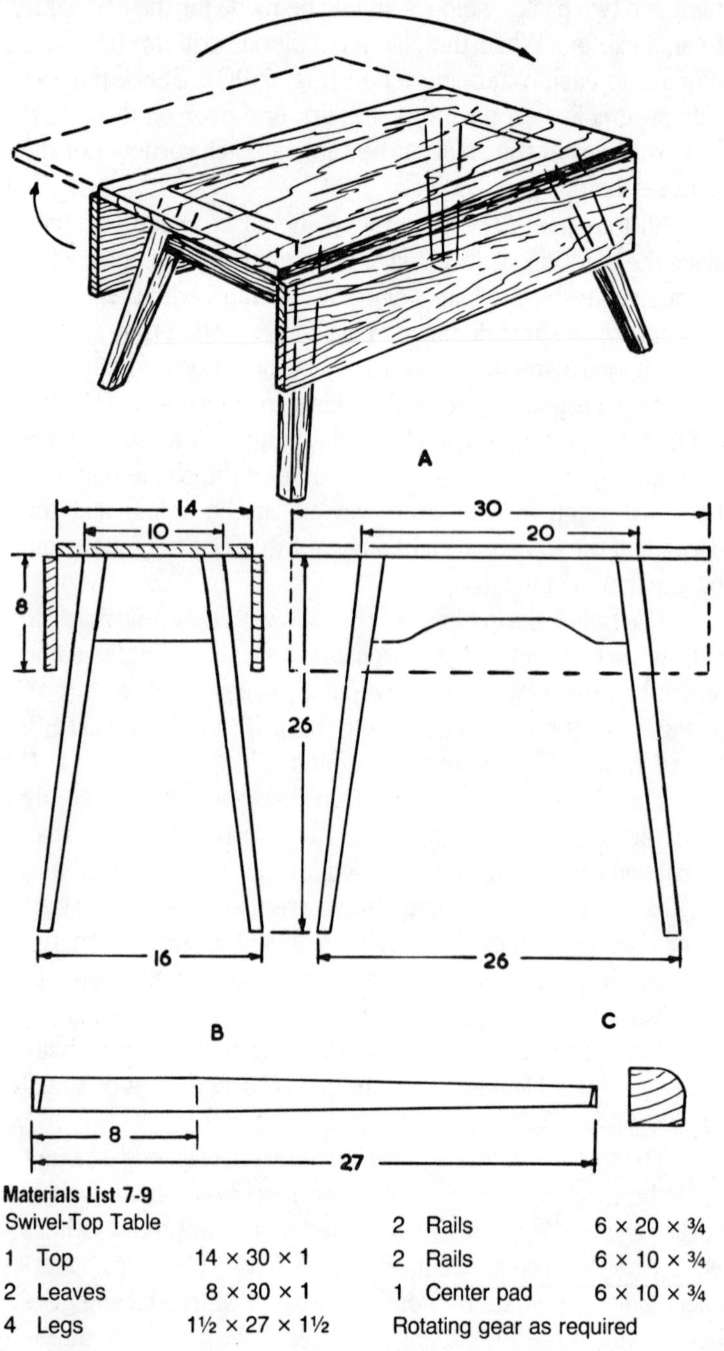


**Materials List 7-9**

Swivel-Top Table

| | | |
|---|---|---|
| 1 | Top | 14 × 30 × 1 |
| 2 | Leaves | 8 × 30 × 1 |
| 4 | Legs | 1½ × 27 × 1½ |
| 2 | Rails | 6 × 20 × ¾ |
| 2 | Rails | 6 × 10 × ¾ |
| 1 | Center pad | 6 × 10 × ¾ |

Rotating gear as required

Fig. 7-9. Swivel top table. (Continued on next page.)

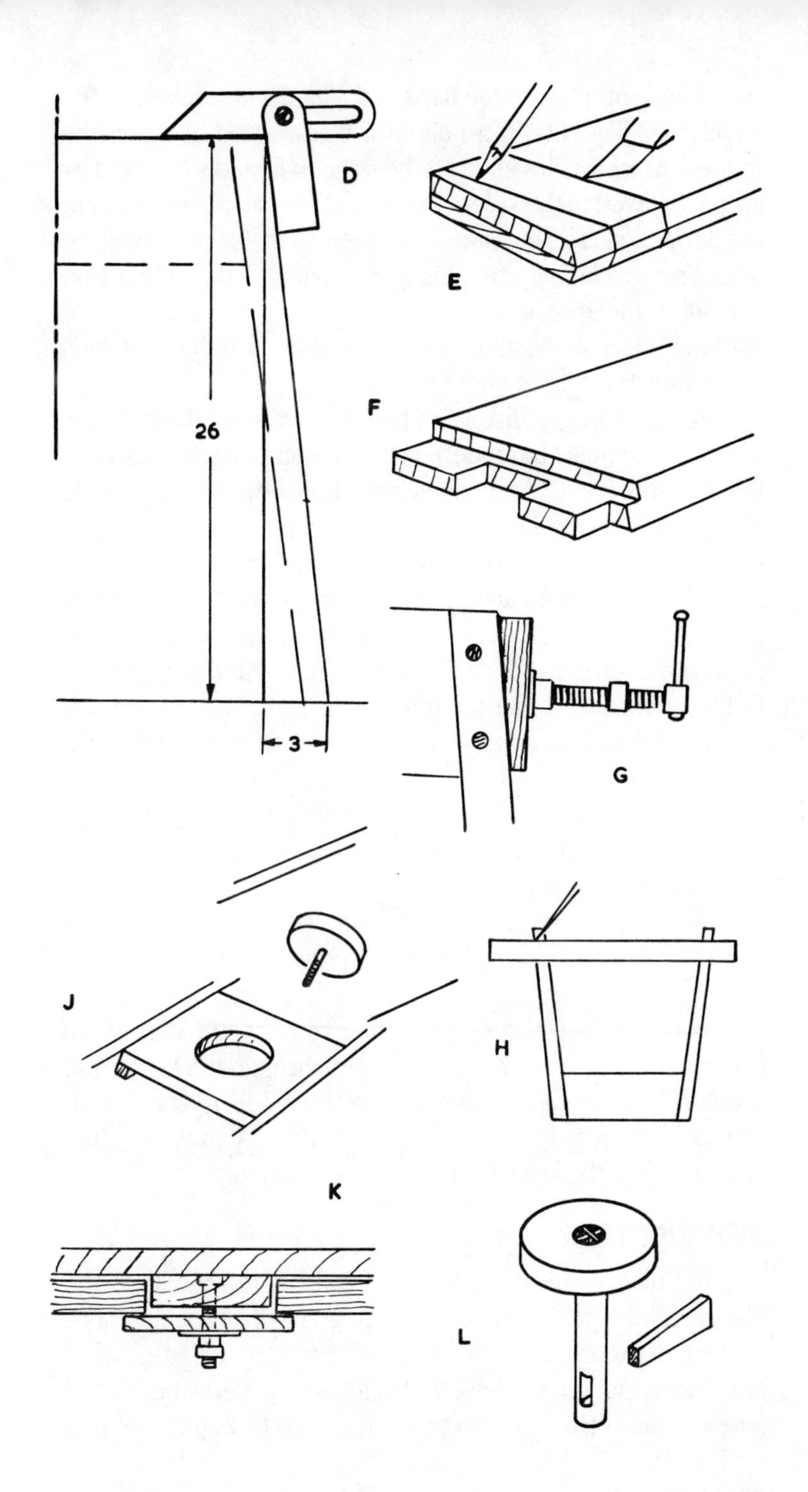
D
26
3
E
F
G
J
H
K
L

The center of the top has a disc glued and screwed to the underside. This fits in a hole in a board fitted between the framework sides. Its ends are beveled to fit and supported by strips screwed to the sides (Fig. 7-9J). The disc can be turned, but perfection in its outline is not essential to its functioning, so a handcut circle will do. This also applies to the hole it fits. Providing the disc will turn in the hole, a small amount of slackness is unimportant and preferable to parts that bind against each other at some points.

Another larger disc goes below the disc in the hole and overlaps the hole. In modern construction this would best be made of plywood. As it does not show, there seems little objection to using plywood, but if complete authenticity is required, it could be any thin wood unlikely to crack or split.

The best way to arrange the pivot is to use a bolt with its head let into the top disc. This goes through both discs to two nuts with a washer (Fig. 7-9K). The disc is glued and screwed to the underside of the top after the bolt has been inserted. The nuts are adjusted to allow the top to turn without undue slackness, then locked by tightening against each other. An original blacksmith-made bolt would have had a square head and square nuts, but modern machine-made screws and nuts may have to be used.

Some of these tables were made with wooden pivots. A stout round wood rod is glued and wedged in a hole in the top disc. This must be secure, and two glued wedges can be driven into the top across each other to resist the downward pull that will come later. The rod goes through the lower disc and is slotted to take a long wedge (Fig. 7-9L). The wedge should be a drive fit in the slot, so it will stay in place when driven to get the best tension on the assembly.

## LIGHT SIDE TABLE

In Colonial times, settled conditions, better facilities, and the skills of specialized craftsmen gradually brought more delicate treatment and tables that were more graceful, particularly those that did not have to stand up to general use. Wood for early furniture was converted from logs by equipment that would not cope with light sections and this wood was often used before it was properly seasoned, so heavy sections also helped to resist warping and splitting. Later on wood had time to season and more advanced milling equipment was available to bring it to lighter sections. Experience with local woods had allowed cabinetmakers to select attractive hardwoods for the better quality furniture, although much softwood was used, probably because of easier working with hand tools.

Lathes were usual in cabinet shops and much decoration was provided by turned parts. This table (Fig. 7-10A) is typical and might have been made of walnut or other available hardwood, or it could have been produced in pine. It uses five identical spindles. The shaped parts would have been worked with a bow saw and spokeshave, but anyone with a bandsaw will find getting accurate outlines much simpler than the earlier woodworker did with his hand tools only.

The four legs must be identical. The spindle forming the bottom rail does not have to be the same length and the turned pattern shown can be lengthened or shortened by modifying the flowing curves. A more complex turning with many shorter patterns would not be so easy to adapt to different lengths.

The spindles are turned with dowel ends (Fig. 7-10B). It is advisable to make a full-size drawing of at least half the profile (Fig. 7-10C). A template can be cut from thin plywood (Fig. 7-10D) and used to check the shapes as they are produced, but test frequently with calipers so diameters at various places are the same on all the parts. For the dowel ends, drill a hole of the size to be used, in a piece of scrap wood and use this to check the turned ends. Taper the extreme ends so they will enter easily. Be careful that overall lengths between the shoulders are exactly the same on the four legs, and the central bead really is central.

The top and bottom blocks have the same overall sizes, so they should be set out together, with the hole positions and the ends matching (Fig. 7-10E). The holes for the dowels are best drilled by machine, but they can be made by hand drilling, with an assistant sighting to check that the drill is upright. Take the holes slightly deeper than the lengths of the dowels.

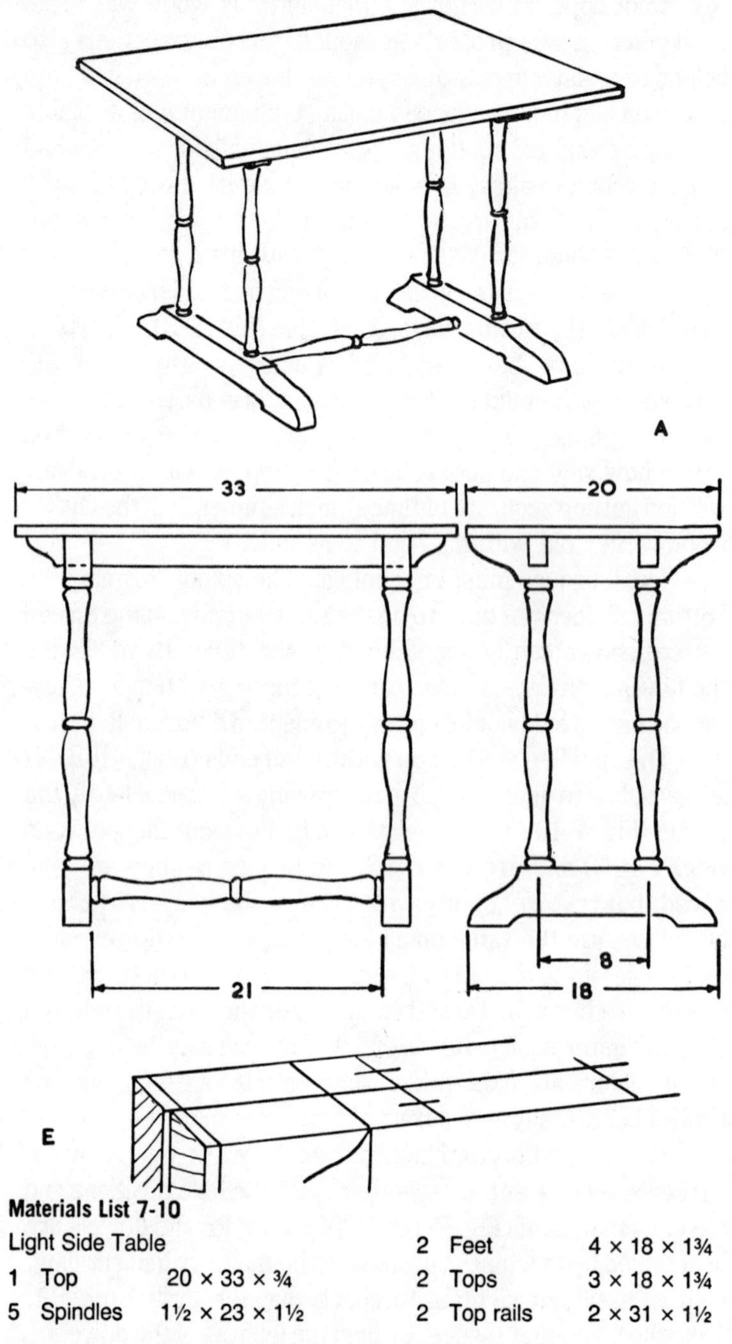


**Materials List 7-10**

Light Side Table

| | | | | | |
|---|---|---|---|---|---|
| 1 | Top | 20 × 33 × ¾ | 2 | Feet | 4 × 18 × 1¾ |
| 5 | Spindles | 1½ × 23 × 1½ | 2 | Tops | 3 × 18 × 1¾ |
| | | | 2 | Top rails | 2 × 31 × 1½ |

Fig. 7-10. Light side table. (Continued on next page.)

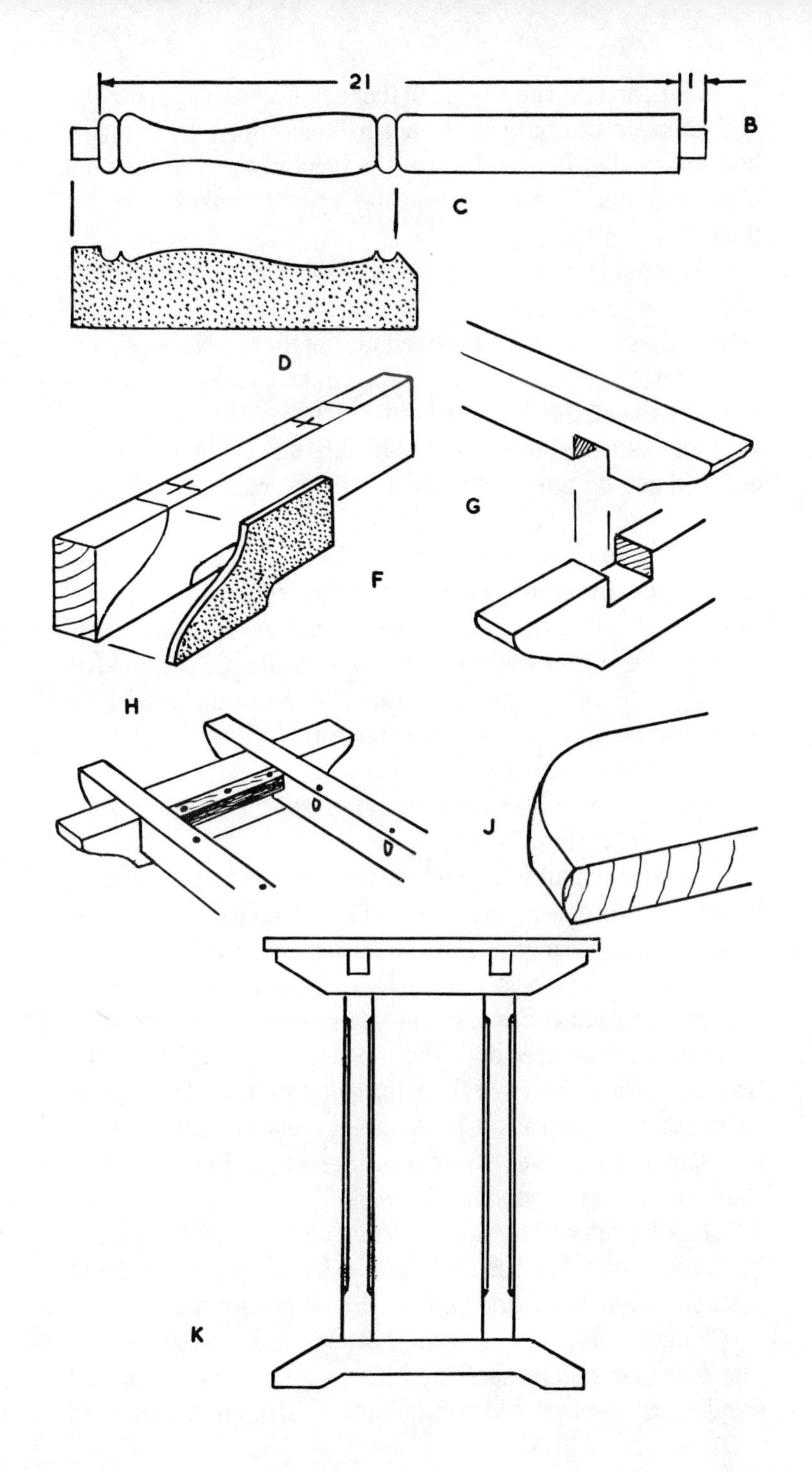
21
1
B
C
D
F
G
H
J
K

Mark and cut the shapes of the feet blocks (Fig. 7-10F). A half template can be used to ensure uniformity. Drill for the bottom spindle. Be careful that the point of the drill does not break through. The dowels on this spindle could be shorter than those on the legs.

The top blocks have to be notched to take the top rails, which fit with a version of a halving joint (Fig. 7-10G). The ends of these rails and the extremities of the top blocks should have similar curves, so their appearance under the top is uniform. Check the distance between the joints in the top rails with the distance between the shoulders in the bottom spindle. If these do not agree, the table will not stand upright.

In some original tables of this type the top was screwed down into the supports, but this necessitates counterboring and plugging the holes. Plugs evenly spaced may be regarded as a decorative feature, but if an unmarked top is preferred there can be pocket screwing from below, although it would be simpler at the ends to have strips inside the top blocks for screws to be driven upwards (Fig. 7-10H).

The top can be made from two or more boards glued together. Corners should be rounded and the edges given a curved section (Fig. 7-10J).

All work should be done on the parts before assembly, including the preparation for pocket screws. Glue the spindles to top and bottom blocks to make up one end. See that it is flat and measure diagonals to check squareness. Make up the opposite end and check it by putting it in the correct relative position over the first end. Put a board and weight over the two assemblies and leave them for glue to set. Fit the bottom spindle and the top rails. Check for squareness, both from the side and from above, by measuring diagonals, as well as standing back and viewing the work.

It will probably be best to leave all this until the glue is hard, then invert the assembly on the table top so the correct position can be seen and screws driven downwards.

Similar tables were made without the use of a lathe. There can be square-sectioned pieces instead of the turned spindles for the legs and central bottom stretcher. Plainness can be relieved by chamfering the edges, either the full length or by using wagon beveling stopped short of the joints (Fig. 7-10K). This type of construction looks better with a more angular treatment of the blocks.

## TRESTLE COFFEE TABLE

The basic type of trestle table goes back a long way before the settlement of America. There are tables of the type in many ancient castles and houses in Europe. Most are quite large and would be unsuitable for modern homes. Even one of dining table size, but otherwise in the usual proportions, might tend to look rather heavy in a small room. Trestle tables of this type were made by early American craftsmen, with larger versions in meeting houses and similar places and others of more modest overall sizes, but still stoutly built, in private homes. Although a full-size trestle table of this type could be built today and might have uses in some circumstances, the example shown, to illustrate the basic method of construction, may be regarded as a model which is of a suitable size to serve as a coffee table (Fig. 7-11A). The proportions can be adapted to suit available wood or the intended purpose. If modifications are made, the feet should be arranged to spread almost as wide as the top, and the central post at each end should be wide enough to have its end joints strong enough to take the considerable leverage that may come on them if the edge of the table top is pressed hard.

Work from a full-size half drawing of an end (Fig. 7-11B). This gives the location of the parts in relation to each other and should be drawn using the actual pieces of wood for sizes. Prepare the wood for the two trestle assemblies first. It is easiest to cut the joints before doing any shaping of these parts.

Mark the lengths and mortise positions on the two feet pieces. The profile and cutaway between the feet can be marked for cutting later (Fig. 7-11C). The crossbars under the top need not be quite as long as the bottom pieces, but similar mortise positions should be marked and the profile can be drawn. In both cases it is advisable to use a card or plywood template to mark the curves. Even if shapes will be cut with a band saw, it is advisable to mark the outlines on both sides to serve as guides when cleaning off the curves with spokeshave, Surform tool, or sandpaper.

Mark the two posts together. Distances between shoulders are the important sizes and these should be cut with a knife all round the wood. Mark where the stretcher will come (Fig. 7-11D).

Strength comes from having the tenons as thick as reasonably possible. As the cross members are wider than the thickness of the post, the rule about having a tenon one-third the thickness of the wood does not apply. Instead, the tenons are cut with narrow shoulders. They should be as long as can be conveniently cut. They need not go right through the cross members, although that would allow wedging for maximum strength. Otherwise they can go about three-quarters of the way through and foxtail wedging be used for security. Do not cut back the tenons from the post edges—the wider the spread of the tenons, the greater will be the resistance to bending loads on the table edge (Fig. 7-11E).

When the tenons and mortises have been cut, the parts can be shaped. Some tables have very ornate outlines cut in the posts, but it is inadvisable to cut away the edges very much. The decoration shown is a form of wagon beveling worked with a chisel (Fig. 7-11F). A similar pattern could be worked on the feet, but with a curved profile it is better to merely sand the sharpness off the edges.

There need be no lengthwise top rails, although some tables had them let into the top crossbars of the trestles. Instead, lengthwise rigidity is partly due to the stiffness of the top and mainly due to the central stretcher. This is of fairly stout section, so its depth resists lengthwise loads, and it was traditionally fixed with what was called a wedged tusk tenon. A wedged tenon probably originated with the need for takedown furniture when families moved on. In medieval England it was usual for the nobility on tour to take much of their furniture with them. In pioneer America it was convenient to dismantle furniture when moving westwards. In this table the wedged tenon does not serve that purpose as the table top does not take off (unless it is merely screwed on), but wedging gets maximum tightness and rigidity in the joint.

A wedged tusk tenon (Fig. 7-11G) is made with the stretcher on edge. Besides the tenon proper, which goes right through, there is a step cut in the shoulder below the tenon and a wedge from the shoulder below the tenon and a wedge from the shoulder line to the same point above the tenon. This has to be matched in the mortise. Such a construction is not really essential, although if the reproduction is to closely match the customary original joints, it should be made. The alternative is to make the joint with the shoulders of the tenoned piece cut straight to butt against the post.

The tenon goes through far enough for a slot to take a wedge, then enough wood outside that for the end grain to resist the pressure due to driving the wedge. So the wedge will pull the stretcher tight when it is driven, its slot is cut so the inner edge is below the surface of the post (Fig. 7-11H). In most tables and other furniture using wedged tenons, the wedge was usually plain, although there are examples with shaped top profiles and some with carved ends. The stretcher may have wagon beveling or its edge can be rounded. A full-size table that had been much used would have its stretcher edges rounded from contact with many boots.

Put together the end assemblies in stages. Make sure each post stands upright in the foot section. A line drawn at right angles to the edge of a piece of plywood can be used as a guide. Diagonals can be measured from the extremities of the cross piece to the center or matching points on the post. Add the top crossbar and clamp the parts tight. If the tenons go right through, drive wedges into saw cuts in their ends. Small foxtail wedges could be used inside for stub tenons. The alternative to wedging is doweling through, but wedges are preferable.

The wedged tusk tenons were traditionally left without glue. It was then possible to draw them tighter if age or shrinkage caused loosening. This is unlikely in the coffee table version, so the joint and wedge could be glued.

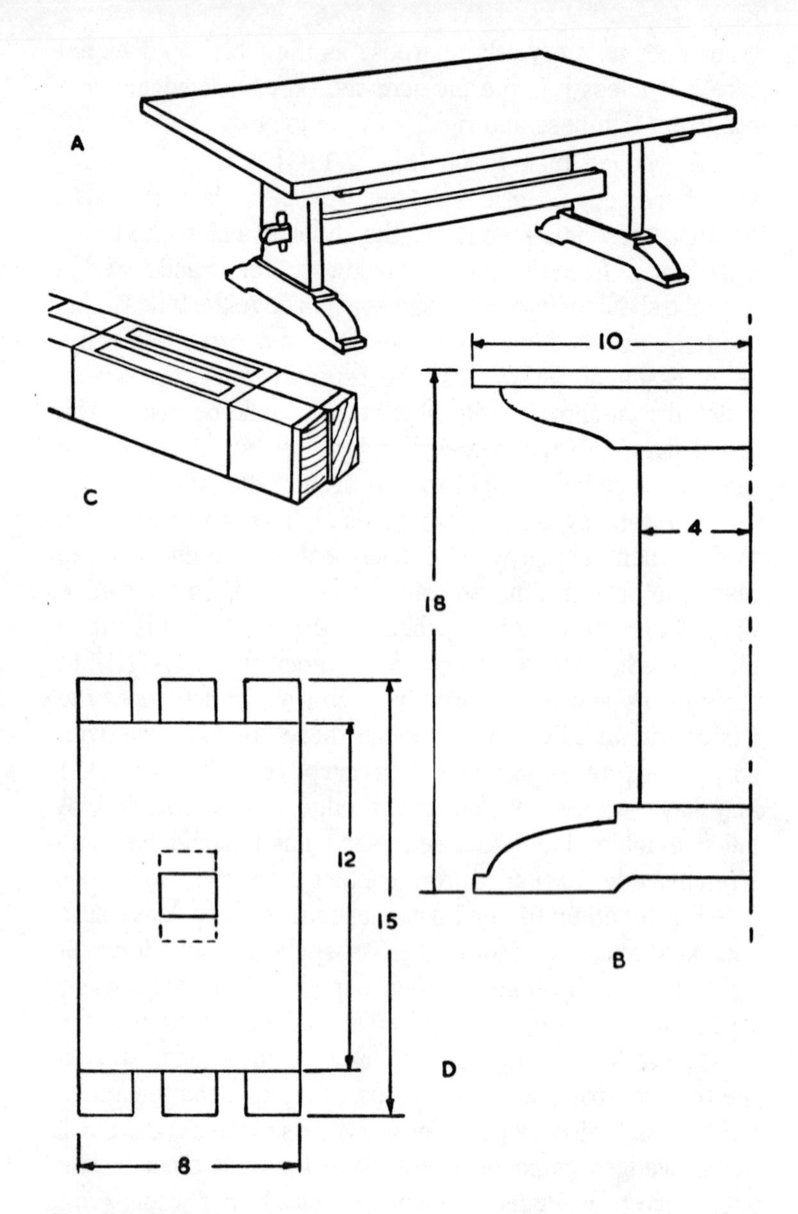


**Materials List 7-11**

| Trestle Coffee Table | | | | | |
|---|---|---|---|---|---|
| 1 | Top | 20 × 30 × ¾ | 2 | Feet | 4 × 20 × 1½ |
| 2 | Top cleats | ¾ × 20 × 2 | 2 | Tops | 3 × 18 × 1½ |
| 2 | Ends | 8 × 15 × 1 | 1 | Stretcher | 3 × 28 × 2 |
| | | | 2 | Wedges | 1 × 5 × ¾ |

Fig. 7-11. Trestle coffee table. (Continued on next page.)

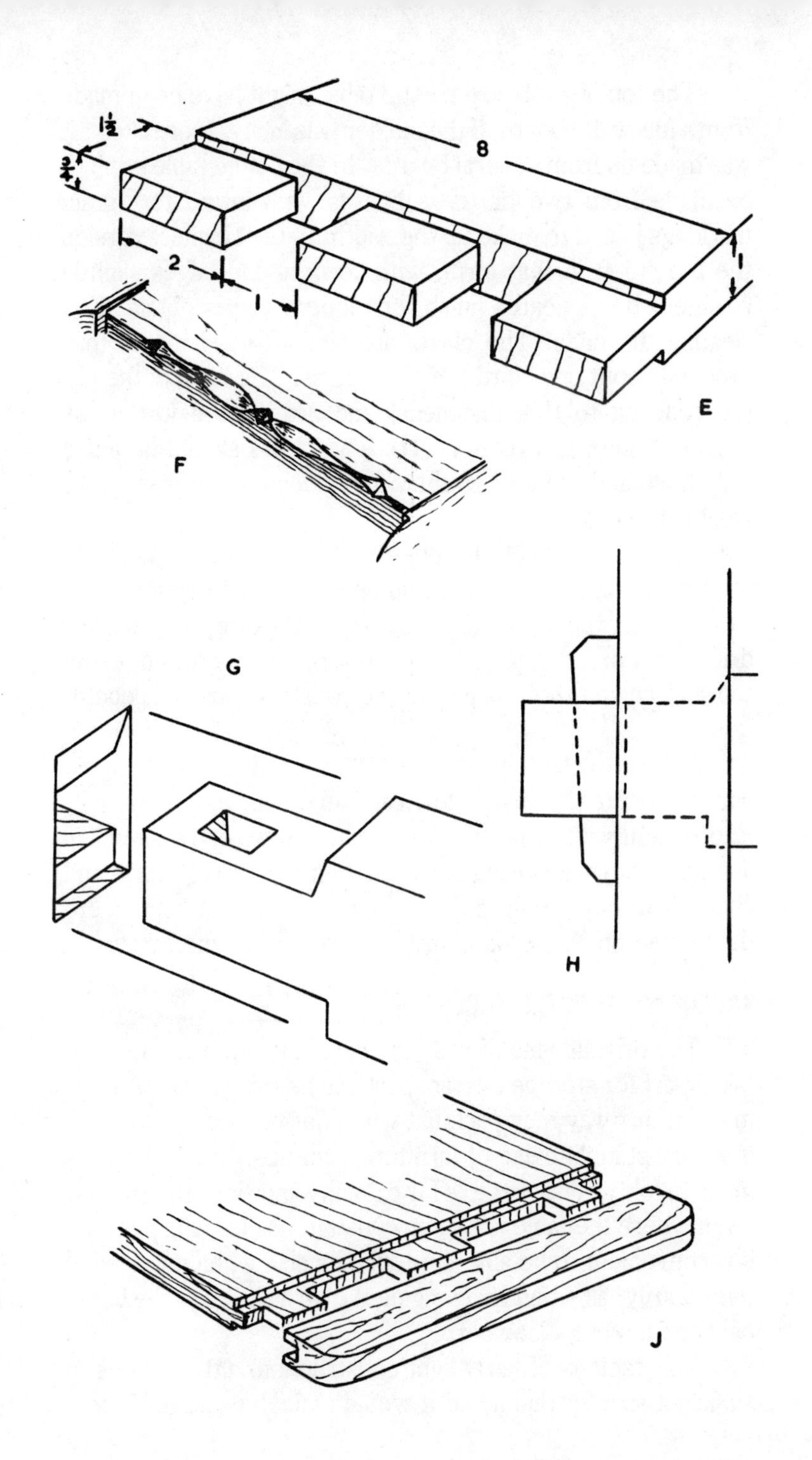
1½
¾
8
2
1
1
E
F
G
H
J

The top of a full-size trestle table might have been made from a full-width board, if the builder was lucky. More likely, it was made up from several boards. In the coffee table it might be made from two or three boards with interesting grain markings joined to make up the width. In the simplest version the top is left in that form, with corners and edges slightly rounded, but a neater finish for modern use is obtained by cleating the ends. The cleats are similar wood to the top, grooved about one-third their thickness. The ends of the top are reduced to this thickness, and are carried further as tenons at intervals (Fig. 7-11J). The cleats should be left a little thick and reduced to their final thickness after the joint has been glued.

Although it would be possible to fix the top by deeply counterboring screws driven upwards through the supports, this is a case where it would be nearer to the original method to drill downwards, so plugs over the screws are leveled on the top surface and show as part of the constructions and decoration.

Draw the stretcher tight to the posts with the wedges. Have the table top upside down and invert the assembly on it. Experiment with its position. See that the two end assemblies are parallel by measuring between their tops and bottoms and check that they are upright on the top before marking where they come on the top and drilling through for the screws.

## TAKEDOWN TRESTLE TABLE

The original idea of making tables and other furniture to take apart for storage or transport can be used today. A table made in this way may pack flat when not needed, yet make a more substantial piece of furniture than many modern tables made to fold or disassemble for camping and similar purposes. Even where the table is kept in constant use for long periods, it is convenient to be able to reduce its size when not needed temporarily, as when rearranging the furnishings of the home or when moving elsewhere.

This table is of fairly light construction, although it is of sufficient size for dining, or it would make a useful table in a children's room. It could be made of hardwood, but if taking down and moving may be frequent, it is better to use a softwood, such as yellow pine, for lightness. Much depends on the intended use. Softwood will have a good life with careful use, but hardwoods will take a better finish and may be needed to match existing furniture. They will also stand up to rougher use. This type of table may be used outdoors on a patio, when a durable wood must be used if it is to stay out in all weathers.

The general construction is very similar to the previous table, although the proportions and profiles are different (Fig. 7-12A). The rail or stretcher provides lengthwise stiffness. The top crossbars of the trestles are not connected directly to the top. Instead, there are braces across the underside of the top against these rails and held to them with pegs, which can be withdrawn for disassembly. The braces also stiffen the top and prevent it warping.

The feet and top rails could have many different outlines. Those shown are easy to cut. Instead of the feet tapering towards the floor directly, they are given an upward curve, then pads are added to bear on the floor. In this way the table is prevented from looking excessively light by an appearance of solidity around the feet (Fig. 7-12B).

Match the uprights with the parts they tenon into. Prepare and cut the joints before doing any shaping (Fig. 7-12C). As with the previous table, keep the tenons thick and let them come to the extreme width of the wood to get the benefit of maximum resistance to bending. The tenons may go through the top rail, or be only taken part way, as in the feet, but a tenon length of about 1½ in. is needed for adequate strength, particularly in softwood. Original tables of this type usually had pegs through the tenons. These were often only roughly rounded from square section, then driven into round holes. Their uneven outline can be seen on the surface of some old furniture. Pegs could still be made and used in this way, but it will be simpler to use pieces of dowel rod (Fig. 7-12D).

The stretcher is fitted above half the height (Fig. 7-12E). Its ends are shaped as wedged tusk tenons, in the same way as described for the trestle coffee table. Fit the joints carefully so

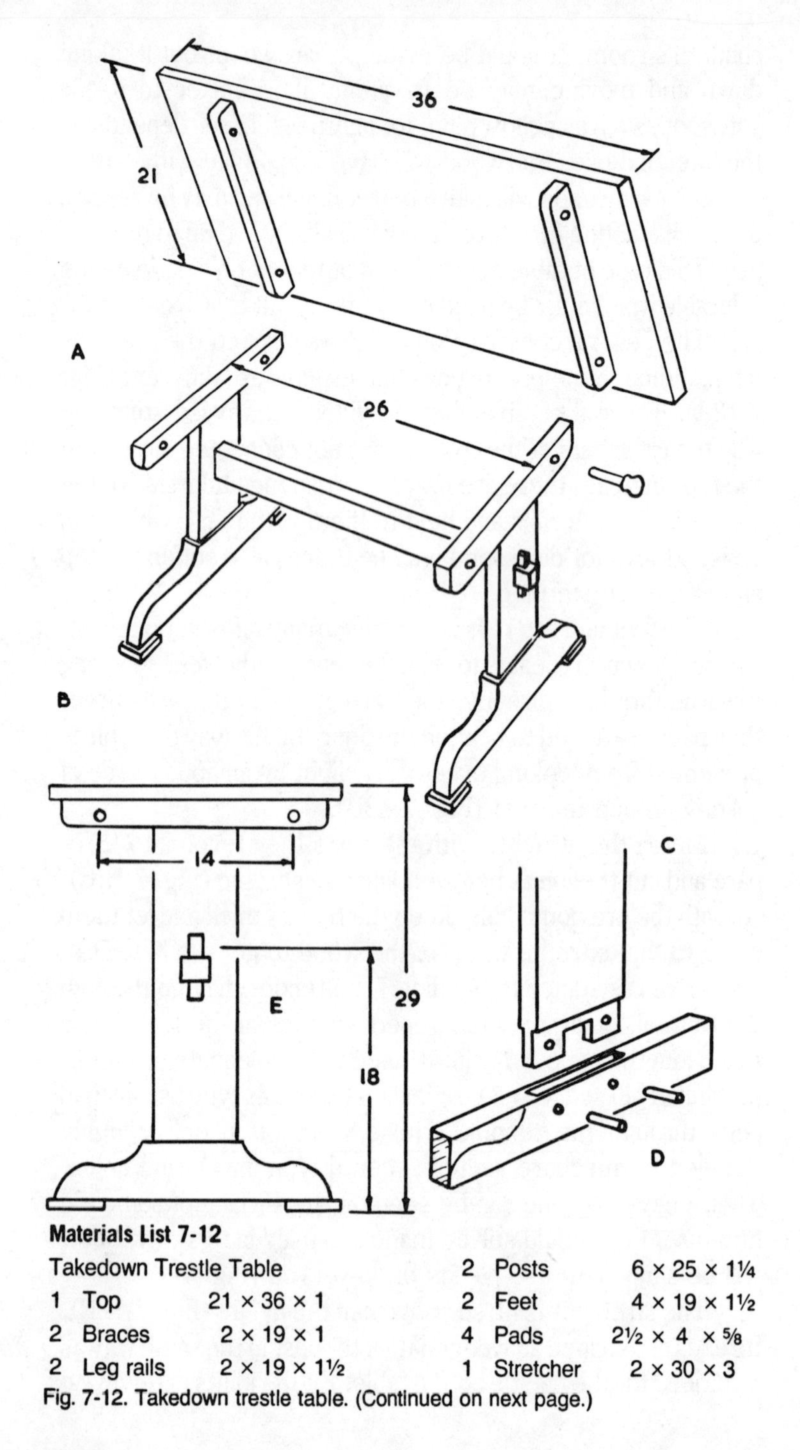


**Materials List 7-12**

Takedown Trestle Table

| Qty | Part | Size | Qty | Part | Size |
|---|---|---|---|---|---|
| 1 | Top | 21 × 36 × 1 | 2 | Posts | 6 × 25 × 1¼ |
| 2 | Braces | 2 × 19 × 1 | 2 | Feet | 4 × 19 × 1½ |
| 2 | Leg rails | 2 × 19 × 1½ | 4 | Pads | 2½ × 4 × ⅝ |
| | | | 1 | Stretcher | 2 × 30 × 3 |

Fig. 7-12. Takedown trestle table. (Continued on next page.)

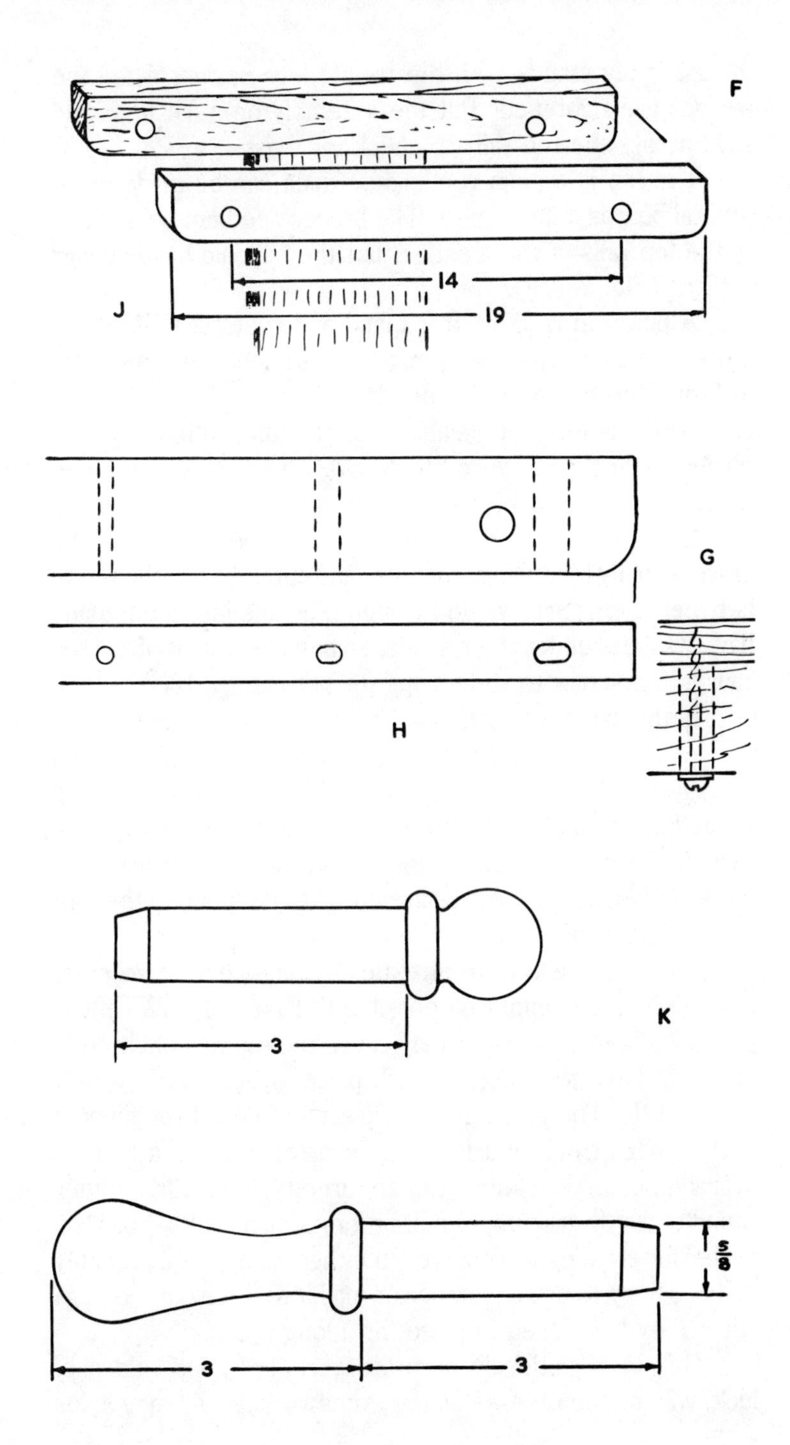
F
14
J
19
G
H
K
3
5/8
3
3

the assembly stands with the trestle legs upright when the wedges are tightened. Put the assembly on a flat floor and sight across the top rails to check for twist.

The top is a plain rectangle, which can be made up of several boards if necessary. The braces need not be as thick as the top rails of the trestles, but they should have similar outlines (Fig. 7-12F).

A pine top is likely to expand and contract in its width more than most hardwoods might. This should be allowed for in fitting the braces by using slot screwing. Expansion and contraction is most noticeable near the full width and is less obvious near the center of the board. This means that movement which has to be allowed for is slightest close to the middle. With slot screwing there are slot holes made in the brace, usually by drilling two holes and cutting away the waste between them. Screws go through the slots into the top and have washers under their heads, so any movement of the top causes the screw to slide along its slot (Fig. 7-12G).

In this table, there is one screw through a round hole at the center, two others with slots about ½ in. long, and two farther out about ¾ in. long (Fig. 7-12H). The braces are located on the underside of the top so they fit easily over the tops of the trestles. Check the whole table for squareness, particularly that the trestles are upright in relation to the top, before fixing the braces.

The top is held to the trestles by pegs, or *trunnel pins*, through holes. It might be possible to have only one central peg at each end, but wear may cause the top to wobble. It is better to have two pegs in each place, spaced fairly widely (Fig. 7-12J). The pegs could be pieces of dowel rod given a slight taper at one end for ease in driving, but if a lathe is available, pegs with knobs can be turned (Fig. 7-12K), either round ends for gripping to pull or longer handles that may be better for twisting to remove. In either case, it will probably be necessary to use a hammer or mallet to drive out the pegs when they have been in place for a long time.

Only in exceptionally accurate work, or by a great deal of luck, will the top reverse on the framework and the peg holes line up properly again. It is better to mark the way the peg holes were drilled, so the table is always assembled the same way An X-cut with two crossing chisel cuts on the adjoining brace and trestle will be better than using a pencil or pen.

## TRESTLE DINING TABLE AND BENCH

Large trestle tables were often of massive construction and a full-size reproduction might be considered rather clumsy for use in a room with normal modern furniture. The design shown here has its sections lightened, but is otherwise made in the same way as many early trestle tables that had to serve for most other purposes as well as dining in the early homes. Although the wedged stretcher, essential to retain the characteristic appearance has been retained, much of the stiffness of the table is due to the deep central lengthwise rail directly under the top (Fig. 7-13A).

Later tables of this type were given decorative outlines on the legs. Some possible designs are shown (Fig. 7-13B). If other outlines are chosen, it is important to keep the wood to its greatest width at the ends, so tenons of the full width can be made. Although it is possible to cut away quite a lot around the centers of the edges, sufficient width should always be left to ensure rigidity. It is also possible to cut decorative holes in the legs, but shaping the edges was more usual.

Decoration of the uprights can also be reflected in similar edge decoration on the stretcher, although this should not be taken too deep, if its stiffening effect is not to be impaired.

The two trestles are laid out, joints cut and the parts assembled in the same way as for the previous two tables. The mortise for the stretcher should be just above half the height for the best appearance. If it is exactly halfway, an optical illusion will make it appear below halfway. On each trestle, the inner surface of the top rail should be level with the leg for ease in fitting the lengthwide rail (Fig. 7-13C).

How the lengthwise rail is fixed to the trestles depends on skill and personal preference. Whatever method is used, the details of the joint will not be apparent in the finished table. The simplest method is to cut the ends of the rail squarely and join it with dowels (Fig. 7-13D). Another way is to have short tenons (Fig. 7-13E). They cannot be very long unless they are to go right through and their ends be left showing. There could be a groove to take the end of the rail (Fig. 7-13F), but this would not have much useful glue area and strength would have to be provided by giving the groove a dovetail form, so the rail entered from the top (Fig. 7-13G).

A broad hardwood table top could have cleated ends. The tendency then for the wood to expand and contract might not be much, and the construction would be satisfactory, but if softwood is used, allowance should be made for changes in the width. There should be firm fastenings along the central rail. There could be counterbored screws driven from above and plugged or pocket screws could be driven upwards from alternate sides (Fig. 7-13H). These screws will keep the top securely in place, but further screws are needed at the extremities of the tops of the trestles to further hold the top and prevent warping. They should be in slots to allow for changes in the top width. The design of the ends could be arranged to allow for slots and inconspicuous countersunk screws (Fig. 7-13J). Another method that was used and is still a good one is to have metal plates with slots. The wood is notched to take the plates, which are screwed on, then round head screws through the slots secure the table top (Fig. 7-13K).

A solid top of good width has to be fairly thick for stiffness, but it can be made to look lighter by beveling around the underside (Fig. 7-13L). Molding the edges of the table top is inappropriate for this traditional table. A small curve at each corner and rounded edges are all that should be done.

Trestle tables date from the days when chairs for all were unusual. The head of the house may have had a chair, but most others sat on stools or benches. It was usual to sit at the table on benches that matched the style of the table. Sizes varied, but a convenient sitting height was between 15 in. and 18 in. for eating off a table top 28 in. to 30 in. high. The higher seat would be preferable now, but only a few generations ago, our ancestors had shorter legs than we have, and seats were generally lower. Their full height was also much less, as you will find when ducking your head to go through a doorway in a very old house.

Benches were made to the same length as the table (Fig. 7-14A). This one has the stretcher and its wedged tusk tenons to give rigidity, but sitters may put considerable strain on a bench, so there are rails under the top, with strips between to give further support to the top (Fig. 7-14B).

Having strips across allows the legs to be made without top pieces tenoned on. There is no need for feet to be made, but the bottoms of the legs should be cut back so only the outer edges rest on the floor (Fig. 7-14C). Any outline shaping of the legs should match the decoration used on the table.

The bench top can be a single board or it can be made up from two or more, and there may be cleated ends similar to the table top. A bench is often lifted by its top, so the joint between top and framing should be secure. Glue can be used, but there should also be screws upwards into the top, arranged to go as deeply as possible, without breaking out the grain on the top surface.

## DROP LEAF TRESTLE TABLE

Trestle tables were not made with flaps to drop at the sides and were certainly not made in a form comparable to a gate leg table. It is possible to arrange a means of supporting side leaves, but trestle tables that could be enlarged were more usual with leaves at one or both ends. Two leaves could be arranged so they almost doubled the length of the top when raised. Usual supports were central swinging brackets and their size was limited by the need to keep with the width of the table top when swung back for folding, so a raised leaf should not extend too far past the bracket if there is to be sufficient strength.

The table shown (Fig. 7-15A) is a suitable size for a side table, for sewing with enough area for laying out patterns, or for occasional dining use. It looks best in hardwood but is equally suitable for pine.

The general construction is very similar to the takedown table. The feet are shaped and cut away to bear at their ends

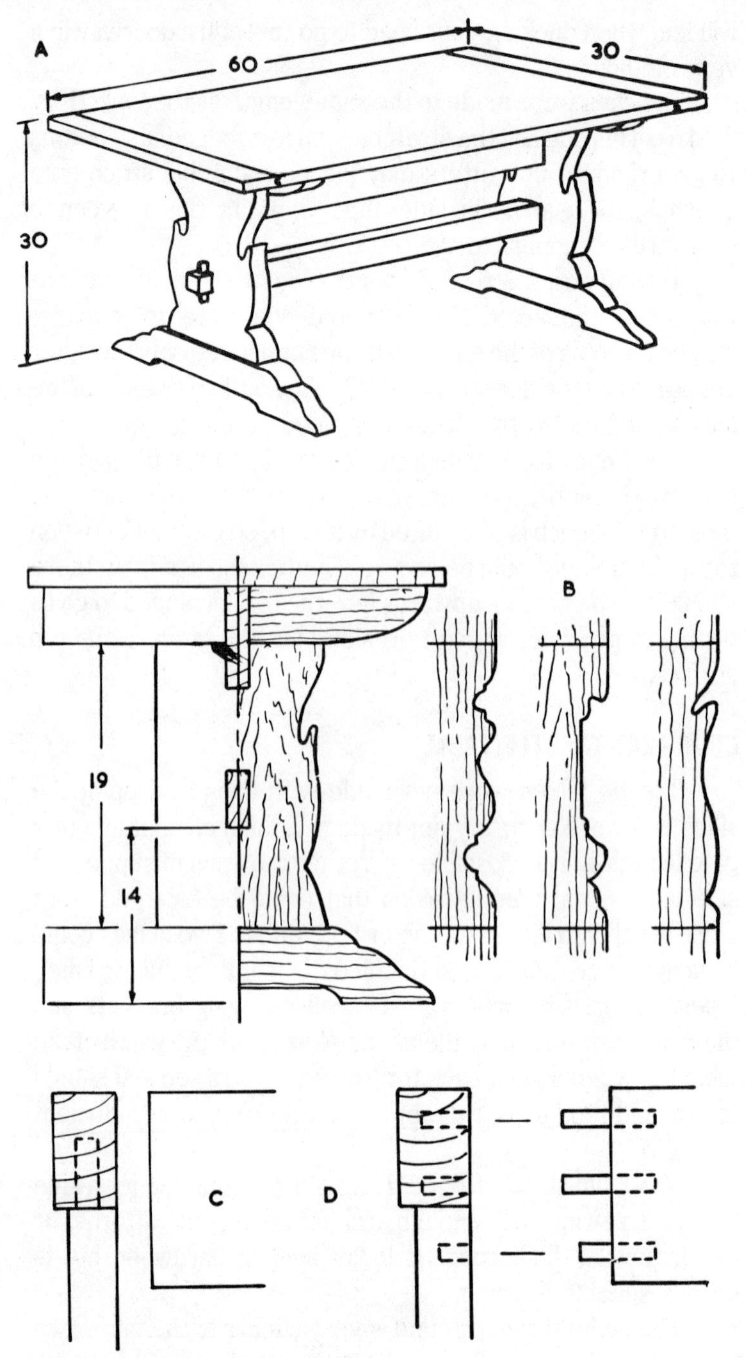


Fig. 7-13. Trestle dining table. (Continued on next page.)

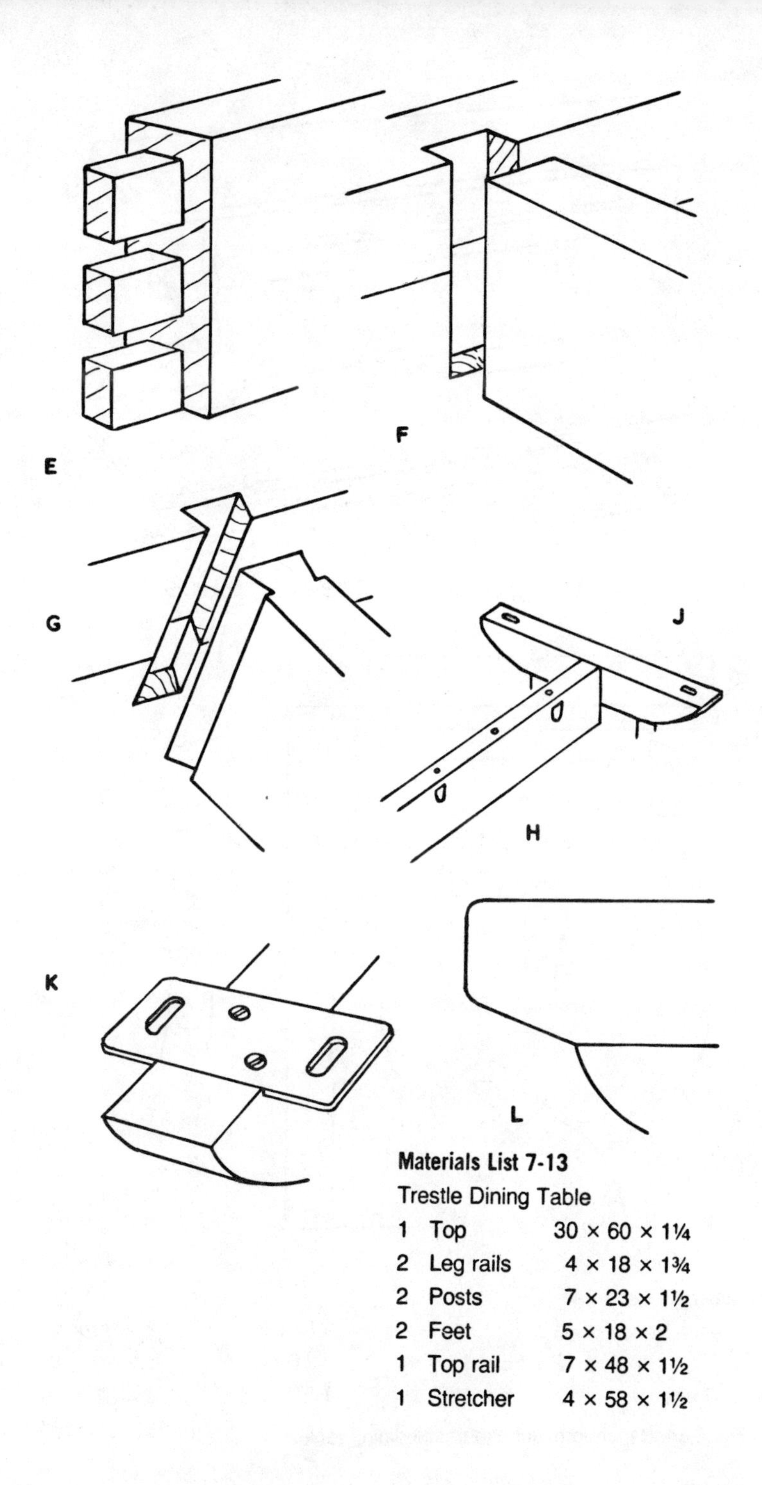


**Materials List 7-13**

Trestle Dining Table

| | | |
|---|---|---|
| 1 | Top | 30 × 60 × 1¼ |
| 2 | Leg rails | 4 × 18 × 1¾ |
| 2 | Posts | 7 × 23 × 1½ |
| 2 | Feet | 5 × 18 × 2 |
| 1 | Top rail | 7 × 48 × 1½ |
| 1 | Stretcher | 4 × 58 × 1½ |

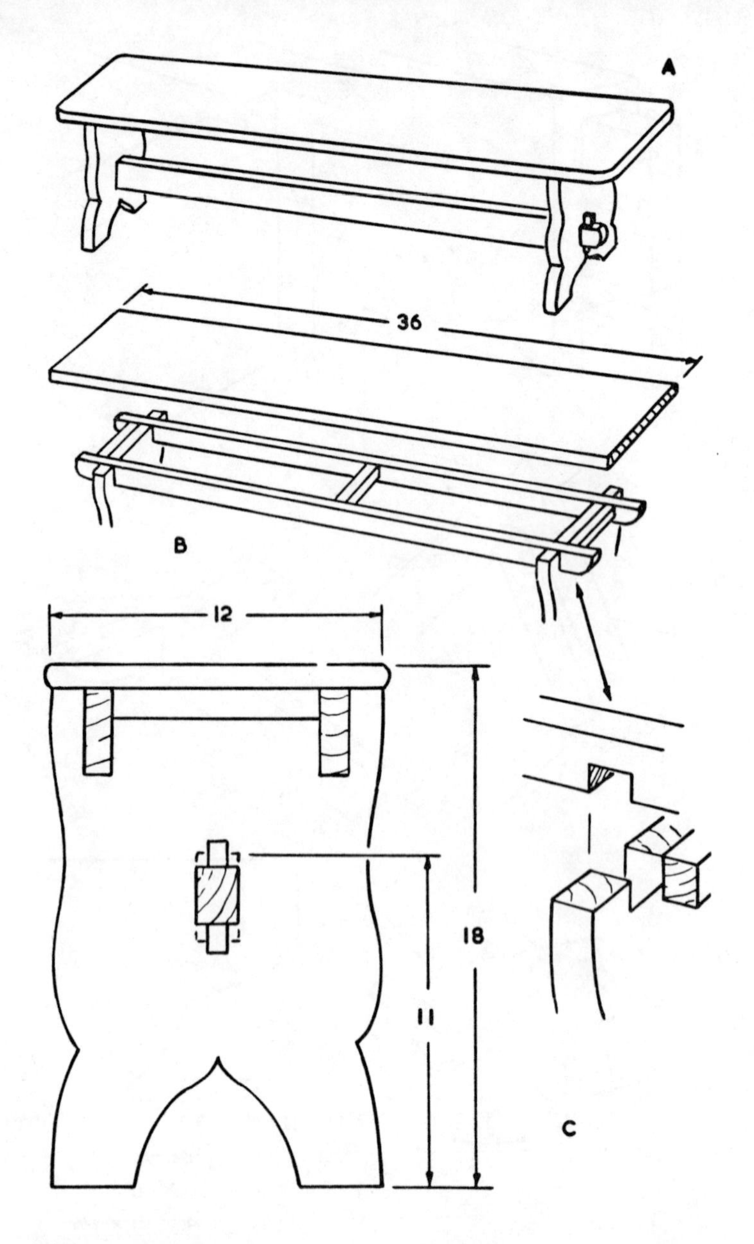


**Materials List 7-14**

Trestle Bench

| | | | | | |
|---|---|---|---|---|---|
| 1 | Top | 12 × 36 × 1 | 2 | Rails | 2 × 33 × 1 |
| 2 | Legs | 12 × 17 × 1½ | 3 | Rails | 1 × 8 × 1 |
| | | | 1 | Stretcher | 3 × 33 × 1½ |

Fig. 7-14. Bench to match the trestle dining table.

on the floor. The top rail of each trestle is kept parallel so it can more easily be used for slot screws. There is a central shallow lengthwise rail that is notched through the trestles to provide a pivot for the bracket at each end. It also adds to stiffness and can be screwed through into the top (Fig. 7-15B). Cut only a little out of the rail to give a positive location in the trestle without weakening the wood (Fig. 7-15C).

The stretcher is above halfway. It supports the bracket and its exact position may have to be arranged to suit the wood available for the bracket. The overhang of the table top at the ends must be enough to allow a leaf to hang down clear of the bracket and the end of the stretcher. It is advisable to draw this detail full-size, to get the dimensions of the parts right (Fig. 7-15D). There has to be enough of the stretcher past the wedge to take a hole for a pivot. It is the extension necessary for this which decides on the amount of projection for other parts. The ends of the lengthwise rail should be allowed to extend as far as possible, so the maximum strength in the end grain outside and pivot hole is obtained.

The bracket has its grain upright. Holes are drilled for pieces of dowel rod on which it pivots (Fig. 7-15E). Even if the main parts of the table are softwood, the dowels should be hardwood and a close-grained hardwood is better for the lengthwise rail than a softwood, because there is considerable load on the short grain outside the pivot dowel at each end. At the ends of the stretcher the loads on the pivot are inwards, so bursting forces are not so great there.

Only the outer part of the bracket is at the supporting height (Fig. 7-15F). The rest of the top is cut back so it does not bind under the table end. There is no need to round the inner edge of the bracket much, except where it might touch another part. Leaving it as near square as possible makes for strength.

The main top and its leaves should be of similar wood and the grain pattern should continue across all three if a wood with prominent grain is chosen. The three parts are best cut from one piece if possible. In any case the grain on the leaves should run in the length of the table. This means that the

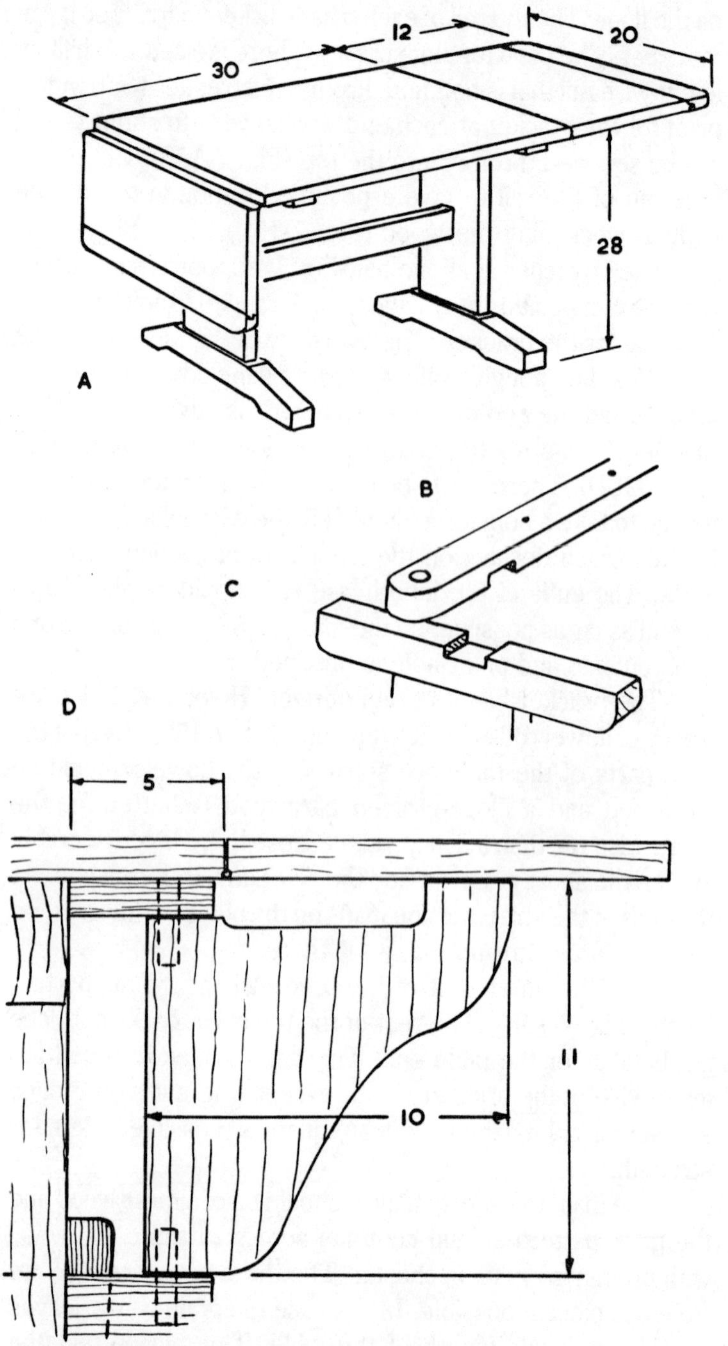


Fig. 7-15. Drop leaf trestle table. (Continued on next page.)

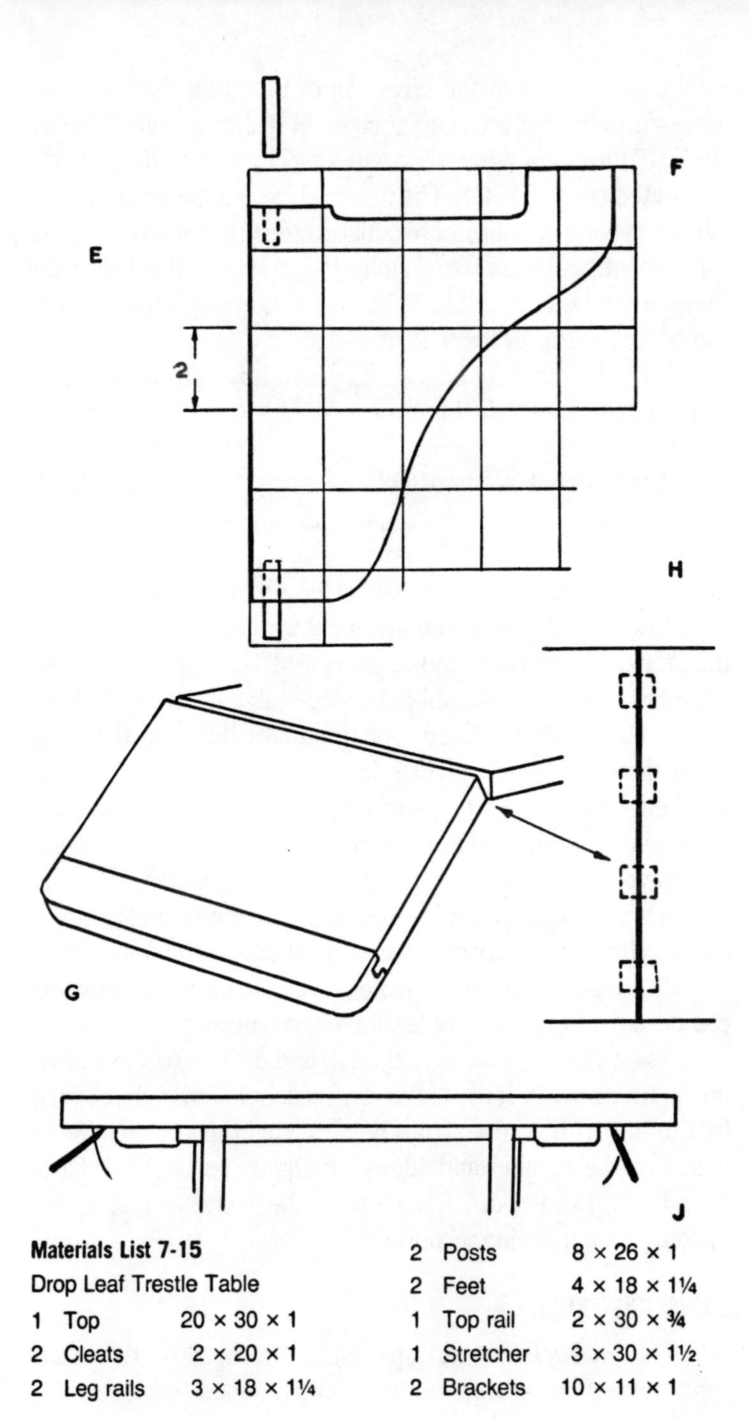


**Materials List 7-15**

Drop Leaf Trestle Table

| | | |
|---|---|---|
| 1 | Top | 20 × 30 × 1 |
| 2 | Cleats | 2 × 20 × 1 |
| 2 | Leg rails | 3 × 18 × 1¼ |
| 2 | Posts | 8 × 26 × 1 |
| 2 | Feet | 4 × 18 × 1¼ |
| 1 | Top rail | 2 × 30 × ¾ |
| 1 | Stretcher | 3 × 30 × 1½ |
| 2 | Brackets | 10 × 11 × 1 |

leaves are smaller in the direction of the grain than they are across it. These are circumstances in which warping is more likely, if nothing is done to prevent it. The outer edges should be cleated (Fig. 7-15G). The inner edges can be supported by using a greater number of backflap hinges than would be usual if the meeting edges were along the grain. In this size table there could be four, let in flush so they do not interfere with the action of the bracket (Fig. 7-15H).

With the meeting edges end grain, it would be difficult to plane a rule joint, so this type of table was allowed square meeting edges.

Although it is as important as always that the table should be properly squared up by testing diagonals, and the trestles should stand upright, the most important consideration, for utility and appearance is for the full length of the top to be level when the leaves are up. To ensure this it is advisable to make the brackets with their ends high at first. The main part of the table framework is assembled completely. Each bracket can have its lower dowel fixed, but the upper dowel is slipped in loose through the top pivot point in the lengthwise rail. The brackets are swung into their support position and a piece of wood with a straightedge put along to represent the table top and leaves. A pencil along this marks the supporting position on the brackets (Fig. 7-15J), which are removed and trimmed to size. If they are correct when tried again, the upper pivot dowels are glued into the brackets. Candle grease or graphite can be put in the pivot holes for easy working.

Assemble the leaves to the top and make a trial assembly on the framework. If the leaves and brackets function properly fix the top with screws from below. This type of table looks best with the corners and edges left square, except for sharpness being sanded off. There could be some rounding, but molding would be inappropriate.

## SAWBUCK TABLE

The *sawbuck table* is American from the similarity of the leg arrangement to the common support used for supporting logs being sawn by hand. The design is European, where a sawbuck is more often called a "sawing trestle" and this name was not applied to tables. It was more likely to be referred to as an "X-leg" or "X-frame" table. These tables may be found in many old houses and castles in Europe, but they are sometimes called "Swedish" tables in America, because many were made by Swedish immigrants who settled in the Pennsylvania area.

The parts used in the constructon of the leg assemblies have to be of fairly substantial section because they are weakened by being cut away to make cross-lap joints and are further cut away for the mortise at the end of the stretcher. Although there were some sawbuck tables made with crossed pieces of straight section, the majority have the legs with shaped outlines. This breaks up the heavy appearance and gives some grace to what would otherwise be a rather clumsy assembly—appropriate to a sawyer's clearing in the woods but unwelcome in a home.

The design shown (Fig. 7-16A) could be made full-size as a dining table. A smaller version could be regarded as a model and used as a coffee table. Benches for use with the table were often made in the same way, so it would be appropriate to use a similar construction for a seat.

An end view should be drawn full-size (Fig. 7-16B) without first considering any shaping. Crossing two straight pieces shows where parts come in relation to each other. Draw on the end view of the stretcher and note where the mortise will be cut, balancing its size between the need for a strong tenon and the need for sufficient wood to be left around it in each of the crossing pieces. The strongest joint comes when the width of the table is about the same as its height (Fig. 7-16C). A table that is much higher than it is wide gets very acute angles in the crosslap joint (Fig. 7-16D). It is also normally best to have the crossing near the middle of the legs. If it is higher or lower, it affects the spread. If the crossing is below the center, the feet do not spread as much as the top, so if carried too far, the table becomes unstable (Fig. 7-16E). If the crossing is to be off-center, it is better to have it slightly higher than the middle, then the feet spread wider than the tops of the

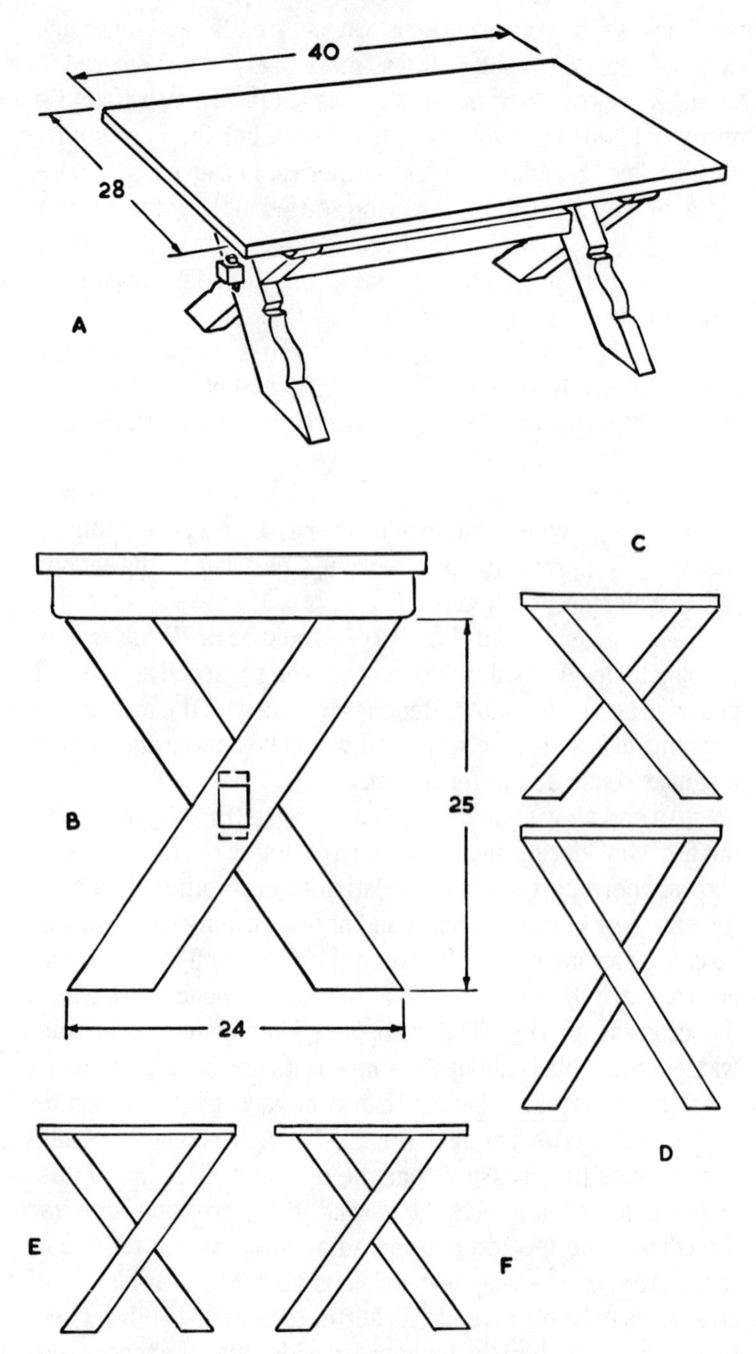


Fig. 7-16. Sawbuck table. (Continued on next page.)

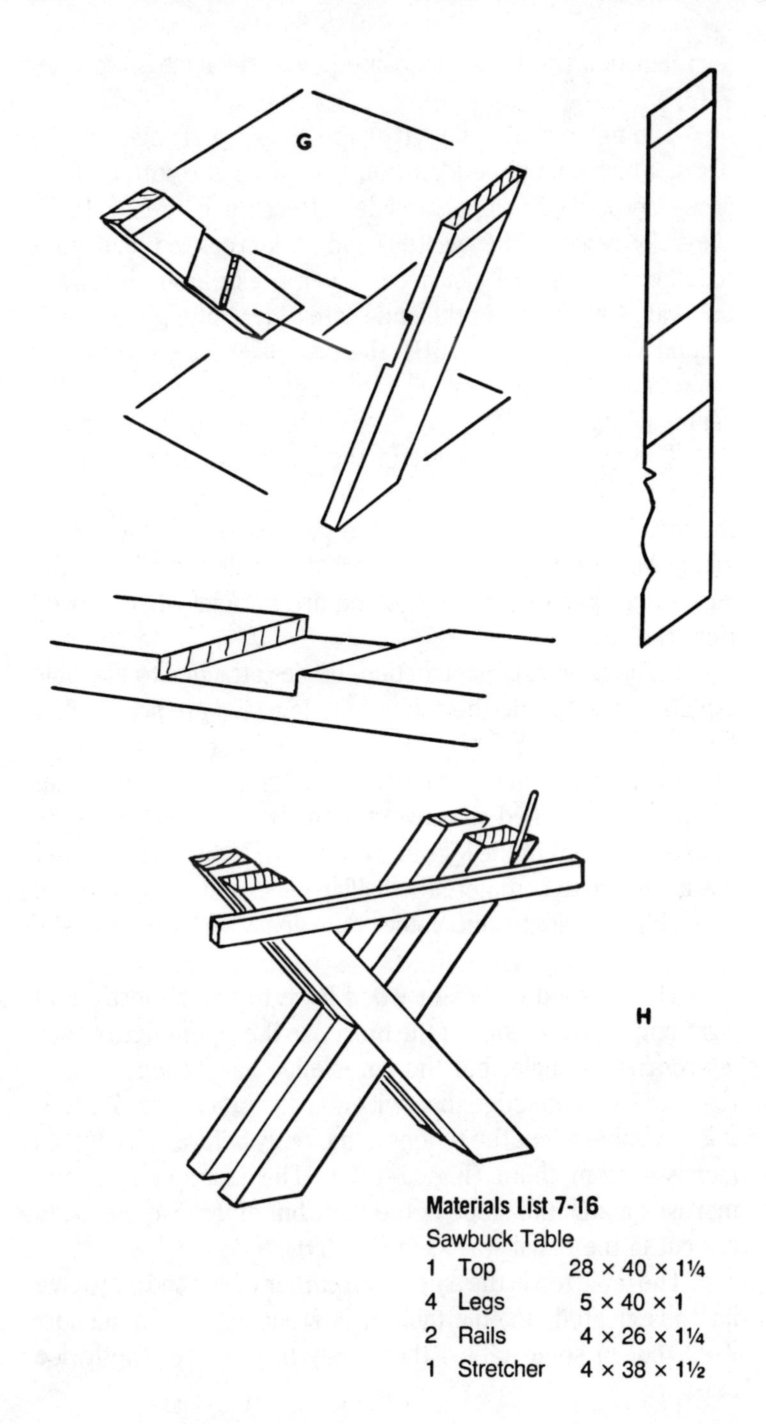


**Materials List 7-16**

Sawbuck Table

| | | |
|---|---|---|
| 1 | Top | 28 × 40 × 1¼ |
| 4 | Legs | 5 × 40 × 1 |
| 2 | Rails | 4 × 26 × 1¼ |
| 1 | Stretcher | 4 × 38 × 1½ |

legs, but that can be compensated by a wider table top (Fig. 7-16F).

The full-size drawing gives the shapes and angles of the parts, which should be identical, except for the cutout of the cross-lap being on opposite sides of each pair (Fig. 7-16G). Carefully remove the waste wood so a cross-lap joint goes together with the two surfaces level. Make up both ends in this way. Check across the ends with a straightedge and mark around all sides (Fig. 7-16H), then cut off the ends. Separate the part and do the shaping to the edges. Glue and clamp the center joints.

The stretcher is made in the same way as for trestle tables, with the ends cut as wedged tusk tenons. Mark and cut the mortises in the legs after the glue has set in the halflap joints. Make a trial assembly, check diagonals and see that the legs stand on all four corners and are upright when viewed from the side.

In the simplest construction, braces attached to the table top go across beside the tops of the legs and are screwed or doweled to them (Fig. 7-17A). This is a satisfactory arrangement and is found in some early examples of these tables, but when a more skilled woodworker made a sawbuck table he tenoned the tops of the legs into the brace. If this is to be done, it is advisable to complete the halflap joints and treat each end assembly as a single unit, rather than deal with loose pieces of wood.

The crossed pieces of wood have to enter mortises at right-angles to the edge of the brace, so the inner edge of each leg retains its angle, but the outer edge has its tenon cut at right angles to the edge that will enter the brace (Fig. 7-17B). It is advisable to cut the tenons completely before marking the mortises from them (Fig. 7-17C). The inner ends of the mortises match the slope of the legs, but otherwise the joints are cut in the usual way (Fig. 7-17D).

The table top is the same as in earlier tables and may have its ends cleated. In this table it is stout enough to support itself, but in some tables there may have to be lengthwise rails.

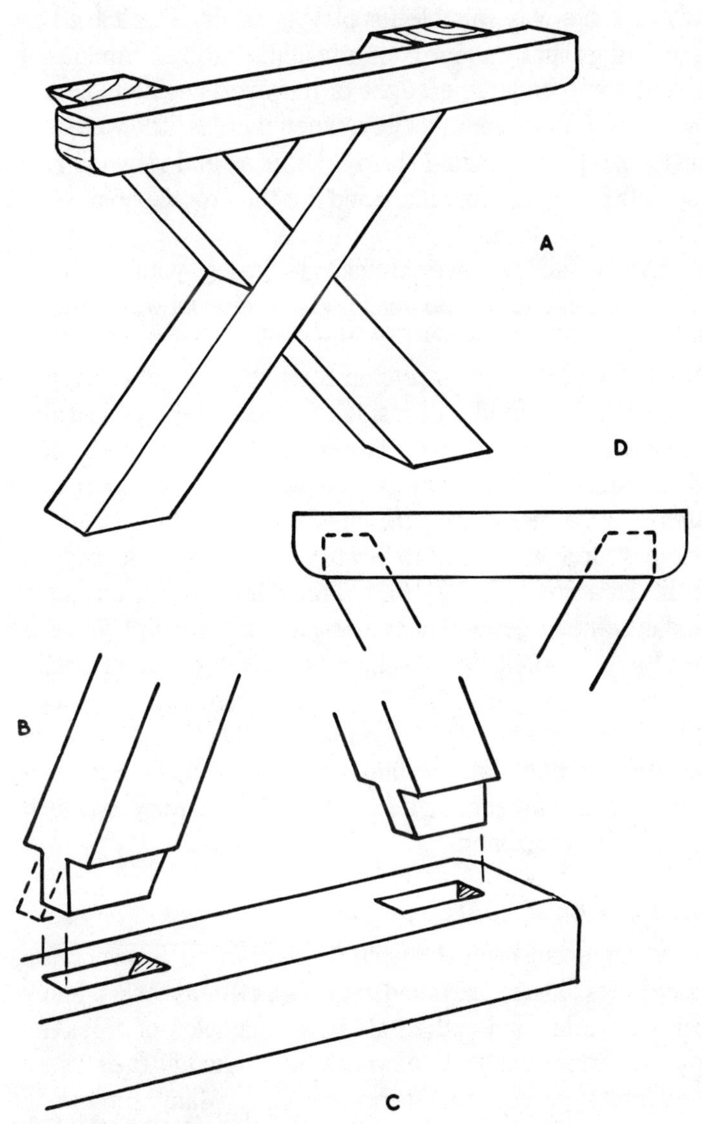

Fig. 7-17. End details of a sawbuck table.

## SAWBUCK SIDE TABLE

Traditional sawbuck tables mostly require wood of quite large section, but the method of construction was used for small tables that were for occasional use, put at the wall for serving from, or used for sewing or writing. A light square sawbuck table was suitable for playing cards. This table has the crossing slightly above center height, so the extremities of the feet come under the edges of the overhanging table top (Fig. 7-18A), for proper stability, when there is little weight to assist in keeping the table steady. Draw an end view full-size (Fig. 7-18B). From this, mark and cut the crosslap joints and the ends ot the legs.

The top rails or braces are fixed to the legs with dowels or tenons. Besides the stretcher fixed in the usual way through the crosslap joint there are two more rails under the top (Fig. 7-18C). They assist the stretcher to provide lengthwise rigidity. They are located just inside of where the legs join the braces and are cross lapped. Lay out the joints in these rails and the stretcher together so distances between the joints match. Notice that in the stretcher joint there is not enough thickness for a wedge slot to be cut vertically and the wedges are driven across (Fig. 7-18D). This direction of wedging is found in some larger and heavier tables, but vertical wedging when there was sufficient thickness of wood was more usual.

Some light sawbuck tables were made with the legs straight, but this one is shown with shaped outlines below the joint. Any method of decorating edges can be used, but when the wood is of light section it should not be cut away too much or it may be weakened.

## HEAVY SAWBUCK TABLE

Much ecclesiastical furniture in Europe incorporates crossed legs. These are found in chairs as well as tables. Many old monasteries and cathedrals have examples of cross leg furniture many hundreds of years old, although their users would not recognize the term *sawbuck*. Many settlers in America would have known these tables and chairs, which were usually large and of quite heavy construction, so then they were faced with the need to make furniture for public buildings, churches, and other communally used places besides private homes, they remembered these designs and reproduced them. A modern reproduction of this type might be regarded as a reproduction of a reproduction.

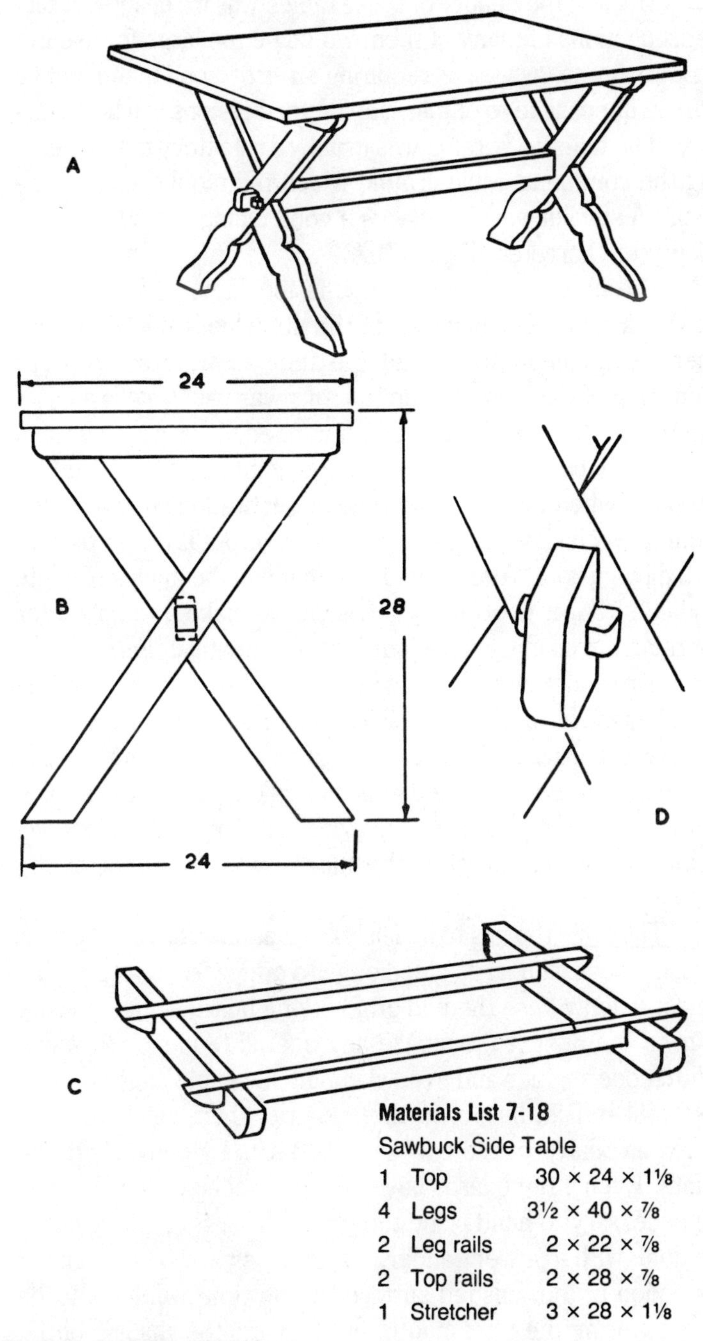


**Materials List 7-18**

Sawbuck Side Table

| Qty | Part | Size |
|---|---|---|
| 1 | Top | 30 × 24 × 1⅛ |
| 4 | Legs | 3½ × 40 × ⅞ |
| 2 | Leg rails | 2 × 22 × ⅞ |
| 2 | Top rails | 2 × 28 × ⅞ |
| 1 | Stretcher | 3 × 28 × 1⅛ |

Fig. 7-18. Sawbuck side table.

Much of the beauty of these tables was in the legs. Exact reproductions of many of them would be too large for use in a modern home, as well as requiring sizes of wood that might be almost impossible to obtain, but lighter versions can be attractive. The full-size version was usually a refectory table, meaning the communal table around which the monks sat to eat a meal. A smaller version makes a good dining room table with plenty of character (Fig. 7-19A).

The method of construction is the same as for the first sawbuck table, but because of the steadiness due to weight there is no need to spread the feet as wide as the top. Tenoning of the legs into the top rails was usual and is advisable today, as maximum strength is needed for a heavy table that could put excessive strain on joints if mishandled or dropped when moving. The type of decoration shown comes from an ecclesiastical table (Fig. 7-19B), but it is appropriate to a dining room. A full-size drawing gives the angles of joints and cuts, but it is probably advisable to make a template for marking the shaping so all four legs are identical (Fig. 7-19C). They are most simply cut with a bandsaw, but you can remember the hard labor and skill of the original craftsmen using hand tools. Make sure all signs of machine sawing are removed from the decorated edges. Besides sanding, scraping with a metal scraper or the edge of a broken piece of glass will remove saw marks from the more awkward parts of the design.

The table top has to be fairly thick and will have to be built up from several boards glued edge to edge. So far as possible select wood where the end grain of one board is the opposite way to the next, to minimize any overall tendency to warp. With modern glues and even clamping, a simple edge-to-edge joint will suffice, but for further security there can be dowels between boards or the edges worked with tongue and groove joints. Even if the boards have all been machine planed, it will be necessary to hand plane the top surface. Something might be done with a power sander, but there should be no signs of its action in the finished surface. Some time will have to be spent getting the top smooth, but this and the shaping of the legs are the outstanding features of the design.

Because of the weight of even this lightened version, it is unwise to depend only on wood screws for holding the top to the leg rails. Instead it is advisable to follow what was customary in the heavier originals. Iron angle brackets go inside the top rails (Fig. 7-19D). Those above the legs should overlap on to them so two or three stout wood screws can be driven. The original brackets would have been made by a blacksmith, but it should be possible to adapt iron shelf brackets that will look sufficiently authentic. The originals would have been black from forging, so bright modern brackets would not look right. The number of brackets depends on their size, but four should be enough.

The top is held by bolting through these brackets, but before drilling any holes it is advisable to invert the assembled legs and stretcher over the reversed top. Get its position correct and check the framework for squareness and the legs for upright. When you are certain everything is as accurate as you can get it, mark through the bolt holes in the brackets. Drill through with an undersize drill from the underside. This will give the location on the top without the risk of grain breaking out, which might happen with a larger drill.

Use carriage bolts to fix the top. Counterbore enough to sink the head far enough below the surface to allow of plugging, then follow through the small pilot hole with a drill to suit the bolt (Fig. 7-19E). Insert all the bolts then tighten progressively all round until the top is tight. The plugs should be made from the same wood as the top and ought to have their grain across to match the top.

Some refectory tables were fitted with shallow drawers for cutlery. As there was no framing between the legs immediately under the top, it was easy to fit. One type of drawer could be opened from either side and this would be useful in a modern dining table version. The drawer is made in the usual way, but with what amounts to two fronts, preferably dovetailed and fitted with handles. This is hung from slides fixed under the table top. Square strips along the top edges of the drawer sides run in rabbeted pieces screwed below the table top (Fig. 7-19F). On a long table there could be more

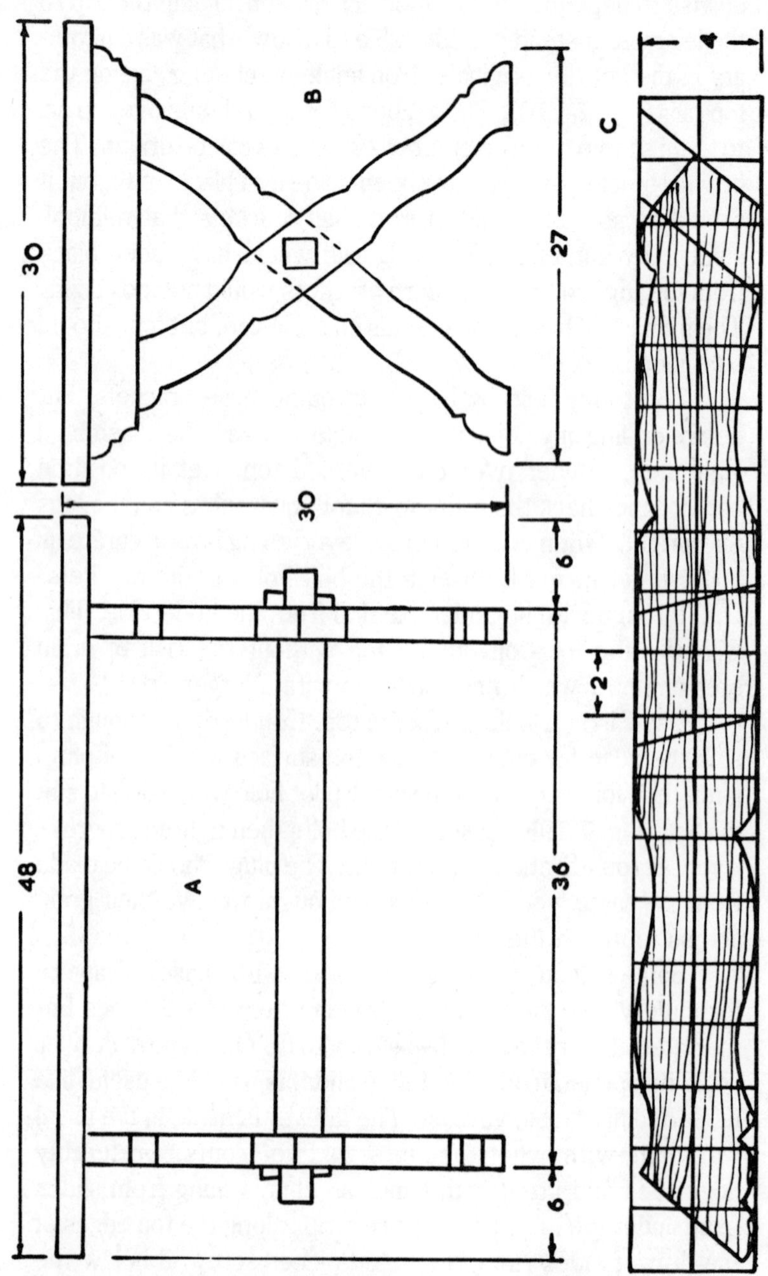


Fig. 7-19. Dimensions and additional features for the sawbuck side table. (Sheet 1 of 2). (Continued on next page.)

D

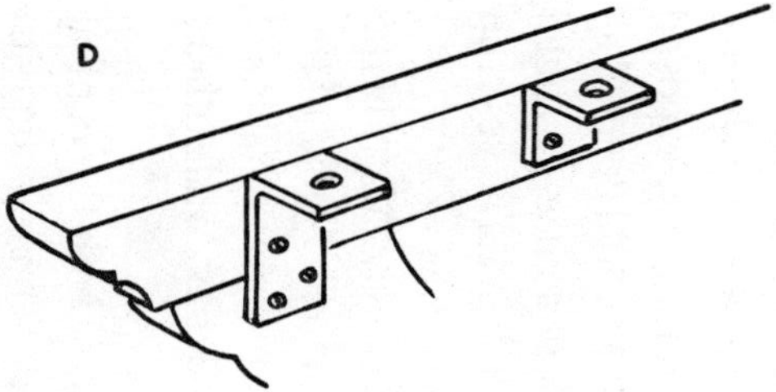

E

**Materials List 7-19**

Heavy Sawbuck Table

| | | |
|---|---|---|
| 1 | Top | 30 × 48 × 1½ |
| 4 | Legs | 4 × 40 × 1¾ |
| 2 | Rails | 3 × 28 × 1¾ |
| 1 | Stretcher | 3 × 42 × 1¾ |

F

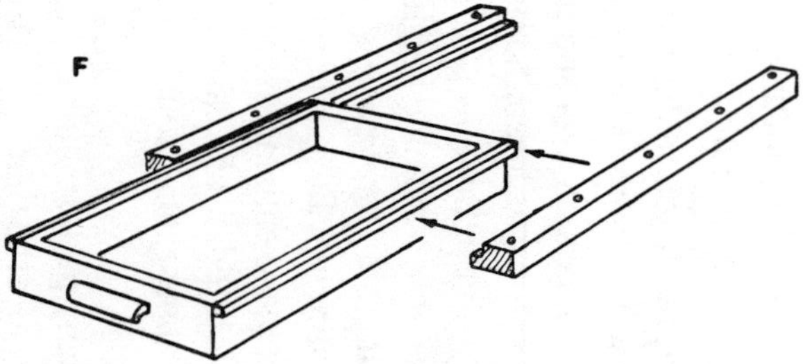

G

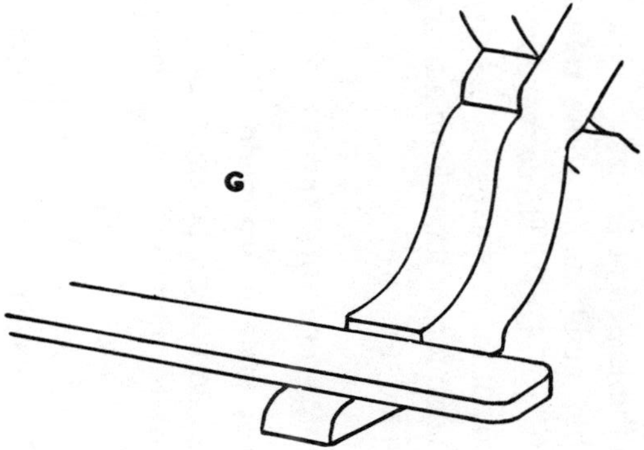

than one drawer, but they should be kept shallow so as not to impede the knees of sitters.

Other additions to some refectory tables were footboards (Fig. 7-19G). These were intended to provide somewhere to put the feet a few inches above the ground. There is no real need for footboards on a reproduction, but they could be provided if desired.

## TILT-TOP AND CANDLE TABLES

Many tables were made so the top could be tilted completely to an upright position. Besides the method being an alternative to a drop leaf table for reducing the size when out of use, this allowed the top to form a screen. A large top might protect occupants of the room from draughts. Some tables had a small flat area exposed when the top was tilted and this would be a place to put a candle, then the tilted top acted as a draught screen and a reflector. As a candle did not spread its light very far, it had to be located where needed, and there were many small tables made to take a candle, alongside a chair, bed, or elsewhere. These serve as atrractive occasional or bedside tables and for use in places too small for a larger table. Even if not needed for supporting a lamp or books, such a table makes a good stand for a plant pot or a vase of flowers.

Large tilt-top tables were often made on a single central pedestal in a similar way to the smaller candle tables. Others were arranged on legs and there was a storage box exposed when the top was lifted. Some of these tables could be used as seats, with the table top forming the back of a chair arranged with a seat at a suitable height between the legs. The seat top might then lift to expose a storage chest.

There may be less need for tilting tops today. Many of the designs make satisfactory tables with fixed tops. Not all of the originals tilted, in any case, and there are examples of tables of similar appearance, some of which had rigid tops, while others tilted.

Many pedestal tables had turned parts, with the central post in patterns that varied from rather basic conic sections to elaborate designs with many beads, quirks and curves. Some of these are adaptable to construction without the use of a lathe, but many of the candle tables, in particular, are attractive turning exercises, well within the capacity of a light lathe. The large tables with turned pedestals may require a rather larger lathe, although most lathes that will accept up to 30 in. between centers can be used.

Pedestal tables were usually made with three legs. Less common were four legs—the reason being the ability of a three-leg assembly to stand firm on any surface, while four legs might wobble (even a slight wobble could be a nuisance or a danger with a candle or oil lamp).

Whatever the method of construction, the arrangement of three equally spaced legs involves the same preparatory geometry. If the three legs are to be correctly positioned, they have to be at 120° to each other around the pedestal (Fig. 7-20A). If a lathe has a dividing head or there are other means of spacing mechanically, the dividing can be done with precision. If a radius is stepped off around a circumference, it goes six times, so on a circle of the size of the pedestal, the leg positions are at alternate marks (Fig. 7-20B). Another way is to wrap a strip of paper around the wood and push a spike through the overlapping parts (Fig. 7-20C). Open the paper and divide the the distance between the holes made by the spike into three (Fig. 7-20D). Put the paper back around the wood and transfer these positions.

Lines have to be drawn along the cylinder to give the positions of the legs. This can be done in the lathe. Bring the toolrest close to and parallel to the wood. Get a mark in position and draw a line along the toolrest with a pencil (Fig. 7-20E). There is another way if joints have to be marked away from the lathe. Join two narrow parallel pieces of wood to an angle—it will probably be a right angle, but it does not matter if it is not. What is important is that the edges are parallel with the joint and with each other. Bevel the edges (Fig. 7-20F). If this tool is put on a cylinder with an edge on a mark, a pencil line along the edge will be parallel with the axis of the cylinder.

The alternative to a cylindrical pedestal with three legs is an hexagonal pillar. The problem then is to get all six faces the same width and all angles of the section the same. Stepping off the radius around the circumference gives the six points of a regular hexagon (Fig. 7-20G). This is one way to get the shape. If you start with a square piece of wood, the size circle to work on is the distance across the flats of the square. The distance across the points of a hexagon is obviously more than the distance across the flats, so you cannot include the existing flat of a square piece, but if you start with wood wider than it is thick, two faces may be used as part of the hexagon. In that case, draw a circle to touch the edges (Fig. 7-20H). Shaping can be done by planing, in the way that would have been used by the original craftsmen, but with the tilting fence of a table saw or jointer, the six faces can be trued with less effort and more precision.

The part of the pedestal where the leg joints come does not have to be parallel, but laying out the joints is easier if it is. There could be a regular slight taper, but decorative beads and other turned shapes are better kept away from the area of the joints.

Joints in original construction were mostly mortise and tenons. Making a full-size drawing of a section of the pedestal will show how deep the tenons can go. They should not meet, as that might weaken the pedestal, but they should go as deep as reasonably possible. This sort of joint cannot be strengthened by dowels across the tenons and it is important to give as large a side-grain glue area as possible (Fig. 7-21A).

Where the shoulders of the tenoned legs come against the pedestal, they may be undercut to make a close fit (Fig. 7-21B). This was sometimes done, but a more usual way was to flatten the pedestal for the width of each leg, so shoulders were cut squarely (Fig. 7-21C). In most cases two narrow tenons are better than one long one on a leg (Fig. 7-21D).

Dowels can be arranged in a similar way to tenons, with the pedestal cut flat to give a good bearing for the leg, which should be planed to fit closely (Fig. 7-21E).

In most constructions the legs meet the pedestal a short distance above its bottom and this should be stronger than having them level with the end. Some originals have the legs

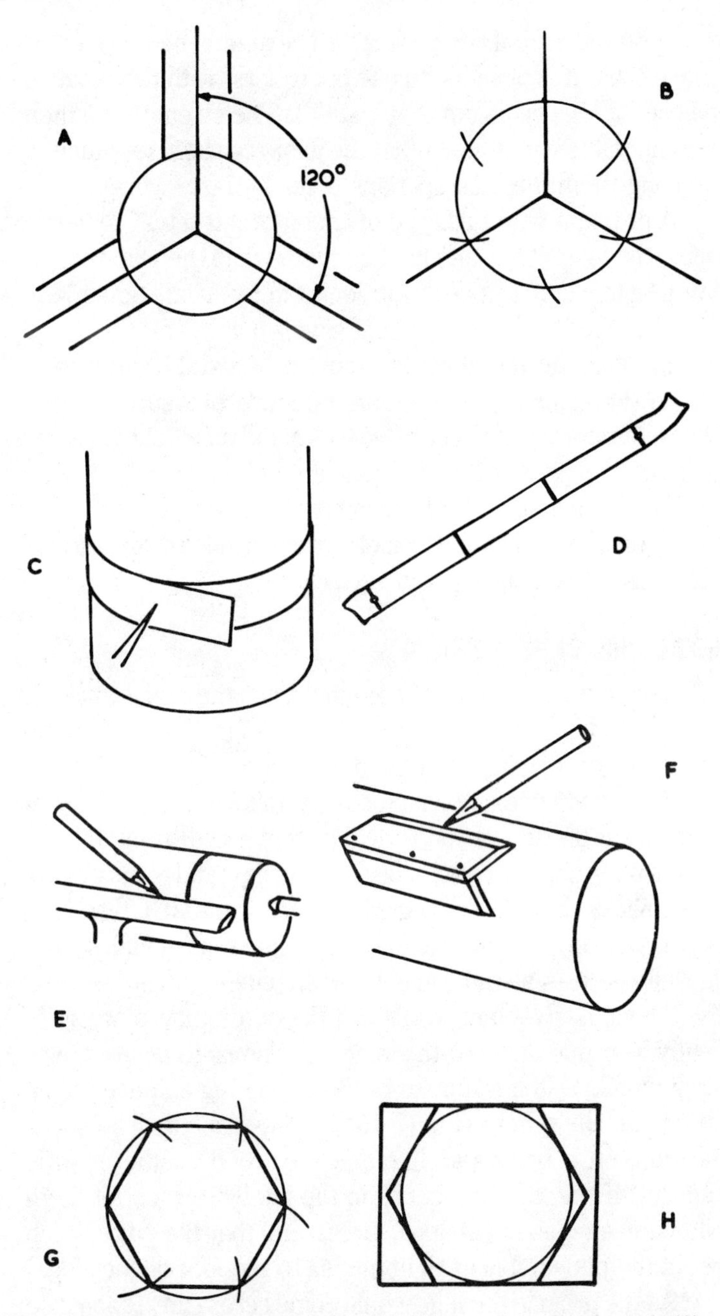


Fig. 7-20. Legs for tilt-top and candle tables have to be spaced evenly (A), obtained by geometry (B) or with a strip of paper (C and D). Lines may be drawn in a lathe (E) or with a jig (F). The pillar can be marked hexagonal (G and H).

level with the end of the pedestal. They could be doweled or tenoned, but it is possible to use open slots, with the reduced ends of the legs sliding in (Fig. 7-21F). The strength will then be comparable with tenons, but the joints can be strengthened by giving them dovetail sections (Fig. 7-21G).

A problem with this type of tripod construction comes in pulling the joints tight and holding them while the glue sets. It may be sufficient to press the joints in by hand. Some legs were designed with patterns that gave a bearing for the pad of a clamp opposite the joint, but most legs had flowing curves with nowhere for a clamp to give effective pressure. Sometimes a temporary block of wood was glued on to take a clamp, but a better way is to leave a small area of the actual leg (Fig. 7-21H). The clamp squeezes against that and it is not difficult to cut it off afterwards and fashion the surface to the final shape when it is known the joint is secure.

## HEXAGONAL CANDLE STAND

This is based on an early original when the cabinetmakers probably did not have access to a lathe (Fig. 7-22A). The top was arranged to tilt, but a fixed alternative is shown.

The central hexagonal piece is parallel in the length, but there is a little decoration provided above and below the leg joints with V-shaped cuts. These are shallow and made by cuts with a backsaw, using two guidelines (Fig. 7-22B). The projecting bottom can be beveled, but the top should be cut carefully so it is at right angles to the sides.

The legs sweep upwards and the outer curves are sufficiently near parallel over the joints for clamps to be used over scrap wood. Use a template or make one leg and use it as a pattern for the others (Fig. 7-22C) if they cannot all be cut at one time on a bandsaw. Arrange the wood so the grain is diagonal. If there is any curve in the lines of grain, let them follow the shapes of the legs. Be careful that the edge which meets the pedestal is at right angles to the foot of each leg.

As the grain in the legs would come across any tenons, so they would not be very strong, it is better to use dowels in these leg joints (Fig. 7-22D). The joints can be prepared, but

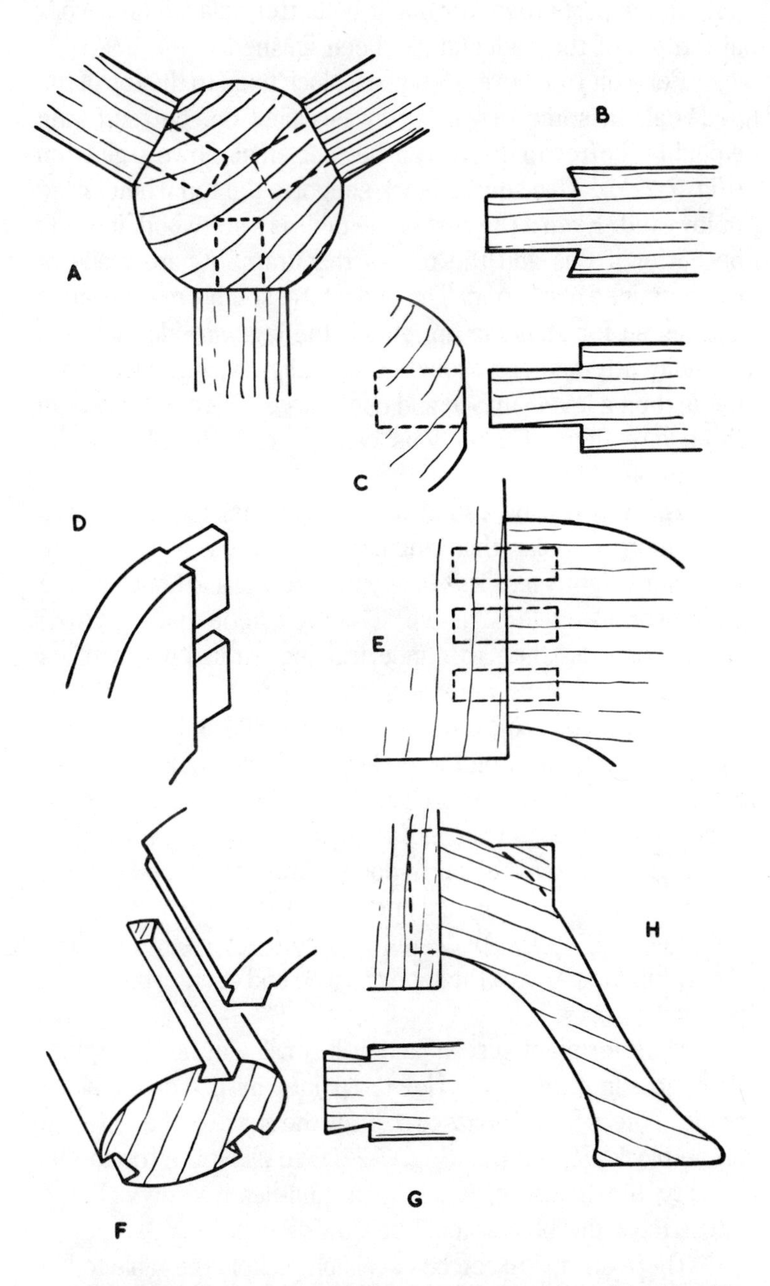


Fig. 7-21. Three legs fitted into a round pillar (A) may have shaped shoulders (B) or fit against flats (C). There may be tenons (D), dowels (E), or grooves (F and G). A temporary piece left on allows clamping (H).

putting the parts together might be better delayed until work at the top of the pedestal has been finished.

For a tilt top there is a square block fixed to the top of the pedestal. In some originals it was nailed on, but screwing would be better or there can be four small dowels glued in (Fig. 7-22E). This square block supports the top when raised or lowered. Even if the rest of the table is a softwood, it would be better if this and the pieces that frame it, are made of close-grained hardwood. The pedestal assembly may be glued and tested for standing upright. If the legs are identical and carefully fitted, there should be no difficulty, but check with the feet on a level surface and use a large try or set square in three directions. Corrections can be made by planing the bottom of a leg.

The top can be round, elliptical or hexagonal. Curves were more popular than angular shapes, possibly because there was slightly less risk of anyone passing and knocking the table over. A circle is shown. The top can be made up from several boards, then the underframing arranged across its grain provides some resistance to warping.

Two braces are fixed to the top, parallel and each side of the supporting block on the pedestal. They should be across the grain of the top and in the same direction as the grain of the pedestal block. Taper the ends almost to nothing, so they are not obvious when the top is down. Another piece between these braces is best tenoned into them (Fig. 7-22F). When the top is central on the pedestal, this comes loosely over the block. Fix the parts to the top with glue and counterbored and plugged screws.

Mark for pivot screws and drill small pilot holes through the braces into the block. Use the points marked on the block as the centers for compasses to draw the curve of the top edge of the block. Round this (Fig. 7-22G) to allow the top to tilt. Enlarge the holes to suit large round-head screws. For a larger table the pivots could be dowels or iron rods.

There are metal catches available to hold the table top in the down position and fittings of this type were available quite early, so using one need not necessarily be a departure from authenticity, but a simpler and older method of locking the top in position was a peg (Fig. 7-22H) pushed into a hole. This could be turned or hand whittled. It may have a hole in the end for a cord to another hole in a brace, so it does not become lost.

For a fixed table top the support does not have to be square, so a round or hexagonal piece of wood can be made to fit on the top of the pedestal. Tapering towards its edges will improve its appearance and allow for screws upwards into the top (Fig. 7-22J).

## SIMPLE ROUND CANDLE TABLE

Many candle tables and their larger counterparts had their pedestals turned. Some also had their tops turned, but this is only possible if the lathe has a sufficient swing. Turned tops usually have raised edges or may be molded around the rims. Leg shapes were related to the turned spindles. The plain turned spindles of a Shaker table had legs in simple curves, while a spindle with a bulbous outline and much turned decorations had legs with more flourishing outlines.

The plainly turned Shaker candle table gets its beauty from its proportions and fitness for purpose. As most of the lines are plain accurate workmanship is important as flaws will show up more than in an intricate design. Sizes may have to be modified to suit materials or the size of lathe, but the drawing is of normal proportions (Fig. 7-23A).

The bottom of the spindle is parallel and should be kept as thick as the wood allows for strength in the joints. After curving in, the taper towards the top is straight, then an enlarged part takes the top bolster on a dowel end (Fig. 7-23B). Make a hole of the size to be used in the bolster as a gauge for the size of the dowel.

The top bolster is also turned. It could be mounted on a faceplate, with the side that will be against the table top towards a plywood pad (Fig. 7-23C), or the hole can be drilled first and pushed on to a temporary mandrel (Fig. 7-23D).

The feet follow simple curves (Fig. 7-23E), with the grain following the long way as far as possible. The best joint is a dovetail, a sliding in from below (Fig. 7-23F).

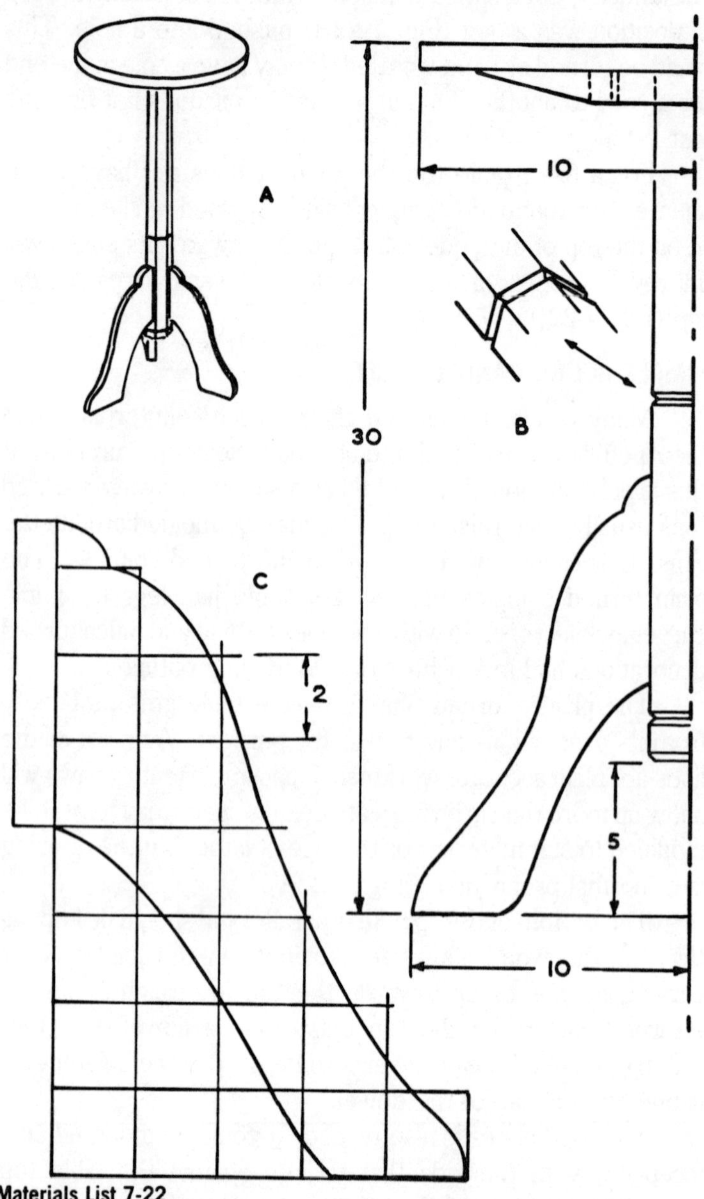


**Materials List 7-22**

Hexagon Candle Stand

| | | | | | |
|---|---|---|---|---|---|
| 1 | Post | 2½ × 25 × 2½ | 1 | Support | 3 × 3 × 1½ |
| 3 | Legs | 6 × 17 × 1 | 2 | Braces | 1½ × 18 × ¾ |
| 1 | To- | 1 × 20 × 1 | 1 | Brace | 1½ × 6 × ¾ |
| | | | 1 | Peg | ⅝ round × 4 |

Fig. 7-22. Hexagon candle stand. (Continued on next page.)

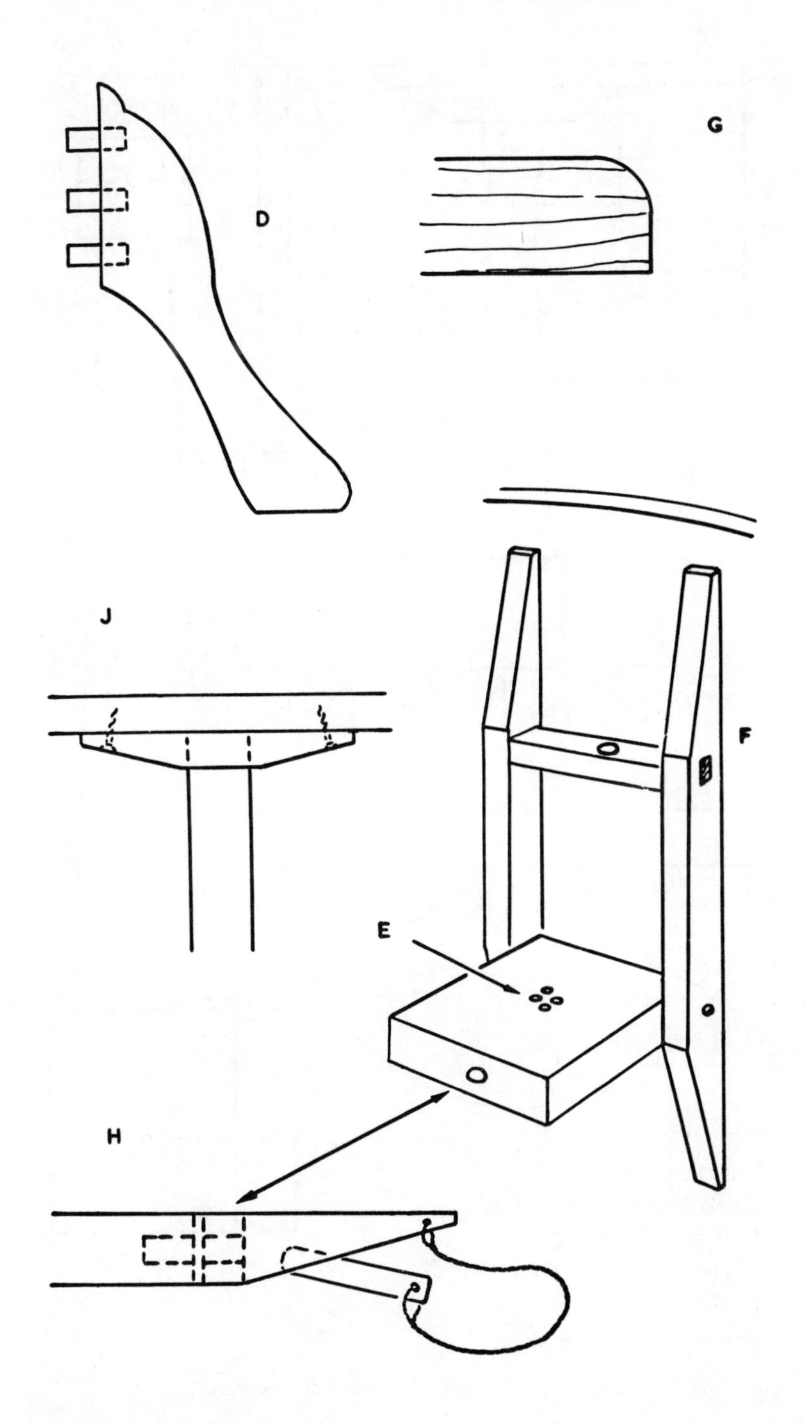
D
G
J
F
E
H

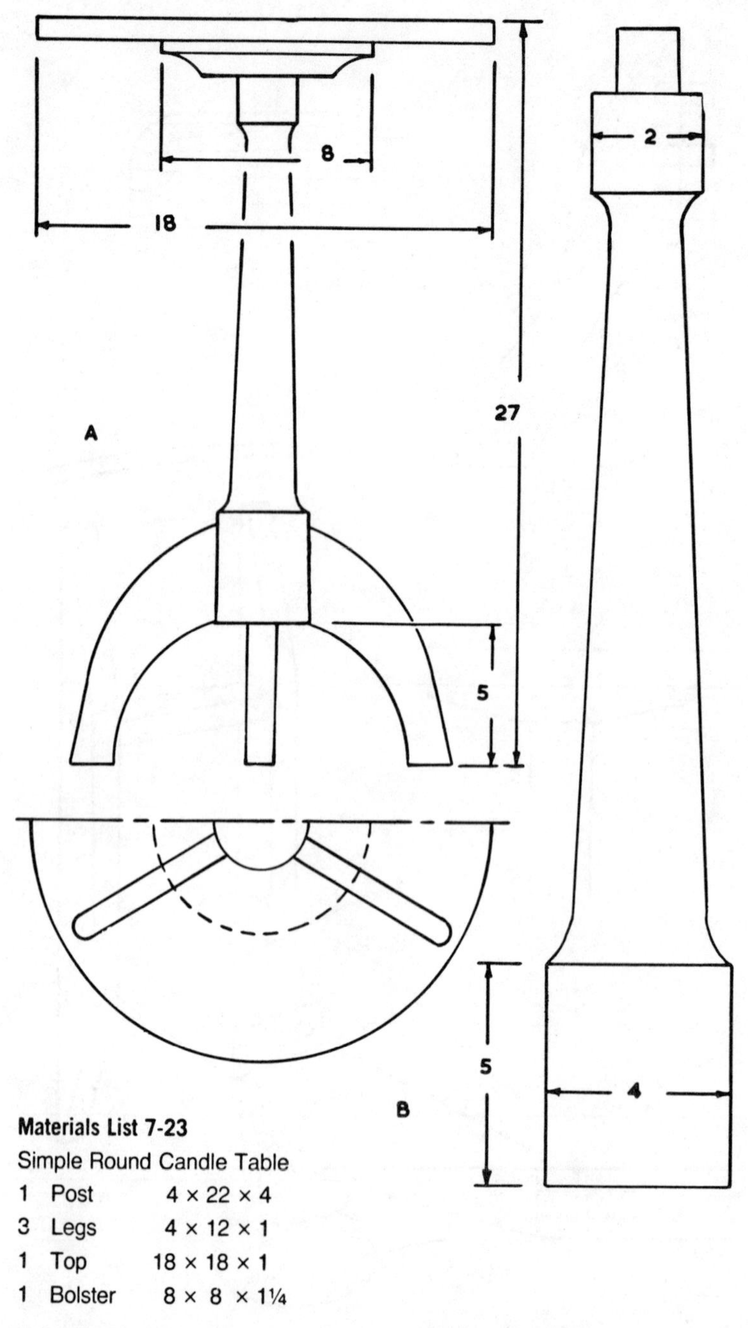


**Materials List 7-23**

Simple Round Candle Table

| | | |
|---|---|---|
| 1 | Post | 4 × 22 × 4 |
| 3 | Legs | 4 × 12 × 1 |
| 1 | Top | 18 × 18 × 1 |
| 1 | Bolster | 8 × 8 × 1¼ |

Fig. 7-23. Simple round candle table. (Continued on next page.)

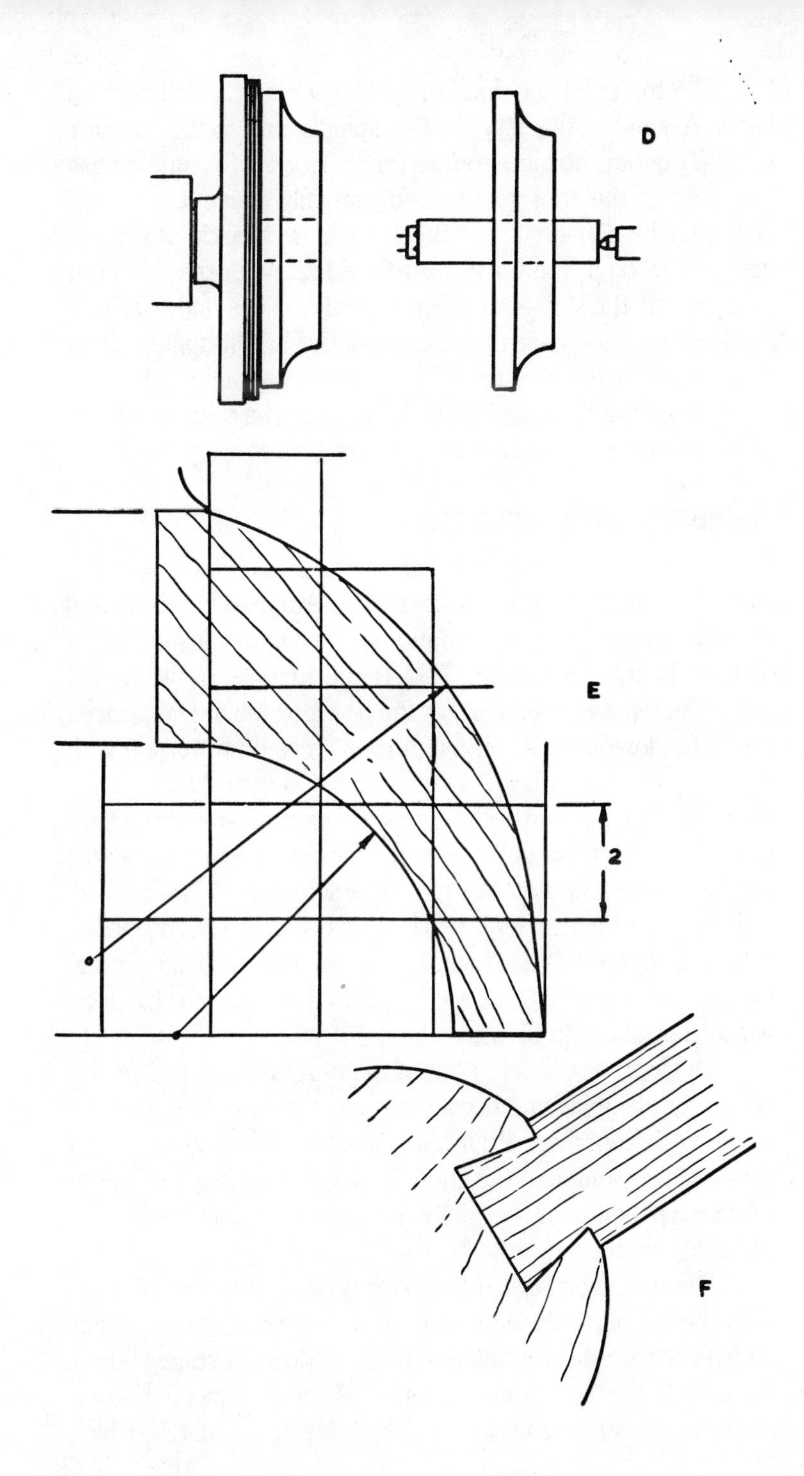
D
E
2
F

The top is a plain disc, either turned or carefully cut by hand. Assemble the legs to the spindle and fix the bolster centrally under the table top. Arrange its grain to come across the grain of the top, so the two mutually prevent warping. Glue may be sufficient, but there could be a circle of screws upwards through the bolster into the top. With the table top inverted, fit the dowel of the pedestal in place and check all round with a try square that the spindle is at right-angles to the top. Leave for the glue to set, then stand the table on its legs to see if it is upright and with the top parallel with the floor. Adjust by planing the bottoms of feet if necessary.

## ROUND TILT-TOP CANDLE TABLE

Most wood turners produced more elaborate spindles than those used by the Shakers. The example is typical and there were a great many variations, but general designs were similar. In this table (Fig. 7-24A) the method of fitting and tilting the top is the same as for the hexagon table. Differences are in the lower parts, although tops were often turned with raised rims when a large-swing lathe was available.

The spindle is at its maximum diameter at three points (Fig. 7-24B): at the bulbous part, just above the part where the legs come, and at the top. The lower part is a parallel cylinder, but the main length follows classical lines. The sweep of the curve towards the top is broken by a single bead. At the top the end is turned to a large dowel to fit into the top block on which the table top pivots.

The legs (Fig. 7-24C) are of the type where a pad should be left for clamping and tenons are the correct joints. Cut the wood to the outlines, then mark and cut the tenons. Chisel flats on the cylinder so the shoulders will come level when the joints are pulled tight. Do all the work on the joints, but do not assemble them yet.

The legs look best if they are given a rounded section. Only the last parts close to the pedestal remain angular. To get an even curve the rounding should be done in stages—first beveling the same amount all round. A notched piece of wood can be used with a pencil to mark the bevel (Fig. 7-24D), which is then worked with chisel, spokeshave or Surform tool. When the bevel is the same all round (Fig. 7-24E), its sharpness is removed and the edges further rounded by sanding (Fig. 7-24F). A suitable cutter in a spindle molder or router would also do the bulk of the shaping, but the final finish should be by hand. Under curves are not as important, but a good smooth flowing curve should be on the outside of each leg and the foot against the floor should show an almost elliptical outline. Get all three to the same shape for a neat finish.

Of course, the clamping pads will delay complete shaping of each leg. Glue the mortise and tenon joints. To avoid damage to the cylinder, make a curved block to go under the clamp (Fig. 7-24G). Although it is possible to glue all three legs in place at the same time, positioning the clamps becomes difficult and it would be better to glue and clamp the legs one at a time (Fig. 7-24H). Cut away the clamping blocks and complete the shaping of the legs.

When the pedestal has been assembled, completion of the table is the same as for the hexagon tilt-top table (Fig. 7-24I).

## OTHER CANDLE TABLES

Although three shaped legs around a central spindle or post made up the usual arrangement for a small table for a candle or lamp, there were other constructions.

Two feet could be cross lapped and the post tenoned or doweled at their center (Fig. 7-25A). With a basically deep section, there was strength and weight at the center, then the extremities were tapered. The underside could be shaped, but it was simpler to put pads under the ends.

With this arrangement of feet it was logical to do the same under a fixed top, although for a tilt top a solid block was used. With four feet the spindle could be just a square post (Fig. 7-25B), it could have wagon beveling, be made octagonal, or be turned.

Four feet are acceptable on modern flat floors, but on the early uneven floors, three feet were almost obligatory and there is an interesting Shaker variation of the cross-lapped

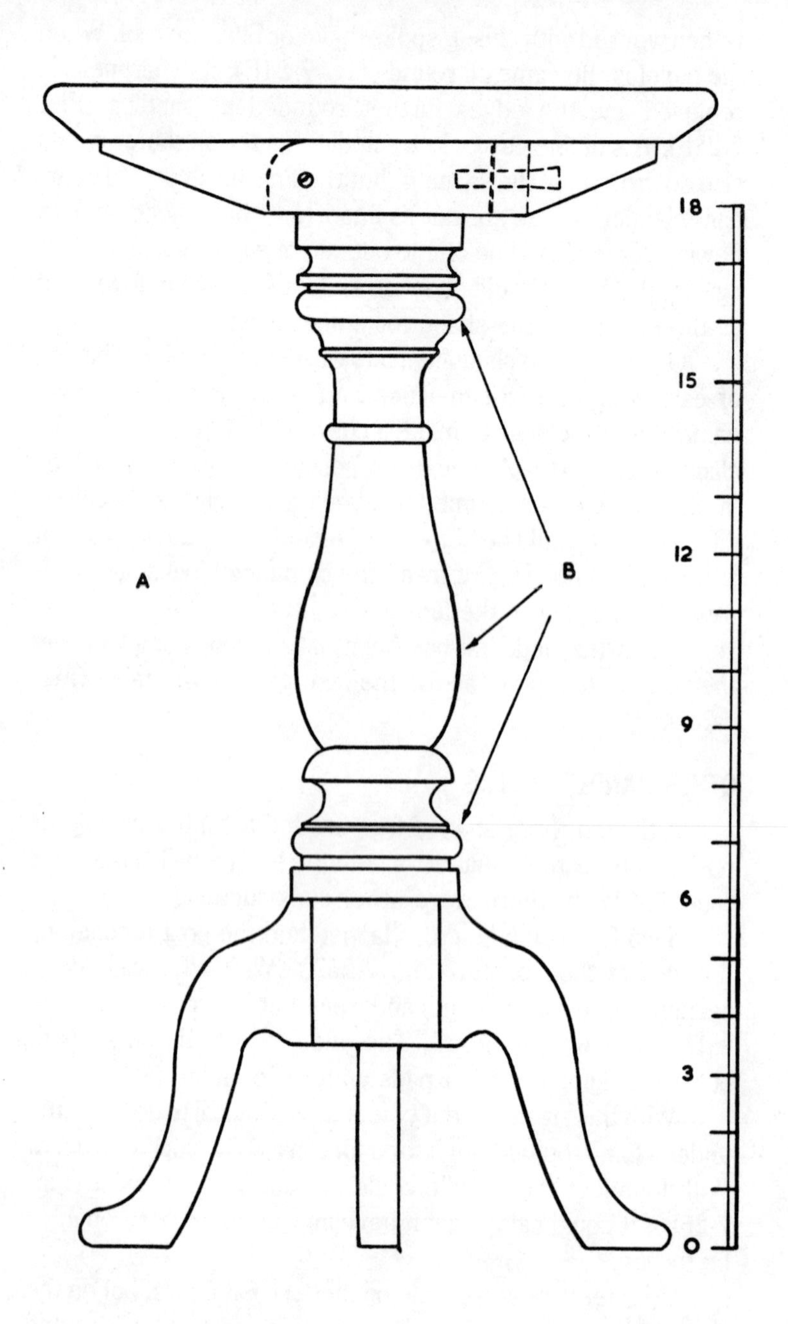


Fig. 7-24 Round tilt-top candle table. (Continued on next page.)

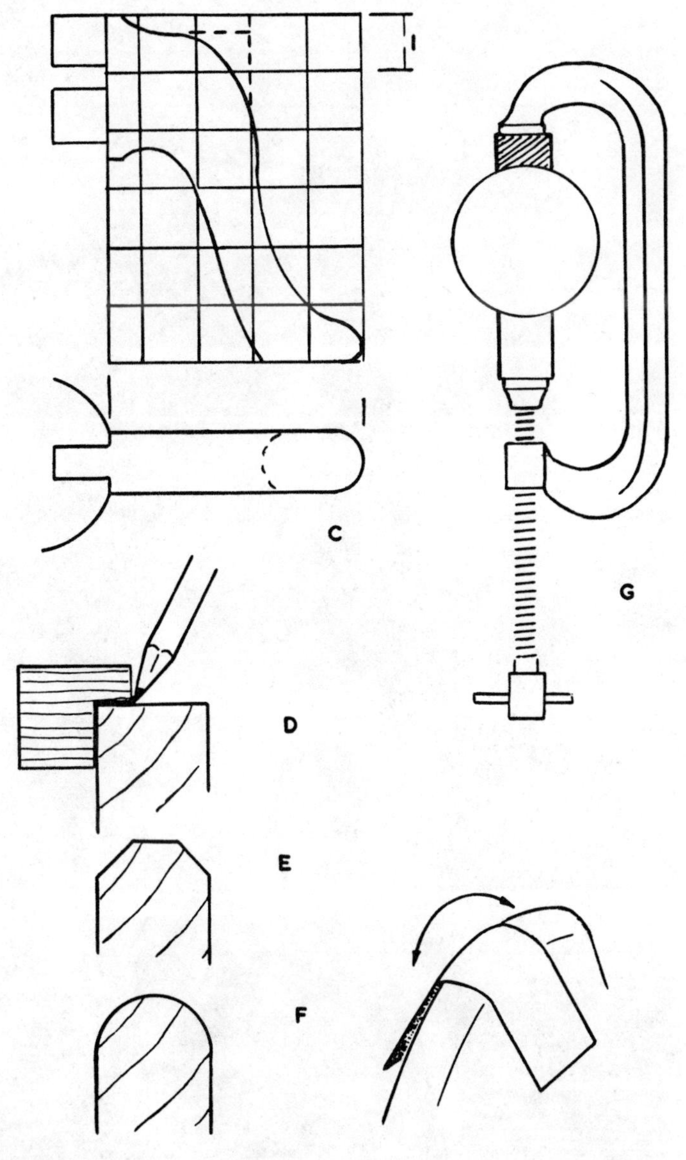


**Materials List 7-24**

Round Tilt-Top Candle Table

| | | |
|---|---|---|
| 1 | Post | 3 × 16 × 3 |
| 3 | Legs | 3½ × 9 × 1 |
| 1 | Top | 12 × 12 × 1 |
| 1 | Support | 4 × 4 × 1½ |
| 2 | Braces | 1½ × 10 × ¾ |
| 1 | Brace | 1½ × 6 × ¾ |
| 1 | Peg | ⅝ round × 4 |

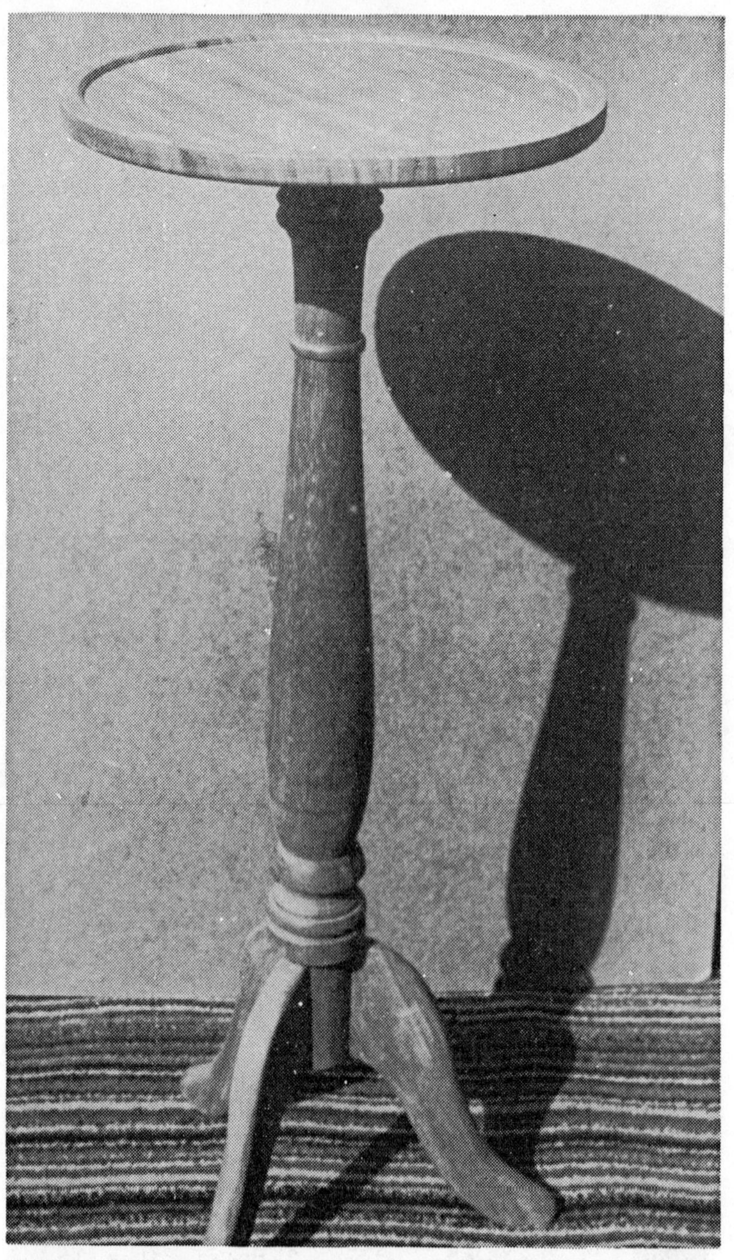

Fig. 7-24H. The parts of a candle stand. The legs have been marked from a template and include clamping pads to be removed after fixing. One leg is clamped in place, with a pad at the other side to prevent damage. The top has a turned pad fixed underneath, with a hole to take the dowel at the top of the pedestal.

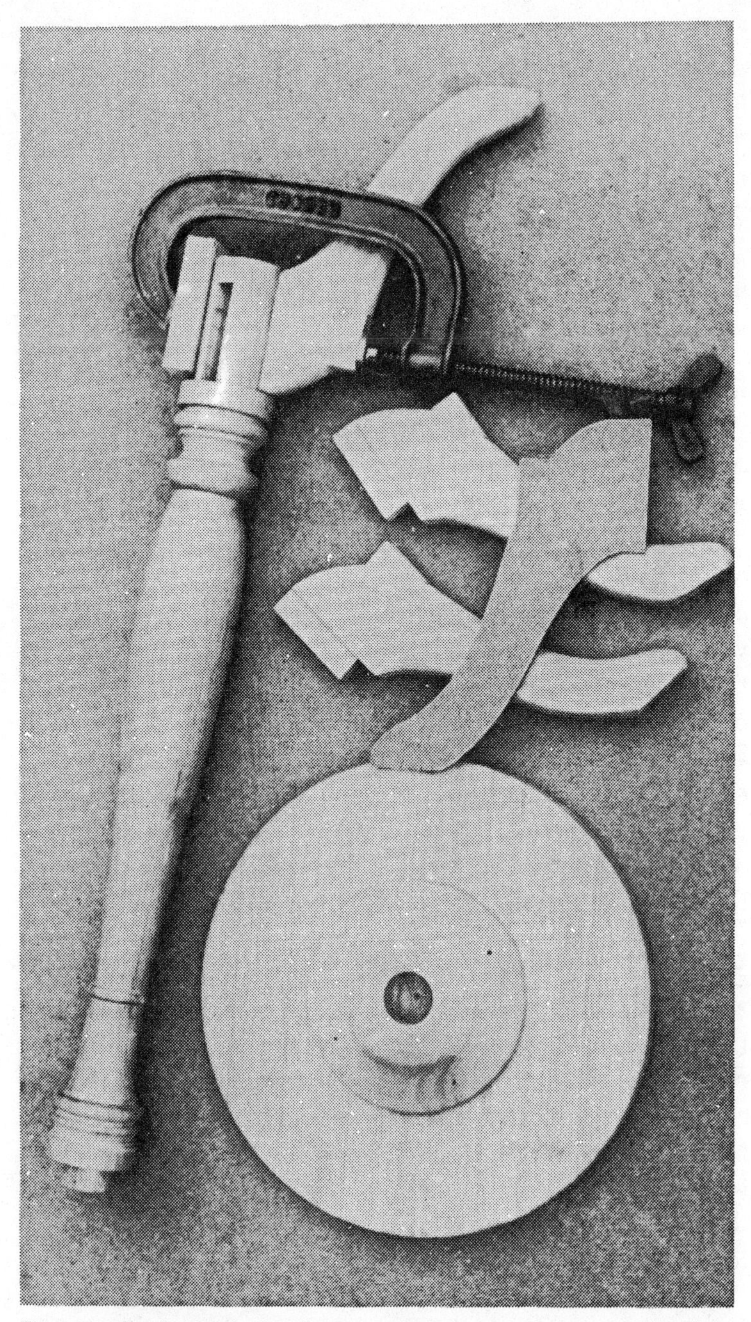

Fig. 7-24I. Candle stand with a fixed top,made in the same way as a small round three-legged table, with the legs tenoned into the pedestal and the pedestal doweled into a pad under the top.

feet to get only three bearing surfaces. This has the two pieces joined in a T-shape, with the spindle or post on the leg of the T (Fig. 7-25C).

The top of a fixed table then has a single bar across the underside, in a direction to control any tendency to warp (Fig. 7-25D). In a Shaker table the turned spindle has no concessions to decoration, except a slight taper, which could be larger at the top or the bottom (Fig. 7-25E), with dowels to make the joints at the ends.

## REVOLVING TILTING TABLE

Tilting tables of many sizes were common in Europe and America, but a type of table that would revolve as well as tilt was more particularly American. This was arranged with a "bird's cage" or "crow's nest" at the top of the pedestal. This consisted of two square pieces with corner posts, that was arranged to revolve on the shaft projecting from the pedestal, while the table top pivoted on the top square piece. Most of the tops were round, and the construction was used for tables of dining size as well as for smaller tables for lamps or candles. The specimen shown (Fig. 7-26A) is of candle table size, but a dining table could be made with a thicker and longer spindle under a larger top.

The feet and the lower part of the pedestal are similar to those in tables already described. The three feet are fitted into dovetail slots or mortises in the post. The turned design is generally similar to a previous table, but the top is turned with a shaft extension in two diameters and a slot is cut through to take a wedge (Fig. 7-26B). To get the slot marked accurately on opposite sides of the shaft, wrap a piece of paper around and push a spike through the overlap. Remove the paper and fold it midway between the spike holes (Fig. 7-26C). This represents half the circumference. Put the paper back around the shaft and mark the spike hole and fold positions. Use these to locate the setting out of the slot.

The bird's cage is made of two boards. One is a plain square, but the other is the same size with two dowels cut to project from it (Fig. 7-26D). Traditionally these were cut in

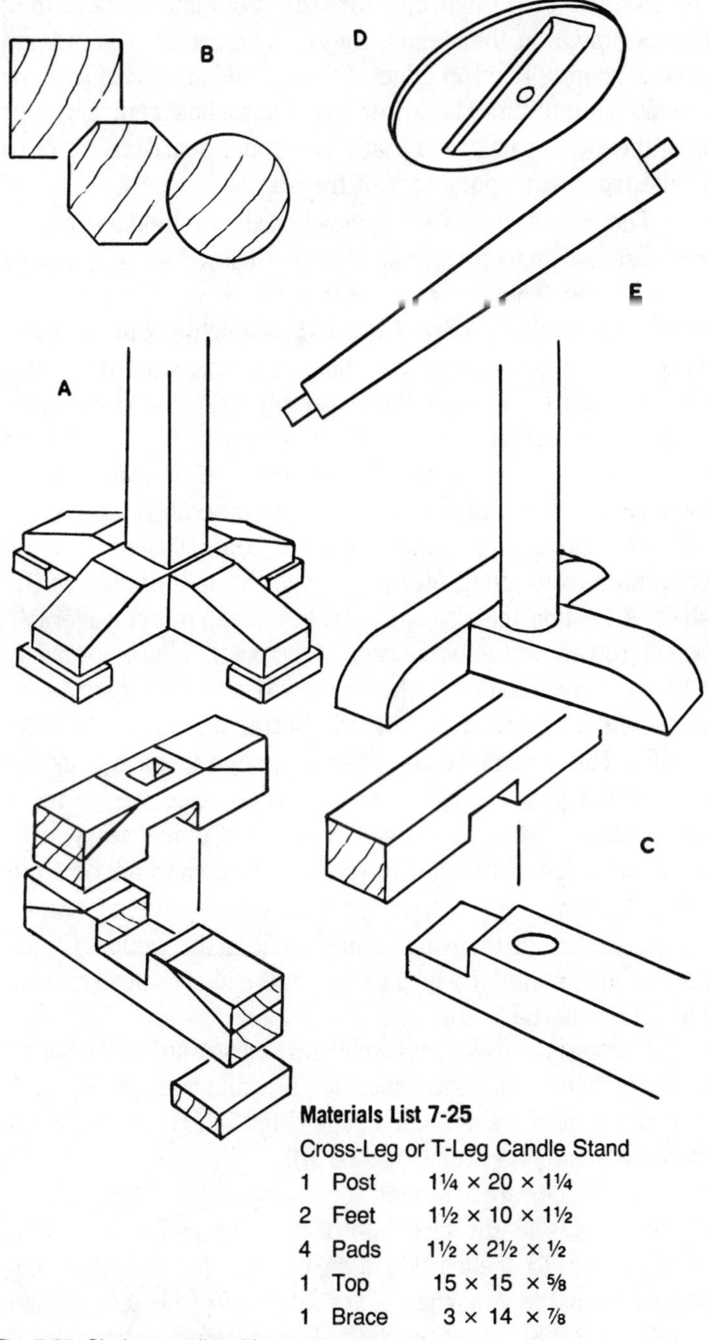


**Materials List 7-25**

Cross-Leg or T-Leg Candle Stand

| | | |
|---|---|---|
| 1 | Post | 1¼ × 20 × 1¼ |
| 2 | Feet | 1½ × 10 × 1½ |
| 4 | Pads | 1½ × 2½ × ½ |
| 1 | Top | 15 × 15 × ⅝ |
| 1 | Brace | 3 × 14 × ⅞ |

Fig. 7-25. Shaker candle table.

the solid wood. If the projections are first made square, then circles drawn on their ends, they can be carefully pared and sanded round. The top edge of the board is rounded to allow the table top to tilt. The lower board has a hole centrally to fit over the lower part of the shaft. The upper board has a hole to fit the narrower upper part of the shaft.

The upper and lower square boards are held at the correct distance apart by four spindles with dowel ends into holes in the boards. These are turned to patterns which match those of the main pedestal (Fig. 7-26E). The heights of the spindles at the corners of the square boards should hold them at a distance apart so when the assembly rests on the central shaft, the top of the shaft does not quite pass through the top board. It will probably be best to make the central shaft too long at first and trim it to length after assembly.

The bird's cage, and the table top attached to it, is prevented from lifting off by a wedge through the slot in the shaft. A load on the rim of the table top can put considerable bending strain on the bird's cage at the pivot. This is spread by a wooden washer under the wedge. It could be a square of wood under the wedge, but it is better if it is turned (Fig. 7-26F). The wedge or key is long enough to pass over the washer and project slightly (Fig. 7-26G). The wedge must thrust against the top of the slot in the shaft. If necessary, trim the lower edge of the slot to give clearance and prevent the wedge binding there instead of pressing on the washer. Make the groove across the washer an easy fit on the wedge. Check the fit and action of the bird's cage on the shaft before making and fitting the table top.

The top is a circle, preferably turned on a lathe. If it has to be cut by hand it may be a plain circle with rounded edges. A turned top can have a molded edge (Fig. 7-26H) or be given a lip and a sunken center (Fig. 7-26J).

Two braces are arranged across the underside of the top, at right angles to the direction of its grain and at a suitable distance apart to fit each side of the bird's cage. The projecting dowels from the top square are level with the surface, so recesses for them must touch the top edges of the braces and are most easily cut by drilling, then trimming with a chisel (Fig. 7-26K). If a catch is bought to hold the table down, the braces can be fixed with glue and screws independently to the top, but if a peg is to be used, add a cross brace (Fig. 7-26L).

Check the action in all positions. If necessary, lubricate with graphite or candle grease. Do not use oil or mineral grease. Disassemble as much as possible for finishing with stain and polish.

## TIER TABLE

Early table makers who had developed their skills with simple treadle lathes expanded their turned work to produce tables with tops at two levels—usually with a smaller top above the main top so the assembly could act as a side table for foods to be served on the main dining table, or as a place for fruit or candies to be eaten between meals. Such a tier table could be made without turned parts, but it has a more graceful appearance if the main parts are made on a lathe.

Several variations are possible. The main support could be a central pedestal with three legs, then a turned pillar continues to support the upper tier. The lower part could be a table made in another way, possibly with three legs, then the central pillar taken up to the upper tier. Some tables had a further turned piece extending a short way above the top tier, to act as a handle for lifting a light table, to serve food to guests. The central pedestal version could be made similar to one of the tables described earlier, then a spindle to the upper tier could be doweled into its center (Fig. 7-27A). The top of the spindle goes into a bolster made like the one below the main table top and the wood above it is made to match the larger piece (Fig. 7-27B).

If a three-legged version is made (Fig. 7-28A), the main feature is the central pillar assembly, but it is logical to also turn the legs. However, some of these tables had the legs made with square or octagonal sections and a moderate taper. If turned legs are used, they are best made with simple outlines, so as not to detract from the central turnings, and given dowel ends to fit into angled blocks at the top (Fig.

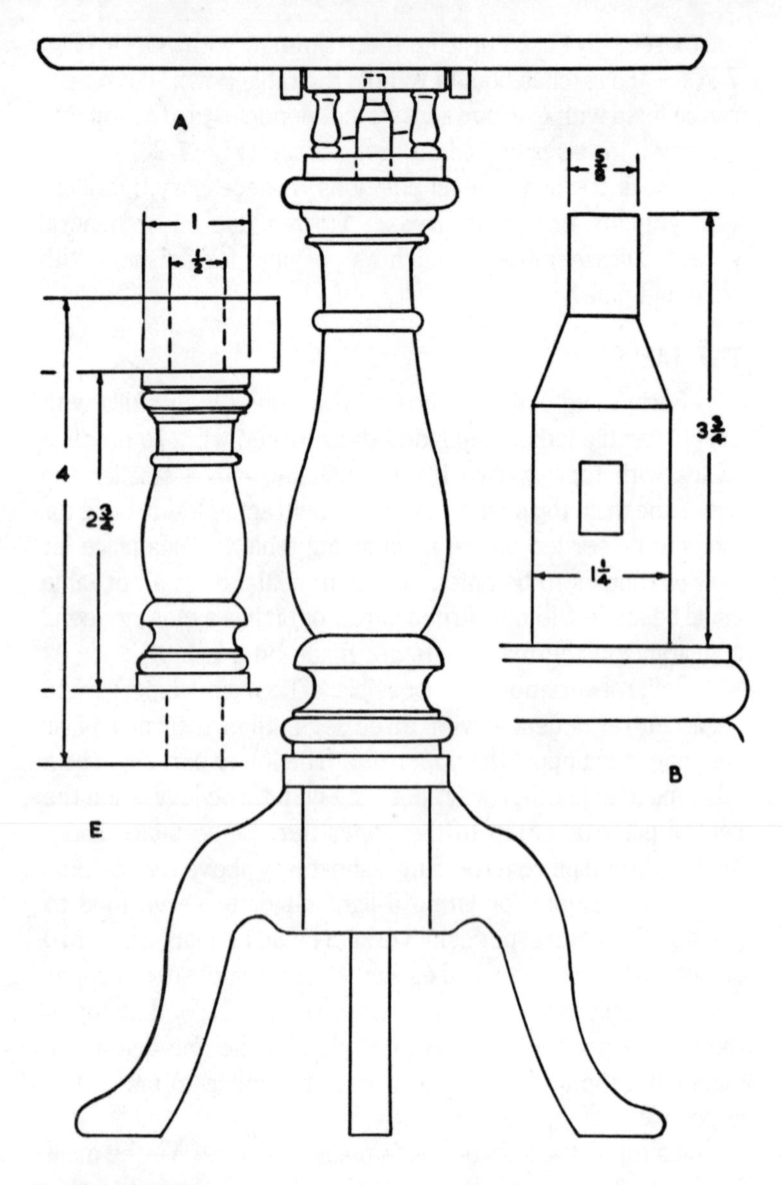


**Materials List 7-26**

| Revolving Tilting Table | | | | | |
|---|---|---|---|---|---|
| 1 | Top | 12 × 12 × 7/8 | 2 | Cages | 5 × 7 × 7/8 |
| 3 | Legs | 5 × 16 × 1 | 4 | Posts | 1 × 4 × 1 |
| 1 | Pedestal | 3 × 16 × 3 | 1 | Wedge | 1 × 4 × 3/8 |
| | | | 2 | Braces | 1¼ × 10 × 7/8 |

Fig. 7-26. Revolving tilting table. (Continued on next page.)

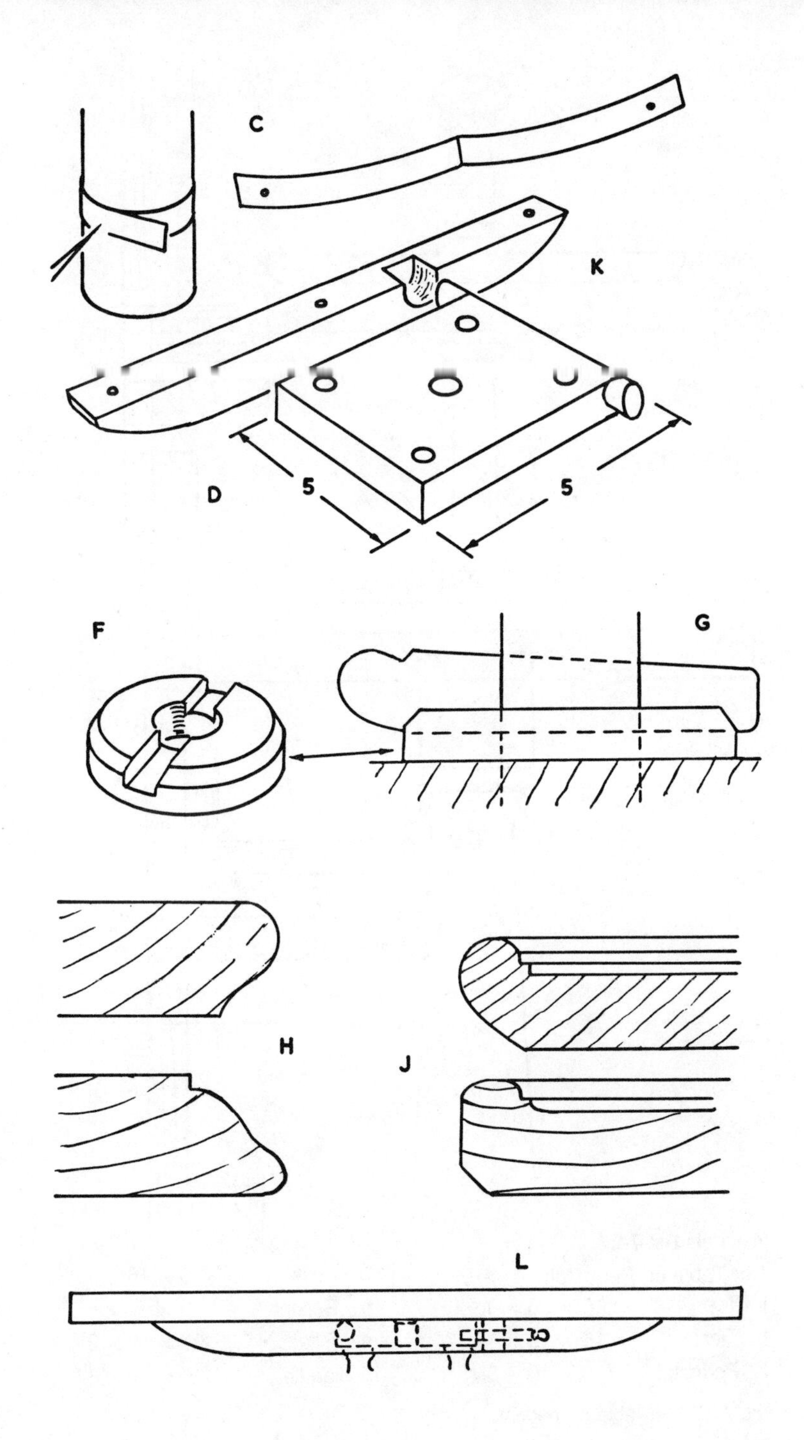
C
K
D
5
5
F
G
H
J
L

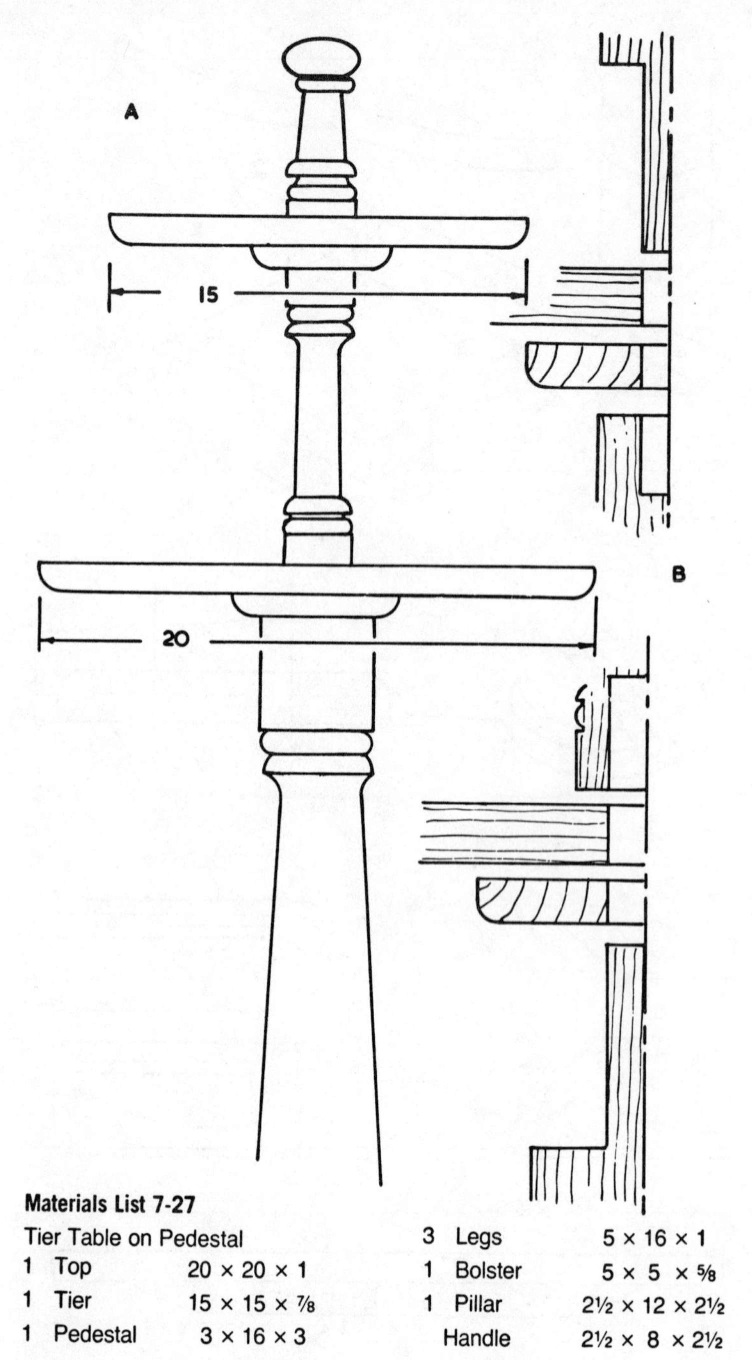


**Materials List 7-27**

Tier Table on Pedestal

| | | |
|---|---|---|
| 1 | Top | 20 × 20 × 1 |
| 1 | Tier | 15 × 15 × 7/8 |
| 1 | Pedestal | 3 × 16 × 3 |
| 3 | Legs | 5 × 16 × 1 |
| 1 | Bolster | 5 × 5 × 5/8 |
| 1 | Pillar | 2½ × 12 × 2½ |
| | Handle | 2½ × 8 × 2½ |

Fig. 7-27. Tier table on pedestal.

7-28B). These angled blocks under the table top allow of accurate setting of the slopes of the legs and make stronger joints than having the doweled ends going directly into holes in the table top. The method also avoids the need to cut the shoulders of the turnings at an angle where they meet the flat wood.

The drawing shows an extension of the central turned pillar above the top tier, for use as a handle, but this can be omitted to give a clear surface if the stand is intended to be used for a large dish or a plant pot. Although the underside of the table is not normally visible, it is good craftsmanship to arrange another turned piece below its center (Fig. 7-28C). This is not essential, but it gives a good finish to the piece of furniture (Fig. 7-28D).

The method of construction depends on facilities available to make the two large diameter discs. If they are too large to be turned on the lathe, they can be given plain outlines, carefully sawn, then the edges rounded or beveled, depending on available tools. A spindle molder can work a pattern, but machine work should be followed by enough hand work to disguise the method used. The alternative for making without a lathe is to cut the wood hexagonal, or twelve sided (Fig. 7-28E).

Central holes through the discs are made to suit dowels turned on the spindle parts. The bearing surfaces of the turned parts should be increased by thin turned discs, otherwise there is a danger of rather narrow jointed areas weakening and becoming loose after some use. These pads or washers need not be round, but they continue the entire theme of the design if they are (Fig. 7-28F). The two are similar to each other, but the upper one can be slightly smaller and thinner.

The main pillar is given a classical taper (Fig. 7-28G). If there will not be a turned part below the lower tier, make a dowel end long enough to go through the tier and pad below. If there is to be a turned part below, it is easier to turn the parts so the main pillar has holes for dowels at both ends. Getting the parts to assemble accurately depends on the fit of the joints and it is wiser to turn the ends of the main spindle so they

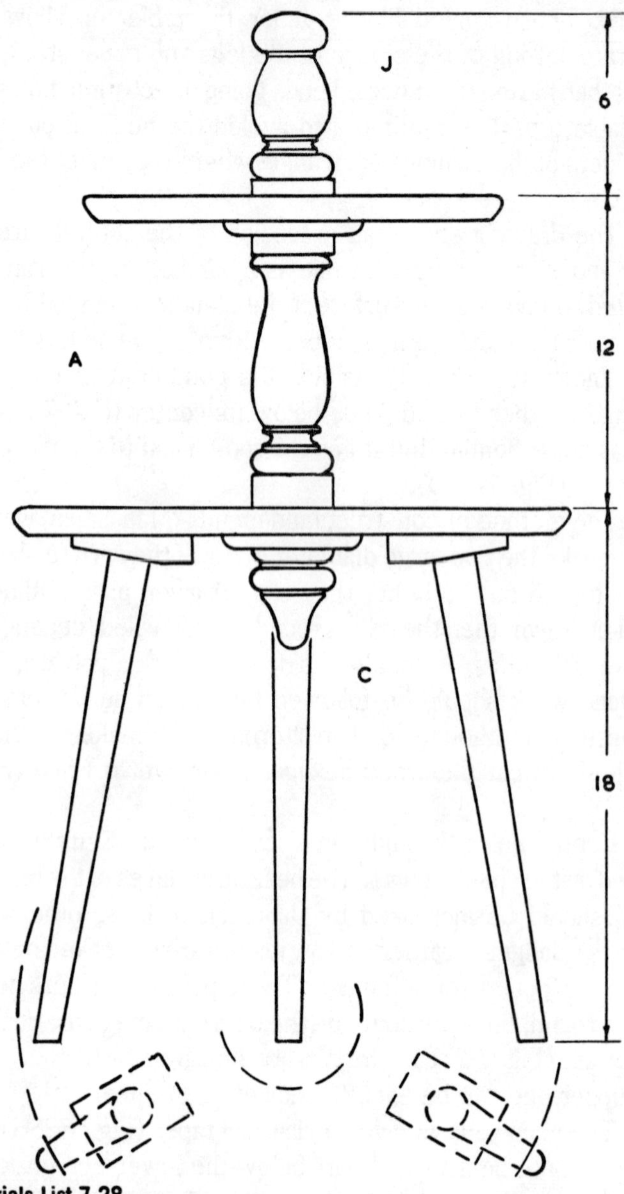


**Materials List 7-28**

Tier Table on Three Legs

| | | | | | |
|---|---|---|---|---|---|
| 1 | Top | 20 × 20 × 1 | 1 | Handle | 2½ × 8 × 2½ |
| 1 | Tier | 15 × 15 × ⅞ | 2 | Bolsters | 5 × 5 × ⅝ |
| 1 | Pillar | 2½ × 12 × 2½ | 3 | Legs | 1½ × 20 × 1½ |

Fig. 7-28. Tier table on three legs. (Continued on next page.)

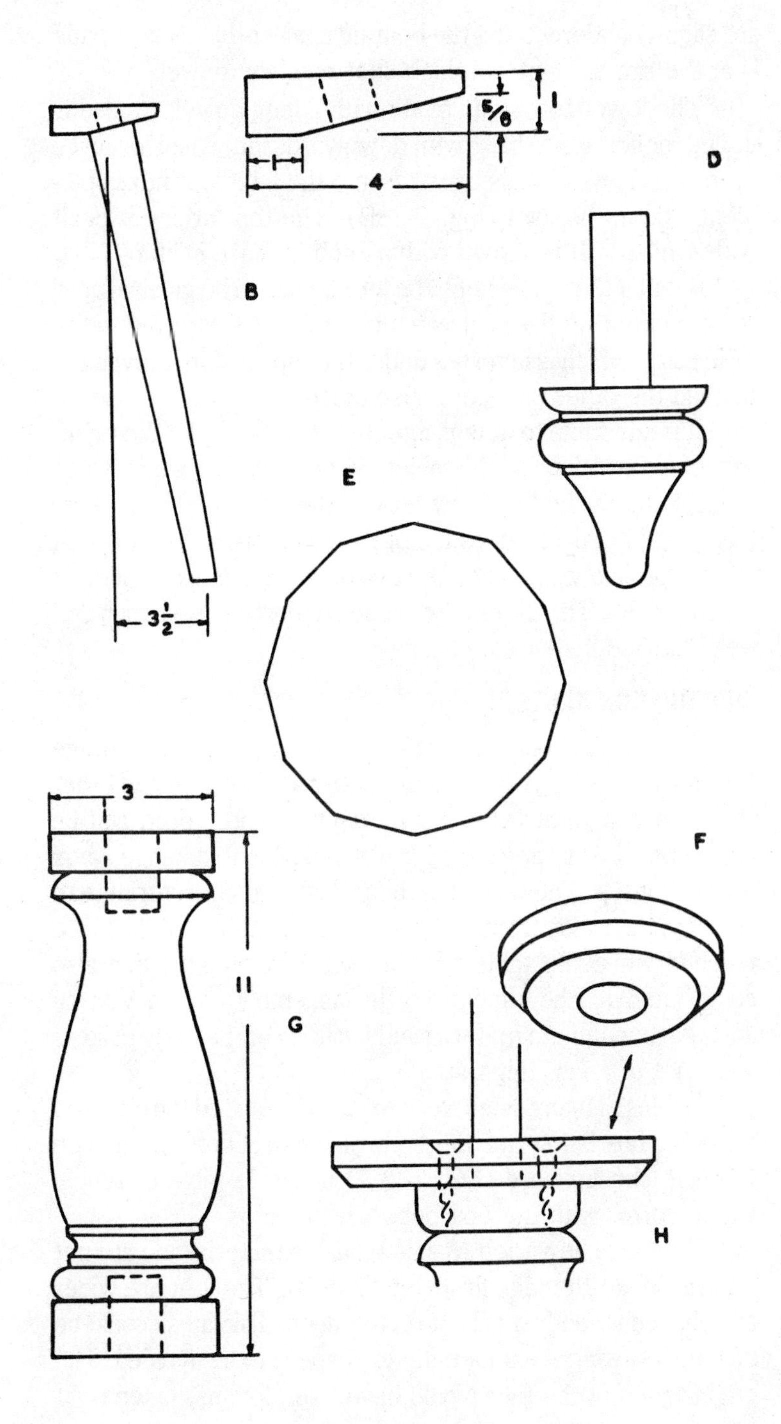

5/8
1
D
1
4
B
3 1/2
E
3
F
11
G
H

are slightly undercut and the bearing against the discs or pads is at the rim and not at a high spot near the dowel.

The lower turning is made with a long dowel. Its pad is drilled for screws to be driven downwards into it and for three or more screws to pass upwards into the tabletop and supplement glue in the joint (Fig. 7-28H). The top turning is dealt with similarly. It is shown with a knob for ease in lifting (Fig. 7-28J), but if the unit is not to be lifted, it could be given a taper or be omitted. In the final assembly the pad is screwed to the main pillar, which is inverted under the top tier for screwing to it, then the other parts are assembled.

It is advisable to fit legs into their blocks and let their glue set before attaching to the tabletop. The central assembly can probably be pushed tight by hand if the joints are a good fit. Clamping is difficult, because of the large discs. The original makers probably squeezed the two doweled joints in a cider or cheese press. The assembly can be supported on a bench and weights used instead of clamps.

## TILT-TOP BOX TABLE

A table that combined its normal purpose with storage had obvious uses. A drawer under allowed cutlery and other things of comparatively shallow depth to be stored and be accessible. For larger things it was possible to arrange a box under a tilt top. The weight of things inside might contribute to stability, but a disadvantage was that the contents could not be reached while the table was in use. Box construction also contributed to the rigidity of the assembly, which was an advantage when the material and facilities of the early makers were not of a very high standard.

Tables of many sizes were made so the tilted top exposed a storage box below and methods of construction varied. The example chosen here (Fig. 7-29A) is a side table of simple trestle form, with the box between the ends.

Sizes can be varied to suit available material and are not critical. Make the legs first (Fig. 7-29B). The feet are wider and shaped so end pads rest on the floor. Thickness could be built up if sawing the underside to shape is to be avoided. The original joint at the feet would have been tenons, taken right through (Fig. 7-29C). In a reproduction table there could be a doweled joint (Fig. 7-29D), if that can be more conveniently worked.

The sides of the box overlap notches in the legs and many early tables were simply nailed or screwed (Fig. 7-29E). A better construction uses a rabbet, so nails can be driven both ways (Fig. 7-29F). Check for squareness when the box parts have been assembled to the legs.

In a modern construction, a plywood bottom could be let into plowed grooves during assembly (Fig. 7-29G). As the edges of the plywood would not be visible, this may be acceptable. In the most primitive construction the bottom was made of boards nailed from below, but for a neater appearance the bottom was made of thin boards with their grain across the box, supported in strips around the sides and ends (Fig. 7-29H).

The top pivots on two pegs or dowels. They could be plain pieces of dowel rod, or they are more authentic if turned (Fig. 7-29J). The pivot corner should be laid out full-size. Keep the holes fairly close to the box sides and at the center or lower on the top braces; otherwise the top will not swing clear and finish in an upright position. If the table is made of softwood, there may be reinforcing strips across inside the tops of the legs. Draw a curve to indicate the swing of the top over the edge (Fig. 7-29K). This shows the amount the back of the box has to be rounded to provide clearance.

The top shown could be a rectangle with rounded corners, but it could be round or elliptical (Fig. 7-29L). The braces are best glued and held with counterbored screws from below. Their distance apart should allow free movement over the box. If a tilt-top metal catch is used, it can be arranged centrally to engage with a slot in the box side. Another method of securing is to drill the opposite side of the leg tops for pegs. To avoid confusion these could be slightly smaller and turned with knobs for ease of withdrawal (Fig. 7-29M).

## SEAT TABLE

When a tilt-top table had the top swung to a vertical position to take up less space against a wall, there was obvi-

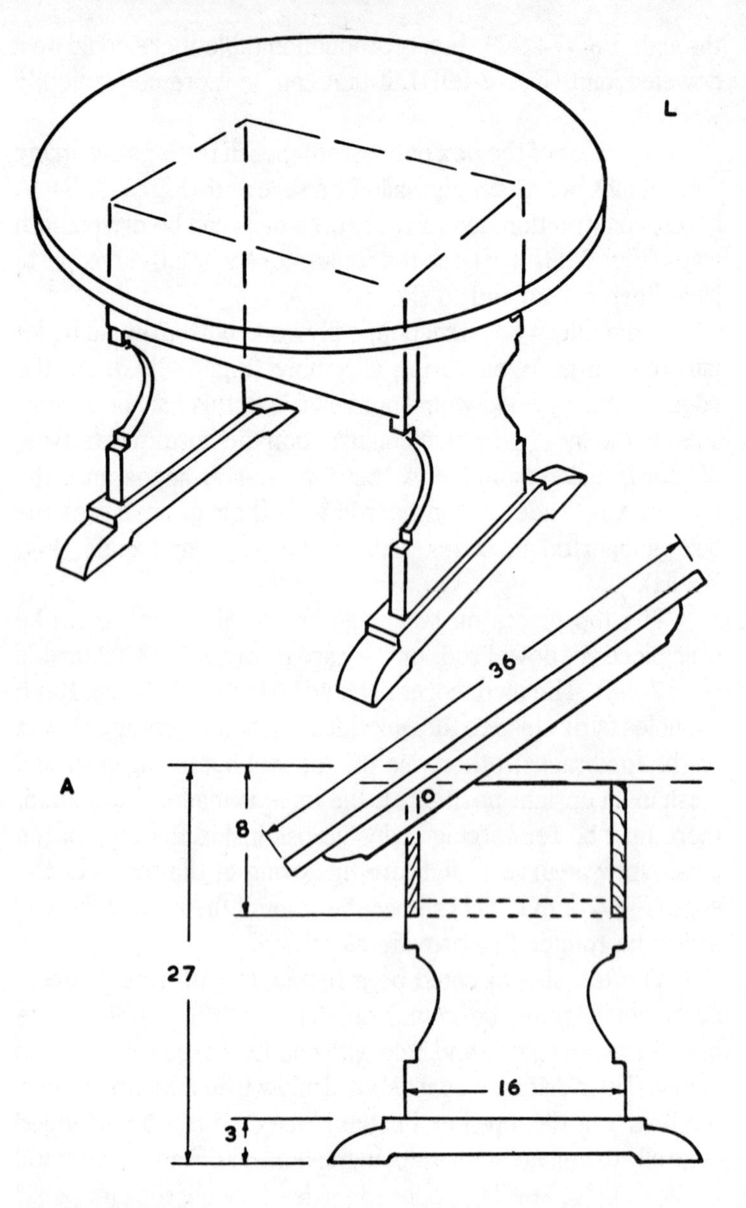


**Materials List 7-29**

| Tilt-Top Box Table | | | | |
|---|---|---|---|---|
| 1 | Top | 36 × 40 × 1¼ | 2 Feet | 3 × 28 × 1¾ |
| 2 | Braces | 3 × 30 × 1¼ | 2 Sides | 8 × 28 × 1 |
| 2 | Legs | 16 × 25 × 1¼ | 1 Bottom | 16 × 28 ply or thin wood |
| | | | Wood for pegs | |

Fig. 7-29. Tilt-top box table. (Continued on next page.)

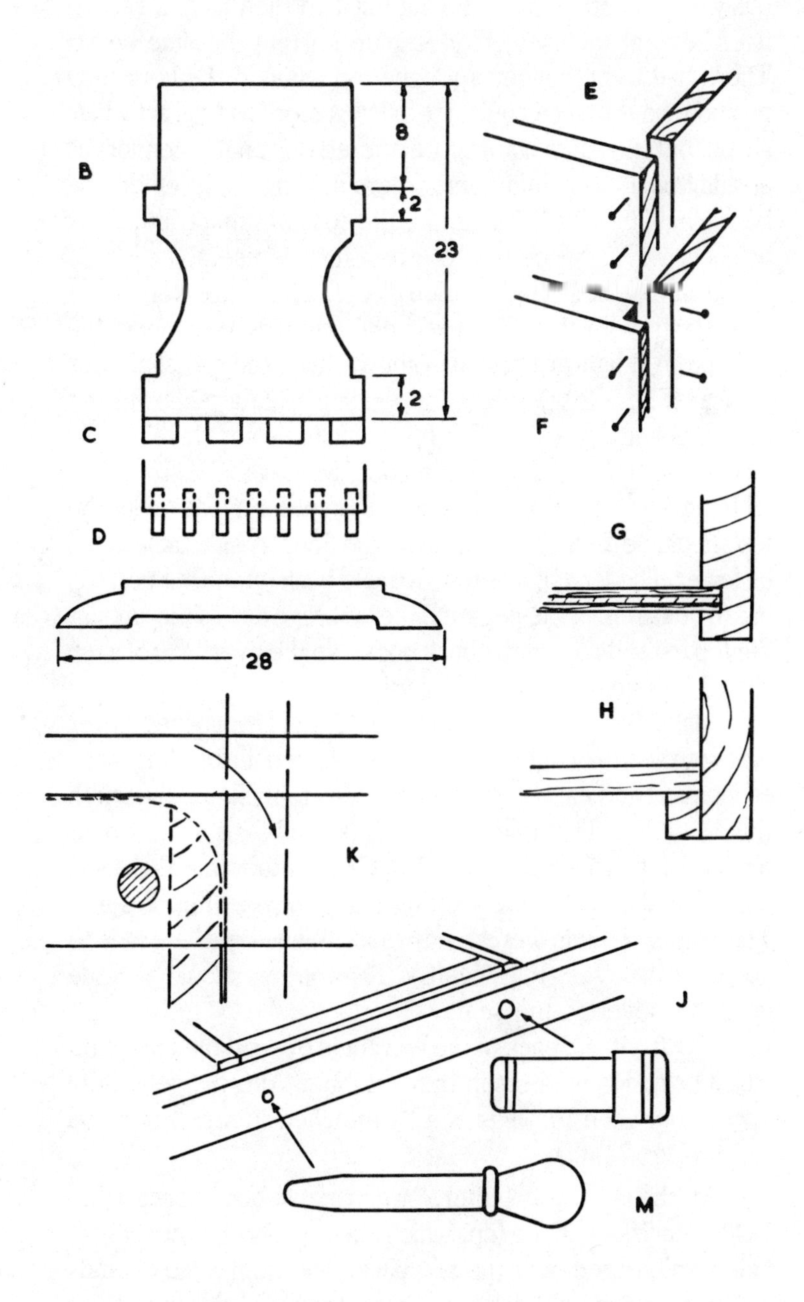
B
8
2
23
2
C
D
28
E
F
G
H
K
J
M

ously an advantage in arranging for it to then have a second use. Several tables were designed so they became seats. There had to be supports for the top when in the horizontal position, so the ends could not follow a more normal armchair shape, but the piece of furniture offered reasonable comfort as an additional chair, in a home where seating might otherwise be inadequate. The space under the seat was made into a box or chest with a lifting top to give a further use.

Some of these combination pieces of furniture were made like chests with the ends extended upwards to support the tilting top. A lighter version is shown, with the box shallower on legs (Fig. 7-30A). Sizes for a dining table are shown, but other sizes are possible. For normal use the seat level should be not less than 14 in. from the floor, whatever the size of the table, unless it is for a child's use. Except for a side table, the top should be 28 in. to 30 in. from the floor. A side table could be lower. The load of a person leaning back on the vertical top has to be taken on the pegs and the leverage due to the amount the top extends down the back posts, so the overhang of a top should be enough to allow for this.

Make the two end assemblies first. The shaped lower parts of the legs could be cut from solid wood, but it is more economical and easier to glue on pieces to make up the width (Fig. 7-30B). The ends of the box could be solid wood, tenoned into the legs (Fig. 7-30C). Another method uses framed ends, with panels fitting into grooves (Fig. 7-30D). The original panels were solid wood, thinned at the edges to go in the grooves (Fig. 7-30E). The top rail should be wide enough to overlap the seat.

The front and back of the box could overlap the legs, with nailed or dado joints, as in the box table. Alternatively, they may fit between the legs and be attached to strips of wood inside (Fig. 7-30F).

At the seat level there are narrow end pieces (Fig. 7-30G) each side of the top, which is a single board with braces below and hinged over the box back. The front edge extends and is rounded, but it is cut back towards the ends (Fig. 7-30H). This makes for comfort and gives a grip for lifting.

The tops of all four legs are out the same with holes for pegs. So the tabletop will swing without binding, the curves of the tops have their centers at the holes.

The tabletop will have to be made up from several boards, and the braces may have slotted screws through to allow for expansion and contraction. The pivot pegs and locking pegs are similar to those for the box table. Check the action with a trial assembly, before sanding and applying a finish.

## JACKSTAND

Many early woodworkers became intrigued with the adjustable action of a carriage jack, many of which used a ratchet and pawl movement. Small tables were made to adjust in height with this action. Candle holders were made with several sockets around the top. Others were made quite tall and arranged to support a hanging lamp. With light sources of only small output, there was a need to be able to adjust them to the best advantage. The jack adjustment provides an interesting design, and the most generally useful form today would be in the form of a small table or candle stand (Fig. 7-31A). The idea obviously predates the modern electric floor lamp, and the jack adjustment could be included in an electric stand, but could hardly be described as a reproduction.

The two posts (Fig. 7-31B) and the center shaft (Fig. 7-31C) are similar sections. The base is made of two fairly heavy-sectioned pieces to provide stability. They should extend a little further than the diameter of the top. Half lap them together. They can be cut back below to form feet, or pieces can be added, if that is easier (Fig. 7-31D).

The top crossbar has the posts tenoned into it and this should be marked with the mortises into the base, to get the spacing the same. Tenons showing through the crossbar may be regarded as a design feature, or they can be shorted stub tenons. Do not assemble these parts yet.

At the bottom of the shaft there is a guide joined on with a mortise and tenon joint (Fig. 7-32A). Its ends are notched to slide easily on the post. There is a mortise slot in the crossbar that lets the shaft slide through. Rigidity of the table depends

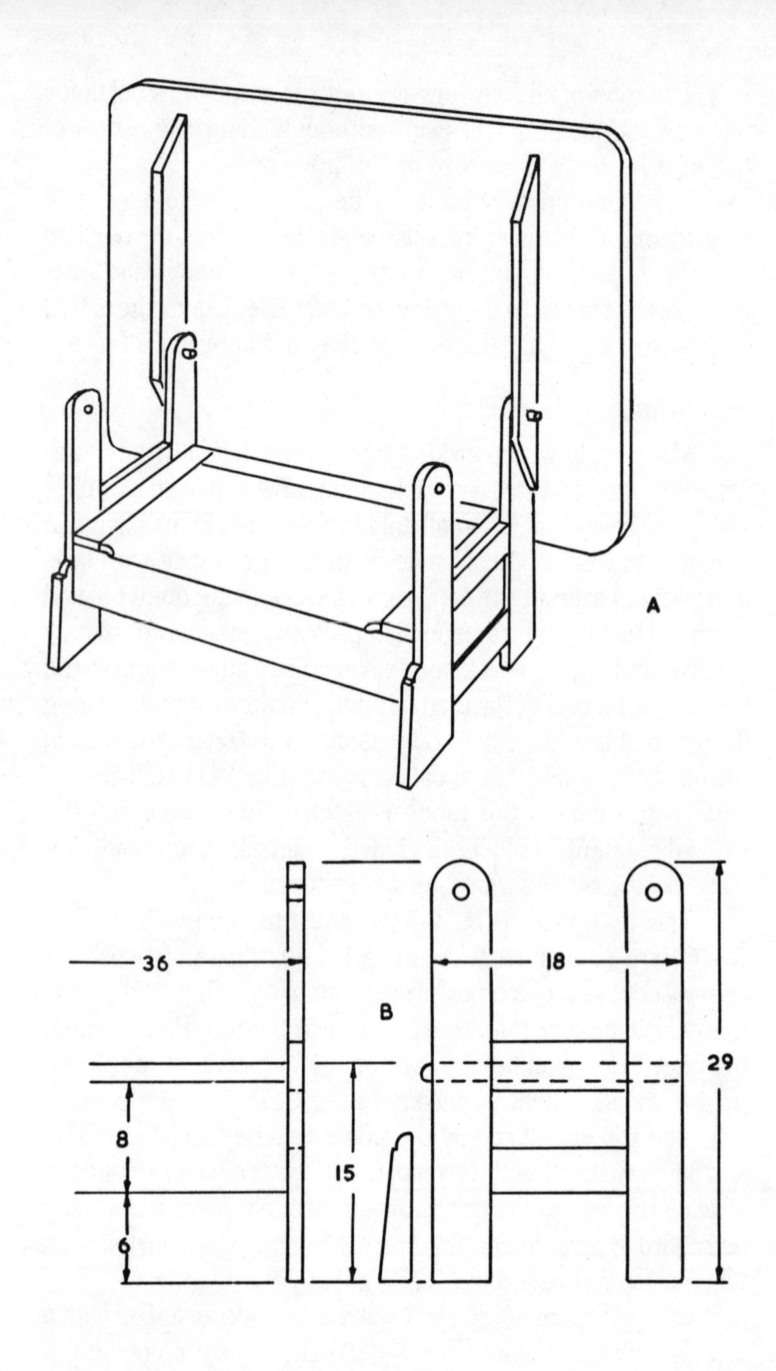


Fig. 7-30. Seat table. (Continued on next page.)

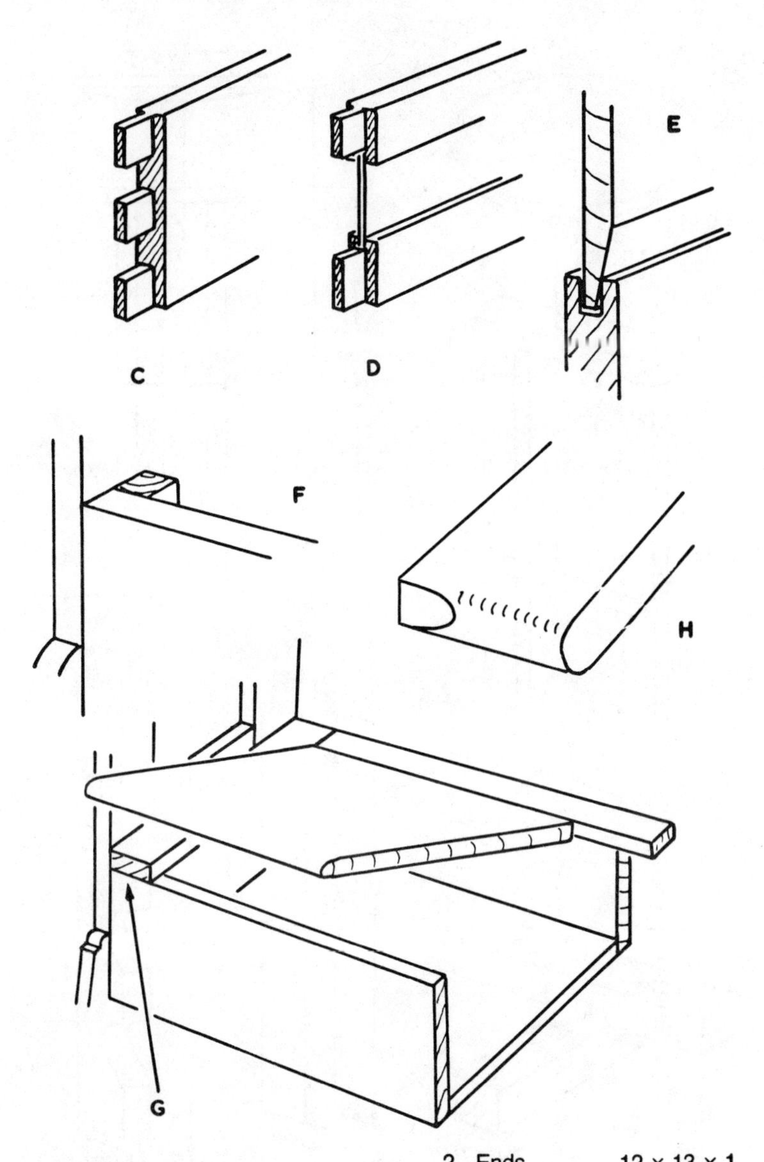


**Materials List 7-30**

Seat Table

| | | |
|---|---|---|
| 1 | Top | 36 × 50 × 1 |
| 2 | Braces | 4 × 30 × 1 |
| 4 | Legs | 4 × 29 × 1 |
| 2 | Legs | 2 × 10 × 1 |
| 2 | Ends | 12 × 13 × 1 |
| | or 2 Ends | 3 × 12 × 3/8 |
| | and 2 Ends | 7 × 12 × 3/8 |
| 1 | Seat | 16 × 30 × 1 |
| 2 | Seat ends | 3 × 18 × 1 |
| 1 | Seat back | 3 × 36 × 1 |
| 3 | Seat braces | 1 × 16 × 1 |

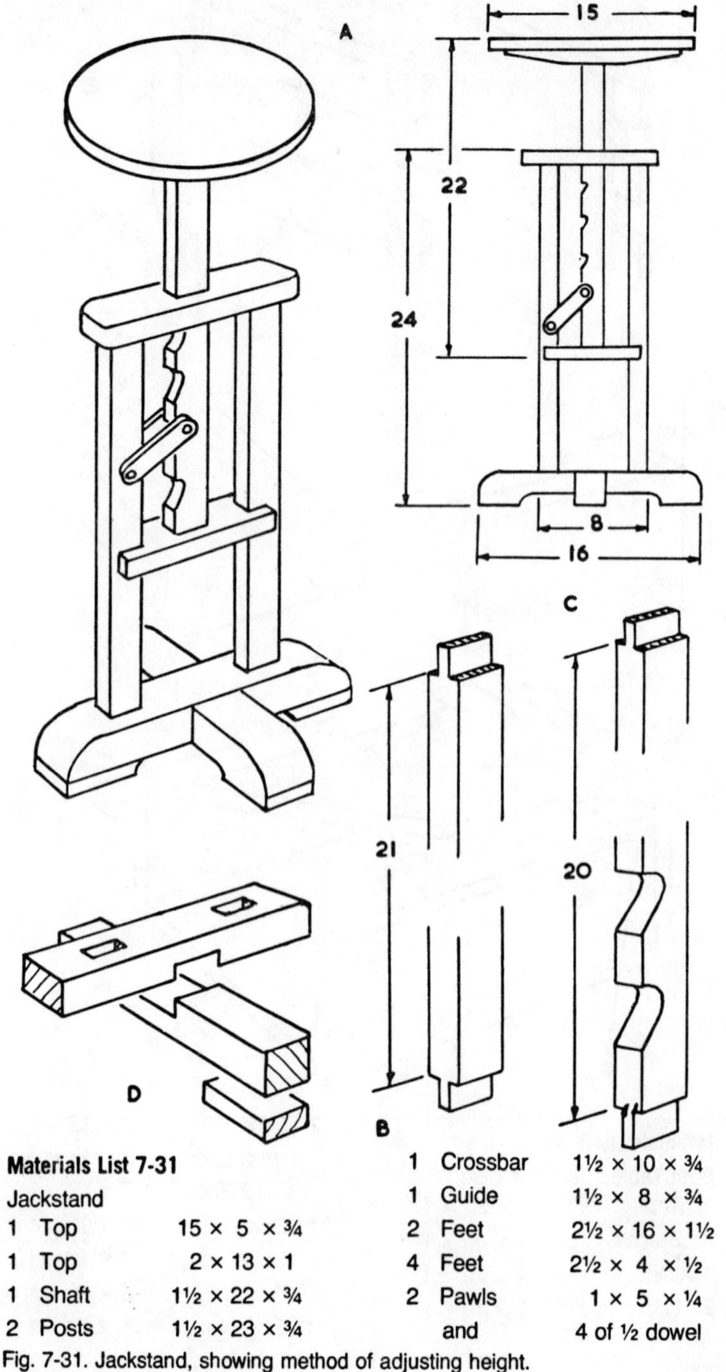


**Materials List 7-31**

Jackstand

| | | |
|---|---|---|
| 1 | Top | 15 × 5 × 3/4 |
| 1 | Top | 2 × 13 × 1 |
| 1 | Shaft | 1½ × 22 × 3/4 |
| 2 | Posts | 1½ × 23 × 3/4 |
| 1 | Crossbar | 1½ × 10 × 3/4 |
| 1 | Guide | 1½ × 8 × 3/4 |
| 2 | Feet | 2½ × 16 × 1½ |
| 4 | Feet | 2½ × 4 × ½ |
| 2 | Pawls | 1 × 5 × ¼ |
| | and | 4 of ½ dowel |

Fig. 7-31. Jackstand, showing method of adjusting height.

on the notched ends of the guide and the fit of the shaft mortise. Mark these parts carefully on both sides of the wood (Fig. 7-32B) and cut away the waste carefully from both sides.

The tabletop may be round or octagonal. Stiffen it with a batten across the grain (Fig. 7-32C), which is mortised to take a tenon on the top of the shaft.

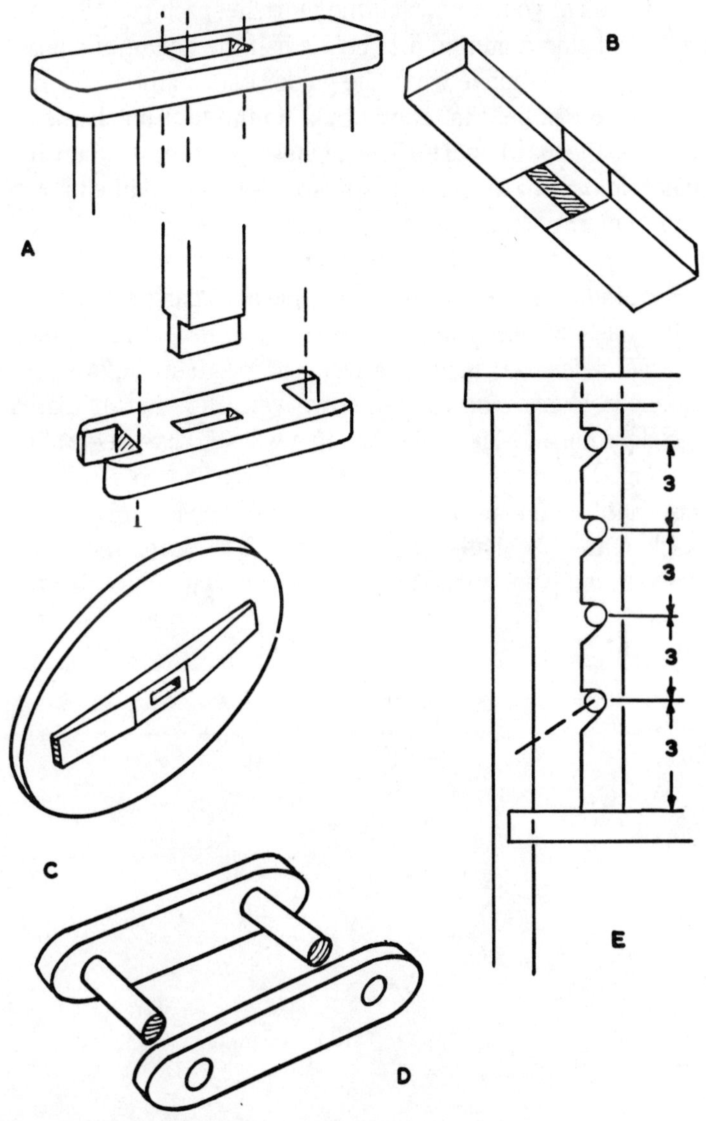


Fig. 7-32. Details of the moving parts of the jackstand.

Some jackstands had the pawl made as a single piece let into a slot in one of the posts, but it is stronger and results in a more rigid assembly if the pawl is made with two cheeks and two dowels (Fig. 7-32D). One dowel goes through the post, while the other engages with the notches.

Draw the center part of the assembly full-size to the actual sizes of your wood and the mortise spacings. Allow for the pawl being mounted just below half the height of a post. The lowest position is when the guide rests on the base. The next move can be 3 in. above this, so the first notch comes opposite the pawl there. The highest position is when the guide almost reaches the pawl, so allow for another notch there. Other notches can be spaced between these points—2 in. to 3 in. intervals should be satisfactory (Fig. 7-32E).

Because of the difficulty of getting at all parts satisfactorily for finishing after complete assembly, it is best to make up subassemblies and paint, varnish, or oil them before final assembly. Waxing on rubbed-down varnish is better than a high gloss finish. Make sure the shaft will still slide freely after finishing. There could be lubrication with candle grease or one of the antifriction sprays. Suitable subassemblies are: the top attached to the shaft, but the guide left loose; the base, crossbar and posts made up; the pawl left with one side off.

# Chairs and Seats

Stools and simple benches that are no more than extended stools may have served for seats while there were things of more importance to occupy early settler craftsmen, but these things do not offer much comfort and there would soon have been a demand for chairs, settles, and other forms of seating that most immigrants would have known in Europe.

Unfortunately, a chair that is to provide a high degree of comfort is not an easy thing to make, and many early craftsmen with high degrees of skill in many aspects of their occupation would have found that making chairs that were fully functional did not come as readily as they may have expected. Chairmaking has always been a specialized branch of furniture making, and many craftsmen are still occupied almost solely in this branch of cabinetmaking. It would have been so, in the days when people from all walks of life decided to try a new home in America.

Consequently there are some examples of early chairs and seats that reflect the inability of their makers to produce something fully up to the standards of what they could remember in their home lands. Whether some of these are worth reproducing or not depends on other aspects of the particular items, which may have artistic merit or features of particular interest, even if they are not as fully functional as their makers had hoped.

Upholstery, as we know it, was uncommon at first. Any softening of seats and backs would have been by draping blankets over them or by having loose cushions. In the later more settled period, when many people expected to live in greater comfort and with more amenities, there were craftsmen making American equivalents of Chippendale chairs and working to the designs of other famous cabinetmakers on the other side of the Atlantic. Gradually the designs were adopted and a local influence became apparent, so chairs and other pieces of furniture could be identified as American and not imports from England. The American chairmaker was also influenced by designs from countries other than England, so features he liked may have been incorporated in something that was basically of English design, to produce the start of a new series of designs.

Chairs that reproduce the better type of style and design of the later period are difficult to make, and it would be inadvisable for the average amateur to attempt them. There are plainer chairs that provide reasonable comfort and are much easier to make. These may be all wood and softening is by loose cushions, or some of them include upholstery of a type that is easy to apply. Anyone new to chairmaking is advised to start with a simple design, before going on to try a reproduction of an advanced type that is contoured to give support at just the right parts of the human anatomy and still be a thing of beauty.

Another consideration may be the number of chairs. Chairs are normally in sets of four or more, possibly with one or more matching armchairs. When a single chair is made, there can be variations due to errors or the need to adapt construction to suit the size of a piece of wood, but there is more skill called for if several chairs are to be completed to be identical.

Some chairs and benches are little more than stools with backs built in. These obviously are a little more comfortable, but better chairs have shaped wooden seats or the part that takes the sitter's weight is either made slightly flexible or is padded. Further steps are contouring of the back and the addition of arms. Early chairs were made in all these ways and can serve as prototypes for reproduction work.

## PEASANT CHAIR

Many European countries, notably Germany, Austria, and Switzerland, favor a stool type of seat with a solid back having its decoration provided by shaping around the edge. The Pennsylvania Dutch remembered their German origin and produced chairs of this type in the early days of settlement when most available wood was in thicker sections. The example chosen here (Fig. 8-1A) should be kept to thick wood to retain authenticity and to provide sufficient strength in the joint between the seat and the back, which would not have sufficient rigidity without additional brackets or other strengthening if thinner wood was used.

The seat is a plain slab with its grain front to back. It may be made parallel or arranged to be slightly wider at the front, then the corners are taken off (Fig. 8-1B). The edges could be left square or be rounded, preferably with more rounding on the top edge than the bottom (Fig. 8-1C), although some chairs were molded (Fig. 8-1D). At this stage, leave the rear edge too wide and untreated.

There can be considerable load on the angle between the seat and the chair back when the sitter leans back, so the joint must be secure. The best is a multiple mortise and tenon, with tenons on the back passing through a series of mortises in the seat. As both parts are meeting with their grains in line, the tenons should be arranged so their greater lengths are in the direction of the grain (Fig. 8-1E). This would be stronger than having the tenons wider. The joint should be marked out and partly cut before the legs are fitted and before the outline of the back is cut.

The back should slope at about 10°. Set an adjustable bevel to this and use it instead of a try square when marking across the edges of both pieces of wood to transfer the joint details to the other sides (Fig. 8-1F). Cut the tenons carefully,

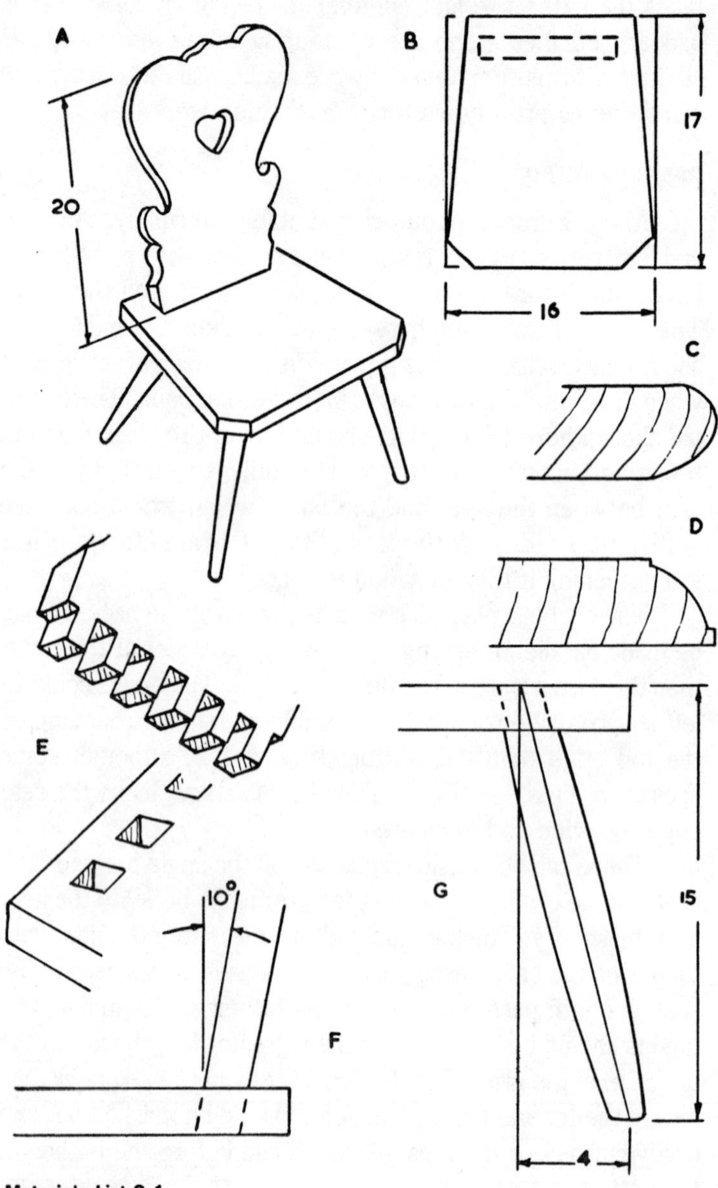


**Materials List 8-1**
Peasant Chair

| | | |
|---|---|---|
| 1 | Seat | 16 × 17 × 1½ |
| 1 | Back | 16 × 22 × 1½ |
| 4 | Legs | 2½ × 16 × 2½ |

Fig. 8-1. Peasant chair. (Continued on next page.)

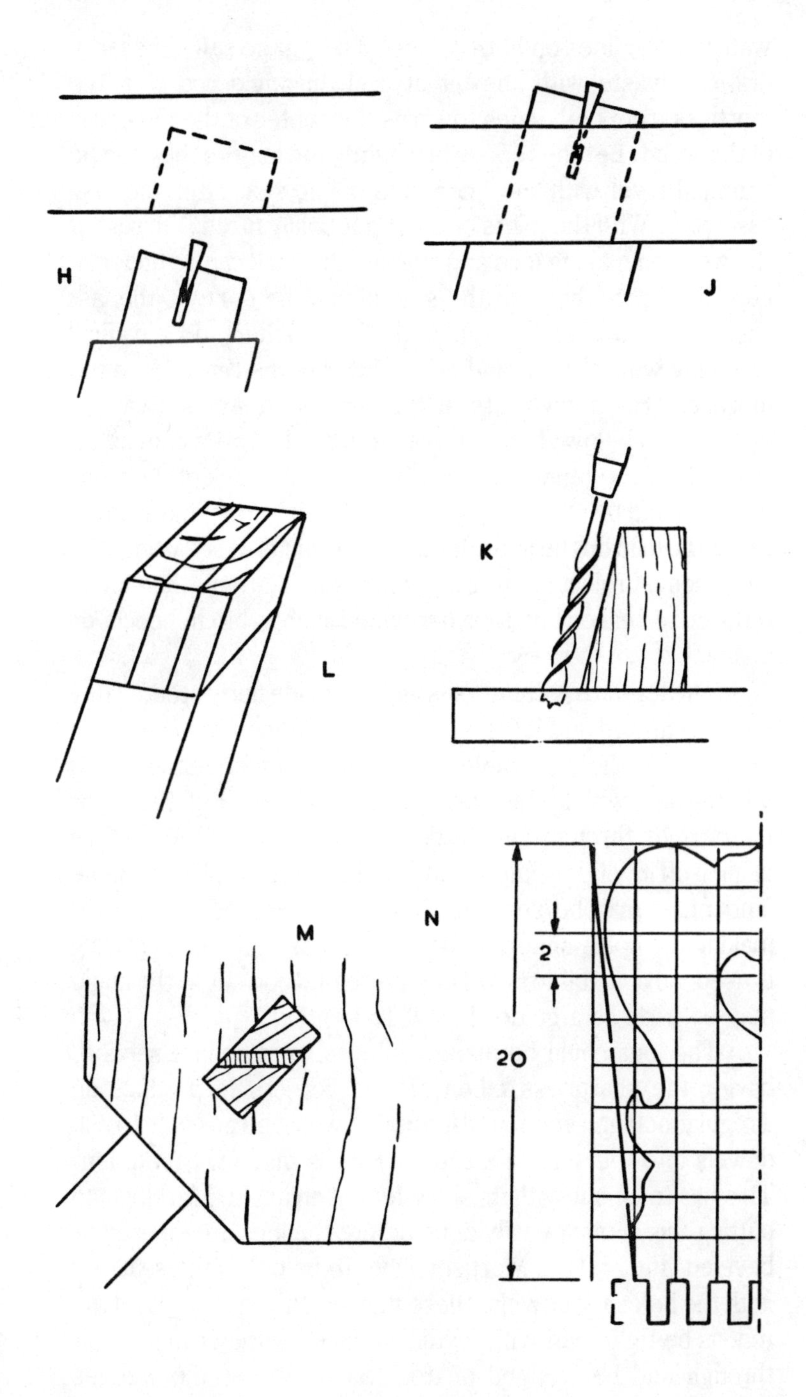
H
J
K
L
M
N
2
20

watching the lines on both sides and tilting the saw. Similarly, drill out waste with the bit at a slight angle and trim the mortises from both sides towards the center of the thickness of the wood. Let the tenons be slightly too long so they can be trimmed level with the underside of the seat after the final assembly. With the joints cut, but not finally fitted, the rest of the work on making legs and shaping the back can be undertaken. Fixing the back to the seat should be done as the last assembly process, but when this is reached, do any final trimming with a chisel and drive and glue the tenons into the mortises. Have saw cuts in the tenons so wedges can be driven from below. Leave the glue to set before trimming off the ends of the tenons and finally truing the back of the seat, which should be allowed to project enough for the end grain to resist the load on the joint. If the chair is made of softwood, the seat should project about 2 in. behind the joint, but this can be reduced to nearer 1 in. for a hardwood such as birch, beech, or maple.

The legs are without rails and are made fairly stout. They could be turned on a lathe with a simple outline and a dowel top (Fig. 8-1G). Early examples made this way were either fitted into the seat with foxtail wedging in blind holes (Fig. 8-1H), or taken right through and wedged on top (Fig. 8-1J), before planing off level. It is important that all four legs splay the same amount. It may be possible to set up a tapered support for making the holes uniformly on a drill press, but if hand drilling is used, an adjustable bevel or a piece of wood cut to the angle may be used as a guide (Fig. 8-1K).

The legs could be make with a tapered square section, having the sharpness taken off the corners to produce an irregular octagon section. Although it would be possible to use dowels into the seat, a stronger joint is made with a tenon. This has to be cut with its shoulders at an angle. Marking and cutting this is most easily done before the legs are tapered or beveled (Fig. 8-1L). Mortises have to be cut in the seat. As with the holes for dowels, these may go only part way and the tenons be tightened with foxtail wedges, or they can go right through and be wedged on top. Saw cuts for the wedges should be at right angles to the grain of the seat and not at right angles to the tenons. This puts the spread of the tenon against the seat in the direction best able to resist it (Fig. 8-1M).

The back is shown with a typical outline (Fig. 8-1N). The hollows suit the cords of cushions tied on. It may be advisable to make a template of half the back so both sides are cut uniformly. The band saw will be the best tool to cut the outline, but the first makers did the work by hand and a bow saw or jigsaw will get around the outline, even if the muscles have to be exercised to the full. Clean the edges with a Surform tool and plenty of sanding. The hole at the center will have to be cut with a jigsaw or saber saw. Many of these chairs have the outline left square across in section with the sharpness taken off the edges. Others have the front edge well rounded. Some have the outline thoroughly rounded to a semicircular section.

When assembly is completed, stand the chair on a level surface and trim the legs so it stands without wobbling and with the seat parallel with the floor. Round the bottoms of the legs so they will not mark carpets or other floor covering.

## LADDERBACK CHAIR

Chairs with slats across the back have been popular for a long time and there are modern versions still being made. The name 'ladderback' is obvious from the ladderlike appearance of the back.

Many early ladderback chairs had the rear posts arranged at right angles to the floor, so the support for the sitter's back was upright. This form was probably easiest to make and assemble, but it gives an unnatural and uncomfortable posture. The design is improved by letting the rear posts slope back at a slight angle. This does not affect stability. Some old chairs, and many new ones, have the rear posts curved, so the part forming the leg below the seat is upright, but the curve above produces a slope. Some posts were steamed and bent around jigs. This would be the only way of producing a bent turned leg, but for a square section it is possible to bandsaw the shape from a flat board.

Many old ladderback chairs had high backs, and all parts except the slats had been turned on a lathe. Some of the old treadle lathes had a long capacity, but many modern lathes will only handle a length about 30 in. and a high-back chair needs more than this—spindles near 4 ft. for the rear posts are usual. The first example shown here (Fig. 8-2A) has a lower back within the capacity of most lathes. The back slopes, and a side view should be drawn full-size to obtain the sizes of the parts (Fig. 8-2B).

The rear posts and the front legs are turned from 2 in. square wood, so the greatest diameters will finish about 1¾ in. The front legs are simple cylinders with the bottoms slightly rounded and the top finished in a shallow knob. While the wood is revolving in the lathe it is helpful for further work to use a pencil on the toolrest to lightly mark around at each position that will have to be drilled for rails. The side rails are at a slightly different level to the front rails. Staggering the holes allows the dowel ends of the rails to penetrate further and produce stronger joints. The top rails have to be at the same level for working the seat (Fig. 8-2C).

The posts are turned parallel up to slightly above seat level, then they are given a slight taper towards the top. Use one of the front legs as a guide to pencil the rail positions while the post is in the lathe. Also pencil the positions of the tops and bottoms of the mortises for the back slats (Fig. 8-2D). The posts are plain turnings, except there can be some decoration at their tops.

The rails can be plain parallel cylinders reduced at the ends to form dowels (Fig. 8-2E). It is unusual in these chairs for the rails to be turned with beads or other decorations. One small amount of shaping that was sometimes used was to have the centers of the rails slightly thicker than the ends (Fig. 8-2F).

Some chairs were made with flat slats and these are shown in this case (Fig. 8-2G), but shaped slats are more comfortable and they could be made (as described in the next example) for this chair. Flat slats are cut to the outline. A template can be used, or one slat made and used to mark the others. Mark the lengths between shoulders of the tenons to match the lenghts of the turned rails for the back (Fig. 8-2H).

Holes can be made on a drill press, with an electric drill or by using a bit brace. A line along a post or leg can be drawn to get all holes in line. Deal with the mortises and the holes across the back and front of the chair first. These are all at right angles. If drilling is by hand, have a try square alongside, and get an assistant to sight the drill, so drilling is as accurate as possible. Drill some of the waste from the slat mortises and trim them to shape with chisels.

Because the chair seat is wider at the front than the back, the other holes have to be drilled at something other than a right angle to the first holes. Draw half a plan view of the seat sufficient to get the angle between front and side rails. Set an adjustable bevel to this (Fig. 8-2J). If a rail is entered in one of the holes, the bevel will give the angle the other holes are to be, using the obtuse angle for the back posts and the acute angle for the front legs (Fig. 8-2K). If a drill press is used, it would be helpful to make up a jig to hold the post or leg with a rail in position as a guide to the angle and an extension each way to allow the jig to be used for obtuse and acute angles (Fig. 8-2L)

The amount the rail holes differ from a right angle at the sides into the rear posts is not enough to matter.

Assemble the chair in stages. Join the legs with their rails. Check squareness with a try square and by measuring diagonals. Check that there is no twist across the assembly by putting it on a flat surface and seeing that it does not wobble. Assemble the two rear posts and their slats and rails. Use the front legs assembly to check the rear assembly by putting it over the matching part. As well as this check the rear assembly for squareness and lack of twist in the same way. Do not do any more assembly until these parts have their glue set.

Fit all the side rails into the front assembly. Put glue on all the joints into the rear assembly, then bring all the parts together. Use bar clamps where necessary to get joints tight, but sight across the chair to see that rails are parallel, then stand the chair on a flat surface and check diagonals across the

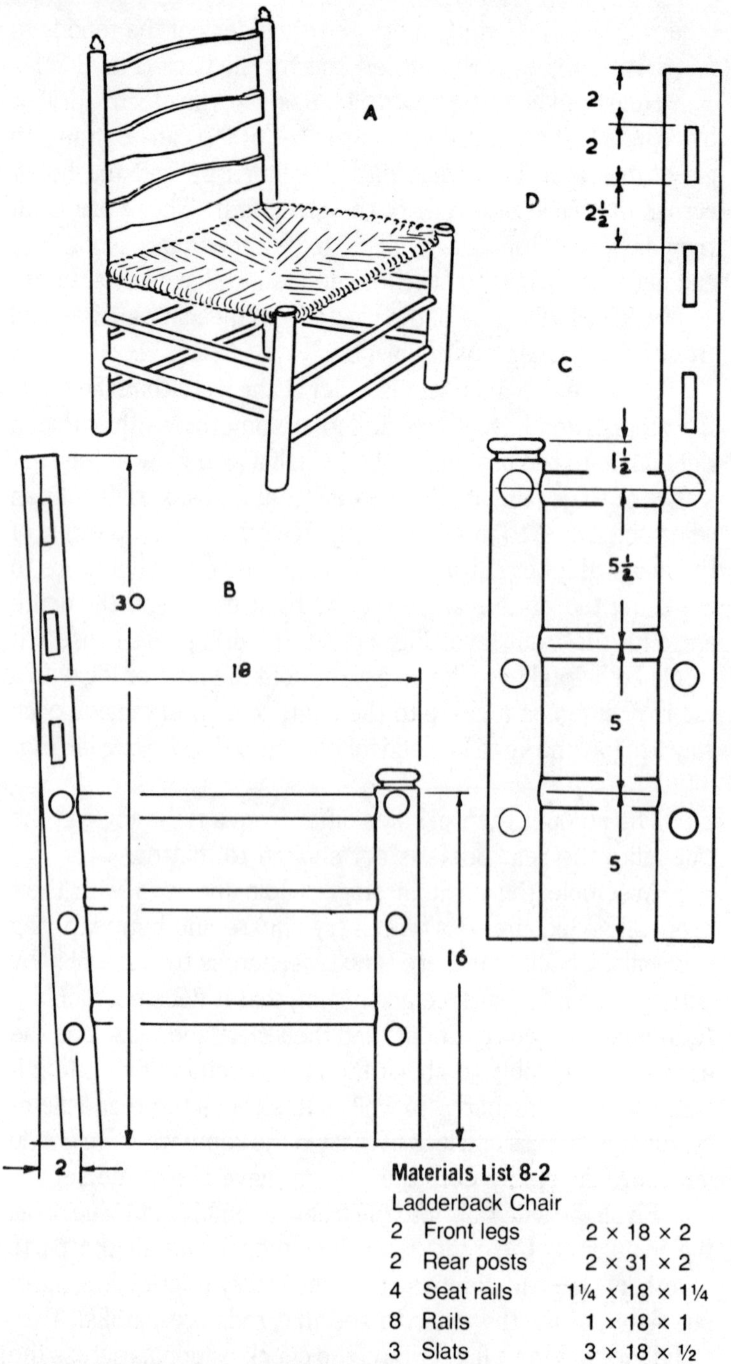


**Materials List 8-2**

Ladderback Chair

| | | |
|---|---|---|
| 2 | Front legs | 2 × 18 × 2 |
| 2 | Rear posts | 2 × 31 × 2 |
| 4 | Seat rails | 1¼ × 18 × 1¼ |
| 8 | Rails | 1 × 18 × 1 |
| 3 | Slats | 3 × 18 × ½ |

Fig. 8-2. Ladderback chair. (Continued on next page.)

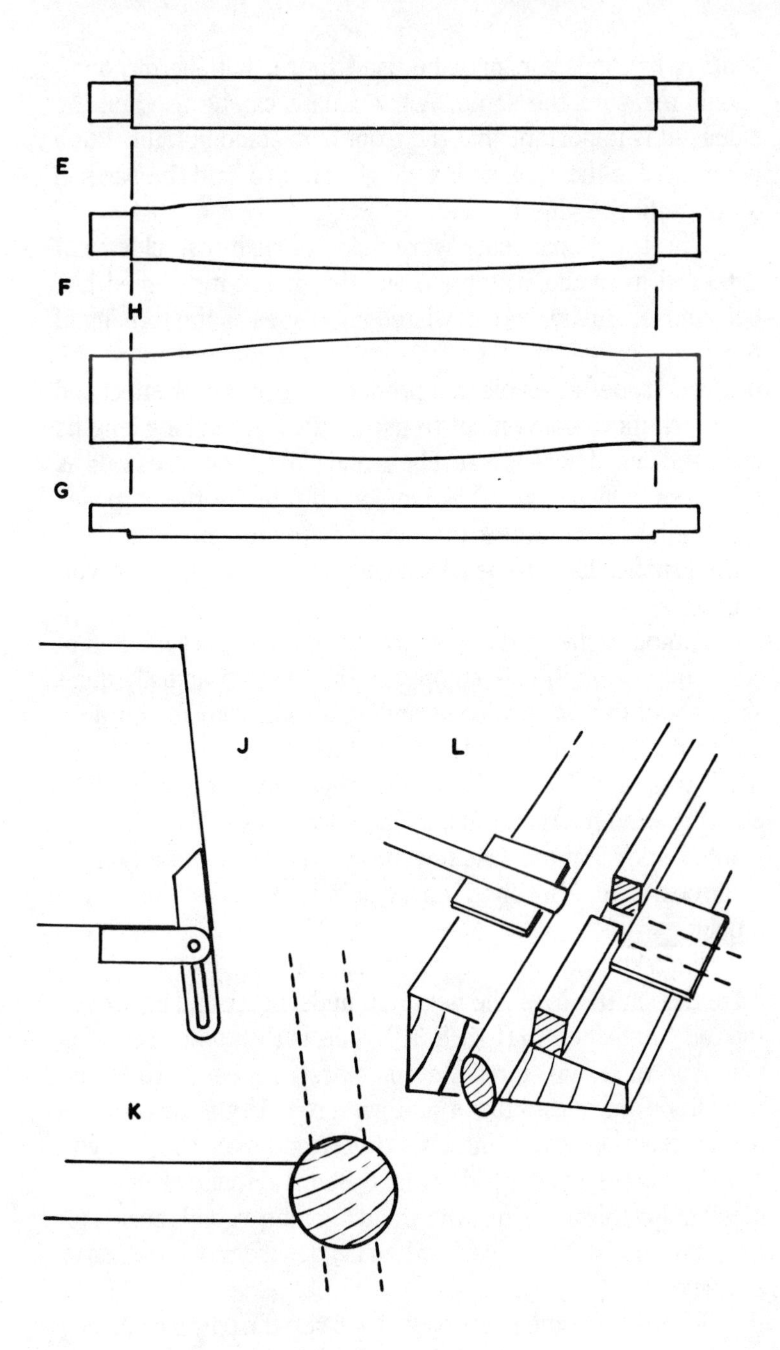
E
F
H
G
J
L
K

seat. A try square cannot be used there, but the diagonals should measure the same. A try square can be used on the sides—it is important that the front legs stand upright. Put a board across the seat with a weight on it to hold the parts in shape until the glue has set.

The traditional seats were made of rush (cattail leaves) gathered from the waterside and dried, but moistened just before use. Rushes were twisted into ropes as the forming of the seat proceeded. This can still be done, but there are prepared ropes available that produce a very similar effect and are much more convenient to use as they are in long lengths and used dry. There are art fibers and plastic ropes, as well as sea grass, which is a rushlike imported rope for the purpose. The method of working is the same whatever material is used, except rushes have to be added constantly and twisted as you go.

Although the traditional form of seat hides its method of construction when it is complete, the work is actually quite simple and the pattern of strands mitered from the corners builds up automatically. If any of the continuous ropes are used, it is helpful to make a few rough wooden spools (Fig. 8-3A) to wind the material on. The only other tool needed is a pointed stick for the last few turns when completing. This could be a square or round rod about ¾ in. across sharpened to a point.

Tie a knot in one end of a strand and tack it inside a rail. Take the shuttle over the next rail, underneath and back over the rail you tacked to (Fig. 8-3B). This is the complete action you need to know—further steps merely repeat it. Keep the tension on that first corner and go across to the next one—over the opposite rail, into the center and over the one you have just crossed alongside (Fig. 8-3C). Continue around the stool, doing this at each corner, and keeping a good tension on the next strand, particularly when it goes from one corner to the next.

After a few times around you will see the pattern building up. It will be the same above and below the seat, and the strands going from one corner to the next will eventually be

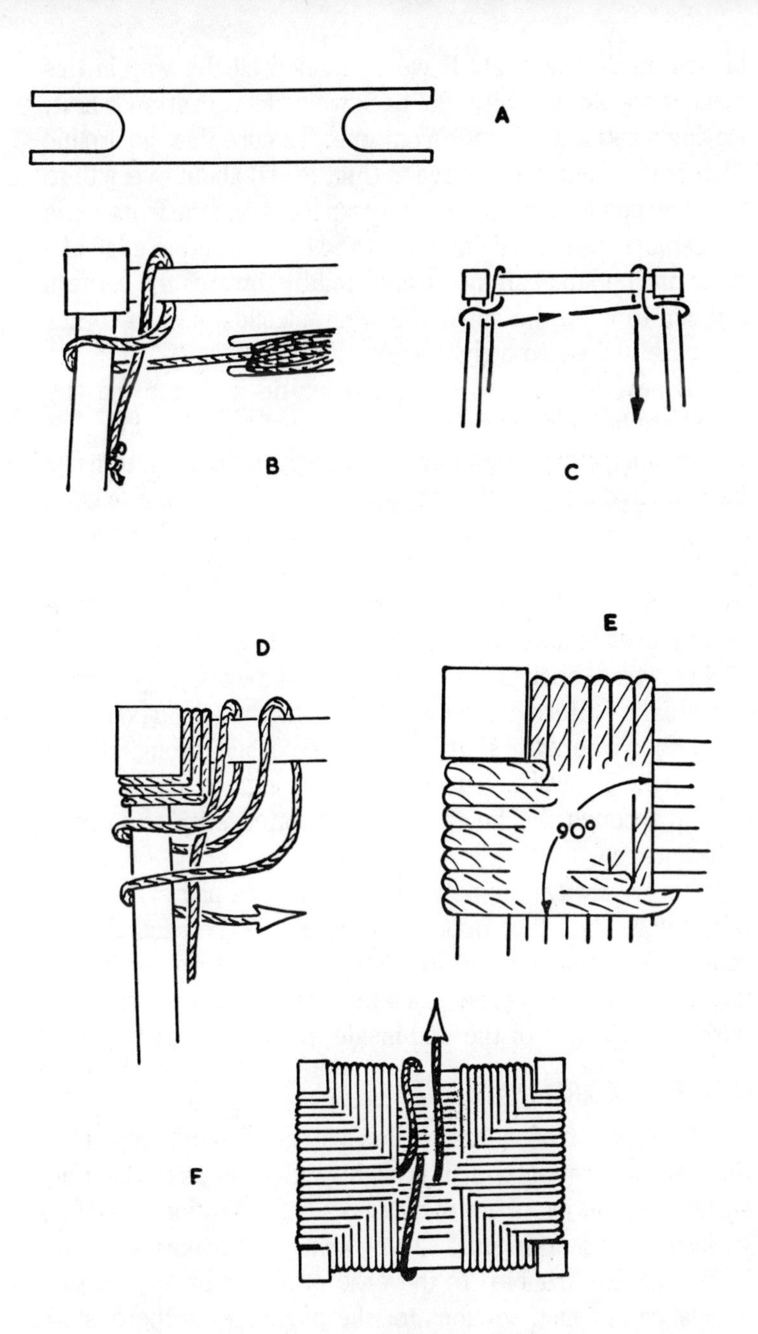


Fig. 8-3. The method of working a rush seat. A shuttle holds the line (A), which is tacked to a rail (B) and worked around the frame (C). For a tapered shape go twice around the corners at the wider part (D) to make up width. Keep the pattern square (E). Make up across the short way by working over and under (F).

hidden inside the seat. If we continued all the way in this manner the narrow rail at the back would fill with strands first, leaving a gap at the wider front one. To cure this, go around each of the front corners twice (Fig. 8-3D) about every third time you come to them, until the gap left along the front rail is the same as the remaining one at the back. Use the edge of a piece of wood to push the strands tightly towards the corners and aim to keep the angles between strands at each corner reasonably close to a right angle (Fig. 8-3E).

If new line has to be joined in, tie it to the old line anywhere between corners. The knot will then be hidden. It will be satisfactory to continue in this way until the pattern fills the seat, and many chairs are finished in this way, but to get a firmer seat, it is possible to stuff the seat with oddments of rush or the material used. When the seat is about half completed, pockets between the top and bottom patterns will be seen. Pieces of the covering material can be pushed into these pockets with a stick and more added as the work progresses.

As the pattern continues towards the middle, a point will be reached where the shuttle cannot be passed through. From here on the line will have to be used in a long length and its end pushed through the hole. Use the pointed stick to force a sufficient gap.

Nearly always the pattern fills up on one pair of opposite rails before the other opposite pair. To fill the second pair, continue to thread through in a figure-eight pattern (Fig. 8-3F) until the rails are covered. Tack the last turn under its rail and push a few inches of the end inside the seat.

## LADDERBACK ARMCHAIR

Using wood of square section instead of round section for the legs and posts of a chair is slightly stronger as the bearing surfaces in the joints are increased a little. Working on a flat surface when marking and cutting joints also makes for accuracy with less trouble. In the case of a high-back chair the avoidance of round sections for the posts means there is no need for a lathe of increased capacity.

This chair (Fig. 8-4A) has the wood of square section throughout for legs, posts and rails. The slats could be flat, as in the previous chair, but they are shown curved in the way most of these chairs were produced. It would be possible to make the chair in the way just described, using turned parts. The overall sizes and the method of construction could be the same.

Joints may be doweled. A doweling tool for use in a bit brace can cut dowels directly on the ends of rails, or there can be pieces of dowel rod glued into holes in the ends of the rails (Fig. 8-4B). Dowel diameters should be about two-thirds of the thickness of the rails. Better joints are made with mortises and tenons. The rails could be shouldered both sides of the tenon, but they are easier to cut if barefaced and the obtuse and acute angles are easier to fit closely (Fig. 8-4C). The tenons should be only slightly less than the thickness of the rail—one-third of the thickness of the legs and post would be about right.

Start with the front legs (Fig. 8-4D). Leave some surplus length at the top until after the mortises have been cut. Mark the positions of the mortises or dowels for the rails. Note that the side and front rail positions are staggered, so the mortises do not meet. For the seat rails the mortises may be cut to meet; then the ends of the tenons or dowels can be mitered. But allow a slight gap (Fig. 8-4E); otherwise it may be difficult to bring the shoulders of the rails tight against the legs.

The rear posts are cut from a wide board, either one post from one board, or it is less wasteful to cut both from a wider board if that is available. The lower part is upright and matches the front legs, then the upper part sweeps back (Fig. 8-4F). The upper part may taper both ways slightly. Each top may finish in a simple rounding or a turned finial could be plugged in (Fig. 8-4G).

The rails on each panel are all the same length. Mark all the side rails together and mark the back and front ones in sets. It is the distance between shoulders that is important. All of the ends of doweling and the shoulders for tenoning may be cut square, except for the best fit and appearance the side rail angles should match the shape of the seat, with the angles found from a full-size drawing (Fig. 8-4H). Round the edges of the seat rails around which the rushes will be wrapped.

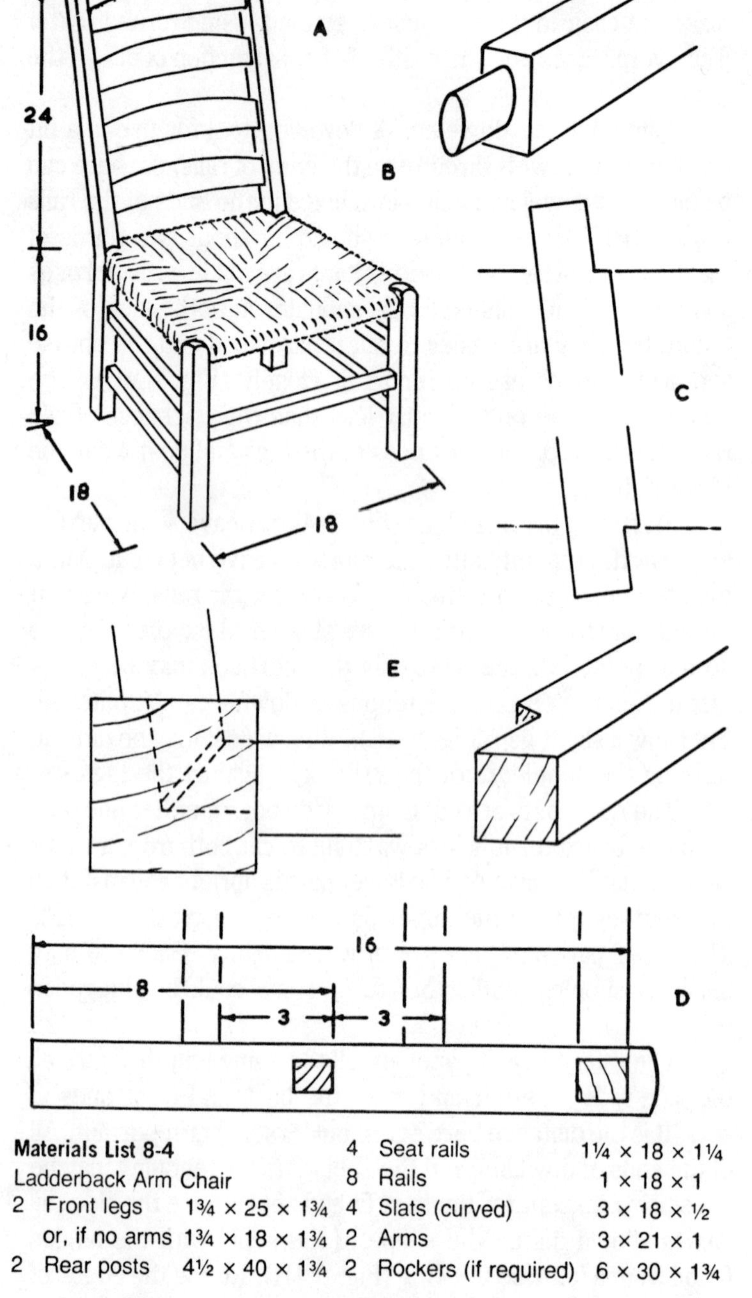


**Materials List 8-4**

Ladderback Arm Chair

| | | |
|---|---|---|
| 2 | Front legs | 1¾ × 25 × 1¾ |
| | or, if no arms | 1¾ × 18 × 1¾ |
| 2 | Rear posts | 4½ × 40 × 1¾ |
| 4 | Seat rails | 1¼ × 18 × 1¼ |
| 8 | Rails | 1 × 18 × 1 |
| 4 | Slats (curved) | 3 × 18 × ½ |
| 2 | Arms | 3 × 21 × 1 |
| 2 | Rockers (if required) | 6 × 30 × 1¾ |

Fig. 8-4. Shaped ladderback chair. (Continued on next page.)

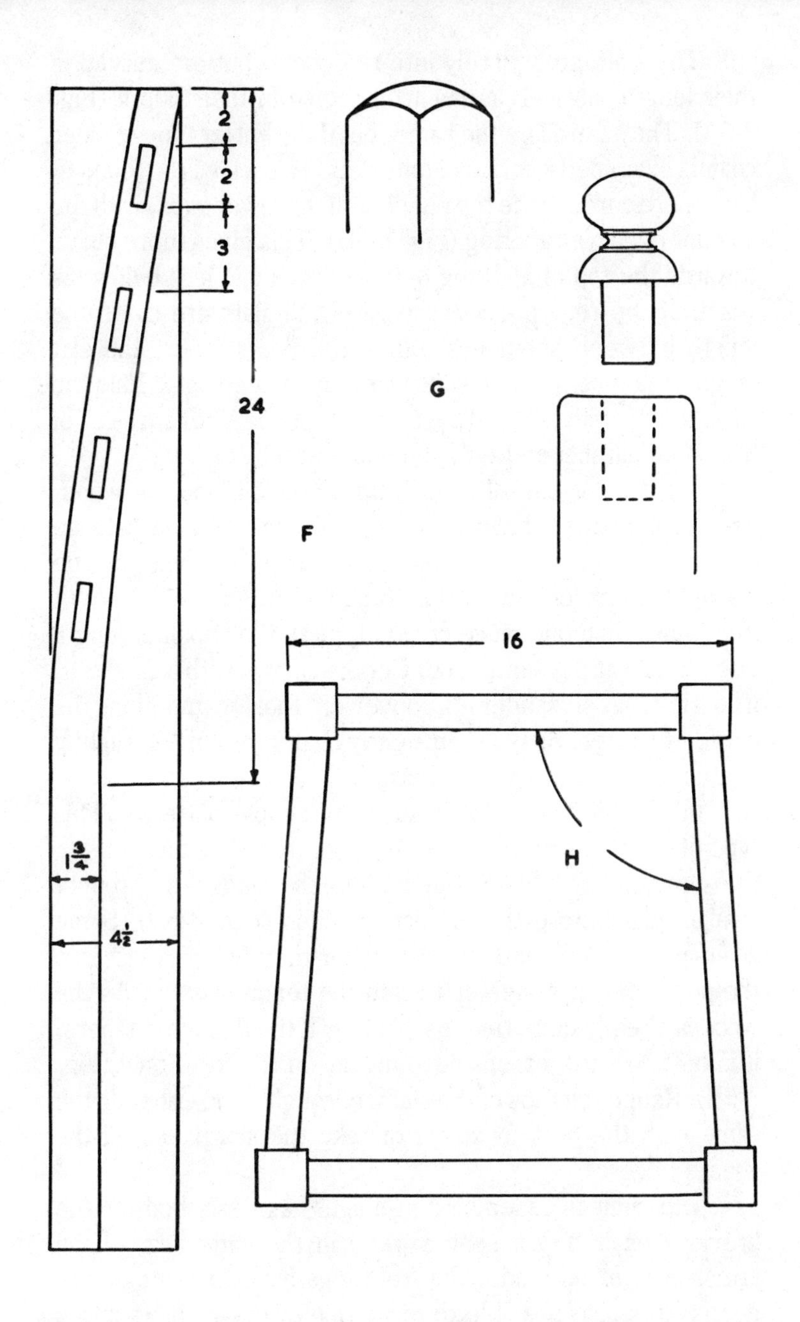
2
2
3
24
1 3/4
4 1/2
G
F
16
H

The slats go squarely into the posts, but are curved in their length, as well as cut to a profile in their depth (Fig. 8-5A). They can all be the same, but if the better type of older chair is examined a series of four slats in a back will be found to have more curve in the top one than in the lower ones, with the amount of curve tapering (Fig. 8-5B). This gives more curve towards the top of a sitting person's back and less below his waist. If the rear posts are parallel, all slats are the same length between shoulders, but if the posts taper, the slat lengths must be made to suit. One way of keeping all slats the same length with tapered posts is to keep the inner surfaces of the posts parallel and only taper the outer surfaces.

If possible, cut all slats from one solid block of wood. Mark around this to indicate the overall length and the distance between shoulders. Draw the curves to be cut with a little waste between for sawing (Fig. 8-5C). If the slats are to be cut from more than one piece of wood, mark the shoulder length on all pieces at the same time. Cut the curves with a bandsaw, if possible. A belt sander is a convenient tool for smoothing the curved surfaces. Slats in some early chairs were made slightly thinner at the top than the bottom.

Profiles for slats followed many simple patterns. This type of chair was not made with elaborate twists and curls to the outlines. Whatever the outline the ends are brought straight just before the projecting tenon (Fig. 8-5D). Some chairs will be found with the slats taken their full thickness into the posts, but it is neater to thin the tenon slightly. As the wood is already quite thin, particularly if the thickness tapers, it is best to cut a barefaced shoulder on the front only (Fig. 8-5E). Round the tops of the slats thoroughly and either do the same with the bottom edges or take the sharpness off the square edges.

The chair is assembled in stages, as described for the previous chair and a seat worked in the same way. If an armchair is to be made, the front legs have to continue upwards. It is also possible to make one of these chairs into a rocker.

For an armchair the front legs continue upwards (Fig. 8-6A), but are otherwise the same as for a plain chair. They

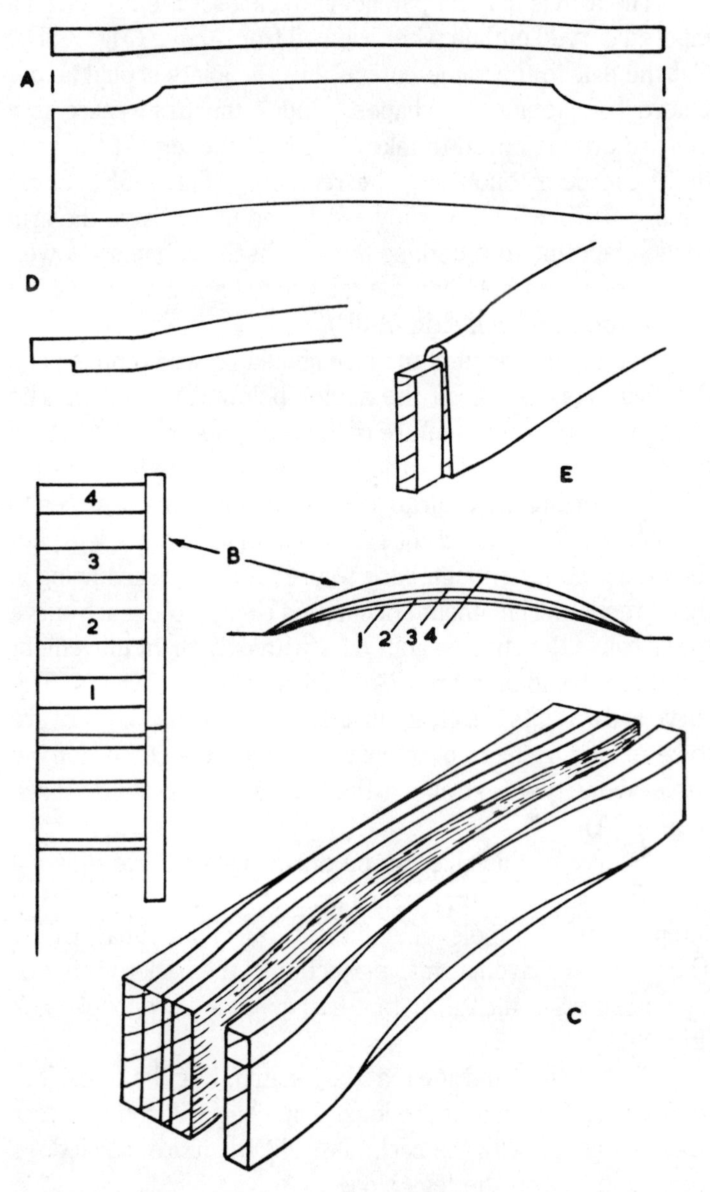


Fig. 8-5. The shaping and methoa of cutting the back rails in a ladderback chair.

could be square and tenoned into the arms (Fig. 8-6B), or the upper part might be turned and finished with a dowel into the arm (Fig. 8-6C).

The arm is flat and parallel in thickness, but it is given a tapered curved outline when viewed from above (Fig. 8-6D). Cut the pair to the same outline, but the joints should be cut before completing the shapes. Under the front there is a mortise or hole bored to take the top of the leg. At the back there can be a tenon into the rear post (Fig. 8-6E). Some arms, particularly when they join round posts, have the arm section tapering to round, so the arm itself becomes a dowel. This goes into a hole and the joint may be reinforced with a screw from the back (Fig. 8-6F).

The upper edges of the arm should be well rounded and the sharpness taken off the angles below (Fig. 8-6G). The arms are a prominent feature of the chair, so care is needed in their shaping, particularly the finish at the front of the chair.

Converting the chair to a rocker involves fixing pieces to the bottom. These need not extend far forward of the legs, but they must go far enough back to prevent the chair tipping in that direction. The amount of curve is slight—too much curve would cause the chair to go too far with only slight movement and there would be more risk of falling over backwards. The curve shown suits the chairs just described. If rocking feet are to be made for chairs of other sizes, choose a center for the curve about two feet above the seat and towards the back (Fig. 8-7A).

A curve of this size can be drawn with a piece of wood turning on an awl, with a pencil against the end (Fig. 8-7B) if compass or trammels of sufficient reach are unavailable. These feet are given a small projection at the back to serve as a stop and warn the sitter that he has gone far enough back (Fig. 8-7C).

Cut both feet and see that they match. Use the actual feet to mark the bottoms of the legs. The chair will come to rest when out of use with the back tilted slightly more than it does when standing on the legs alone.

Transfer the sloping lines of the shoulders of the leg tenons around the wood (Fig. 8-7D) and cut the tenons. This can be done on a completed chair, but if it is being built as a rocker, the pair of sides of the chair can be assembled and the

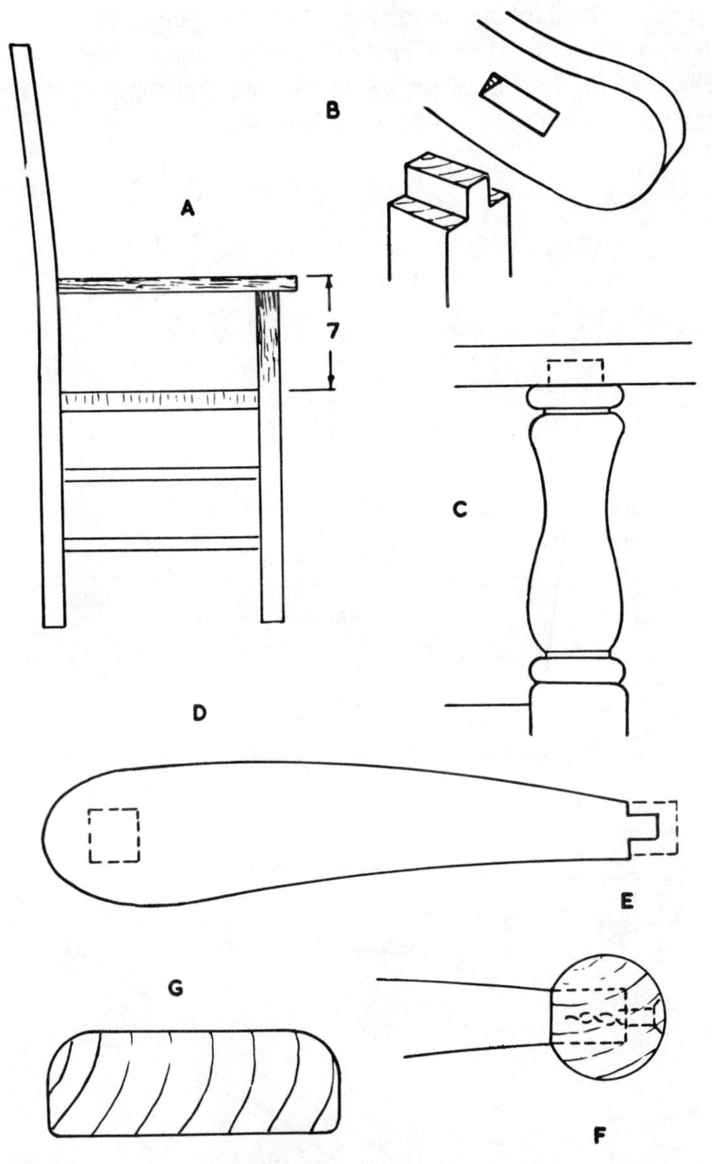


Fig. 8-6. Converting a ladderback chair to an armchair, with square or turned posts.

feet added before the chair is finally assembled with the other crossing rails and slats.

Locate and mark the mortises on the feet. The tenons go fairly deeply into the feet and a modern glue may be all that is needed to hold them securely, but dowels or pegs through the joints were usual (Fig. 8-7E) and may be added. Round the edges of the feet between joints and see that the bottom is smooth, with no sharp edges to mark floor covering.

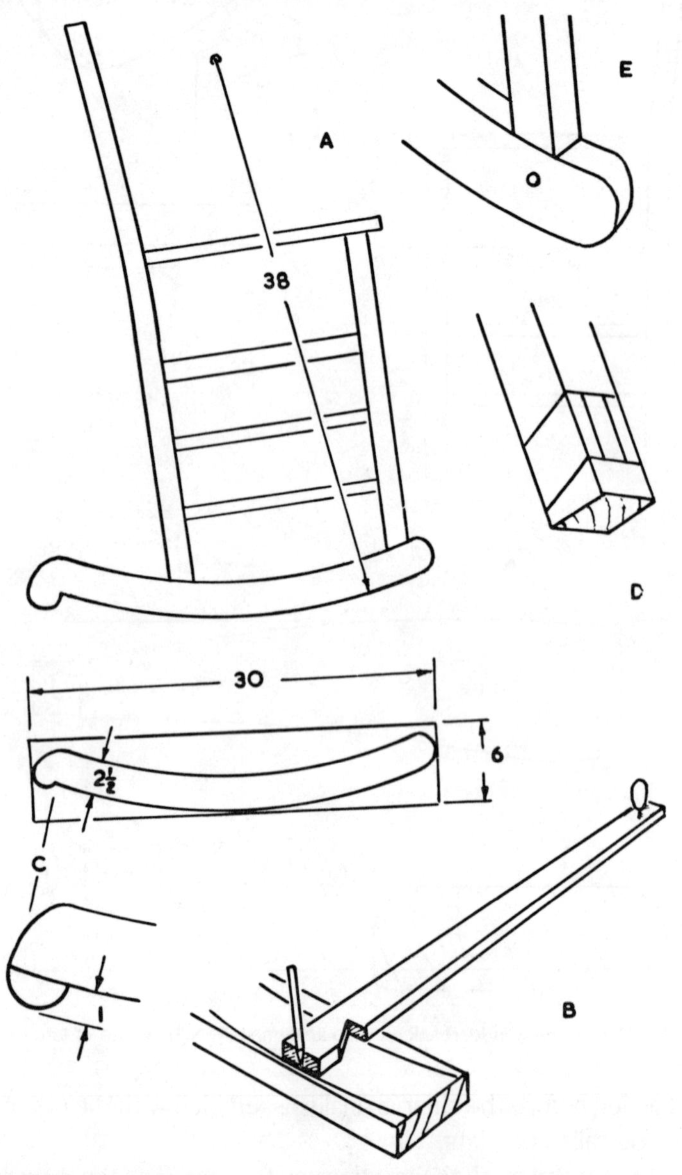


Fig. 8-7. Steps in making a chair into a rocker, with an improvised compass for the curve.

## SPINDLE CHAIR

Many Colonial chairs were made almost entirely by turning the parts on a lathe. It seems that having bought or made lathes the furniture makers looked for projects that would make the fullest use of them. Probably a point in favor of turning was the comparative ease with which a competent craftsman could produce a good surface on round work, yet getting as good a surface with the planes and sanding equipment of the day was much more difficult. This applied particularly to wood that had not been fully dried during seasoning. Turned work in "green" lumber may be brought to a reasonable finish, yet the same wood worked under a plane would be liable to tear up and leave a poor surface, no matter what direction it was planed. As sufficient time could not be allowed between felling trees and converting their wood into furniture, these qualities associated with the lathe must have had considerable appeal.

The ladderback chairs have turned parts, but their outlines are plain and utilitarian. Other chairs were given decorative turnings along the lengths of spindles. If made in attractive hardwood and polished, these chairs were attractive pieces in a dining room and could still be used for that purpose. Most followed the early tendency to make the backs upright. Seats were often rush, worked in the manner described for the ladderback chairs, or some were given lift-out panels that either supported a cushion or were upholstered. The example shown (Fig. 8-8A) has this type of seat, but giving it a rush seat instead would only involve the substitution of suitable seat rails.

The main motif in all the turned parts is a series of large beads, with very few small quirks of angular sections. The lower parts of the rear posts were left plain, except for the feet, but they could be turned like the front legs if the back of the chair was likely to be visible in normal use.

Make the front legs. Note that the parts that will be drilled for rails are parallel (Fig. 8-8B). Mark the rail positions with lightly penciled rings while the wood is rotating in the lathe. Make the rear posts (Fig. 8-8C), using the front legs as a guide to the centers for drilling rails. As with the legs, keep the parts which will be drilled parallel. Some of these chairs had quite tall spindles projecting at the tops of the posts, but the more squat finial shown (Fig. 8-8D) was typical of a more compact decoration. This should be turned as part of the post, but if the post length is near the capacity of the lathe, its end could be drilled and the finial made separately with a dowel for plugging in.

The front legs and rear posts stand upright, so the side joints are at right angles. When viewed from above the front of the chair is wider than the back. This means that care is needed when drilling to always have the drill at right angles to the length of the spindle being drilled, although it may have to be a few degrees away from a right angle in relation to other holes, due to the taper of the seat. As with the ladderback chairs, draw the seat shape full-size to get the corner angles (Fig. 8-8E).

Instead of slats, the back is made up of two horizontal spindles and four upright ones (Fig. 8-8F). Make the horizontal spindles with the same distance between shoulders as the lower rails, and space the beads to suit the upright spindles (Fig. 8-8G). Pencil around where the holes are to come, although some chairs have a line cut around with the long point of a turning chisel.

The upright spindles are turned without shoulders at their ends (Fig. 8-8H). In this way, there can be some adjustment in the joints to allow for slight errors in the diameters of the horizontal spindles or the spacing between the holes for them in the posts.

If the horizontal spindles are drilled by hand, the wood should be held in a vise and a try square stood beside each hole in turn so the drill is always as near upright as possible. If the spindles are drilled in a drill press, it is helpful to use V-blocks. These may be a metal engineering type or they can be made of wood. Accuracy in the V is not important, so long as both blocks are identical, as they should be if cut together on a bandsaw (Fig. 8-8J).

The holes in the legs and posts are drilled at the correct angles in relation to each other, either with an adjustable bevel alongside for hand drilling or on a drill press using a similar jig to that suggested for the ladderback chairs (Fig. 8-2L).

The chair rails could be rabbeted square section (Fig. 8-9A) to take the seat panel. An alternative is to fasten one piece inside another (Fig. 8-9B). If a turned effect is wanted alongside the seat, a split turning can be used.

Two opposite parts are made at the same time. Prepare two strips that will make up a square when put together (Fig. 8-9C). Glue them with paper between (Fig. 8-9D) and let the glue set. Turn this spindle to the pattern for the seat rails. Avoid very great differences in diameter between parts of the spindle (Fig. 8-9E). Let the ends of the design be straight and leave a little excess length for trimming to make joints. Remove the wood from the lathe and split the pieces apart along the paper line with a knife or chisel. Scrape and sand away any remaining paper.

Glue on a strip to form the ledge inside the turned part (Fig. 8-9F). Whatever type of seat rails are used, join them to the legs and posts with mortise and tenon joints. Assemble the chair in a similar way to the ladderback chairs. Make up the assembly of spindles in the back and join these to the posts with the lower rails before the glue in any joint has set, then the upright back spindles can adjust to the other parts. Check diagonals and flatness, then allow to set—under weights if necessary. Do the same with the chair front, then join with the side rails, checking that the chair stands upright and does not wobble.

In its simplest form the seat is a plain board, making a loose fit on the rails (Fig. 8-10A). In modern furniture it would be plywood, but if a board is used, as it would have been in an original chair, there can be battens across the grain below and cut back to fit inside the rail frame.

The plain wooden seat can support a loose cushion or it may be given its own padding. This would have been sheep wool or pieces of cloth, but a modern version would be better with plastic or rubber foam. Cloth is stretched over and tacked underneath (Fig. 8-10B), with the corners of the cloth neatly folded around the corners of the board.

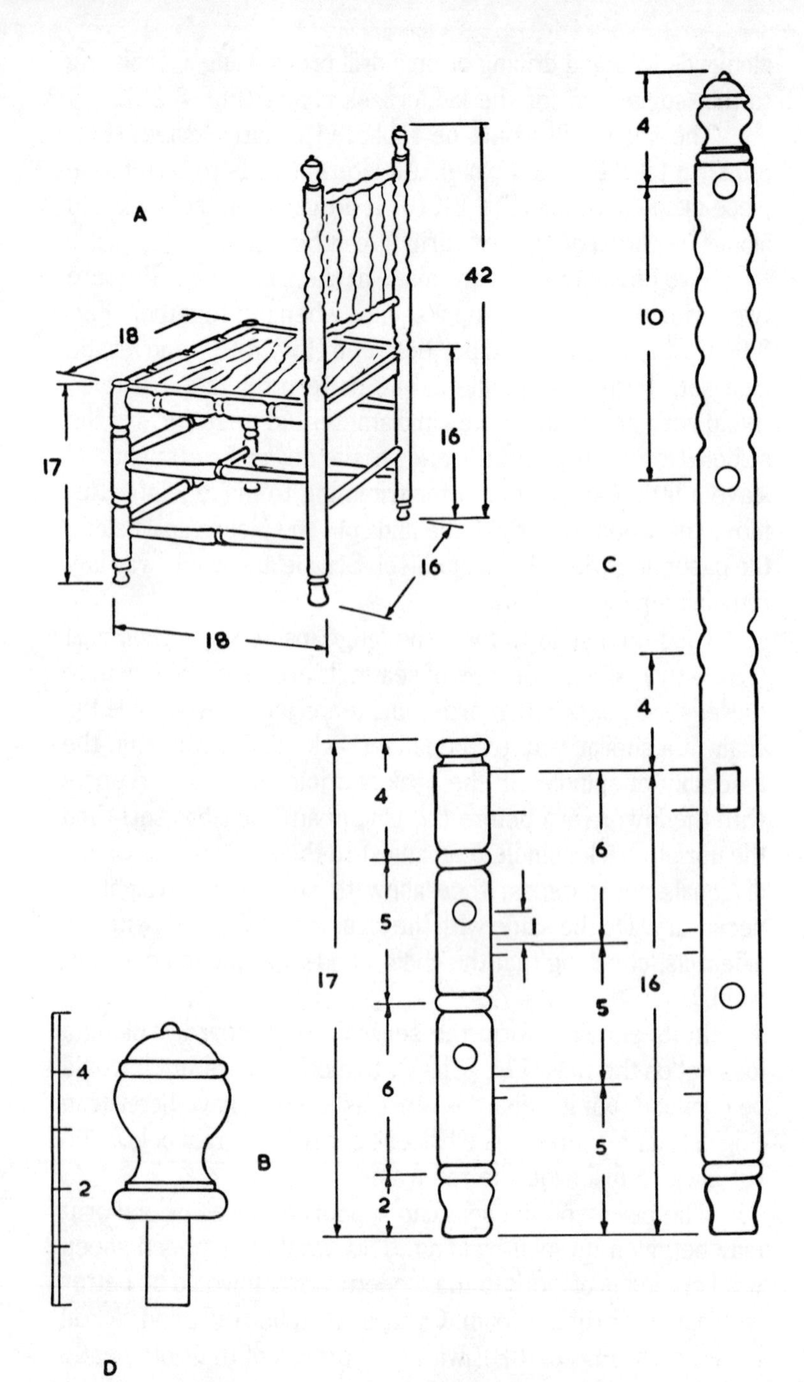


Fig. 8-8. Spindle chair. (Continued on next page.)

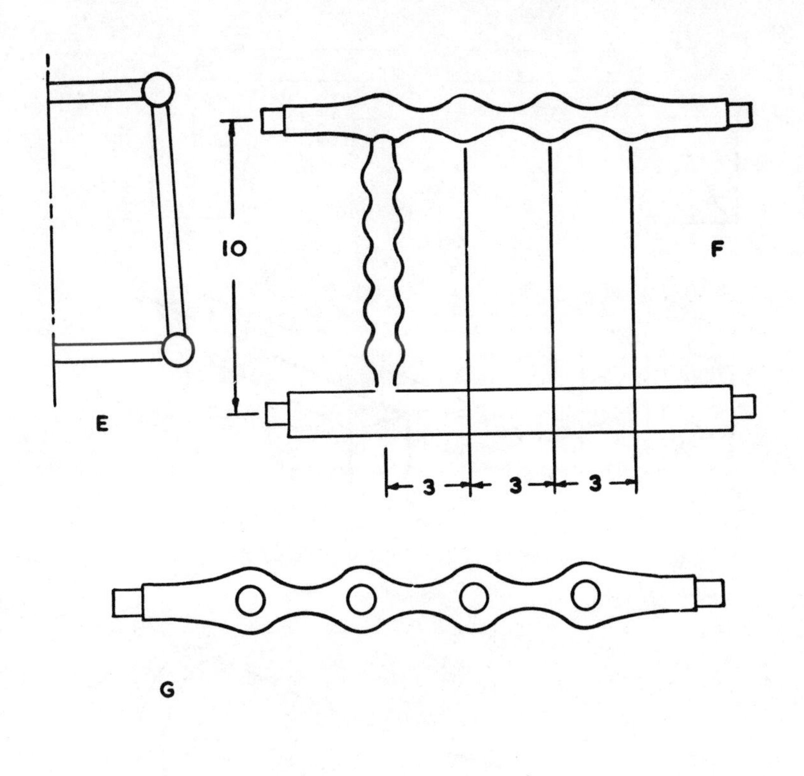


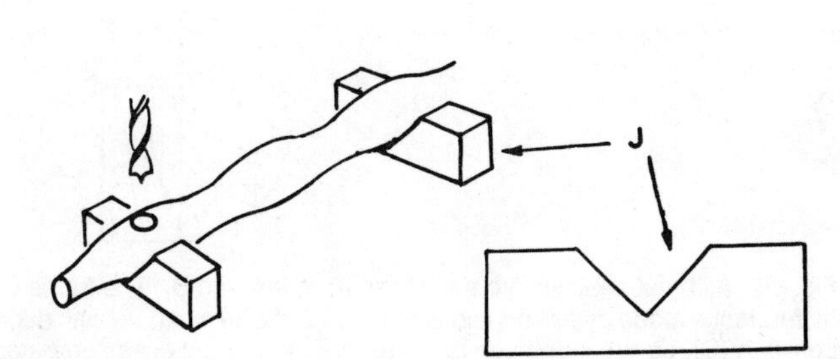


**Materials List 8-8**

Spindle Chair

| | | |
|---|---|---|
| 2 | Legs | 1¾ × 17 × 1¾ |
| 2 | Posts | 1¾ × 42 × 1¾ |
| 7 | Rails | 1¼ × 18 × 1¼ |
| 2 | Back rails | 1¼ × 16 × 1¼ |
| 4 | Back rails | 1¼ × 10 × 1¼ |
| 4 | Seat rails from | 1½ × 18 × ¾ |
| 1 | Seat | 18 × 18 × ½ |
| or 4 | | 1½ × 18 × ⅝ |

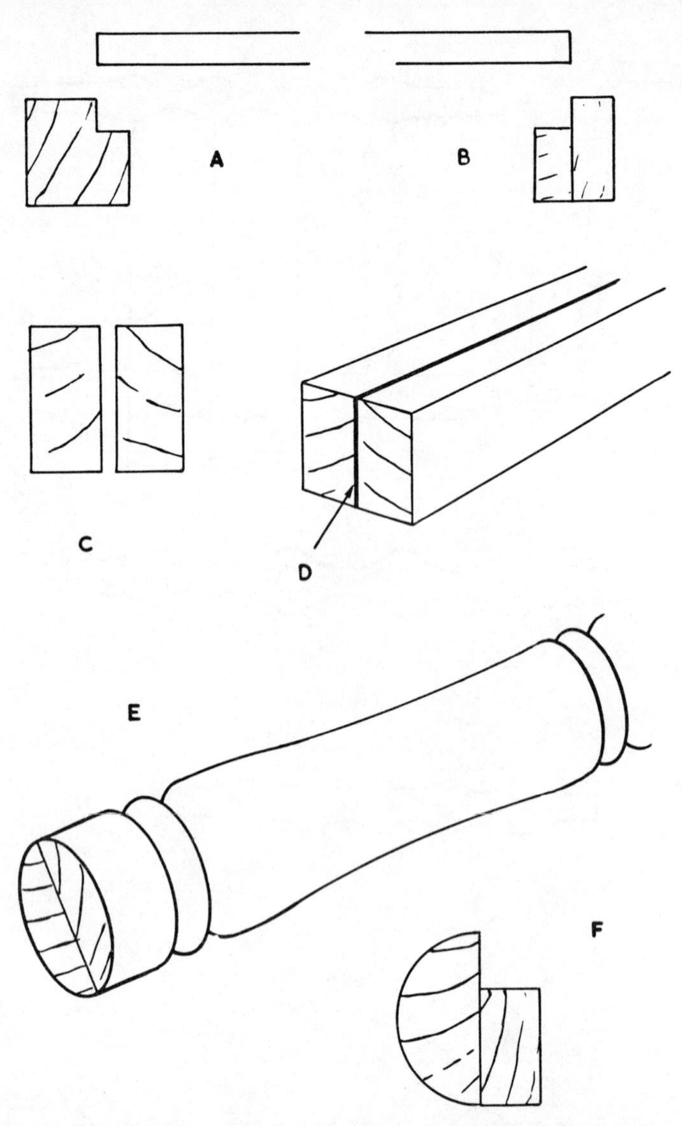


Fig. 8-9. A lift-out seat fits into a notched frame (A and B). The frame can have half-turnings made by joining two pieces (C) to make a square with paper glued between (D), so the wood can be turned (E) and the pieces separated (F).

Such padding only gives limited comfort and a further step was to use an open frame with the padding supported on strips of canvas, webbing or leather. The frame is made a loose fit in the recess, and the corners may be cross lapped (Fig. 8-10C) or joined with open mortise and tenon joints, sometimes called "brindle joints" (Fig. 8-10D). The straps are interlaced tightly and tacked below (Fig. 8-10E). Tension can be put on with one of the modern types of upholstery webbing stretchers, but the simplest way was the original one, levering

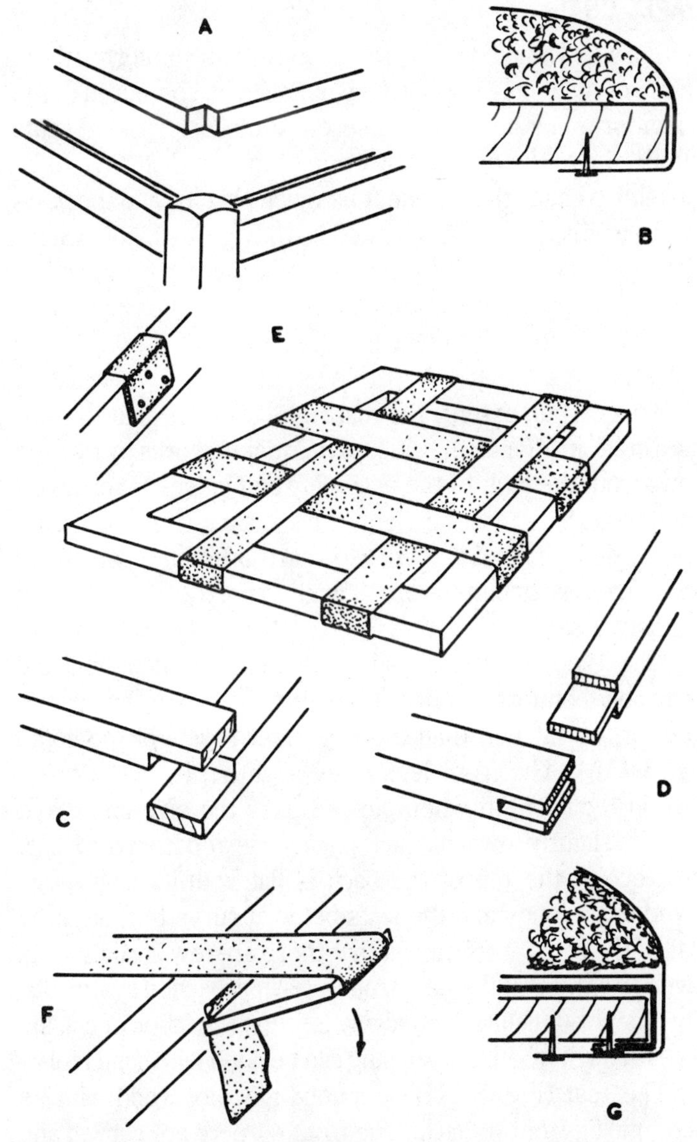


Fig. 8-10. A lift-out seat (A) can be solid and padded (B) or a frame covered with webbing (C-F) and then upholstered (G).

with a piece of wood (Fig. 8-10F). A piece of cloth, such as burlap, is tacked above the webbing, then the padding put on and the cloth cover pulled over and tacked in the same way as for a plain board bottom (Fig. 8-10G).

## SHAPED CHAIR

If a wooden chair is to provide maximum comfort without the use of cushions or upholstery, it has to be contoured to the human form in many ways. There are modern molded seats that blend into the figure, but when strips of wood have to be made into a chair, there cannot be much shaping and the parts have to be disposed and arranged so they give support where they touch the body and other parts of the construction are arranged to contribute to this. Some curving of parts may be possible, but to avoid complications, most of the parts are straight.

To a certain extent, the making of chairs is an art rather than a craft, insofar as the skilled chairmaker works by eye and knows from the look of the assembly and judges by previous experience that it will be right. This makes working from a drawing difficult, mainly because there are some compound curves involved and these are difficult to portray and interpret on a flat piece of paper.

One type of solid wood chair that was common and reasonably comfortable had a beauty in its form, but it was more for the kitchen than the important rooms of the home (Fig. 8-11A). The front legs splay slightly. The back posts curve in their length when viewed from the side and curve outwards slightly towards the top when viewed from the front. The piece at the top of the back is flat with its front edge curved to the body and the slats below it curve to fit into the small of the back. This means that there are few straight lines to work from, but if the construction is approached systematically it is not difficult. A bandsaw lessens the labor of cutting curves in thick wood, but shaping can be done with hand tools.

The seat (Fig. 8-11B) is a solid piece of wood with its grain running front to back. The front corners are curved and the sides may have a slight curve. The top could be flat, but these seats were hollowed to a shape something like the human posterior (Fig. 8-11C). This was done with an adze or a curved drawknife. It could be done with a broad gouge. The depth does not have to be great, but care is needed to keep the two halves matching. Work towards the deepest parts from a penciled outline. A curved scraper will remove tool marks and this can be followed by a coarse abrasive paper, followed by a finishing grade.

The two front legs are simple turnings. Keep the diameters near parallel for the parts that will be drilled to take the rails (Fig. 8-11D). The dowel tops usually go through the seat and are wedged on top. The exact amount of splay is not so important as getting both legs splayed the same amount. An adjustable bevel alongside the drill will guide it correctly.

The rear posts are first cut from a wide board (Fig. 8-11E), and the two planed to match in side view. Their thickness is then modified so they form parallel legs up to the seat level, then flare outwards slightly towards their tops (Fig. 8-11F).

Remove all signs of saw marks and clean up the posts. See that they finish with their surfaces at right angles to each other in cross section. The upper parts should retain the same width all the way to the top. This type of chair does not have tapered posts.

The rails are either plain cylindrical ones or turned with a thicker part at the center. It was usual to not shoulder the ends, but turn them parallel with a slight chamfer to push into the holes (Fig. 8-11G). This allows adjustment. It would be difficult to get every shouldered rail correct when dealing with flared and curved legs and posts. Holes are drilled slightly too deep to allow for this. Although some guidance may come from the use of an adjustable bevel, there has to be a certain amount of judgement of the angle to hold the drill for some holes. If there are slight errors, holes may be modified with a gouge or the end of a rail pared with a chisel. However, joints should make tight fits. Glues are not sufficiently gap-filling to retain their strength if required to fill spaces. Sawdust can be mixed with glue that has to go into a space. Many old chairs that have

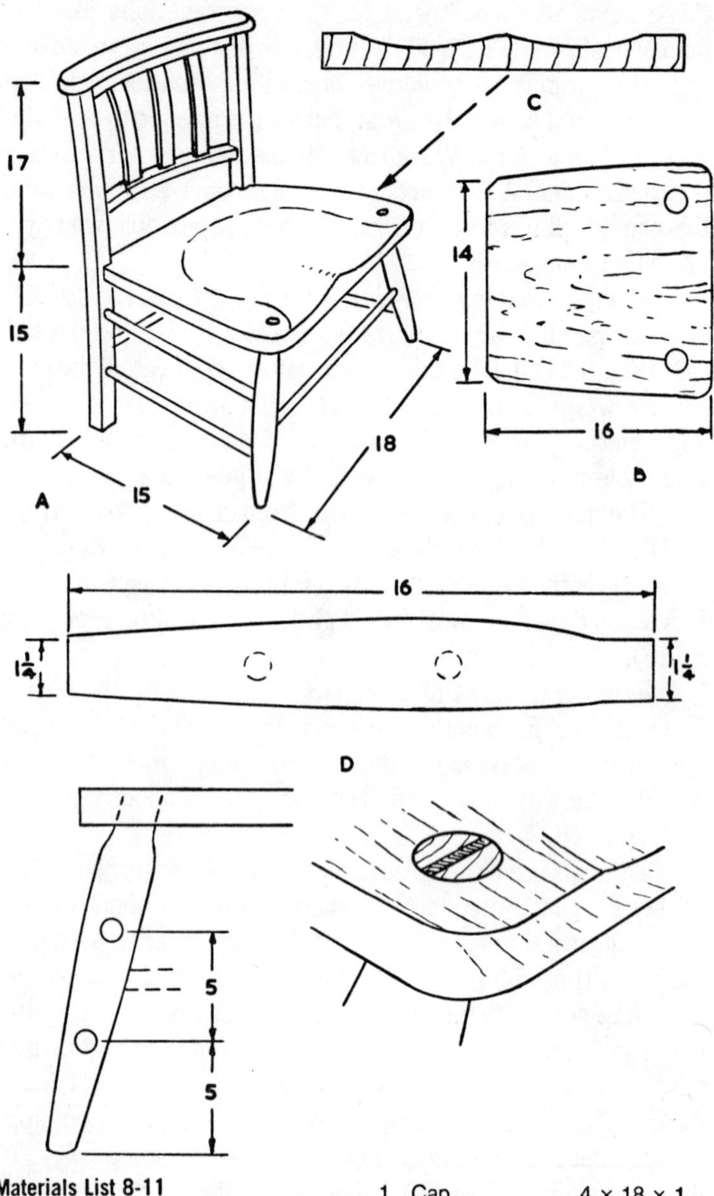


**Materials List 8-11**
Shaped Chair

| | | |
|---|---|---|
| 2 | Legs | 2 × 16 × 2 |
| 2 | Posts from | 4 × 32 × 4 |
| 6 | Rails | 1 × 18 × 1 |
| 1 | Cap | 4 × 18 × 1 |
| 1 | Cap rail | 1¾ × 14 × 1¾ |
| 1 | Back rail | 1¾ × 14 × 1¼ |
| 3 | Slats | 1¼ × 11 × ⅜ |
| 1 | Seat | 18 × 18 × 1½ |

Fig. 8-11. Shaped chair. (Continued on next page.)

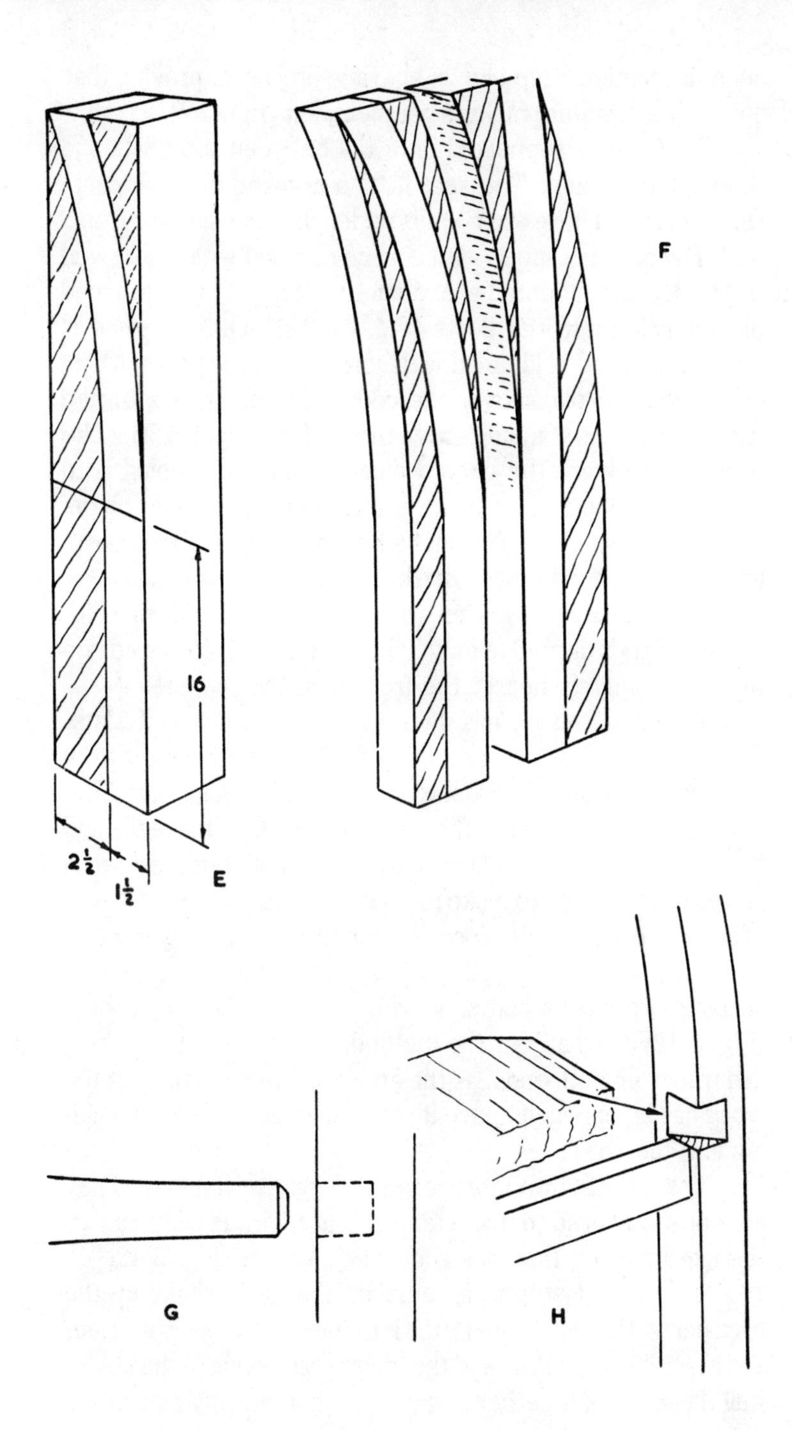
F
16
2 1/2
1 1/2
E
G
H

been dismantled have shown shavings in joints, proving that not all early furniture makers got their joints right every time.

The seat is supported on a rail between the posts and tenoned into them. The seat is also notched into the posts (Fig. 8-11H). There are no rails under the seat sides or front.

The back is capped with a piece of wood with a hollowed front edge and mounted above another curved piece tenoned or dovetailed into the posts (Fig. 8-12A). The top piece is glued to this and held down with screws into the posts. Many chairs had the plugs over the counterbored screws turned with curved tops standing above the surface (Fig. 8-12B). The best way to mark the curved piece under the capping is to make it too long, then make a temporary assembly of the lower parts, so the wood can be held against the flared posts and the compound angles marked.

Another rail crosses between the posts lower down (Fig. 8-12C). This is curved to match the top one and is tenoned into the posts, slightly nearer the front than the top one.

Between these rails there are narrow curved slats. There are two ways of making them. They could be cut from thick wood with a band saw or alternative handsaw (Fig. 8-12D). In original chairs they were more likely made flat and bent. Larger pieces would have to be steamed, but these small pieces can be boiled to make them sufficiently pliable. One way of bending is to use one piece of wood to push a slat against two more in a vise (Fig. 8-12E). A better curve is obtained by shaping two blocks and squeezing the wood between them (Fig. 8-12F). Whatever the method, make the slats too long and trim from both ends, as the ends tend to straighten. If the wood has been boiled, leave it to dry completely before building into the chair.

The slats fit into mortises in the two curved rails. They are not shouldered to make tenons, but their full width fits in. A slight taper on the back allows adjustment (Fig. 8-12G).

As the first step in assembling the chair, make up the back parts. Put the curved laths into their mortises, with glue, and assemble their rails and the lower rails between the posts. Pull these parts together and check symmetry by measuring

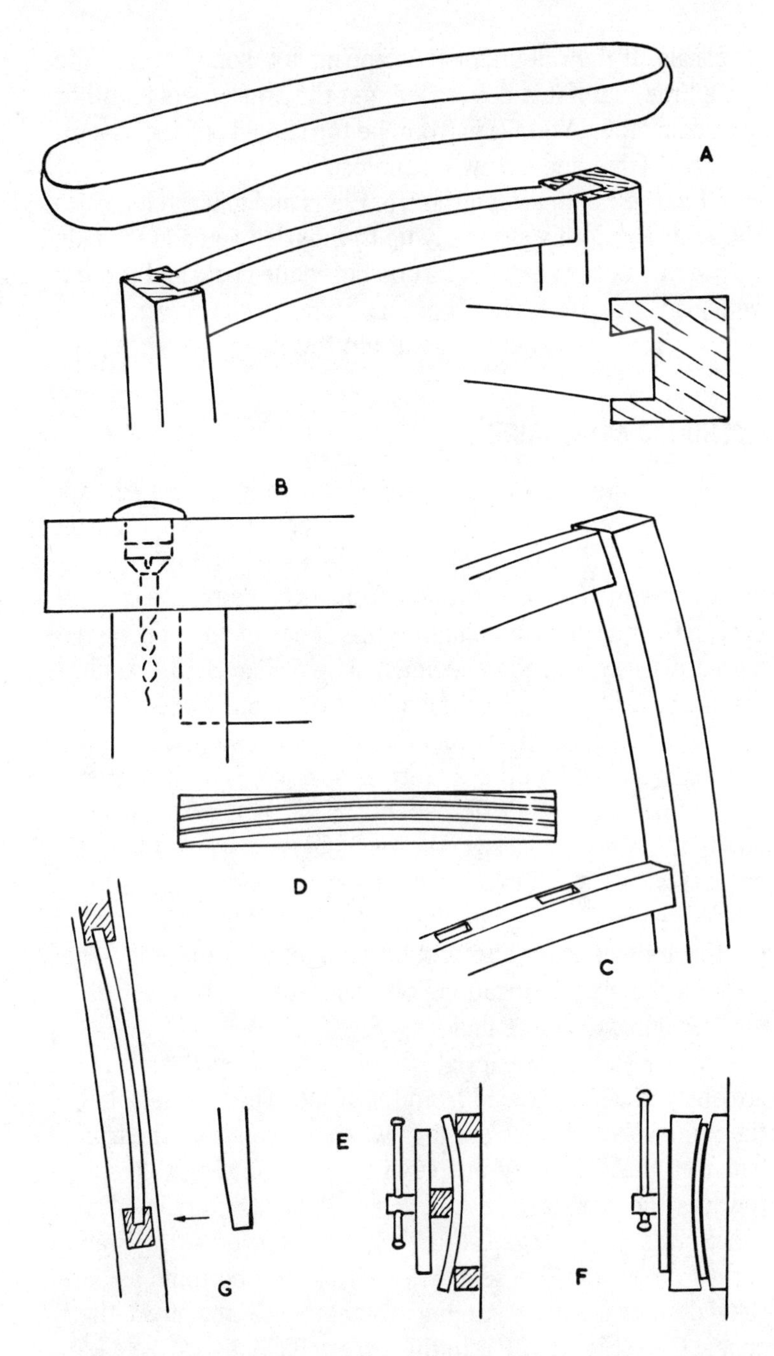


Fig. 8-12. Details of construction of the back of a shaped chair with a top (A and B) fitted above curved rails (C-G).

diagonals. If the rail under the capping is tenoned fit it at the same time, but if it is dovetailed, get the other parts together and sliding the dovetails in from the top should pull the assembly tight. Glue and screw on the capping.

Fix the rail between the front legs and join the legs into the seat. Bring this assembly up to the back and add the side rails as you fit the seat into its notches in the posts and settle it with glue on its back rail. There may have to be a few counterbored screws through the seat into the rail.

## FIREHOUSE ARMCHAIR

Armchairs shaped to fit around the body are sometimes loosely referred to as "Windsor chairs," but the true Windsor chair has an arched back (see the next example). The firehouse armchair gets its name from its common use in early days in the quarters of volunteer fire departments. There are a great variety, but the specimen shown (Fig. 8-13A) is chosen because it can be made without steaming wood.

Some chairs had flat seats, others were shaped as in the last example, while others were shaped from back to front, while remaining straight across (Fig. 8-13B). The front edge is straight, the grain is across the seat and the back is a part of a circle (Fig. 8-13C). The seat is the key member of the assembly. Make this first. Locate the leg positions on the underside. On the top, pencil a line around parallel with the edge and position the spindle locations on this. Note there is an even number and spacing is uniform (Fig. 8-13D).

The front legs are upright when viewed from the side, but are splayed when viewed from the front. The rear legs have the same splay as the front legs when viewed from the front, but from the side they are seen to have considerable splay towards the rear (Fig. 8-13E). It is difficult to arrive at the exact sizes of the legs, so the tops are turned with parallel parts to adjust in the seat holes, while the bottoms are arranged so that final trimming to length will not affect their appearance (Fig. 8-13F). In this case the front legs are decorated with beads, but the rear legs are plainer.

The spindles are turned with thicker centers and there may be beads to match the front legs (Fig. 8-13G). In effect the under assembly and seat may be regarded as a stool and can be put together without reference to the parts above the seat. This can be done before proceeding with the arms and spindles, if you wish.

The combined arms and back is laminated with two or three thicknesses. The shape must match the seat, and the inner edge should be just within the outline of the seat (Fig. 8-14A). Use any convenient lengths of wood. Let them butt together and arrange joints to come at different places in each layer (Fig. 8-14B). Cut each piece to shape with a little to spare. Glue the part together and put them under pressure until set. After that you can treat the laminated part as a single piece of wood. Trim its profile, but do not do any cross-sectional shaping at this stage.

Transfer the spindle locations from the seat to the arm. The spindles will flare out slightly. Let the front pair flare in the width, but be upright when viewed from the side, then space the hole positions for the others around the centerline of the arm piece (Fig. 8-14C).

The eight spindles are all the same. Allow a little excess length and keep the ends parallel and to the hole size, so they will still fit if trimmed to length.

The armchair can be completed at this stage, but many chairs were given an extension backrest. A modern method of making would be to laminate many thin pieces of wood around a mold, but the older glues were not suitable for this method, so the backrests were built up by laminating more flat pieces in a similar way to the making of the arm piece (Fig. 8-14D). This can be worked with spokeshave and plane to a comfortable section to mount on top of the arm piece (Fig. 8-14E), with dowels or screws from below.

This method of mounting does not give high support to the back and another method of mounting the backrest is to use short spindles located above and between the main spindles (Fig. 8-14F). These are turned with dowel ends (Fig. 8-14G) and stand upright between the two parts.

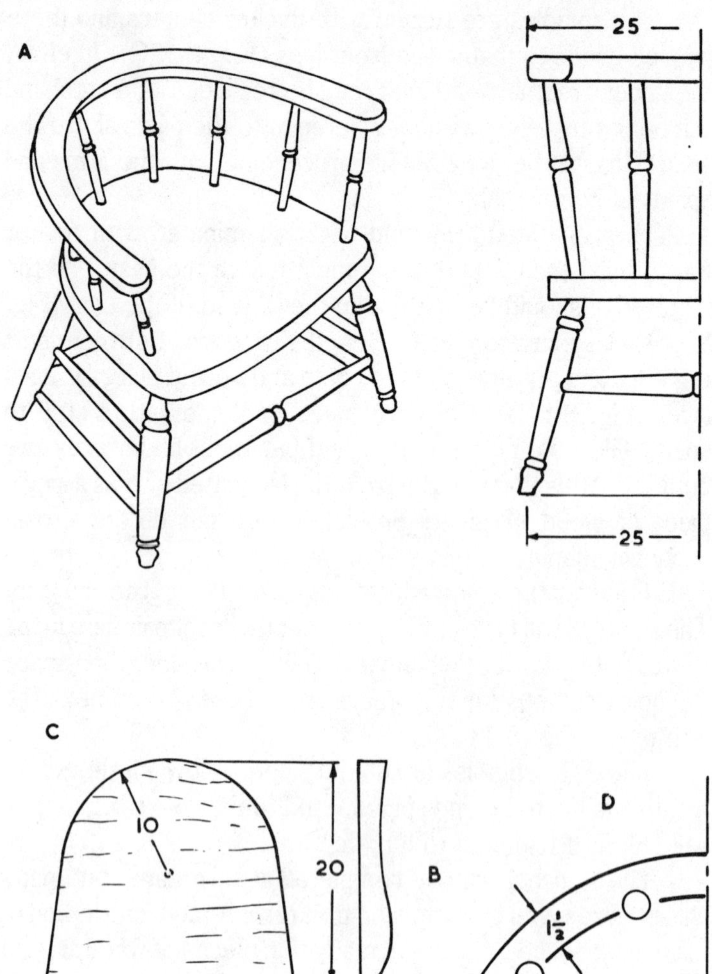


Fig. 8-13. Firehouse armchair. (Continued on next page.)

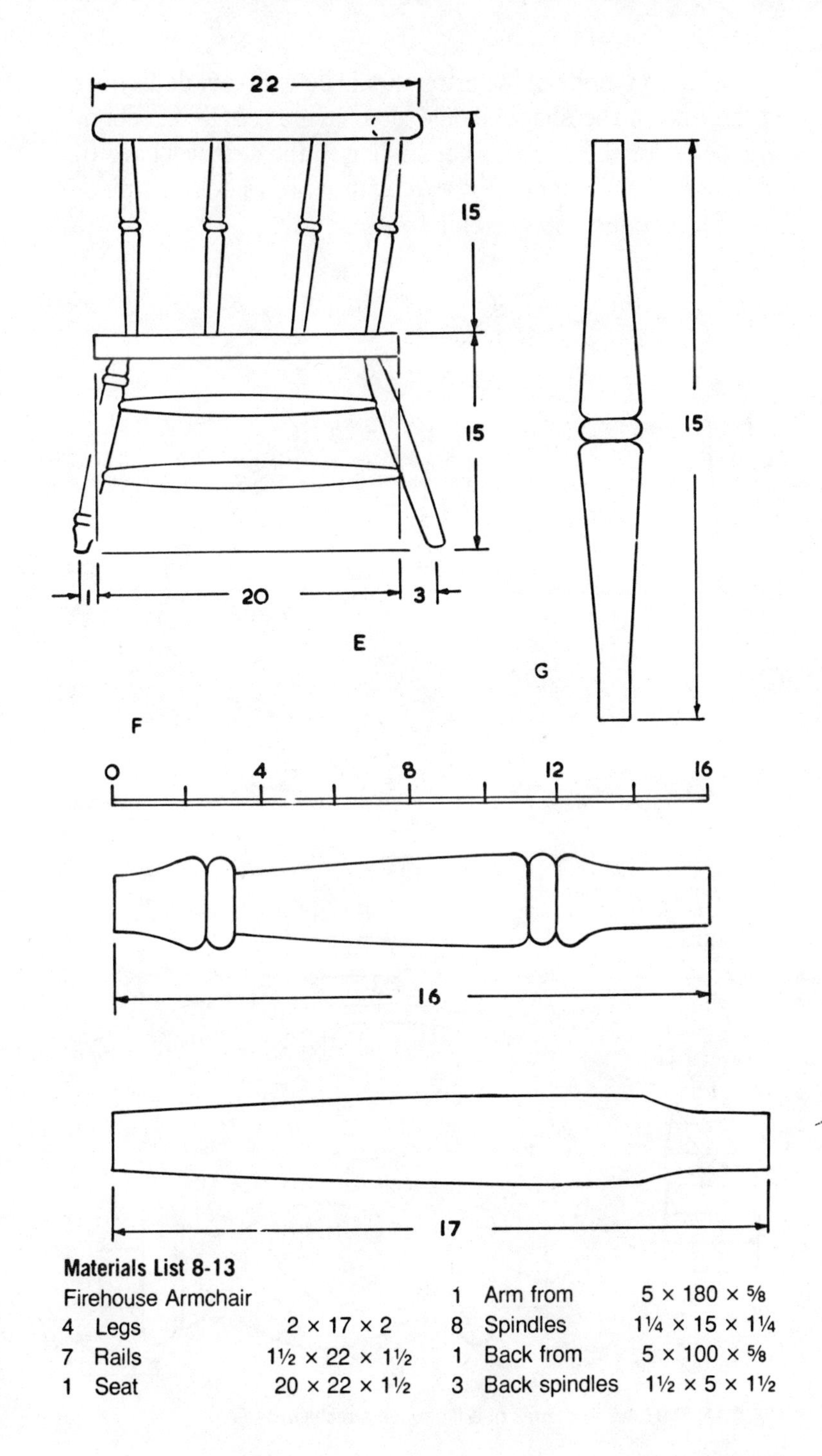


**Materials List 8-13**

Firehouse Armchair

| | | | | | |
|---|---|---|---|---|---|
| 4 | Legs | 2 × 17 × 2 | 1 | Arm from | 5 × 180 × ⅝ |
| 7 | Rails | 1½ × 22 × 1½ | 8 | Spindles | 1¼ × 15 × 1¼ |
| 1 | Seat | 20 × 22 × 1½ | 1 | Back from | 5 × 100 × ⅝ |
| | | | 3 | Back spindles | 1½ × 5 × 1½ |

The front ends of the arms should be well rounded. Most of the rest of the shape should also have a rounded section. The holes for the spindles connecting to the seat will have to be drilled at angles judged by eye, with appropriate adjustment later with gouge and chisel if necessary.

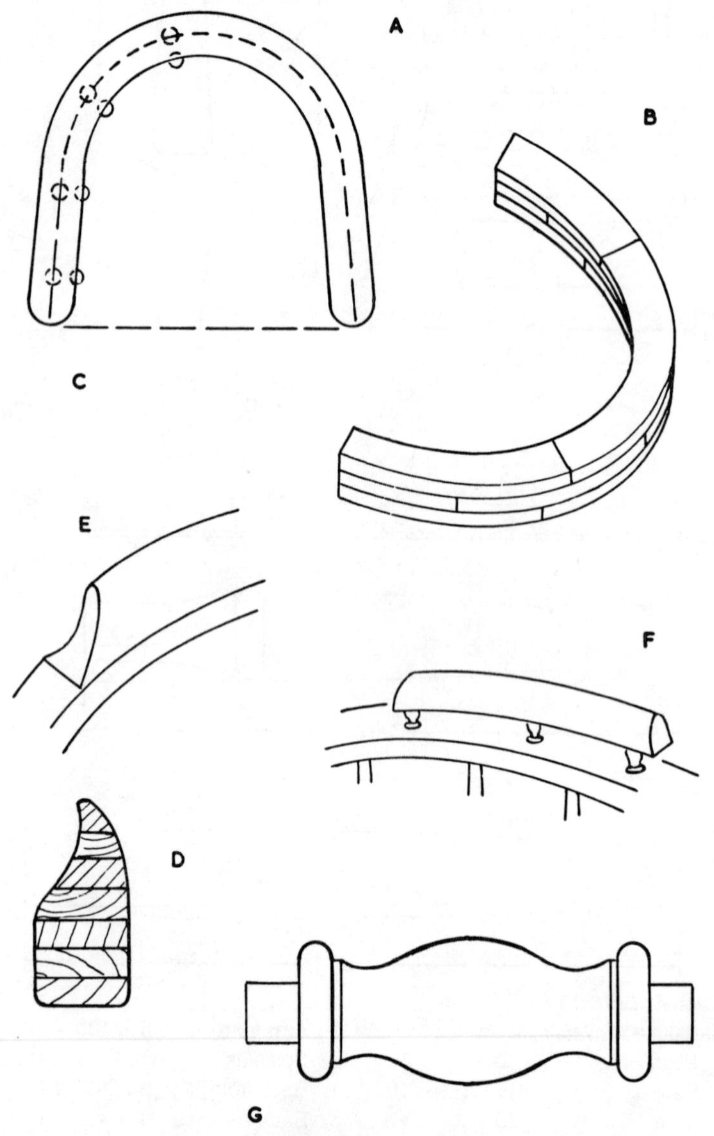


Fig. 8-14. The back and arms of a firehouse armchair.

When the arm is to be attached to the seat, have all the spindle ends glued and lightly inserted in place in the seat. Bring the arm into place and get the spindle ends located in their holes. Use a piece of scrap wood under a hammer or mallet to work around the arm a little at a time driving the parts together. When all of the spindles have entered a short distance, check that the arm is parallel with the seat and the assembly when viewed from the front is not flaring more one way than the other. Continue driving progressively around the arm until all the joints are fully closed and the chair is seen to be symmetrical.

## WINDSOR CHAIR

This type of chair originated at High Wycombe in Buckinghamshire, England, a town which is still situated amid beech woods. The main parts of the chairs were made from this wood, with the arched bow of the back made of yew. The name comes from nearby Windsor, with its Royal Castle, and a medieval monarch who used the chairs gave them this name. The type was well known to those who sailed to America, and many chairmakers produced local variations from very different woods. No British Windsor chairs were made of softwoods, but some American versions were. There are a great many designs of Windsor chairs, but all have the characteristic bow back and a number of upright rods or spindles. Many British Windsor chairs had a central "plat" in the back, decorated with profiling and fretting. This was less common in American Windsor chairs. The ordinary Windsor chair does not come high enough to provide a headrest. Some chairs were made with some of the rods extending through the bow to a shaped top high enough to come behind the head. These were "comb back" Windsor chairs.

Some of the best Windsor chairs are examples of a high degree of craftsmanship, and it is unlikely that even the most skilled amateur woodworker could make one, as these chairs are the result of years of experience making nothing else. Even the more basic types are complex to the extent that much of the work has to be done without guides and only experience will show if the action was right. Consequently, the first attempt at a full Windsor chair may not be successful.

The bow at the back of many Windsor chairs continues to make arm rests. This complication can be avoided if a version without arms is made (Fig. 8-15A). Up to seat level the chair can be made with splayed legs as described for the firehouse chair, or with almost any arrangement of rails. The top is traditionally hollowed to suit the sitter's posterior, but some specimens were made with shaping back to front only in a "plank" seat.

The example has turned legs doweled into the seat and single rails between back and front legs, then a stretcher between them (Fig. 8-15B). The rails should be thickened at their centers to allow for a hole deep enough to provide strength in the joints.

The bow can be made of solid wood, such as hickory or ash, if it can be steamed. A steam chest is made of four boards nailed together into a box, a little longer than the wood for the bow. Some sort of water container and a source of heat are provided and a tube led into one end of the box. This should be surrounded by cloth or other packing, with more at the other end, except for a small space for steam to escape. The wood has to steam long enough to become flexible without risk of breaking. This may take an hour.

Make a mold from scrap wood to the intended outline. Have blocks of wood screwed on and wedged ready for tightening (Fig. 8-15C). With the help of an assistant get the wood from the steam chest and pull it around the mold as quickly as possible, working from the center towards the ends (Fig. 8-15D). Leave this for at least a day.

A modern way of making the bow without steaming is to laminate from three thin pieces. They should be full length, coated with glue and pulled around the same mold, then wedged in the same way as for steaming. This would not be authentic, but when cleaned up and rounded the glue joints would not be obvious to the casual viewer.

The ends of the bow could be tenoned into the seat, but many ends were rounded and pushed into holes like dowels.

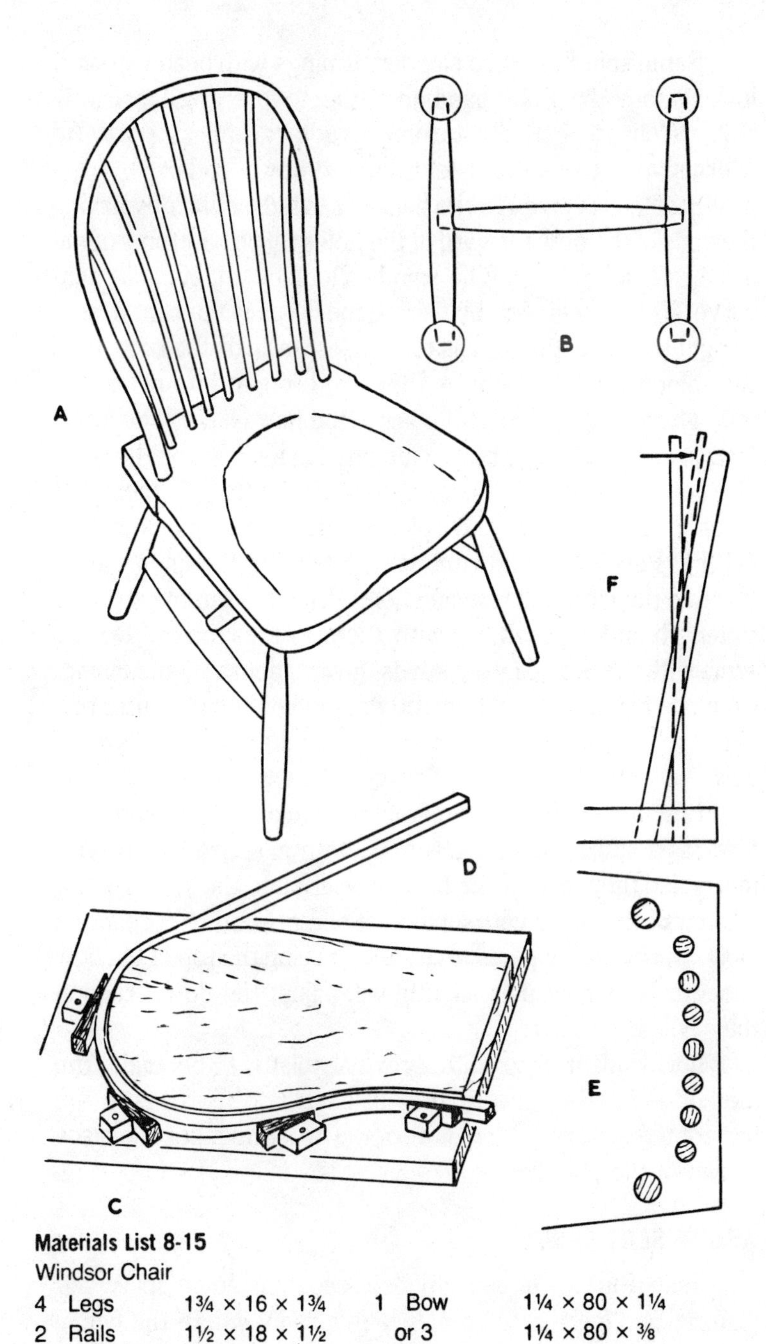


**Materials List 8-15**

Windsor Chair

| | | | | | |
|---|---|---|---|---|---|
| 4 | Legs | $1\frac{3}{4} \times 16 \times 1\frac{3}{4}$ | 1 | Bow | $1\frac{1}{4} \times 80 \times 1\frac{1}{4}$ |
| 2 | Rails | $1\frac{1}{2} \times 18 \times 1\frac{1}{2}$ | | or 3 | $1\frac{1}{4} \times 80 \times \frac{3}{8}$ |
| 1 | Seat | $20 \times 20 \times 1\frac{1}{2}$ | 7 | Spindles | $\frac{5}{8} \times 30 \times \frac{5}{8}$ |

Fig. 8-15. Windsor chair, showing how to bend the back.

Some spindles were slender turnings with beads around, looking something like bamboo. Others were given a slightly bulbous shape. Slender turning needs careful support. An alternative is to use parallel prepared dowel rods.

Stiffness is given to the back of a Windsor chair by having the ends of the bow forward of the holes for the bottoms of the spindles (Fig. 8-15E). The spindles look best if given a slight curve. This is achieved by drilling the holes in the seat nearer upright than is estimated as the angles towards the bow, then the spindles will be bent as they are brought into place.

The actual positions of holes in the bows have to be found by trial and error. The bow is mounted in its holes on the seat. The center spindles are easy to locate. Put them in their seat holes and pull them back to a pleasing position on the bow (Fig. 8-15F). Pencil this and remove the bow so the lines can be taken to the inner surface and holes drilled. Trim the spindles to length and reassemble with them in their holes. Do the same with the next pair outwards, giving them a slight fanning. Continue in this way with the other spindles. As the outer pair are reached the holes will have to be taken acutely into the bow.

Round the edges of the bow, particularly parts that come towards a sitter's back. Assemble with glue and check symmetry and the slope of the back in relation to the seat. Hitting the top of the bow, with a piece of scrap wood to spread the blow, will bring the parts together. Forcing the top of the bow backwards or forwards slightly will adjust the dowel rods in their holes.

If a Windsor chair with a central splat is to be made, the method is similar, except the splat fits into mortises in the back of the seat and the center of the bow and takes the place of two of the spindles.

## WAGON SEAT BENCH

Seats for two or more people economized on space and material and were a convenience in a room where the family gathered around a fire. A bench like an extended stool had its uses, but for comfort there had to be a back of a reasonable height. Farm wagons were often equipped with bench seats across their width and this idea was adapted in a variety of ways to broad seats for use in the home. Wagon seat benches were popular for use on an exterior porch. Those for use indoors acquired refinements as they developed later into settees and love seats.

The majority of early seats of this type were made of wide boards nailed together with only elementary joints. Better seats had screws counterbored and plugged, and this would be the best method for a reproduction wagon bench seat. The example (Fig. 8-16A) is built this way. Sizes can be altered to suit available boards, but if the design is modified take care to see that the legs extend to near the full length of the seat and go out to at least its width to minimize the risk of tipping.

Draw a full-size front view of one end (Fig. 8-16B) to get the angles for the legs and arms. Overall sizes are governed by the size of the board which makes the seat.

Make the two legs and check that they match and angles on their edges are the same (Fig. 8-16C). Notch them for the rails, but these need not be let in for their full thickness (Fig. 8-16D). The rails look best if their lower edges are shaped (Fig. 8-16E), although the back rail can be left parallel if the bench is to go against a wall.

Assemble the rails to the legs and check squareness and that the feet stand level. Do not fit to the seat board yet, although that can be cut to size and tried in position.

Note that the back comes between the arms, so the load of anyone leaning against it is taken across the screws and not in a direction that would pull them endwise. The back board is planed at an angle to fit on the seat and the arms also given a slight flare. Shape the fronts of the arms. Their tops can be rounded, or they can be made more comfortable by widening with top pieces (Fig. 8-16F).

The ends can be pierced for two reasons. The holes may be decorative, but they also serve as hand grips when two persons want to move the bench about (Fig. 8-16G). Many outlines of holes were used, so piercing can be shaped to suit personal preference.

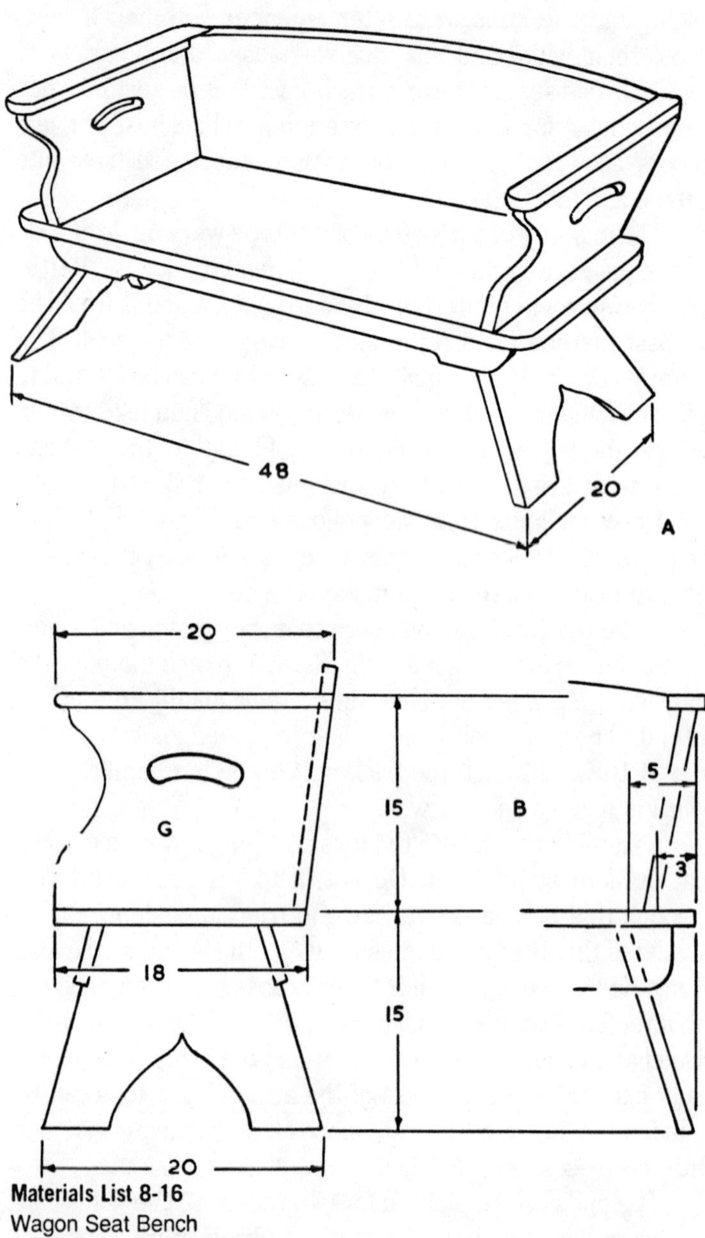


**Materials List 8-16**

Wagon Seat Bench

| | | | | | |
|---|---|---|---|---|---|
| 1 | Seat | 20 × 48 × 1¼ | 2 | Arms | 4 × 20 × 1¼ |
| 1 | Back | 18 × 48 × 1¼ | 2 | Legs | 20 × 16 × 1¼ |
| 2 | Arms | 14 × 20 × 1¼ | 2 | Rails | 4 × 46 × 1¼ |

Fig. 8-16. Wagon seat bench, arm details and assembly. (Continued on next page.)

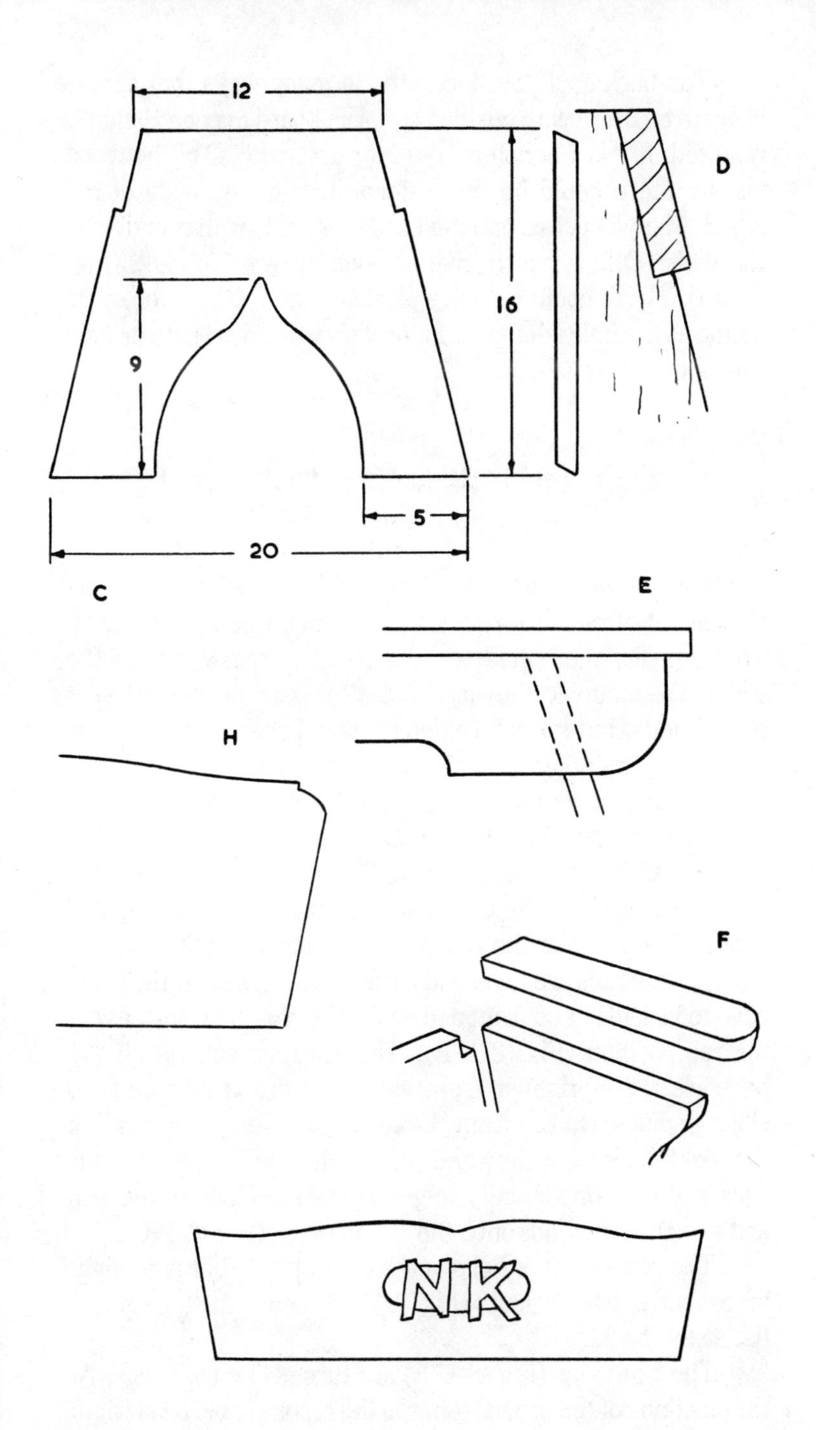
12
16
9
5
20
C
D
E
H
F
NK

The back could be decorated in many ways, but as it is likely to be fitted with cushions, a plain board may be all that is required. If it is a bench for outdoor use, with all of the wood visible, there could be more decoration to the body of the board. Many benches had the backs straight, with rounding at the ends. Others were given a slightly wavy outline (Fig. 8-16H). There could be holes pierced that continue the same theme as the holes in the ends, or it may be possible to include initials or a date (Fig. 8-16J).

## LOVE SEAT

Many seats were really double-width chairs, and some of the chairs already described could be widened in this way. The broader seat and larger load meant there was some tendency to strain the construction in the width, so although the arrangement of rails from back to front might be little different from a chair, there had to be stronger bracing across the width. The example shown (Fig. 8-17A) is a double-width seat on four legs, but it is of a Pennsylvania Dutch style that was finished by painting brightly, and others were made wide enough for four people, with support below coming from as many as eight legs. For that number of legs to stand firmly, the floor has to be absolutely flat.

In the example the front legs stand upright, when viewed in any direction, but the rear legs are splayed both ways. So that the side rails are level and parallel with the seat, the parts have to be laid out so front and back legs cross in front view at the rail position (Fig. 8-17B). The spindles supporting the back are also upright in front view, but the arms spread to sloping spindles at the front. Drawing two views of the end of the seat full-size will show the angles which will have to be cut. This is also an opportunity to get a pleasing shape to the arm and see that it blends into the other parts (Fig. 8-17C).

The plank seat is hollowed back to front, but is straight across and flat underneath (Fig. 8-17D). Leave the top surface flat at the back.

The front legs (Fig. 8-17E) are turned like table legs. At the positions of the broad front rail the taper should be straight so the mortise and tenon joints can be most simply made. The rear legs are plainer (Fig. 8-17F). Since the front legs are upright, their tops can have a definite shoulder where they are doweled into the seat, but because of the flare of the rear legs it is better for the shaping to blend into the dowel end, so there is no need for hand work cutting a sloping shoulder across the turned wood. The positions of the rails can be marked with pencil while the front legs are revolved in the lathe, but the rail positions on the rear legs are best found during a trial assembly. With the legs temporarily plugged into the seat, the wood for the rails can be held in position parallel with the seat and the joint positions marked on rails and legs.

Holes are drilled for the side rails, at right angles into the front legs, but at estimated angles, using the full-size drawing as a guide, into the rear legs.

For the flat rails the joints are mortise and tenons, but it is advisable to flatten the legs in each place for an area to match the section of the rail, then cut and fit the joints (Fig. 8-17G). Without this flattening it would be necessary to cut the tenon shoulders to a curve to get a close fit.

Above the seat there are spindles supporting the back and the arm. The back is straight in its length, but its front should be curved (Fig. 8-18A). Some originals had the rear surface hollowed, but this is difficult to do and is not essential.

The spindles go squarely into the back with dowel ends (Fig. 8-18B). The lower ends taper into thicker dowels, long enough to go right through the seat, for maximum strength.

The back rail fits to the spindles in the same way as the flat rails between the legs, but it looks best and is most comfortable if the front surface is rounded, with the shaping carried over its edges (Fig. 8-18C).

It is advisable to make the arm spindles (Fig. 8-18D) before making the arm. Care is needed to get the holes into the seat drilled at a matching pair of angles. The exact angles are not so critical as the need to get them the same both ways. Use templates cut to the intended angles, as seen from front and side, as a guide to drilling (Fig. 8-18E). With the arm

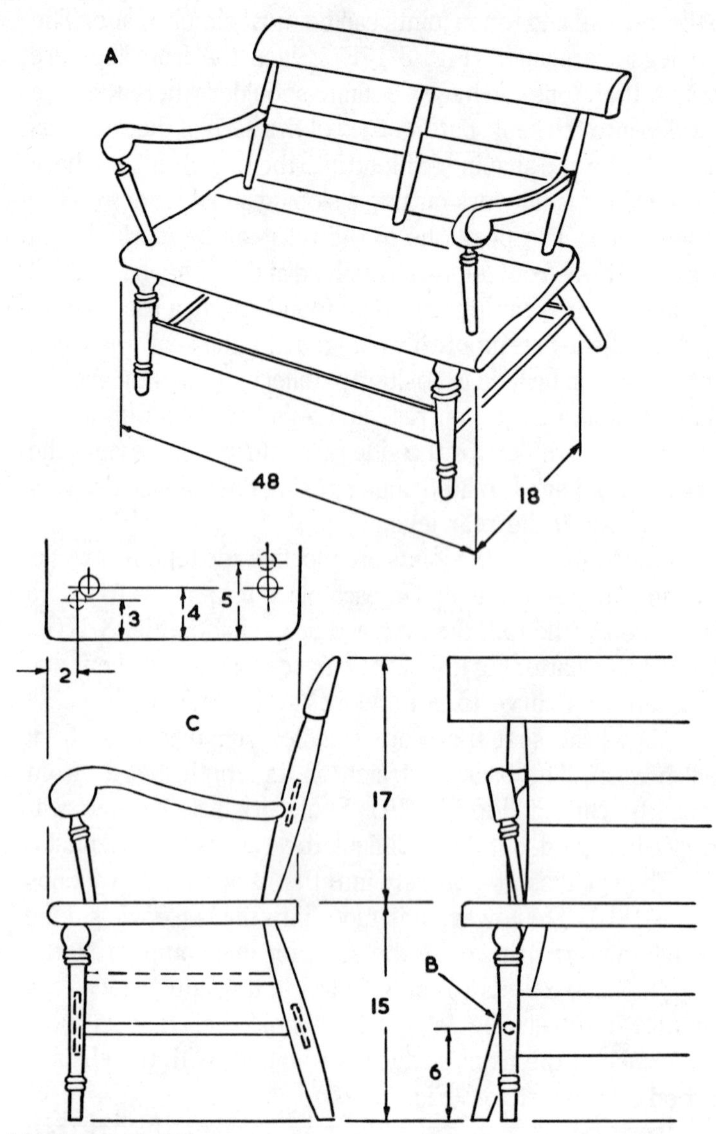


**Materials List 8-17**

Love Seat

| | | | | | |
|---|---|---|---|---|---|
| 1 | Seat | 18 × 48 × 1¼ | 1 | Rear rail | 3 × 44 × ¾ |
| 1 | Back | 4 × 48 × 1½ | 2 | Side rails | ¾ × 20 × ¾ |
| 2 | Legs | 3 × 15 × 3 | 3 | Back posts | 1¾ × 17 × 1¾ |
| 2 | Legs | 3 × 17 × 3 | 2 | Back rails | 3 × 24 × ¾ |
| 1 | Front rail | 4 × 43 × ¾ | 2 | Arms | 4 × 17 × 1½ |
| | | | 2 | Arm posts | 1¾ × 15 × 1¾ |

Fig. 8-17. Love seat. (Continued on next page.)

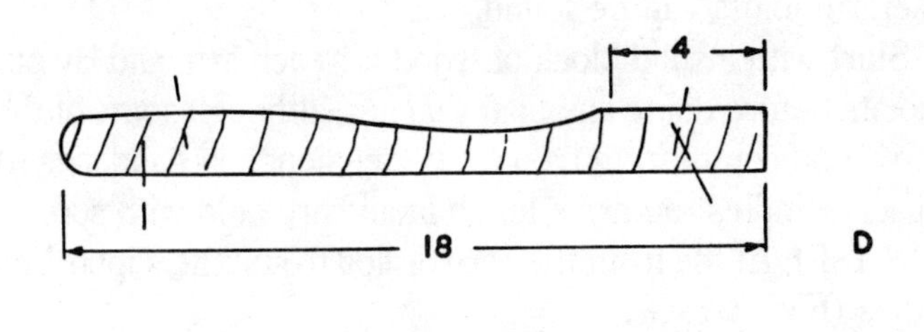
4
1
1
18
D

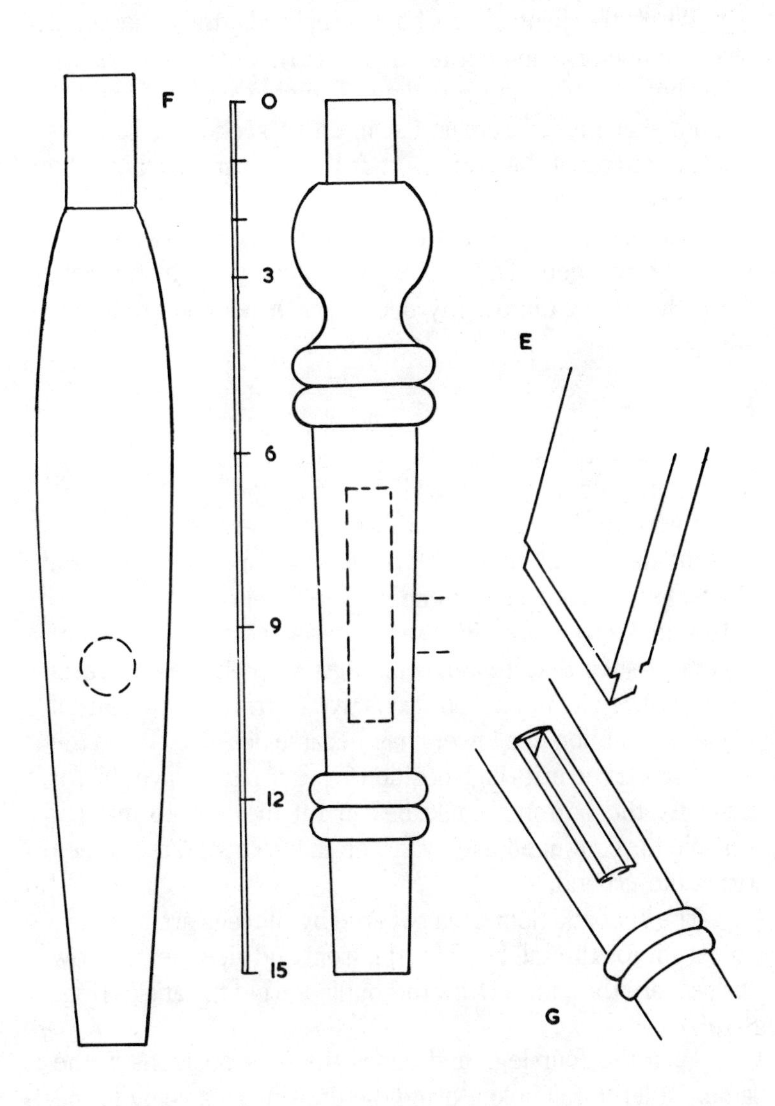
F
0
3
6
9
12
15
E
G

spindles mounted temporarily in position, the exact locations of the arm joints can be found.

Start with a solid block of wood for each arm and lay out the joints before doing any final shaping, although some of the waste wood can be removed for convenience in handling. At the back spindles the arms notch in and are held with screws (Fig. 8-18F). At the front they are drilled to suit the supporting spindles (Fig. 8-18G).

When the joints have been prepared, draw the scroll shape of one arm and cut it (Fig. 8-18H). Use it to mark the other before doing any rounding. The side surfaces and the bottom shaping can remain flat in cross section, except for slight rounding of the corners, but the top surface should be domed (Fig. 8-18J).

For maximum strength the parts attached to the seat should be wedged. Those downwards can go right through, while the legs go into fairly deep blind holes and are foxtail wedged.

## HIGH CHAIR

A high chair for a baby needs to stand on a broad base to prevent tipping and be provided with a footrest. Many versions were made and some of them have carried over to the present day. The simplest form is made like many normal chairs, but with the legs extended. The specimen chosen (Fig. 8-19A) makes use of plainly turned parts and a simple outline. Its size is such that it would suit a growing child as well as a baby. By keeping the rail positions well up from the bottoms of the legs, adaption to a lower chair became possible. When the chair had served in its high position for each successive child of a family, the bottoms could be cut off the legs to make it suitable for continued use by larger children, who could then reach the ground.

The seat and floor area covered by the legs are squares, so except for the rail heights, the front and side views below the seat are the same. Draw this outline to get the angles (Fig. 8-19B).

Turn the four legs and pencil the hole positions in the lathe. Drill the rail holes, using the drawing as a guide to the

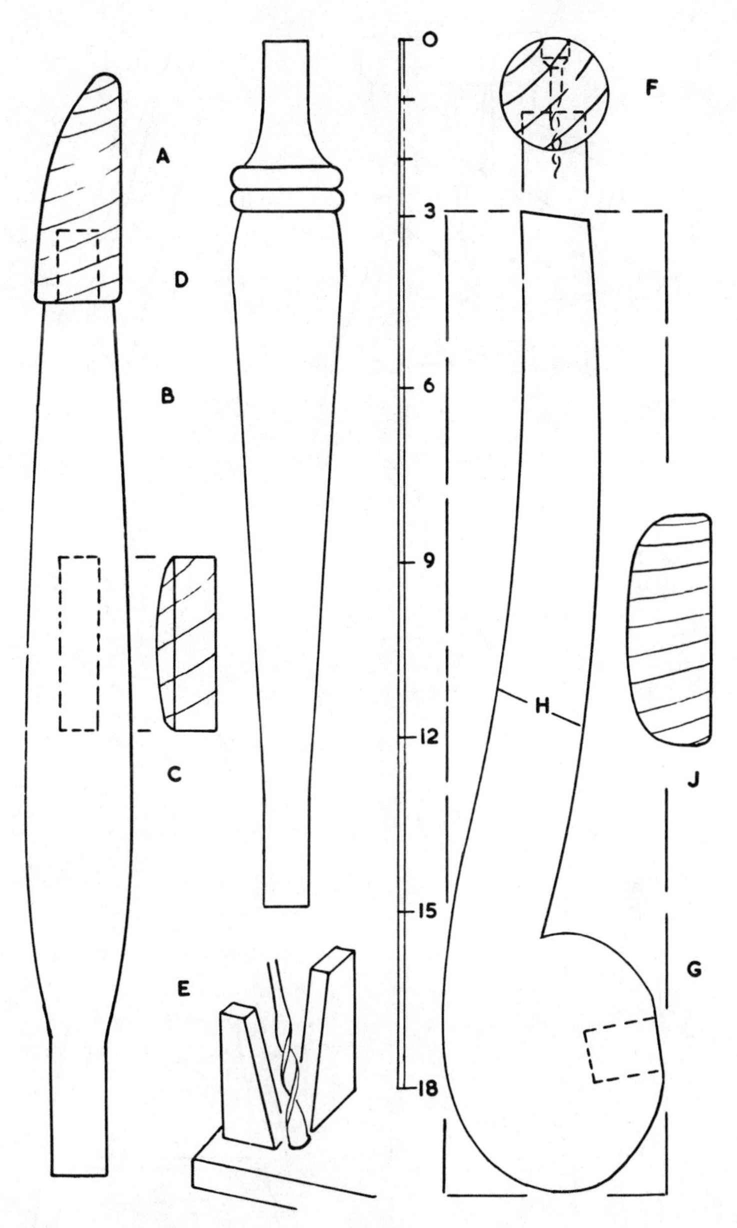


Fig. 8-18. Arm and back details for love seat.

angles. The seat is a square board with the front edge well rounded. Make and drill this, so there can be a trial assembly of the under framing.

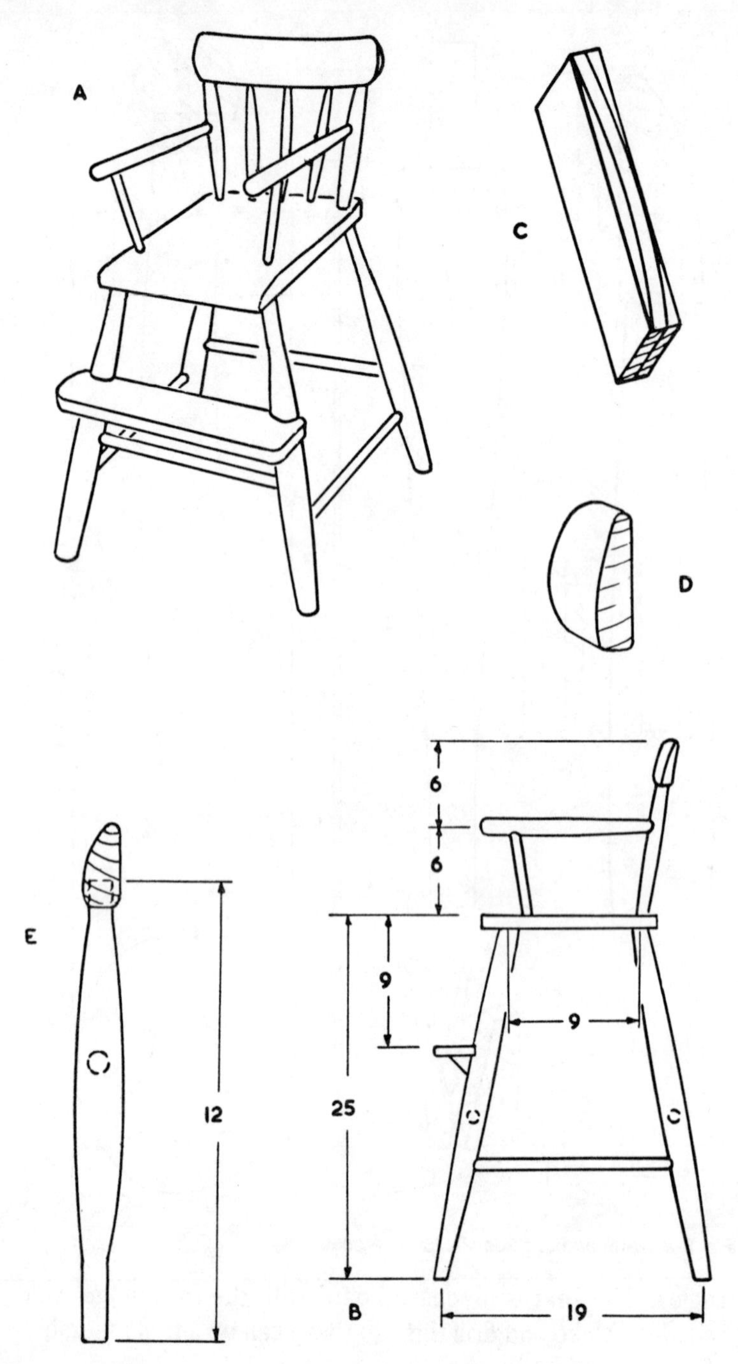


Fig. 8-19. High chair. (Continued on next page.)

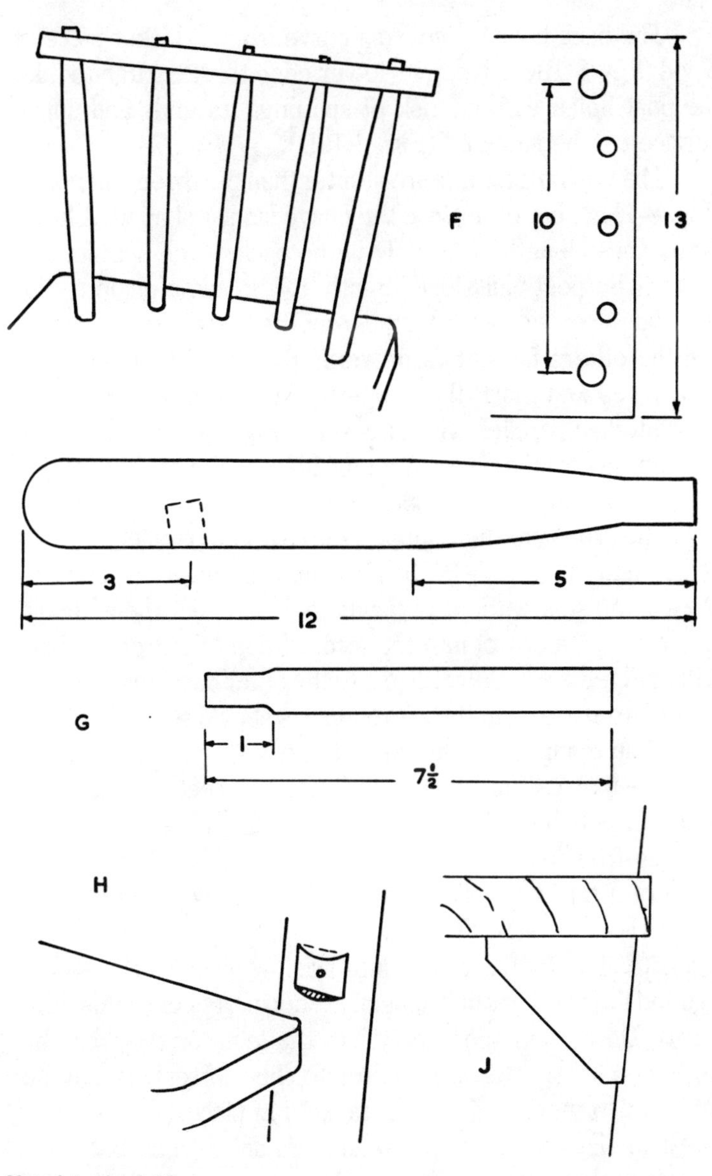


**Materials List 8-19**

High Chair

| | | |
|---|---|---|
| 1 | Seat | 13 × 13 × 1 |
| 4 | Legs | 1¾ × 25 × 1¾ |
| 4 | Rails | ¾ × 19 × ¾ |
| 1 | Back | 2½ × 14 × 1¼ |
| 2 | Back posts | 1¼ × 12 × 1¼ |
| 3 | Back posts | ⅞ × 12 × ⅞ |
| 2 | Arms | 1 × 12 × 1 |
| 2 | Arm supports | ⅞ × 8 × ⅞ |
| 1 | Footrest | 3 × 17 × ⅝ |

The back board is cut to a curve from a thicker piece of wood (Fig. 8-19C). Keep its lower edge thick enough to take the post holes without risk of splitting. Its ends and upper surface can be rounded (Fig. 8-19D).

The two outer posts are stouter than the three inner ones (Fig. 8-19E), but otherwise they have similar shapes. Allow a little excess length at first. Drill the back of the seat for the posts. The posts all slope slightly to the same angle to the rear, but when viewed from the front the center post is upright and the others fan outwards very slightly. Put the posts in their holes and mark their tops to the same heights with a straightedge parallel with the seat (Fig. 8-19F). Use this assembly to get the positions of the holes in the back board and it will also indicate the angles to drill them.

The arms and their supports are turned parallel for most of their lengths (Fig. 8-19G). The supports can go directly into holes in the seat without reducing their size, but there should be a taper to a dowel into the arms. Round the fronts of the arms and reduce to dowel size into the outer back posts. When viewed from the front the arm supports should slope outwards at the same angles as the outer back posts.

The footrest may be left until after the rest of the chair is finally assembled. This reduces any risk of error due to changes from measurements taken at a trial assembly and those of a final one. The footrest has rounded corners and edges (Fig. 8-19H). It is supported by two small wooden brackets. The footrest goes into shallow grooves across the legs and the brackets fit against flattened parts below this (Fig. 8-19J). Do not cut too deeply into the legs, or they may be weakened. If screws are taken into the footrest, it may be sufficient to merely glue the brackets in place.

The sizes given were taken from an original, but obviously there is scope for variation. Much depends on the size of the child and table height. In particular positioning of the footrest is best related to the leg length of the child who will use the seat, with due allowance for growth in the time the chair will be needed.

# Cupboards and Cabinets

Chests and open shelves have their uses, but for the better and more attractive storage of the great many household items that accumulate, furniture that can be opened and closed from the front is more convenient. This meant that some early furniture took the form of cupboards and closets, either standing free or attached to the wall, while other items were like tables enclosed with storage space below, to form dry sinks and similar kitchen and domestic furniture, some of which developed into better cabinetwork pieces for use in bedrooms and the more important rooms of the house.

Open storage does not have to involve great precision in its making, but when this is developed into a form of closed storage by the addition of doors there has to be more careful fitting and the better forms of furniture with doors was usually the product of a specialist craftsman. One problem that came with the fitting of doors was the provision of hinges and catches or fasteners.

Blacksmith-made hinges were usually large in relation to the door and mounted on the surface. A clumsy appearance was avoided by giving the hinges decorative shapes. Reproductions of these hinges are obtainable and may be chosen for any reproduction doors (Fig. 9-1A). Hinges that went between the door and its stile were not long in coming into use and these "butt" hinges could be used for many reproduction doors. Some of the more primitive hinges were made from interlocking pieces of bent wire or by nailing on strips of leather.

With any hinge it is the center of the knuckle which is the pivot point. The door swings on this. In most assemblies the knuckle can be centrally over the gap between the door and its stile (Fig. 9-1B) and it will swing clear without trouble. If some old cabinets are examined, the very close fit of the doors may be admired, yet they swing clear without binding on the frame. Having the knuckle slightly towards the stile (Fig. 9-1C) helps in bringing the other side of the door clear of the frame as soon as it starts moving and allows a closer fit.

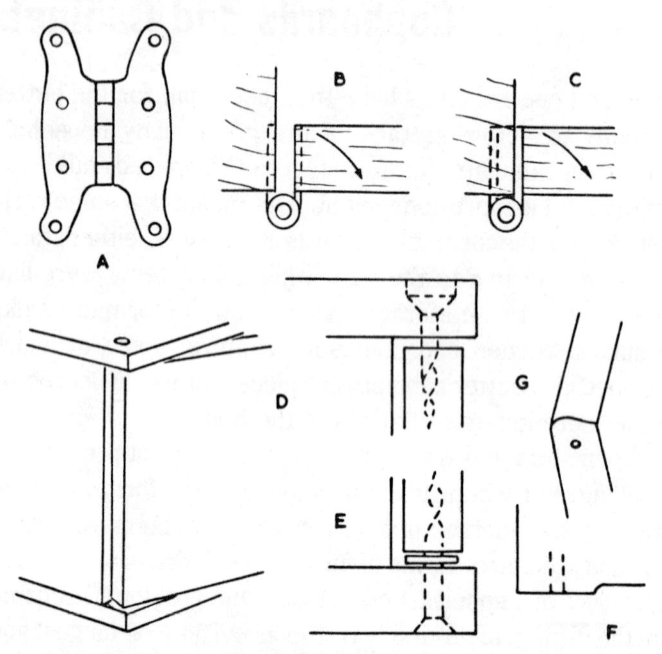


Fig. 9-1. Many early hinges were put on the surface (A). The position of the knuckle affects the way a door swings (B and C). A door may pivot on screws or dowels (D and E). Shaping the bottom avoids a washer (F). The door corner is rounded for clearance (G).

Hinges can be avoided if the door is arranged to pivot on nails, screws or dowels. Top and bottom of the cabinet should overlap and the pivots go through these overlaps into the doors (Fig. 9-1D). For the majority of pieces of furniture the pivots are best made of stout screws, with the top one counterbored and plugged if the upper surface will be visible in the finished work. The bottom of the door has to be lifted slightly so it swings into place without rubbing. It could be done with a washer on the screw (Fig. 9-1E), although this was avoided in some old doors by cutting the bottom of the door away, except for a small area around the screw (Fig. 9-1F). To give clearance as the door swung its edge had to be rounded enough to clear the cupboard side (Fig. 9-1G).

The simplest arrangement of a door is to have a flat board overlapping all round (Fig. 9-2A), with hinges on the edge or between the door and frame. This could be modified to let the top and bottom overlap the door (Fig. 9-2B), providing some protection against dust entering. A further step was to set the door inside the framework (Fig. 9-2C) and this is the customary way of mounting doors in most good quality furniture, where there is no reason for using any other method, but it calls for the exercise of more care and skill in handing the door.

When a door overlaps the carcase it is automatically stopped in the closed position. If it fits inside there has to be a stop. This may be a single small block of wood near the center of the door (Fig. 9-2D) or pieces top and bottom for a tall door. Sometimes a shelf was arranged to be at a width that would also act as a door stop, but it was more usual for shelves to be set back a short distance.

In cabinets with a pair of doors these might be arranged to meet at the center (Fig. 9-2E). Top and bottom stops brought the closed doors to the same level, then one door was secured with a bolt or catch to the frame (top and bottom usually) and the other door closed to it with a catch.

Many old double-door arrangements had a post between the doors (Fig. 9-2F), so each door was treated like a single one. The simplest catch then was a wooden turnbutton turning on a screw (Fig. 9-2G), with a single long one closing both doors, or a smaller one for each door. Turnbuttons varied from unadorned plain wood to others that were whittled into decorative patterns or given shaped beveled edges (F 9-2H).

Metal catches of simple form were imported or manufa tured locally. One common method of holding an overlappir door was with a metal hook and screw eye (Fig. 9-2J). Smɛ sliding bolts would be appropriate in a reproduction and door could be fastened with catches operated by a knob. However the more ingenious type of modern door fasteners would b inappropriate, particularly if of plated metal or plastic.

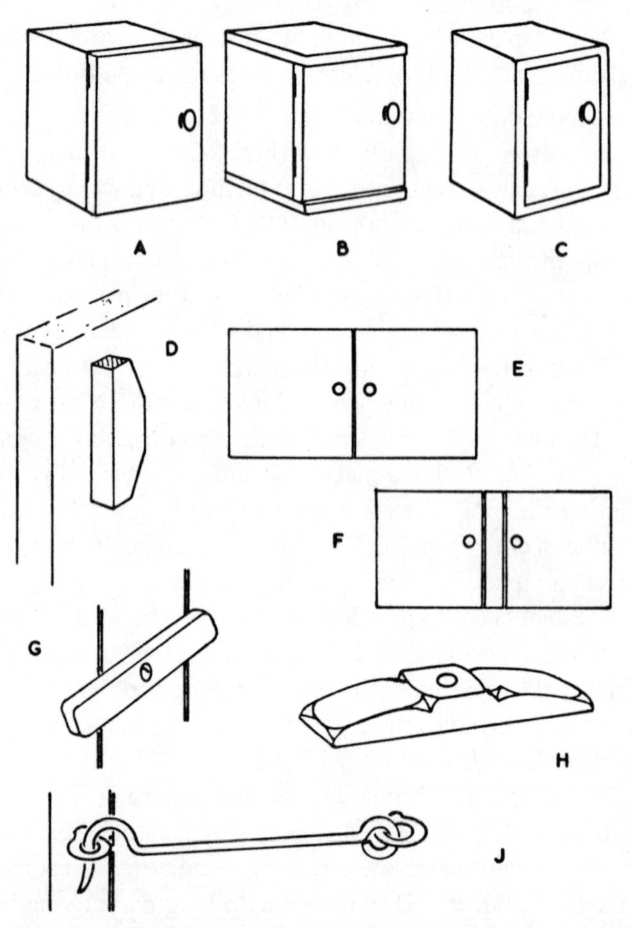


Fig. 9-2. Doors may be on the surface (A), the top and bottom may overlap (B) or the door be fully enclosed (C). A stop goes inside the case (D). Doors may meet (E) or have a post between (F). Turnbuttons were used to secure doors (G and H) or there were hooks at the side (J).

The simplest door is a plain piece of wood. If the risk of warping is to be avoided as far as possible, it should be radially cut, so the end grain lines are across the thickness of the wood (Fig. 9-3A). If the width of a door is enough to need boards glued edge to edge, it is advisable to put battens across inside (Fig. 9-3B). They may be slot screwed, to allow for expansion and contraction or glued and screwed directly with a wood not expected to vary. Variation in the width of a door is undesirable and may have to be accepted if the door overlaps, but would affect fit of a door within its frame, so a different method of construction would be preferable.

In many items for kitchen or wash house, wide doors were made of many boards tongued and grooved together without glue (Fig. 9-3C). This allowed movement in the width of each board without affecting the overall width of the door enough to matter. To give rigidity the door was ledged and braced inside (Fig. 9-3D). The brace sloped upwards from the hinged side and prevented the door sagging. To do this it had to be related to the braces as well as the boards and it was usual to notch its ends into them (Fig. 9-3E). The natural tendency of the boards to settle, caused the notched joints to be pushed tighter. If the brace was arranged the other way, the joints would tend to open. Ledges and braces were kept back from the door edges. Shelves or divisions had to be set back to give clearance inside. If strap or T-hinges were used on the outside, their positions were arranged so screws went through into the ledges.

A design consideration to be noted is the poor appearance of arranging hinges the same distance from top and bottom of a door (Fig. 9-3F) and the improved appearance if the lower distance from the edge is more than the top one (Fig. 9-3G). It is reasonable to make the bottom measurement about 1½ times the top one, which should be one fifth or one fourth of the total depth.

Better doors were framed and paneled. A smaller door had a frame enclosing one panel (Fig. 9-4A), but dividing a larger door into two or more panels provided strength members between the outer solid wood framing, as well as keeping

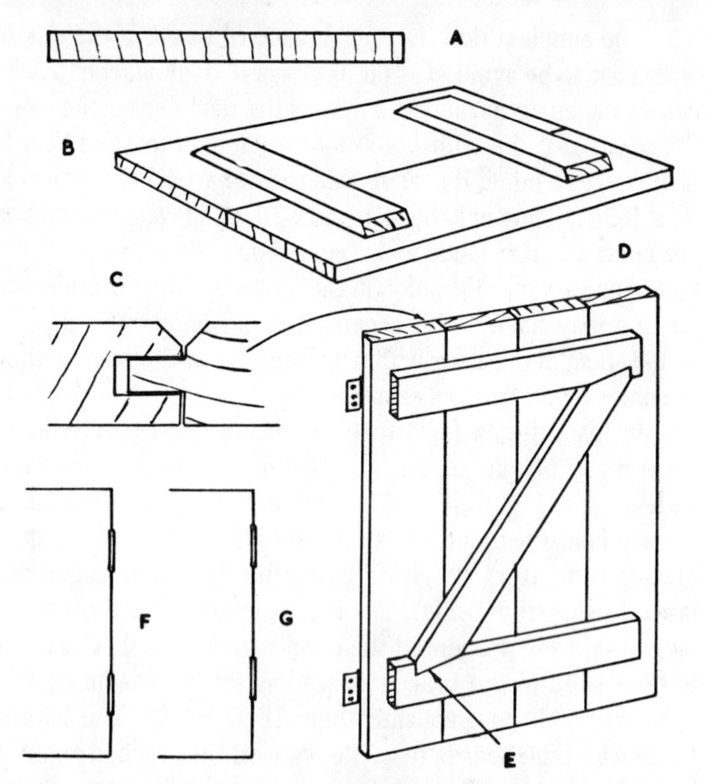


Fig. 9-3. Boards for doors are best chosen with end grain across to reduce the risk of warping (A). Battens inside must clear the frame (B). Wider doors are made of tongued and grooved boards (C), ledged and braced inside (D and E). The appearance of hinges is improved if lifted from equal spacing (F) to a wider gap at the bottom (G).

the panels down to a size more suitable for available wood. If there were two panels, the upper one was usually smaller than the lower one (Fig. 9-4B) as this looked better than two equal panels. Four panels might be similarly arranged, although some doors had the sides wider at the lower panels to give strength lower down (Fig. 9-4C).

The traditional cabinetmaking method of making a framed door had grooves plowed in the wood and the tenons in the horizontal members going into mortises in the uprights. In thin wood the tenons were the same width as the grooves, but usually they were thicker and the inner edge was cut back to the bottom of the groove, while the outer edge had a haunch projecting the depth of the groove (Fig. 9-4D). The mortise

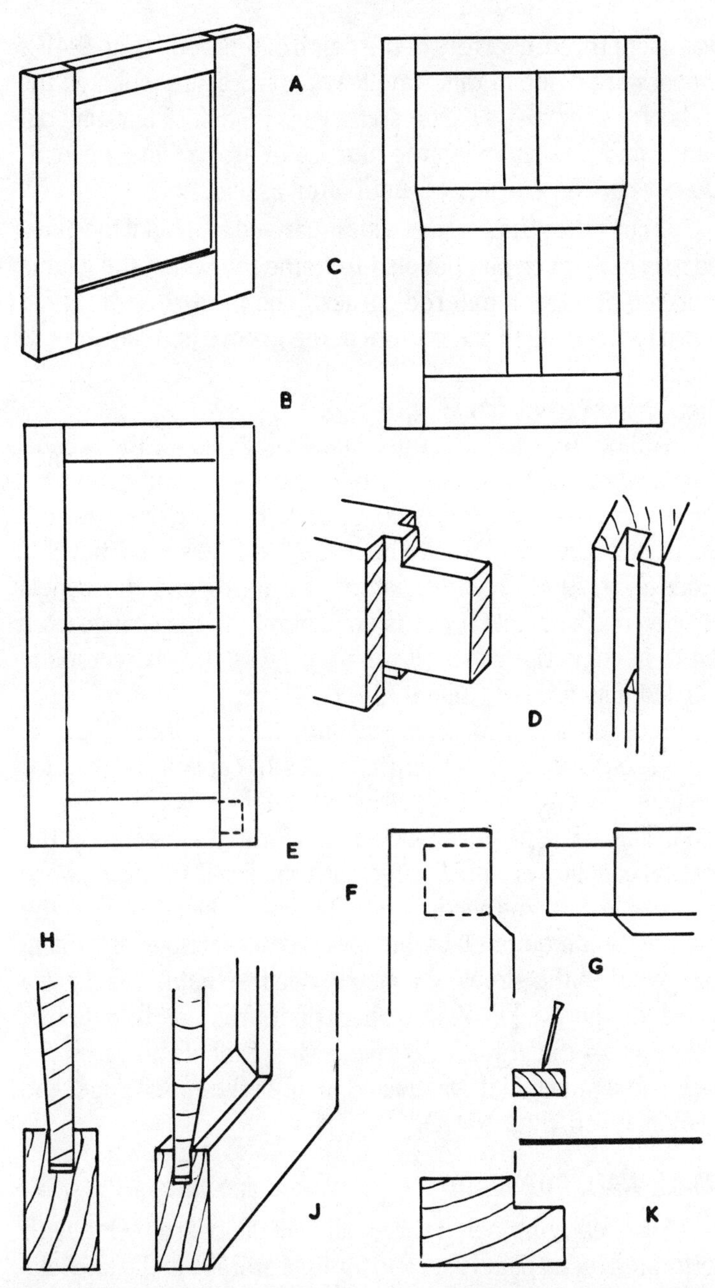


Fig. 9-4. If a door is framed (A) a tall one can have an extra rail (B), which is stronger if the stiles widen (C). Corners are tenoned (D and E), with any molding mitered (F and G). A beveled panel may show a flat surface outside (H) or use the shaping as decoration (J). Pertorated zinc panels are held with fillets (K).

was about three-quarters of the depth of the wood (Fig. 9-4E). If doors are made in this way, leave some spare wood on the ends of the mortised parts, so there is no risk of bursting out end grain when chopping the mortise or assembling the joint. Do not cut the surplus off until after assembly.

That joint suits a frame with square edges, but if the inner edge is molded or just beveled to frame the panel, the joint is modified to allow a mitered corner. The mortised part is cut down to the level of the bottom of the groove and the corners standing above it cut at 45° (Fig. 9-4F). The tenoned part is then shaped to match (Fig. 9-4G).

Although a modern panel would be plywood, the original panels were solid wood cut as thin as possible, but even then thicker than the grooves. Two methods of fitting were used. If the front of the panel was to be level, the edges were beveled inside (Fig. 9-4H), but most old furniture has the panels beveled on the front. If this is done neatly so the change from flat to bevel is the same all round, it gives the characteristic paneled appearance (Fig. 9-4J).

A development of a paneled door was the fitting of perforated sheet metal panels in the doors of cupboards used for food, in the days before refrigerators. Zinc was commonly used. There is a modern machine-perforated version, but the original panels were perforated with a nail and the holes were arranged in patterns according to the artistic inclinations of the makers. Some quite elaborate pierced decorations are still in existence. In the simplest construction the metal was merely nailed to the backs of the open door frames. In a better construction the frame was made with rabbets towards the back and a small fillet was nailed in after the metal panel had been inserted (Fig. 9-4K).

## SMALL WALL CUPBOARD

Most early homes used small wall cupboards. One with perforated metal panels served for food storage in the kitchen, while others with solid doors served in living and bed rooms. Many developed from hanging shelves, to which a door was added in front. The example here is typical of many variations on a basic theme (Fig. 9-5A). In effect it is a box with a door at the front.

The sides may have rabbets for a rear panel and the shelves fit into dados, either cut through or stopped for neatness at the front (Fig. 9-5B). The main load when hanging is taken by a bar across the inside at the top and the sides have their rabbets deepened to take it (Fig. 9-5C). Screws through this into the wall support the cupboard, although there may be one or two other screws to supplement them through the back panel lower down.

The top overlaps the sides. The bottom may overlap, but it is stronger if it fits between the sides and is notched around, with a mitered strip at each side (Fig. 9-5D). There are stiles each side of the door which can have nails or screws through them, either covered with stopping or plugs, but if a smooth front appearance is to be maintained they can be glued with small fillets added to increase glue area inside (Fig. 9-5E). When assembling the cupboard be careful to check squareness. The door opening must be true; a door only slightly out of square becomes very obvious.

To break up the plainness of the cupboard, a shaped piece is fitted above the front of the top (Fig. 9-5F). This can be held by glue and screws from below. There may be a glued fillet behind it.

A single-paneled door is shown with fairly wide framing for stiffness. The corners are mortise and tenoned in the way just described and the panel shows the bevels at the front (Fig. 9-5G).

The hinges may be set on the surface for a kitchen cupboard or into the edges if the cupboard is made of attractive hardwood and polished. Traditionally hinges were let into both surfaces (Fig. 9-5H), but it is less trouble to let into one edge only, adjusting the depth to suit the clearance needed. There is usually some fitting to be done when a door is hung. Make the door near to its final size, but hang it with one screw in each hinge. Note what needs to be planed off, then remove the door, plane it and try again, until the clearance all round is the same and all the hinge screws can be driven.

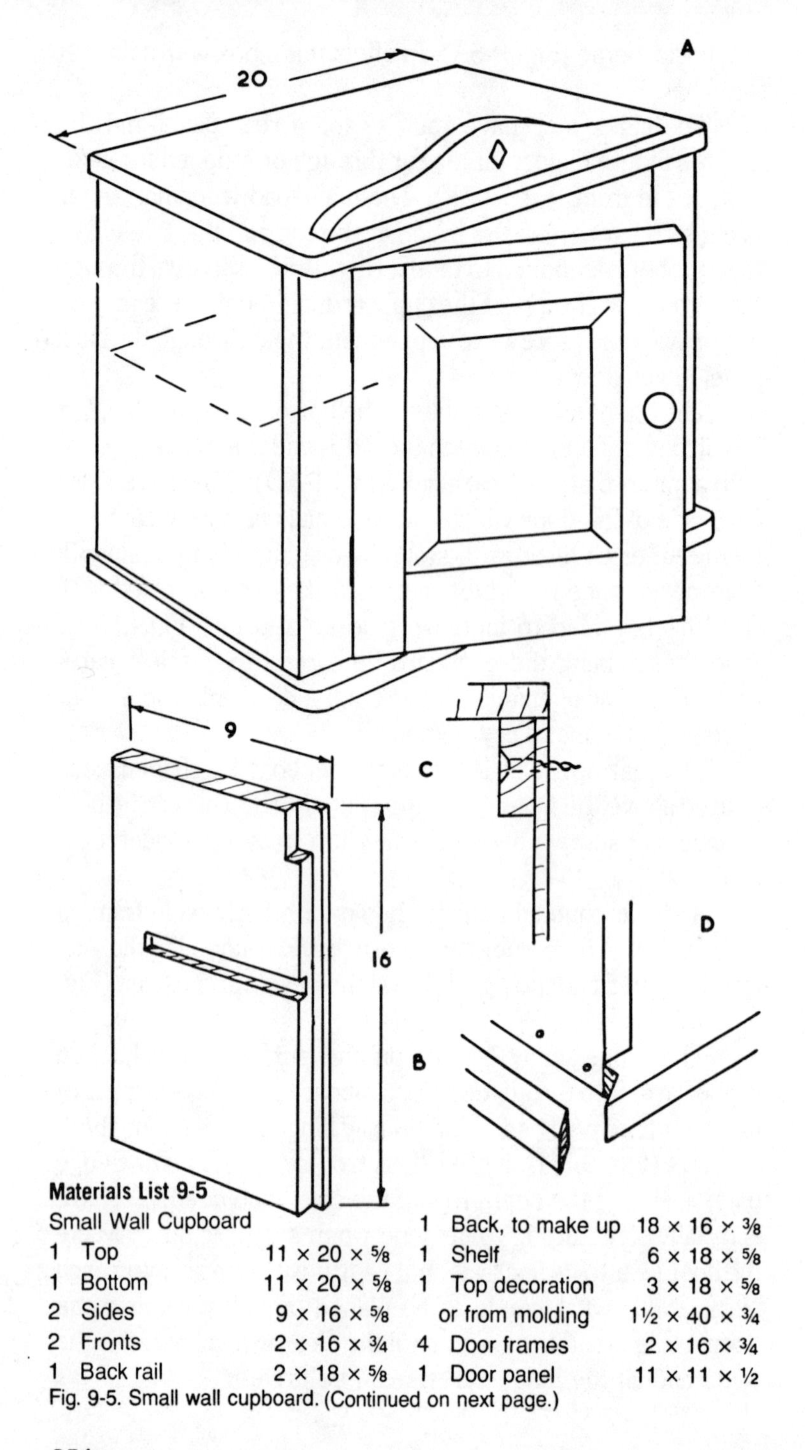


**Materials List 9-5**

Small Wall Cupboard

| Qty | Part | Size |
|---|---|---|
| 1 | Top | 11 × 20 × 5/8 |
| 1 | Bottom | 11 × 20 × 5/8 |
| 2 | Sides | 9 × 16 × 5/8 |
| 2 | Fronts | 2 × 16 × 3/4 |
| 1 | Back rail | 2 × 18 × 5/8 |
| 1 | Back, to make up | 18 × 16 × 3/8 |
| 1 | Shelf | 6 × 18 × 5/8 |
| 1 | Top decoration | 3 × 18 × 5/8 |
| | or from molding | 1½ × 40 × 3/4 |
| 4 | Door frames | 2 × 16 × 3/4 |
| 1 | Door panel | 11 × 11 × ½ |

Fig. 9-5. Small wall cupboard. (Continued on next page.)

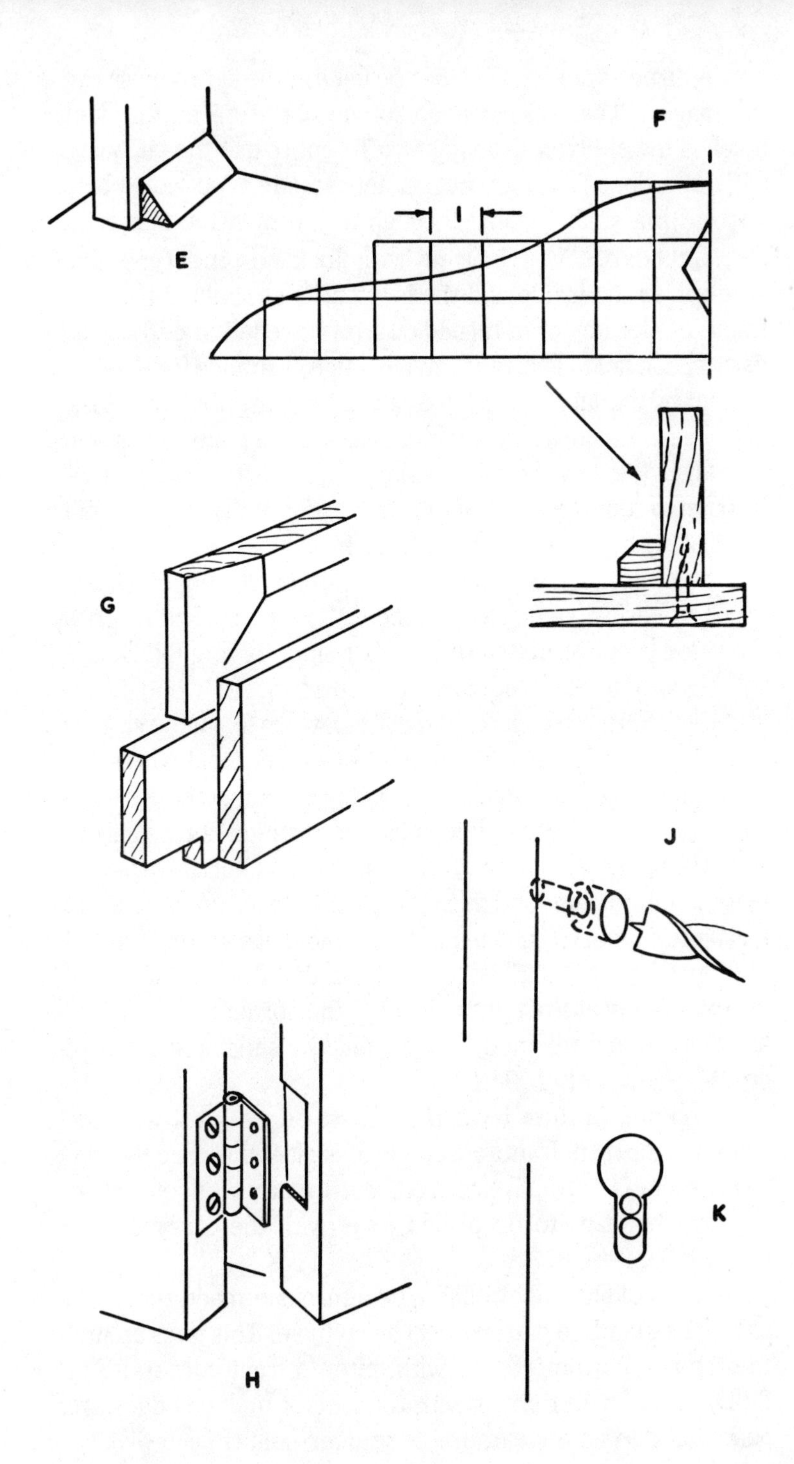
F
1
E
G
J
K
H

A turned wooden knob can be used at the side opposite to the hinges. There is no need for a door stop, as the door touches the shelves. It may be sufficient to use the cupboard without a door fastener, but an appropriate type would be a knob with a shaft passing through to a turnbutton inside.

Cupboards were fitted with locks of the type that screwed to the inside and the lock bolt went behind the door frame as the key was turned. Care is needed in cutting the escutcheon hole. This must give enough clearance for the key, yet not be too large or it looks ugly. Measure the size of the key. Press the lock into position inside. The point of the post on which the key fits will make a dent in the wood. Drill through to remove some of the waste (Fig. 9-5J) and clean out the slot with a chisel and file (Fig. 9-5K).

Some locks are supplied with a brass escutcheon liner, which makes a neat finish to the hole. This has a slight taper. If the wood is cut to match the smaller side, forcing the liner in will tighten it as it compresses surrounding wood fibers slightly. There are escutcheon plates, which fix on the surface over the keyhole, usually made of brass and held with small brass pins. For good quality work there are matching sets of hinges, knob, and escutcheon plate in an antique brass finish.

There was a furniture fashion in early Victorian days, and before, for moldings and this was felt in America. A variation of this basic cupboard can be made with moldings around top and bottom (Fig. 9-6A). The framing at the front is all round instead of only at the edges. Ideally, the corners of the frame are mortise and tenoned, but it would be satisfactory to use cross lap joints (Fig. 9-6B).

Top and bottom have their front edges level with the sides and the front frame assembly fits aginst this. See that the front frame is carefully squared, but its outer edges can be slightly oversize, to be planed level with the carcase after fitting (Fig. 9-6C).

The molding will probably be a machine-made type, and any of the standard patterns will be suitable. This goes around the top and bottom edges, with mitered front corners (Fig. 9-6D), then further strips with rounded or molded edges are added to give an appearance of greater bulk (Fig. 9-6E).

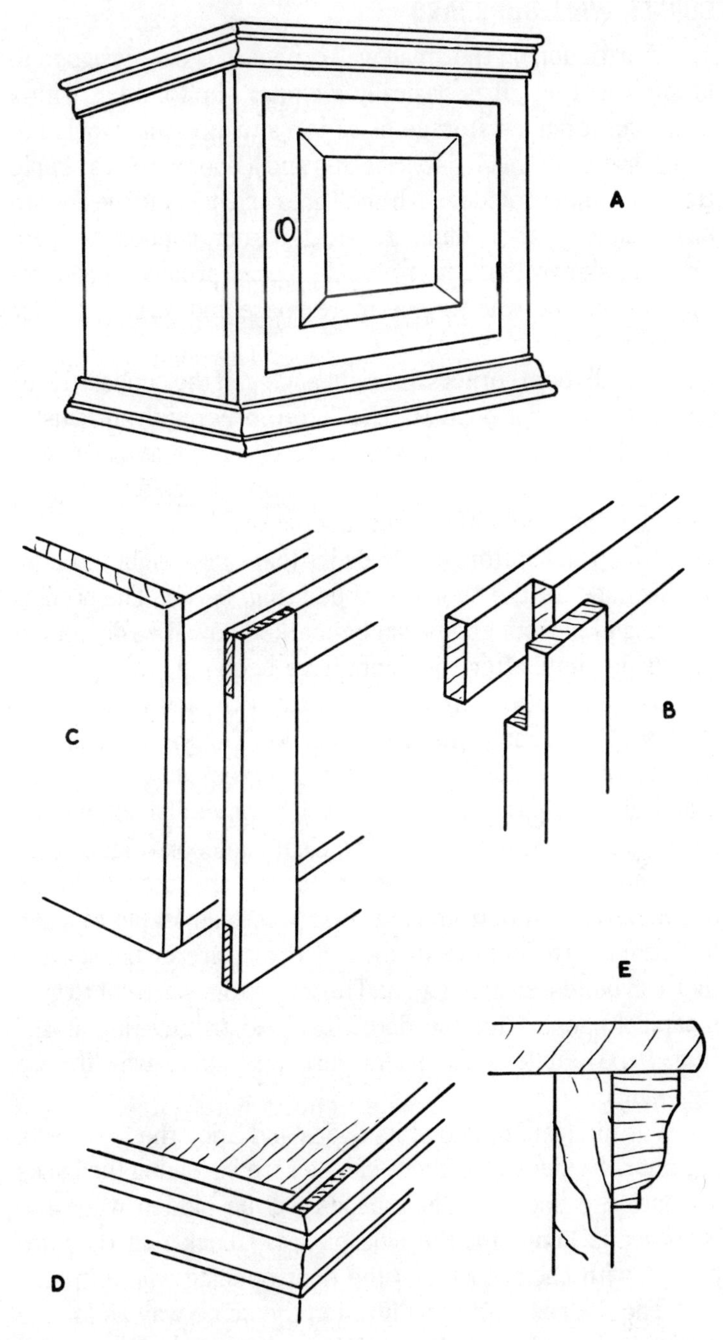


Fig. 9-6. Molded wall cupboard.

## CORNER WALL CUPBOARD

A variation on the small wall cupboard is one designed to fit into a corner. It is basically a corner shelf fitment with a door, but it makes storage place in a situation that would not otherwise be of much use. Shelves and a door across a simple triangle do not provide much shelf area and hanging the door to swing clear is then difficult. Most corner cupboards were made as shown, with narrow side pieces projecting at right angles from the wall to give more space and make the door action better (Fig. 9-7A).

Not all room corners are right angles. If the cupboard is to go into a particular position, check the corner with an adjustable bevel and make the parts to suit this if it is not a right angle.

Prepare the wood for the two back pieces first. One is narrower than the other by the amount that one overlaps (Fig. 9-7B). Top and bottom fit into dados that can go right through, but the dado for the shelf is stopped (Fig. 9-7C). The profiles for top and bottom edges can be marked now, but do not cut the shapes until after the joints have been cut.

Top and bottom are the same, cut with their grain across (Fig. 9-7D). Prepare these parts and use them to check the marking of the dados before cutting the grooves. Use them as a guide for marking out the shelf, which comes against the side pieces, but is cut back enough to clear the door (Fig. 9-7E).

The side pieces overlap the backs and are cut to fit closely between top and bottom (Fig. 9-7F). It is advisable to leave final trimming to length until the other parts are assembled and they can be tested in position. The inner edges are cut to give a parallel opening for the door. This means beveling at 45° (Fig. 9-7G), unless the room corner is some way from a right-angle.

Put the shelf in one of its dados and bring the two backs together. Besides glue there can be screws joining the backs and into the shelf, as their heads will be hidden when the cupboard is hung. Fit the side pieces. Check that they are parallel with each other and the door opening will be true.

The door is made and fitted in the same way as for the earlier wall cupboard. It could have its panel showing the bevels on the front or it could have a level surface on the front with some sort of decoration at its center. For Pennsylvania Dutch finishing, it could have a painted design. For another theme it could have a curved design mounted on it.

Hanging is by screws through the backs inside and just below the top. A variation could be without any projection of the backs below the bottom. The cupboard could then stand on a corner table or be attached to the wall just above it.

## STANDING CUPBOARD

A cupboard with a top at a suitable height for use as a table when standing can be made to match the hanging cupboards (Fig. 9-8A). Sizes are not critical and can be adapted to suit available wood. In a cupboard of this size it is usually more convenient to arrange shelves to rest on battens so they can be lifted out than to fix them into dados or in any other permanent manner. Most of the parts are plain rectangles, but the door is shown with tapered sides, although they could be made parallel. Note that appearance is improved by having the bottom door rail wider than the other two.

If the back is to be made traditionally, it will have to be several boards, preferably tongued and grooved together. The alternative is plywood. In any case, the back overlaps the bottom and is set into rabbets in the sides.

Mark out one side and use this as a guide to the sizes of other parts (Fig. 9-8B). Make the two front pieces (Fig. 9-8C). They are shaped at the bottom to form feet and the sides are similarly cut (Fig. 9-8D). There may be square corners, but a stopped chamfer enhances appearance (Fig. 9-8E). The bottom fits between the front pieces. For the strongest construction it fits into dados in them (Fig. 9-8F). It could go into dados in the sides, but it is simpler and stronger to put battens across underneath (Fig. 9-8G). The top goes above the sides and front. A batten is put across the back and more battens at the sides. At the front a batten is cut to fit across between the upright parts. Assemble all these parts and screw upwards into the top (Fig. 9-8H).

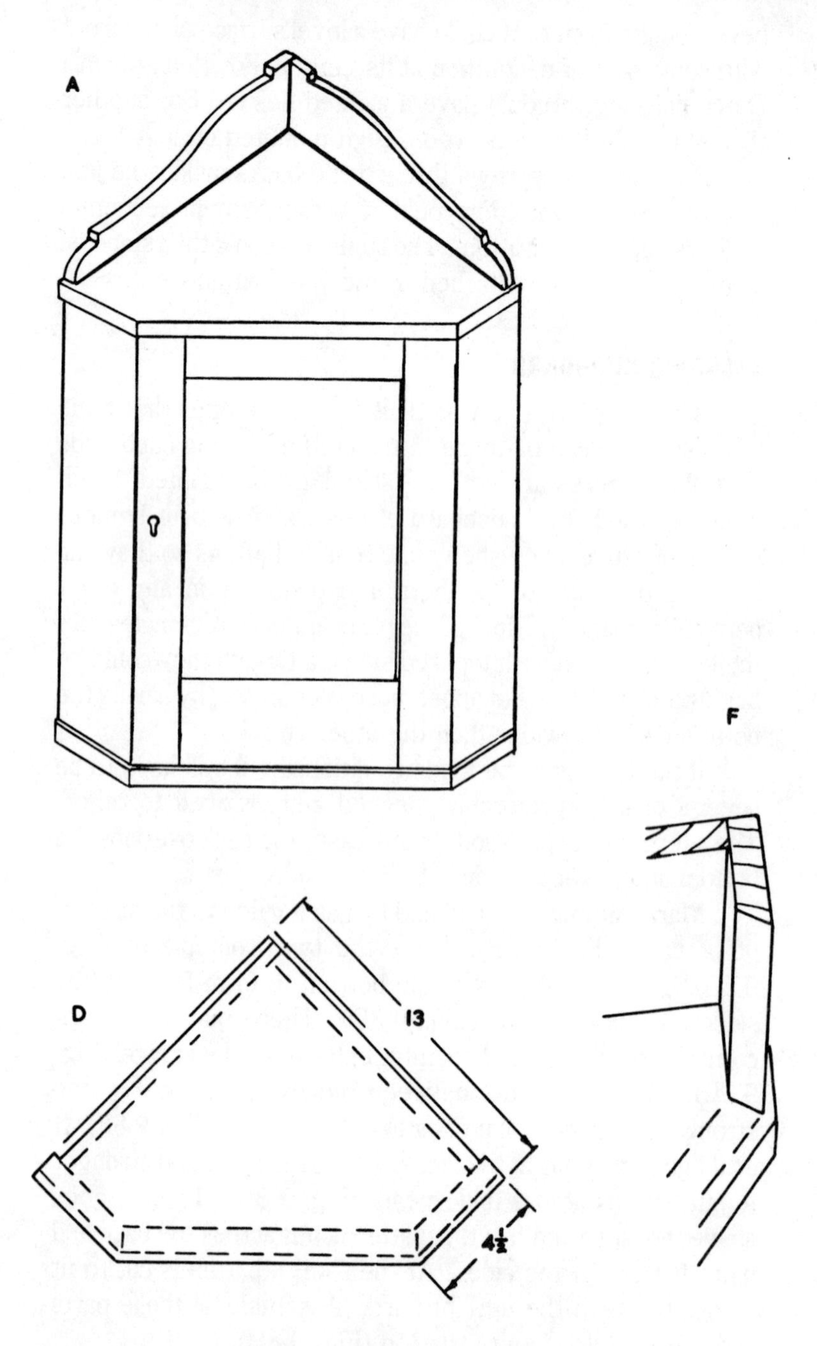


Fig. 9-7. Corner wall cupboard. (Continued on next page.)

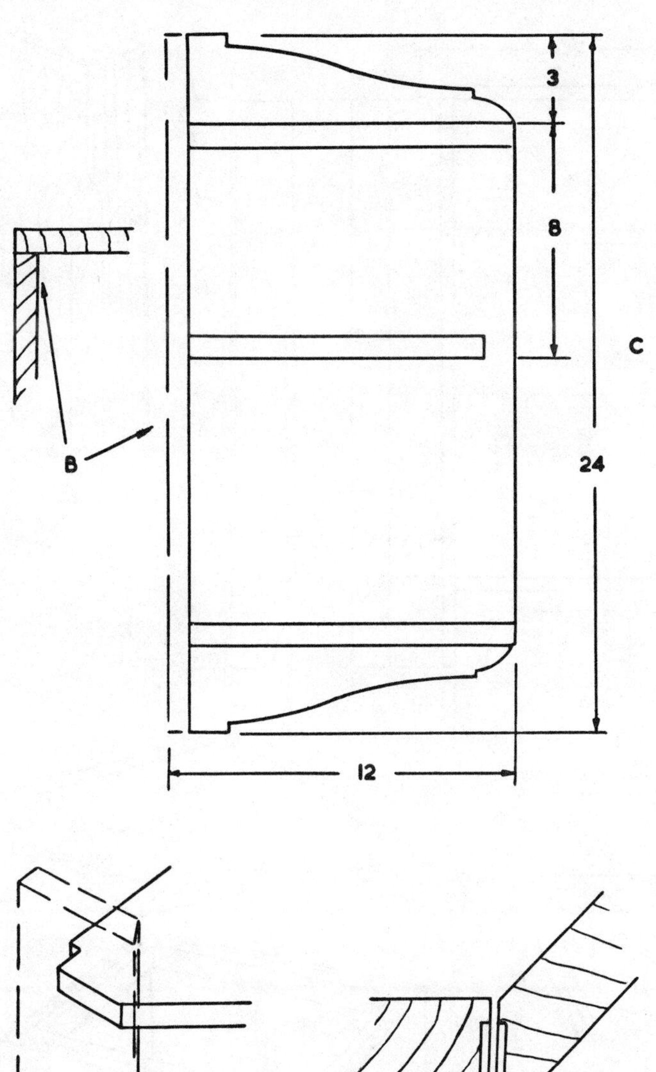


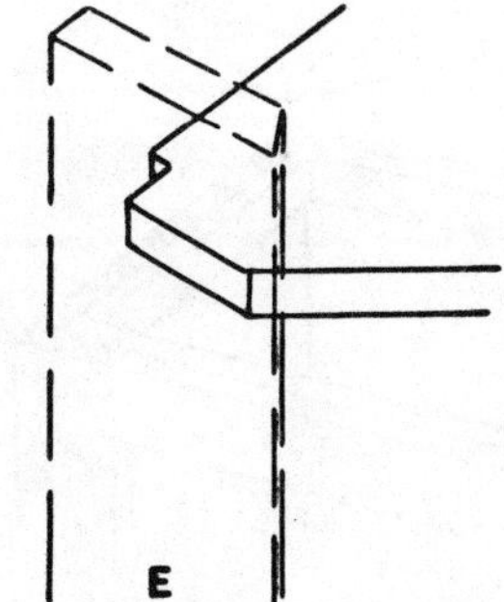


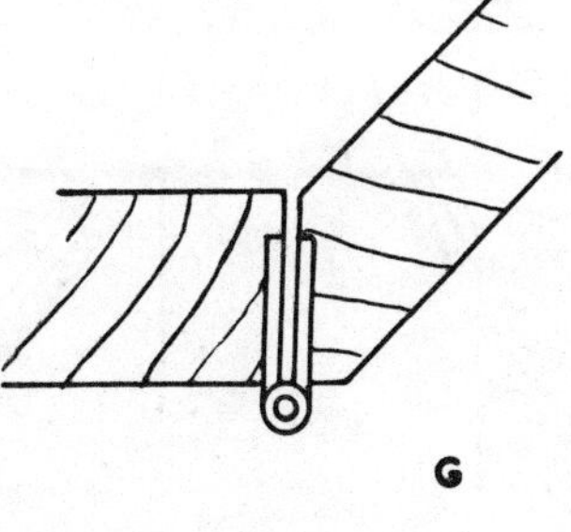


**Materials List 9-7**

Corner Wall Cupboard

| | | |
|---|---|---|
| 2 | Backs | 12 × 24 × ⅝ |
| 2 | Sides | 4½ × 18 × ⅝ |
| 1 | Top | 13 × 20 × ⅝ |
| 1 | Bottom | 13 × 20 × ⅝ |
| 1 | Shelf | 11 × 18 × ⅝ |
| 2 | Door sides | 2 × 18 × ¾ |
| 2 | Door rails | 2 × 10 × ¾ |

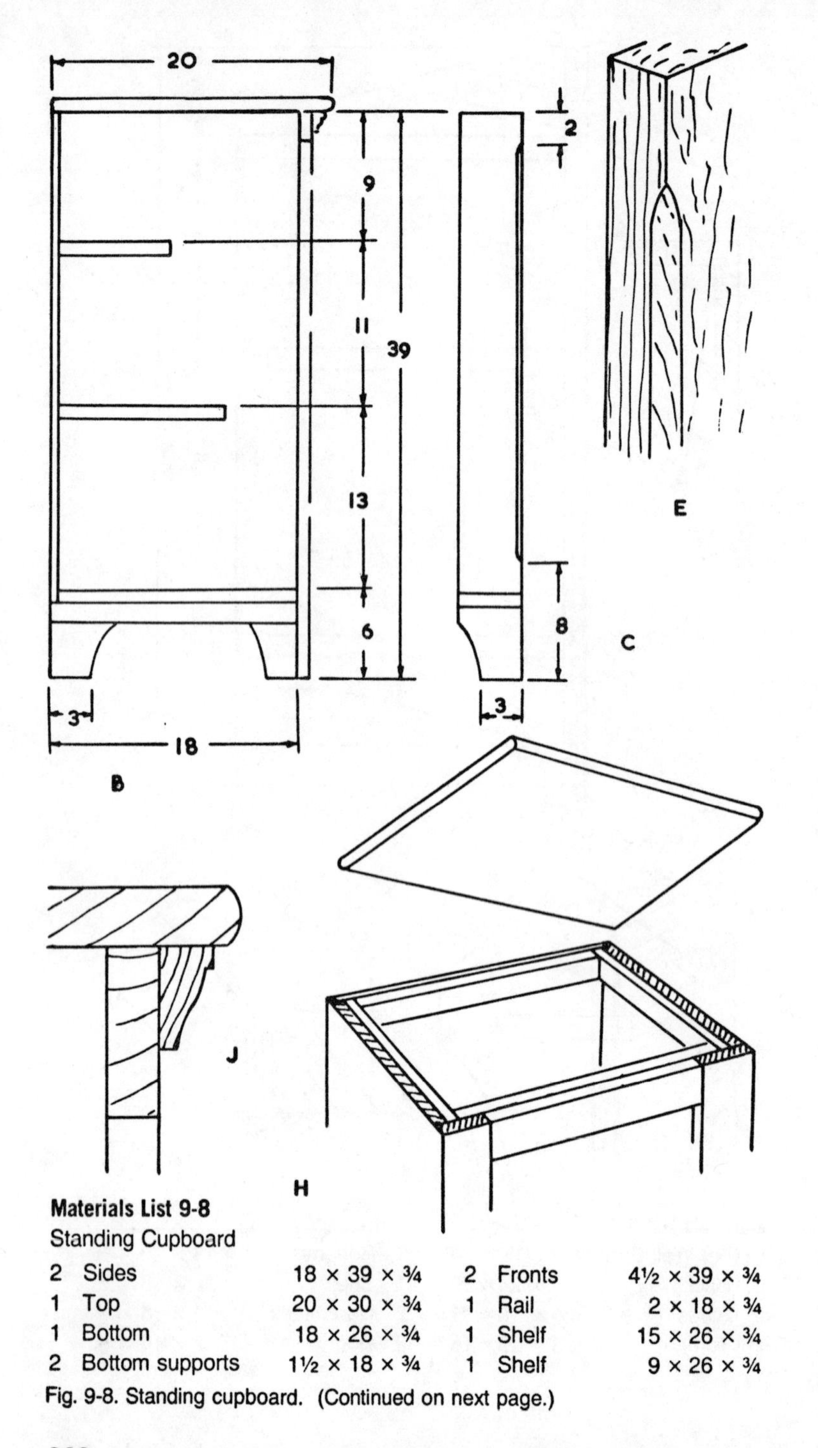


**Materials List 9-8**
Standing Cupboard

| | | | | | |
|---|---|---|---|---|---|
| 2 | Sides | 18 × 39 × ¾ | 2 | Fronts | 4½ × 39 × ¾ |
| 1 | Top | 20 × 30 × ¾ | 1 | Rail | 2 × 18 × ¾ |
| 1 | Bottom | 18 × 26 × ¾ | 1 | Shelf | 15 × 26 × ¾ |
| 2 | Bottom supports | 1½ × 18 × ¾ | 1 | Shelf | 9 × 26 × ¾ |

Fig. 9-8. Standing cupboard. (Continued on next page.)

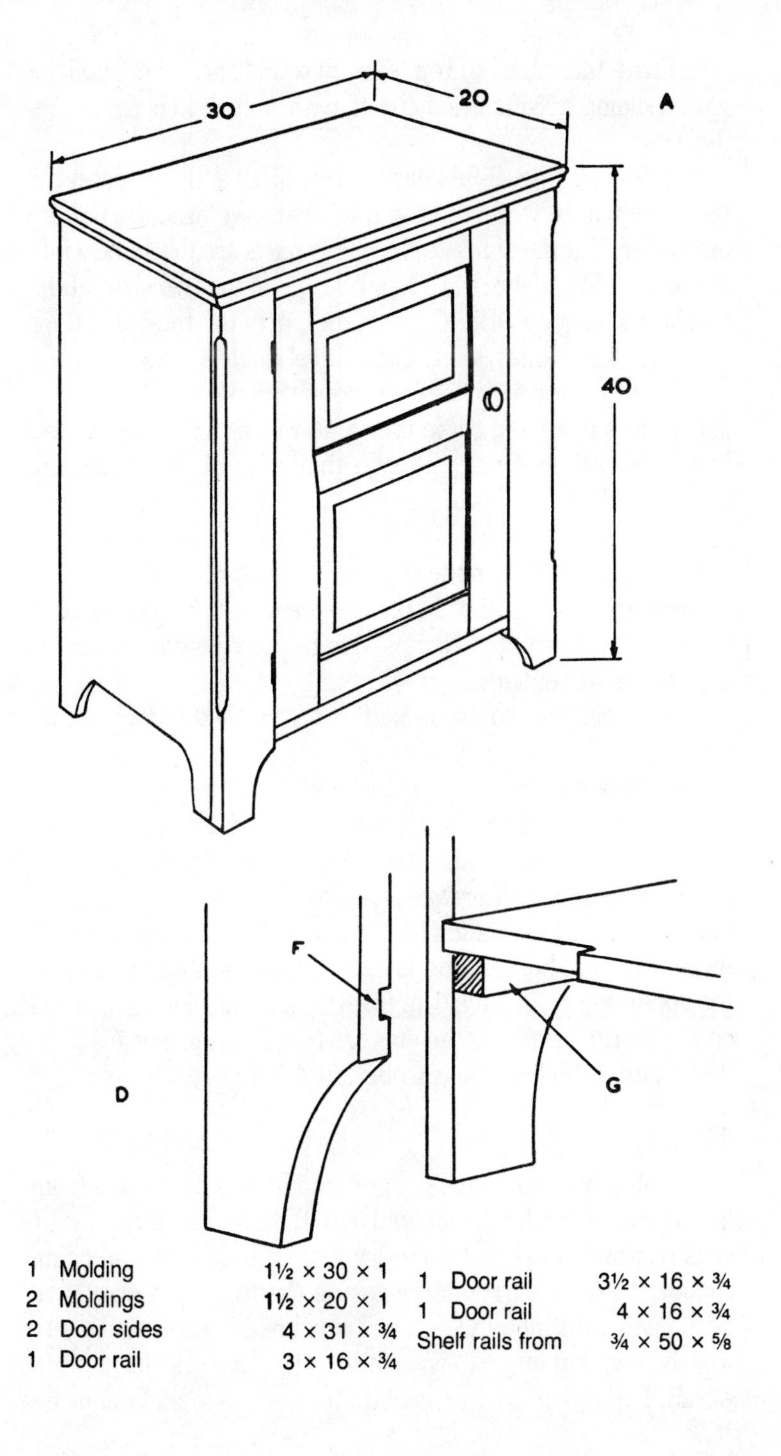


| | | |
|---|---|---|
| 1 | Molding | 1½ × 30 × 1 |
| 2 | Moldings | 1½ × 20 × 1 |
| 2 | Door sides | 4 × 31 × ¾ |
| 1 | Door rail | 3 × 16 × ¾ |
| 1 | Door rail | 3½ × 16 × ¾ |
| 1 | Door rail | 4 × 16 × ¾ |
| Shelf rails from | | ¾ × 50 × ⅝ |

Plane the edges of top level all round and cover the joint with molding at sides and front, with mitered corners (Fig. 9-8J).

The door (Fig. 9-9A) has the two sides and the center rail the same width, while the top rail is narrower and the bottom one wider. Cut the sides so the upper parts are the same width as the top rail and there is a taper between the two sizes at the middle rail (Fig. 9-9B). Groove the parts for the panels.

The top corner joints may have single tenons, but the others are better with double tenons (Fig. 9-9C). The corner joints are laid out and cut in the same way as for earlier doors. In the central beveled joints the shoulders of the tenons are cut to match the angles of the uprights. The ends of the tenons could be at the same angles or cut squarely. The sides of the tenons are parallel with the edges of the rail, not at right angles to the slope (Fig. 9-9D). Make the door slightly ovesize. Pull the joints tight with bar clamps. There could be dowels across the tenons for extra security.

Two hinges should be sufficient, but if the door shows signs of flexing there could be a third. Be careful that all the hinge knuckles are in line if the door is to swing smoothly. Arrange door stops at top and bottom and fit a knob and catch.

In a cupboard of this size it is inadvisable to have the shelves too wide; otherwise it is difficult to see what is at the bottom or on a lower shelf from the usual standing position. If there are two shelves, the lower is set back about 6 in., and the upper one is set back 6 in. from that. Small blocks mounted on the battens prevent the shelves from sliding forward (Fig. 9-9E) but still allow them to be lifted out.

## DRY SINK

Water was not usually piped and had to be carried from the well or pump for household use. The basins, pitchers, or pans of water were put on a dry sink, which was a standing cupboard with a surround enclosing the top. This may have been lined with metal to prevent any spilled water finding its way below, although it was more often merely planked in wood. The lower part provided storage space and might be

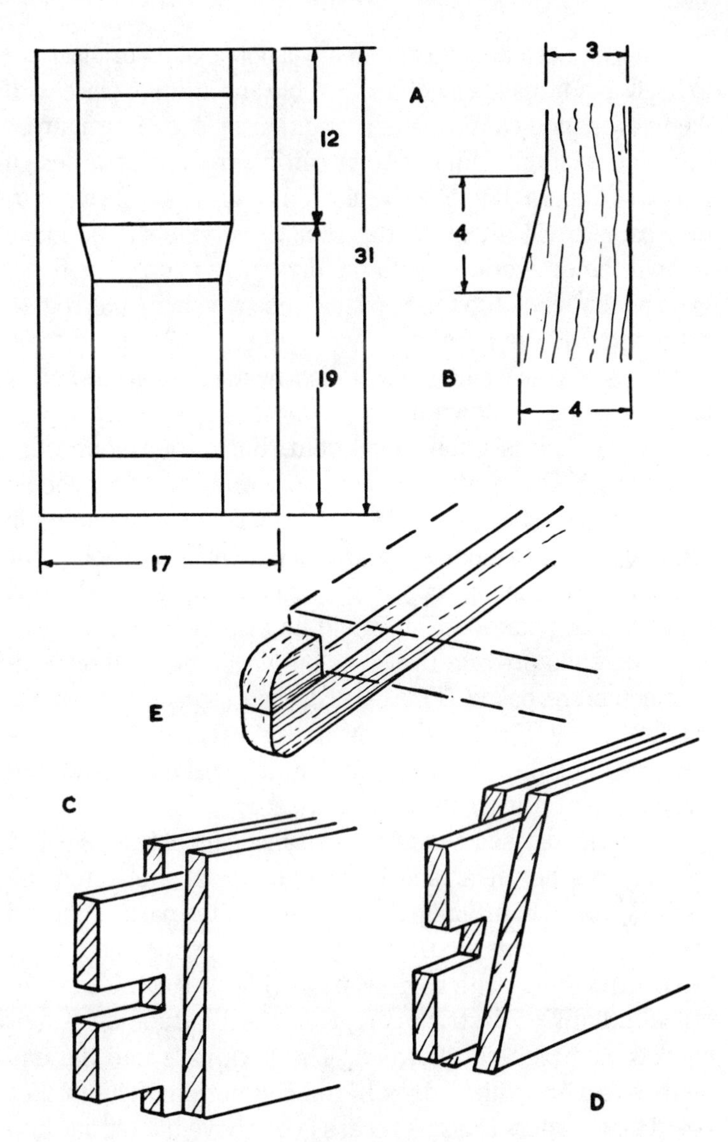


Fig. 9-9. Door and shelf details for a standing cupboard.

enclosed with doors, although some longer dry sinks had a block of drawers as well. This was the form of the basic dry sink, but some were given upper cupboards as well, and the whole assembly served the women of the house in much the same way as the sink, working tops, and cupboards of a modern kitchen do today.

In a modern home a dry sink will not have its original use to fulfill, but it makes a good side table and storage place with the interest and character of a traditional piece of furniture.

The example (Fig. 9-10A) can be treated as a design typical of the era, but it can be altered to suit available wood or the space it will occupy and a smaller version can be made without the drawers, or with the drawers and only one door. In some dry sinks the top border is the same height all round, but others had the front cut down. If the reproduction is to be made to serve as a side table or display stand, it will be better made with the cutdown front.

A dry sink is a functional item. Early specimens were very plain. Nailed joints were common. Any decoration should be confined to shaping edges. The usual construction was in softwood, such as pine, which was occasionally scrubbed. For modern use in a living room, the grain should be sealed, but a high gloss or painted finish would be inappropriate.

The ends provide the sizes on which most other measurements are based (Fig. 9-10B). The top and bottom are parallel boards (Fig. 9-10C), which may rest on battens across the ends, but the top, in particular, will make a neater and stronger joint if it also goes into a dado.

In many dry sinks the back was made up of boards nailed on, but for a better arrangement the ends are rabbeted and thin wood used to make up the main area of the back. Tongued and grooved boards would be appropriate, on the joints could be covered inside with narrow strips (Fig. 9-10D). The modern alternative, if strict compliance with tradition is not needed, is a piece of plywood. The back nails into the end rabbets and on to the edges of top and bottom. The thicker board that borders the sink recess goes above the top and into deeper rabbets in the ends (Fig. 9-10E).

The division between the drawers and the cupboard fits between the top and the bottom. In the simplest construction it would be nailed in place, but using dado joints is better craftsmanship as the grooves prevent the board warping (Fig. 9-10F), which could cause trouble with the running of the drawers.

The drawer runners can be glued and screwed in place, but allow for the front rails, which are strongest if they come behind the front uprights and meet the runners (Fig. 9-10G).

The front assembly is best treated as a unit that will be screwed to the front of the carcase (Fig. 9-11A). The board across the bottom is cut away to match the ends. The board at the top is cut down and the edges well rounded. Its lower edge is level with the underside of the top, so the top drawer comes against the top of the sink.

The vertical pieces that come between doors and door and drawers, as well as at the ends, could be joined to the horizontal members with short tenons (Fig. 9-11B), although with thinner wood it would be simpler to use cross lap joints (Fig. 9-11C), glued and strengthened with screws from inside. The most critical measurements are around the drawers. The edge of the intermediate upright must be level with the divider between drawers and cupboard, and the two posts should make a truly parallel space for the drawers. Outer edges can be slightly oversize for trimming after fittng.

The rails between the drawers are notched to fit behind the front uprights at a suitable spacing to suit the drawers and to fit closely against the runners (Fig. 9-10G).

The doors are made up with panels as previously described. Stops are provided at top and bottom (Fig. 9-11D). Locks can be put inside with keyholes below the knobs

The drawers can be made in one of the ways already described. Many of the original ones had dovetails at the front. There may have been dovetails at the back, or the back could fit into dados in the sides (Fig. 9-11E). Bottoms were made of pieces of thin wood with their grain across the drawer and fitting into grooves, either in the drawer sides or in strips fitted inside. These gave a broader bearing surface, which was worth having to reduce wear, particularly when a softwood was used (Fig. 9-11F).

A variation sometimes seen, took the block of drawers higher, so the sunk part to contain pans of water was over the part enclosed by doors, then the surface over the drawers could be used as a dry place for towels or cups and dippers.

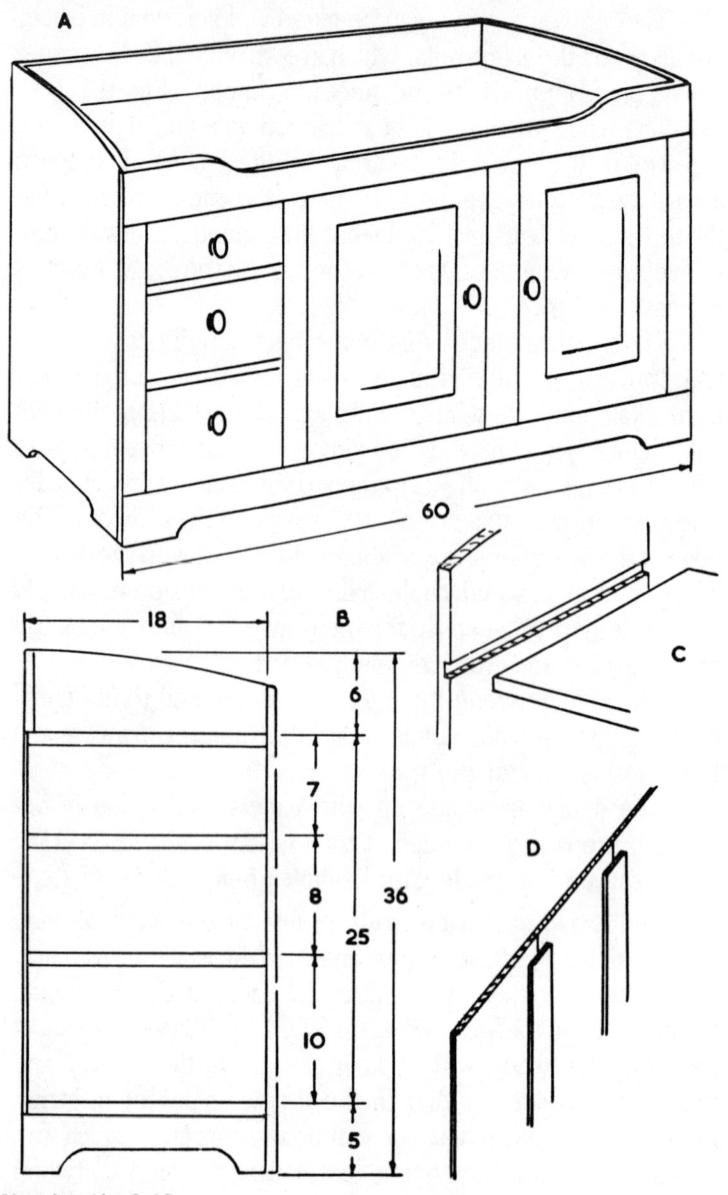


**Materials List 9-10**

Dry Sink

| | | | | | |
|---|---|---|---|---|---|
| 1 | Top | 18 × 60 × ¾ | 1 | Rim | 4 × 60 × ¾ |
| 2 | Ends | 18 × 36 × ¾ | 1 | Plinth | 5 × 60 × ¾ |
| 1 | Rim | 6 × 60 × ¾ | 4 | Uprights | 2 × 25 × ¾ |

Fig. 9-10. Dry sink. (Continued on next page.)

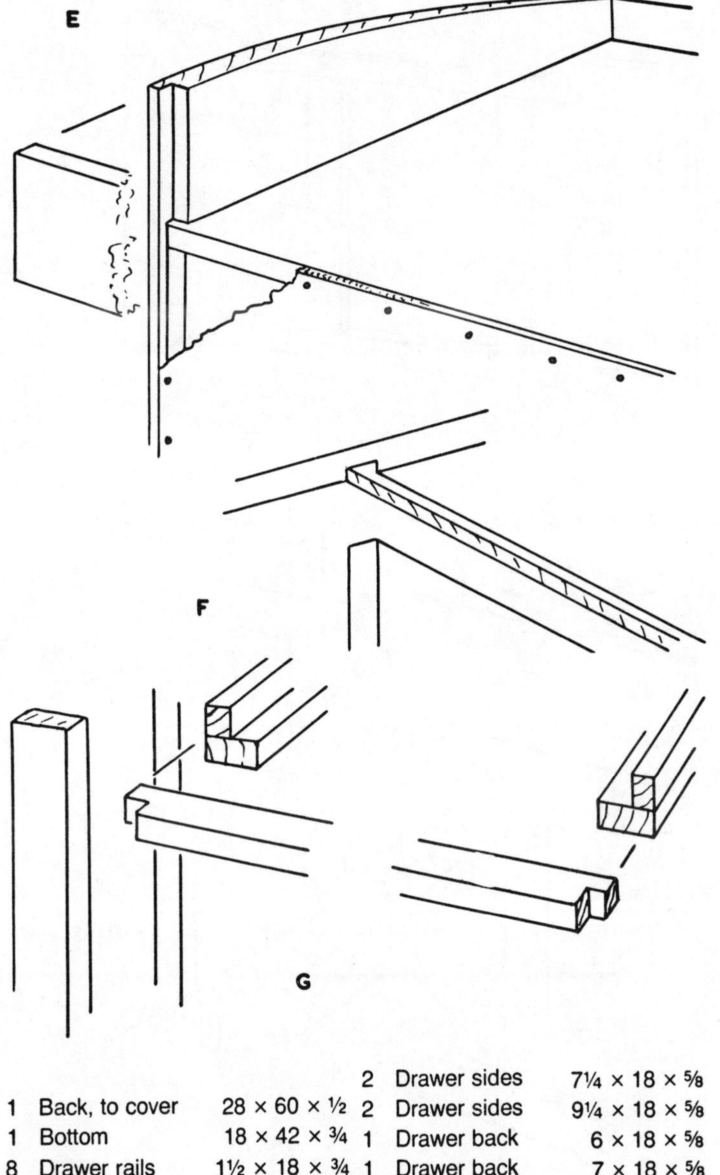


| | | | | | |
|---|---|---|---|---|---|
| | | | 2 | Drawer sides | 7¼ × 18 × ⅝ |
| 1 | Back, to cover | 28 × 60 × ½ | 2 | Drawer sides | 9¼ × 18 × ⅝ |
| 1 | Bottom | 18 × 42 × ¾ | 1 | Drawer back | 6 × 18 × ⅝ |
| 8 | Drawer rails | 1½ × 18 × ¾ | 1 | Drawer back | 7 × 18 × ⅝ |
| 6 | Drawer guides | ¾ × 18 × ¾ | 1 | Drawer back | 9 × 18 × ⅝ |
| 1 | Drawer front | 6¼ × 18 × ¾ | 3 | Drawer bottoms | 18 × 18 × ⅜ |
| 1 | Drawer front | 7¼ × 18 × ¾ | 4 | Door Sides | 3 × 25 × ¾ |
| 1 | Drawer front | 9¼ × 18 × ¾ | 4 | Door rails | 3 × 20 × ¾ |
| 2 | Drawer sides | 6¼ × 18 × ⅝ | 2 | Door panels | 18 × 23 × ½ |

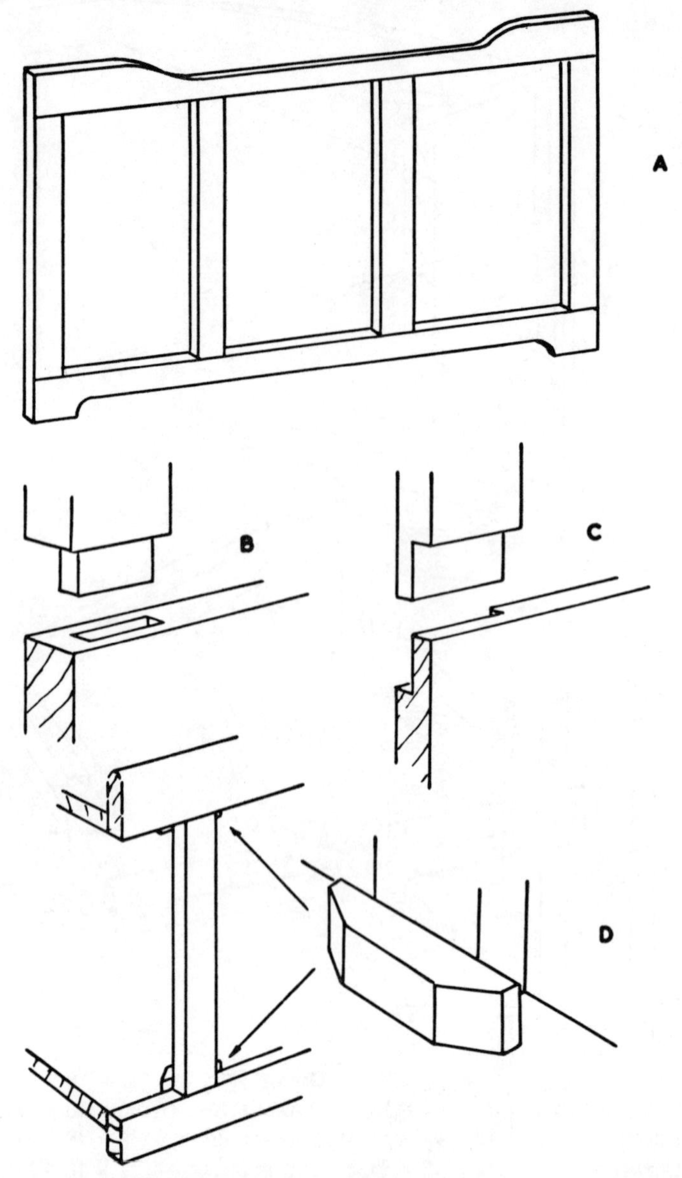


Fig. 9-11. Dry sink front details. (Continued on next page.)

For that construction the division between the drawers and the cupboard has to be taken higher, with the sink top fitting into dados in it and another top provided at the higher level (Fig. 9-11G).

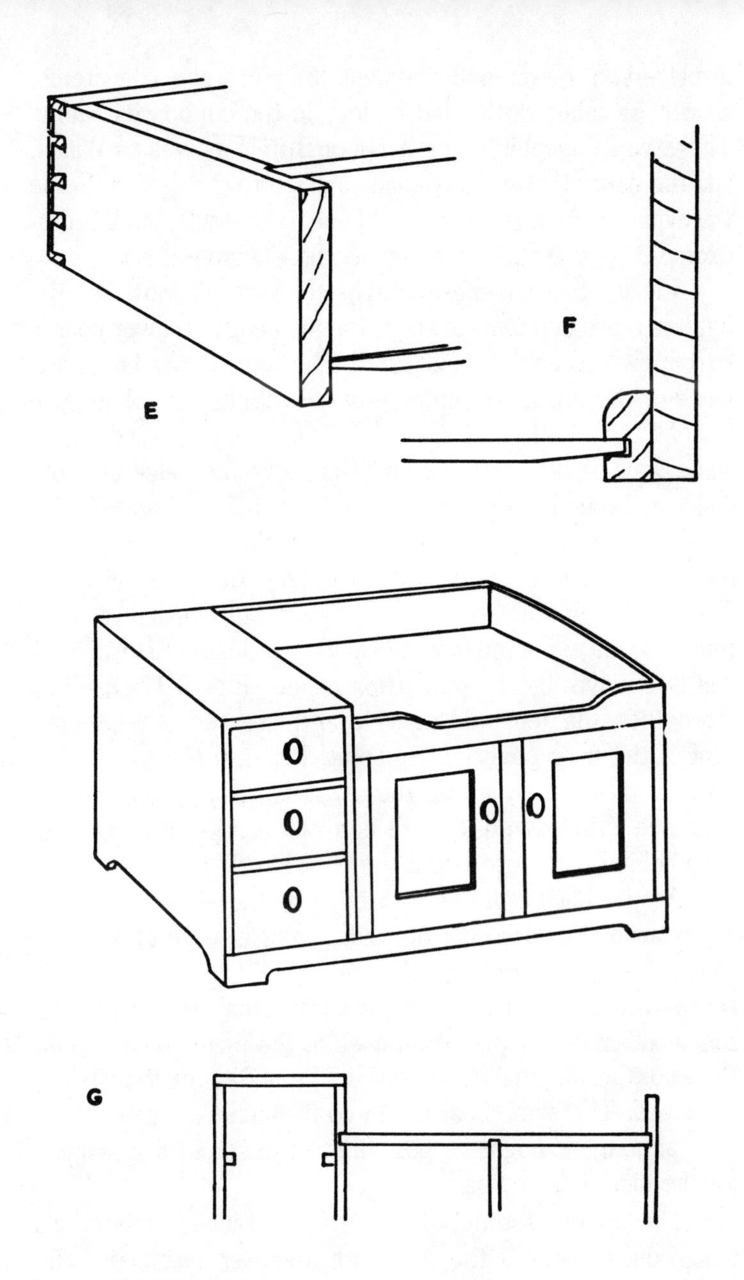


## WELSH CUPBOARD

Settlers from Britain would have known the Welsh dresser or cupboard, which often acted as the main center of interest in a living room, with the best plates and other china displayed on the open shelves and the more everyday items, as well as table cloths and cutlery in the cupboards below. These were usual in many parts of Britain as well as Wales, and the name *Welsh* was usually applied to the design. Some were quite elaborate and made of fine hardwoods, but this first example (Fig. 9-12A) is a simple and effective design.

Ideally, the two ends might be cut from full-width boards, but it is more economical and a way of using narrower boards to join two pieces (Fig. 9-12B). The edges may be simply glued or there can be reinforcements with dowels. The table top of the enclosed part may have to be made up in width the same way. It fits over the short parts of the sides and into dados in the ends, with reinforcing strips below (Fig. 9-12C).

The bottom is also notched into the ends with strips below, then the front uprights cover the edges (Fig. 9-12D). The doors come between the uprights, but overlap the bottom. The ends and the front uprights are shaped to form feet, and it is advisable to put strips inside (Fig. 9-12E). They strengthen the feet and provide an increased bearing area against the floor covering. In some furniture the tops of the doors come directly under the overhang of the top, but appearance is improved if there is a rail across, with another strip behind it to screw into the top (Fig. 9-12F).

As the back will show through at the shelf levels, its appearance should be considered. A single piece of plywood would be inappropriate. Tongued and grooved matched boards with a bead over each joint was usual (Fig. 9-12G). If this wood matches the wood used in the main construction, the whole setting makes a good background to the thing being displayed. The same boards can go through from top to bottom, although it might be possible to use something simpler for the hidden lower part.

The upper assembly has shelves arranged at intervals that reduce towards the top, with a space clear above the tabletop for anything expected to be put on it (Fig. 9-13A). The front edges are framed around with strips of wood that look best with molded or beaded edges. A beaded strip can be applied (Fig. 9-13B) or the edge molded (Fig. 9-13C). The top strip goes across and any molding is mitered (Fig. 9-13D).

The shelves could fit into dados in the ends, but the cover strips on the front edges hide supporting battens and it would be sufficient to fit the shelves to them (Fig. 9-13E). This method also allows shelves to be removed later if ever necessary. However, for the security of valuable china so that accidental knocking could not dislodge the shelves, they should be screwed to the battens.

Those shelves which will support plates should be grooved a short distance from the back (Fig. 9-13F) or strips could be fitted to prevent plates slipping (Fig. 9-13G). For further safety there could be thin pieces of wood put across inside the front pieces.

What is done at the extreme top depends on the intended appearance. A simple overhang with rounded edges (Fig. 9-13H) will be appropriate to the generally simple outlines, but there could be molding included (Fig. 9-13J). The top comes above the normal eye level, so any decoration there should suit an upward view.

Doors for the lower part could be made from boards ledged and braced, or framed and paneled.

## FINE WELSH DRESSER

This type of furniture continued to play an important part in the equipment of kitchen and dining room. With the coming of more settled conditions and the availability of specialist craftsmen with more time at their disposal there came Welsh dressers of good quality, that served as main features of dining rooms, as well as being functional. A characteristic of some Welsh dressers, is a curved top, but others kept to a generally square outline and got their decoration from shaped edges. The specimen described here is of this type and the method of construction given is of cabinetmaking quality (Fig. 9-14A). The same general appearance could be obtained with a simpler construction, but a cabinetmaker always preferred fitted and glued joints to nailed or screwed ones. Although counterboring and plugging over screw heads may be found in some early furniture, the better pieces normally had no sign of this having been done, except where there was no alternative. Instead,

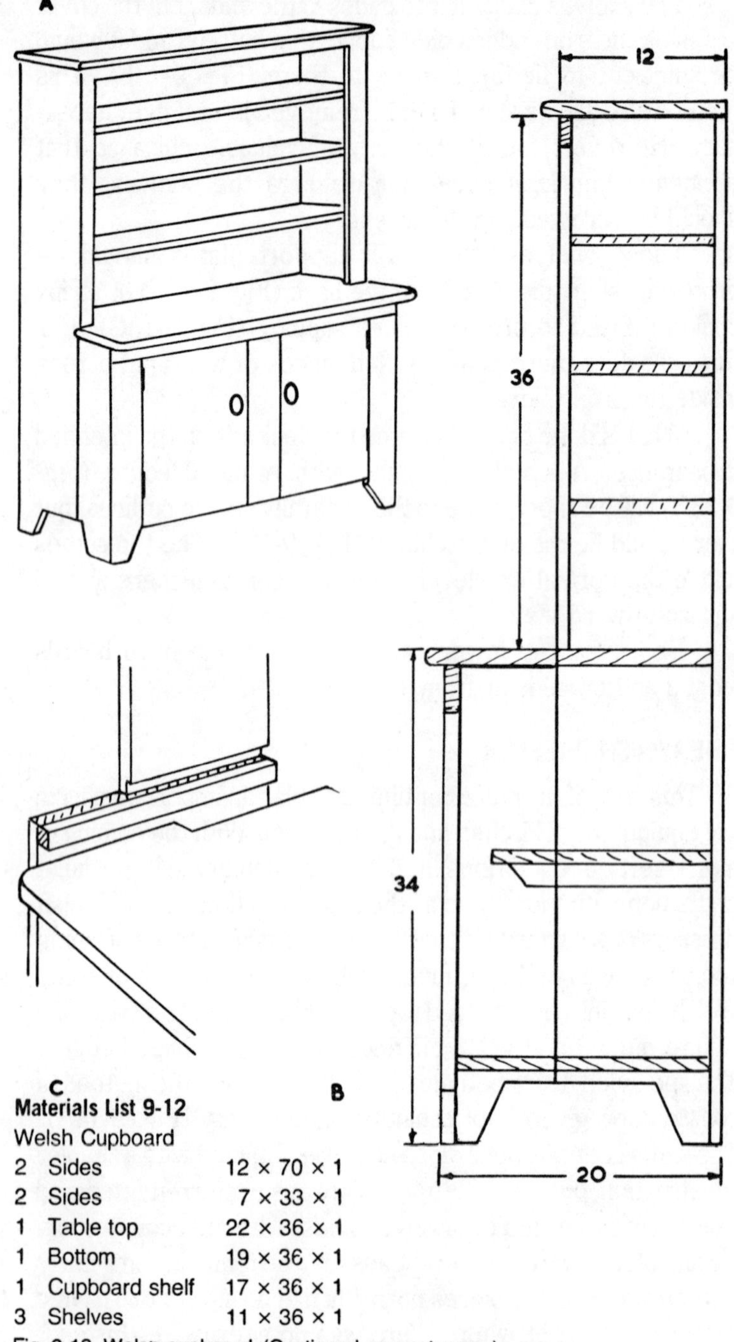


**Materials List 9-12**

Welsh Cupboard

| | | |
|---|---|---|
| 2 | Sides | 12 × 70 × 1 |
| 2 | Sides | 7 × 33 × 1 |
| 1 | Table top | 22 × 36 × 1 |
| 1 | Bottom | 19 × 36 × 1 |
| 1 | Cupboard shelf | 17 × 36 × 1 |
| 3 | Shelves | 11 × 36 × 1 |

Fig. 9-12. Welsn cupboard (Continued on next page.)

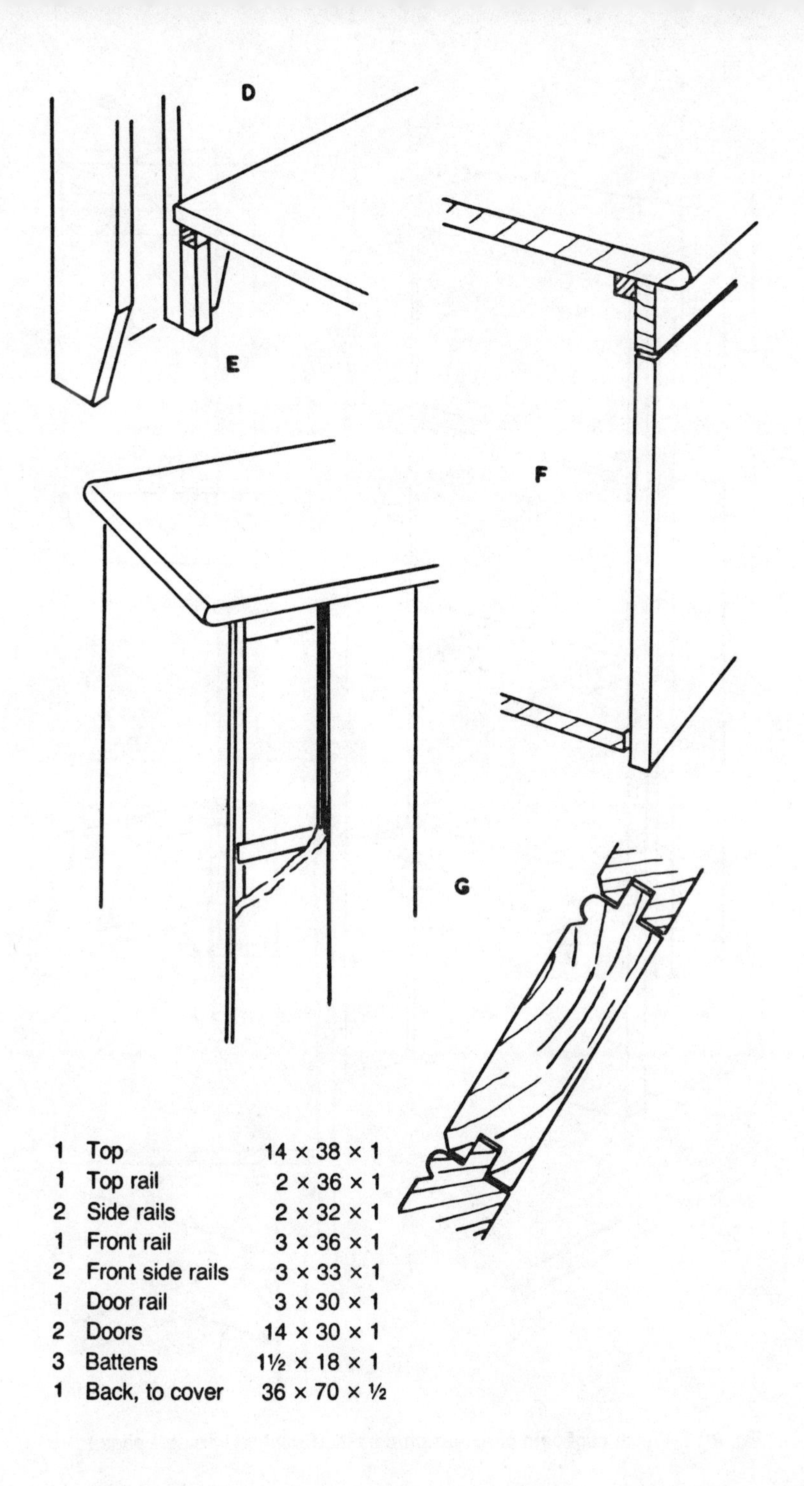


| | | |
|---|---|---|
| 1 | Top | 14 × 38 × 1 |
| 1 | Top rail | 2 × 36 × 1 |
| 2 | Side rails | 2 × 32 × 1 |
| 1 | Front rail | 3 × 36 × 1 |
| 2 | Front side rails | 3 × 33 × 1 |
| 1 | Door rail | 3 × 30 × 1 |
| 2 | Doors | 14 × 30 × 1 |
| 3 | Battens | 1½ × 18 × 1 |
| 1 | Back, to cover | 36 × 70 × ½ |

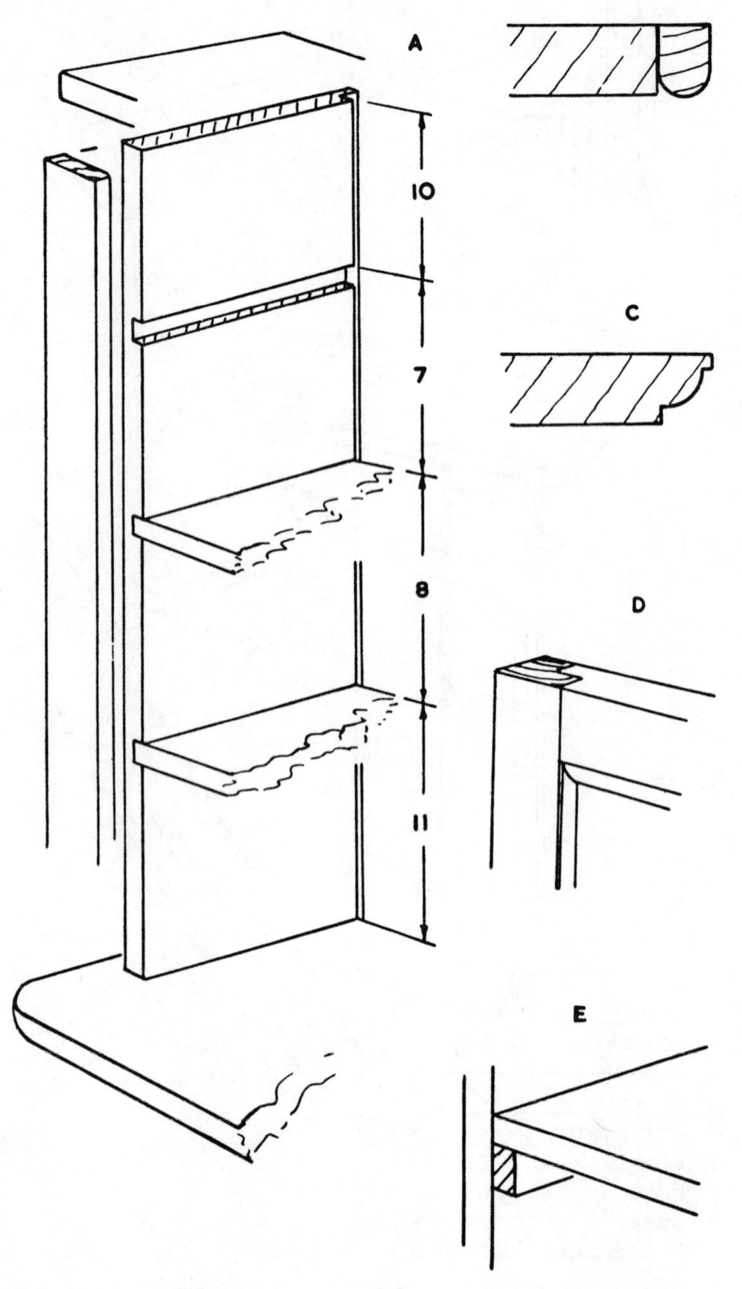


Fig. 9-13. Welsh cupboard construction details. (Continued on next page.)

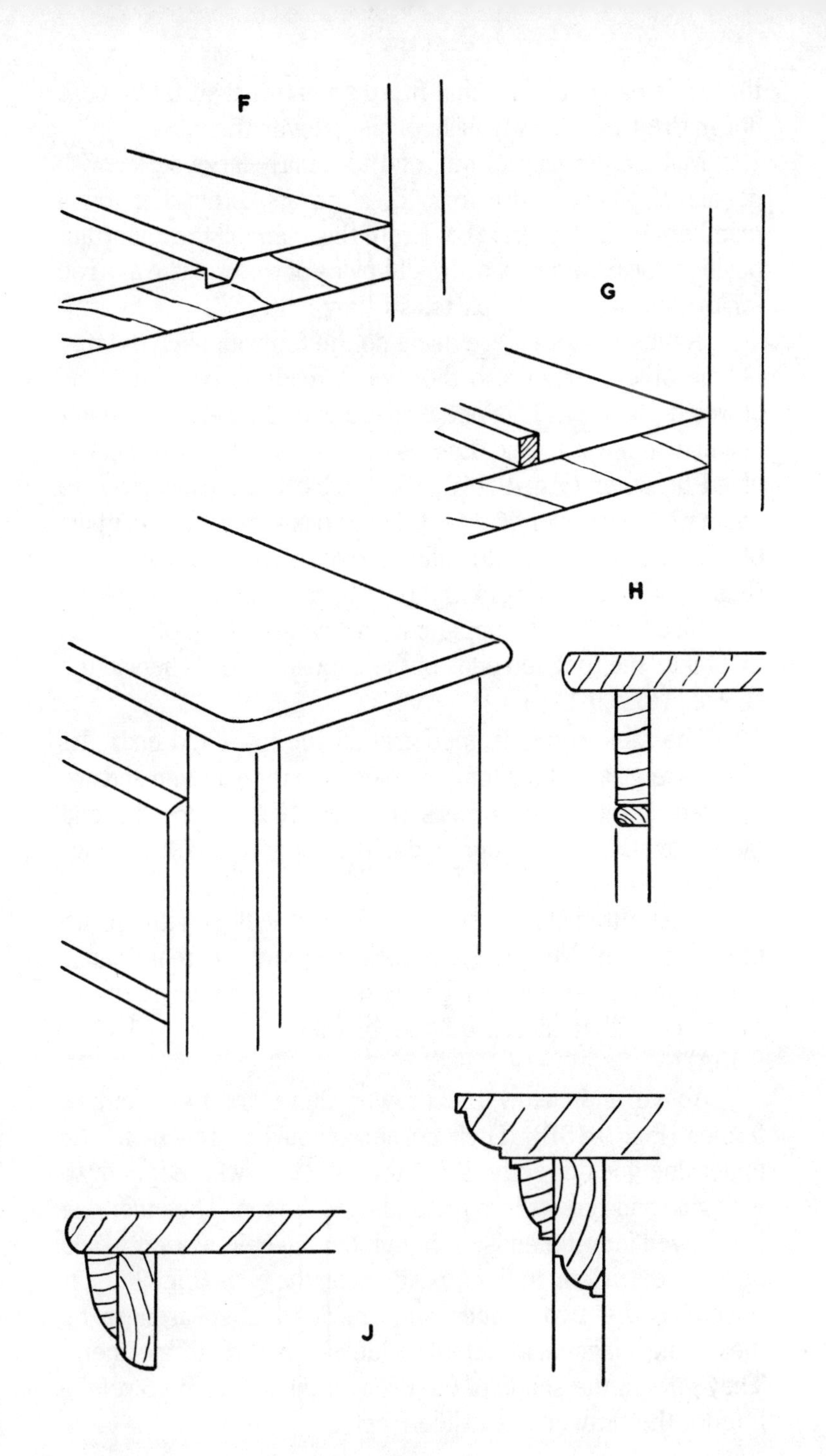
F
G
H
J

the craftsman cut joints that fitted so external surfaces were not marred by screws, nails or plugs over them.

Make a drawing of one end to a fairly large scale, with details of shelves, drawers, dividers and other horizontal members on it (Fig. 9-14B). From this mark all the important positions on the edge of a straight piece of wood to use as a rod for marking all upright parts, so they match.

Some dressers were made so the top with shelves lifted off the other part, or so they were made in two parts and doweled together. This one is made with the sides to the full height without a break. Each side is made from two boards glued together (Fig. 9-14C). The table top is also glued to width from narrower boards. Its ends pass over the lower part of the sides, but it fits into dado grooves across the higher part (Fig. 9-14D). At the back the boards covering the lower part are nailed to it, but the upper part is covered by a molded strip that takes the tongued ends of the exposed boards behind the shelves (Fig. 9-14E).

The table top is framed around the front and ends. Its edges are grooved for tongued pieces that go around and are mitered at the front corners (Fig. 9-14F). Where the end pieces overlap the higher ends, the tongue is cut off (Fig. 9-14G).

The bottom of this dresser is flat on the floor with a plinth fitted around it. No part is cut back, although the rear edge is not continued to the floor. The bottom of the cupboard fits on to battens, that increased the bearing area as well (Fig. 9-15A).

Above and below the drawer there are two identical frames (Fig. 9-15B). Their corners should be tenoned. The upper one goes directly under the tabletop, where it is fixed with glue and screws into the ends and the top. The other one is screwed into the ends, although for the best work it would be made extra long to fit into dadoes on the ends (Fig. 9-15C). Assemble the two frames and check their squareness by measuring diagonals. Let the glue set before fitting them. They govern the shape of the drawer and should be carefully fitted if the drawer is to slide freely.

The shelf in the cupboard rests on battens (Fig. 9-15D) and is probably best left loose so it can be removed for cleaning. There could be other shelf arrangements to suit individual needs.

At the front the edges of the frames above and below the drawer and the edge of the bottom come level with the edges of the side (Fig. 9-16A). The plinth is set back under the bottom (Fig. 9-16B) and will carry a decorative overlay. The ends of the plinth fit against the ends of the battens under the bottom, which are cut back to suit. The plinth could be notched into the sides or cut to fit closely in the final assembly.

Check dimensions and squareness of the lower body, but do not assemble yet. A trial assembly should be avoided, as this may cause loosening of joints. The overlay on the plinth may be given an undulating edge pattern or be made to a similar shape to the rail under the top. When the dresser is finished, this may be stained darker than the rest of the wood to emphasize its shape.

The upper part of the dresser is decorated by scalloped edges. Some early furniture makers drew curves with a compass and left the shape at that (Fig. 9-17A). A step between reversed curves was usual. A better artistic appreciation is shown by assymetrical curves between the shelves (Fig. 9-17B), with comparable curves around the fronts. A paper template is helpful.

The shelves have rounded front edges and are cut back to fit into stopped dado grooves (Fig. 9-17C). They are grooved to hold plates. At the top there is a rail with a shaped lower edge (Fig. 9-17D). Its ends are shouldered to fit into grooves in the sides (Fig. 9-17E).

The top is one part where a skilled furnituremaker might resort to screws, as this is not normally visible, but the best way of attaching it would be with a series of short tenons (Fig. 9-17F). In this case the dresser is capped with a fairly wide overhang of top.

The back is made of several vertical boards, which may be tongued and grooved, or thin boards may be only halved

**Materials List 9-14**

Fine Welsh Dresser

| | | | | | |
|---|---|---|---|---|---|
| 2 | Sides | 12 × 72 × 1 | 1 | Cupboard shelf | 18 × 36 × 1 |
| 2 | Sides | 12 × 36 × 1 | 2 | Shelves | 11 × 36 × 1 |
| 1 | Table top | 26 × 36 × 1 | 1 | Top | 14 × 38 × 1 |
| 1 | Table top | 2 × 40 × 1 | 1 | Top rail | 2 × 36 × 1 |
| 2 | Table tops | 2 × 26 × 1 | 4 | Drawer dividers | 1½ × 36 × 1 |
| 1 | Bottom | 24 × 36 × 1 | 4 | Drawer dividers | 1½ × 24 × 1 |

Fig. 9-14. Fine Welsh dresser. (Continued on next page.)

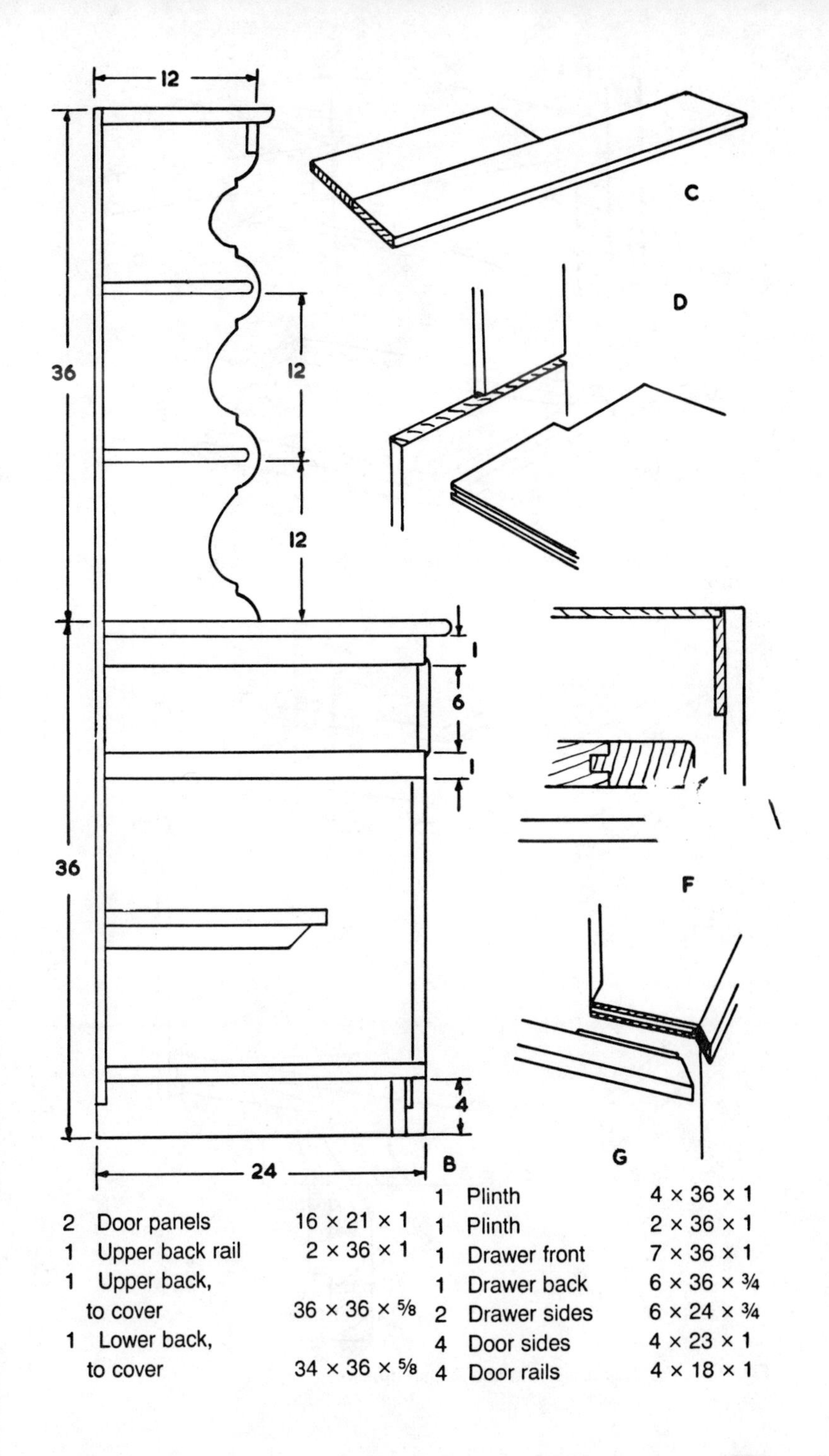


| Qty | Part | Size |
|---|---|---|
| 2 | Door panels | 16 × 21 × 1 |
| 1 | Upper back rail | 2 × 36 × 1 |
| 1 | Upper back, to cover | 36 × 36 × 5/8 |
| 1 | Lower back, to cover | 34 × 36 × 5/8 |

| Qty | Part | Size |
|---|---|---|
| 1 | Plinth | 4 × 36 × 1 |
| 1 | Plinth | 2 × 36 × 1 |
| 1 | Drawer front | 7 × 36 × 1 |
| 1 | Drawer back | 6 × 36 × 3/4 |
| 2 | Drawer sides | 6 × 24 × 3/4 |
| 4 | Door sides | 4 × 23 × 1 |
| 4 | Door rails | 4 × 18 × 1 |

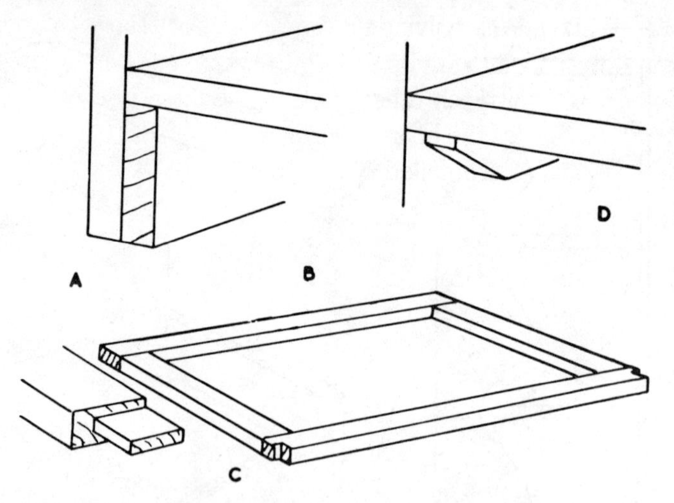


Fig. 9-15. Bottom (A), shelf (B) and drawer divider (C) details of the fine Welsh dresser.

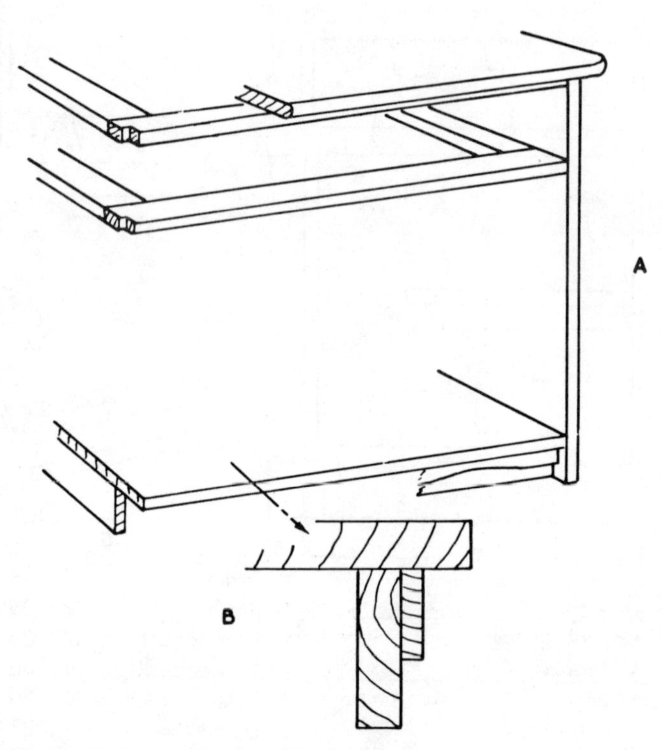


Fig. 9-16. Front details of the fine Welsh dresser.

(Fig. 9-17G). With halving there is a risk that a board warping may open its joint with its neighbor, but tongued and grooved boards will limit each other's warping tendencies.

At the sides the boards fit into rabbets in the ends. At the top the boards are nailed or screwed to the back of the top

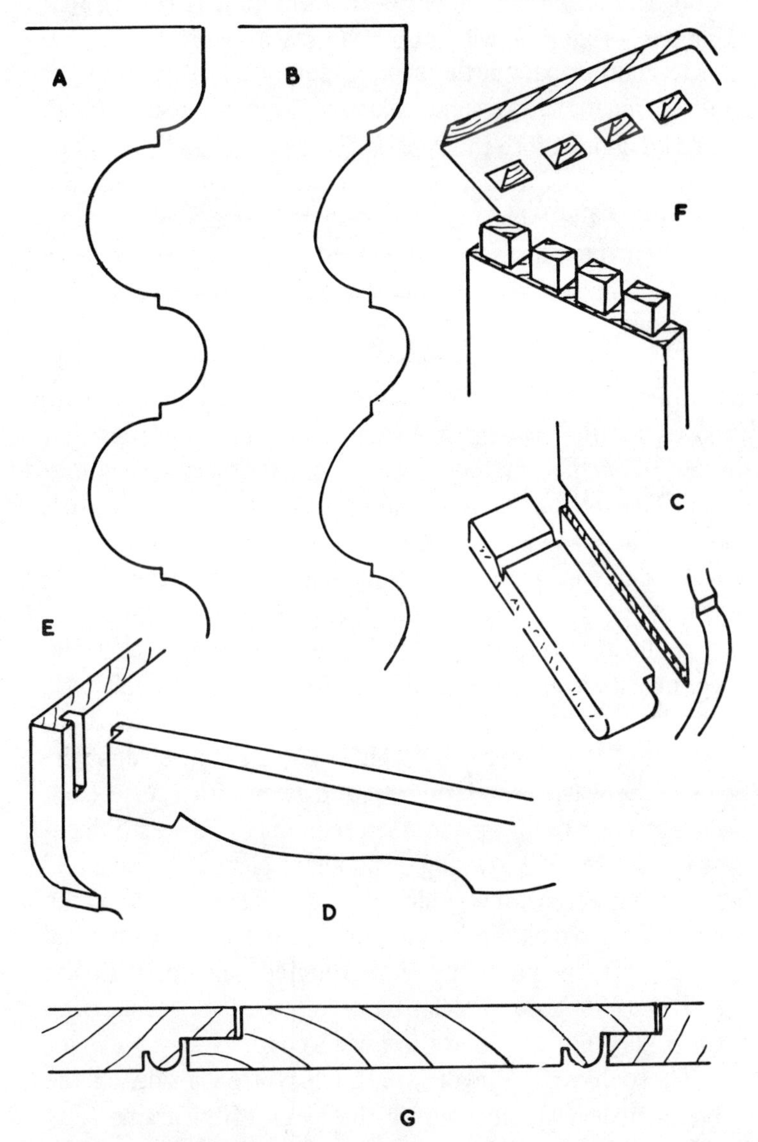


Fig. 9-17. Side shaping (A and B), shelf assembly (C), top joint (D-F) and back joints (G) in the fine Welsh dresser.

board. At their bottoms the boards are tongued into the strip across the table top. These are the only parts that are not glued in the final assembly, as they must be able to expand and contract.

Up to this stage certain subassemblies can be made up, but no final assembly should be done until it is certain that fixing parts together will not interfere with work to be done later to another part of the same assembly. For instance, all the grooving for shelves and making of joints for the upper part should be done before the cupboard is assembled. The frames and the bottom of the cupboard should be fitted between the sides before the table top or upper shelves are added.

When the carcase has been assembled, check it in all directions for squareness, and leave it standing level for the glue to set.

The pair of doors are made in the same way as previously described, with the frame joints mortise and tenon, with grooves for the panels. In better work the panels are not merely thinned to fit the grooves, but they are *fielded and raised*. This means that the center part has a definite edge so it shows a clean line instead of a blend from flat to a bevel (Fig. 9-18A). This can be done with a suitable tool in a power spindle or router, but to make a panel by hand the outline of the raised part is cut in, either with a cutting gauge working from the edge, or with a sharp knife along a steel straightedge. This is important if disfiguring by grain tearing out is to be avoided. The amount of raising can be slight—1/16 in. may be enough. Some of the waste wood can be pared away with a chisel (Fig. 9-18B), then a rabbet plane used to reduce the waste thickness (Fig. 9-18C). A low-angled shoulder plane is the best tool for working across the grain. With the depth worked, the plane is tilted to make the bevel (Fig. 9-18D). The lowered and tapered part should then be thoroughly sanded, with the abrasive paper around a flat piece of wood to get an even surface. Try not to round the raised edge.

There have to be drawer guides fitted inside on the runners, which are formed by the sides of the frame (Fig. 9-18E), otherwise there are no special preparations to take the drawer. Fit stops for the drawers.

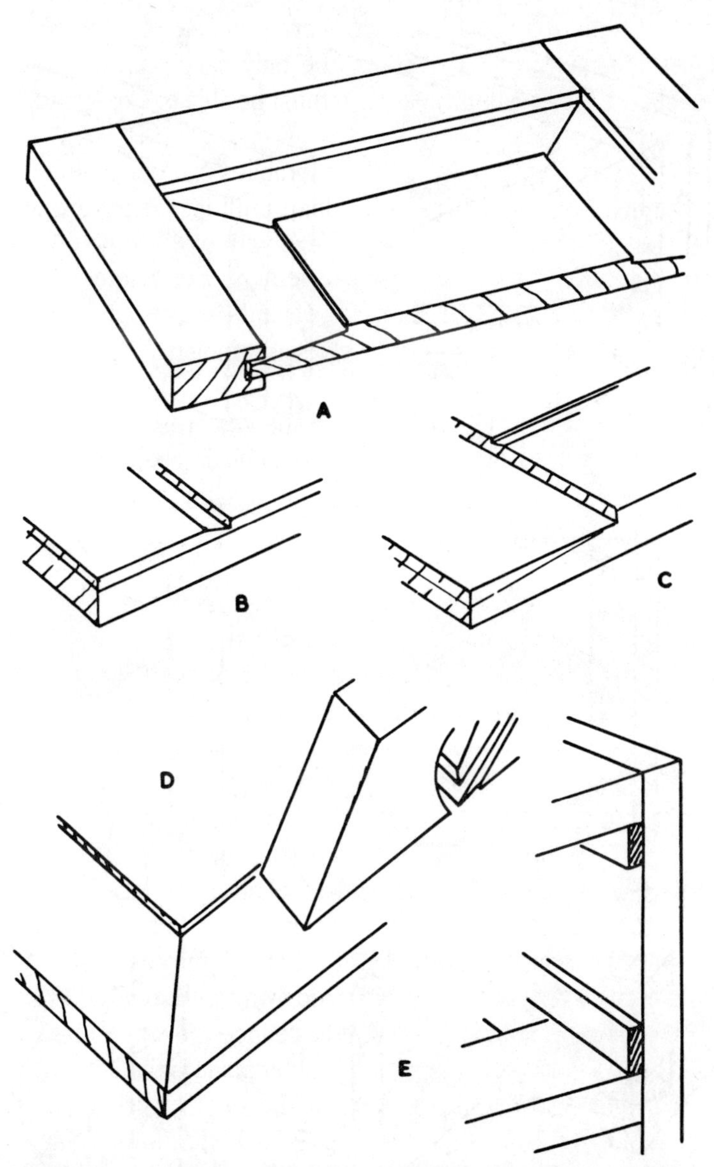


Fig. 9-18. Steps in fielding panels (A-D) and arranging drawer guides in the fine Welsh dresser.

The drawer for this piece of furniture has an overlapping front (Fig. 9-19A), otherwise its construction is similar to drawers described for earlier items. The front is prepared by working rabbets across the top edge and the ends (Fig.

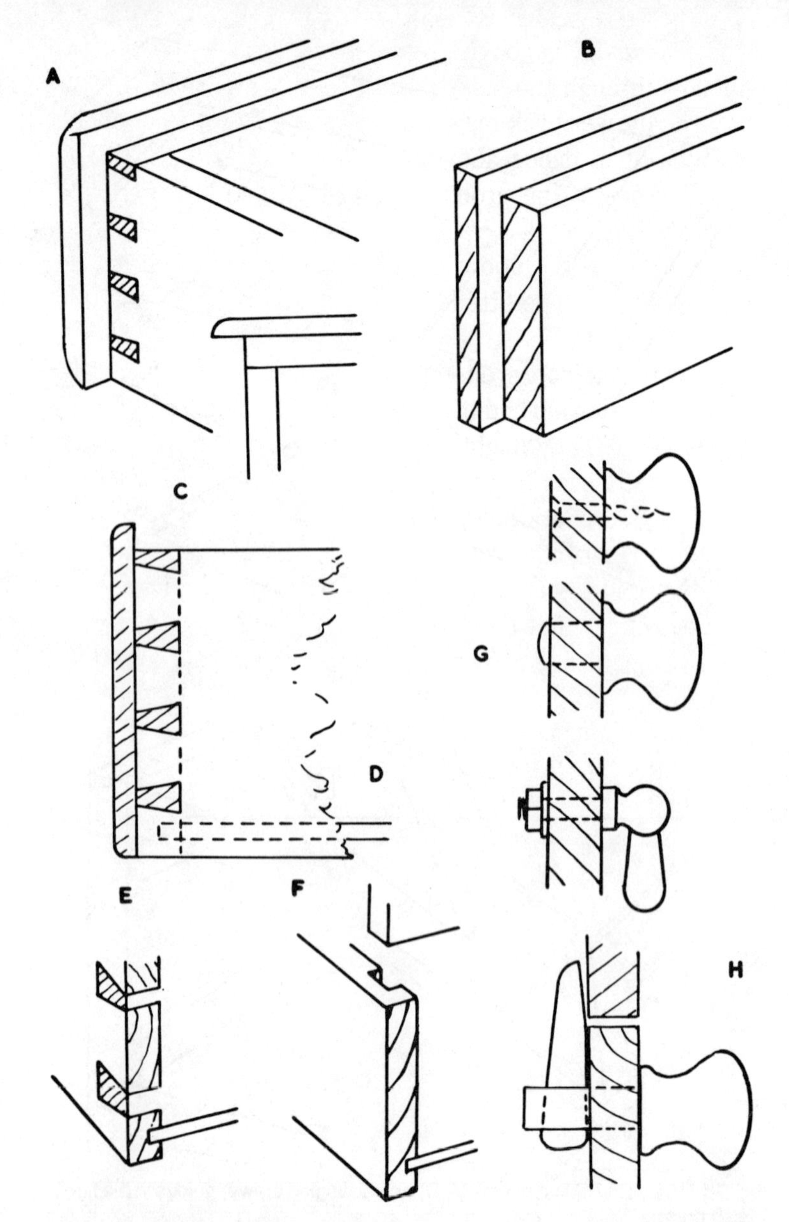


Fig. 9-19. Drawer construction (A-F), with suitable knobs and catches (G and H) for the fine Welsh dresser.

9-19B). When this has been done the projecting part of the back surface should fit in the opening in the carcase. The drawer sides dovetail into the front (Fig. 9-19C). The bottom dovetail is cut high enough to allow for a groove for the bottom to follow through the sides into the front (Fig. 9-19D).

The drawer back may be dovetailed (Fig. 9-19E) or the back can fit in dados above the bottom (Fig. 9-19F). The bottom slides in the groove from the back and is screwed under the back.

Hinges for the doors could be ornamental ones on the surface, or butt type fitted into the space between the doors and their stiles.

Knobs for doors on this type of dresser were nearly always turned wood and they followed a fairly uniform pattern (Fig. 9-19G). They might be screwed from the inside of the drawer, but it was more usual for them to be turned with a dowel to glue into a hole.

Separate catches could be provided for the doors, but one original wooden combined catch and knob was used. The dowel extends inside the door and is mortised to take a wedge, which can be turned to overlap the stile and hold the door (Fig. 9-19H).

# Finishing

Most modern furniture has surfaces brought to near perfection, and these are covered by hard protective coatings, most of which have a synthetic base. Some of the first furniture made in Colonial days was probably put into use without much surface finishing and no applied protective coating. Later furniture was given a better finish, but since the bulk of the work was done by hand, there was not the mechanical perfection that comes from power tools and the applied protection was all with natural bases.

In reproduction work, the maker will have to decide what finish to use. If complete authenticity is aimed at, there should be an attempt to reproduce the original maker's methods. If the furniture is to take its place alongside modern furniture and reproduced original finish is not regarded as important, any modern finishing system of lacquer, polish or paint can be used.

Much genuinely old furniture has acquired a patina of age, usually with a satin feel and appearance that has come from long handling and usage. There is no quick way of reproducing this, but it is possible to use modern finishes to fill the grain and provide protection to the surface, then rub this to a flat appearance and follow with wax or oil to give something of the old appearance. This mixture of new and old techniques is probably the best way to deal with most reproductions.

Another thing to consider is what effect is expected. Should the finished article look like its counterpart did when first made, or should it look more like that item does today after maybe two centuries of wear? The author favors aiming at the quality of the thing as it was and leaving it at that, but it is possible to indulge in furniture *faking* or *distressing*. This is not an attempt to pass off the reproduction as a genuine antique, but there is an attractiveness about an old appearance, and the wood can be finished to simulate old age if desired.

## WOOD PREPARATION

How well the wood was finished depends on the age of the original, but nearly all of the furniture considered in this book would have had nearly all the work on it done with hand tools. Consequently, one of the first requirements is the removal of any signs of machine work. This applies particularly to machine planing. Even after sanding, the characteristic marks across the grain from this process may show through a clear varnish or lacquer. It is wiser to go over all machine-planed surfaces with a smoothing plane. Heavy power sanding should be avoided. It is better to follow hand planing with hand sanding. If this does not completely remove all signs of planing and the final surface is not perfect, that would be more like early Colonial furniture than a more perfect surface.

A scraper has its uses. Early furniture makers used steel scrapers or the broken edge of a piece of glass after planing. A scraper surface, with only light sanding, is a good finish. For hand sanding a flat surface, wrap the abrasive paper around a block of wood and work only in the direction of the grain. A shaped surface may have to be worked across, but finish with the grain. Some of the early sanding was done with sand or pumice powder, used with a wet or oiled cloth, and this is a technique valuable today, either for the bare wood or taking the gloss off an applied finish. Steel wool can also be used, but this was not available to the early cabinetmaker.

Wood may have to be stopped or filled. *Stopping* is the filling of holes or cracks, while *filling* is the treatment of the grain so it is less absorbent and woods with very open grain patterns present a level surface for paint or varnish.

There are many prepared stoppings, and it will be simplest to get something in a tube to squeeze in a hole, rather than mix your own. If the wood is to be stained or given a clear finish, the stopping must take stain to the same intensity as the wood or be the same color. For a painted finish the color of the stopping is less important. Plastic water putty can be pressed into a hole with a screwdriver or knife. Wood plastic is more like wood when it sets. Both will take stain. Stick shellac will not take stain, but can be bought colored and is intended to be used after wood has been stained.

Not all woods require filling. Spruce, redwood, and pine are softwoods that do not need filling. Some of the close-grained hardwoods to not need the treatment. At the other extreme, open-grained woods, such as ash, oak, chestnut, elm, and hickory, need a paste filler. Between these are mahogany, walnut, cedar, sycamore, and similar woods. They can have a liquid filler.

Most modern fillers are a finely ground crystal, called silex, which is mixed with linseed oil or other binder into a thick paste. Liquid filler is made by thinning this.

The filler may be used before staining and take the color with the wood, or it can be dyed and used after staining. Staining before filling achieves a better penetration. Paste filler is rubbed on across the grain with coarse cloth, such as burlap, then the surplus rubbed off. An old hair brush can be used instead of a cloth. Liquid filler can be put on with a paint brush. Cloth or a paint brush will get filler into shaped parts. Rub smooth and leave for at least a day before the next stage.

## PRIMING COATS

Even woods that do not need filling may be very absorbent. There may be no need to do anything to get a level surface, but it is advisable to seal the grain so too much of the applied finish has to be used. If finishing coats are put directly on some bare wood, they will soak in, often unevenly, and many coats will be needed to get a good result. If the wood is sealed, fewer finishing coats are needed. Any staining should be done before sealing. Sealing may follow filling and stopping.

There are prepared sealers, but shellac is convenient. Shellac is imported in flakes, which are dissolved in denatured alcohol. The dissolved shellac can be bought in many concentrations, described by their *cut*, denoting the amount of shellac dissolved in one gallon of alcohol. A *5 lb. cut* means 5 lb. of shellac dissolved in one gallon. There are weaker cuts, but stronger solutions can always be diluted. For use as a sealer, a 5 lb. cut might be diluted with about six times as much alcohol, then brushed on and left about twelve hours.

Common shellac has a slightly orange color. This does not matter on most woods, and in its very dilute form for filling it may not have any appreciable effect on the color of the near white woods. However, for light color woods there is bleached shellac, which is clear. Bleached shellac does not have as good a storage slife as orange shellac.

## STAINS

Much early furniture was left in its natural color. Darkening or coloring may have been due to age and exposure to light. For most reproduction furniture, staining is not required, although copies of later pieces may be stained, particularly to hasten the effect of age-darkening. In general, staining should empasize the existing color. The brownness of oak and walnut may be darkened. The redness of mahogany is made more intense. There may have to be staining of one wood to match another, but trying to make one wood look like another by coloring it is usually unsuccessful. Grains vary and something like pine stained to look like mahogany would not deceive anyone with a little knowledge of woods. Stains alter the color of wood without hiding the appearance of its grain.

Stains consist of a pigment in a solvent, which enters the grain. There are several solvents used, but oil and water are commonest. Both can be bought in prepared form and may be diluted, but the two types cannot be mixed and one should not be used after the other.

Oil stains use a light oil, such as benzene or turpentine. They spread evenly and should dry without brush marks.

Plenty of stain should be applied fairly quickly, then the surplus can be wiped off with a cloth. There can be a second coat to darken the color. Under most clear finishes the color tends to appear lighter than its does when first applied. End grain absorbs more than side grain and finishes darker. This can be limited by using sealer on the end grain.

Water stains are bought as powders to dissolve in hot water and used cold. They brush on, but do not have as good a penetration as oil stains, nor are they so easy to apply without risk of brush marks. Two or more coats of a light stain are easier to get even than one coat of a dark stain. Stain all over a piece of furniture quickly and do not wipe with a cloth, unless there is an obvious excess anywhere.

There are chemical ways of coloring wood and some of these would have been used on the original furniture. Acetic acid (cider vinegar), which has been left overnight to react with iron filings, can be used on pine to give it a weathered grey effect. Household lye and some domestic cleaning powders will turn some woods brown. Permanganate of potash crystals dissolved in water will turn many woods a medium brown.

Spirit stains are best avoided. These use alcohol as a solvent and dry so rapidly that it is difficult to brush them on evenly. They are of some use for narrow parts, such as molding or for touching up damaged work.

## PAINTING

While most early settlers found beauty in the natural appearance of wood, some, notably the Pennsylvania Dutch, preferred to paint it. Colors were bright, and besides overall painting there were patterns and motifs in contrasting colors. Such designs are best seen on the actual furniture, and anyone wanting to decorate in this way will be guided by furniture in museums and elsewhere.

Paints were compounded mainly from natural materials, using lacs and resins and various pigments. Paint continued to be made in this way until after World War II when synthetic resins and other ingredients began to take the place of the older materials. The result has been to improve paints, both in their ease of application and in their subsequent appearance and wearing qualities.

The word *paint* refers to an opaque finish. If the grain shows through, it is a *stain*. Paint may be *enamel* or lacquer. Enamel is durable and nearer to the traditional finishes. Lacquer dries quicker and is not really applicable to traditional furniture. Fortunately there is little to distinguish modern synthetic paints for the earlier paints from natural materials once they have dried, so any good modern paint would be acceptable on reproduction furniture. Paints come in flat, semigloss and gloss finishes. Water-base paints are unsuitable for furniture. Oil-base paints are the type to choose.

It is advisable to select the products of one paint maker and follow the directions he provides. The traditional sequence of painting a sealed or filled surface is: one or more priming coats that form a base for the other paints; one or more undercoats that have a color related to the top coat, for which they form a base; a top coat that provides the final visible surface. There are some paints that do not require all these steps. Primer and undercoat may be the same thing.

Most paints require rubbing down between coats. This is a light sanding with medium abrasive. If more than one top gloss coat is applied, the shine should be rubbed off the first before applying the second. *Wet-and-dry* abrasive paper is a special grade to be used wet for this purpose. Dust from sanding should be removed with a damp cloth or a prepared *tack rag*.

Many modern paints should not be stirred—check the directions. Otherwise, make sure all pigment is thoroughly mixed before starting painting. Natural bristle brushes are best, but there are other satisfactory ones with nylon and other bristles. Flat brushes are graded according to their width and thickness. A thick brush gives a better result on a broad surface than a thin one. Sometimes best brushes are described as *varnish brushes*. This indicates quality, not that the brush is only for varnish. Besides paint, have a solvent for storing and cleaning brushes. It may be linseed oil, but this may not be compatible with all synthetic paints, so check the maker's recommendations.

Paint the long way of a surface, which is usually with the grain, and make final strokes towards a part already done, lifting the brush as it passes over it, to reduce the risk of brush marks. Paint may be applied in several directions to get good spread and coverage, but finish with the grain. Brush towards an edge, not from it—which may cause drips. Be careful that each brushful of paint is spread. An excess on a vertical surface may run and dry as *curtains*. It is usually best to paint shaped parts such as molding, before going over broader flat surfaces.

A modern help which the original painters did not have, is masking tape. If two colors are to meet, masking tape along the line prevents the paint being applied going over on to the other paint. However, make sure a paint surface is hard before applying masking tape to it.

Paint is easiest to apply on a horizontal surface. It is usually best to manipulate a piece of furniture so you are working on near horizontal surfaces as much as possible. Usually the least important parts are done first, then visible parts like legs and ends, before finally dealing with the top.

## VARNISH AND WAX

Much early polishing was done with oils and wax. They may have been the only suitable materials available, but getting a finish with them can be tedious and laborious. Many oils can be used. Some early oil polishes may have been incidental to animal fats being wiped on kitchen tables. Linseed oil was used.

To polish bare wood there have to be many coats of linseed oil, wiped on and polished off with a coarse cloth, at long intervals of time. Heating the oil makes it penetrate. It is the heat generated by the friction of rubbing that produces the polish.

Wax was applied in a similar way—beeswax being usual. This produced a harder surface than oil, but applications at weekly intervals over a long period made results slow. Wax is still used as a finishing or reviving coat. The hardest wax is carnauba. It is too brittle to use alone, but it forms the base of most modern wax polishes, mixed with paraffin, ceresine or beeswax.

Varnish may be regarded as paint without coloring matter. Traditional varnish was made with natural ingredients and some of it was rather difficult to apply. In damp or humid conditions or if applied too late for it to dry before nightfall, it might "bloom," become cloudy and remain sticky for a long time. It also tended to attract dust for some time after brushing on. Modern synthetic varnishes are not so much affected by atmospheric conditions, but they are still best applied in dry warm conditions. They become tack-free in a short time, so dust is not such a problem.

Varnish should not be stirred, as this causes bubbles, which transfer to the surface and dry out as blemishes. The instructions on some cans advise "flowing on." This means applying with the minimum of brushing, so each brushful should get enough working to spread it, but with no unnecessary strokes. Too much brushing may cause the brush to suddenly drag and lift varnish to leave a rough surface. This has to be left and sanded after drying, to start again.

For most reproduction furniture a pure varnish finish might not be appropriate, although it can be used to match other furniture or for the greatest protection in damp or exterior conditions. Instead, it is better to apply two or three coats of varnish to build up a protective coating, then finish with wax.

Varnish dries with a gloss and this should be rubbed down between coats. The top coat of varnish should be left to get really hard before rubbing down and waxing. Instructions with the varnish will indicate the time, but synthetic varnishes tend to harden to a state when they can be handled, but hardness builds up over further days. Take the gloss off the varnish. Steel wool could be used, but pumice powder on a damp cloth or piece of felt, or mixed with a thin oil, such as lemon oil, will produce the necessary flat surface. Try to get rid of the shine, but do not rub away varnish unnecessarily.

With the varnish as a base, instead of bare wood, wax can be used to build up a satin gloss with only a moderate amount of hand rubbing. The result after a few applications will be satisfactory, but further polishing at intervals of a month or so will establish the finish to look very similar to one on furniture a century or more old. Further treatment may be with a wax or cream sold for reviving furniture finishes, including any sold as 'no-rub," although even they benefit from a rub with a light cloth. Any cloth used for polishing should be lint-free—well-washed cloth has usually lost all of its lint, in any case.

## SHELLAC

Shellac in alcohol, of fairly strong concentration, has a consistency and appearance very like varnish. It can be used in the same way by brushing. The effect can have a similar appearance to varnish, but it does not have such a good resistance to abrasion and many solvents. In any case, it would not be appropriate for reproduction furniture. It could be used instead of varnish as a base for waxing, as just described, but better results are likely with varnish.

Although a 5 lb. cut may be used, better results are obtained by applying more coats of a thinner mixutre, such as 2 lb. cut or 5 lb. diluted with an equal amount of alcohol. As drying is rapid, it is possible to apply coats at about two-hour intervals, making five coats in a day possible. Do not brush excessively and avoid going over one part frequently. Use long single strokes. Lightly sand between coats. Hard shellac sands as a white powder. If it does not, it may not be fully hardened.

On reproduction furniture shellac is more likely to be used for French polishing. This would not have been used in early Colonial days, but it became the accepted finish for the good quality furnituremakers and designers of the late eighteenth and early nineteenth century on both sides of the Atlantic. The glowing surface obtained by French polishing is considered superior to any other gloss finish. There is a certain amount of labor involved, but it is a skill that improves with practice. It is patience as much as skill that gets good results.

French polishing is done with thin shellac in denatured alcohol, of about 2½ lb. cut. However, some alcohol contains a resin, making it less suitable for French polishing, and shellac sold as French polish is to be preferred. French polish is normally used without coloring, with bleached shellac polish for the lightest color woods.

Polishing is done with a pad. Outside is an old piece of cotton cloth. Inside is a pad of cotton batting. The cloth is drawn around the pad and screwed around on top. Its bottom surface should be up to 3 in. across, so it can be gripped in the hand. Work is done on the bare wood which has been brought to a good surface. It may be filled. French polishing brings out the quality of the grain. It also emphasizes any flaws, so a good finish to the wood is necessary.

There are three stages in French polishing: bodying in, building up, and spiriting out. Of course, the wood has to be brought to a good surface, as described earlier, then stained and filled. If anything, French polishing emphasizes the quality of the wood surface. This is not a finish for disguising imperfections.

Bodying in is the process that puts a skin of shellac on the wood. Sprinkle shellac on the inner pad and cover it with the cloth. Twist the cloth up so the shellac oozes through. Rub across the grain and then with it. Cover every part of the surface, particularly the corners. Do not stop on the surface. Change to a circular motion or a figure-eight action. Continue rubbing until all the polish in the pad is exhausted. Allow the surface to harden, then recharge the pad and repeat.

Try to cover the whole surface with an even film. It is the corners that suffer. Usually if you concentrate on the corners, the center or a panel will take care of itself. Recharging and rubbing may be repeated as many times as needed to give the whole surface a good protective coating. Leave the work in a dust-free room for about a day.

Follow this by examining the surface in a light. There may be unevenness. Use fine steel wool lightly to remove this then change the pad and apply more polish. If the pad sticks when moved over the surface, add a few drops of linseed oil to the outside of the pad. Get an even depth of polish, then wait for another day. If flaws are still there, the process and waiting should be repeated.

The building up stage is next. Lightly rub the surface with steel wool and wipe off the dust. Prepare the pad with polish, but not as much as for bodying in. The smaller amount of polish will cause the pad to drag, and this has to be prevented with a few drops of oil. Do not use any more oil than necessary. To check the pad, press it on paper. Oil will make a mark if present. If none is shown, the pad is ready for a few more drops of oil. The same test will show how wet the pad is with polish. If there is a definite wet trail when the pad is drawn lightly across the bodied-in surface, there is too much polish on the pad. If the pad marks are shiny, there is too much oil.

Work over the surface with circular or figure-eight movements in the same way as when bodying in. Stroke lightly. Do not rub hard. Make sure the whole area is covered. Do not put down or take up the pad from the center of the surface. Slide on or off at an edge. Do not stop on the surface. It is not swift rubbing that produces a good polish. There is no need to rush.

Recharge with polish as necessary and add spots of oil when needed. Continue until there is a good layer of polish over the surface of the wood. The layer need not have much of a shine or a very even gloss. Next, apply a coat of polish diluted with an equal quantity of alcohol. The result may look smeary, but it does not matter at this stage. Leave the work for at least five hours.

The next stage is spiriting out. Use a fresh pad with a double outer cloth. Dampen this with a little alcohol. Put the pad into an airtight jar for a short time so the alcohol permeates the pad. Wipe the surface with very light strokes. This should remove smears. Change to a dry clean pad and go over the whole surface, first with circular strokes and then with the grain. This burnishing action should bring up an even glow to the surface. Be careful not to use too much alcohol. This would dissolve too much of the surface that has been applied. The polished work should be left for two or three days to fully harden.

French polishing is a process for dealing with large areas. There are many fretted, carved, or molded parts that cannot be treated with a pad. Simple molding can be rubbed lengthwise, but shellac will have to be applied by brush to most other shaped parts, even if adjoining flat surfaces are polished with a pad.

## OTHER FINISHES

Several special finishes have been used at various times, but most of these are comparatively recent. Bleaching, liming, and other special effects do not go as far back as the furniture described in this book. Spraying is fairly recent. It may be a good way to apply lacquer, but reproduction furniture ought not to be treated that way.

More information on wood finishing may be found in the author's book, Do-It-Yourselfer's Guide to Furniture Repair and Refinishing (TAB book No. 894).

## DISTRESSING

If there is to be a simulation of age in a piece of furniture it is necessary to visualize the effect normal wear may have on it over a long period. Table legs may have been knocked by a chair or seat. Rails may have become hollowed and rounded by boots rubbing on them. Tops may have their edges worn and hollows developed in their surfaces. Exposed surfaces may have taken knocks from things dropped on them. There may be a general denting of a surface that was once flat. There may be cracks developed in varnish or French polish. The finish may have become unevenly colored due to partial exposure to sun or the effect of a solvent spilled at some time.

Any applied "wear" should not be too regular. Abrasive paper over a curved piece of wood may be used like a file to form footwear hollows or other dents, but avoid too symmetrical a shape and round all edges. Surface dents can be made in several ways. A piece of chain may be wrapped into a ball and pounded on the wood. Rocks, such as coral, can be used in the same way. An iron rod can simulate dents caused by knocking. Use restraint. It is unlikely that owners would have allowed indiscriminate damage. Dents tend to darken, so stain may be rubbed in them and waxed over.

Sometimes there small dark dots on an old finish. This can be done by "splattering." Have dark stain in a brush. Rest a stick across the wood and knock the brush against it to cause drops of stain to fly on the wood. Obviously, practice on scrap wood first. If an old finish cracks, this will show as haphazard fine lines, which have been polished over. They can be painted on with artists' brushes.

In general, distressing is best done at an intermediate stage during finishing. Apply some varnish or polish, do the distressing, and continue with more finish.

*Antiquing* is a name applied to a process that gives a certain effect that some people find attractive, but only in the broadest sense can it be regarded as a way of simulating old age. It does not make anything look antique, so is not really appropriate to reproduction furniture, unless the finish appeals to the user. Kits are available. A colored glaze is put over an existing surface—usually painted—and some of it is rubbed away before it dries. Usually moldings and other surrounding parts finish dark, with a lightening towards the centers of panels. Carved parts are dark in their recesses, while high parts are rubbed lighter.

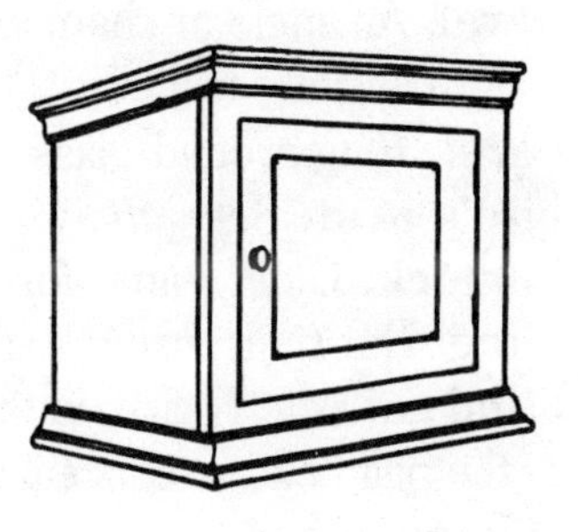

# Glossary

**annular rings.** The concentric rings which form the grain in a tree.

**annulet.** A turned raised bead or flat molding around a cylindrical part.

**apron.** A piece of wood below a drawer, which may have its lower edge decorated by shaping.

**arch back.** An armchair with the arms continuing to an arched back, as in a Windsor chair.

**architrave.** Outer moldings around a door.

**arris.** A sharp angle between two surfaces.

**astragal.** A raised molding or bead on a flat surface.

**backboard.** The piece of wood closing the back of a cabinet.

**back-flap hinge.** A hinge that can swing back further than a normal hinge, particularly used under a drop leaf on a table.

**bail.** A swinging loop handle.

**ball foot.** A turned round or elliptical ball on the bottom of a leg.

**baluster, balluster.** Pillar to support a rail.

**banding.** A strip of inlay laid around edges of drawers, cabinets and table tops.

**barefaced tenon.** A tenon shouldered on one side.

**batten.** A strip of wood which may be fixed across boards to join them or cover a gap.

**baulk, balk.** Roughly squared lumber.

**beetle.** Heavy mallet or cudgel, particularly used with a froe.

**bench stop.** A wood or metal stop on a bench top, against which wood is planed.

**bevel.** An angle or chamfer planed along an edge. Also a tool for checking angles.

**bezel.** Ring around glass over clock face.

**bird's nest.** See *gallery*.

**bitstock.** Older name for a brace or bit brace.

**blind.** Not right through, as with a drilled hole or a mortise.

**blind nailing.** Nailing in the rabbet at the edge of a board, so the nail head is concealed by the next board.

**bolster.** A pad to take a thrust.

**bonnet.** Decorative shaping and molding or carving at the top of a piece of furniture, particularly a clock.

**Boston rocker.** A version of the Windsor chair with the rear of the seat raised where it is bored for the spindles.

**bow back.** A chair back with a curved bow and spindles enclosed in it.

**bow saw.** See *frame saw.*

**bracket.** An angular support, particularly for a shelf or under a drop leaf on a table.

**bullnose plane.** A plane with its iron very close to the front of the body and usually of the rabbet type, for getting close to the end of a stopped rabbet.

**bureau.** A writing desk with a closing front and storage places inside.

**burl, burr.** Very twisted grain, often due to a lump on the tree. Cut into veneers for its decorative value.

**cable molding.** Molding with part carved to look like stranded rope.

**cabriole leg.** Leg with a flourish so it curves out from a corner and finished in a small foot.

**cant.** Sloping surface, as around the edge of a panel to fit a groove.

**carcase.** The main assembly of parts that make up the skeleton of a piece of furniture, such as the framework of a table or a chest of drawers.

**cast** Twisted or "winding" wood.

**chamfer.** An angle planed on an edge. Also *bevel* or *splay*. A *stopped chamfer* extends only part way along an edge.

**check.** Rabbet, particularly in a joint.

**claw and ball.** A form of carved foot in the appearance of a bird's claw holdng a ball.

**cleat.** A strip of wood fixed across other boards to prevent them warping, particularly when mortise and tenoned across their ends.

**cock head.** A strip with a rounded edge, fitted around a drawer front or other edge.

**cockshead hinge.** An ornamental hinge with narrow knuckles.

**comb.** An undulating edge, particularly on a chair back.

**cornice.** A molding above eye level, projecting around the top of a cabinet.

**counterbore.** Let a screw head below the surface.

**countersink.** Let a screw head in level with the surface.

**cross-lap joint.** Cutting two pieces of wood to fit into each other where they cross.

**crotch, crook.** Wood at the point where a branch leaves the trunk of a tree. Cut to take advantage of the strength of the curved grain or for decoration.

**crow's nest.** See *gallery*.

**cup shake.** Defect in lumber, with crack around annular rings.

**curly grain.** Pattern caused by cutting across uneven grain.

**dado.** Groove.

**dead pin.** A wedge.

**deal.** Trade name sometimes used for wood from softwood trees, such as pine and fir. More particularly applied to these woods imported from Baltic countries.

**distressing.** Intentionally damaging furniture to make it look old.

**door pull.** Handle on door.

**double-quirk bead.** A rounded bead worked along an edge to disguise its joint to another board.

**dovetail joint**. Joint with fan-shaped pieces on one part fitting between "pins" in the other part.

**dowel**. Round wood rod, either a separate piece or worked on the end of another part. Commonly used glued into holes to make joints.

**draw bore or draw pin**. A dowel or roughly shaped peg driven through holes across a mortise and tenon joint to draw the parts together.

**drop leaf**. A flap which swings down at the edge of a table and which can be supported when raised to enlarge the table top.

**Dutch foot**. A turned tapered leg finishing in a foot extending outwards.

**escutcheon**. A keyhole or the plate covering or surrounding it.

**face marks**. Marks to denote the face side and edge of planed wood.

**fall front**. A flap that lets down to be supported in a horizontal position, particularly the writing surface of a bureau.

**fasteners, fastenings**. Anything, such as nails, used for joining.

**feather crotch**. See *crotch*.

**fiddle back**. Pattern when some wood is quarter sawn, particularly mahogany used for violin backs, but also seen in sycamore and maple.

**figure**. Decorative pattern, particularly that shown when the medullary rays are prominent in quarter-sawn wood.

**fillister**. A rabbet plane with fences to control depth and width of cut. Sometimes confused with a *plow*, which has a similar appearance, but cuts grooves.

**finial**. A turned end to a post.

**flap**. See *drop leaf*.

**flap hinge**. See *back-flap hinge*.

**flush bead molding**. A bead worked in a surface instead of standing up as in an astragal.

**fluting**. Rounded grooves, the reverse of beads.

**folding wedges**. Two similar wedges used overlapping each other to apply pressure.

**foxtail wedging.** Using a wedge in a saw cut in the end of a tenon so it spreads the wood as it is driven into a blind mortise.

**frame saw.** A narrow saw for cutting curves, tensioned in a frame, traditionally of wood with a twisted cord for tightening.

**fretwork.** Pierced work, done with a very fine frame saw.

**froe.** Wedge-sectioned knife with an end handle at right angles used to split or "rive" wood.

**gage, gauge.** A marking tool or a definition of size, as in screws.

**gallery.** A shelf often bordered with turned spindles. On a table, the bird's cage or crow's nest at the top of a pedestal which allows the table top to turn and pivot.

**gate leg table.** Table with drop leaves held up by swinging legs like gates.

**glazier's points.** Small steel triangles used as nails to hold glass in a frame.

**grain.** The stripes seen in wood, due to the annular rings.

**groove.** Any slot in wood. Less commonly a rabbet.

**gunstock stile.** The upright at the side of a paneled door which is wider beside the lower panel than beside the upper one.

**halving joint.** See *cross-lap joint.*

**hand screw.** A wooden clamp.

**handed.** Made in pairs.

**hanging stile.** The stile on which hinges are fixed.

**haunch.** A short part of a tenon in a corner joint.

**housing joint.** Grooved surface to take the end of another part, such as a shelf.

**inlaying.** Setting one piece of wood in another, either solid wood or veneers.

**joinery.** Woodworking concerned with the making of jointed parts, such as window frames, but not furniture, which is cabinetmaking.

**joint.** Any means of fitting one piece of wood to another.

**kerf.** The slot made by a saw.

**keying.** Fitting veneer into saw kerfs, particularly to strengthen a miter joint.

**knot.** Fault in wood, due to where a branch left the trunk of the tree.

**knuckle.** The pivot part of a hinge.

**knuckle end.** A carved end to the arm of a chair, like several curled fingers.

**ladder back.** A chair back with several cross-members between uprights.

**laminate.** Use several pieces of wood to build up a thickness, particulary in curved work.

**lap joint.** General name for several types of joints in which one piece of wood overlaps another.

**lattice work.** Pierced strapwork.

**laying out.** See *marking out.*

**lineal.** Length only.

**listel.** See *annulet.*

**locking stile.** The upright against which a door locks.

**lunette.** Semi-circular carving in a bonnet.

**marking out.** Marking sizes on wood for cutting and shaping.

**marquetry.** A system of inlaying using many woods to produce a pattern, either in solid wood or veneer.

**matched boarding.** Joining boards edge to edge with matching tongue and groove joints.

**miter, mitre.** Corner joint, as in a picture frame.

**miter box or board.** Guide for the saw when cutting miters.

**miter square.** A testing tool similar to a try square, but with its blade at 45°.

**molding, moulding.** Decorative edge or border, which may be a simple rounding or an intricate section of curves and quirks. There are many classical forms often used in furniture.

**mortise, mortice.** The rectangular socket cut to take a tenon.

**mortise and tenon joint.** A method of joining the end of one piece of wood into the side of another with the tenon projecting like a tongue to fit into the mortise cut in the other piece. There are many variations. This is the commonest joint in traditional furniture.

**mullet**. A groove block used for testing an edge of a panel or drawer bottom to fit a groove.

**muntin**. An internal rail in a framed structure, as between panes in a window frame.

**necking**. Turned bead or mold on the upper part of a pillar, pedestal or finial.

**ogee**. A molding section with a convex curve above a concave one, named for its likeness to a combination of the letters *O* and *G*.

**onion foot**. A squat version of a ball foot.

**orbital sander**. Power sander in which the flat sanding pad makes small orbital movements. Used for finishing.

**ovolo**. A molding like a raised bead.

**patina**. Surface texture, particularly that due to age.

**pedestal**. A supporting post.

**pediment**. A top shaped and molded and carved. Larger than a bonnet.

**pegging**. Dowels or pegs through joints.

**pendant, pendil, pennant**. A hanging turned or carved decoration. The reverse of a finial.

**piercing**. Decorative pattern made by cutting through the wood, as in a splat of a chair back.

**pigeon hole**. Storage compartments, particularly in a bureau.

**pilaster**. A decorative column, fitted on a flat surface.

**pilot hole**. A small hole drilled as a guide before using a larger drill.

**pintle**. A dowel or peg on which parts pivot. Name taken from the pivot for a boat's rudder.

**plain sawn**. Lumber cut across a log in slices.

**planted**. Applied piece, such as a planted molding fitted to a surface or edge.

**plinth**. The base part around the bottom of a piece of furniture.

**plow, plough.** A plane for cutting grooves. The traditional type has a general appearance similar to a fillister, with which it may be confused.

**pluck up**. Tear up the surface of the wood by planing against the grain.

**punchwork**. Background to carving made with punches having patterned ends.

**quartered, quarter-sawn**. Boards cut radially from a log. In some woods this shows a decorative figure.

**quirk**. A bead worked into joining parts to form a cover or disguise for the joint. A raised part between patterns in turned work.

**rail**. Horizontal member of a carcase framing.

**relief**. Cut back, usually to gain emphasis in appearance.

**rift sawn**. See *plain sawn*.

**ripples**. Series of rays showing in the grain of some woods.

**riven, rive**. Split boards from a log instead of sawing them. Traditionally with a froe and beetle.

**rod back**. Type of Windsor chair with many spindles and the arms joined to back spindles.

**rolled arm**. Arm of a chair shaped for comfort and the front finished in a scroll.

**router**. Tool for leveling the bottom of a groove, hand or power.

**rule**. Measuring rod. Not spelled *ruler*.

**rule joint**. Molded joint used between a table top and a drop leaf with back-flap hinges. Named for its similarity in section to the joint of a two-fold rule.

**run**. In a long length. Particularly a molding worked direct on an edge and not "stuck" as a separate piece. Lengths of lumber may be quoted as so many feet run.

**saddling**. Scooping a chair seat to a comfortable shape.

**sapwood**. The wood nearest the outside of a log. In many woods this is liable to rot.

**sash**. Molded and rabbeted edge of a window frame. A *sash plane* cuts the rabbet and molding in one pass.

**sausage and ball molding**. Long and short curved shapes in a molding.

**saw buck**. Crossed sawing trestle. Name is applied to table legs arranged in a similar way.

**scratch molding**. Small molded edge cut with a "scratch stock" having a cutter made like a scraper.

**scroll**. Carved shape like end view of loosely rolled paper.

**set**. Punch a nail below the surface. The bending of saw teeth in alternate directions.

**setting out**. See *marking out*.

**shooting board, shuting board**. Holding device for wood having its edge planed or molded.

**shot joint**. Planed edges glued together.

**shoulder piece**. Extra bracket at the top of a leg, extending under the rail or framing.

**skirt**. Wood to form a border.

**slat**. Narrow thin wood, particularly across a chair back.

**snipe or staple hinge**. Crude hinge made by linking loops of wire.

**spandrail, spandrel**. Shaped rail between upright parts of a piece of furniture.

**spindle.** Rounded slender part, usually vertical as in a chair back.

**splat**. Central upright member in a chair back. Usually decorated by shaping, piercing or carving.

**splay**. See *chamfer*. Also to spread out.

**spline**. Narrow strip fitted into two facing grooves in boards being joined.

**split turning**. A piece with a semi-circular section, made by turning two pieces of wood glued together and separating them.

**square**. Cabinetmaking term meaning true or at right angles and not necessarily a square section.

**square turning**. Wood of square section, but with lengthwise shaping similar to a turned outline.

**star shakes**. Radial splits in the end of a log.

**stile**. Vertical part at edge of furniture framing to which horizontal rails are joined.

**stop fluting**. Flutes cut in a surface, but not taken through to the end of the wood.

**stock knife**. Early means of shaping wood. A knife loosely pivoted at one end to a block of wood, with a long handle so it could cut in many directions.

**strap work**. Carving that looks like interwoven crossing straps.

**stretcher**. Lengthwise rail between the lower parts of a chair or table.

**stuff**. General term for wood gathered to be made into something.

**tang**. The tapered end of a tool to fit into a handle.

**template, templet**. Shaped pattern for marking parts.

**tenon**. The projecting tongue on the end of one piece of wood to fit into a mortise in another piece.

**tester**. The roof over a four-poster bed.

**thread escutcheon**. A metal liner for a keyhole.

**thumb molding**. Curved edge below a small rabbetted step.

**thumb plane**. Any very small plane.

**tote**. A handle, particularly on a plane.

**trunnel, treenail**. Peg or dowel driven through a joint.

**tusk tenon**. A tenon projecting beyond its mortise and cross wedged.

**veneer**. Thin layer of wood, usually of decorative type glued to a solid backing.

**wainscot**. Strictly paneling around a room, but applied to quarter-sawn wood that shows figuring.

**wany edge**. The edge of a board that still has bark or the pattern of the outside of a log.

**warping**. Twisting or curving of a board due to unequal shrinkage.

**wavy grain**. See *fiddle back*.

**winding**. An assembled frame is in winding when it is not flat and a twist can be seen when sighted from one end.

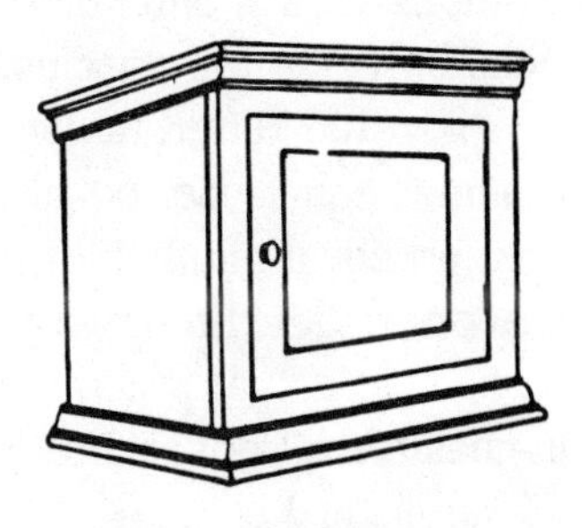

# Appendix
# Wood Characteristics

This appendix will help you select the right wood species for specific furniture-making projects. Here you'll find information on important wood properties and species, information that you can use not only in the creation of fine furniture but in *any* kind of wood construction.

The choice of one wood species in preference to another for any use should seldom be based on a single vital property. Usually a favorable combination of two or more basic qualities or characteristics should determine the selection.

In Table A-1 the various woods are classified according to a number of these important properties. Class A, in Table A-1, includes woods that are relatively high in the specific property or characteristic listed; class B woods are intermediate in the specific property or characteristic listed; and class C woods are relatively low.

For example, Class A in columns 2 to 16 indicates species that are generally the most desirable from the standpoint of working and behavior characteristics and strength. In columns 17 to 21, class A indicates species with the most desirable qualities because it designates greater freedom from knots and other characteristics, and greater acceptability as to their size.

Such a general classification necessarily ignores small differences and sacrifices detail in favor of the simplicity desired by the ordinary user. All woods in the same class are by no means equal, and no attempt is made to draw fine distinctions between the species.

For the different kinds (species) of wood, Table A-1 assumes equal size, equal dryness, and, for strength properties, an equal number of knots and other strength-reducing characteristics. So far as cross-sectional dimensions are concerned, in actual practice the different species of softwood lumber are all governed by trade standards.

Standard sizes for boards and dimension are larger for lumber surfaced green than lumber surfaced dry. When lumber surfaced green dries to the standard dry moisture content, it will shrink to approximately the standard dry surfaced size.

Most hardwoods differ substantially from softwoods in their properties (basic characteristics) and in their uses. As a class, hardwoods are heavier, harder, shrink more, and are tougher. Hardwoods and softwoods are similar in stiffness, so on a weight basis the softwoods are actually much stiffer. In strength as a post and in bending strength the two groups are more directly comparable than they are in weight, toughness, and hardness; nevertheless, more commercial hardwoods than softwoods can be rated high in bending strength.

The various properties and characteristics as designated in Table 1 are more fully described in the following sections.

## HARDNESS

Hardness (Table A-1, column 2) is the property that makes a surface difficult to dent, scratch, or cut. Generally, the harder the wood, the better it resists wear, the less it crushes or mashes under loads, and the better it can be polished. On the other hand, the harder wood is more difficult to cut with tools, harder to nail, and more likely to split in nailing.

There is a pronounced difference in hardness between the springwood and the summerwood of woods such as southern yellow pine and Douglas-fir. In these woods the summerwood is the denser, darker colored portion of the annual growth ring. Differences in surface hardness thus occur at close intervals on a piece of such wood depending on whether springwood or summerwood is encountered. In woods like maple, which do not have pronounced springwood and summerwood, the hardness of the surface is quite uniform.

The classification of a species as a hardwood or softwood is not based on actual hardness of wood. Technically, softwoods are those cut from coniferous or evergreen trees, whereas hardwoods are those cut from broad-leaved and deciduous trees. Actually, some of the softwoods are harder than some of the hardwoods.

As a group, the hardwoods can be divided into (a) dense and (b) less dense. The softwoods can also be divided into two groups: (a) medium-density and (b) low-density.

Differences in hardness are great enough to affect the choice of woods for such uses as flooring and furniture on one hand, and for siding, millwork, and cabinets on the other.

## WEIGHT

Weight, in addition to being important in itself, is generally a reliable index of strength. A heavy piece of wood is generally stronger than a lighter piece of the same moisture content and size, whether it is of the same or of a different species.

Wood weights, as commonly expressed, are either in the green or in the air-dry condition. Green weight of wood is the weight before any drying takes place; air-dry weight of wood refers to the weight after drying by exposure to atmospheric conditions for a time, either outdoors or in unheated sheds. The classification in Table A-1, column 3, is based on the air-dry condition.

## FREEDOM FROM SHRINKAGE AND SWELLING

Most materials change in dimension with changes in temperature or moisture. Wood, like many other fibrous

TABLE A-1. Broad classification of woods according to characteristics and properties A, woods relatively high in the particular respect listed; B, woods intermediate in that respect; C, woods relatively low in that respect. (Letters do not refer to lumber grades.)

| Kind of wood | Working and behavior characteristics | | | | | | | | | | | Strength properties | | | |
|---|---|---|---|---|---|---|---|---|---|---|---|---|---|---|---|
| | Hardness | Weight, dry | Freedom from shrinkage and swelling | Freedom from warping | Ease of working | Paint holding[4] | Nail holding | Decay resistance of heartwood | Proportion of heartwood | Amount of figure | Freedom from odor and taste (dry) | Bending strength | Stiffness | Strength as a post | Toughness |
| 1 | 2 | 3 | 4 | 5 | 6 | 7 | 8 | 9 | 10 | 11 | 12 | 13 | 14 | 15 | 16 |
| Ash: Black | B | B | C | B | C | C | A | C | C | A | A | B | B | C | A |
| White | A | A | B | B | C | C | A | C | C | A | A | A | A | A | A |
| Aspen | C | C | B | B | A | A | C | C | B | C | A | C | B | C | C |
| Basswood | C | C | C | B | A | A | C | C | C | C | A | C | B | C | C |
| Beech | A | A | C | C | C | B | A | C | B | B | A | A | A | B | A |
| Birch | B | A | C | B | C | B | A | C | C | B | A | A | A | B | A |
| Cedar: Eastern red | B | B | A | A | B | A | B | A | B | B | C | B | C | B | B |
| Northern white | C | C | A | A | A | A | C | A | A | C | B | C | C | C | C |
| Southern white | C | C | A | A | A | A | C | A | A | C | B | C | C | C | C |
| Western red | C | C | A | A | A | A | C | A | A | B | C | C | C | B | C |
| Cherry | B | B | B | A | B | B | A | C | B | B | B | A | A | A | B |
| Cottonwood | C | C | B | C | B | A | C | C | C | C | B | C | B | C | C |
| Cypress | B | B | A | B | B | A | B | A | B | A | B | B | B | B | C |
| Douglas-fir | B | B | B | B | B | B | A | B | A | A | C | A | A | A | B |
| Elm: Rock | A | A | B | B | C | C | A | C | B | A | A | A | A | A | A |
| Soft | B | B | B | C | C | C | A | C | B | A | A | B | B | B | A |

| | | | | | | | | | | | | | | | |
|---|---|---|---|---|---|---|---|---|---|---|---|---|---|---|---|
| Fir: Balsam | C | C | B | B | B | C | C | C | B | C | A | C | C | C | C |
| White | C | C | A | B | B | C | C | C | C | C | A | B | A | B | C |
| Gum | B | B | C | C | B | C | A | B | B | B | B | B | A | B | B |
| Hackberry | B | B | C | B | C | C | A | C | C | A | A | B | C | C | A |
| Hemlock: Eastern | B | C | A | B | B | B | B | C | B | B | A | B | B | B | C |
| West coast | B | C | B | B | B | B | B | C | B | B | A | B | A | B | B |
| Hickory | A | A | C | B | C | C | A | C | B | B | B | A | A | A | A |
| Larch: Western | B | A | B | B | C | C | A | B | A | A | C | A | A | A | B |
| Locust | A | A | A | B | C | C | A | A | A | A | B | A | A | A | A |
| Magnolia | B | B | B | B | B | B | A | C | B | B | B | B | B | B | B |
| Maple: Hard | A | A | C | B | C | B | A | C | C | B | A | A | A | A | A |
| Soft | B | B | B | B | C | B | A | C | C | B | A | B | B | B | B |
| Oak: Red | A | A | B | B | C | C | A | C | B | A | B | A | A | B | A |
| White | A | A | C | B | C | C | A | A | B | A | B | A | A | B | A |
| Pecan. | A | A | B | B | C | C | A | C | B | B | B | A | A | A | A |
| Pine: Idaho white (western) | C | C | B | A | A | A | C | C | B | C | C | B | B | B | C |
| Lodgepole | C | C | B | C | B | C | B | C | B | C | C | B | B | B | C |
| Northern white (eastern) | C | C | A | A | A | A | C | B | B | C | C | C | C | C | C |
| Ponderosa | C | C | A | A | A | B | B | C | C | C | C | C | C | C | C |
| Southern yellow | B | A | B | B | B | C | A | B | C | A | C | A | A | A | B |
| Sugar | C | C | A | A | A | A | C | C | B | C | C | C | C | C | C |
| Poplar | C | B | B | A | B | A | B | C | B | B | A | B | B | B | B |
| Redwood | B | C | A | A | B | A | B | A | A | B | A | B | B | A | C |
| Spruce: Eastern | C | C | B | A | B | B | B | C | C | B | A | B | B | B | C |
| Engelmann | C | C | A | A | B | B | C | C | C | B | A | C | C | C | C |
| Sitka | C | C | B | A | B | B | B | C | C | B | A | B | A | B | B |
| Sycamore | B | B | B | C | C | B | A | C | B | B | A | B | B | B | B |
| Tupelo | B | B | B | C | C | B | A | C | C | C | A | B | B | B | B |
| Walnut | B | A | B | A | B | C | A | A | B | B | A | A | A | A | A |

[4] Indicates general paintability and performance characteristics of edge-grained surfaces exposed to the weather.

TABLE A-1. Con't.

| Kind of wood | Surface characteristics of common grades | | | | | Distinctive and principal uses |
|---|---|---|---|---|---|---|
| | Knots | | Pitch defects | Other defects | | |
| | Freedom from | Acceptance as to size | Freedom from | Freedom from | Acceptance as to size | |
| 1 | 17 | 18 | 19 | 20 | 21 | 22 |
| Ash: Black | A | B | A | B | B | Implements, cooperage, containers |
| White | A | B | A | B | B | Implements, containers, furniture |
| Aspen | A | A | A | B | B | Boxes, lumber, pulp, excelsior |
| Basswood | A | B | A | A | A | Woodenware, boxes, veneer |
| Beech | B | B | A | C | C | Flooring, furniture, woodenware |
| Birch | A | B | A | B | B | Flooring, furniture, millwork |
| Cedar: Eastern red | C | A | A | A | A | Posts, paneling, wardrobes, chests |
| Northern white | B | B | A | B | B | Poles, posts, tanks, woodenware |
| Southern white | A | B | A | A | A | Posts, poles, boat and tank stock |
| Western red | A | C | A | B | B | Shingles, siding, poles, millwork |
| Cherry | A | B | A | B | B | Furniture, woodenware, paneling |
| Cottonwood | A | A | A | A | A | Pulpwood, excelsior, containers |
| Cypress | A | B | A | B | B | Millwork, siding, tanks |
| Douglas-fir | B | B | B | B | B | Construction, plywood, millwork |
| Elm: Rock | B | B | A | B | B | Furniture, containers, veneer |
| Soft | B | B | A | C | C | Containers, furniture, veneer |

| | | | | | | |
|---|---|---|---|---|---|---|
| Fir: Balsam | C | A | A | B | B | Light construction, pulpwood |
| White | B | B | A | B | C | Light construction, containers |
| Gum | A | B | A | A | A | Millwork, containers, furniture |
| Hackberry | A | C | A | B | B | Furniture, veneer, containers |
| Hemlock: Eastern | B | B | A | C | C | Construction, containers |
| West coast | B | B | A | B | B | Construction, pulpwood, containers |
| Hickory | B | C | A | B | B | Handles, athletic goods, implements |
| Larch: Western | C | A | A | C | A | Construction, poles, ties, millwork |
| Locust | B | B | A | B | B | Poles, posts, insulator pins, ties, fuel |
| Magnolia | A | B | A | B | B | Furniture, veneer, containers |
| Maple: Hard | B | B | A | B | B | Flooring, furniture, veneer |
| Soft | A | B | A | A | A | Furniture, woodenware, fuel |
| Oak: Red | A | C | A | B | B | Flooring, furniture, veneer, posts |
| White | A | C | A | B | B | Furniture, cooperage, millwork, veneer |
| Pecan | A | C | A | C | C | Implement handles, flooring, pallets |
| Pine: Idaho white (western) | C | A | A | C | A | Millwork, construction, siding, paneling |
| Lodgepole | C | B | A | B | B | Poles, lumber, ties, mine timbers |
| Northern white (eastern) | C | A | A | B | B | Millwork, furniture, containers |
| Ponderosa | B | B | B | B | B | Millwork, construction, poles, veneer |
| Southern yellow | A | C | C | B | B | Construction, poles, siding, cooperage |
| Sugar | C | B | A | B | A | Millwork, patterns, construction |
| Poplar | A | B | A | A | A | Furniture, plywood, containers |
| Redwood | A | C | A | A | B | Siding, tanks, millwork |
| Spruce: Eastern | C | A | A | B | B | Construction, pulpwood |
| Engelmann | C | A | A | B | B | Light construction, poles, pulpwood |
| Sitka | B | B | A | B | B | Construction, millwork, containers |
| Sycamore | A | B | A | B | B | Furniture, veneer, cooperage |
| Tupelo | A | A | A | A | A | Containers, furniture, veneer |
| Walnut | A | B | A | A | A | Furniture, gunstocks, interior finish |

materials, shrinks as it dries and swells as it absorbs moisture. As a rule, however, much shrinking and swelling of wood in structures can be avoided by using wood that has been dried to a suitable moisture content.

For most species, the shrinkage or swelling in width of a flat-grained or plainsawed board is often approximately twice that of an edge-grained or quartersawed board of the same width (see Fig. A-1). Edge-grained boards or other items cut from a species with high shrinkage characteristics will therefore prove as satisfactory as flat-grained boards or items cut from species with lower shrinkage characteristics. The normal wood of all species shrinks or swells very slightly along the grain (lengthwise).

The classification according to the amount of shrinkage (Table A-1, column 4) generally compares the performance of woods of various species. It does not tell the user the whole

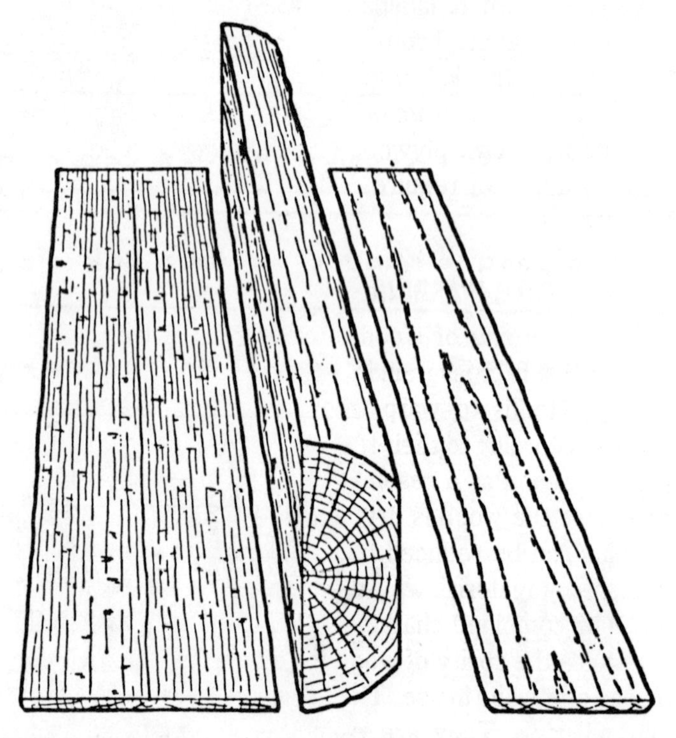

Fig. A-1. Grain depends on how lumber is cut from log. Board A is quartersawed or edge-grained. Board B is plainsawed or flat-grained.

story of the shrinking and swelling of different species in service. Shrinkage of wood begins when moisture in the wood is removed by drying below the fiber saturation point (approximately 30 percent moisture content). When wood reaches a moisture content of 15 percent, about one-half of the total shrinkage has occurred. The moisture content of wood in service constantly changes since it adjusts to corresponding changes in surrounding atmospheric conditions.

The moisture content of woodwork installed within heated buildings reaches a low point during the heating season and a high point during the summer. The moisture content at the time of installation should be near the midpoint of this range. If this rule is followed, slight shrinkage will occur during some seasons and a slight swelling during others.

Plywood is relatively free from shrinkage and swelling as compared to solid wood because its construction generally consists of alternate laminations of veneers laid with grain at 90° to each other. From soaked to overdry condition, the shrinkage of plywood in length and width is generally quite uniform and ranges from only about 0.2 to about 1.2 percent. After manufacture, plywood has a low moisture content and normally does not require drying out before use.

## FREEDOM FROM WARPING

The warping of wood is closely allied with shrinkage. Lumber that is crossgrained, or is from near the pith (core) of the tree, tends to warp when it shrinks. Classification of species according to their tendencies to warp and twist during seasoning, and as a result of changes in atmospheric conditions once the wood is dry, is listed in Table A-1, column 5. Warping can be reduced to a minimum by the use of edge-grained dry material.

The combined characteristics of warping and shrinkage determine the ability of wood to remain flat, straight, and not change size while in use. These qualities are desired in practically all uses. They are especially important in furniture, cabinetwork, window sash and frames, doors, and siding.

## EASE OF WORKING

Wood is generally easy to cut, shape, and fasten with ordinary tools. For some purposes the difference between woods in ease of working is negligible, but for others it may decidedly affect the quality and cost of the finished job. In general, ease of working is of first importance to the worker.

Harder and denser woods with high load-carrying capacity and wear resistance should not be passed over just because softer woods are easier to work; rather, a reasonable balance must be drawn in selecting wood for a specific use.

A skilled carpenter working with lumber that is well seasoned and manufactured can get good results from even the more difficult-to-work woods. An unskilled worker is more likely to get good results only from the softer woods. However, with portable power tools, jigs for installation of hinges and door locks, and other modern labor-saving methods, skill is no longer the major factor it was when hand tools were the only means of cutting and fitting on the job.

The classification of the more common woods according to their working qualities (Table A-1, column 6) is based on a combination of the hardness, texture, and character of the surfaces obtainable. Woods in the A class have soft, uniform textures and finish to smooth surfaces; woods in the C class are hard or nonuniform in texture and more difficult to surface without chipping the grain, fuzzing, or grain raising. The B class is intermediate.

## PAINT HOLDING

Good paint performance or ability of a wood surface to hold paint depends on three factors: (1) the kind of paint, (2) surface conditions and application factors, and (3) the kind of wood.

Different woods vary considerably in painting characteristics, particularly for outdoor exposure. The ratings of the species in Table A-1, column 7, indicate generally their abilities to hold paint under exposure to the weather.

Paint is more durable on edge-grained surfaces than on flat-grained surfaces. The edge-grained boards in B class woods usually have a better surface for painting than the flat-grained surfaces of A class woods.

Knots, particularly resinous ones, do not hold paint well and contribute to abnormally early paint failure. High content of pitch and resin will also detract from the paintability of wood unless the pitch is set adequately by proper high-temperature seasoning of the wood.

Class B and class C woods and plywood are best finished with pigmented stains that penetrate the wood surface and do not form a continuous film on the surface. Such stain finishes do not fail by cracking and peeling of the coating from the wood as does paint.

## NAIL HOLDING

As a rule, fastenings are the weakest link in all forms of construction and in all materials; therefore the resistance offered by the wood to the withdrawal of nails is important. Usually, the denser and harder the wood, the greater is the inherent nail-holding ability, assuming the wood does not split. The grouping of the commercial woods (Table A-1, column 8) according to their inherent nail-holding ability is based on tests that measured the force required to pull nails from wood.

The size, type, and number of nails have a marked effect on the strength of a joint. Correct placement of the nails is as important as the size and number.

The resistance of nails to withdrawal increases almost directly with their diameter; if the diameter of the nail is doubled, the holding strength is doubled, providing the nail does not split the wood when it is driven. The lateral resistance of nails increases as the 1½ power of the diameter.

The splitting of wood by nails greatly reduces their holding ability. Even if the wood is split only slightly around the nail, considerably holding strength is lost. Because of hardness and texture characteristics, some woods split more in nailing than do others. The heavy, dense woods, such as maple, oak, and hickory, split more in nailing than do the light-weight woods such as basswood, spruce, and balsam and white fir.

Predrilling is good practice in dense woods, especially when large diameter nails are used. The drilled hole should be about 75 percent of the nail diameter.

Woods without a uniform texture, like southern yellow pine and Douglas-fir, split more than do such uniform-textured woods as northern and Idaho white pine, sugar pine, or ponderosa pine.

In addition to predrilling, the most common means taken to reduce splitting is the use of small diameter nails. The number of small nails must be increased to maintain the same gross holding strength as with larger nails. Slightly blunt-pointed nails have less tendency to split wood than do sharp-pointed nails. Too much blunting, however, results in a loss of holding ability.

## DECAY RESISTANCE

Every material has its distinctive way of deteriorating under adverse conditions. With wood it is decay. Wood will never decay if kept continuously dry or continuously under water. Fortunately, most wood in ordinary buildings is in dry situations and therefore not in danger of decay. It is only in certain parts of the buildings that decay resistance is important, such as areas where wood may become damp or where it touches or is embedded in the ground.

The different kinds of wood are classified in accordance with their natural decay resistance in Table A-1, column 9. This classification applies solely to the heartwood, because sapwood of all species in the untreated condition has low decay resistance. Also, this classification deals only with averages, and exceptions frequently occur because of variations in the wood itself and because of differences in the kinds of fungi that cause the decay.

## PROPORTION OF HEARTWOOD

When selecting untreated wood for use where the decay hazard is high, one must consider the heartwood content, because only the heartwood is decay resistant. When the sapwood of the species of tree is normally narrow, as it is in the woods rated as class A in Table A-1, column 10, the lumber runs high in heartwood content even without special selection. When the sapwood is normally wide, as in woods rated as class C and even in class B in column 10, the commercial run of lumber contains considerable sapwood.

## FIGURE

Figure is due to various causes in different woods. In woods like southern yellow pine and Douglas-fir, it results from the contrast between springwood and summerwood in growth rings; in oak, beech, or sycamore, it results from the flakes or rays in addition to the growth rings; in maple, walnut, and birch it results from wavy or curly grain; and in gum it results from infiltrated coloring matter.

Except where the figure in wood results from flakes or rays, it is more pronounced in flat-grained lumber than in edge-grained. Figure resulting from wavy or curly grain or from infiltrated color does not occur in all lumber of a given species, but only in lumber from occasional logs. To be certain of getting figured lumber in maple, walnut, or gum, special selection is necessary.

Woods with outstanding knots, such as pine and cedar, or with other unique characteristics such as those of pecky cypress, or "white speck" Douglas-fir, are often selected because of their novel patterns. The finish selected for these types of wood tends to accentuate rather than obscure the knots or other features.

The color of the wood has a decided influence on the figure. However, stains are so commonly and easily applied to most woods that natural color is usually not the first consideration, except where a very light color is desired.

A broad classification of the important kinds of lumber, from the standpoint of the amount of figure they contain, is shown in Table A-1, column 11. Woods classed as A are highly figured, and ordinary commercial run will have a pronounced figure. Class B woods have more modulated figures and sometimes require special selection to obtain the desired figure.

Class C woods are seldom satisfactory where figure is desired.

## BENDING STRENGTH

Bending strength is a measure of the load-carrying capacity of wood.

Even though a species is low in bending strength, it may still be selected for uses where this property is essential. However, larger sizes are then required to obtain the same load-carrying capacity.

The hardwoods in classes A and B in Table A-1 are often used in furniture, flooring, and veneers in plywood.

## STIFFNESS

Stiffness is a measure of the resistance to bending or deflection under a load. Stiffness is important in shelving, ladder rails, beams, and long, slender columns.

Differences in stiffness between species may be compensated for by changing the size of members. Depth and length of members have a greater effect on their stiffness than on other strength properties. For example, a change of 1/32 inch in the thickness of a 25/32-inch board produces a change of 12 percent in the stiffness of the board laid flat in a floor.

The species are classified by stiffness in Table A-1, column 14. Softwoods in class A and class B dominate the uses where stiffness is the most important requirement. When woods in class C are used where stiffness is desired, it is because other properties are more important. The woods in class A have the highest stiffness, but they are heavier and harder than those in Class B.

Light weight is quite commonly desired in combination with stiffness. The softwoods meet this requirement much better than the hardwoods, and softwoods in class B are often chosen in preference to those in class A because the weight of the latter excludes them.

## TOUGHNESS

Toughness is a measure of the capacity to withstand suddenly applied loads. Hence, woods high in shock resistance are adapted to withstand repeated shocks, jars, jolts, and blows, such as are given ax handles and other tool handles. The heavier hardwoods—hickory, birch, oak, maple, and ash—are so much higher in shock resistance than the toughest of the softwoods that these hardwoods are used almost exclusively where an exceptionally tough wood is required.

None of the softwoods in Table A-1, column 16, is grouped in class A in toughness, and few hardwoods (aspen, cottonwood, and basswood) fall in class C. The woods in class A completely dominate the uses where toughness is the outstanding requirement, and hickory dominates class A.

# Index

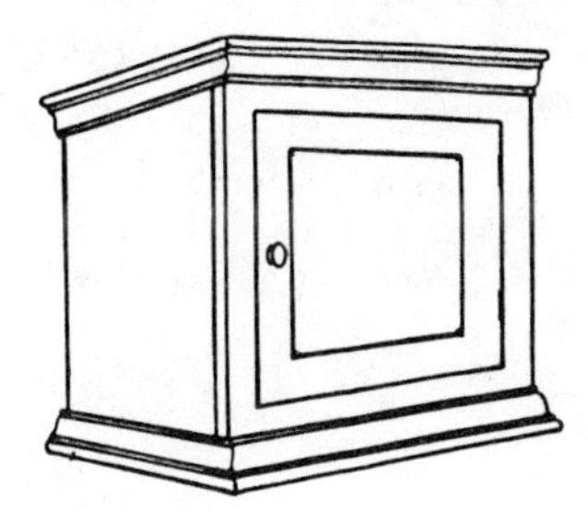

# Index